The Best Things to Do in NEW YORK

in

1001 IDEAS

The Best Things to Do
in NEW YORK

1001 IDEAS

Second Edition
By Caitlin Leffel and Jacob Lehman

UNIVERSE PUBLISHING

A Division of

Rizzoli International Publications, Inc.

This edition first published in the United States of America in 2010
by Rizzoli International Publications, Inc.
300 Park Avenue South
New York, NY 10010
www.rizzoliusa.com

2014 2015 2016 / 15 14 13 12
Second edition

Distributed in the U.S. trade by Random House, New York

Printed in the United States of America

ISBN-13: 978-0-7893-2026-1
Library of Congress Control Number: 2010920186

DEDICATION

CL

To my dad, who's been showing me great things about New York all my life; Alex, the best thing I found in New York; and in memory of my mom, whom New York will always miss.

JL

To David and Melanie, Michael and Rosa, and Maryana, all of whom made New York my second home.

TABLE OF CONTENTS

Acknowledgments: **p. 9** *Preface* **p. 10** *Introduction:* **p. 11** *How to use this book:* **p. 14**

Chapter 1: **The Classics** p. 17
Historic Sites • Good Old Haunts • Signature activities • Places We Miss Most • Expert Contributor Ric Bell: *My Five Favorite Classic Buildings in New York*

Chapter 2: **Views & Sights** p. 57
Rooftop Bars & Restaurants • Views from Buildings • Views from Monuments • Water Views • Promenades & Esplanades • Views from Bridges & Subways • People Watching • Expert Contributor Joseph O. Holmes: *My Five Favorite Spots to Photograph—and Photograph from—in New York*

Chapter 3: **On the Street & Underground** p. 84
Street Fairs & Festivals • Parades • Flea Markets • Walking Tours • Interesting Houses & Beautiful Blocks • Subways & Subway Stations • Street Features & Fun • Street Food • Favorite Movie Locations • Expert Contributor Bret Watson: *My Five Favorite Places to Visit in New York*

Chapter 4: **Arts & Culture** p. 118
Museums • Art • Music & Dance • Theater & Performance • Film • Expert Contributor David Masello: *My Five Favorite Artworks in New York*

Chapter 5: **Eating & Drinking** p. 161
New York Chefs • Incredible Meals • Remarkable Holes-in-the-Wall • Famous Food Wars • Food Festivals • Gourmet Markets • Ethnic Eats • Great Bars • Pizza! • Expert Contributor Andrea Strong: *My Five Favorite Restaurants in New York*

Chapter 6: **The Great Outdoors** p. 209
Parks & Gardens • Cinema al Fresco • Outdoor Music • Central & Prospect Parks • Water Fun • Nature & Wildlife • Outdoor Yoga • Tai Chi & Other Activities • Expert Contributor Francisco Liuzzi: *My Five Favorite Outdoor Sports in New York*

Chapter 7: **Bargains & Splurges** p. 242

Department Stores • Sample Sales • Boutiques & Specialty Shops • Record Stores • 5 Ways to Live Rich on the Sly • Shopping Excursions • On the Cheap & All Out • Cheap Thrills • Deluxe Treatment • Expert Contributor Laura Dave: *My Five Favorite Bookstores in New York*

Chapter 8: **Enrichment & Renewal** p. 290

Literature & Spoken Word • Classes & Courses • Lectures • Dance & Martial Arts • Meditation • Spas • Baths & Acupuncture • Expert Contributor Pavia Rosati: *My Five Favorite Retreats in New York*

Chapter 9: **24-Hour Fun** p. 315

24-Hour Services & Destinations • Early Bird and Night Owl Shopping • New Year's Fun • Clubs & Live Music Venues • 24-Hour Spas & Gyms • All-Night Diners & Other Eateries • Midnight Movies • Expert Contributor Wendy Mitchell: *My Five Favorite Dive Bars in New York*

Chapter 10: **Only in New York** p. 345

Unique Sites & Activities • Coney Island • The Best Bathrooms • Famous Faces at the Bar • One-of-a-kind Restaurants • Favorite New York Characters • Expert Contributor AJ Jacobs: *My Five Favorite Facts I Learned about New York from Reading the Encyclopedia*

Indexes and more:

The Best New York Websites: **p. 372** *Main Index:* **p. 375** *Index by Neighborhood:* **p. 386** *Calendar of Annual Events:* **p. 394** *Free Activities:* **p. 395** *Kid-friendly Activities:* **p. 396** *Restaurants, Food Markets, and Bars:* **p. 398** *About the Authors:* **p. 400**

ACKNOWLEDGMENTS

Whatever the body of work, acknowledgments often begin from the premise that it would not have been possible to create it without the people named. This book is no different, except that in this case, it's true in more ways than one.

The first thanks goes to the people at Universe who trusted us with this book in the first place—Charles Miers, Ellen Nidy, and Kathleen Jayes. Another thanks to Kathleen, our editor, for helping us persevere through this wonderful but unwieldy project with her hard work, patience, and encouragement. Also thanks to Nancy King, Elizabeth Smith, and Sylvia Karchmar, our copyeditors, and Tricia Levi, whose contributions included a mastery of the subway system for which we are extremely grateful.

We would especially like to thank our expert contributors— Rick Bell, Joseph O. Holmes, Bret Watson, David Masello, Andrea Strong, Francisco Liuzzi, Laura Dave, Pavia Rosati, Wendy Mitchell, and A. J. Jacobs—for their expertise, generosity, and enthusiasm when we contacted them (or, in one case, accosted them at the gym) about contributing to this book. We'd also like to thank Alison Lowenstein, who also generously shared her NYC expertise with us, and Allan Ishac, whose ideas for great things to do in New York are limitless.

Finally, we would like to thank all of the people—friends, family members, acquaintances, and a few that we never even met—who shared their personal lists of bests with us over the last year and a half. Your tips were invaluable, and through them we discovered many, many wonderful things about New York. There are too many of you to name, but you know who you are, and you can find your suggestions all over the book.

PREFACE TO THE SECOND EDITION

It took a two-week autumn vacation for the English half of this writing partnership to fall in love with New York and move here. But before that came twenty-five years of getting to know the city from afar, the way the rest of the world gets to know it—through the movies, the music, the photographs, the books, the T-shirts, the crossing signs, and all the icons of landscape and kinks of character that have come to define New York more by reputation alone than any other city on the planet.

That "the city's really changed" is a belief voiced frequently by lifelong New Yorkers. In this city, perhaps more than in any other, it's true: things change quickly here, whether you're talking politics, demographics, economics, or the best place to get a grilled cheese sandwich. What's also true is that along with all the inherent gripes—eulogies for times past, laments for landmarks lost—this refrain is an implicit acknowledgment of what keeps the city alive. As the character of one neighborhood moves in a new direction, so the character of the next goes another. The constant regeneration is what keeps New Yorkers on their toes, what inspires them to continue to explore, and what requires them continually to renew their enthusiasm for the city. As easily as the relics of the way things used to be fade into memories, new ways become the norm, and in New York, "the way things used to be" might only mean last week.

To love New York, you must love old and new in equal doses. You've got to be able to embrace change while keeping an affectionate grip on the past. You have to lament CBGB's, hope that Chumley's reopens, but take a cue from Florent as his restaurant went softly, chicly into the night. You must respect legends, but be too cool for sentimentality—though not cool like a faux-cool that sends you charging blindly into every Brand New Thing. You have to be able to hold on until you need to let go. This isn't easy—but true love never is, and anyway, easy is never what New York's been about.

If you do manage to toe the line, to flirt with both muses, oh how you'll be rewarded. In every place, through all of your senses, at every hour of the day. Because on top of the variety, on top of the electricity, on top of the steamy pressure, the adventure, and the insouciance that comes from being the city that all others compare themselves with is a mix of intimacy and desire that anyone who's ever put a foot down has gotten a whiff of, and that keeps those of us who live here faithful and enamored, committed to our city, and endlessly inspired by it.

- Jacob Lehman and Caitlin Leffel

INTRODUCTION

New York is the ultimate metropolis, a true melting pot, a city with an ocean, rivers, lakes, islands, and the sound; home to some of the world's premier art and culture, the restaurant capital of the world, and the city that never sleeps. Yes, there's a lot you can do here. But with so many activities, across so many areas, all the time, it is no small task to wrap your head around the infinite number of offerings, and to uncover all the treats hidden in the city's nooks and crannies. Plus, among all the possible things that one can do, there are some that are better than others, and more than a few (1,001, as we found out) that are truly, unequivocally great. In *The Best Things to Do in New York*, we have crossed genres and boroughs to find the city's best offerings. A city guide like no other, we have gone beyond locations and events to tap into the variety of experiences in this city, from $10 manicures to $700 dinners; subterranean wonders to views from staggering heights; edifying classes and offbeat activities to classic haunts and historic landmarks—and everything in between.

When Jacob and I were first approached about doing this book, I remember thinking "One thousand and one—how are we ever going to come up with that many really good things to do?" Having grown up in New York, I was acutely aware of the city's riches—world-class museums, historic sites, glamorous shops, restaurants of every shape, size, and taste—and I certainly appreciated my proximity to such largesse. But despite their elite status in guidebooks and tour itineraries, great treasures alone do not best things make. As anyone who has fought crowds, stood in interminable lines, or borne unsubstantiated attitude can tell you, it is the quality of the overall experience that catapults an activity over the bar of the simply impressive and into the realm of the supremely special and indisputably enjoyable. As I happily discovered, there are plenty of the latter type of experiences to be had here, things that are wonderful, incredible, and exceptional in more ways than I could have imagined. In this book, we have drawn from months of research and hundreds of visits to select what we believe are the best experiences of this city, and laid them out as specifically as possible. Visiting the Met, for instance, *can* be a wonderful experience—but, frankly, it can also be frightfully overwhelming. So instead of simply telling you to visit, we've suggested taking a museum highlights tour, and making an appointment for a private viewing of the drawings collections, a special amenity offered by the museum that is easily overlooked in the shadow of its grandeur. We also aimed to be both open-minded and critical, which meant trying things that may not have been to our particular taste, and not including entries for stock New York activities unless they satisfied our exacting criteria for a "best thing." Certain things, which will remain nameless, did not make the cut because—despite their fame or reputation or longevity—they were not exceedingly pleasant experiences when viewed objectively. In other cities, fame or longevity might have carried more weight but in New York, the competition is stiff.

Also contributing to my initial feeling of being daunted by the scope of the project was that, in my adult life, I confess, I had become lazy. My New York was a city within the city, existing inside a ten-block radius from my apartment in Manhattan to my office, both downtown, with occasional, activity-specific forays uptown and to Brooklyn—plus vivid memories of certain things that I loved as a kid. But when we started this project, I began carting out those memories—like watching chess at Washington Square Park with my dad, and being excited and intimidated by those fast-handed renegades; or standing transfixed for as long as my mom would let me in front of the marbles at the Forbes Gallery; or school field trips to the Queens Hall of Science—and I was eager to see whether they were still as magical as I remembered (they all were, only more so). Then I realized that there were dozens of things that I did daily, weekly, or in season—bike rides along the Hudson River, literary readings at bars and bookstores, great meals at all sorts of different places, walks around new neighborhoods—that, while not necessarily standard guidebook fare, were special, often idiosyncratic experiences, each terrific in its own right. And from there, I started to think about all the things that I had wanted to do, was curious about trying, or that I had heard about but had never gotten around to, like taking a continuing-education class at NYU or the New School, visiting the Lower East Side Tenement Museum, or going to that Bohemian beer garden in Queens that people kept telling me about. At that point, I was convinced that not only were there 1,001 really, really great things to do here, but that there was also a need for someone to pluck them out from the rest of the city's offerings. Jacob and I accepted the challenge.

Of course, that was only the beginning. Many of the entries we ended up with are things that a year ago, I hadn't even heard of. That is in large part thanks to Jacob's pioneering spirit and infectious enthusiasm about the city. A relatively recent transplant to New York, Jacob awed me with his breadth of knowledge about my hometown (you can touch Cole Porter's piano in the Waldorf lobby? Who knew?), and earned his stripes many times over with his remarkable eagerness to explore (you have him to thank for all of the entries on City Island). We also hunted down treasures through research and tips from friends and family (so as not to confine readers to the range of our tastes). I can't tell you how surprised I was to learn that there is a real, working farm in Queens, or how often I used Hopstop.com to plan a fact-finding excursion, and one of the nicest evenings I spent all year was the class I took at the Miette Culinary Studio with my cousins.

Ultimately, this book changed from being a seemingly insurmountable task to a true labor of love, stoking my fascination with New York anew with every chapter. I have deepened my affection for this city, and my appreciation for its unique character and multitude of amazing and unexpected facets. Throughout the process, Jacob and I were wowed again and again by new discoveries and the delectable treats we unearthed from place to place. We hope that you will have as much fun as we did.

—Caitlin Leffel

HOW TO USE THIS BOOK

O ur book is intended to be inspirational and informative, livelier than a regular guidebook but with the same practical information that will allow you, our readers, to get up and go. Our only base requirement for consideration was that something be a legitimately great thing to do, regardless of reputation, sentimental value, or location. For our research, we scoured New York City to its farthest reaches for its best offerings, and then tried to pare these down to only the truly, indisputably wonderful. Our primary goal (and challenge) was to inspire without overwhelming, and rouse you from your home, hotel room, or subway car to partake of New York's most special offerings.

In keeping with this "inspirational" objective, we have divided the book by theme rather than by specific activity or location. We chose not to rank entries, because after narrowing down all of the best things to do, it seemed beside the point to compare whether the view from the top of the Empire State Building was better than, say, a meal at one of the city's best restaurants. The themes of the chapters are what we deemed to be, broadly speaking, the ten best categories of things to do in New York, including one for all of the idiosyncratic features that can't quite be categorized as anything but "Only in New York." We have delved into every place, site, activity, and service listed in each of these chapters—large and small, famous and unknown—to find the things that make each one particularly great. Most of the time, we centered the entries around a special facet of the place or activity, but occasionally, for certain large entities (the Empire State Building, Grand Central Terminal, Central and Prospect Parks, for example), we divided the sites into different entries according to features that we felt were special and distinct enough to stand on their own. We have tried our best to keep our delineations clear, and not subdivide specific places too much, but to help you, our readers, we've meticulously cross-referenced the book, so if you are reading about, for instance, the New Year's Eve run at Central or Prospect Parks in the "24-Hour Fun" chapter, you'll be able to easily find the main entry for each park in "The Great Outdoors." In the back, we've also included indexes that will make it easier to find activities in certain locations or categories. Also, to bridge the gap between a printed book and the constantly changing city, we've also included our favorite Web sites for local information and services. We would also like to note that the Internet is a perfect chronicler for the city that never sleeps, and we strongly recommend using it as much as possible when planning outings and events. Although we have included the most up-to-date information for every entry, providing phone numbers, subway directions, and more, details on prices, hours, and other specifics are always subject to change. Not only do Web sites reliably deliver the most current information (and as we found out, usually more efficiently than a phone call), they also provide updates on new features, exhibits, and offerings.

The best way to use this book is to read it. Sure, you could just use it to look things up, and yes, if you check the index, you will be able to find the page where we list, for instance, the opening hours for MoMA. But if you merely glance at the main entry for the museum, you'd miss what a local art critic considers his favorite painting there, a tip about the view from the fifth-floor café, and reading about the museum's incredible film program. Instead, we suggest that you spend some time with this book—read entire chapters, flip through different sections, follow our cross-references. There's a lot more in here than just general overviews and practical info, and so much to discover about places you are thinking of going—as well as places you've already been. In addition to the entries themselves, we've also included little-known facts we discovered called "Did you knows?", historical notes about famous people and places, and a section in each chapter in which local experts share "five bests" in their area of expertise.

Several times during the process, we were asked whom the book was for—tourists or residents. The answer is both—really. Even if you are a New Yorker who can remember when riding the subway cost a dime, you'll find plenty of things to take advantage of in these pages, including special delivery services, continuing education classes, and all-night gyms. And for those of you who are visiting, there is a wealth of activities to enjoy, many not covered by other guidebooks and all with the logistical information you need to enjoy them. Both groups of readers will, we hope, relish discovering, remembering, and experiencing the city's finest treasures.

CHAPTER 1:

The Classics

W hen thinking about the best things to do anywhere, it's easy to ignore the obvious and hunt for the obscure. This is even easier in a place with the diverse character and the trendsetting inclinations of New York City. With so much that's new, unusual, and ephemeral, there is a tendency to seek out the cutting edge and to discount anything that might be on the itinerary of a high school field trip. Yet, though they're well known, easy to spot, and often very crowded, places like the Statue of Liberty, the Empire State Building, and the Brooklyn Bridge are undeniably among New York's greatest assets. They are symbols of the city, representing the magnificence, the power, and the imagination for which New York prides itself.

But, of course, it's not only the celebrated sites across the city skyline that have made New York what it is today. There are shops, hotels, bars and restaurants, sporting events, and even grocery stores with influential provenances, each full of treasured relics and forgotten secrets that point to the rich and eclectic history of the tastes, fashions, lifestyles, and achievements of New Yorkers through the ages. What makes a place or an experience "a classic" has to do more with its history than its fame or age. Sites of memorable events, yearly rituals, or remnants of bygone eras also symbolize significant facets of our city, from the historic to the idiosyncratic. Moreover, these iconic tidbits come from many periods of the city's history, both recent and long-gone—from the colonial years, through the Roaring Twenties and Prohibition, to the high-rolling eighties and then on into their current incarnations. In this chapter, you'll find places of all kinds that have figured prominently in the development of the city's character, from the sites of famous events to legendary old haunts and some good, old-fashioned New York activities worth waiting in line for.

Sadly, some of these spots have surely seen better days. Places like the Ziegfeld Theater or Tavern on the Green are no longer in their heydays, but because of their colorful history we feel that they still merit an entry. The fact that something is still standing is not necessarily enough to make it a "best," but since so many legendary places are gone without a trace (Max's Kansas City, the famous '60s hangout, is a deli; both Ebbets Field and the Polo Grounds are now the sites of apartment complexes), any place that was a stomping ground for so many New York characters in its heyday—and hasn't been turned into a luxury condo development or a Starbucks—deserves a salute.

1. Climb to the top of the **Statue of Liberty**–again!

Consider this: it took France twenty years, 450,000 pounds of steel and copper, multiple national fundraising campaigns, and 214 shipping crates to get the Statue of Liberty to her home in Manhattan harbor—all as a gift to us. It is no wonder then that the Statue of Liberty is such an inspiring landmark. The enormity of the project aside (including the extra year, additional 27,000 tons of concrete for the pedestal, and exhaustive fundraising efforts it took on our shores before she was presented to the public), Lady Liberty has stood sentry before the city of New York since 1886, and she has become a symbol of both the city and the nation, of freedom and friendship. Viewing her from across the Hudson River, you can appreciate how she watches over the city with a strong, unwavering gaze; viewing her from up close and inside, you can appreciate the magnificent feat of engineering, cooperation, and patriotism that brought her here. After September 11, 2001, visitation to the statue was restricted for security reasons. In 2004, the pedestal, base, and observation deck were reopened, but the crown remained off limits to visitors. On July 4, 2009, the crown reopened to the public, and visitors to Liberty Island with adequate stamina (it's a 354-stair climb, and the inside can get very hot) can now make the journey to the top. (The crown visit requires an extra ticket, and reservations must be made in advance.) You don't have to go nearly so high to see the torch—the statue's original torch is located in the lobby. (The torch was replaced in 1986.) Also located closer to ground level is the Statue of Liberty Museum, which features exhibits on the construction, history, and influence of one of the most recognizable artifacts in the world. Afterward, you can continue on to **Ellis Island** (see below) on the same ferry that you arrived on.

Open daily, except Christmas Day. Admission to the pedestal, base, and museum is free, but there is a fee for the ferry. Crown reservations are $3 per person. Reservations for the ferry are recommended, and can be made by visiting www.statuecruises.com or calling 1-877-LADY-TIX. A limited number of same-day reservations may be available at the ferries on a first-come/first-served basis. Ferries depart from Battery Park in lower Manhattan and from Liberty State Park in New Jersey. For more information on the statue, call 212-363-3200 or visit www.nps.gov/stli.

2. Look for your ancestors at **Ellis Island**.

Almost half of all Americans can trace their roots through the doors of Ellis Island. Ellis Island was designated as the national immigration station at the end of the nineteenth century, when control of immigration was taken over by the federal government. Some 2 million people passed through it on their way to becoming Americans between its opening in 1892 and its closing in 1954, sometimes thousands a day. (And despite its reputation as the "Island of Tears," most immigrants made it through in a couple of hours, and only 2 percent were sent back.) The Ellis Island Museum is located in a beautifully restored Beaux-Arts–style building, where the immigrants were processed and examined before being given permission to enter the country. There are exhibits, artifacts, documents, and oral histories about Ellis Island and the immigration experience, plus many resources for tracing your genealogy. You can browse through the immigration records at the American Family Immigration History Center, and then go outside to see the Wall of Honor, on which are inscribed the names of more than 600,000 courageous immigrants.

Open daily, except Christmas Day. Admission is free. Ellis Island is accessible by the same ferries that serve the Statue of Liberty; see previous page for details. For more information on the museum, call 212-363-3206 or visit www.ellisisland.org.

3. Go to the top (or almost to the top) of the **Empire State Building**.

The Empire State building is the quintessential skyscraper, and its illuminated figure is the centerpiece of the Manhattan skyline. Constructed in the early 1930s as part of a contest to build the world's tallest building, the Empire State Building eclipsed the Chrysler Building by a few hundred feet. (And, perhaps more impressive to New Yorkers, was completed ahead of schedule, in just one year and forty-five days.) After the Depression, the Empire State Building came to define Midtown Manhattan as modern, exciting, and full of promise, inspiring the building of other skyscrapers around town. It remained the tallest building in the world for more than four decades, until the World Trade Center towers were built in the mid-1970s. Between its grand Art Deco style and its astonishing size, the ESB (as it's sometimes known) is an incredible site, both to behold and to look down from. If the additional $15 admission fee to the observatory on the 102nd floor seems steep, the view from the eighty-sixth floor is more than spectacular.

350 FIFTH AVENUE BETWEEN 33RD AND 34TH STREETS IN MANHATTAN. Subway: 6 to 33rd Street; B, D, F, V, N, R, Q, W to 34th Street-Herald Square. Eighty-sixth-floor observatory open daily (see page 81); tickets to the 102nd floor must be purchased in person on the day of visitation. For more information on hours and ticket prices, visit www.esbnyc.com. For Empire State Building lights, see page 317. For Empire State Building Run, see page 360.

4. Take a trip to a foreign land at the **United Nations**.

The eighteen-acre UN complex along the East River is designated international terri-tory, outside of the jurisdiction of the city and the state (though we don't advise try-ing to hide out there to evade a parking violation). On the tour, which is offered, not surprisingly, in dozens of different languages, you'll see the General Assembly Hall, as well as special exhibits and a collection of art and artifacts from member nations. (Because of construction, tours of the conference building, which includes the cham-bers of the Security Council, are currently suspended.) Afterward, you can sample the local cuisine in the **Delegates Dining Room** (see page 205), and then send a postcard from the UN post office, with a special United Nations stamp from its land of origin.

FIRST AVENUE BETWEEN 42ND AND 48TH STREETS IN MANHATTAN. Subway: 4, 5, 6, 7 to Grand Central-42nd Street. Tours offered daily, about every half hour. For more information, sched-ules, and ticket prices, call 212-963-TOUR or visit www.un.org/tours.

→ *DID YOU KNOW? When New York City was chosen to host the early Security Council meetings of the United Nations, it was in far less formal surroundings than the UN complex: the swimming pool of the Bronx campus of Hunter College served as a postwar assembly hall for the young diplomatic organization, and is responsible for bringing Winston Churchill to the Bronx for the first time.*

5. Walk (or bike) across the **Brooklyn Bridge**.

For a real treat, time your trip so that you can see the sunset. When you make it to (or back to) the Brooklyn side, stop in for some coal-oven pizza at **Grimaldi's** (a Sinatra favorite—see page 206).

Subway: (for Manhattan) 2, 3, J, M, Z to Fulton Street, 4, 5, 6 to Brooklyn Bridge-City Hall, A, C to Broadway-Nassau Street; (for Brooklyn) A, C to High Street.

6. Pretend to be a World War II flying ace at the *Intrepid*.

If you think the skyscrapers make you feel puny, try looking up at the *Intrepid* from the pier below. Commissioned for action during World War II, the aircraft carrier also served during the Vietnam and Cold wars, and later was used by NASA as a recovery vessel. Inside, the museum has some great interactive exhibits (such as flight simula-tors and naval navigation demonstrations), but to really feel like you're part of the crew, head to the hangar and flight decks. There, you can see and explore the museum's collection of vintage and modern aircraft, from actual fighter planes that landed on the carrier during World War II to a retired British Airways Concorde jet. After that, head to the Growler, a Cold War–era submarine and the only one left in existence that has fired nuclear missiles. Particularly, well, intrepid couples can even have their weddings on board.

PIER 86 BY 46TH STREET AND THE HUDSON RIVER IN MANHATTAN. Subway: A, C, E to 42nd Street-Port Authority Bus Terminal. For more information, ticket prices, and operating hours, call 877-957-SHIP or visit www.intrepidmuseum.org.

7. Take refuge in St. Patrick's Cathedral...

Part of this church's spiritual majesty comes from its location: it's right in the middle of one of the most famous shopping strips in the world, its great Gothic spires towering above Fifth Avenue. The contrast between its architectural magnificence and the surrounding retail extravagance is stark, and rather awe-inspiring. Mass is held every day of the week (the church seats a congregation of 2,200), but you can come in between masses to explore the church's many fine details, such as the great rose stained-glass window and, fittingly, an altar designed by Tiffany & Co. Even when the cathedral is as crowded as the department stores across the street, there's a solemnity that takes you away from the earthly chaos outside.

14 EAST 51ST STREET AT FIFTH AVENUE IN MANHATTAN. Subway: B, D, F, V to 47th-50th Streets-Rockefeller Center. 212-753-2261. wwwsaintpatrickscathedral.org.

→ **DID YOU KNOW?** *The first televised midnight mass was broadcast from Saint Patrick's Cathedral on Christmas Eve, 1948. Today, televised masses at Saint Patrick's are broadcast daily on local channels.*

8. ...or be humbled at the Cathedral of Saint John the Divine.

Saint John the Divine is considered the largest cathedral in the world and is one of the most drawn-out construction projects in the country. The cathedral has been under construction on and off since the cornerstone was laid in 1892, and it's still not quite "finished." However, despite the ongoing work, it remains one of the city's most remarkable sites, as well as a powerful and moving spiritual center. In addition to the grand, Gothic-style features, such as the famous nave, which is the size of two football fields, what is particularly uplifting about the cathedral is its unmistakably ecumenical spirit. The Chapel of the Seven Tongues, for instance, is an homage to New York's diversity, made up of special chapels dedicated to seven saints, each chapel representing a country or ethnicity of the people that helped build the church. Saint John's also glorifies the arts; it is home to a gold triptych by the artist Keith Haring (his only religious work) as well as numerous concerts, performances, and literary events. Visiting Saint John's is a stirring experience no matter what your faith, and its glorious, unfinished state is a poignant metaphor for our own lives.

1047 AMSTERDAM AVENUE NEAR 110TH STREET IN MANHATTAN. Subway: 1 to 110th Street (Cathedral Parkway); B, C to Cathedral Parkway (110th Street). 212-316-7490. www.stjohndivine.org.

9. Check out the tombstones in the churchyard at **Trinity Church**...

Alexander Hamilton and Robert Fulton are among the notable early Americans buried in the churchyard of this historic neo-Gothic church. One of the oldest churches in the country, it was built in 1697 as an Anglican church chartered by the king of England. During the period of the Revolution, some of the parishioners took part in the Continental Congresses, while the clergy remained with the Crown, and Trinity's destiny mirrored that of the country as a whole. After the war, the church's charter was ratified by the newly independent state of New York, freeing it from paying dues and declaring loyalty to the British monarchy, and in 1789, its rector was appointed the first bishop of the new diocese of New York. The church building, having burned down in 1776, was rebuilt and reopened in 1788. (This second structure was destroyed in 1839 and rebuilt for a third time.) In between the construction of the first church and the second, services were held at nearby Saint Paul's Chapel, part of the Trinity parish, including a thanksgiving service for George Washington after his inauguration as president.

Open daily. 74 BROADWAY AT WALL STREET IN MANHATTAN. Subway: 1, N, R, W to Rector Street; 4, 5 to Wall Street. 212-602-0800. www.trinitywallstreet.org.

→ **DID YOU KNOW?** *Saint Paul's Chapel, located at Broadway and Fulton, is the oldest public building in continuous use in New York City.*

10. ...and at **Trinity Cemetery**.

Confusingly, the main burial ground of Trinity Church is located all the way uptown, on a plot of land that was part of the former Audubon estate. (Trinity parish bought the land from the family in 1842, when an ordinance was passed prohibiting burials in lower Manhattan.) It is the only active burial ground in the borough of Manhattan, although burials are now restricted to direct descendants of those already interred there. In addition to John James Audubon, the naturalist, the cemetery contains the graves of John Jacob Astor and Clement Clarke Moore (author of the poem "A Visit from Saint Nicholas"), as well as beautiful and elaborate mausoleums, vaults, and tombs of many one-time prominent and affluent New Yorkers.

Open daily. 770 RIVERSIDE DRIVE IN MANHATTAN. Subway: 1 to 157th Street; C to 155th Street. 212-368-1600.

11. See the Rockettes at **Radio City Music Hall**.

Originally a dance troupe from St. Louis called the "Missouri Rockets," the Rockettes captivated audiences with their flying kicks when they performed at Radio City Music Hall's opening night in 1932, and they have been dancing there ever since. If you think that what today's pop stars do on stage is dancing, then you're in for a treat. Performing in the traditional Radio City Christmas Spectacular, as well as other events during the year, their acts consist of intricately choreographed routines of eye-high kicks performed in perfect tandem. The costumes are more beautiful than ever, and thanks to modern technologies like Lycra and spandex, have only gotten shorter and tighter. This is one of the few venues where it's entirely appropriate (and practically inevitable) to ogle the girls' legs.

SIXTH AVENUE, BETWEEN 50TH AND 51ST STREETS IN MANHATTAN. Subway: B, D, F, V to 47th-50th Streets-Rockefeller Center; N, R, W to 49th Street. 212-307-7171. (Christmas Hotline is 212-307-1000.) www.radiocity.com.

12. See the city from the **Circle Line**.

Of all the traditional tourist attractions, this is one that plenty of New Yorkers agree is a pretty great thing to do, and unlike some other famous activities, something that many have actually done themselves. The three-hour Full Island cruise gets you a view of all five boroughs, plus three rivers, seven bridges, and two dozen major landmarks; the two-hour Harbor Lights cruise does a semicircle around Manhattan in the evening. You can sit and listen to the jaunty commentary, or get some wine, and toast the city from the deck.

Sightseeing cruises leave from PIER 83, 42ND STREET AND THE HUDSON RIVER IN MANHATTAN. Subway: A, C, E to 42nd Street-Port Authority Bus Terminal. For information, schedules, and prices, call 212-563-3200 or visit www.circleline42.com.

Grand Central.

Grand Central Terminal has stood in the heart of New York City for nearly a century, and its presence and influence have shaped the development of the city's Midtown area. Constructed over a decade between 1903 and 1913 through the combined efforts of two architecture firms (Reed and Stern, and Warren and Wetmore), the terminal came to embody the dashing, cosmopolitan lifestyle of the city as much as the Empire State Building, the Chrysler Building, the Waldorf-Astoria, and the other buildings that grew up around it.

Though it is nominally a train station, anyone who's ever been to Grand Central knows that it is so much more. Over the course of its existence, Grand Central has been home not only to trains but also to a host of other distractions: an art gallery, an art school, various exhibitions, a museum, bars, restaurants, stores, and shoeshine stands. On top of this, the building itself is full of secrets and stories that will forever be part of New York legend (Franklin Delano Roosevelt's secret passage from the station to the Waldorf-Astoria, for one). Declared a National Historic Landmark in 1978, and beautifully restored to its original glory in 1998, the terminal is both a mine of New York history and a very real part of New York life today.

42ND STREET BETWEEN LEXINGTON AVENUE AND PARK AVENUE IN MANHATTAN. Subway: 4, 5, 6, 7, S to Grand Central-42nd Street.

13. *Find your way to the Campbell Apartment, the "secret" bar upstairs at Grand Central Terminal.* This warm, oak-paneled, stone hall was formerly the property of John W. Campbell, the fabulously wealthy business tycoon who bought the corner of the railway station in the 1920s and transformed the space into a distinguished Renaissance-style apartment, which served as his office by day and a club for private parties by night. The bar is grand, old-fashioned, and cozy, and the bartenders know how to mix a very strong martini. There is an entrance to the bar from Vanderbilt Avenue, but the real aficionado will seek out the elegant Art Deco elevator down in the station concourse.

15 VANDERBILT AVENUE AT GRAND CENTRAL TERMINAL. 212-953-0409. www.hospitalityholdings.com.

14. *Tell a secret to someone on the other side of the room at the whispering gallery.* Standing in opposite corners of the concourse, you can face the wall and have your voice travel across the curve of the domed roof. The faintest whisper will sound on the other side as if you were only a foot away.

WHISPERING GALLERY, DINING CONCOURSE.

15. *Get your shoes shined outside Grand Central.* You can't get into the **Campbell Apartment** without good, shiny shoes. Take a chair outside the main entrances on 42nd Street and enjoy people-watching in one of the busiest parts of Midtown.

16. *Have an old-fashioned lunch at the Oyster Bar.* This landmark restaurant has been located "below sea level" in Grand Central since 1913, the year the terminal opened. Today, the Oyster Bar is a bastion of lunchtime civility, surrounded as it is by an entire dining concourse of fast-food options. So when "working lunches" and toss-your-own salads get you down, retreat to the Oyster Bar, and enjoy some of New York's best seafood (including nearly thirty kinds of oysters)—and maybe a martini or two— before heading back to the office.
LOWER LEVEL. 212-490-6650.www.oysterbarny.com.

17. Welcome Eloise back to **the Plaza**.

This eminent hotel (and National Historic Landmark) figures prominently in the collective memory of New Yorkers and people from around the world. This is where Eloise played, Macauley Culkin hid out, Cary Grant was kidnapped, and Tony Soprano had some crazy dreams. The Plaza (so named because of its location across from Grand Army Plaza) has been a fixture on Fifth Avenue for more than a hundred years; when the hotel opened in 1907, rooms cost less than the tip you'd leave today for a drink at the famed Oak Bar. In April 2005, the Plaza checked out itself, closing for a $400-million renovation. The Plaza reopened in 2008, and in May of that year, after an extended vacation in a storage facility in New Jersey, the famous Eloise portrait returned to its official residence opposite the Palm Court for what is hopefully another long stay.
FIFTH AVENUE AT CENTRAL PARK SOUTH IN MANHATTAN. 212-759-3000. www.theplaza.com.

18. Bounce on the keyboard at **FAO Schwarz**.

It was a nightmare right out of the Brothers Grimm when FAO Schwarz buckled to the pressure of the toy chain behemoths and closed its beloved Fifth Avenue playground, to the horror of kids, New Yorkers, and doll collectors and Lego fans around the world. But there's a happy ending, at least for now: in December 2004, the iconic Fifth Avenue store was reopened, and it's still stuffed to the seams and piled high with every toy, game, doll, or amusement imaginable. But as big kids know, a trip to FAO Schwarz is more about the experience than what you bring home, and they will be happy to hear that FAO hasn't dispensed with all of the old favorites—you can still dance on the electric keyboard just like Tom Hanks did in *Big*.
767 FIFTH AVENUE AT 58TH STREET IN MANHATTAN. Subway: F to 57th Street; N, R, W to Fifth Avenue/59th Street. 212-644-9400 ext. 4242. www.fao.com.

19. Go ring shopping (or pretend to) at **Tiffany**.

Between the little blue box, the diamond setting that bears its name, and the ubiquitous image of Holly Golightly eating a pastry in front of its Fifth Avenue window, Tiffany is one of the most well-recognized stores in the world. It is a grand old establishment whose rarefied status has perhaps been taken down a notch by an influx of tourists buying $100 signature key chains, but this increased popularity has in fact only enhanced its image as *the* New York jewelry store. And though there are now outlets in shopping malls all over the world, that hasn't stopped thousands of couples from making the trip to the original Fifth Avenue location to buy their engagement rings. (Not to mention the ones who come in asking for Cracker Jack rings to be engraved.)
FIFTH AVENUE AT 57TH STREET IN MANHATTAN. Subway: E, V to Fifth Avenue/53rd Street; N, R, W to Fifth Avenue/59th Street. 212-755-8000. www.tiffany.com. For more on jewelry stores, see Chapter 7.

Watch the Fourth of July Fireworks.

Macy's Fourth of July Fireworks is the biggest fireworks show in the country; it uses more than fifty times the number of fireworks than the average American display. Each year, tens of thousands of fireworks are set off from river barges in a spectacularly choreographed show. The barges are usually docked in the East River, but in 2009 were moved to the Hudson in honor of the 400th anniversary of Henry Hudson's voyage to New York. In the past, fireworks displays have also taken place simultaneously on the East and Hudson rivers, by South Street Seaport, and in front of the Statue of Liberty. Exactly where the best spots to watch will be depends on where the fireworks happen, but here are some reliable standbys.
Macy's Fourth of July Fireworks show starts at 9:00 p.m. on July 4. For specific information on the show, check newspapers or visit www.macys.com.

20. The FDR Drive: When the show is on the East River, the traditional Manhattan viewing point is on the FDR Drive, between 14th and 42nd Streets. If you want a good seat, you'll have to get there a few hours before the fireworks start, and be prepared for crowds, security checks, and a lot of sitting around (use the bathroom before you go). However, this is the best view you can get of the fireworks; they go off right above your head.
The fireworks can be viewed from the southbound lane of the FDR Drive between 14th and 42nd Streets. Accessible by taking the ramp at 23rd, 38th, and 42nd streets, starting at 7:00 p.m. Subway: 6 to 23rd Street, 33rd Street, and 4, 5, 6 to Grand Central-42nd Street.

>>> **TIP:** *If you can't (or don't want to) get to the FDR Drive early enough to get a seat, try heading to Midtown around when the fireworks begin and walk east. You can get a good view of the show overhead from anywhere east of First Avenue from the 20s through the 40s.*

21. Gantry Plaza State Park: At this waterfront park, you can get a clear, unobstructed view of the fireworks that are sent off the barges on the East River, set against the Manhattan skyline.
474 FORTY-EIGHTH AVENUE ALONG THE EAST RIVER IN QUEENS. Subway: 7 to Vernon Boulevard-Jackson Avenue; E, V to 23rd Street-Ely Avenue.

22. Brooklyn Heights Promenade: In years when there are shows on both the East River and by South Street Seaport, this is a cool place to watch because you can see them both. Crowds are sizable but not unmanageable. If you're lucky enough to be on top of a building, depending on where you are in the area, you can even see the display coming from Liberty State Park, too.
BETWEEN MONTAGUE AND MIDDAGH STREETS ALONG THE EAST RIVER IN BROOKLYN. Subway: 2, 3 to Clark Street; A, C to High Street; M to Court Street; N, R to Court Street-Borough Hall.

23. Hudson River Park: If fireworks return to the Hudson River, the lower portion of Hudson River Park is a good place to watch them. And if you aren't too far uptown, you'll also be able to get a view if there are fireworks being set off by South Street Seaport.
WEST SIDE OF MANHATTAN ALONG THE HUDSON RIVER. For best fireworks viewing, check location of barges.

24. Take a carriage ride in **Central Park.**

Though plenty of New Yorkers wouldn't be caught dead in one of these, millions of happy couples have made this tourist-heavy attraction a bona fide classic. It's no secret that riding through Central Park in a horse-drawn carriage is one of the most romantic things you can do in the city, and if statistics were kept on the city's most popular spots for a proposal, these buggies might easily top the list. The prices for rides aren't exorbitant ($34 for the first half hour, and $10 for each additional fifteen minutes), and it's not hard to do: the carriages are usually lined up on the south end of the park, waiting for customers. The ride is even more romantic in the winter, when you can cuddle under blankets with your beloved. Just be sure you like your companion, and the cold.

NORTH SIDE OF 59TH STREET BETWEEN FIFTH AND SIXTH AVENUES IN MANHATTAN. *Subway: 1, A, C, B, D to 59th Street-Columbus Circle; F to 57th Street; N, R, W to Fifth Avenue/59th Street; Q to Midtown-57th Street.*

25. See a **Broadway show**.

Not sure what's playing? ***Playbill's* official Web site** has synopses, performances times, and theater locations for all Broadway shows. Also on the Web site is information about and listings for shows with standing room or lottery policies. These are special tickets available at the box office on the day of the performance, from the time the box office opens until it sells out. The policies vary from show to show (some give preference to students; some give only one ticket per person; many are cash only), the availability is completely unpredictable, and waits are inevitable—however, if you have time to wait in line and don't mind standing, this is a great way to see a sold-out show that you wouldn't be able to catch otherwise.

    If you don't have your heart set on a certain show and have some time, you can also try your luck at one of the three **TKTS booths**. At the Times Square booth, you can buy tickets for shows on the same day; the South Street Seaport and Brooklyn locations have same-day tickets for evening performances, and next-day tickets for matinees. These tickets can be up to half the price of what you'd pay at the box office. If you don't want to leave your show all up to chance, visit www.broadway.box.com. The discounts offered on this Web site are typically more modest than those at TKTS, but the selection is better, and you don't have to wait until the day of.

    For a completely authentic Broadway experience, pair your evening with a meal at one of the joints on "Restaurant Row," the famous strip of restaurants lining 46th Street between Eighth and Ninth Avenues. **Joe Allen** is a reliable place to see the stars when they're not on stage—and the food is good, too. (Tip: Go after the shows let out.) *Playbill's official Web site is www.playbill.com. For information on the TKTS booths, visit the Theater Development Fund's Web site, www.tdf.org. For tickets through Broadway Box, visit www.broadwaybox.com. Joe Allen is at 326 West 46th Street between Eighth and Ninth Avenues. 212-581-6464. www.joeallenrestaurant.com. Subway (for both): 1, 2, 3, 7, N, Q, R, W, S to Times Square-42nd Street; A, C, E to 42nd Street-Port Authority Bus Terminal.*

→ **DID YOU KNOW?** *Many Broadway shows adopted lottery policies after the '90s hit musical* Rent *started reserving the first two rows of the orchestra for $20 day-of tickets to accommodate students and other young people who made up a big part of the show's fan base.*

26. Watch the **New York City Marathon**.

The New York City Marathon has grown from a modest, low-budget race around Central Park to the premier long-distance running event in the country. For the first incarnation, in 1970, only a small crowd of people showed up to watch 127 runners compete for old bowling trophies (the marathon's entire budget was $1,000). Today the race attracts tens of thousands of runners—who compete for more than $500,000 in prize money—as well as millions of spectators. And the competition begins long before race day: nearly 100,000 athletes from around the world vie for 35,000 spots that are selected by lottery. The course was expanded in 1976 and now travels through all five boroughs, starting from the Staten Island side of the **Verrazano-Narrows Bridge** (see page 68), then passing through Brooklyn, Queens, across Manhattan to the Bronx, and back into Manhattan to finish in Central Park. The marathon has been the site of record-setting victories, stunning accomplishments and upsets, and even played a part in the most infamous episode in the history of modern footraces. Rosie Ruiz, who received a respectable finish time of 2:56:29 in the 1979 marathon, was later revealed to have traveled part of the course on the subway. (The hoax was uncovered six months later, when she completed the Boston Marathon in record time, after jumping into the race from the crowd a few miles before the finish line.)

Since we're not in good enough shape to attempt it ourselves, we can't vouch for how great running the marathon actually is. Watching it in person, however, is an exciting way to soak up New York spirit. Seeing this great spectacle from the street is exhilarating and breeds heartwarming camaraderie, as everyone cheers the athletes as they go by. Check the map—you can pick any spot along the route and cheer for free. For the best view of the finish line, you can purchase tickets for bleacher seats adjacent to it, which also have a view of a big-screen broadcast of the runners as they approach.

First Sunday in November. VIP seating (bleacher seats) costs $75; members of New York Road Runners are eligible for a discount. For more information, call 212-423-2249 or visit www.ingnycmarathon.org.

27. Watch the **U.S. Open**.

The U.S. Open, which will celebrate its 130th anniversary in 2010, has grown from humble beginnings as an amateur singles championship in 1881 into the biggest grand slam event on the tennis world circuit. It is to New York what Wimbledon is to London, capturing the character of its locale, enjoyed by tennis fans and non-tennis fans alike. Watched by millions around the world on television, it is a great event to see up close. The USTA's magnificent National Tennis Center is in Flushing Meadows Corona Park, the large and beautiful park in Queens that has hosted two World's Fairs (1939 and 1964) and is home to the Unisphere, the globe sculpture from the 1964 fair, and **Citi**

Field (see below). Whether you have seats in the Arthur Ashe Stadium for the final, or you're strolling around the park watching the games on giant TV screens outside the grounds, the Open is as much a New York event as a sporting one.

USTA NATIONAL TENNIS CENTER, FLUSHING MEADOWS CORONA PARK IN QUEENS. Subway: 7 to Willets Point-Shea Stadium. www.usopen.org.

28. Get to a Yankee game early, and visit **Monument Park**.

Even the most rabid Boston fan will grudgingly admit that the Yankees have a monumental history. Since 1932, the team has honored its many greats with a collection of plaques and monuments known as Monument Park. Originally, these plaques were located on the outfield wall of the original Yankee Stadium. In the '70s, when that stadium was remodeled, the monuments were moved to a fenced-in area by the bullpens and christened Monument Park. When the team moved into its new home before the 2009 season, the park came with them, and before the game starts, you can still pay tribute to Yankee heroes like Babe Ruth, Lou Gehrig, Mickey Mantle, and Joe DiMaggio, Yogi Berra, Phil Rizzuto, and longtime Yankee broadcaster, Mel Allen.

161ST STREET AT RIVER AVENUE IN THE BRONX. Monument Park is open to ticket holders on game days, from the time gates open until forty-five minutes before the game starts. Subway: 4, B, D to 161st Street-Yankee Stadium. For more information on batting practice, directions, and hours, call 718-293-4300 or visit newyork.yankees.mlb.com.

29. Take in a game at Shea—er, **Citi Field**.

Mets fans have long had a tough lot in the major leagues. The team is prone to promising starts followed by stupendous late-season collapses, and Shea Stadium, their home for forty years, was, to put it charitably, a very quirky place to visit. Citi Field, which opened in the shadow of Shea in 2009, is a vast improvement on the team's former digs. It's easy to navigate, boasts good sight lines, and is full of pleasant distractions for when the Amazins aren't looking so hot. The main attraction (besides the game) is behind center field: Taste of the City is a pleasant, open-air food court, with an outpost of **Shake Shack** (see page 166), a Mexican taquería, a fish place, and plenty of picnic tables and other comfortable spots to stand and watch the action while you eat. But fear not, Citi Field still has plenty of quirks. You still hear planes overhead from nearby LaGuardia airport, and an apple still pops up when the Mets hits a home run. (It's a new apple, though the original has been imported from Shea and is on view by the bullpen.) And strangest of all is the grand entryway to the stadium, called the Jackie Robinson Rotunda, which features a memorial to Robinson's career—even though he wasn't a Met.

123-01 ROOSEVELT AVENUE IN QUEENS. Subway: 7 to Willets Point-Shea Stadium. For more information, directions, and practice schedule, call 718-507-TIXX or visit www.mets.scom.

30. Watch the New York Knicks play at **Madison Square Garden**.

This may be one of the more difficult things to do in New York: however well (or poorly) the Knicks are doing, tickets to games are always in demand, and with good reason. The Garden is New York's most famous arena, and the Knicks have played basketball there since its opening in 1968; its status in basketball and city history was cemented when the team won its very first championship there in 1970. If you manage to get seats, you can expect to rub shoulders with the cream of New York celebrity. Of course, the Knicks aren't the only game in town—the Garden is also the home stadium to the Rangers and the WNBA team, the New York Liberty, as well as serving as the premier rock concert site in Manhattan, a legendary boxing venue, and the place to see the circus when it comes to town.

SEVENTH AVENUE BETWEEN 31ST AND 33RD STREETS IN MANHATTAN. Subway: 1, 2, 3, A, C, E to 34th Street-Penn Station. 212-465-MSG1. www.thegarden.com/sports_knicks.jsp.

31. Hear tonight's jokes before anyone else at a **late night talk show**.

New York has been home to the nation's sharpest bedtime storytellers since Steve Allen charmed the nation with the first *Tonight Show* in 1954, a late-night companion to one of the longest-running television shows in history, NBC's *Today Show*. Since then, New York's evening comperes have been the best loved in the business, with legendary hosts like Ed Sullivan and Johnny Carson bringing the biggest stars to the city, launching the careers of countless actors and comics, and cementing the city's reputation as the cultural mouthpiece of the nation. While Johnny, Jay, and Conan have been lured out west to Hollywood, New York City still boasts the hosts with the most—David Letterman and Jon Stewart.

N.B.: Age restrictions apply to all three, so bring your ID and don't get your hopes up if you're under eighteen—they make no exceptions. LATE SHOW WITH DAVID LETTERMAN: 1697 BROADWAY BETWEEN WEST 53RD AND WEST 54TH STREETS. Subway: B, D, E to Seventh Avenue. www.cbs.com. THE DAILY SHOW WITH JON STEWART: 733 ELEVENTH AVENUE BETWEEN 51ST AND 52ND STREETS. Subway: C, E to 50th Street; 1, A, C, B, D to 59th Street-Columbus Circle. www.comedycentral.com.

32. Check out the **Christmas windows**.

It's a grand old New York tradition, and each store has its own look, so visit them all for the full seasonal effect. (Tip: escape the crowds by going at night, after the stores have closed.)

Start downtown with Macy's. The annual window displays aren't as lavish as those at some of the other stores, but the annual Miracle on 34th Street windows that line 34th Street are nice to stop by after a visit to **Santaland** (see page 346).

Then move over to Fifth Avenue to Lord & Taylor. Lord & Taylor was the first of the department stores to do themed Christmas windows, a legacy that they take very seriously. Their windows are poised on freight elevators, so they can be lowered and assembled in the basement (as opposed to the other stores, who must cover their windows while they are being dressed). The most traditional of all the holiday displays, their windows use elaborate décor and intricate details, usually to tell an explicitly Christmas-themed story.

From there, it's a few blocks up to Saks Fifth Avenue, whose windows are often just as packed as those at Lord & Taylor. Their windows also tend toward popular classic Christmas themes, and their location just across from the Christmas tree at Rockefeller Center (see below) doesn't hurt.

Then wander up to **Bergdorf Goodman** (see page 243) for the elegant and fashion-forward creations overseen by window-dresser extraordinaire, Linda Fargo.

Finally, head over to Madison Avenue for Simon Doonan's whimsical display at **Barneys** (see pages 244–245). The cheekiest of the bunch, Doonan's windows are naughty and nice, with humorous or satirical twists mixed into the holiday spirit. (Doonan's windows are crowd-pleasers all year round and always worth checking out.)

Christmas windows are usually unveiled in November and stay up until just after New Year's. All of the following locations are in Manhattan:

Macy's: 151 WEST 34TH STREET BETWEEN BROADWAY AND SEVENTH AVENUE. Subway: 1, 2, 3, A, C, E to 34th Street-Penn Station; B, D, F, V, N, Q, R, W to 34th Street-Herald Square.

Lord & Taylor: 424 FIFTH AVENUE AT 39TH STREET. Subway: B, D, F, V to 42nd Street-Bryant Park; 7 to Fifth Avenue-Bryant Park.

Saks Fifth Avenue: 611 FIFTH AVENUE AT 50TH STREET. Subway: B, D, F, V to 47th-50th Streets-Rockefeller Center.

Bergdorf Goodman: 754 FIFTH AVENUE AT 57TH STREET. Subway: F to 57th Street. Barneys: 660 MADISON AVENUE AT 60TH STREET. Subway: N, R, W to Fifth Avenue-59th Street.

33. Visit the Christmas tree in **Rockefeller Center**...

For the most pleasant visit, try going at night. There'll still be plenty of tree-viewers around (unless there's a blizzard!), but at least you won't have to contend with the regular daytime pedestrians. Plus, the tree is that much more dazzling against the night sky. *The tree is up from the end of November through New Year's and is lit from 5:30 a.m. to 11:30 p.m. Best viewing is from Fifth Avenue between 47th and 50th Streets. Subway: B, D, F, V to 47th-50th Streets-Rockefeller Center. For more information, visit www.rockefellercenter.com.*

34. ...or go skating underneath it.

There's no need to visit this tiny rink (it can accommodate only 150 skaters at a time) except at Christmastime, when you can skate right up close to the famous Rockefeller Center Christmas tree. If you go at prime times, you will pay handsomely for the privilege of twirling around underneath the nearly 100-foot-tall tree, but the rink also offers discounted admissions at certain times on weekdays.

The rink is open daily, October through April, and is located in the middle of Rockefeller Center. Subway: B, D, F, V to 47th-50th Streets-Rockefeller Center. Call 212-332-7654 for information, prices, and schedules. www.therinkatrockcenter.com.

35. Learn about Revolutionary War—era history at **Fraunces Tavern**.

Though there's no plaque, it's very possible that at some point George Washington slept here. He certainly did plenty of other things here, including, most famously, giving his troops a farewell address after the Revolutionary War before returning to Mount Vernon. But the modest three-story building on Pearl Street is much more than just the place where the founding fathers came to drink. Founded as the Queen's Head by Samuel Fraunces in 1762 (the name was changed after the Revolution), this tavern played many parts during the nation's formative years. The New York Chamber of Commerce was founded here in 1768, and after the Revolution it was used as the offices for the Departments of Treasury, War, and Foreign Affairs. Operated by the fraternal organization Sons of the Revolution, the museum displays a collection of American art and artifacts from colonial, revolutionary, and early federal years, such as paintings, furniture, weapons, documents, personal artifacts, and flags. You can also visit the Long Room, where Washington delivered his farewell address. Downstairs, have a bite or a drink at the colonial-themed bar and restaurant. And if you end up there on a whim, fear not: staying true to our founding fathers' spirit of freedom, the restaurant does not enforce a dress code.

54 PEARL STREET AT BROAD STREET IN MANHATTAN. Subway: 2, 3 to Wall Street; 4, 5 to Bowling Green; J, M, Z to Broad Street. For more information, hours, schedules, and prices, call 212-425-1778 or visit www.frauncestavernmuseum.org.

→ **DID YOU KNOW?** *Before the building that became the tavern was erected, this was the site of the city's first landfill.*

36. Get a custom-flavored prescription filled at **C.O. Bigelow**.

Bigelow, the oldest apothecary in the country—Mark Twain used to fill his prescriptions here—is a New York institution par excellence. (Mr. Bigelow, the store cat, had his obituary in the *New York Times*.) Shopping at Bigelow feels like an experience out of another, chain-free world, not only because of the old-fashioned wooden counters from which chemists fetch the products you want, but also because of the eclectic selection of goods. In addition to the staples available at mainstream drugstores, you'll find homeopathic products, lots of hard-to-find and high-end international brands, and all sorts of gorgeous accessories, particularly for hair. At the pharmacy, you can get your medicine custom flavored and then delivered to your door.

414 SIXTH AVENUE, BETWEEN 8TH AND 9TH STREETS IN MANHATTAN. Subway: A, C, E, B, D, F, V to West 4th Street. 212-533-2700. www.bigelowchemists.com.

---

37. Get a straight-razor shave at the **Paul Molé Barber Shop**.

A proper straight-razor shave is a dying art—and a luxurious treat. Paul Molé has been in business in the same narrow barbershop on the Upper East Side for close to a century, and getting a shave here hasn't changed much since then. An authentic experience from the warm, steamed towels down to the sharp silver blade, the barbers are reassuringly experienced and deliver the best shave in the city. You'll leave looking and feeling a better man.

1031 LEXINGTON AVENUE BETWEEN 73RD AND 74TH STREETS IN MANHATTAN. Subway: 6 to 77th Street. 212-535-8461.

---

38. Look for famous faces (part 1) at **Elaine's**.

Celebrity is never far from this legendary Upper East Side restaurant, where the imperious Elaine Kaufman has been shielding the likes of Woody Allen, Michael Caine, Candace Bushnell, and other famous New Yorkers from oglers since its opening in 1963. Elaine's reputation as a legendary hostess has grown from her generosity toward irregularly paying writer friends and from her ruthless efforts to keep out the riffraff—she has been known to have fistfights with unwanted diners and to eject more common customers in favor of a big name or two. While other restaurants run hot and cold like a bad brownstone faucet, Elaine's has remained a refuge for a certain veteran celebrity set, who've been going there since before anyone knew their names.

1703 SECOND AVENUE BETWEEN 88TH AND 89TH STREETS IN MANHATTAN. Subway: 4, 5, 6 to 86th Street. 212-534-8114.

---

39. Look for famous faces (part 2) at **Sardi's**.

Plenty of theater-district restaurants have a regular roster of famous patrons, but the only one that can truly guarantee that you'll see stars is Sardi's. Started in 1921 as The Little Restaurant by Vincent Sardi, it quickly became a clubhouse for Broadway stars.

At the first Tony Awards in 1947, Sardi was honored for "providing a…home and comfort for the theater folk at Sardi's for twenty years." The restaurant's claim to fame is the collection of caricatures, an idea that Sardi got from a well-known restaurant in Paris. Some 1,300 portraits line the wall, drawn in a harsh, exaggerated caricature style that has famously angered some of the models. (Maureen Stapleton allegedly stole her portrait and burned it and didn't come back to the restaurant until Vincent Sardi Jr. took it over and wrote her a note saying that all was forgiven. She returned, and a new portrait of her was done in 1996.) The current house caricaturist, Richard Baratz, does around twenty new portraits each year. Before it is hung, each new caricature is unveiled privately before the "honoree" over a champagne toast, presumably to prevent any further Stapleton-style disappearances. (Though even theft may not do the trick—rumor has it that the restaurant keeps duplicates of each drawing, a measure taken after James Cagney's portrait was stolen after his death.)

234 WEST 44TH STREET, BETWEEN BROADWAY AND EIGHTH AVENUE IN MANHATTAN. Subway: 1, 2, 3, 7, N, Q, R, W, S to Times Square-42nd Street; A, C, E to 42nd Street-Port Authority Bus Terminal. 212-221-8440. www.sardis.com.

→ **DID YOU KNOW?** *The first Sardi's caricaturist, Alex Gard, refused to be paid for his work, and instead drew in exchange for meals. According to legend, to maintain a good working relationship, Sardi couldn't criticize the portraits, and Gard couldn't criticize the food.*

40. Visit **Tavern on the Green?**

Tavern on the Green, the ornate glittering palace in Central Park, has perhaps the most humble provenance of any restaurant in New York: it originally housed the sheep that grazed on Sheep Meadow. Now a solid fixture of New York history, the tavern's unpretentious start in the late nineteenth century was just the beginning of its long and bumpy journey to becoming one of the most well-known restaurants in the world. It has opened, shut down, and reopened, always to much fanfare; it has been used for movie scenes, hosted premiere parties, and is the New York wedding cliché; and its illuminated façade peeking out of the park is one of the most familiar images of New York. A $10 million renovation in the mid-1970s turned it into the over-the-top wonderland, full of the decorative features that New Yorkers loved to hate. The crystal chandeliers, hand-painted murals, abundant floral bouquets, carved mirrors, and copper and gold-leaf weather vanes gave it an opulent if slightly anachronistic feel, kind of like a Mad Hatter's tea party on an unlimited budget. Alas, the restaurant fell on hard times again, and in August 2009, it was announced that Dean J. Boll, the proprietor of the restaurant at the Central Park Boathouse, would take over Tavern from the Le Roy family, which had operated it since the seventies. At time of press, plans are being hammered out for a renovation of the sprawling prically, the food has been, well, what you might expect from a lavishly ...action, but going to Tavern on the Green for the food would be like walk-...p of the Eiffel Tower for exercise—theoretically possible, but entirely beside ...ut who knows what the next incarnation will bring?

CENTRAL PARK WEST AT 67TH STREET IN MANHATTAN. Subway: B, C to 72nd Street; 1 to 66th Street-Lincoln Center; A, C, B, D to 59th Street-Columbus Circle. 212-873-3200. www.tavernonthegreen.com.

→ ***DID YOU KNOW?*** *In 1934, when the legendary New York Parks Commissioner Robert Moses decided that the old sheepfold should be turned into a restaurant, he shipped the sheep out to* **Prospect Park** *(see pages 222–223), and reassigned their shepherd to the lion house in the Central Park Zoo.*

41. Have a "Red Snapper" at the St. Regis Hotel's **King Cole Bar.**

Named for the Maxfield Parrish mural depicting the Mother Goose character that graces the wall, this bar occupies an important part of cocktail history: it claims to be the birthplace of the Bloody Mary—though here they still call it by its "real" name, the Red Snapper. (The bartender who invented the drink also worked at a bar in Paris; "Bloody Mary" was what they called it there.) Order a Red Snapper, and then hunker down in one of the leather club chairs with a fancy tray of nuts and bar snacks, and you'll feel classy and authentically big-time.

2 EAST 55ᵀᴴ STREET AT FIFTH AVENUE IN MANHATTAN. Subway: E, V to Fifth Avenue/53ʳᵈ Street. 212-753-4500. www.stregis.com.

→ ***DID YOU KNOW?*** *The bar's namesake mural was actually made for another hotel, the Knickerbocker, on Broadway and 42ⁿᵈ Street, where it originally hung after it was completed in 1906. When the Knickerbocker closed during Prohibition, the mural was saved and eventually relocated to the St. Regis in 1935.*

Make time for tea.

For a glimpse into the civilized city of yesteryear, there's no more effective way to do it than with afternoon tea. Though not the institution that it is in London, afternoon tea here is an uncommonly decadent pleasure, a vestige of an old-fashioned, high-class world where people with the means didn't think twice about pausing to enjoy an extra meal. In addition, tea is a fitting way to take in the legendary grandeur of some of the city's longstanding bastions of high society. The following hotels are themselves classic New York haunts from this lost era of leisure and refinement, and enjoying an authentic, well-appointed afternoon tea at one of them is the best way we can think of to appreciate their legacy and be transported back to their glory days.

42. *The Lounge at the Pierre Hotel.* For years, the Pierre and the Plaza engaged in a subtle rivalry across Fifth Avenue, each proudly standing as its own version of the grand New York hotel. The Plaza was the showier of the two, while the Pierre exuded a more discreet kind of charm. Each has undergone recent renovations, but at the moment, the subdued grandeur of the Pierre is the surer bet for tea. If you can summon up the courage to penetrate the hotel's forbiddingly posh exterior (Tip: the main entrance is on 60th Street, not under the canopy on Fifth Avenue), tea in the comfortable, renovated lobby lounge is a nice reward. (Tea is served every day from 3 to 5 p.m.) Before you leave, make sure to take a peek inside the hotel's famous Rotunda room, a visual feast of romance and sumptuous color, and lavish trompe l'oeil murals depicting gods and goddesses along a perfect blue sky. Some of the figures in the murals depict the hotel's former patrons; see if you can find the one that's supposed to be Jackie O.
FIFTH AVENUE AT 61ST STREET IN MANHATTAN. Subway: N, R, W to Fifth Avenue/59th Street. 212-838-8000. www.tajhotels.com.

43. *Astor Court at the St. Regis Hotel.* Right across from **King Cole's Bar** (see opposite) is the posh Astor Court restaurant. Afternoon tea at Astor Court (served daily from 3:00 p.m. to 5:00 p.m.) is more elegant than decadent, with abundant flowers, the requisite trompe l'oeil ceiling, and first-class table settings. The harpist who often plays during teatime adds an additional touch of refinement.
2 EAST 55TH STREET AT FIFTH AVENUE IN MANHATTAN. Subway: E, V to Fifth Avenue/53rd Street. 212-753-4500. www.stregis.com.

44. *The Cocktail Terrace at the Waldorf-Astoria.* Since its inception, many famous figures have resided at this grand Art Deco hotel, among them Cole Porter, who immortalized one of the hotel's other well-known features, the Waldorf salad, in his song "You're the Top," from the musical *Anything Goes.* Porter wrote many of his most famous lyrics at the Waldorf Towers, where he lived in style for a quarter of a century, from the late 1930s until near his death in 1964. Porter's light-colored Steinway—covered in his own coffee cup circles and cigarette burns—still sits in a balcony lounge called the Cocktail Terrace. They won't let you play it, but they do have someone playing when the lounge is open (Wednesday through Sunday), and during breaks, you can go up and inspect it. You can have a drink here in the early evenings, as the name implies, but they'll send you across the lobby to Sir Harry's Bar when they start to close up around 8:00 p.m., so afternoon tea is the way to go. Served until 5:30 p.m., tea at the Cocktail Terrace is light, gay, and relatively laid-back as teatime goes. Instead of sitting up straight at well-appointed tables, you can languish in plush sofas or sink into easy chairs and, shielded from onlookers, dip your scones to your heart's content.

WALDORF-ASTORIA HOTEL, PARK AVENUE LOBBY, 301 PARK AVENUE BETWEEN 49TH AND 50TH STREETS IN MANHATTAN. Subway: 6 to 51st Street; E, V to Lexington Avenue/53rd Street. 212-872-4818. www.waldorfastoria.com.

→ **DON'T MISS:** The Wheel of Life, *the enormous mosaic on the floor of the lobby, just inside the Park Avenue entrance, below the cocktail terrace. The mosaic depicts six stages in the life of man in colorful, stunning detail.*

45. *Lady Mendl's Tea Salon at the Inn on Irving Place.* Though not technically a classic spot (the inn has been open only since 1994), this exquisite salon exudes a formal air that recalls another time and comes with an excellent provenance. The inn is housed in two connected nineteenth-century townhouses, whose original architectural details have been preserved. As befitting its namesake (Lady Mendl was the title acquired by the turn-of-the-century decorator Elsie de Wolfe when she married), the salon is resplendent and impeccably furnished with Victorian accoutrements. Lady Mendl's serves a proper high tea seven days a week: a dainty feast comprises five courses of salads, sandwiches, scones, and sweets.

56 IRVING PLACE, BETWEEN 17TH AND 18TH STREETS IN MANHATTAN. Subway: 4, 5, 6, L, N, Q, R, W to 14th Street-Union Square. For reservations, call 212-533-4466. www.innatirving.com.

46. Hobnob with the jet set at **Harry Cipriani**.

Opened in 1985 by the son of Giuseppe Cipriani, a Venetian restaurateur from the early-to-mid-twentieth century, Harry Cipriani is a duplicate of Harry's Bar Venice, the famous ex-pat hangout patronized by Ernest Hemingway, Orson Welles, the Aga Kahn, and Peggy Guggenheim. The list of regulars at the New York restaurant is nearly as luminous (though it would be uncivilized to name names). The restaurant is physically connected to the Sherry-Netherland, an exquisite residential hotel, and shares with it the same charmed and clubby atmosphere. It's the kind of place where people have regular tables, a meeting ground of the well known and the well-to-do. **Cipriani Downtown** is a less formal version of Harry Cipriani and a perpetual socialite hangout. It's where young heirs and heiresses go after they've fine-tuned their social skills at the Fifth Avenue location. *718 FIFTH AVENUE AT 59ᵀᴴ STREET IN MANHATTAN. Subway: N, R, W to Fifth Avenue/59ᵗʰ Street. 212-753-5566. Cipriani Downtown, 376 WEST BROADWAY AT BROOME STREET IN MANHATTAN. Subway: C, E to Spring Street. 212-343-0999. www.cipriani.com.*

47. See Woody Allen play at the **Carlyle Hotel**.

Many people come to the Carlyle to see **Ludwig Bemelmans's *Madeline* murals** (see page 39) in the bar that bears his name. But a slightly less-well-known feature of the Carlyle is the fact that Woody Allen has a regular Monday night gig at certain times of the year at the Café Carlyle supper club. For a $100 cover, you can see New York's most famous living native son pick up the clarinet and perform with the Eddie Davis New Orleans Jazz Band.

35 EAST 76ᵀᴴ STREET AT MADISON AVENUE IN MANHATTAN. Subway: 6 to 77ᵗʰ Street. 212-744-1600. Visit www.thecarlyle.com for current performance schedule.

48. Drink a martini at the **Washington Square Hotel**.

There are not many places in the world that can be said to be equally evocative of Bob Dylan and Henry James, but the Washington Square Hotel looks and feels spiritually connected to all eras of Washington Square's vivid cultural history, from the beautiful and anachronistic wrought-iron awning to the dark, speakeasylike cellar bar. (Dylan, in fact, is reported to have been a resident during his Village days.) The heavy mahogany practically screams for a cigarette and a martini, and while the lack of the former will remind you what century you're in, the latter, when sipped in this secret, windowless nook, will transport you to a New York of another time.

103 WAVERLY PLACE AT MACDOUGAL STREET IN MANHATTAN. Subway: A, C, E, B, D, F, V to West 4ᵗʰ Street. 212-254-1200. www.northsquareny.com.

→ ***DID YOU KNOW?*** *Before it was a park, chess mecca, and the symbol of NYU, Washington Square Park was the site of a potters' fields and several church burial grounds. The city estimates that the remains of nearly 20,000 bodies buried between 1797 and 1825 may still be lurking underneath the park—an estimate corroborated by the unearthing of a 200-year-old tombstone during the park's 2008 renovation.*

49. Hang out in the lobby of the **Hotel Chelsea**.

If New York City is a place where the unconventional retreat from all corners of the world, then the Chelsea Hotel is their temple. This bastion of eccentricity on West 23rd Street has a long and checkered history as a home, hangout, and refuge for some of the most radical artists of the past century. This is where Sid killed Nancy (and then himself), where Dylan Thomas lived out his last booze-filled year, where William Burroughs wrote *Naked Lunch*, and where Andy Warhol filmed *Chelsea Girls*. Built in 1883 in what was then the city's burgeoning theater district, it was New York's first cooperative apartment complex and was the tallest building in the city until 1902. After the theater district migrated uptown around the turn of the century, 23rd Street quickly became commercialized, the residential building folded, and in 1905, it was turned into a hotel. Mark Twain and members of the Ashcan School were among the early guests and tenants who established the Chelsea's reputation as a haven for artists. More recently, the hotel had a featured role in Joseph O'Neill's award-winning 2008 novel, *Netherland*. (The author and his family live in the hotel.) These days, it still attracts an offbeat and arty crowd, both in the guest rooms and the apartments. Evidence of the hotel's illustrious past can be seen in the lobby, which displays an art collection that rivals those of the **galleries** (see page 143) that have cropped up a few blocks west. Tours of the hotel are offered several times a year by veteran front-desk manager Jerry Weinstein.

222 WEST 23RD STREET BETWEEN SEVENTH AND EIGHTH AVENUES IN MANHATTAN. Subway: C, E to 23rd Street. 212-243-3700. www.hotelchelsea.com.

---

50. See an arty movie at the **Paris Theater**.

Sandwiched between Bergdorf Goodman and the Plaza stands this little one-screen movie theater. Before the **Angelika,** the **Sunshine**, and **Film Forum** (see pages 158–160), the Paris was showing foreign and other outside-of-Hollywood movies, many of them the films that we consider classics today. This fifty-year-old theater has stood its ground against multiplexes and skyrocketing rents; it's known for its unusual programming (including some famous long runs—Franco Zeffirelli's *Romeo and Juliet* played here for over a year) and old-fashioned movie-theater sensibility (one screen, no concession stand, no waiting area). Yet despite its anachronisms, and the fact that plenty of "arty" movies can now be seen at other forward-thinking multiplexes, the Paris can still attract a crowd. No matter what the season, people who don't look like they've ever been below 59th Street patiently wait in line for showings of first-run movies like Kenneth Branagh's four-hour *Hamlet* or Merchant Ivory's *Howards End*.

4 WEST 58TH STREET BETWEEN FIFTH AND SIXTH AVENUES IN MANHATTAN. Subway: N, R, W to Fifth Avenue/59th Street. 212-688-3800.

---

51. See an epic movie at the **Ziegfeld**.

Though it doesn't have the same intense nostalgia as the **Paris** (see above), seeing a movie at the Ziegfeld still feels special. There's nothing small or independent about it—it's currently operated by Clearview Cinemas—but this 1,131-seat theater is New

York's last remaining movie palace. The current theater was built in the 1960s on the site of Florenz Ziegfeld's original Ziegfeld Theater. Though the red carpet lining the interior is not as plush as it once was, the theater itself still exudes majesty and large stature. Intimate it's not, but it's a grand old place for a spectacle movie.

141 WEST 54TH STREET BETWEEN SIXTH AND SEVENTH AVENUES IN MANHATTAN. Subway: E, V to Fifth Avenue/53rd Street; F to 57th Street; N, Q, R, W to 57th Street. For showtimes and tickets, call 212-307-1862, or visit www.clearviewcinemas.com.

Shop like they did in the old days.

How—and where—New Yorkers shop for food is both a relic of old-fashioned urban ways and a facet of our intensely pedestrian and cosmopolitan lifestyle. Unlike most of the rest of the country, many New Yorkers still do at least part of their food shopping in family-owned groceries, specialty stores, and local markets. It is an experience broadened by the number of places one passes on a given day and limited only by what can be carried in two hands while walking.

This way of shopping was also perpetuated by the assumption that these types of stores had fresher and more interesting products than the bigger supermarkets. This conviction has been challenged by the arrival of Whole Foods, Trader Joe's, and other specialty food chains—places that many New Yorkers have ambivalent feelings about. Still, even if the stock at places like the stores below is no longer as unusual as it once was, people still seek them out for their reliable quality, knowledgeable proprietors, and idiosyncratic specialties.

The stores below have all achieved unofficial landmark status for their contributions to the city's food shopping. Today, in an increasingly homogenized retail landscape, they are monuments to a unique feature of the New York lifestyle, and something to savor as much as the food they sell. (For more gourmet food markets, see pages 177–178.)

52. Dean & DeLuca. The products may not seem particularly exotic today, but before Dean & DeLuca, most New Yorkers wouldn't have known a loaf of artisan bread if it hit them on the head. The original SoHo branch of this fine-food emporium pioneered the idea of a gourmet grocery store and introduced the city to sundried tomatoes, truffles, and extra-virgin olive oil. Those who shopped at Dean & DeLuca during its early years in the '70s and '80s may fondly remember the generous samples of imported cheeses, decadent pastries, and flavored breads, which previously were attainable only by flying to Europe. (It's also a great place to pick up a delectable free nibble; for more, see pages 285–286.) Today, it is still a reliable source for imported and domestic fine foods and ingredients, and it carries products from other countries that are hard to find elsewhere. It is not an exaggeration to say that Dean & DeLuca played a significant role in shaping the palate of many Americans in the last decades of the twentieth century (as well as defining the neighborhood of SoHo as a cool and cosmopolitan place to be). So take a trip downtown and have an espresso toast to this prominent place in New York's gastronomic development.

The SoHo store is located at 560 BROADWAY AT PRINCE STREET IN MANHATTAN. Subway: N, R, W to Prince Street. 212-226-6800. Additional Manhattan locations can be found at www.deandeluca.com.

53. Zabar's. Zabar's is the granddad of the big Upper West Side food markets. The 80th Street behemoth was born out of a single smoked-fish counter operated by Louis and Lillian Zabar in 1934. Their reputation for high-quality fish at reasonable prices earned them a strong following, and eventually the Zabars took over the entire market. Today, you can buy everything from caviar to coffee appliances here. It's not always the most pleasant place to shop, but consider the crowds and commotion positive signs that it's not going to be turned into a Best Buy anytime soon. Grab some sandwiches and salads to go, and take them over to nearby Riverside Park for a picnic.

2245 BROADWAY AT 80TH STREET IN MANHATTAN. Subway: 1 to 79th Street. 212-787-2000. www.zabars.com.

54. Russ & Daughters. Another family-owned business that started out as a smoked-meat operation is Russ & Daughters. Instead of expanding into other foods and commodities as **Zabar's** did, this beloved Lower East Side institution has largely stuck to fish. You can buy breads, salads, and cookies as well, but it's the herrings, caviar, and smoked and cured meats that have kept people coming for four generations.

179 EAST HOUSTON STREET BETWEEN ORCHARD AND ALLEN STREETS IN MANHATTAN. Subway: F, V to Lower East Side-Second Avenue. 212-475-4880. www.russanddaughters.com.

55. Faicco's Pork Butcher. Situated on the quiet, western end of Bleecker Street, Faicco's has been serving wonderful Italian meats to its Greenwich Village neighbors for more than a hundred years. Treats made from delicious, fresh cuts of pork fill every counter: there are meatballs, cutlets, cured meats, casseroles, pasta sauces, sausages, and special delicacies like the arancini—crispy breaded rice balls stuffed with prosciutto and cheese. The place is always busy and retains a real neighborhood feel: crowds of old Italian women come in for the pastas, meats, and other Italian groceries, while working lunchers stop in to order a sandwich made with Faicco's amazing pork loin. Faicco's makes its own sausage and mozzarella daily and will cut any kind of pork any way you choose.

260 BLEECKER STREET BETWEEN MORTON STREET AND LEROY STREET IN MANHATTAN. Subway: 1 to Christopher Street-Sheridan Square; A, C, E, B, D, F, V to West 4th Street. 212-243-1974.

56. Visit the candles at **John's** of 12th Street.

In 2008, this Italian restaurant in the East Village celebrated its 100th birthday, which is quite a feat in a neighborhood where plenty of restaurants don't make it past five. John's certainly didn't last that long by trying anything cutting edge—the menu is classic, family-style red-sauce Italian and has probably changed little since its opening. (Neither have the payment policies: it's cash only.) To get some sense of what a lengthy tenure the restaurant has had, check out the candles in the restaurant's back room. The cascades of wax have been collecting there since 1937, and serve as a beautiful reminder that new isn't always improved.

302 EAST 12TH STREET, BETWEEN FIRST AND SECOND AVENUES. Subway: L to First Avenue. 212-475-9531. www.johnsof12thstreet.com.

57. Grumble about gentrification at **Pete's Tavern**.

"The tavern that O. Henry made famous" also claims to hold the designation of New York City's longest continuously operating bar. They started serving in 1864 and haven't stopped since, not even during Prohibition, when disguised as a flower shop, Pete's served as a popular speakeasy. O. Henry famously wrote "The Gift of the Magi" seated at one of the booths up front, and despite the fanfare for Ludwig Bemelmans at the **Carlyle Hotel** (see page 279), it was at Pete's that Bemelmans allegedly wrote the first *Madeline* book. But Pete's greatest accomplishment is that nearly 150 years after it opened, it is still a popular neighborhood watering hole.

129 EAST 18TH STREET AT IRVING PLACE IN MANHATTAN. Subway: 4, 5, 6, L, N, Q, R, W to 14th Street-Union Square. 212-473-7676. www.petestavern.com.

58. Get the giggles at **Caroline's**.

Only thirty years old, Caroline's has quickly become Manhattan's busiest and most famous comedy club, hosting new and famous stand-up comics seven nights a week. In 1989, a whole night at the club was filmed for posterity and released as the movie

Caroline's Comedy Hour, which was turned into a hit series on the A&E network. Now in its third locale in Times Square (featuring a décor that earned an award from the American Institute of Architecture), Caroline's attracts the biggest names in today's comedy world, from Jerry Seinfeld to Rosie O'Donnell and Dave Chappelle—and serves a good supper, too.

1626 BROADWAY BETWEEN 49TH AND 50TH STREETS IN MANHATTAN. Subway: 1 to 50th Street; N, R, W to 49th Street. 212-757-4100. www.carolines.com.

See a set at a famous jazz club.

Jazz and New York have gone hand in hand since Duke Ellington, Count Basie, and Billie Holiday lit up the clubs during the Harlem Renaissance of the 1920s and 1930s. As the popularity and reputation of jazz grew through the twentieth century, and as tastes and styles came to shape the districts of the city, jazz venues became beloved fixtures of New York, and the Big Apple became the beloved home of jazz musicians from around the world. Although many of the older establishments are long gone, there still remains a thriving jazz circuit in New York, in the grand revue halls of Harlem, the sophisticated supper clubs of Midtown west, and the underground bars of Greenwich Village. If you stick to these three neighborhoods, good jazz and the remnants of a golden musical age will never be far away. Below are some of our favorites, but it's also a good idea to keep an eye on the local listings for performers, concerts, and new venues.

59. The Lenox Lounge has been a pillar of Harlem's musical community for seventy years. As one of the finer bars and restaurants in the neighborhood it has always attracted locals and tourists alike, and as one of the city's most prestigious venues it has hosted all the legends of jazz through the decades, from Billie Holiday and John Coltrane to Roy Meriwether and Jimmy McGriff. When there isn't a big-name performer onstage, the house bands keep the place jumping with Latin, big band, and jam nights.

288 MALCOLM X BOULEVARD BETWEEN 124TH AND 125TH STREETS IN MANHATTAN. Subway: 2, 3 to 125th Street. 212-427-0253. www.lenoxlounge.com.

60. Birdland. Named for Charlie Parker, who called the original club the "jazz corner of the world," Birdland remains an institution of the Midtown jazz scene that lit up Manhattan in the 1950s and 1960s. Every big name in the history of jazz has played here, and the club's walls are covered in memorabilia of everyone from Duke Ellington to John Coltrane.

315 WEST 44ᵀᴴ STREET BETWEEN EIGHTH AND NINTH AVENUES IN MANHATTAN. Subway: A, C, E to 42ⁿᵈ Street-Port Authority Bus Terminal. 212-581-3080. www.birdlandjazz.com.

61. *Village Vanguard.* On Valentine's Day 2010, this West Village jazz mecca celebrated its seventy-fifth year at the forefront of the New York scene. Since its inception in 1935, this West Village club has hosted some of the all-time greats, from Miles Davis and Thelonius Monk to the masters of modern jazz. Today, the Vanguard still books the best players around, and its acoustics are so revered by the musicians who play here that many have recorded albums on its stage. Go on a Monday night to hear the renowned Vanguard Jazz Orchestra, the house band that has played here for nearly thirty-five years. Note: downtown jazz fans should also have a drink and a listen at **55**, a classic jazz dive that has featured great musicians onstage— and retained a Prohibition-era feel—since 1919.
VILLAGE VANGUARD: *178 SEVENTH AVENUE AT WEST 11ᵀᴴ STREET IN MANHATTAN. Subway: 1, 2, 3 to 14ᵗʰ Street. 212-255-4037. www.villagevanguard.com.*
55: *55 CHRISTOPHER STREET BETWEEN SEVENTH AVENUE AND WAVERLY PLACE IN MANHATTAN. Subway: 1 to Christopher Street-Sheridan Square. 212-929-9883. www.55bar.com*

62. *St. Nick's Pub* is probably the most authentic—and unpretentious— jazz club in the city. Located deep in Harlem's Sugar Hill district, the club is friendly and cheap and the music is always great. Choose the long bar for free over a table on the floor ($20), and you can enjoy simple drinks and great music for old–New York prices. There's live music every night of the week, and local artists frequently come to sit in on a session. Even Stevie Wonder has been known to drop in.
773 SAINT NICHOLAS AVENUE BETWEEN 146ᵀᴴ AND 148ᵀᴴ STREETS IN MANHATTAN. Subway: A, C, B, D to 145ᵗʰ Street. 212-283-9728. www.stnicksjazzpub.net

63. *Vote for the winner at Amateur Night at the Apollo Theater*, the night that helped launch the careers of Ella Fitzgerald, James Brown, and Lauryn Hill. On Wednesday nights, the most famous soul and Motown theater in the world offers its stage to new musicians who might one day become legends—just like the ones you see on the walls of the Walk of Fame, the photographic exhibit of the theater's history set in the hallways backstage.
253 WEST 125ᵀᴴ STREET BETWEEN FREDERICK DOUGLASS BOULEVARD AND MANHATTAN AVENUE IN MANHATTAN. Subway: A, C, B, D to 125ᵗʰ Street. 212-531¬5300. www.apollotheater.com.

64. Feast on design at **Lever House Restaurant**.

Now more than fifty years old, this Park Avenue monument to modern architecture appropriately houses one of the most interesting-looking contemporary restaurants in the city. When it was built in 1952, Lever House was Park Avenue's first glass-covered office high-rise; half a century later, acclaimed designer Mark Newson's modish interior ensures the restaurant's singularity among Midtown's working-lunch spots. Set in a cool, airy room whose décor is at once retro and modern, with a bright bar at one end and booths along one wall, the restaurant's ambience is uniquely quiet and laid-back. The menu is a mix of French and American cuisine, and the fish and poultry dishes are always good. While this is a great (and unusually relaxed) place for an evening meal, Lever House livens up on weekday afternoons, when Midtown hotshots descend in droves for its lunchtime menu.

390 PARK AVENUE AT 53RD STREET IN MANHATTAN. Subway: 6 to 51st Street; E, V to Lexington Avenue/53rd Street. 212-888-2700. www.leverhouse.com.

65. Toast Dylan Thomas at the **White Horse Tavern**.

This West Village pub is New York's quintessential literary haunt—in addition to Thomas, Norman Mailer, James Baldwin, Allen Ginsberg, and Jack Kerouac all drank here. It's a nice old-fashioned place to have a drink, no matter what your passion, but all aspiring writers and poets should make the pilgrimage. If the portraits of Thomas don't get your creative juices flowing, then perhaps the whiskey will.

567 HUDSON STREET BETWEEN PERRY STREET AND WEST 11TH STREET IN MANHATTAN. Subway: A, C, E to 14th Street; L to Eighth Avenue. 212-243-9260.

66. Pass up Pastis for **Odeon**.

Many of today's cool, celebrity-packed restaurants pay homage to Odeon, the Tribeca pioneer immortalized in *Bright Lights, Big City*. This is perhaps because, unlikely as it is, Odeon has managed an enviable feat in the world of New York dining and nightlife: going from hot spot to classic. (The original owner was **Keith McNally**, a restaurateur famously adept at creating sought-after spots, including **Pastis**. For more on McNally, see pages 163–164.) The transition hasn't been seamless, but as many once impenetrable destinations have come and gone, Odeon has hung on by its legendary reputation—and it helps that good bistro food never goes out of style.

145 WEST BROADWAY AT THOMAS STREET IN MANHATTAN. Subway: 1, 2, 3, A, C to Chambers Street. 212-233-0507. www.odeonrestaurant.com.

67. See and be seen at **Indochine**.

This exotic-looking NoHo restaurant was a fixture of the Warhol scene, and just about everyone who's been cool and beautiful in New York in the '80s, '90s, or early 2000s has crossed its threshold. The cuisine is perhaps not the most politically correct (Asian–French Colonial), but that slight anachronism boosts its credibility as a stalwart from another era. Stargazing is still possible, especially if you want to see Warhol's children, all grown up.

430 LAFAYETTE STREET, BETWEEN ASTOR PLACE AND EAST 4TH STREET IN MANHATTAN. Subways: N, R, W to 8th Street. 212-505-5111. www.indochinenyc.com.

68. Drink at the Round Table at the **Algonquin Hotel**.

The Algonquin has long been a celebrated haunt of New York literary types, from the Round Table's origins as a meeting place for such figures as Dorothy Parker and George Kaufman. Since the 1930s, the hotel has allowed a cat free run of the place: look out for the current resident feline at your feet in the Oak Room.

59 WEST 44TH STREET BETWEEN FIFTH AND SIXTH AVENUES IN MANHATTAN. Subway: 7 to Fifth Avenue-Bryant Park; B, D, F, V to 42nd Street-Bryant Park. 212-840-6800. www.algonquinhotel.com.

69. Ogle the interior at the **Four Seasons**.

You may never lead the kind of life where you have a regular lunch table at the Four Seasons, but that shouldn't stop you from eating there on a special occasion. This restaurant defines timeless style. Opened in 1950, the Four Seasons is the only architecturally landmarked interior in New York, but Philip Johnson's modernist design still looks cutting-edge. For lunch, the famed Grill Room is the place to be seated to see the crème de la crème of Midtown working society, but at night, when the movers and shakers have cleared out, the exquisite Pool Room, with its eponymous marble pool and color-changing trees, is the apex of elegant dining.

99 EAST 52ND STREET BETWEEN LEXINGTON AND PARK AVENUES IN MANHATTAN. Subway: 6 to 51st Street; E, V to Lexington Avenue/53rd Street. 212-754-9494. www.fourseasonsrestaurant.com.

70. Eat pizza at **Lombardi's** in Little Italy, at America's very first pizzeria.

Many pizza joints in this town boast that they are "original," but after more than one hundred years on Spring Street, Lombardi's, New York's true original pizzeria, still serves up some of the most delicious pies in the city. Founded in 1905 by Gennaro Lombardi, the restaurant plays the part perfectly: red-and-white checked tablecloths, giant pizzas on silver pedestals, and stuffed calzones—all the good stuff. The lines that run out-side the restaurant most nights of the week testify to its enduring popularity. Although it faces stiff competition from the other **great pizzerias** of the city (see pages 206–208 for a rundown of the best pizza places), Lombardi's remains a favorite, with a warm and lively atmosphere and a menu that defines the American pizza joint. The food here hasn't changed much over the course of a century—the toppings are traditional, the sauces are simple, and the mozzarella is thick and fresh—but why should it? This is pizza the way it is supposed to be.

32 SPRING STREET BETWEEN MOTT AND MULBERRY STREETS IN MANHATTAN. Subway: 6 to Spring Street. 212-941-7994. www.firstpizza.com.

71. Order a frrrozen hot chocolate at **Serendipity**.

Despite woefully tongue-in-cheek touches like "Catcher in the Rye" sandwiches and Andy Warhol look-alike contests (he was once a regular), this eccentric New York insti-tution still charms, a legendary eatery that has hosted celebrities, tourists, families, and sweet-toothed New Yorkers ever since it opened half a century ago. Although you could eat a whole meal here, Serendipity is better known as the home of some of the most delicious and indulgent desserts in the city—enormous chocolate fudge cake sundaes, peanut butter and chocolate ice creams, and banana splits like you wouldn't believe. The trademark dish is the frrrozen hot chocolate, a giant bowl of sweetness that seems bottomless until you finish it and wish you had another. Try sipping one of these from two straws with a sweetheart—it's like being at a classic American soda fountain dreamed up by Warhol.

225 EAST 60TH STREET BETWEEN SECOND AND THIRD AVENUES IN MANHATTAN. Subway: 4, 5, 6 to 59th Street; N, R, W, to Lexington Avenue/59th Street. 212-838-3531. www.serendipity3.com.

72. Have a cannoli (or two) at **Veniero's**.

For more than a century, this has been the place for Italian sweets in the East Village. Opened in 1894 as a pool hall with pastries, the shop and café still has many of its orig-inal architectural details, and a dizzying amount of good, old-fashioned calorie- and cream-laden treats to enjoy. Get a cappuccino and a cannoli (regular or chocolate-dipped), and relax in the cozy café, where you can admire the etched glass doors, exquisite marble floors, and the old-fashioned décor. Then take a number at the counter and get another cannoli to take home for later.

342 EAST 11TH STREET, BETWEEN FIRST AND SECOND AVENUES IN MANHATTAN. Subway: L to First Avenue. 212-674-7070. www.venierospastry.com.

73. Get a table at **Rao's**.

With a long-standing reputation as one of the hardest restaurants in the city to get into, Rao's is a quaint and authentic little Italian restaurant hidden away in East Harlem. A century ago, Rao's was the neighborhood favorite for the local Italian community, and it has since found favor with celebrities, in-the-know uptowners, and lovers of authentic southern Italian cooking all over the city. Call early to reserve a table, or else prop up the bar until there's one available—it can be done.

455 EAST 114TH STREET AT PLEASANT AVENUE IN MANHATTAN. N.B.: Open Monday through Friday for dinner only. Subway: 6 to 116th Street. 212-722-6709. www.raos.com.

74. Power breakfast at **Michael's**.

For a trip back to the glamorous, high-rolling times of the late twentieth century, have breakfast at Michael's. When it opened it the mid-'80s, Michael's was known for its then-exotic California cuisine, stylish contemporary art, and the business breakfast scene. Aside from the hairstyles and shoulder pads, not too much has changed, and you can still see executives hashing out deals over egg-white omelets.

24 WEST 55TH STREET, BETWEEN FIFTH AND SIXTH AVENUES IN MANHATTAN. Subway: E, V to Fifth Avenue/53rd Street. 212-767-0555. www.michaelsnewyork.com.

75. Power lunch at the **Palm**.

Though you can now go to the Palm in Los Angeles, Miami, and Mexico City, the original Second Avenue location has classic New York written all over it—literally. Considered the country's oldest family-owned sit-down restaurant chain, the Palm was opened in 1926 by two Italian immigrants from Parma—which was the restaurant's intended name. However, a language barrier between the owners and the city register resulted in its being known as "the Palm." The cuisine was originally Italian, too, but they started serving steaks at the request of the executives, newsmen, and journalists who worked in the neighborhood. Those steaks—originally purchased from a butcher a few blocks up and carried to the kitchen by hand—garnered a large and loyal following. Eventually they made it onto the menu, and the rest is history. Back when lunch meant sirloins and stiff drinks, and businessmen meant, well, men, the Palm was the place to go. As the rest of Midtown popped up around it, the Second Avenue stalwart held its own for almost fifty years until 1972, when at the behest of then-ambassador to the UN George Bush, they opened their first branch in Washington, D.C. Today, there are more than twenty-five branches, but aside from the addition of lobster to the menu in 1965, nothing much has changed at the New York location.

837 SECOND AVENUE, BETWEEN 44TH AND 45TH STREETS IN MANHATTAN. Subway: 4, 5, 6, 7 to Grand Central-42nd Street. 212-687-2953. www.thepalm.com.

→ **DID YOU KNOW?** *Because they had no money to decorate, the original owners struck a deal with the newspaper artists and cartoonists who frequented the Palm: they could draw on the walls in exchange for a plate of spaghetti. Today, you can see cartoons of Batman, Popeye, and Beetle Bailey by their original artists, and regulars such as Yogi Berra, Francis Ford Coppola, Hugh Hefner, and J. Edgar Hoover immortalized on the walls.*

76. Get a bottle from the wine cellar at **One If by Land, Two If by Sea**.

This cozy West Village restaurant has been a favorite spot for lovebirds and Casanovas for more than thirty years—which in this city of rapid turnover is a feat of longevity in itself. The building's history, however, really dates back another two hundred years. Originally part of Richmond Hill, George Washington's headquarters, the building was first used as a carriage house during the defense of Manhattan in the mid-1700s; after the war, it was purchased by Aaron Burr as his private carriage house. Underneath the restaurant, where the wine cellar is now located, is a series of tunnels that once led all the way to the Hudson River. These tunnels are believed to have been used to smuggle in contraband during the Revolutionary War and were later part of the Underground Railroad.

17 BARROW STREET BETWEEN BLEECKER AND WEST 4TH STREETS IN MANHATTAN. Subway: A, C, E, B, D, F, V to West 4th Street. 212-255-8649. www.oneifbyland.com.

77. Choose between light and dark at **McSorley's Old Ale House**.

Opened in 1854, McSorley's is one of the oldest bars in New York, and it's defiantly old-fashioned. They started letting in women in the '70s; aside from that, everything else is pretty much the same as it was 150 years ago. Drinking at McSorley's is a good antidote to the city's high-pressure, cutting-edge, here-today-gone-tomorrow bar culture. Just don't expect a fancy beer menu: they brew only two types of ale, and you have to buy your drinks in pairs.

15 EAST 7TH STREET BETWEEN BOWERY AND SECOND AVENUE IN MANHATTAN. Subway: F, V to Lower East Side-Second Avenue. 212-473-9148.

78. Drink to New York under the shadow of the Brooklyn Bridge at the **Bridge Café** the oldest business in New York. (The restaurant eclipses

Chase Manhattan, the runner-up, by five years.) The Bridge Café has been operating out of a beautiful old building on Water Street since 1794, when the area around the South Street Seaport was altogether unsavory. These days, the building is much the same and you can still get a rum if you'd like, but the clientele is more city than sailor, and a good wine might go better with the excellent seafood-focused menu.

279 WATER STREET BETWEEN DOVER STREET AND PECK SLIP IN MANHATTAN. Subway: 6 to Brooklyn Bridge-City Hall. 212-227-3344.

Lament a legendary New York landmark that's passed.

Sadly, not every great spot in the city has made it to the present. Gentrifying neighborhoods, skyrocketing rents, changing tastes, and just plain time has brought on the demise of some truly great New York places. Here, we take a moment to remember some of the city's beloved institutions that are no longer with us (and one that's teetering on death's door...):

79. *The Polo Grounds.* Technically, there were four incarnations of the Polo Grounds, the historic baseball field that was home at different points to three New York baseball teams. The first one, where the New York Giants played between 1883 and 1888, was located at the northern tip of Central Park, so called because it had been converted from a polo ground to a baseball field. Polo Grounds II, III, and IV were all located around 155th Street and Frederick Douglass Boulevard, on a site overlooking Coogan's Bluff that is now a housing project. Although Polo Grounds IV is the only one anyone living today might have been to, collectively, the Polo Grounds are a local legend of glory and rebuff. The Polo Grounds are where "the greatest game ever played" was played on October 2, 1951, and where "the shot heard round the world" was hit (ending that same game). It was the longtime home of the Giants, before they left for San Francisco, and it was the first home of the Mets during their first two seasons, before they left for Shea Stadium and the rejected field was laid to rest in 1964. Still, the Polo Grounds may have gotten the last laugh. Who knows what kind of glorious future these two teams might've had if they hadn't left?

Formerly located at 155TH STREET AND FREDERICK DOUGLASS BOULEVARD IN MANHATTAN.

80. *Ebbets Field.* No other lost landmark in the city can more easily bring tears to a grown man's eyes than Ebbets Field, and plenty of baseball fans and longtime New Yorkers are still hurt by the demise of this stadium and the way their team left them. Opened in 1913, the stadium was home to the beloved Brooklyn Dodgers until 1957, when the team's owner made good on a threat to move them out West. The stadium was demolished in 1960 and now is the site of a group of apartment buildings known as the Jackie Robinson Apartments, after the Dodger great.

Formerly located at 55 SULLIVAN PLACE IN BROOKLYN.

81. *CBGB.* CBGB was responsible for bringing punk music to the forefront of the music scene in the 1970s, and it was home to some of the best and most influential bands of that generation. Opened in 1973 by country-music obsessive Hilly Kristal, the club on the Bowery was originally intended to be a bluegrass venue, until the prevailing tastes of the Lower East Side took the music and CBGB in a new direction. Everyone from East Coast favorites like the Ramones, the Modern Lovers, and the Cars, to Television, Patti Smith, Deborah Harry, the Stilettos, and the Sex Pistols graced (and disgraced) its stages, and it boasted the most notoriously abused bathrooms in the city. Sadly for everyone, the club closed with a triumphant final concert led by Patti Smith. In 2007, men's designer John Varvatos moved into the hallowed space, where he's done what he can to keep the surviving details intact—you can still check out the original graffiti in the bathrooms.

Formerly located at 315 BOWERY BETWEEN 1ST AND 2ND STREETS IN MANHATTAN. Subway: 6 to Bleecker Street; F, V to Lower East Side-Second Avenue. 212-982-4052. www.cbgb.com.

82. *Max's Kansas City.* This legendary hangout frequented by artists and performers was a cauldron of creativity that churned with some of the late-twentieth century's great artistic figures. Max's was where everyone came—when everyone was Andy Warhol, Roy Lichtenstein, Patti Smith, Bob Dylan, Bruce Springsteen, and Abbie Hoffman. Deborah Harry waited tables there; the Velvet Underground produced a live album there; both the B-52s and Bob Marley and the Wailers made their New York debuts there. Owner Mickey Ruskin offered advice, fostered creativity, and championed future stars for a few magical years until the '70s, when the magic faded, and Max's disappeared.

Formerly located at 213 PARK AVENUE SOUTH BETWEEN 17TH AND 18TH STREETS IN MANHATTAN.

83. *Kim's Video:* Famously thorough and infamously unpleasant, Kim's Video was a landmark of fine cinema, scrappy service, and wide variety. In an impressive twist on a familiar New York story, Korean immigrant Youngman Kim built his local video rental empire (and a movie collection sought out by cineastes around the world) on a beginning of his renting movies out of a dry cleaners he owned previously. At the height of its reign, Kim's had locations in the East and West Villages and Morningside Heights, but the multilevel location on St Mark's Place was the heart of the minichain. By the late '00s, Kim realized that he was losing a battle to the Internet, Netflix, and iTunes, and announced he was closing his stores. However, his 55,000-copy video collection lives on—intact—in, of all places, a small town in Sicily. When Kim decided to close the stores, he offered to donate his collection on three conditions: that the collection be kept together; that it would be updated; and that it would be available to the public. The only takers who fit the bill were an Italian couple, who are getting the collection up and running in a town called Salemi, which is poised to become something of an artists' and creative colony of the twenty-first century. At time of press, rental privileges for former Kim's members are in the works.

Formerly located at 6 St. Marks Place, between Second and Third Avenues in Manhattan. Subway: 6 to Astor Place.

84. *Chumley's.* Buried in the twists and turns of the far West Village and infamously hard to find, this signless, sawdust-covered dive was one of the city's greatest places for drinking on the sly any time of the year. With a fine selection of ales, excellent pub grub, a working fireplace, and an impressive collection of literary memorabilia from some famous former patrons, Chumley's was an institution whose name spread well beyond the neighborhood. The phrase to "86 it" comes from Chumley's: during Prohibition, patrons were told to "86 it" before a raid, which meant they were to leave by the anonymous front entrance at 86 Bedford Street, and not by the courtyard exit on Barrow. Chumley's closed in 2007, projecting dim hopes of reopening after long-term and major structural repair to the building; it seems unlikely, but all of New York's savvier drinkers still cross their fingers for a miracle.

86 BEDFORD STREET BETWEEN BARROW AND GROVE STREETS IN MANHATTAN. Subway: 1 to Christopher Street-Sheridan Square; A, C, E, B, D, F, V to West 4th Street.

85. *Café des Artistes.* One of the oldest restaurants in Manhattan, Café des Artistes served the well-heeled and bon vivants of the city from 1917 until 2009, when its last owners, having supported the restaurant with millions of their own dollars in its last years, decided to shut it down. Once frequented by artists and creatives like Marcel Duchamp and Isadora Duncan, the café resisted the temptation to innovate, and the old New York feeling was preserved perfectly, right down to the deliberately classic French cuisine (no tofu or lemongrass here). Just after the turn of the century, the neighborhood was largely populated by artists, and the café was opened to serve the residents of the Hotel des Artistes in the building above it. (The rooms didn't have full kitchens, so tenants sent down ingredients and cooking instructions to the kitchen by dumbwaiter.) Even long after the hotel closed, the café retained a bit of an insider feel, catering to cliques of visiting performers from nearby Lincoln Center (the struggling ones had long since been priced out of living in the neighborhood). The atmosphere, however, remained largely unchanged to its last days; the dining rooms were cradled by Howard Chandler Christy's murals of frolicking nymphs, which, nearly a century later, still seemed a little risqué.

1 WEST 67TH STREET BETWEEN COLUMBUS AND CENTRAL PARK WEST IN MANHATTAN. Subway: 1 to 66th Street-Lincoln Center. 212-877-3500. www.cafenyc.com.

Expert Contributor: Ric Bell

THE BEST THINGS TO DO IN NEW YORK

Ric Bell, FAIA, is the Executive Director of the New York chapter of the American Institute of Architects, housed in the Center for Architecture (see page 303).

86. *McGraw-Hill Building*

When completed in 1931, Raymond Hood's horizontally banded McGraw-Hill Building towered over 42nd Street between Eighth and Ninth avenues and the adjacent elevated subway. I worked here for fifteen years, in an open studio with views to the horizon in four directions. A block west of "America's crossroads" at Times Square, its location was linked to New York's zoning regulations—the mixed-use of printing presses and editorial offices was tolerated in Hell's Kitchen. At thirty-three stories tall, it stood alone as Midtown expanded east and north. The distinctive green terracotta sign-band top proclaiming the publishing house's name was illuminated for one night only in the early 1990s.

330 WEST 42ND STREET BETWEEN EIGHTH AND NINTH AVENUES IN MANHATTAN. Subway: 1, 2, 3, 7, N, Q, R, S to Times Square-42nd Street; A, C, E to 42nd Street-Port Authority Bus Terminal.

87. *Municipal Building*

For fifteen months I worked as an architectural bureaucrat in Manhattan's Municipal Building, across the street from City Hall Park. Completed in 1913, the building is the beautiful result of a competition won by McKim Mead & White; seeing photographs and film of "Civic Fame" being reinstalled atop its peak is as close to Fellini as one gets in Manhattan. With over a million square feet of office space for administrators and elected officials, the Municipal Building allowed the diminutive 1812 City Hall to remain the ceremonial center of political power. And with wedding-cake frills and operable windows, the building from the start was a combination of excess and practicality. Straddling Chambers Street, its monumental arch stands as a portal between Manhattan and Brooklyn.

1 CENTRE STREET AT CHAMBERS STREET IN MANHATTAN. Subway: 4, 5, 6 to Brooklyn Bridge-City Hall; J, M to Chambers Street; N, R, W to City Hall.

88. *Lever House*

Seen as a fraternal twin tower to the Seagram Building, Lever House, by Gordon Bunshaft of Skidmore Owings & Merrill, shook up stodgy Park Avenue in ways that the more sober Seagram did not. Lever House is excruciatingly beautiful, elegant in the way that the Rat Pack was elegant and refined in the way that cars of the period are in-your-face. The now-classic use of green glass and the animated creation of an elevated garden and asymmetric open plaza expressed an openness of spirit, an urbanistic clarity befitting the Liverpudlian soap conglomerates' headquarters. With a narrow floorplate assuring that almost every occupant of the building would be near a window and have a view, Lever House expressed premature ambitions toward green architecture; that expression continued in 2008 with a head-to-toe renovation by the Polshek Partnership.

390 PARK AVENUE AT 53ᴿᴰ STREET IN MANHATTAN. Subway: 6 to 51ˢᵗ Street; E, V to Lexington Avenue/53ʳᵈ Street.

89. *Lipstick Building*

John Burgee and Philip Johnson—with help from high-fashion architect Ronnette Riley—took chances at Third Avenue and 43rd Street that they could not take on Fifth Avenue. They created the most feminine of skyscrapers, the so-called Lipstick Building—given its natty nickname for reasons that go beyond its purple-brown urban lipshade. The slender and curving shape of each office floor evokes the form of a cosmetic department purchase, a visible lipstick that you might find hidden among the miniature model towers in Riley's collection. The Lipstick Building—more than 2 Columbus Circle, AT&T, or any other pretender—points out that modernism in New York is skin-deep, and has fun doing so.

885 THIRD AVENUE BETWEEN 53ᴿᴰ AND 54ᵀᴴ STREETS IN MANHATTAN. Subway: 6 to 51ˢᵗ Street; E, V to Lexington Avenue/53ʳᵈ Street.

90. *7WTC*

The new 7WTC tower by David Childs of Skidmore Owings & Merrill (opened in May 2006) replaces its namesake, destroyed on September 11, 2001. It is a superb building that reminds me of Danny DeVito in *Twins*—all dressed up, and waiting for the bigger sibling. Where previously there was a roadblock, the new building permits a Greenwich Street–view corridor to the World Trade Center site. Reconstructed elements at the building's base are masked by the twinkling exterior wall art of James Carpenter, and the words of Jenny Holzer's moving installation in the lobby keep visitors thinking. Innovative stairway design assures that building safety is taken very seriously in the first new building to be completed in lower Manhattan since the 2001 terrorist attack. One of the wisest urban planners in the history of New York has called it "the first building of the twenty-first century."

250 GREENWICH STREET AT MURRAY STREET IN MANHATTAN. Subway: 2, 3 to Park Place; E to World Trade Center.

CHAPTER 2:

Views & Sights

Look up, look down, look around—no matter where you look in this city, you're guaranteed to see something remarkable. On the streets, there's always something new to gaze upon—a restaurant that has suddenly opened in a spot that was long vacant, a movie shoot, a street performer attracting a crowd. The constantly changing and unpredictable nature of the city gives every outing the potential for unexpected excitement. But there are also plenty of places—obvious and unlikely—with reliably spectacular views. This chapter has the best sites worth seeking out.

The panorama of the city seen from the top of a building is the quintessential New York view. The top of the Empire State Building is the city's signature vantage point, but it's not only the skyscrapers that have stellar views. The top of every building offers its own special glimpse of the city, revealing a perspective visible only from overhead. Of course, many of these buildings are private residences, so only occupants and their invitees are privy to them, but plenty are open to the public—including a whole host of rooftop bars and lounges, where you can comfortably drink in the view for as long as you please (as long as you keep drinking).

Then there are the waterfronts and all the glorious vistas they afford—river views, ocean views from boardwalks and beaches, island views, and of course the sunrises and sunsets over the water. Here, the transit department has helped us quite a bit, offering some of the city's best water views courtesy of its bridges, subways, ferries, and the Roosevelt Island Tram.

Of course, the best views aren't always of the city's natural or man-made landscapes. Watching human dramas unfold in some of New York's colorful locales can be fascinating and surprising, whether for the pleasurable juxtaposition of so many different people at a single crossroads or the uniformity of a specific milieu so complete, you'd think you were in a different country (or world). And don't forget the buildings themselves—feats of architecture and engineering are yours to admire and wonder at, as long as you keep your eyes open.

Enjoy the views!

Rooftop Bars.

Though they used to be as subtle as speakeasies, over the past couple of years, rooftop bars have gone mainstream, and nowadays they seem to be cropping up faster than ATMs. Hotels are one of the few kinds of buildings with an incentive to turn their roofs into lively public spaces, so that's where most rooftop bars are located. Some have been around for ages but were traditionally frequented only by hotel guests and not really thought of as a destination for anyone not staying there. However, after the advent of the hip luxury and boutique hotels came a new spate of rooftops with high profiles, built-in cachet, and excellent views. Note: Except for two (which we've specified), all of these bars are open to the public; however, some of them are open only during the warmer months, so it's best to call before heading out.

91. Fly to the "Paris of the East" at Salon de Ning, the new Shanghai-inspired bar atop the roof of the Peninsula Hotel. For the price of a cocktail (a hefty $23), you get to luxuriate in a setting inspired by 1930s Shanghai, as well as quite a view. From there you can see up the length of Central Park all the way to Harlem, and down below to the throngs of tourists on Fifth Avenue, who seem very, very far away…
700 FIFTH AVENUE AT 55TH STREET IN MANHATTAN. Subway: E, V to Fifth Avenue/53rd Street; F to 57th Street. 212-956-2888. www.newyork.peninsula.com.

92. Vertigo, voyeurism, or both will keep you glued to the railing at the Top of the Tower, the discreet Art Deco bar on the roof of the Beekman Tower Hotel in Midtown. The wall around this penthouse bar is so low you can lean over and look straight down First Avenue. To the west is New Jersey, and to the east you can see Roosevelt Island and the neon lights of the Long Island and Pepsi-Cola signs. Voyeurs take note: you can easily pass many hours staring through a martini into the well-lit rooms of several neighboring apartment buildings.
FIRST AVENUE AND 49TH STREET IN MANHATTAN. Subway: 6 to 51st Street; E, V to Lexington Avenue/53rd Street. 212-980-4796. For more information, see the listing for Beekman Tower Hotel at www.thebeekmanhotel.com.

93. Look up at the two most impressive buildings of Midtown—the Empire State Building and the Chrysler Building—from the Rare View.
This aptly named bar and restaurant ("rare" is a play on the view and the burgers they serve) on top of the sixteen-floor Shelburne Hotel puts you face-to-midsection with

the Midtown skyscrapers. The tropical-looking trees and lounge chairs make it feel like an elevated beach in the middle of the city.

303 LEXINGTON AVENUE AT 37TH STREET IN MANHATTAN. Subway: 6 to 33rd Street. 212-481-8439. www.rarebarandgrill.com.

94. Bask in the shadow of the Empire State Building at the Hotel Metro Rooftop Bar.

This small, humble roof deck has an exclusive yet amateurish feel—drinks are served in plastic glasses full of ice from a small cart—and offers an excellent close-up of the city's tallest building.

45 WEST 35TH STREET BETWEEN FIFTH AND SIXTH AVENUES IN MANHATTAN. Subway: B, D, F, V, N, Q, R, W to 34th Street-Herald Square. 212-947-2500. www.hotelmetronyc.com.

95. It's not part of a hotel, but one of the city's best rooftop treats is to drink champagne on the rooftop terrace of the Metropolitan Museum.

There's a new sculpture installed here each year, but the real thing to admire is the incredible view of Central Park—the same one that people living on Fifth Avenue pay millions for. (The views of those buildings are great to look at as well—try to find some of the lovely private gardens on the rooftops.)

1000 FIFTH AVENUE AT 82ND STREET IN MANHATTAN. Subway: 4, 5, 6 to 86th Street. 212-535-7710. www.met.org. See pages 119–121 for more information on the museum.

96. Look down on Soho House members–literally–from the top of the Hotel Gansevoort.

The spectacular lounge on top of this chic Meatpacking District hotel lets you gaze out from all four sides of the building. You can see the towers of Midtown facing the Hudson River, and in the right light, the New Jersey coast looks positively sun-kissed. You can also watch the hammock swing by the pool on the famously lavish roof of the elite private club, Soho House, a few floors lower down. The Gansevoort has a rooftop pool, too, and one-ups the rival Soho House's with an underwater music system. But this pool's just for hotel guests, so lest you forget your place in the social pecking order and try to take a dip, the friendly hotel enforcers will escort you back to the lounge.

18 NINTH AVENUE AT 13TH STREET IN MANHATTAN. Subway: A, C, E to 14th Street; L to Eighth Avenue. 212-206-6700. www.hotelgansevoort.com.

97. See the city in a 360-degree panorama at the **View Lounge**.

It's worth the trip to the top of the Marriott Marquis in Times Square to experience New York's only revolving restaurant and bar. An overhaul several years ago improved the food and drink—and removed the dance floor—but the view is as stellar as it has always been. The clientele hasn't changed much either, so you'll be admiring the skyline with business travelers and couples in town for the evening to celebrate an anniversary or a birthday.

1535 BROADWAY BETWEEN 45TH AND 46TH STREETS, 48TH FLOOR, IN MANHATTAN. Subway: 1, 2, 3, 7, N, Q, R, W, S to Times Square-42nd Street. 212-398-1900. www.nymarriottmarquis.com.

98. Another place with a great Times Square view is **Ava Lounge** on top of the **Dream Hotel**.

The crazy décor inside the bar is hard to ignore, but don't let it distract you from going to the windows to look Times Square straight in the eye (the hotel is only fifteen stories high, which makes for an almost eerie close-up of the neon billboards). For a more panoramic view, go out to the impeccably manicured garden terrace (open spring through fall, weather permitting), and try to make out the Hudson River behind the steely buildings and the pulsating lights. More surreal views can be found in the hotel's lobby—there's a wild copper statue of Catherine the Great, and a 4,000-gallon fish tank, the largest indoor aquarium in North America.

210 WEST 55TH STREET BETWEEN BROADWAY AND SEVENTH AVENUE IN MANHATTAN. Subway: 1 to 50th Street; E, V to Fifth Avenue/53rd Street. 212-956-7020. www.avaloungenyc.com.

NOTE: The following two bars are technically reserved for hotel guests and not open to the public. But the views are so lovely, we couldn't resist including them. Either splurge and make an overnight of it, or pose as guests who have lost their key (at your own risk).

99. *Hudson Hotel Sky Terrace:* Jersey's not quite Monaco, but this beachy rooftop bar feels just like an elevated café on the Riviera.

356 WEST 58TH STREET BETWEEN EIGHTH AND NINTH AVENUES IN MANHATTAN. Subway: 1, A, C, B, D to 59th Street-Columbus Circle. 212-554-6000. www.hudsonhotel.com.

100. *A60 at 60 Thompson Hotel:* A great cityscape view from an unusual vantage point, right in the middle of SoHo.

60 THOMPSON STREET BETWEEN SPRING AND BROOME STREETS IN MANHATTAN. Subway: C, E to Spring Street. 877-431-0400. www.60thompson.com.

More rooms with a view.

A restaurant is a trickier venture to pull off on a roof (though there are some—see below), but that doesn't mean that the city lacks for restaurants with impressive views. Whether high up, on the water, or right in the middle of a bustling locale, the following restaurants offer built-in ambience that equals (or exceeds) the quality of the food they serve.

101. Check out northern Manhattan at **Terrace in the Sky**.

Eating at this indoor/outdoor rooftop restaurant nestled on the sixteenth floor of a building by Columbia University, is like dining in a bird's nest with very fancy food.
400 WEST 119TH STREET BETWEEN AMSTERDAM AVENUE AND MORNINGSIDE DRIVE IN MAN-HATTAN. Subway: 1 to 116th Street-Columbia University. 212-666-9490. www.terraceinthesky.com.

102. Check out lower Manhattan at **Alma**.

You wouldn't know it from its modest brick exterior, but this second-floor Mexican joint in Brooklyn has a rooftop deck (open in season) with glorious views of the lower Manhattan skyline. Waits for prime-view tables can be long at prime times, so after you put your name on the list upstairs, grab a stool at **B61**, the bar on the ground floor—the river views from the bay windows aren't bad either.
187 COLUMBIA STREET AT DEGRAW STREET IN BROOKLYN. Subway: F, G to Carroll Street. 718-643-5400. www.almarestaurant.com. N.B.: Alma and B61 share an address but have different hours.

103. View MoMA's sculpture garden from above at **Terrace 5**.

If you make it all the way to the Museum of Modern Art's top floor, you'll be rewarded by this lovely (and relatively calm) seasonal café. You'll need to pay admission to the museum, but the view and the treats—snacks and desserts from **Danny Meyer**'s hospitality group (see pages 165–166)—are worth it.
11 WEST 53RD STREET, FIFTH FLOOR, BETWEEN FIFTH AND SIXTH AVENUES IN MANHATTAN. Subway: E, V to Fifth Avenue/53rd Street. 212-708-9400. www.moma.org. For more information on the museum, see page 122.

104. See Manhattan in a different way at the **River Café**.

When you see the view, it's hard to believe that this restaurant hasn't been around forever. But when founder Michael "Buzzy" O'Keefe decided in the late '70s to open a restaurant under the Brooklyn Bridge, everyone thought he was crazy to consider such a desolate area. How times have changed. Go to this Brooklyn waterfront pioneer for dinner, lunch, brunch, whatever—just don't forget to look out the window.

1 WATER STREET IN BROOKLYN. Subway: 2, 3 to Clark Street; A, C to High Street. 718-522-5200. www.rivercafe.com.

---

105. Get ferried to the **Water's Edge**.

The comparisons are inevitable: they're both in boroughs, both on barges, and both boast exquisite waterfront views of Manhattan. But this Long Island City restaurant overlooking the East River has one feature that the River Café lacks: it offers free ferry service from Manhattan.

EAST RIVER AT 44TH DRIVE IN QUEENS. Ferry service available Wednesday through Sunday from 34th Street pier in Manhattan; ferries depart from Manhattan on the hour from 6:00 p.m. to 10:00 p.m. 718-482-0033. www.watersedgenyc.com.

---

106. Pretend you're on a (semi-) private yacht at the **Water Club**.

Manhattan's answer to Brooklyn's River Café and Queen's Water's Edge is this fancy barge-top restaurant in the East River. Looking out from the enclosed dining room or the seasonal Crow's Nest bar on the upper deck, you can gaze across the river to Queens and at the sparkling lights of Midtown Manhattan right in front of you.

EAST RIVER NEAR 30TH STREET IN MANHATTAN. For more information and directions, call 212-683-3333 or visit www.thewaterclub.com.

---

107. See the sun set over New Jersey from the **Boat Basin Café**.

Though it hasn't been around as long as some, this seasonal riverside bar and restaurant fits right in on the Upper West Side and is something of a warm-weather institution. Located above the 79th Street Boat Basin in Riverside Park, in a series of stone structures that look like Roman ruins, the café has endeared itself to its notoriously opinionated neighbors with excellent burgers, a baby- and dog-friendly attitude, and casual riverside atmosphere.

WEST 79TH STREET AND THE HUDSON RIVER IN MANHATTAN. Open April through October, weather permitting. Subway: 1 to 79th Street. 212-496-5542. www.boatbasincafe.com.

---

108. See Manhattan in panorama from **Giando on the Water**.

Located near the Brooklyn foot of the Williamsburg Bridge, Giando is an extravagant Italian restaurant with a lavish dining room and walls of floor-to-ceiling windows facing the East River. Its location affords one of the broadest panoramas of the city, looking south beyond the Manhattan Bridge to downtown Manhattan and north beyond the Williamsburg Bridge to Midtown. In warmer months, you can have dessert or drinks on the terrace, without any glass coming between you and the view.

400 KENT AVENUE BETWEEN BROADWAY AND SOUTH 8TH STREET IN BROOKLYN. 718-387-7000. www.giandoonthewater.com.

---

109. One-up the beer garden on the roof of Berry Park.

If you find this garagelike space on a barren strip of street just west of McCarren Park in Williamsburg suspiciously empty on a nice evening, it's probably because everyone's up top. The place calls itself a beer garden, and while the first half is correct (it's run by an alum of the longstanding East Village beer hall, Zum Schneider), the atmospheric draw is actually a 3,000-square-foot roof deck. There's a cozy nook on the roof's westernmost side that offers a killer view of Manhattan's most glamorous skyscraper, the Chrysler Building.

4 Berry Street at N. 14TH Street IN BROOKLYN. Subway: L to Bedford Avenue. 718-782-2829.

---

104. Watch the action at Grand Central at Metrazur or Cipriani Dolce.

Both of these restaurants—which face each other from balconies across the terminal—are like indoor urban terraces. They overlook Grand Central's famous main hall, with its lovely, recently restored ceiling shining above, and some of the most dynamic people-watching in the city just below. Come for drinks in the late afternoon and watch commuters of all shapes and sizes scurry to make their trains.

GRAND CENTRAL TERMINAL. *42ND STREET BETWEEN LEXINGTON AND MADISON AVENUES IN MANHATTAN. Subway: 4, 5, 6, 7, S to Grand Central-42nd Street. Metrazur is on the east balcony; Cipriani Dolce is on the west.*

METRAZUR: *212-687-4600. www.charliepalmer.com/metrazur.*

CIPRIANI DOLCE: *212-973-0999. www.cipriani.com. For more on Cipriani, see entry on pages 38–39.*

For full entry on Grand Central Terminal, see pages 23–25.

Time Warner Center.

This enormous complex boasts more vistas from a single site than any-where else in the city. Located right on Columbus Circle, at the foot of Central Park, pretty much everywhere in the two-building glass-fronted complex has a good view of something. (Except for the **Whole Foods** in the basement—see page 71 for a Whole Foods with a view.)

10 COLUMBUS CIRCLE AT 59TH STREET IN MANHATTAN. Subway: 1, A, C, B, D to 59th Street-Columbus Circle.

Starting from the top...

111. Asiate. At this Franco-Japanese restaurant in the Mandarin Oriental Hotel, the main decorative element is the spectacular Central Park panorama presented through sixteen-foot-tall windows. The wall of wine—their 1,300-bottle collection displayed by the entryway—is also an impressive sight.
Mandarin Oriental Hotel, Thirty-fifth floor. 212-805-8881.
www.mandarinoriental.com.

112. Lobby Lounge. Clever name. Yes, it's adjacent to the Mandarin Orien-tal's lobby—but that lobby is 280 feet above street level! Enjoy the view of Broadway over drinks, snacks, or afternoon tea.
Mandarin Oriental Hotel, Thirty-fifth floor. 212-805-8881.
www.mandarinoriental.com.

113. A little farther down, **Dizzy's Jazz Club Coca-Cola** on the fifth floor offers great close-ups of Columbus Circle and the foot of Central Park—as well as the street performers.
Dizzy's is part of Jazz at Lincoln Center; for more information, see pages 148–149, call 212-258-9595, or visit www.jalc.org.

114. The dining rooms in the fourth-floor "restaurant collection"—which include **Per Se** and **Masa** (for full entries, see pages 168–169) all have excellent views. But take note: these are some of the most expensive (and exclusive) restaurants in the city, so advance planning is advised.
Fourth floor.

115. Ride the Wonder Wheel at **Coney Island**.

Thanks to Mayor Bloomberg, who bought the site in 2008 to prevent it being destroyed in the redevelopment of Coney Island, you can still sit in one of the cars that don't swing to take in breathtaking views of the Atlantic Ocean in one direction and the Manhattan skyline in another.

ASTROLAND, 1000 SURF AVENUE AT WEST 10TH STREET IN BROOKLYN. Open March through October. Subway: D, F, N, Q to Coney Island-Stillwell Avenue. www.astroland.com. See also pages 348–349.

116. Watch the sun set from the roof deck of the arch in **Wagner Park**.

Watching the sun go down from anywhere along the boardwalk of Battery Park is beautiful, but the unobstructed views of Lady Liberty and the small islands below Manhattan from Wagner Park are amazing.

OFF BATTERY PLACE, JUST NORTH OF BATTERY PARK IN MANHATTAN. Subway: 1 to South Ferry.

117. See the stars (the real ones) at Columbia University's **Rutherford Observatory**.

Seeing the constellations with the naked eye is one of the few things you can't do in New York. But Columbia University's observatory periodically opens its doors to the public for stargazing, usually one Friday a month. Under the guidance of a professor or grad student, you can use the observatory's equipment to break through the city's "light pollution" and admire the vast night sky.

PUPIN HALL, COLUMBIA UNIVERSITY. 120TH STREET BETWEEN BROADWAY AND AMSTERDAM AVENUE IN MANHATTAN. (The public must enter through the Columbia campus.) Subway: 1 to 116th Street. Schedule and frequency of open nights vary; call 212-854-6864 or visit http://outreach.astro.columbia.edu/ for current information.

→ **DID YOU KNOW?** *Pupin Hall is where the first atomic bomb was developed, hence the name "Manhattan Project."*

118. Make your way to the tip of **Far Rockaway** and stand on the beach at nightfall.

The coasts of Brooklyn, Queens, and New Jersey light up like a long, drawn-out fireworks display.

FAR ROCKAWAY IN QUEENS. Subway: A to Rockaway Park/Beach 116th Street or Far Rockaway-Mott Avenue.

Esplanades & Promenades.

The city's waterfront walkways offer lovely views of different parts of the city from afar, and a stroll along one of them is a pleasant reminder that no matter where you are in the concrete jungle, you're never landlocked.

119. *Brooklyn Heights Promenade.*

A walk along the esplanade in one of Brooklyn's oldest neighborhoods is impressive and romantic, any time of day or night. On one side are views of lower Manhattan, and on the other, complementary views of tranquil streets lined with beautiful brownstones.

BETWEEN MONTAGUE STREET AND MIDDAGH STREET AT THE WATER'S EDGE IN BROOKLYN. Subway: 2, 3 to Clark Street.

120. *Battery Park Promenade.*

From here, at the southern tip of Manhattan, you have an unobstructed view of the waters in front of you—a good way to pass the time while waiting in line for the ferry to the **Statue of Liberty** and **Ellis Island** (see pages 18–19).

BATTERY PARK, NEAR THE CASTLE CLINTON MONUMENT IN MANHATTAN. Subway: 1 to South Ferry; 4, 5 to Bowling Green.

121. *Coney Island/Brighton Beach Boardwalks.*

Walk off your hot dog from **Nathan's** or **Ruby's** (see page 170) by strolling from the vendors at Coney Island to the Russian cafés of Brighton Beach on the huge, wooden boardwalk by the sea.

FROM SURF AVENUE TO BRIGHTON BEACH AVENUE AND THE OCEAN IN BROOKLYN. Subway: B, Q to Brighton Beach; D, F, N, Q to Coney Island-Stillwell Avenue.

122. *FDR Boardwalk.*

This beach, and the two-and-a-half-mile boardwalk (the fourth-largest in the world) that runs along it, look out toward the Atlantic on one side and toward lower Manhattan and Liberty, Governor, and Ellis islands from the other. Come at sunset and watch the city turn pink and orange as the sun drops behind it. During the day, the boardwalk is surprisingly pleasant to bike along, because while it's still not quite as smooth as a paved road, it's generally not as clogged with pedestrians as some of the city's other boardwalks, and cyclists are well tolerated. You can also enjoy ocean breezes and a killer view of the Verrazano-Narrows Bridge.

SOUTH BEACH IN STATEN ISLAND. Staten Island Ferry to St. George; then bus S51 to Father Capodanno Boulevard.

123. *Bobby Wagner Walk and Carl Schurz Park.*

The West Side doesn't have a monopoly on the best waterfront views in Manhattan. Bobby Wagner Walk is the three-mile esplanade that extends from 63rd to 125th Street along the East River. Between 81st and 90th Streets, there is an elevated portion (also known as the John Finley Walk) adjacent to Carl Schurz Park, which offers a wonderful uninterrupted panorama of the East River and its landmarks. True, it's not as pastoral as, say, the Palisades across the Hudson, but you get a good urban mix of islands (Randall's, Ward's, and Roosevelt), bridges (the Triborough and the Hells Gate), the lighthouse at the tip of **Roosevelt Island** (see page 237), and usually a tugboat or two. The park itself is uncommonly pretty, with winding pathways overlooking idyllic clearings dotted with benches and fountains, an unusually pleasant dog run with a river view, and hidden among the trees, Gracie Mansion.

BETWEEN 63ᴿᴰ AND 125ᵀᴴ STREETS ALONG THE EAST RIVER IN MANHATTAN. Subway: 4, 5, 6 to 86ᵗʰ Street. www.nycgovparks.org/parks/M108T, www.carlschurzparknyc.org.

Bridges & Tunnels.

Thank goodness for the water. Without it, the dramatic scenery that separates different pieces of the city would be gone, and interborough transportation would be limited to views of streets and the insides of dark tunnels. Fortunately, geography and the transit department have blessed us with some incredible vistas at various crossings. Try some of these great transportation options, and enjoy the views that those lucky enough to commute that way get to experience every day.

BRIDGES:

Many of the bridges that connect the boroughs of New York to each other and to their neighboring state, New Jersey, are not only feats of modern engineering in their own right (the Verrazano-Narrows Bridge, to give one example, was until recently the longest suspension bridge in the world) but also offer some of the most spectacular views of the city. From the right vantage point—whether it's from the window of a moving train, through the rear windshield of a speeding cab, or from a bench in the middle of the bridge itself—looking at New York from its bridges can be one of the most revealing, exciting, and romantic things to do.

124. *The Brooklyn Bridge.*

Stretching across the East River between City Hall in lower Manhattan and Brooklyn Heights, the Brooklyn Bridge is the most famous of the city's bridges and by far the most beautiful. Walk across at dawn or at dusk and stop at one of the benches along the way for a breathtaking sunrise or sunset view. Look north toward the skyscrapers of Midtown or gaze south across the water toward the Atlantic Ocean and the Statue of Liberty.

125. *Manhattan Bridge.*
Reaching from the easternmost end of Canal Street in Manhattan to DUMBO in west Brooklyn, the best thing to see from the Manhattan Bridge is its neighbor, the Brooklyn Bridge. There are cutaways in the structure of the bridge that let pedestrians look out over the water at the lower tips of Brooklyn and Manhattan, and north toward the Williamsburg Bridge and the towers of Midtown. The views can be enjoyed in both directions by riding one of the subways (B, D, N, Q—see opposite for more information) that use the bridge to travel between the boroughs.

126. *George Washington Bridge.*
Although crossing the George Washington Bridge means stepping out of New York—it runs from 178th Street in Manhattan over the Hudson River to Fort Lee in New Jersey—a walk over the southern side of this mighty suspension bridge offers unbeatable views of Manhattan.

127. *Verrazano-Narrows Bridge.*
Connecting the boroughs of Brooklyn and Staten Island by stretching across the Narrows from Bay Ridge to the Staten Island Expressway, the Verrazano-Narrows Bridge is now the second-longest suspension bridge in the world (and still the largest in the U.S.), and an amazing sight to see. Although plans have been in the works since the bridge's construction in 1964, there is still no pedestrian walkway, so you have to drive across to see the glittering lights of the outer boroughs. But if that's not an option, the bridge is an equally impressive sight from the ground, so it's worth finding a spot on the coast of Brooklyn or Staten Island from which to take it in.

TRAINS:
Subways are well known as efficient and convenient ways to get from point A to point B, but often overlooked (or unknown) is the fact that certain train rides are scenic as well. At different points along the subway system, the trains emerge from underground and cross bridges, climb elevated tracks, or ride alongside the ocean, routinely treating passengers to a picturesque diversion on top of the transportation they paid for.
(For information on individual subway lines and locations, visit www.mta.info.)

128. *7 train into Queens:*
As you enter the borough, the train curves and gives you amazing views of the Manhattan skyline and an aerial tour of the graffiti art at 5Pointz (see page 139).

129. *4 train into the Bronx:*

Ride right to the end of the line on a weekend for the most bucolic views of any of the five boroughs—and catch the West Indian cricket teams in authentic whites as the train goes by Van Cortland Park.

130. *Q train in Brooklyn:*

Survey the beach scene before you plop your blanket down. For a quick tour of the Brooklyn beaches, let the Q train take you from Sheepshead Bay and Brighton Beach all the way around to Coney Island (see pages 348–349) and the New York Aquarium (see page 227).

131. *F train to Brooklyn:*

A few stops into Brooklyn, the F train emerges from its tunnel into the picturesque neighborhood of Carroll Gardens, where it rises and runs elevated over Park Slope. Get out at Smith-9th Streets and enjoy the views across Brooklyn to Manhattan and the Statue of Liberty from the platform—the highest elevated point of New York's train system.

132. *B, D, N, Q train over the Manhattan Bridge:*

Whichever direction you travel, you get an exquisite view of the Brooklyn Bridge, suspended between the water and the sky.

---

133. Look at the fall foliage in Central Park from BG at **Bergdorf Goodman**.

If you can't make it upstate, the view from the store's seventh-floor café can satisfy yearnings for autumnal beauty. (The Kelly Wearstler décor inside isn't bad to look at, either.)
754 FIFTH AVENUE AT 57TH STREET IN MANHATTAN. Subway: N, R, W to Fifth Avenue/59th Street. 212-753-7300. www.bergdorfgoodman.com. See full entry page 243.

---

134. Take the ferry to **Staten Island** and enjoy a twenty-five-minute tour of

great New York vistas. On the way over, you'll roll by the Statue of Liberty, Ellis Island, and Governors Island; on the way back, you'll get a glorious view of the Manhattan skyline—all for free.
The Staten Island ferry runs between Whitehall Terminal in Manhattan and St. George Terminal on Staten Island. For more information and ferry schedules, visit www.siferry.com or www.nyc.gov/html/dot/html/ferrybus/statfery.shtml#info

135. Ride the tram to **Roosevelt Island** and back, and catch a tantalizing glimpse up and down the East River and over Manhattan, Brooklyn, and Queens while you glide through the air.

59TH STREET AND SECOND AVENUE IN MANHATTAN. Subway: 4, 5, 6 to 59th Street; N, R, W to Lexington Avenue/59th Street. For more information, call 212-832-4543, or visit www.ny.com/transportation/ri_tramway.html.

136. Stretching from Manhattan to the **Verrazano-Narrows Bridge** (see page 68), **the view of New York Harbor from the grounds of the Alice Austen House** is an unexpected treat at this spectacular historic house (once lived in by the nineteenth-century photographer) and museum. In addition to the breathtaking panorama, you can also enjoy Austen's lovely gardens and a collection of her photographs that document the social history of her time.

2 HYLAN BOULEVARD IN STATEN ISLAND. Grounds open daily until dusk; museum open Thursdays through Sundays from noon to 5:00 p.m., except January and February and major holidays. Staten Island Ferry to St. George Terminal; then S51 bus to Hylan Boulevard. For more information, call 718-816-4506 or visit http://www.aliceausten.org/museum/index.html

137. Even as the area around it continues to develop into one of Brooklyn's most coveted neighborhoods, **the views at Empire-Fulton Ferry State Park (also known as Brooklyn Bridge Park)** are already some of the most incredible vantages in the city. The combination of the distant buildings of lower Manhattan across the water and the Brooklyn Bridge looming overhead makes for an unusual and exquisite mix of urban architecture and natural beauty. These once-desolate former dockyards are now home to one of the city's prettiest parks—and one of the most popular spots for a picturesque wedding reception. With plans for piers, floating bridges, and restored marshlands, the surrounding neighborhood will only become more extraordinary.

EAST RIVER BETWEEN THE BROOKLYN AND MANHATTAN BRIDGES IN BROOKLYN. Subway: 2, 3 to Clark Street; A, C to High Street; F to York Street. For more information on the park and development project, call 718-802-0603 or visit www.bbpc.net. For information on outdoor programs in the park, see Chapter 6, "The Great Outdoors."

138. Check out the Bronx, the aqueducts, and the oldest interborough bridge from the top of the **High Bridge Water Tower**.

OK, we'll slow down. First, the High Bridge Water Tower is that scary-looking tower that stands all by itself in upper Manhattan—the one you see on the way to Yankee

Stadium. Second, yes, those stone arches really are aqueducts, and yes, they really were once used to bring water into the city. Third, the bridge—built to bring water to the city from the aqueducts—is older than the Brooklyn Bridge by a good forty years. The water tower is not regularly open to the public but can be climbed and toured on various dates throughout the year (one of which is **OpenHouseNewYork**; see page 143), and the complete restoration of the bridge and revitalization of surrounding Highbridge Park are part of Mayor Bloomberg's PlaNYC.

HIGHBRIDGE PARK, WEST 155TH AND DYCKMAN STREETS BETWEEN EDGECOMBE AND AMSTERDAM AVENUES IN MANHATTAN. Subway: 1 to 157th Street; C to 155th Street. For more information and scheduled visiting days, call 212-304-2365, or visit http://www.nycgov-parks.org/sub_your_park/highbridge/html/highbridge_water_tower.html

---

139. The view of Union Square from the local **Whole Foods'** sit-down café upstairs

is the only reason we'd recommend visiting this store. The upstairs seating area has perfect views of the plaza on the 14th Street side of the park and whatever happens to be going on there: protests, demonstrations, skaters doing tricks, or temporary art displays. But checkout lines on the first floor frequently snake around the entire take-out area, creating gourmet urban chaos. Our advice: skip the maddening crowds below and eat before you come.

4 UNION SQUARE BETWEEN BROADWAY AND UNIVERSITY PLACE IN MANHATTAN. Subway: 4, 5, 6, L, N, Q, R, W to 14th Street-Union Square. 212-673-5388. www.wholefoods.com.

---

140. Stop for a look at the Cloisters from **Margaret Corbin Drive**.

One of the most pleasurable things about visiting the **Cloisters** (see page 121) is the walk along Margaret Corbin Drive to the museum's entrance, high up in Fort Tryon Park. The walkway leads straight through one of the city's most beautifully landscaped flower gardens, beyond which lies the Hudson River and magnificent views of the valley extending north toward the Bronx and south toward the distant Midtown skyline. And once you reach the Cloisters, the views from all sides of the museum are astonishing.

FORT TRYON PARK IN MANHATTAN. Subway: A to 190th Street. 212-923-3700. For more information on the museum, see entry on page 121.

---

141. The view of Manhattan, Brooklyn, Ellis Island, the Statue of Liberty, and more...from **Governors Island**.

More than two centuries after we gave Governors Island to the government to use as a military training ground, it was finally returned to us in 2003. Since then, the city and the park service have been in the process of converting its grounds, historic structures (including two massive nineteenth-century fortifications), and waterfront promenade for public access. Despite a flurry of amenities including outdoor art, mini-golf, bike rental, and a **water taxi beach** (see next entry), much of Governor's Island feels exotically unexplored. The island is currently open for visitors during the warmer months and visiting hours are limited, but when you can get there (by ferry, a free ten-minute ride from lower Manhattan), you'll be treated to striking views of the city all around you. *The Governors Island ferry departs from the Battery Maritime Building at 10 SOUTH STREET IN MANHATTAN. Subway: 1 to South Ferry; 4, 5 to Bowling Green; R, W to Whitehall Street-South Ferry. For current visiting hours, call 212-825-3045 or visit www.nps.gov or www.govisland.com.*

142. We don't know where the idea came from, but the Long Island City **Water Taxi Beach** is one of the most fun places to get a view in the New York area. It started when New York Water Taxi carted in 400 tons of sand and a couple of picnic tables and turned the Hunter's Point water taxi stop into a beach. The spectacular built-in waterfront views of Midtown are best enjoyed from a lounge chair (included) or from a beach towel (bring your own), with a tropical drink from the beachy concession shack. Though there are now Water Taxi beaches at South Street Seaport and on Governor's Island, those locations are more susceptible to overcrowding due to their tourist-itinerary-friendly locations. The Manhattan and Queens beaches are easily accessible by subway, bus, car, and, of course, water taxi. (Governor's Island is currently only accessible by the Governor's Island ferry.) *The Long Island City beach is located at Hunter's Point Pier, 2 BORDEN STREET AND THE EAST RIVER IN QUEENS. Subway: 7 to Vernon Boulevard-Jackson Avenue; G to 21st Street. Water Taxi beaches are open from summer through early October, weather permitting. For more information and directions to other Water Taxi Beach locations, visit www.watertaxibeach.com.*

143. Peek into other people's houses during OpenHouseNewYork.

One weekend a year, nearly 200 private buildings and structures around the five boroughs open their doors to the public. Most offer free guided tours highlighting each site's history or notable features. The roster includes a variety of monuments, historic buildings, parks, and even private homes (it also includes several places listed in this chapter, such as High Bridge Tower, the Highline, and Governors Island), many of which are seldom or never open at any other time of the year. Our suggestion: browse the schedule online around the time of the festival, then try to check out as many as you can. *OpenHouseNewYork is held annually for one weekend in early October. For more information, call 212-991-6470, or visit www.ohny.org.*

144. Get a bird's-eye view of the city on a **helicopter tour**.

Nervous? The tours last between two and seventeen minutes, so by the time you actu-ally remember to be scared, you'll already be on your way down.

Liberty Helicopters operates one heliport in Manhattan: PIER 6 ON THE EAST RIVER. For infor-mation on tours, schedules, and prices, call 212-967-6464 or visit www.libertyhelicopters.com.

145. Enjoy medieval views of Central Park from the highest points of **Belvedere Castle**, a fantastical folly from whose towers and balconies visitors can gaze down upon Turtle Pond, the Great Lawn, and into the Delacorte Theater, where **Shakespeare in the Park** (see page 155) takes place every summer.

MID-PARK AT 81ST STREET IN MANHATTAN. For more information on Central Park, see entry on page 219. Subway: 6 to 77th Street; B, C to 81st Street-Museum of Natural History.

146. Time your climb up the **bell tower at Riverside Church** so that you arrive on the hour. Then look out across the whole city as some of the largest (and loudest) bells in the world ring out.

490 RIVERSIDE DRIVE AT CLAREMONT AVENUE IN MANHATTAN. Subway: 1 to 116th Street-Columbia University. 212-870-6700. www.theriversidechurchny.org.

147. Sit on a bench below Pier 17 at **South Street Seaport** and look across the river. You can while away an afternoon watching the busy waters between you and the bor-ough of Brooklyn, which looks close enough to swim to (not something we'd recommend).

SOUTH STREET AND WATER STREET IN MANHATTAN. Subway: 1 to South Ferry; 2, 3 to Wall Street; 4, 5 to Bowling Green; J, M, Z to Broad Street; R, W to Whitehall Street-South Ferry.

148. See Manhattan from the *Shearwater*.

The traditional way to see the island in detail is the **Circle Line** (see page 23), but a classy alternative is this elegant, vintage, 82-foot, 49-person schooner that gives water tours. You'll cruise by the sights of New York harbor, including the Statue of Liberty, Ellis and Governors islands, and the Brooklyn and Manhattan bridges. When you dock next to the other yachts at the Battery Park marina, who will know that it's not yours?

The Shearwater sails from April through October. NORTH COVE YACHT HARBOR (HUDSON RIVER, IN FRONT OF THE WORLD FINANCIAL CENTER) IN MANHATTAN. Subway: 1 to Rector Street; E to World Trade Center; R, W to Cortlandt Street. Public sails are offered daily. For more information, schedules, and prices, call 212-619-0885 or visit www.shearwatersailing.com.

149. Look out over downtown from the **New Museum terrace**.

When the New Museum opened on the Bowery in 2007, it brought more than a new venue for contemporary art to Nolita. The icing on the cake of this spectacular building—the only structure in the city designed by the award-winning Japanese architecture firm SANAA—is the glorious (and happily underused) terrace on the seventh floor, which affords amazing views across SoHo, the Lower East Side, and Chinatown, all the way down to the Financial District. Although the terrace is occasionally reserved for openings and other events, and is naturally a deservedly popular spot during summer weekends, we think that heading up there on a weekday evening for a quiet sunset is worth the price of admission alone.

235 BOWERY AT PRINCE STREET IN MANHATTAN. Subway: 6 to Spring Street; J, M, Z to Bowery. For more information call 212-219-1222, or go to www.newmuseum.org. For full entry on the museum, see page 125.

150. Watch the sun set behind the **Colgate Clock**, an often-overlooked New

Jersey attraction that you get a great view of from Hudson River Park. Pick a spot on a grassy pier and watch the sun go down behind the clock's giant octagonal face. Try Pier 45 by Perry Street.

HUDSON RIVER PARK IN MANHATTAN. Subway: 1 to Rector Street.

151. Stand by the lighthouse at the northern tip of **Roosevelt Island** for a

breathtaking view of Midtown and uptown Manhattan.

LIGHTHOUSE PARK ON ROOSEVELT ISLAND. Subway: F to Roosevelt Island; Roosevelt Island Tram.

152. Find the lighthouse under the **George Washington Bridge**.

From next to the forty-foot-high Little Red Lighthouse, you can see all the way up the Hudson River to the north, the Palisades to the west, and the bridge directly overhead.

178TH STREET AND THE HUDSON RIVER IN MANHATTAN. Subway: A to 175th Street.

→ **DID YOU KNOW?** *This lighthouse (whose official name is the Jeffrey's Hook Lighthouse) was the subject of a popular 1942 children's book by Hildegarde H. Smith called* The Little Red Lighthouse and the Great Gray Bridge. *When the lighthouse was decommissioned in 1947, it was supposed to be torn down, but outcry from fans of the book prevented it, and it was turned into a National Historic Landmark.*

153. Enjoy the picture-perfect view of Central Park from **Bow Bridge**.

This low-lying cast-iron bridge delicately meanders across the lake, offering a scenic view of Manhattan's bucolic center. You'll see rowboaters bobbing along between the flowering fields of Cherry Hills and the wild green landscape of the Ramble.

WEST OF BETHESDA TERRACE BY 74TH STREET IN MANHATTAN'S CENTRAL PARK. Subway: B, C to 72nd Street. For more information on the park, see entry on pages 219–222. N.B.: There are thirty-six bridges and arches all over Central Park, many of which offer unusual views of particular areas. Check out a map before you visit the park.

154. See across state lines from **Lafayette's feet**.

At the 9th Street entrance to Prospect Park, a monument commemorates New York's favorite Frenchman. Follow his gaze down 9th Street and you'll see all the way to the edge of Brooklyn, across lower Manhattan to the Jersey hills on the horizon. Go on a pleasant day and you might understand why Jack Kerouac said, "Whenever spring comes to New York, I can't stand the suggestion of the land that comes blowing over the river from New Jersey, and I've got to go."

PROSPECT PARK WEST AND 9TH STREET IN BROOKLYN. For more information on the park, see entry on page 222. Subway: F to 15th Street-Prospect Park or Seventh Avenue.

155. See where Manhattan ends and the Bronx begins at the Half Moon Overlook.

At the southwesternmost tip of the Bronx, the hillside neighborhood of Marble Hill ascends to a natural vantage point known as Spuyten Duyvil, whose views of the Hudson River and upper Manhattan are unrivaled. Named for the creek that used to run into the mainland from the Hudson, Spuyten Duyvil is the meeting point of the two boroughs, offering dramatic scenery that makes it a wonderful place to walk. Start from the Spuyten Duyvil Metro-North rail station and walk south along the shorefront park. Just south of Palisade Avenue, the path takes you up to the Half Moon Overlook, a quiet semicircular viewing point with the perfect perspective over the river.

SPUYTEN DUYVIL SHOREFRONT PARK IN MANHATTAN. Subway: 1 to Marble Hill-225th Street or Metro-North Railroad (Hudson Link) to Spuyten Duyvil.

→ *DID YOU KNOW* **(part 1)?** *Spuyten Duyvil takes its name from the Dutch-American folk legend of Anthony Van Corlaer, the loyal trumpeter of Peter Stuyvesant (a Dutchman who was mayor of New York in the early seventeenth century), who drowned swimming across the creek to warn his countrymen of attack from the British. With no ferry to take him across, Van Corlaer tried to swim "en spijt den Duyvil" (in spite of the Devil). Locals still say you can hear his trumpet sounding out across the water on windy nights.*

→ **DID YOU KNOW** (part 2)**?** *The neighborhood of Marble Hill is the only part of the borough of Manhattan physically connected to the mainland. It was originally the northernmost tip of Manhattan, but the construction of the Harlem River Ship Canal in 1895 severed it from the island. For the next twenty years, Marble Hill was an island until the small creek that separated it from the mainland was filled. Despite being geographically joined to the Bronx, however, Marble Hill is still considered part of Manhattan.*

156. Sit on **Grant's Tomb**.

The impressive memorial for General Grant (it contains the tombs of both him and his wife) is situated in the middle of a stretch of park that offers some of the prettiest views of the Hudson River and the old stone buildings along Riverside Drive. Sit on the wall and look down over Riverside Park to the water, or walk north behind the memorial to the road bridge that extends into Harlem, where semicircular viewing points are built into the stonework so you can look across Harlem and the Hudson.

RIVERSIDE DRIVE AT 122ND STREET IN MANHATTAN. Subway: 1, A, C, B, D to 125th Street.

157. Take a free ferry to the **Red Hook waterfront**.

One hundred and fifty years ago, before the construction of the Brooklyn-Queens Expressway overwhelmed the neighborhood, Red Hook was one of the busiest ports in the world. Today, the quaint waterfront is less quiet than it used to be, as the neighborhood grows into the last refuge of the Brooklyn hipster, but it still boasts wonderful views across the East River to Governors Island and to the Atlantic. Even with the arrival of the much-contested Ikea store—and the residence in 2009 of the cast of *Real World Brooklyn*—walking along the docks and back streets at the port of Red Hook is like stepping back in time. And as compensation for invading the area, Ikea offers free water taxis from downtown Manhattan to Red Hook and back on weekends. Even if you're not out for affordable Scandinavian housewares, it's worth the ride for the views alone.

CONOVER STREET AND BEARD STREET, RED HOOK IN BROOKLYN. Subway: F to Smith-9th Streets.

158. Go to the top of the **Rock**.

After nearly twenty years and a $75 million renovation, the spectacular roof on the seventieth floor of Rockefeller Center reopened in 2005. Though a good deal shorter than the **Empire State Building** (see page 76), the roof of the Rock has one great advantage: it doesn't have a spire, so there's no structure in the middle blocking your view from one side to another. This means that the top of this mighty Midtown skyscraper offers the clearest north-south views of New York by a long shot. The Rock is right in the middle of Manhattan, ten blocks south of Central Park and pretty much in the center of the island. You can look south and see straight down over Liberty Island, and turn around to see past Central Park all the way to Harlem. Make reservations in advance, and you won't have to wait in line for hours like at the Empire State Building. *30 ROCKEFELLER PLAZA, 49TH STREET BETWEEN FIFTH AND SIXTH AVENUES IN MANHATTAN. Subway: B, D, F, V to 47th-50th Streets-Rockefeller Center.*

159. Rise above the city on the **Chelsea Highline**.

Proof that in New York, everything old becomes new again: the dilapidated remains of the Chelsea Highline, an elevated Depression-era transport system that runs along Tenth Avenue, has been turned into an elevated park. Inspired by Paris's Promenade Plantée, a three-mile stretch of elevated viaducts that was converted into a planted pedestrian walkway in the 1990s, the Chelsea Highline is a unique public space that is removed from the city streets and decorated in a clean and modernist style with plantings, sunken glass-walled viewing areas, and ingenious wooden lounge chairs that can slide up and down the old train tracks. Because the highline runs over the middle of blocks (instead of directly over the avenue), in addition to exquisite views of the Hudson River to the west and the Manhattan skyline to the east, you will also be privy to a bird's-eye view of the passages, gardens, and streets of the Meatpacking District below. The park runs between Gansevoort and West 30th Streets; entrances are located at Gansevoort Street, 14th, 16th, 18th, and 20th Streets, with elevators at the 14th and 16th Street access points.

TENTH AVENUE BETWEEN GANSEVOORT AND WEST 30TH STREETS IN MANHATTAN. Subway: for southern end, A, C, E to 14th Street; L to Eighth Avenue; for northern end, 1, 2, 3, A, C, E to 34th Street-Penn Station. For more information on the highline and the restoration project, call 212-206-9922, or visit www.thehighline.org.

160. Get an aerial view of New York without leaving the ground at the **New York Panorama**.

This permanent exhibit at the Queens Museum of Art is a popular destination for school groups, but it's guaranteed to knock the socks off visitors of all ages. This 9,335-square-foot bird's-eye model of New York City lays out 320 miles of terrain, including nearly 900,000 buildings, and accurately depicts the topography to scale (1 inch = 100 feet). A longtime favorite attraction, the panorama was built for the 1964 World's Fair. Between 1992 and 1994 and again for a few months between 2006 and 2007, it was closed and updated to reflect the changes in landscape during the three decades since its construction. It's quite a sight to behold, both for the view of the land and the mind-boggling detail in which it is depicted. The most shocking feature: how diminutive Manhattan is compared to the other boroughs.

QUEENS MUSEUM OF ART, NEW YORK CITY BUILDING, FLUSHING MEADOWS CORONA PARK IN QUEENS. Subway: 7 to Willets Point-Shea Stadium. The museum is open Wednesday through Sunday; free guided tours of the panorama are offered on Saturday at 3:30 p.m. For more information on hours, directions, and exhibits, call 718-592-9700 or visit www.queens-museum.org.

161. Stand at the top of **Park Avenue** and look downtown.

Flanked on either side by distinguished buildings like the Armory and the Waldorf-Astoria, as well as some of the city's most exclusive addresses, the view down Park Avenue is the ultimate cosmopolitan vista. The planted gardens on the mall lead the way down to 42nd Street, where the graceful Helmsley Building straddles the avenue and sucks the traffic away.

PARK AVENUE BETWEEN 42ND AND 96TH STREETS IN MANHATTAN. Best places to stand are in the 70s and 80s. Subway: 4, 5, 6 to 86th Street; 6 to 77th Street.

162. Look down on Amsterdam Avenue from the **overpass**.

Crossing Amsterdam Avenue at 117th Street, this landscaped extension of Columbia University's main campus is a delightful little perch from which to gaze at the city. Manhattan is laid out in front of you, from the beautiful university buildings and the nearby **Cathedral of Saint John the Divine** (see page 21) all the way downtown. Also on the overpass is Henry Moore's famous *Three Way Piece* sculpture, which spins when you push it (see page 144).

ACROSS AMSTERDAM AVENUE, ACCESSIBLE BETWEEN 116TH AND 118TH STREETS IN MANHATTAN. Subway: 1 to 116th Street-Columbia University.

People-Watching

People are among the most prominent features in the city—and can be some of the most interesting things to look at. In addition to Metrazur and Cipriani Dolce in Grand Central (see page 63), here are some particularly good vantage points for human sightseeing of all genres:

163. *For a mix:* Large enough that you can relax but well-trafficked enough to make it interesting, *the stairs in front of the Metropolitan Museum of Art* is the best place to see a wide variety of people all at once. While most of the other places listed here are good for niche sightings, the steps in front of the Met are the crossroads of so many different kinds of people—foreign tourists, tony art patrons, warring hot-dog vendors, prep-school kids hanging out during free periods—that the possibilities are limitless.

1000 FIFTH AVENUE BETWEEN 82ND AND 84TH STREETS IN MANHATTAN. Subway: 4, 5, 6 to 86th Street.

164. For celebrities: Pastis has the optimal conditions for celebrity sighting: it draws a collection of famous people at pretty much every meal, and it's big enough and has been open long enough that you actually have a chance of getting in. (Most of the time. If you wait long enough.) Though most celebrity hot spots are tepid long before regular people can get in the door, Pastis's relative longevity (it opened in 2000) and its provenance (it was opened by **Keith McNally**, the city's most trusted scene-maker in the restaurant business; see pages 163–164) have established for Pastis the unlikely dual identity of celebrity clubhouse and neighborhood institution. At breakfast, lunch, and dinner (and brunch), this is the place to go to see the somebodies off screen.

9 NINTH AVENUE AT LITTLE WEST 12TH STREET IN MANHATTAN. Subway: A, C, E to 14th Street; L to Eighth Avenue. 212-929-4844. www.pastisny.com.

165. For athletes: From near-professional cyclists to souped-up weekend warriors, **Central Park Drive** is ideal for active-people watching. The benches along the drive are great places to take a break from whatever you're doing and watch the people whiz by on foot, bike, rollerblade, unicycle, or what-have-you. Some benches are established hangouts for different recreational communities, so novices should look before they sit.

Central Park Drive is closed to traffic on weekends and on weekdays between 7:00 p.m. and 10:00 p.m.; much of it is also closed between 10 a.m. and 3 p.m. For more information on Central Park, see entry on pages 219–222.

166. For a picture-perfect ethnic enclave: the Brighton Beach boardwalk is a people-watching dream: a comfortable public place where you can watch endless scenes from another world play out without anyone taking notice of you. From the boardwalk, you have front-row seats of the main set of Little Odessa—the beach, the restaurants, the nightclubs—and all of its vivid characters.

BRIDGEWATER AVENUE IN BROOKLYN. Subway: B, Q to Brighton Beach.

167. *For wild costumes:* Nothing beats **the Eighth Avenue catwalk post-Gay Pride Parade.** Typically, warm weather plus flamboyant dressers turn the strip between 14th and 23rd Streets into a veritable costume parade of its own, where you can see cowboys chatting up fairy princesses, and much more. Actually, it's pretty much a block party all weekend long, so anytime you go should be quite a display. (Just don't try to camp out at one of the open-front bars unless you really want to party. The window seats at Better Burger on the corner of 19th and the bench in front of the Tasti D-Lite between 21st and 22nd are good alternative viewing locations.)

Last Sunday in June. EIGHTH AVENUE BETWEEN 14TH AND 23RD STREETS IN MANHATTAN. Subway: A, C, E to 14th Street; L to Eighth Avenue; C, E to 23rd Street. For more information on the parade, see entry on page 92

.

168. *For the unemployed and aspiring (uptown):* Once the preserve of aristocrats and the literati, reading and writing over innumerable cappuccinos is how many New Yorkers now spend their days. Certain coffee shops and cafés attract a steady crowd during traditional working hours—they toil away on their laptops, working on their next novel, screenplay, or business plan. **The Hungarian Pastry Shop** is a long-standing favorite of the Upper West Side intelligentsia—its walls are plastered with the jackets of the many successful books that have been penned here over the years. It is the perfect place to see writers (professional or otherwise) and Columbia University students having impassioned discussions about existentialism.

1030 AMSTERDAM AVENUE BETWEEN 110TH AND 111TH STREETS IN MANHATTAN. Subway: 1, B, C to 110th Street (Cathedral Parkway).

169. *For the unemployed and aspiring (downtown): Café Doma on Perry Street* is the place to be. Everybody is writing, reading, or mouthing words from a script, and if the customers aren't enough to keep you entertained, the endless stream of West Village characters strolling by the corner windows should do it.

17 PERRY STREET AT SEVENTH AVENUE IN MANHATTAN. Subway: 1 to Christopher Street-Sheridan Square; A, C, E, B, D, F, V to West 4th Street.

170. *For shoppers (uptown):* Find a seat around **the fountains at Columbus Circle** and watch the teeming crowds of uptown shoppers converge from all sides on this popular resting place. Everyone from museum-going tourists to upscale Fifth Avenue department store regulars schlep their bags to the bottom of the park for a breather.

COLUMBUS CIRCLE AT THE SOUTHWEST CORNER OF CENTRAL PARK IN MANHAT-TAN. Subway: 1, A, C, B, D to 59th Street-Columbus Circle.

171. *For shoppers (downtown):* Take a seat on one of the benches that line the *playground on Thompson Street* (at Spring Street) and educate yourself about the different Greenwich Village and SoHo boutiques by observing who's carrying which shopping bag.

Thompson Street at Spring Street in Manhattan. Subway: C, E to Spring Street.

172. *For high fashion (sometimes to a ridiculous degree):* Hang out by the *tents in Bryant Park during Fashion Week.* You'll see editors, models, stylists, and celebrities all dolled up in the season's best, plus a press stunt here and there. If you can manage to get an invite to a show (or offer your services to a PR company as an usher), you'll be privy to some front-row voyeurism inside the tents, and you can partake in the abundant swag that sponsors generously dole out to those cool enough to make it in. Fashion Week is held in September and February, but unless you really want to see cranky fashionistas in heels slip on the ice, September is the more pleasant option.

TENT ENTRANCE ON SIXTH AVENUE BY 41ST STREET IN MANHATTAN. Subway: 7 to Fifth Avenue-Bryant Park; B, D, F, V to 42nd Street-Bryant Park.

And of course, for the grand finale, no list of New York's best views would be complete without a mention of...

173. ...a trip to the top of the Empire State Building.

Pay the entry fee, take the elevator to the eighty-sixth-floor observation deck, and look around. That's New York for you.

350 FIFTH AVENUE BETWEEN 33RD AND 34TH STREETS IN MANHATTAN. www.esbnyc.org. For more information on the building and its history, see entry on page 19.

Expert contributor: Joseph O. Holmes

Joseph O. Holmes is a fine-art photographer based in Brooklyn. He teaches photography at New York University and exhibits his photos in New York and around the United States. He posts a new photo of New York City every day at http://joes-nyc.streetnine.com.

MY FIVE FAVORITE SPOTS TO PHOTOGRAPH— AND PHOTOGRAPH FROM—IN NEW YORK

174. *The walkway of the Manhattan Bridge:*

The Brooklyn Bridge may be more popular with pedestrians, but the best view of the bridge itself is from up the East River a bit, from the less-well-known walkway of the Manhattan Bridge. Accessible from DUMBO in Brooklyn and Chinatown in Manhattan, the walkway has spectacular views south. The best views are on the Manhattan end, where you can look down toward Chinatown and the Lower East Side. (The Brooklyn end looks down into the streets of DUMBO.) Every now and then, a subway train will rumble by, just a few feet from the walkway. Photo tip: use your widest-angle lens to capture the vistas.

ENTER FROM CANAL STREET AT BOWERY IN MANHATTAN, OR AT JAY STREET NEAR SANDS STREET IN BROOKLYN. Subway (Manhattan): J, M, Z to Essex Street or F to Delancey Street; (Brooklyn) A, C to High Street or F to York Street.

175. *The Brooklyn Botanic Garden:*

I visit the BBG all year, and there's never a time when I don't come home with stunning photos. The Japanese Garden is serene after a snowfall, and gorgeous daffodils cover entire hillsides in the spring. The lily ponds are home to dragonflies and huge orange koi (a type of carp). Late in the day is the best time for gorgeous light and beautiful shadows. Photo tip: use a macro lens to shoot the inside of a backlit flower for magnificent color images.

1000 WASHINGTON AVENUE IN BROOKLYN. Subway: B, Q to Prospect Park; 2, 3 to Eastern Parkway-Brooklyn Museum. 718-623-7200. www.bbg.org.

176. *DUMBO:*

The neighborhood under the Manhattan Bridge (the acronym stands for Down Under the Manhattan Bridge Overpass) on the Brooklyn waterfront is slowly being gentrified, but it's still a fabulous spot to find some of the city's best examples of serious graffiti and street art along Water Street between the Manhattan and Brooklyn bridges, as well as picturesque warehouses and abandoned industrial buildings.

There are also some incredible views looking up at the bridges from the Empire-

Fulton Ferry State Park, and it's all just a short walk south to the Brooklyn Heights Promenade, with the city's most famous views of the Manhattan skyline. Photo tip: with the sun setting toward the southwest, dusk often brings breathtaking sunset views of the Manhattan skyline; take a tripod to the promenade and shoot until dark.

Subway: A, C to High Street; F to York Street, and then a short walk toward the water.

177. *Times Square:*

It's been photographed so many times that it's nearly impossible to get a fresh shot of the signs and buildings of Times Square, but that's not why I head there on a regular basis with my camera. Times Square turns out to be a terrific place to photograph people: tourists, of course, but also street musicians, office workers, occasional con artists, and the crowds that gather outside the upstairs MTV studios or the ground-level *Good Morning America* studio, both near 44th Street and Broadway. Photo tip: find whatever attraction is drawing a crowd—then turn around and snap the people watching it.

42ND STREET BETWEEN SIXTH AND NINTH AVENUES IN MANHATTAN. Subway: 1, 2, 3, 7, A, C, E, N, Q, R, W, S to 42nd Street-Times Square.

178. *The subway:*

Contrary to popular belief, it's perfectly legal to take photos in the New York City subway. As a street photographer, I love to get candid shots of train riders, including the *street musicians and performers who sometimes pass through the cars* (see page 370). But check out the Times Square station—particularly the tunnels connecting the A, C, and E lines with the 1, 2, and 3—for the best variety of street performers and artists. Photo tip: always, always tip the performers at least a dollar before shooting.

For subway maps and route information, visit www.mta.info.

CHAPTER 3:

On the Street & Underground

This chapter is devoted to one of New York's unique, idiosyncratic treasures: its streets (and what's underneath them). Difficult to quantify but precious to many inhabitants, New York's street culture is varied, vibrant, and full of possibility—a cherished feature that the city both flaunts and guards, and that is truly accessible only by foot. To its pedestrians, New York offers secret gardens off the driven path, glorious displays of art and architecture, spontaneous entertainment, and edible treasures galore—and it punishes motorists with one-way streets, Byzantine parking restrictions, and uncooperative traffic lights. While in most other places—even major metropolitan areas—walking has gone the way of shoeshines and telephone booths, in New York (thanks to active community groups and falling crime rates), the streets are better than ever.

This chapter also celebrates the city's wonderful subterranean culture. Averaging over five million rides every weekday (and over two million every weekend day) across 468 stations, the subway system is its own underground neighborhood, one that unites New Yorkers from all boroughs, who are as familiar with the twists and turns of their home stations and regular routes as they are with their apartments. And just like every New York neighborhood, the subway system has its own quirks and character, with historic sites, glorious architecture, and more than 200 works of original art.

Perhaps more than any other chapter in the book, this one encourages you to explore, and to be excited by the possibility of discovery. In this chapter, you'll find plenty of things worth seeking out—street festivals, parades, flea markets, and famous movie sites—but many of the entries are for curiosities or charming details that you may have passed many times without knowing where to look or what is special about them. Wonderful things to see and do abound, so keep your eyes open and your feet on the ground.

Street Fairs & Festivals

179. Bump into a **street fair**.

Although there are no official rules distinguishing them, street fairs differ from flea markets in that they move from place to place, and most of the merchandise is new and manufactured rather than secondhand, antique, or handmade crafts. The street-fair "season" runs from April to Thanksgiving, and there's at least one (often more), rain or shine, every weekend during that period. Although each street fair is ostensibly different and tied to a particular neighborhood group or organization, the merchandise and food at most fairs are pretty much the same because almost every fair is produced by the same company that lines up the vendors. (The fairs also all have the same hours: Saturday or Sunday, 10:00 a.m. to 6:00 p.m.) While some of the offerings do change from year to year, you can count on finding discontinued Gap clothing, socks, ties and scarves, cheap sunglasses, jewelry, cosmetics, handbags (mostly designer knock-offs), other cheap clothing, incense and spices, a couple of gadgets that look like they'd be sold on an infomercial, quickie back rubs, and, for food, crêpes, kebabs, grilled corn, fruit shakes, and kettle corn. We recommend them as a diversion, rather than as a destination: a trip to a street fair probably won't have the same sense of discovery as a planned outing to a flea market, but if you happen to bump into one, it can give a little variety to a regular walk and is a dependable source for **cheap back rubs** (see page 283) and free samples of kettle corn.

For list of upcoming fairs, visit www.nycstreetfairs.com/sched.html.

180. Feast at **San Gennaro,** New York's oldest and biggest street festival. Each fall, the streets of Little Italy host a lively eleven-day block party to salute the patron saint of Naples. People of all ethnicities come to partake in the festivities, which include live concerts, several parades, religious processions, and the International Cannoli Eating Championship (the record in 2005: twenty-six cannolis in six minutes).

September. THE FEAST RUNS ALONG MULBERRY STREET BETWEEN CANAL STREET AND HOUSTON STREET, AND ON GRAND STREET AND HESTER STREET BETWEEN MOTT STREET AND BAXTER STREET IN MANHATTAN. Subway: 6, N, Q, R, W, J, M, Z to Canal Street; B, D to Grand Street. For dates and a schedule of events, visit www.sangennaro.org.

181. Celebrate Brooklyn at the **Atlantic Antic**.

On one Sunday in early fall, there is a one-and-a-half-mile outpouring of Brooklyn pride called the Atlantic Antic, which is one of the best street fairs of the year, in any borough. The thirty-five-year-old fair is produced by the Atlantic Avenue Local Development Corporation and very unlike the street fairs described earlier in this chapter; you'll find that the majority of the booths are hosted by local businesses. Instead of crêpes, kettle corn, and cheap sunglasses, there's food from **Sahadi's** (see page 178) and neighborhood restaurants, plus books, jewelry boutiques, live music, martial arts demonstrations, a bounce castle, and pony rides. There's definitely a heavy local flavor to this fair and the neighborhood spirit is contagious; it's a lot of fun no matter what borough (or state) you're from.

September or early October. ATLANTIC AVENUE BETWEEN FOURTH AVENUE AND HICKS STREET IN BROOKLYN. Subway: 2, 3, 4, 5, B, Q to Atlantic Avenue; A, C, G to Hoyt-Schermerhorn Street; D, M, R to Atlantic Avenue-Pacific Street; N to Pacific Street. For more information, the date of this year's fair, and an event schedule, visit www.atlanticave.org.

182. Pig out at the **Big Apple Barbeque Block Party**.

At this two-day urban cookout, award-winning pit masters from all over the country fire up their barbeques in Madison Square Park. You can feast on brisket, ribs, and pork barbequed to perfection while enjoying musical performances, book signings, seminars and guests appearances and other events throughout the day. It's a block party, so admission is free, but you have to buy the food ($8 per plate, with one side). For $100, you can buy a FastPass, which lets you and a guest bypass the lines at the pit masters' stations and is redeemable for the equivalent value of 'cue and merchandise. Proceeds benefit the Madison Park Conservancy, which oversees the maintenance and programming of the park.

June. MADISON SQUARE PARK, 23RD TO 26TH STREETS BETWEEN FIFTH AND MADISON AVENUES IN MANHATTAN. Subway: 6 to 23rd Street; N, R, W to 23rd Street. www.bigapplebbq.org.

183. Visit–for free!–the nine museums that call Fifth Avenue home during the **Museum Mile Festival**.

This annual high-culture block party, held on a Tuesday evening each June, celebrates New York's historic "museum mile," a consortium of the museums that line upper Fifth Avenue. For more than twenty-five years, some of New York's finest museums— including the Met, the Neue Galerie, El Museo del Barrio, the Cooper-Hewitt, the Guggenheim, and the Museum of the City of New York (for more information, see Chapter

4)—have opened their doors to the public and brought together uptown, downtown, and out-of-town for a night of art and revelry. In addition to access to the museums, there are also free performances, music, and displays all along Fifth Avenue between 82nd and 105th Streets, which is closed to traffic during the festival.

June. FIFTH AVENUE BETWEEN 82ND AND 105TH STREETS IN MANHATTAN.

Subway: 4, 5, 6 to 86th Street; 6 to 77th or 96th Streets. For a schedule of events and a list of participating museums, visit www.museummilefestival.org.

---

184. Visit your favorite authors at **New York is Book Country**...

After a brief hiatus, this beloved outdoor book fair is returning to the city in 2010, with a full day of literary-focused events, games, performances, food, and of course, author appearances. It's a celebration of literature and books, so the atmosphere is lively— more like a carnival than a library.

In 2010, New York is Book Country will be held on May 16 in Union Square Park. For schedules, and location and information on fairs in future years, visit www.newyorkisbookcountry.com.

---

185. ...or check in with the city's best independent publishers at the **Brooklyn Book Festival.**

For one weekend in September each year, Columbus Park and the square beside Borough Hall are taken over with stalls, stands, and installations representing Brooklyn's great and diverse literary scene. While book lovers browse books from independent and larger presses alike outside, local and international cultural voices hold panels and debates on the hot literary topics of the day.

September. Borough Hall at Joralemon Street in Brooklyn. Subway: 2, 3, 4, 5, A, C, F to Borough Hall. For more information, visit www. visitbrooklyn.org/BookFestival/festival.html.

---

186. Enjoy the East Village during the **Howl! Festival**.

For one week toward the end of summer, the bars, clubs, cafés, bookstores, and parks of the East Village turn themselves over to the countercultural legacies that have colored their streets since the 1950s. Named for the seminal poem by Allen Ginsberg, the festival preserves the spirit of the Beat Generation that did so much to define the reputation of New York's Lower East Side. Poetry readings, jazz performances, avant-garde dramatics, political debates, and screenings of independent movies spring up on every corner and in every dingy basement, and the whole neighborhood buzzes with its biggest crowds of the year. The highlights of the week are invariably the free events in Tompkins Square Park, the heart of the East Village, where live music, readings, and dance performances take place throughout each day, and where festival-goers can join impromptu classes in art, sculpture, or writing. There are always appearances, scheduled or otherwise, by indie stalwarts such as Chloe Sevigny and John Waters, but it's the spirit of the week and the energy of the artists, performers, and visitors that make the Howl! Festival so special.

Late summer/early fall. TOMPKINS SQUARE PARK IN MANHATTAN. Subway: F, V to Lower East Side-Second Avenue; L to First Avenue. For dates and a schedule of events, check local papers or www.howlfestival.com.

187. Go back in time at the **Cloisters' Medieval Festival**.

What more fitting setting for a Renaissance festival than the **Cloisters** (see page 121)? This annual event, held each autumn, has all of the requisite Renaissance-fair trappings: lavish costumes, minstrels, jugglers, jesters, and, of course, a joust.

Fall. FORT TRYON PARK IN MANHATTAN. Subway: A to 190th Street. 212-923-3700. www.met-museum.org.

188. Celebrate **Bastille Day** (part 1).

The annual Bastille Day Festival held by the **Alliance Française** (see page 301) is the most official way to celebrate France's national holiday. It features music, dancing, performances, and plenty of food.

Sunday near Bastille Day (July 14th). 60TH STREET BETWEEN FIFTH AND LEXINGTON AVENUES IN MANHATTAN. Subway: 4, 5, 6 to 59th Street; N, R, W to Fifth Avenue/59th Street or Lexington Avenue/59th Street. For more information and the date of next year's festival, visit www.fiaf.org or call 212-355-6100.

189. Celebrate **Bastille Day** (part 2): Pétanque.

Thought bocce was the only kind of lawn bowling around? Brooklyn boasts a de facto French *quartier* of restaurants and bars, and at this annual Bastille Day celebration on Smith Street, you can try your hand at the quintessential French street sport, pétanque. For the event, temporary courts are set up and filled with the traditional mounds of sand to prevent anyone from confusing it with that other European street game. Local stores and restaurants join in the celebration, and the street is filled with stalls selling food, drink, and other treats.

Sunday near Bastille Day, 9:00 a.m. to 8:00 p.m. SMITH STREET BETWEEN PACIFIC AND BERGEN STREETS IN BROOKLYN. Subway: F, G to Bergen Street.

190. Take a kid on the haunted carousel at the **Prospect Park Halloween Carnival**.

Walking through the ravine of Prospect Park on a windy fall day can be scary even without the monsters, witches, skeletons, and ghosts that populate its woods on Halloween. But every year, local volunteers transform the park into a great Halloween party, with walks through the decorated woods, events, rides, games, and frights spread out across the park. Kids can enhance their costumes with an expert face-painter or help carve spectacular pumpkins on the grass in Nethermead. Fair games are flavored with a ghoulish twist—here you throw balls at skulls, not cans—and the snacks are warm and seasonal, from spicy pumpkin pie to mulled wine for the grown-ups. Gather round for scary stories of the ghosts of Brooklyn past at the Lefferts Homestead or walk through the creepy haunted barn at the zoo. The highlight of the day is a frightening ride on the haunted carousel: the lights go down and evil laughter booms out as bats, spiders, and ghosts drift around the spinning children's heads.

Saturday before Halloween, usually from noon to 3:00 p.m. PROSPECT PARK IN BROOKLYN. Subway: 2, 3 to Grand Army Plaza or Eastern Parkway-Brooklyn Museum; F to Seventh Avenue or 15th Street-Prospect Park; B, Q to Prospect Park. For details, visit www.prospect-park.org.

191. Paint your face and samba down Sixth Avenue at the **Brazil Day Festival**.

On September 7, 1822, Brazil won independence from Portugal, and on the first Sunday in September, New York celebrates this victory. The northern end of Sixth Avenue, from 43rd Street up to Central Park, is lined with stages, stalls, and bandstands. The Brazil Day Festival is one of the most colorful, sexy, and lively of the city's street fairs: teams of footballers in the patriotic yellow and green stripes play games in the street; troupes of amazing dancers perform up and down the avenue; and Brazilian restaurants and food stores sell delicious snacks and exotic fruit juices.

First Sunday in September, 10:00 a.m. to 7:00 p.m. SIXTH AVENUE BETWEEN 42ND AND 56TH STREETS IN MANHATTAN. Subway: B, D, F, V to 47th-50th Streets-Rockefeller Center. Check local listings for festival details.

192. Sing the "Dachs Song" along with the dogs at the **Washington Square Park Dachshund Festival**.

On the first Saturday in October ("Dachtober Fest") and the last Saturday in April ("the Dachshund Spring Fiesta"), proud dachshund owners (don't call them hot dogs!) congregate under the arch in Washington Square Park for the singing of the "Dach Song."

Many of the dogs come in costume, although the festival coordinators stress that fancy dress isn't mandatory, and they welcome those outside the dachshund family to join them as well. The song is pretty much it for organized activities—the "festival" is intended as a social event for dogs and their owners—but the spectacle of dozens of tiny pups all dressed up as their glowing parents show them off is too precious to miss. As a bulldog-owning passerby once lamented, "You don't get that kind of camaraderie among bulldog owners."

First Saturday in October and last Saturday in April. Meet under the arch in Washington Square Park; singing starts at noon. FIFTH AVENUE AT WASHINGTON SQUARE NORTH IN MANHATTAN. Subway: A, C, E, B, D, F, V to West 4th Street. For more information and upcoming festival dates, visit www.nycgovparks.org/washingtonsquarepark/events or www.dachshundfriendshipclub.com/events.

Parades

193. Sit on the street and watch the **Macy's Thanksgiving Day Parade...**

Yes, it's early in the morning, and yes, it's usually pretty cold (it might even snow), but watching the Macy's Thanksgiving Day Parade is something that everyone should do at least once, preferably with (or as) a kid. Even if you've watched it on TV every year, the enormous balloons, the elaborate floats, and the choreography of the marching bands are truly exciting to see in person, and it feels a lot more like a parade without the commentary or commercial breaks. Go early (i.e., well before 9:00 a.m., when the parade starts) and grab a spot on the street. Our favorite viewing spots are on Central Park West, where the streets are a bit wider (the parade starts at 77th Street). Wherever you go, the crowd is pretty deep, but if you've got little kids, they can sit underneath the police barriers and have a front-row view of the parade going by. You can't bring folding chairs, but hot chocolate is a must.

Thanksgiving morning at 9:00 a.m. THE PARADE STARTS AT 77TH STREET AND CENTRAL PARK WEST, CROSSES TO BROADWAY AT COLUMBUS CIRCLE, AND THEN PROCEEDS DOWN BROADWAY TO MACY'S AT 34TH STREET IN MANHATTAN. Subways: 1, A, C, B, D to 59th Street-Columbus Circle; B, C to 72nd Street or 81st Street-Museum of Natural History; N, R, W to 49th Street or 57th Street. For more information and a map of the parade route, visit www.macy.com.

→ **DID YOU KNOW?** *The parade was started in 1924 and has been held every year since (except between 1942 and 1944 when Macy's donated the balloons to the war effort).*

194. ...but first, watch the **balloons being inflated** the night before.

The night before Thanksgiving, you can watch the balloons being blown up between 77th and 81st streets by the American Museum of Natural History. The view is best from above, but if you can't snag one of the luxury apartments in the vicinity (or don't have a friend who lives in one), you can watch the annual spectacle for free on the street below.

Balloons are inflated outside the Museum of Natural History on the Wednesday before Thanksgiving Day from 3:00 p.m. to 10:00 p.m. 77ᵀᴴ TO 81ˢᵀ STREETS BETWEEN CENTRAL PARK WEST AND COLUMBUS AVENUE IN MANHATTAN. Subway: B, C to 81ˢᵗ Street-Museum of Natural History.

195. Celebrate the beginning of summer at the **Mermaid Parade**.

The Mermaid Parade has the festive spirit of the Macy's Thanksgiving Day Parade, the flamboyant style of the Halloween Parade, and exudes New York pride like none other. Every year, to mark the beginning of beach season, a King Neptune and Queen Mermaid lead a dazzling, vaguely maritime-themed costume parade along Coney Island's Surf Avenue, with elaborate floats, swimsuit-clad marchers, and assorted sea creatures waving to bystanders from the top of antique cars. If you've got a gorgeous costume, you can march, but you must register in advance on the Coney Island Web site (see below) and pay a small fee. Watching is free, however, and the experience is priceless. This is truly New York at its best—an event where people of different types and ages come together just to have fun. It's a spectacle like none other and should not be missed.

First Saturday after the summer solstice. SURF AVENUE, CONEY ISLAND, BROOKLYN. Subway: F, D, N, Q to Coney Island-Stillwell Avenue. For more information, exact parade location, and the date of this year's parade, visit www.coneyisland.com/mermaid. For more information on Coney Island and its attractions, see pages 348–349.

196. Spend the last day of the summer at the **West Indian-American Day Parade & Carnival**.

For most of the country, the first Monday in September is Labor Day, a bittersweet national holiday signaling the end of summer and a day off from work. Here, it's West Indian-American Day, the day of the city's biggest parade. The parade, which travels down Eastern Parkway to Grand Army Plaza, tops off a four-day celebration of West Indian and Caribbean culture. The parade itself is an all-day affair, drawing more than three million people who come to see the elaborate floats and masquerade performers, listen to steel drums and calypso music, and gorge on food from all different parts of the Caribbean.

Labor Day, 11:00 a.m. to 6:00 p.m. EASTERN PARKWAY FROM ROCHESTER STREET TO GRAND ARMY PLAZA IN BROOKLYN. Subway: 2, 3 to Grand Army Plaza or 3, 4 to Utica Avenue. For more information, visit www.wiadca.org.

197. Check out **PrideFest** & the **Gay Pride Parade**.

The Lesbian, Gay, Bisexual, and Transgender (LGBT) Pride March (commonly known as the Gay Pride Parade) tops off a weeklong commemoration of the historic Stonewall raid in 1969, the event that set off a nationwide gay rights movement. The parade, held the last Sunday in June, starts at 52nd Street and goes down Fifth Avenue, then Sixth, then over to Christopher Street, ending by the Stonewall Bar, where it feeds into an enormous block party called PrideFest that lasts into the wee hours of the night. There is a moment of silence at 2:00 p.m. to honor those who have died of AIDS, but otherwise, the parade and PrideFest are upbeat, inspiring festivals that, in the spirit of inclusion, welcome anyone and everyone to celebrate. If you're anywhere in the area, the parade is hard to miss—and it's nearly impossible not to get swept up in its lively, good-humored spirit—but it's from Union Square south that is the most fun to watch from.

Last Sunday in June. Parade starts at noon; PrideFest starts at 11:00 a.m. and continues until 10:00 p.m. FIFTH AVENUE FROM 52ND STREET TO 8TH STREET, ACROSS 8TH STREET TO CHRISTOPHER STREET, CHRISTOPHER STREET TO GREENWICH STREET IN MANHATTAN. Subway: 4, 5, 6, L, N, Q, R, W to 14th Street-Union Square; 1 to Christopher Street-Sheridan Square (for Pride-Fest). For more information and to view schedules and exact parade route, visit www.nycpride.org.

198. Show off your costume at the **Village Halloween Parade**.

In most places, there aren't many good things to do on Halloween once you've aged out of trick-or-treating. But in New York, you can march in the Village Halloween Parade, the nation's largest and most famous Halloween celebration and the city's most inclusive parade. No need to be a member of a certain group or organization or to apply far in advance—all you have to do is show up at the starting point, pick a spot, and march! (If you like, you can let the parade organizers know beforehand what you'll be dressing as through their Web site.) If you don't want to come in costume, you can also volunteer to man one of the many elaborate puppets that are made for the parade each year. You can watch it from the streets, but because most of the action is pretty low to the ground (there are no big floats or balloons), it can be hard to get a good view from behind the crowds—and besides, once the music gets going and the costumes start rolling out, we bet you'll be sorry if you've left yours at home.

Halloween. The line to march begins at 6:30 p.m. (and accepts marchers until 8:30 p.m.) at Sixth Avenue between Broome and Spring. The parade starts at 7:00 p.m. UP SIXTH AVENUE

FROM SPRING STREET TO 23RD STREET IN MANHATTAN. Subways: C, E to Spring Street; A, C, E, B, D, F, V to West 4th Streets; F, V to 14th Street; L to Sixth Avenue. For more information, visit www.halloween-nyc.com.

→ **DID YOU KNOW?** *The Village Halloween Parade—now the largest organized Halloween celebration in the country—was started by one man in 1973. A puppeteer and mask-maker, he started doing it as a walk with his own and other neighborhood children.*

199. Watch the Lion Dance at the **Chinese New Year** celebration.

The traditional Chinese New Year celebration begins on the first day of the new lunar year and lasts for two weeks until the full moon. During this time, hundreds of people brave the cold for days and come out to Chinatown for performances, ceremonial dances, firecracker displays, and a big parade. See the troupes of dancers perform traditional Lion Dances, where several members join to form a lion's body and dance through the streets.

Chinese New Year occurs in January or February; the parade in Chinatown is usually held on a Sunday during the New Year celebration. CHINATOWN AROUND MOTT, CANAL, AND BAYARD STREETS IN MANHATTAN. Subway: 6, N, Q, R, W, J, M, Z to Canal. Check local listings for parade date.

Give your debit card a break and shop at a **flea market.**

Like many cities, New York has a vibrant flea-market culture, with a ceaseless supply of crafts and antiques and a continuous demand of dedicated shoppers. But unlike the never-ending bazaars of Portobello Road or Camden Town in London, or Clignancourt in Paris, most of the flea markets here are the more manageable "boutiquestyle." They are relatively small, with a comparatively well-edited selection of vendors, and though the merchandise doesn't vary that much from market to market (i.e., clothes, jewelry, collectibles, furniture), each has its own devoted clientele. All of the following markets are easy to navigate and can be visited in a morning or an afternoon. And most are open year-round—a testament both to the appeal of the goods as well as to the devotion of the people who operate and frequent them.

200. *The Brooklyn Flea:* The biggest and best thing to happen to the city's flea market culture (and to local shopping as a whole) has been this market, now held on both weekend days in two different locations. What makes the Flea so great is a simple equation: great vendors + great food + great atmosphere = a guaranteed fabulously enjoyable afternoon of shopping and wandering. Most of the wares are handmade, many by local artists, though vendors selling everything from vintage clothing to furniture to bicycles turn up as well. The borough's reputation as a foodie paradise shows up on the snack side as well. There's everything from homemade pickles and lobster rolls to artisanal ice cream and mini cupcakes, and whatever you fancy, it's going to be great. On Saturdays, the Flea takes place in its original location in Fort Greene in the playground of the Bishop Loughlin Memorial High School. On Sundays, many of the same vendors head over to the Brooklyn Bridge for the DUMBO edition. The Fleas take place rain or shine, and in the winter, the markets move to nearby indoor space.

The Saturday Market takes place from 10 a.m. until 5 p.m. at Bishop Loughlin Memorial High School. LAFAYETTE AVENUE BETWEEN CLERMONT AND VANDERBILT AVENUES. Subway: G to Clinton-Washington Avenues. The Sunday Flea runs from 11 a.m. until 6 p.m. by the Brooklyn Bridge at WATER STREET BY EMPIRE FULTON FERRY STATE PARK. For more information and a vendor list, visit www.brownstoner.com/brooklynflea.

201. *Annex/Hell's Kitchen:* Formerly known as the 26th Street Market, the Annex was long the most popular flea market in the city, and most weekends you were likely to see as many celebrities as antique clocks. Several years ago, the Annex vendors migrated a few blocks north to join the budding Hell's Kitchen Market in a closed-to-traffic area on 39th Street between Tenth and Eleventh Avenues. Flea market purists may at first feel disoriented with the new layout, which looks more like a street fair than the traditional flea market square, but they will quickly feel at home when they see the mix of vintage wares, next to the jewelry, clothing, and craft makers.

Saturday and Sunday, year-round. 39TH STREET BETWEEN NINTH AND TENTH AVENUES IN MANHATTAN. Subway: 1, 2, 3, 7, N, Q, R, W, S to Times Square-42nd Street; A, C, E to 42nd Street-Port Authority Bus Terminal. 212-243-5343. www.hellskitchenfleamarket.com.

202. *25th Street Market/Garage:* These two markets, which take place every weekend on 25th Street on opposite sides of Sixth Avenue, are the last fleas standing in a neighborhood that used to be the heart of the industry. The wares here range from true vintage to stuff that's a (small) step above what you'd see at suburban garage sale. Still, treasures can be had for those who are willing to dig, rummage, and haggle—in other words, for people who want an authentic flea market experience. N.B: The Garage is indoors.

Saturdays and Sundays, year-round. Both locations in Manhattan. West 25th Street market is located on WEST 25TH STREET BETWEEN BROADWAY AND SIXTH AVENUE. The Garage is located at 112 WEST 25TH STREET, BETWEEN SIXTH AND SEVENTH AVENUES.

203. *Greenflea Market:* The Upper West Side's answer to the Annex is Greenflea, an indoor/outdoor market held every Sunday (and occasional Saturdays) at MS 44, a middle school near the Museum of Natural History. Outside in the playground, the vendors are a mix of secondhand vendors selling crafts, jewelry, and clothing, and a small **Green-**

market (see page 334) on the northern end. Inside, mostly antiques, vintage clothing, and collectibles are sold. Greenflea is operated by the parent's association of two neighborhood public schools, and the money it generates goes toward enrichment programs at the two schools. There is also a sister location in the West Village on Saturdays at PS 41. *Greenflea Market is held Sundays year round, and occasional Saturdays (visit market's Web site for dates of upcoming Saturday markets). COLUMBUS AVENUE BETWEEN 76ᵀᴴ AND 77ᵀᴴ STREETS IN MANHATTAN. Subway: 1 to 79ᵗʰ Street or B, C to 81ˢᵗ Street-Museum of Natural History. Downtown: Saturdays. GREENWICH AVENUE AT CHARLES STREET IN MANHATTAN. Subway: 1, 2, 3 to 14ᵗʰ Street; A,C, E, B, D, F, V to West 4ᵗʰ Street. 212-239-3025. www.greenfleamarkets.com.*

204. Park Slope Flea Market: The parent's association of PS 321 in Brooklyn's Park Slope operates a flea market in the school's playground every Saturday and Sunday. The vendors sell antique, vintage, and homemade wares, and like Greenflea, the proceeds fund enrichment programs at the school.
Saturdays and Sundays. 180 SEVENTH AVENUE BETWEEN 1ST AND 2ND STREETS IN BROOKLYN. Subway: F to Seventh Avenue. 718-330-9395. www.ps321.org.

205. Saint Patrick's Old Cathedral Outdoor Market: There's no used merchandise at this NoLita market held at New York's first cathedral church (it became Saint Patrick's Old Cathedral when the new **Saint Patrick's Cathedral** opened in 1879—see page 21), so the selection is a little more upscale than most. Instead of antique and secondhand vendors, artists and craftspeople sell original art, jewelry, and accessories similar to what is sold at the boutiques in the surrounding area.
Friday through Sunday, April through December. PRINCE STREET BETWEEN MOTT AND MULBERRY STREETS IN MANHATTAN. Subway: 6 to Spring Street; B, D, F, V to Broadway-Lafayette Street; N, R, W to Prince Street. www.oldstpatricksmarket.com.

206. Union Square Holiday Market: Just after Thanksgiving, when the fall harvest of the Greenmarket is over and winter is approaching, the lower plaza in front of Union Square turns into a holiday bazaar, with dozens of craftspeople and artists hawking their wares. The goods are on the crafty and creative side—carved wooden boxes, jewelry, woven scarves—and not all of them are as cheap as you might think. However, it is a convenient place to find a holiday gift, and though it gets packed on weekends, it's a nice place to walk around on weekdays if the weather isn't too harsh (the stalls provide cover from the elements but little warmth). N.B. A similar outdoor market is now held in Columbus Circle during the holiday season.
Late November through Christmas. UNION SQUARE AND 14ᵀᴴ STREET IN MANHATTAN. Subway: 4, 5, 6, L, N, Q, R, W to 14ᵗʰ Street-Union Square. Columbus Circle market is held by the SOUTHWEST ENTRANCE OF CENTRAL PARK. Subway: A,B,C,D,1 to 59ᵗʰ Street-Columbus Circle.

207. Check out **stoop sales** in Brooklyn:

The Big Apple version of the yard sale is the seasonal stoop sales that happen along the quiet, brownstone-lined streets in the neighborhoods of Brooklyn. On weekends, you can usually count on seeing several on residential streets in neighborhoods like Brooklyn Heights, Carroll Gardens, Cobble Hill, and Park Slope. People usually advertise by putting up flyers around the neighborhoods, and directions can be found inscribed on the sidewalks in chalk. N.B. Stoop sales have been known to migrate across the river and into some neighborhoods in downtown Manhattan. Brooklyn is still the industry heart, but on warm days—especially ones near the end of the month, when people are getting ready to move—you may bump into some on the other side of the bridge. *Various locations, Brooklyn. Serendipity is part of the stoop sale's charm, but the Web site www.bklynstoop.com can be used as a general guide to some upcoming sales.*

Go on a **walking tour**...

Whether you've been here a few hours or forty years, a walking tour can be an edifying way to see the city. There are literally hundreds to choose from, and they run the gamut from historical sightseeing excursions, to the urbane Brooklyn house tours, to more specialized jaunts focused on gastronomy, art, and architecture. Here are some suggestions:

208. *Big Onion Walking Tours:* A nearly twenty-year veteran of the city touring industry, the Big Onion tours are considered the most comprehensive and intelligent tours in the city. The vast range of outings on offer includes expeditions through ethnic neighborhoods like Chinatown and Little Italy, walks through celebrated artistic communities such as Greenwich Village and SoHo, treks through the oldest parts of the city from Harlem through Central Park to the South Street Seaport, and much, much more. Led by doctoral students, historians, and longtime local residents—people who know their stuff—the tours are well thought-out and extremely informative, encompassing all that's of interest in each district and sometimes focusing on one aspect in particular. A tour might, for instance, highlight the unique architecture of old Brooklyn brownstones in Park Slope, the history of the New York intelligentsia on the Upper West Side, or the visible legacies of immigrant communities on the Lower East Side. Tours almost always start at 1:00 p.m., but check the Web site or call the tour hotline for up-to-date schedules and information. *For current offerings and schedules, call 212-439-1090, or visit www.bigonion.com.*

209. *Eat your way through the city on a food-focused walking tour.* Any notions you may have of walking tours as hokey field trips will disappear when you experience the gourmet expeditions offered by the **Institute of Culinary Education**

(see page 297). Each season, they offer more than a dozen different tours, including ethnic explorations of enclaves such as Chinatown, Curry Hill, the Lower East Side, and, via the 7 train, the many ex-pat cuisines of Queens; specialty- and ingredient-focused tours on wine or chocolate; and tours of markets and Greenmarkets. The schedule changes each season, so check online to see what's currently on offer. Reservations are required, and these tours do fill up, so it's a good idea to reserve early.

Tour times and departure points vary; see online schedule for specifics. Tours are held on weekends and cost between $75 and $110 per person. To register, call 1-800-522-4610 or e-mail RecreationalDivision@iceculinary.com. For more information, visit www.iceculinary.com/recreational/walking_tours.shtml. For address and additional information about ICE, see page 297.

210. *Municipal Art Society Walking Tours:* The Municipal Art Society of New York, a formidably accomplished civic group dedicated to the instigation and preservation of creative, useful, and beautiful works of public art in the city, has been sponsoring architectural tours of the five boroughs for fifty years. Led by a mix of architectural historians, urban planners, geographers, and writers, the walking tours are organized around districts whose streets and buildings reflect periods of particular political, artistic, or social interest, so there is a real coherence to the walk and the tour guide's patter. Subjects include "Art Deco Midtown," which takes in the Waldorf-Astoria and Rockefeller Center, among other examples of the period; a tour chronicling the history of the New York skyscraper; and an exploration of the architectural remnants of old middle-European communities on the Upper East Side. The MAS now offers bus tours, too, including a drive around the historic north shore of Staten Island. The tours are popular, so check their Web site or hotline for schedules and tour details ahead of time. *Walking tours are $15 ($10 for members of MAS); bus tours $15. 212-935-3960. www.mas.org.*

211. *Brooklyn House Tours.* Brooklyn residents never tire of regaling people with the residential beauty of their borough, and they've got good reason to be so house-proud. Brooklyn has many enclaves with grand, notable, and interesting houses and brownstones, and the natural curiosity about what lies inside these private treasures has evolved into a rigorous enterprise of house tours. In the spring and fall, many neighborhood organizations (Brooklyn is nothing if not neighborhood-oriented) offer inside-and-outside tours of some of the area's prominent private homes and gardens. The Brooklyn Heights Association Landmarks House and Garden Tour (in early May) is among the most popular, which takes pie-eyed visitors through different homes in the historic district, showing off the neighborhood's celebrated and diverse nineteenth- and early-twentieth-century architecture. Other areas that can be explored on tours are Clinton Hill, with its glorious turn-of-the-century mansions; Cobble Hill and Prospect Heights, otherwise known as "Brownstone Brooklyn," with their exquisite private gardens; and Flatbush, which has a stunning array of Victorian-era houses. Even those familiar with Brooklyn may be shocked by the grandeur of the houses in certain areas, and it's interesting to see how the current owners coexist within their exalted habitats. Of course, the voyeuristic pleasure of nosing around a stranger's house goes without saying.

For more information about the Landmarks House and Garden tour, visit the Brooklyn Heights Association's Web site at www.brooklynheightsassociation.com. Check local listings or publications such as Time Out *for information and dates of other tours.*

212. *Forgotten NY walking tours:* These irregular, informal walking tours are as fantastic and as quirky as the Web site they are affiliated with (see entry below or pages 105–106), allowing participants to see for themselves the secrets in the city's nooks and crannies. Itineraries range from close inspections of well-trodden areas to intrepid jaunts to far-flung areas at the borough's edges. There's no regular schedule, so we can't guarantee when they'll take place or where they will cover, only that no matter where you go, you will see things you didn't know existed.

Forgotten NY tours take place six to eight times a year, and are announced on the Web site, www.forgotten-ny.com.

...or take **your own walking tour,** guided by one of these two excellent city chroniclers:

213: *Songlines.* Jim Naureckas's "virtual walking tour" of Manhattan is truly one of the city's greatest treasures, and using his online street map is one of the best things to do in New York. Go to his modest, unflashy Web site, and you will find a meticulous point-by-point history of New York City streets, with an entry for nearly every address (yes, you read that right). On the homepage, he explains his inspiration for the site, and then provides a list of streets and avenues to view. Choose one, and you'll be taken to a page where you can cruise from one end to the other (west to east for streets; north to south for avenues), reading the eclectic histories of each block, both real (historic and current) and imagined (from literature, movies, and comic books). As of this writing, he's mapped from the Financial District to 59th Street, and from Avenue D to Eleventh Avenue, plus many of those streets in the West Village that go "off the grid." But what is perhaps even more impressive than the fact that Naureckas took the time to put this together is that he's still working—not only are new streets added regularly but existing streets are updated and expanded upon.

www.nysonglines.com.

214. *Forgotten NY:* Kevin Walsh, a Brooklyn native who's been around long enough to have witnessed the construction of the Verrazano-Narrows Bridge as a child, created and maintains a wonderful Web site devoted to the exploration of New York past

and present. With amazing patience, a keen eye for detail, and an unriν
for the secrets of the city, Walsh continues to scour the five boroughs
points of historical interest that range from little-known lighthouses to a
trading sites, from buried landmarks to rooftop views, and from overlc
spots to rusted-over signposts. The Web site is updated regularly and is illustrated with
hundreds of photographs that reveal a city within a city, the remains of a metropolis
hidden by the New York we know today.
www.forgotten-ny.com.

Interesting Houses & Beautiful Blocks

215. Walk down the "**Block Beautiful...**"

A.k.a 19th Street between Third Avenue and Irving Place. The name comes from an
issue of *House Beautiful* from the turn of the twentieth century, praising Frederick J.
Sterner's remodeling of the block's nineteenth-century row houses. Ironically, the name
stuck and refers today to those same well-preserved early twentieth-century houses
Sterner praised then for their modernity. The buildings on this quiet block are truly
interesting; even architecture neophytes will delight in the eclectic and colorful houses
and brownstones. Look out for the four figurines of jockeys in front of no. 139, the lion
gargoyles in front of no. 145, the surprising brick exterior of no. 130, and the beautiful
gable on top of no. 124. Famous past residents of the block include George Bellows,
Oleg Cassini, Ethel Barrymore, and the painter Cecilia Beaux; the ivy-covered four-story
mansion on the northeast corner (80 Irving Place) was also used as the home of Sigourney Weaver's character in *Working Girl*.
*19TH STREET BETWEEN THIRD AVENUE AND IRVING PLACE IN MANHATTAN. Subway: 4, 5, 6,
L, N, Q, R, W to 14th Street-Union Square.*

...or walk down a **beautiful block**.

Though they don't boast 19th Street's official title, the following blocks and areas are
all lovely to wander:

216. *The Village*. Bohemian history and celebrated residents aside, the parts of the West
Village that lie between the Hudson River and Seventh Avenue South, where the streets
break the mold of Manhattan's grid system, are among the most charming in the city.
Spend an afternoon walking along Bank, Commerce, Perry, Gay, Barrow, Charles, and Morton Streets, and you will find not only some of the most beautiful and eccentric houses
in New York but also some pleasant surprises in hidden bookshops, bars, restaurants, and

alleyways. Can you find Left Bank Books, a beloved used-books store? And can you discover all the entrances to the old speakeasy formerly known as Chumley's (see page 53)? In spring, the blossoming trees that line the blocks are stunning; in winter, it is one of the few neighborhoods where the smell of wood-burning stoves still fills the evening air.

MANHATTAN. Subway: 1 to Christopher Street-Sheridan Square; A, C, E, B, D, F, V to West 4th Street.

217. *Brooklyn Heights.* Although much of Brooklyn Heights can be admired for its architecture and for its value as a historic district of old Brooklyn, there are a few blocks that stand out as some of the prettiest and most romantic streets in New York. Build up to a stroll along the Promenade (see page 66) by walking around Willow Street, Love Lane, Joralemon Street, Pierrepont Place, and the "fruit" streets (Cranberry Street, Orange Street, and Pineapple Street)—all roads that extend into Brooklyn Heights between the Promenade, Atlantic Avenue, and Cadman Plaza. Be sure to find Grace Court Alley and Hunt's Lane, two of the smallest streets in the neighborhood, whose buildings were formerly stables for Brooklyn's more-well-to-do residents. At night, the light drifting over the East River and flickering from the gas lamps outside the houses makes you feel like you've stepped into another time.

BROOKLYN. Subway: 2, 3 to Clark Street; M, R to Court Street-Borough Hall.

218. *Central Park West:* The Upper East Side may have been considered New York's "Gold Coast," but for the city's best urban castles, you've got to head across the park. Central Park West boasts several palatial apartment buildings, the grandeur of which will be striking to even the most jaded New Yorker. Highlights include the Beresford (211 CPW at 81st Street), a majestic building that wraps around to 81st Street and overlooks the Museum of Natural History, affording its residents the Holy Grail of New York real estate: green exposure on both sides (it's also the best place from which to watch the balloons being blown up for the **Macy's Thanksgiving Day Parade**; see page 90); the Kenilworth (151 CPW), distinguished by its ornate two-tone brick and limestone façade; the San Remo (145 CPW between 74th and 75th Streets), a twin-towered Art Deco masterpiece that has been home to Rita Hayworth, Dustin Hoffman, and Diane Keaton; the handsome Langham, with its pyramids and elegant entry marquee (135 CPW between 73rd and 74th Streets), and of course, the Dakota (1 West 72nd Street at CPW). Farther north is the El Dorado (300 CPW between 90th and 91st), another twin-towered behemoth designed by the same architect who did the San Remo.

MANHATTAN. Subway: 1, A, C, B, D to 59th Street-Columbus Circle; B, C to 72nd Street, 81st Street-Museum of Natural History, 86th or 96th Streets.

219. *Washington Square North:* This well-preserved stretch of townhouses, known as "the Row," looks like it hasn't changed since Henry James was around. But unless you're thinking of going into academia, you'll have to content yourself with admiring the buildings from the park. Like many pieces of desirable downtown real estate, these houses are owned by New York University and are mostly inhabited by deans and professors. Speaking of the NYU monopoly, just around the corner from the Row is **Washington Mews** (see page 189), a quaint cobblestone street between University Place and Fifth Avenue just north of the park. Although it is officially a private street, nobody will notice if you walk through it, provided you keep your mouth shut—the Mews is home to NYU's La Maison Française, and French is the lingua franca here.

BETWEEN UNIVERSITY PLACE AND FIFTH AVENUE IN MANHATTAN, ONE BLOCK NORTH OF WASHINGTON SQUARE PARK. Subway: A, C, E, B, D, F, V to West 4th Street.

220. *Historic Park Slope:* The part of Park Slope that runs from Prospect Park to Seventh Avenue between Grand Army Plaza and 3rd Street is among the more austere and beautiful parts of Brooklyn. Walk the "extra block" (a small block that disrupts the otherwise meticulously gridded area) that runs between Garfield Place, Polhemus Place, Carroll Street, and Fiske Place, for a true sense of the history of the neighborhood's buildings; and 3rd Street, one of the widest and prettiest blocks in the neighborhood and the epitome of quiet, tree-lined Brooklyn.

BETWEEN GRAND ARMY PLAZA, PROSPECT PARK, AND 3RD STREET IN BROOKLYN. Subway: 2, 3 to Grand Army Plaza; D, M, N, R to Union Street or 9th Street; F to Seventh Avenue.

While you're walking the streets, check out a house of distinction.

Whether for their history, their tenants, or their architecture, the following houses and buildings are all worth seeking out if you find yourself in the neighborhood. (Note: These are some of our favorites, but New York is filled with interesting buildings. A good way to find out about them is by looking at Songlines—see page 98. If you happen to see a remarkable house, note its address, and then check the site and read the entry that accompanies it.)

221. Find the plaque for **Bela Bartók**.

For the last five years of his life—1940 to 1945, the happiest period of his self-imposed exile in the United States—influential composer Bela Bartók lived with his pianist wife in relative poverty on West 57th Street. A plaque commemorates his time at the building.

309 WEST 57TH STREET BETWEEN FIFTH AND SIXTH AVENUES IN MANHATTAN. Subway: F, V to 57th Street; N, Q, R, W to 57th Street.

Don't blink or you'll miss the **narrowest house** in the city.

This little house is quite distinguished despite its size. Built in 1873, it was originally used as the carriage entrance for the house next door, no. 77, also known as the Isaacs-Hendricks House, which is the oldest house in the Village (it was built in 1799). At just 9½ feet wide, no. 75½ is now considered the narrowest house in the city. But its diminutive size hasn't prevented it from attracting some big-name tenants: John Barrymore once lived there, as did the poet Edna St. Vincent Millay.

75½ BEDFORD STREET BETWEEN COMMERCE AND MORTON STREETS IN MANHATTAN. Subway: 1 to Christopher Street-Sheridan Square.

223. Stand on **Allen Ginsberg's stoop**.

From the mid-1950s until shortly before his death in 1997, legendary Beat poet and hero of the East Village Allen Ginsberg lived in a humble apartment at 206 East 7th Street. His rooms were the meeting place of many influential poets and musicians, and everyone acquainted with Ginsberg from Bob Dylan to Jack Kerouac visited him here.

206 EAST 7TH STREET BETWEEN AVENUES B AND C IN MANHATTAN. Subway: L to First Avenue; F, V to Lower East Side-Second Avenue.

224. Salute the Union Jack at **10 Downing Street**.

A restaurant, a condo, and a dry cleaner share New York's equivalent of the Prime Minister's address. Hence the cleaner's incongruous Union Jack awning.

10 DOWNING STREET AT SIXTH AVENUE IN MANHATTAN. Subway: A, B, C, D, E, F, V to West 4th Street.

225. Find country in the city at the **Mount Vernon Hotel Museum and Garden**.

The appearance of this nineteenth-century mansion hidden smack in the middle of the city is a sight in itself. Originally built as a retreat for New Yorkers when this part of the city was rural, the mansion has been preserved, and despite the changes that have taken place around it, it remains pretty much as it was two centuries ago. Stand at the foot of the quaint little path and look up through the pretty flower garden to its front door. You'll enjoy the rare sight of a country cottage in Midtown (and film buffs will recognize it as one of the treats of Manhattan that Sam Waterston's character shows off in Woody Allen's *Hannah and Her Sisters*).

421 EAST 61ST STREET BETWEEN FIRST AND YORK AVENUES IN MANHATTAN. Subway: 4, 5, 6 to 59th Street; N, R, W to Lexington Avenue/59th Street. www.mvhm.org.

Subways & Subway Stations

→ **DID YOU KNOW?** *The number of subway stations within the New York City transit system (468) is only 35 fewer than the number of stations of all other subway systems in the country combined.*

226. Visit the **subterranean art gallery**.

If you think that the New York City subway system isn't much to look at, think again. Our subway stations boast many interesting temporary and permanent works of art, more than 200 in all, including some by renowned artists such as Roy Lichtenstein, Romare Bearden, and Elizabeth Murray. These works take different forms and ornament everything from the tiles on the walls to the benches on the platform. Keep your eyes open on your next trip to see what you pass by, or plan a route to see specific works using www.NYCSubway.org, which keeps a running list of artwork in the stations.

227. Hide or bribe a train conductor to let you stay on the 6 train and see the abandoned **City Hall Station**.

This one is a bit of a cheat, since we're sure our readers are upstanding citizens who wouldn't dream of flouting the MTA. However, we thought this was just too cool to leave out. If you stay on the 6 train going downtown after Brooklyn Bridge/City Hall—the last stop—you'll get to loop around through the original, abandoned City Hall station (it was closed in 1945 because it was structurally unable to accommodate newer, longer trains) as the train returns to the uptown platform. The station has been preserved architecturally and is surprisingly elegant, with beautiful tiled arches and chandeliers. If you don't want to tempt the law, the **MTA Transit Museum** occasionally conducts tours of the station (see following entry, and page 135).

BROOKLYN BRIDGE/CITY HALL STATION IN MANHATTAN. Subway: 6 train to Brooklyn Bridge-City Hall.

228. Take a ride with the **Transit Museum**.

You can explore hidden parts of the subway system with one of the many excellent subway tours led by the **Transit Museum** (see full entry on page 135). During the tours, which are offered regularly throughout the year, you'll learn about the transit system history and operation, and see things like the abandoned City Hall station mentioned above, decommissioned subway cars, power stations, and control centers.

Reservations required. Note: Tours require MetroCard fare in addition to the tour price. For a list of upcoming programs, call 718-694-1600 or visit www.mta.nyc.ny.us/mta/museum.

229. Use solar power in the **Coney Island-Stillwell Avenue Terminal**.

The train ride to Coney Island's Stillwell Avenue station, the terminus of the D, F, N, and Q lines, used to be known as "the scariest ride at Coney Island," a reference to the station's dilapidated and seedy state by the second half of the twentieth century. In May 2005—after two years of construction and service changes—the MTA unveiled a brand-new, European-style (think Germany's *bahnhofs*) terminal, a handsome glass-and-steel structure that is the city's largest aboveground subway station. But the design isn't just for looks—the glass canopy takes in sunlight that is used to provide power for the station and connected stores and businesses (though not the subway itself). It is the only subway terminal in the system that uses solar power—which is fitting, considering the station's proximity to the beach.

D, F, N, Q to Coney Island-Stillwell Avenue in Brooklyn.

230. Go on an **urban scavenger hunt**.

You'll see the city in a new way when you're scouring streets, parks, and even museums for answers to cryptic riddles on a Watson Adventures scavenger hunt. Teams of up to six people (you can participate as a group or be assigned to one) compete against one another to come up with answers to riddles, trivia, and arcane New York knowledge as they travel from site to site. Clues are cryptic and humorous and ask players to find things like a saint who looks like Mick Jagger in the Metropolitan Museum. They offer hunts in more than a dozen historic areas and neighborhoods, including Central Park, the Bronx Zoo, Lower Manhattan, Chinatown, and Little Italy, as well as indoor hunts at the Met, the Museum of Natural History, MoMA, and the Cloisters. Pick an area or place that you're interested in learning more about (or one you know well, if you want to test your knowledge), and put on your thinking cap!

Hunts are held on weekends, year-round, and last between two and three hours. Prices vary. To sign up, call 877-946-4868 or e-mail rsvp@watsonadventures.com. For more information and a schedule, visit www.watsonadventures.com.

231. Blend fact and fiction on the streets in **Accomplice**.

There's very little we can tell about this scavenger hunt-meets-improv show-meets-walking tour; the first rule of Accomplice is that you can't talk about Accomplice. (And that includes the organizers—the meeting point is communicated by a cryptic cell phone call the day before the show.) What we can tell you is that in the course of an afternoon, you will see the streets of lower Manhattan as you never had before. It'll be hard to tell what's real and what's part of the show, but that's part of the fun—as is not knowing who you'll meet or where you'll end up.

Accomplice runs tours in the Village and in Lower Manhattan on Saturdays and Sundays. Groups leave every half hour from 1 p.m. to 5 p.m. Tickets are $65 for the Lower Manhattan show (three and a half hours) and $55 for the Village show (two and a half hours). Tickets must be purchased in advance by phone or online. 212-209-3370. www.accomplicetheshow.com.

232. Play **capture the flag** on the city streets...

In 2005, an enterprising college student and Long Island native brought the public games he'd started in Toronto to the streets of New York. By the end of the summer, he was running weekly group games of capture the flag, each time within different designated streets. The rules of the game are too complicated to review here, but suffice it to say, it's a lot different than the game you played at summer camp. Because it's played on the streets (and not in parks), the whole thing has a bit of an underground, vaguely subversive feel, but it is (as far as we know) perfectly legal. Since 2005, the offerings on his Web site have expanded to include other public playground games, such as pillow fights, bubble battles, and Big Wheel races. All events are open to the public and require only that you bring your inner child.

For more information and upcoming events, visit www.newmindspace.com.

233. ...or be an **Assassin**.

Is New York feeling a little too safe to you these days? Then sign up for StreetWars, a three-week water-gun Assassin tournament that takes place on the city streets each summer, where the object is to "shoot" as many living targets as you can without getting shot yourself. Each participant is provided with the name and picture of their initial target, plus the target's home and work addresses. Once you shoot your target, you take on their target, and keep going until you are either shot by your killer or are the last one standing. (The winner gets a cash prize.) The game is run by a mysterious "Shadow Government" that invisibly oversees the entire campaign.

For more information, visit www.streetwars.net.

234. Step on private property on **Christopher Street**.

In front of the Village Cigar Shop, there is a small plaque in the sidewalk, which, if you look very closely, says "Property of the Hess Estate Which has Never been Designated for Public Purpose." According to **Forgotten NY** (see pages 98–99), the plaque came from a former owner of the property, who was forced to give up his building to accommodate the Seventh Avenue subway in the early twentieth century. He held on to this small parcel of land—how, we're not sure—and marked it with this plaque when they laid the new sidewalk.

CHRISTOPHER STREET AND SEVENTH AVENUE SOUTH IN MANHATTAN. Subway: 1 to Christopher Street-Sheridan Square.

235. Imagine what the Financial District looked like in the Dutch days at **85 Broad Street.**

In front and behind the Goldman Sachs HQ are two identical plaques set in the sidewalk that show a map of the area from 1660. The plaques commemorate the site of the seat of the Dutch Colonial government, where the Stadt Huys ("State House") once stood.

85 BROAD STREET BETWEEN PEARL AND SOUTH WILLIAM IN MANHATTAN. Subway: J, M, Z to Broad Street; 2, 3 to Wall Street; 4, 5 to Bowling Green; R, W, to Whitehall-South Ferry.

236. Look up at the Lenin statue on the roof of the **Red Square building**.

Built during a period of Soviet nostalgia in the late 1980s, this large bronze statue of Vladimir Ilyich Ulyanov Lenin is easy to miss if you don't know it's there, but strangely reassuring to see once you know it is.

250 EAST HOUSTON STREET BETWEEN AVENUES A AND B IN MANHATTAN. Subway: F, V to Lower East Side-Second Avenue.

237. Follow the names in the **"Canyon of Heroes"** downtown.

Set into the sidewalk on Broadway, from Bowling Green up to Park Place by City Hall, is a series of granite plaques that commemorate all the heroes—politicians, singers, astronauts, actors, diplomats, and baseball players—who have been honored with ticker-tape parades down Broadway. "Canyon" is the name given to the stretch of Broadway overshadowed by the early skyscrapers of the Financial District. The plaques mark the dates of each of the nearly two hundred historic parades that have taken place here, from the dedication of the Statue of Liberty in 1886 to the Yankees' World Series celebration in 2000, and they touch on everyone from Charles Lindbergh to President John F. Kennedy and Pope John Paul II.

BROADWAY FROM BOWLING GREEN TO PARK PLACE IN MANHATTAN. Subway: 4, 5, 6 to Brooklyn Bridge-City Hall; J, M, Z to Chambers Street.

238. Keep your eye on the street at the **Library Walk.**

On 41st Street between Madison and Fifth Avenues, there is a line of plaques in the sidewalk honoring literature. Each plaque bears a quote from an author or historic figure on the pleasure of reading and has its own design motif (a quote comparing reading to a good drink, for instance, is in the shape of a martini glass). Not all of the authors or works immortalized are well known, but the path leads up to the entrance of the **New York Public Library** (see page 292), where you can do further research, if you like. *41ST STREET BETWEEN FIFTH AND MADISON AVENUES IN MANHATTAN. Subway: 7 to Fifth Avenue-Bryant Park; B, D, F, V to 42nd Street-Bryant Park.*

239. Discover the **African Burial Ground.**

In 1991, the construction of a federal office building on the cusp of the Financial District downtown unearthed boxes containing the remains of more than four hundred Africans. The 6.6-acre burial ground is thought to be the only pre-Revolutionary African cemetery in the country and was in use during the eighteenth century. In the 1700s, after **Trinity Church** (see page 22) banned Africans from its cemetery, the African community was forced to move south, to the land we know now as lower Manhattan, to bury their dead. The discovery of the burial ground provided key, definitive information about New York's early African community. The site of the African Burial Ground has become a designated landmark and national monument, frequented by many with an interest in or a link to New York's ancestry. On display inside the federal office building built above the site are artifacts recovered from the burial ground—a carved wooden African coffin, some skeletal remains, and photographs and illustrations depicting the burial site as it might have looked centuries ago—and a permanent monument designed by Rodney Léon opened in 2007.
Memorial is located at DUANE STREET AND ELK STREET IN MANHATTAN. Visitor's Center is located one block away, in the Tom Weiss Federal Building, at 290 BROADWAY, AT DUANE STREET. Subway: 2, 3 to Park Place; 4, 5, 6 to Brooklyn Bridge-City Hall; J, M, Z to Chambers Street. www.africanburialground.gov or www.nps.gov/afbg.

240. Remember John Lennon at **Strawberry Fields.**

Just inside Central Park, across from his erstwhile home at the Dakota, a memorial plaque is set into the pathway honoring John Lennon. The spot is said to have been a favorite of John and Yoko Ono, who lived in New York for several years before John's death in 1980. Almost every day you'll find devoted fans sitting around the plaque, singing Lennon songs, or leaving wreaths, cards, and flowers in his memory. If you're in New York on December 8, you can join the crowds that gather here to mark the anniversary of his assassination, which took place just yards away across Central Park West.

CENTRAL PARK BY THE 72ND STREET ENTRANCE IN MANHATTAN. Subway: 1, 2, 3, B, C to 72nd Street.

241. Look down on the city's **biggest subway map in SoHo.**

Laid into the sidewalk on Greene Street, outside the SoHo building, is Belgian artist Françoise Schein's interpretation of the city's transportation system. Created in 1986, *Subway Map Floating on a New York Sidewalk* uses stainless-steel rods for tracks and small lights for the SoHo stations and won the City Art Commission for the best piece of work that year. Stretching the length of the block between Prince and Spring Streets, the map covers only trains in Manhattan because the sidewalk width wasn't able to accommodate the other boroughs. Dulled over time and worn under-foot, it's not easy to recognize that you're walking on a map in the bustle of SoHo, but finding it will make you think of the MTA in a whole new way.

GREENE STREET BETWEEN PRINCE AND SPRING STREETS IN MANHATTAN. Subway: 6 to Spring Street; B, D, F, V to Broadway-Lafayette Street.

Time to look at the street

The furniture of New York streets—its benches, subway entrances, street lamps, and signposts—is as much a part of the city's character as its sky-line. From the 1860s on, oversize cast-iron clocks were a ubiquitous feature of the streets, manufactured by the great clockmakers of the East Coast and often endorsed by the stores they stood in front of. But, like checkered taxicabs and "WALK/DON'T WALK" pedestrian crossing signs, over time they have been phased out, and now only a few remain. Below is a list of some of the city's remaining public timepieces, both new and old, that are worth taking the time to notice.

242. *Metronome.* High on a building wall at the south side of Union Square, this work of art by Kristin Jones tells the time to the second in fifteen brightly lit numbers. Read the numbers from left to right to see the time as it ticks toward midnight; read from right to left to see the time count down to midnight.

14TH STREET BETWEEN FOURTH AVENUE AND BROADWAY IN MANHATTAN. Subway: 4, 5, 6, L, N, Q, R, W to 14th Street-Union Square.

243. *The sidewalk clock:* Buried in the sidewalk at the intersection of Broadway and Maiden Lane is a clock that has told the right time since 1899—the only clock of its kind in the country.

BROADWAY AT MAIDEN LANE IN MANHATTAN. Subway: 4, 5, A, C to Broadway-Nassau Street.

244. The Yorkville Clock on Third Avenue at 85th Street is a designated landmark, a classic street clock designed to resemble a giant pocket watch, right down to the fob ring.
THIRD AVENUE AT 85TH STREET IN MANHATTAN. Subway: 4, 5, 6 to 86th Street.

245. The New York Sun Clock at Broadway and Chambers Street is the last surviving piece from the building that once housed the newspaper.
BROADWAY AT CHAMBERS STREET IN MANHATTAN. Subway: 1, 2, 3, A, C to Chambers Street.

246. The Tribeca Grand Clock, outside the hotel on Sixth Avenue and Church Street, is a recent revival of the cast-iron timepiece.
TRIBECA GRAND HOTEL, SIXTH AVENUE AT CHURCH STREET IN MANHATTAN. Subway: 1 to Franklin Street; A, C, E to Canal Street.

247. The Seth Thomas Clock at Fifth Avenue and 44th Street is a grand street clock, made by the manufacturer of the Grand Central ceiling clock.
FIFTH AVENUE AT 44TH STREET IN MANHATTAN. Subway: 7 to Fifth Avenue-Bryant Park; B, D, F, V to 42nd Street-Bryant Park.

248. The Golden Clock on Fifth Avenue at Madison Square Park is one of the most picturesque, set in the sidewalk in line with the Flatiron building.
FIFTH AVENUE AT 23RD STREET IN MANHATTAN. Subway: F, V, N, R, W to 23rd Street.

249. The Williamsburg Bank building's giant four-faced clock, on Atlantic Avenue and Fourth Avenue, was the largest clock in the world until 1929 and is big enough to see from all over downtown Brooklyn.
ATLANTIC AVENUE AT FOURTH AVENUE IN BROOKLYN. Subway: 2, 3, 4, 5, B, N, Q to Atlantic Avenue; D, M, R to Atlantic Avenue-Pacific Street; N to Pacific Street.

250. The clock on the Schwarzenbach Building on Park Avenue South has two little mechanical gnomes who signal the turning of the hour by what looks like one beating the other with a stick.
470 PARK AVENUE SOUTH BETWEEN 30TH AND 31ST STREETS IN MANHATTAN. Subway: 6 to 28th Street.

251. Cruise the **vendors at Union Square**.

As former mayor Rudolph Giuliani no doubt found out in his efforts to sweep the streets clean, street vendors are an inextricable part of the city's landscape. From Canal Street to Harlem, Brooklyn, the Bronx and beyond, there is no shortage of places to buy knock-off purses, cheap sunglasses, incense, jewelry, and books and DVDs of dubious provenance, and though they're spread around the city, many of the offerings seem to come from the same place. That's not the case in Union Square, where most of the vendors are craftsmen selling their own works. The offerings in this area (roughly the southwest end of the park, including Union Square West between 14th and 16th Streets) range from Xeroxed movie scripts and mediocre paintings to beautiful handmade jewelry and clothing, fairly accomplished paintings and photographs, really interesting magnets, and printed T-shirts that range from tacky to legitimately cool. Our favorite "vendors" here are the Mighty Mutts volunteers, who stand at the south end of the park on weekends (by the Gandhi statue). You can buy T-shirts and tank tops with the adorable "Mighty Mutts" logo to benefit this no-kill animal shelter and volunteer rescue organization, or perhaps take home one of the adorable rescued cats or dogs that they have with them. The vendors are in the park every day, even when the Greenmarket (see page 165) is in session (Monday, Wednesday, Friday, and Saturday), but on those days they all cluster by 14th Street.

UNION SQUARE BY 14TH STREET IN MANHATTAN. Subway: 4, 5, 6, L, N, Q, R, W to 14th Street-Union Square. For more information on Mighty Mutts, visit http://mightymutts.tripod.com.

252. Go to the **Park Avenue Christmas Tree Lighting Ceremony**.

On the first Sunday in December, a ceremony is held on Park Avenue at 91st Street for the lighting of the trees that line the 2 ½ miles of the avenue's mall (from 97th Street to 48th Street). There are carols and choir performances, followed by a moment of silence before all of the trees are simultaneously illuminated.

First Sunday in December. PARK AVENUE AT 91ST STREET IN MANHATTAN. Subway: 4, 5, 6 to 86th Street. For more information, contact the Brick Church, www.brickchurch.org.

253. Dare to go in **Billy's Antiques & Props**.

"We buy apartment contents" proclaims the sign on the front. Inside this dark, covered eyesore on Houston Street, you'll find all sorts of unusual things, like old carnival games and science class–style skeletons, along with secondhand furniture and paintings.

76 EAST HOUSTON STREET BETWEEN ELIZABETH STREET AND THE BOWERY IN MANHATTAN. Subway: F, V to Lower East Side-Second Avenue. www.billysantiques.com.

254. Watch out for **the trucks!**

Eating at a food truck used to be something New Yorkers boasted about only when recounting trips to California taco trucks. Wallflowers no more, local food-truck culture has jumped into the spotlight, and offerings have expanded from coffee and kebabs to a transitory cornucopia. These days, you can get pretty much any kind of gourmet sweet, treat, or chow imaginable handed to you through the windows of tricked-out resto-mobiles with splashy paint jobs. While new ones appear without warning all the time, and some are sure to make their way to the big parking lot in the sky, our favorites to stay the course are the Dessert Truck (for molten chocolate cake), the Wafels and Dinges Truck (for authentic addictive Belgian waffles), the Treats Truck (for homemade Oreos that should be illegal), and the soothing yellow Van Leeuwen ice cream truck (for scoops so fresh you practically hear the cows mooing). Most trucks post their upcoming itineraries on Facebook or Twitter, but in our opinion, the serendipity of finding is the frosting on the cupcake. N.B: The city has traditionally enjoyed its street eats from **pushcarts** rather than trucks. For more on those specific, delectable offerings, see below.

Various locations—keep your eyes open!

Eat on the Street!

Eating street food is one of life's most delectable guilty pleasures. It's usually messy, often unhealthy, and you don't really know where it's been. As the most pedestrian city in the country (and arguably the world), New York has the best and most varied street-food selection, from the traditional hot dog to a darn good dosa. Here are our favorites. (Vendors can be found throughout the city, unless otherwise noted.)

255. *Hot dogs:* Always a classic. Best topped with sauerkraut, then doused with mustard.

256. *Pretzels:* The hot dog cart's vegetarian alternative. Best with mustard.

257. *Knishes:* Good when you need something dense and starchy to fill you up. Also excellent with mustard.

258. *Roasted nuts:* The smell alone is one of the best things about New York.

259. *Coffee from the Mud Trucks:* How do they get such good coffee from those little trucks? *(Check the Web site for times and locations: www.the-mudtruck.com)*

260. *Exotic fruit:* Look for mangoes, lychees, and rambutans from the vendors on the southeast corner of Mulberry and Canal Streets.

261. *Carved mango flowers:* Refreshing, and a fresh alternative to ice cream or smoothies. *(By Union Square, often by the northeast corner of 14th Street and University Place.)*

262. *Gelato from the Otto gelato cart in Washington Square Park:* Try the olive oil flavor.

263. *Dosas from New York Dosa:* Like a crêpe, only better. *(Washington Square Park.)*

264. *Mister Softee ice cream cone:* Check the name on the truck before you buy. There are plenty of Softee imposters, but the real Mister Softee has them all beat.

Expert Contributor: Bret Watson of Watson Adventures

Bret Watson is the founder and president of Watson Adventures Scavenger Hunts, which stages fun, informative hunts for the public every weekend. He also puts out a monthly e-newsletter called the "Culture Vulture" filled with New York trivia, quotes, and more. You can find out about the hunts and see the newsletter at www.watsonadventures.com.

MY FIVE FAVORITE PLACES TO VISIT IN NEW YORK

265. *Satchmo's "office" in the Louis Armstrong House:*

Step into this time machine and set the dial for 1971, the year Armstrong died. His homey second-floor "office" looks untouched since he departed, but there's one special addition: the docent can touch a button and trigger a recording of the gravel-voiced great chatting in this very room. You'll feel like you have a personal audience with the king of jazz.

34-56 107TH STREET AT 37TH AVENUE IN QUEENS. Subway: 7 to 111th Street. 718-478-8274. www.satchmo.net.

266. *Dyker Heights, Brooklyn:*

The most lavish, outrageous Christmas-light extravaganzas can be found on the minia-ture *palazzi* crammed into this largely Italian neighborhood. Sign up for the walking tour led by tour guide nonpareil Justin Ferate. The highlight: a house so decked out that the explosion of lights and characters continues up the front steps and into the living room—go ahead, have a look inside. Ferate will also show you the best place for pastry and hot chocolate along the way.

82ND TO 84TH STREETS BETWEEN TENTH AND ELEVENTH AVENUES IN BROOKLYN. Subway: D to 79th Street. For more information about Justin Ferate and his tours, visit www.justin-snewyork.com.

267. *That dark patch on the ceiling of Grand Central:* Stand in the main hall of

the terminal, facing the track entrances. Look up at the ceiling constellation, with its parade of Zodiac figures. Over by the crab, straddling the ceiling and the molding along the edge, find a dark rectangle that seems about the size of an envelope. During the 1990s cleaning, this patch was left untouched to show how dingy the ceiling used to be.

For more information on Grand Central and other things to do there, see entry on pages 23–24. 42ND STREET BETWEEN LEXINGTON AND MADISON AVENUES IN MANHATTAN. Subway: 4, 5, 6, 7, S to Grand Central-42nd Street.

268. *Congo Gorilla Forest at the Bronx Zoo:* This time you are the caged animal,

gazing through large, panoramic windows at a forest glade populated with gorillas great and small. Unlike a lot of zoo exhibits, these primates stay close to the windows, and you can watch simian soap operas playing out in grimaces, grooming, games, and wild tussles. The newer Tiger Mountain exhibit follows the same idea, offering a close-up view of feline muscles rippling under sleek pelts. However, the tigers often don't come quite as close; leave it to cats to act aloof.

FORDHAM ROAD AT THE BRONX RIVER PARKWAY IN THE BRONX. Subway: 2, 5 to West Farms Square-East Tremont Avenue; 2 to Pelham Parkway. 718-367-1010. www.bronxzoo.com.

269. *Staten Island Yankees game:* Here's the perfect place to be on a summer

night: the third-base-side stands in the smaller Yankee stadium, with a beer and a hot dog, watching a ball game played before the backdrop of New York harbor and the lighted spires of Manhattan glistening like Oz in the distance. The seats are cheap and usually still available at game time, and the stadium is steps away from the ferry, so you can bookend the game with free cruises. Sweet as the summer breeze.

75 RICHMOND TERRACE AT ST. GEORGE IN STATEN ISLAND. Take the Staten Island ferry and follow signs from the ferry to the ballpark. 718-720-9265. www.siyanks.com.

The Best Famous Movie Sites.

Some of the most iconic moments in American cinema have taken place on our streets, and many filmmakers have cast the city as their backdrop over and over again (we could easily have given Woody Allen's movies an entire chapter). From gritty to romantic, colossal to comedic, New York has played a wide range of parts. Here are our favorites of the city's starring roles:

270. *Strut down Brooklyn's 86th Street just like John Travolta did in Saturday Night Fever.* The dance club used in the movie, called "The Spectrum," is still there, too—it's a popular gay disco.
802 64TH STREET AT EIGHTH AVENUE IN BROOKLYN. Subway: N to Eighth Avenue.

271. *Have a treat at the bakery where Cher was* Moonstruck. Its current incarnation, an offshoot of the Park Slope café Naidre's, has treats as good as the Cammareri brothers used to make.
502 HENRY STREET AT SACKETT STREET IN BROOKLYN. Subway: F to Carroll Street.

272. *Stand over the subway grate that made Marilyn famous.* From *The Seven Year Itch*, the image that launched a million tchotchkes.
52ND STREET AND LEXINGTON AVENUE IN MANHATTAN. Subway: 6 to 51st Street; E, V to Lexington Avenue/53rd Street.

273. *Look for love at the "MacDowell's" on Queens Boulevard in Elmhurst.* It's a Wendy's now but otherwise pretty much the same as when Eddie Murphy worked there in *Coming to America*.
85-07 QUEENS BOULEVARD IN QUEENS. Subway: R to Grand Avenue/Newtown.

274. *Speak in funny voices at the Temple of Dendur like in* When Harry Met Sally. The most famous scene from this movie takes place in Katz's (see page 170), but the sounds the actors make at the temple are a little easier for most people to pull off.
Metropolitan Museum of Art. 1000 FIFTH AVENUE AT 82ND STREET IN MANHATTAN. Subway: 4, 5, 6 to 86th Street. 212-535-7710. www.met.org. See entry on pages 119–121 for more information on the museum.

275. *Channel Meryl channeling Clarissa at the flower shop from* The Hours. Though you're more likely to emerge with a lamp than with a bouquet—in real life, it's an antiques store.

370 BLEECKER STREET BETWEEN CHARLES AND PERRY STREETS IN MANHATTAN. Subway: 1 to Christopher Street.

276. *Check your patriotism at Bloomingdale's* right where Robin Williams defects from the Soviet Union in *Moscow on the Hudson*.
LEXINGTON AVENUE BETWEEN 59TH AND 60TH STREETS IN MANHATTAN. Subway: 4, 5, 6 to 59th Street; N, R, W to Lexington Avenue/59th Street.

277. *Visit the fire station from* Ghostbusters. On display are photos of the cast taken during the shoot.
14 NORTH MOORE STREET AT VARICK STREET IN MANHATTAN. Subway: 1 to Franklin Street.

278. *Look for Jason Bourne in the East River.* Let's face it, he probably already made it to Belize—but make your way to John Jay Park on the East River at 77th Street and you can see the building from which Matt Damon plummets in the final seconds of *The Bourne Ultimatum*.
370 BLEECKER STREET BETWEEN CHARLES AND PERRY STREETS IN MANHATTAN. Subway:1 to Christopher Street.

279. *Run around the reservoir as fast as Dustin Hoffman did in Marathon Man* (or walk slowly around the wrong way as Woody Allen did in *Hannah and Her Sisters*).
CENTRAL PARK NEAR 91ST STREET IN MANHATTAN. Subway: 6 to 96th Street; B, C to 96th Street.

280. *Take in an art movie at the Thalia.* The theater where Woody Allen took Diane Keaton in *Annie Hall* to see *The Sorrow and the Pity* is now part of Symphony Space, but you can still catch an arty flick in its renovated digs.
2537 BROADWAY AT 95TH STREET IN MANHATTAN. Subway: 1, 2, 3 to 96th Street. 212-864-5400. www.symphonyspace.org.

281. *Break into song at Harry Winston, just like Edward Norton in Everyone Says I Love You.*
718 FIFTH AVENUE AT 56TH STREET IN MANHATTAN. Subway: E, V to Fifth Avenue/53rd Street; N, R, W to Fifth Avenue/59th Street. 212-245-2006. www.harry-winston.com.

282. *Impress a girl (or two) with Sam Waterston's architectural tour of New York from* **Hannah and Her Sisters.** With Carrie Fisher in the front seat and a fuming Dianne Wiest in the back, Waterston's character, an architect, takes them on a late-night drive past his favorite buildings in Manhattan, including the Dakota and the Mount Vernon Hotel Museum and Garden (see page 102).

Dakota: 1 WEST 72ND STREET AT CPW IN MANHATTAN. Subway: B, C to 72nd Street. Mount Vernon Hotel Museum and Garden: 421 EAST 61ST STREET BETWEEN FIRST AND YORK AVENUES IN MANHATTAN. Subway: 4, 5, 6, N, R, W to Lexington Avenue/51st Street. www.mvhm.org.

283. *Check for hijackers on the 28th Street subway platform as in* **The Taking of the Pelham One Two Three.** (The original, not the remake.) Also, stick around until the end of the film, when the last hijacker climbs out of the manhole, and you'll see what Union Square looked like pre-gentrification.

28TH STREET AND LEXINGTON AVENUE (6 subway station); and UNION SQUARE IN MANHATTAN.

284. *Watch out for witches in the courtyard of the Dakota.* Along with Mia Farrow and John Cassavetes, the Dakota stars in the 1968 occult classic, *Rosemary's Baby.* Only a handful of scenes occur outside of its famous walls, and though the building has been home to many celebrities, this is one of the very few movies actually shot here.

1 WEST 72ND STREET AT CPW IN MANHATTAN. Subway: B, C to 72nd Street.

285. *Whisper conspiratorially over breakfast at the Clinton Diner in Maspeth.* This is where Robert De Niro smashes up a phone booth and Henry says, "That's when I knew Jimmy was gonna get whacked" in *Goodfellas.*

56-26 MASPETH AVENUE AT 56TH ROAD IN QUEENS. Call restaurant for directions by MTA bus. 718-894-1566.

286. *Wait for a date at Café Lalo* like Meg Ryan did in *You've Got Mail.* There are more than one hundred different pies, cakes, and other desserts, so unless you're really indecisive, it's a better choice than Starbucks, where "people with no decision-making ability whatsoever make six decisions to get one cup of coffee," as Tom Hank's character says in the same movie.

201 WEST 83RD STREET BETWEEN BROADWAY AND AMSTERDAM AVENUE IN MANHATTAN. Subway: 1 to 79th Street or 86th Street. 212-496-6031.

287.*Walk around the childhood haunts of Noodles, Max, Cockeye, and Dominic* from *Once Upon a Time in America* in Williamsburg and DUMBO, Brooklyn. The westernmost stretch of 8th Street South leading up to the Williamsburg Bridge is where Max and Noodles meet, and the junction of Water Street and Washington Street beneath the Manhattan Bridge is the iconic location where Dominic "slipped" and was shot by Bugsy.

Both locations in Brooklyn. 8TH STREET SOUTH. Subway: L to Bedford Avenue. WATER STREET AND WASHINGTON STREET. Subway: A, C to Jay Street-Borough Hall; F to York Street.

CHAPTER 4:

Arts & Culture

here are cities that are older, bigger, and more populated, but none surpass New York in terms of art and culture. From world-class museums to outdoor art shows; from glorious Broadway theaters to hole-in-the-wall performance spaces; from classical ballet and opera as grand as can be to movie theaters showing classic, independent, and limited-release features that are nearly impossible to find elsewhere—New York has superior art and creative performances of every size, shape, and genre. With so much that's beautiful, entertaining, and worthwhile happening all over—from venerable institutions famed for their first-class offerings to experimental ventures that challenge patrons with innovative art forms—we've tried (with great difficulty) to narrow them down a little, and give you only the best of the best for museums, visual art, music, dance, theater, and film. In the process, we discovered how much wonderful, rewarding art there really is here, in both the established venues and outside the mainstream. This discovery proves the point that New York is the ultimate crucible for the arts, as it can produce both the classic and the new in inspired ways, and it always delivers a hungry yet critical audience. If you explore the following offerings, you will be pleased to see how thoroughly the city's cultural institutions excel at presenting arts in all mediums, and at nurturing those yet to be discovered.

Museums

Note: Many of the museums listed here that charge admission have designated free or pay-what-you-wish hours or days, some of which feature special programs and performances. For more information, please see page 284 or contact the museums directly.

288. Face the T-rex and the big blue whale at the
American Museum of Natural History...

One of New York's best-loved museums, the American Museum of Natural History is the most impressive museum of its kind in the world, and one of the most enjoyable. Installed in a mammoth complex along Central Park West that includes both the distinguished old halls and the spectacular new Rose Center, the museum's world-renowned permanent collections are exhibited in beautiful spaces with cutting-edge media. In the fossil halls, the famous Tyrannosaurus rex crouches aggressively over the largest single collection of dinosaur fossils in the world. In the Milstein Hall of Ocean Life, the popular 94-foot model of a blue whale hangs suspended over a room of amazing exhibits about the history of aquatic evolution and the technology used in marine biology today. The mammal, bird, and culture halls are filled with so many eye-catching dioramas and artifacts that everyone learns something new with each trip to the museum, and the traveling exhibits—which recently included the stunning and enduringly popular *Frogs: A Chorus of Colors*—are always amazing.

289. ...and make sure to leave time to visit the **Rose Center for Earth and Space,** the stunning glass structure that houses the new Hayden Planetarium. The awesome collection of photographs, displays, and interactive exhibits reveals as much as we know of the history and beauty of the universe. Go in the afternoon for the space show—currently *Journey to the Stars*, narrated by Whoopi Goldberg—or on Friday evenings for Starry Nights, when the Rose Center's spectacular ceiling lights provide the perfect setting for live jazz and light refreshments.

American Museum of Natural History & Rose Center for Earth and Space. 79TH STREET AND CENTRAL PARK WEST IN MANHATTAN. (Rose Center entrance is at 81st Street between Central Park West and Columbus Avenue.) Subway: 1, 9 to 79th Street; B, C to 81st Street-Museum of Natural History. Open daily, 10:00 a.m. to 5:45 p.m. (Rose Center remains open until 8:45 p.m. on Friday). Admission to both (suggested): $14 for adults, $8 for children. Additional fees may apply for space shows and other presentations. 212-769-5100. www.amnh.org.

290. Take the "**museum highlights tour**" at the Met (or use ours).

The city's most prestigious museum suffers from what you might call an embarrassment of riches: it's simply too much, too many, too good. From ancient Egyptian, Islamic, Asian, Oceanic, Greek, and Roman art and artifacts, to European painting and sculpture, modern art, furniture, decorative arts, and costumes and textiles, the Metropolitan Museum of Art is an inexhaustible repository of incredible, original, must-see treasures, displayed in a seemingly infinite number of exquisite galleries. It's more than anyone— tourist or native—could see in a week, and the overwhelming number of masterpieces would intimidate any visitor. Of course, there may be a single gallery, collection, period or show that draws you, so by all means, go on in. But if not, the hour-long museum highlights tour (free with admission) is a wonderful way to get an overview of the Met's many treasures. However, we could not resist putting in some of our personal highlights, so if guided tours aren't your thing, here are our picks:

American Decorative Arts (first floor): Now reopened after a two-year redesign that features beautiful new signage, the American wing includes a wealth of traditional American decorative arts that ranges from Tiffany stained glass to New England cabinet-making, Baroque-style silver pieces, and thousands of examples of pewter, ceramics, and textiles.

Egyptian Galleries (first floor): A large and exciting collection of Egyptian art and artifacts includes hieroglyphics and paintings on papyrus, sphinxes, jewelry, and tombs. The centerpiece is the Temple of Dendur, an enormous Nubian sandstone temple from 15 B.C. that stands in a glass-enclosed room.

Arms & Armor (first floor): The Met's collection of suits of armor, weapons, firearms, and other military paraphernalia dates from 400 B.C. through the nineteenth century. There are pieces from Europe, Asia, the Middle East, India, and North America, including the largest collection of Japanese arms outside of Japan.

European & American Paintings (first and second floors): The Met's paintings galleries present the *crème de la crème* of European painting, from works by the Old Masters through the nineteenth century. And though it's thought of as a more historic and classical museum, the Met also has a nice collection of modern works, with paintings by Picasso, Matisse, Miró, and Balthus's incredible *The Mountain*.

Drawings Collection: This is a really neat one. Because of their fragility, only a small fraction of the museum's collection of drawings and prints are on display at any one time, either in the rotating selection displayed in the department's gallery, or as part of other exhibitions. However, you can view the collection—an incredible holding of 11,000 drawings and 1.5 million prints focused on West European and American works on paper made after the fifteenth century—privately, by appointment, Tuesday through Friday. During the appointment, you'll browse through the catalog of holdings and select the works you want to see, which are then brought out for you to view up close by the museum staff.
Appointments are scheduled Tuesday through Friday, from 10:00 a.m. to 12:30 p.m., and 2:00 p.m. to 4:30 p.m. Call the museum for more information.

The rooftop sculpture garden: See page 59 for information.

1000 FIFTH AVENUE AT 82ND STREET IN MANHATTAN. Open Tuesday through Sunday, 9:30 a.m. to 5:30 p.m. (until 9:00 p.m. on Friday and Saturday). Admission (suggested): $20 for adults, $15 for seniors, $10 for students, free for children under 12. Subway: 4, 5, 6 to 86th Street. 212-535-7710. www.metmuseum.org.

291. See the Unicorn Tapestries at **the Cloisters**.

Set deep in Fort Tryon Park, surrounded by beautiful landscaped gardens overlooking the Hudson, the Cloisters, part of the Metropolitan Museum, is a glittering treasury of European medieval art. The stunning permanent collection of paintings, triptychs, sculptures, armor, furniture, stained glass, and other artifacts is housed in a building made up of original stonework from medieval French cloisters. Perhaps the most impressive objects in the whole collection are the seven "Unicorn Tapestries," a series of fifteenth-century Netherlandish masterpieces of woven wool and silk and among the most beautiful and complex medieval tapestries that survive today. (One of them even had a cameo in *Harry Potter and the Half-Blood Prince!*) Make sure to leave enough time to enjoy the walk along Margaret Corbin Drive through Fort Tryon Park and up the ancient stone steps to the museum.

FORT TRYON PARK IN MANHATTAN. Open (November to February) Tuesday through Sunday, 9:30 a.m. to 4:45 p.m.; (March to October) Tuesday through Sunday, 9:30 a.m. to 5:15 p.m. Admission (suggested): $20 for adults, $15 for seniors, $10 for students, free for children under 12. Subway: A to 190th Street. Bus: M4 bus to Fort Tryon Park/The Cloisters. 212-923-3700. www.metmuseum.org.

292. Relax and recharge at the **Brooklyn Museum**.

Now nearly eighty years old, the Brooklyn Museum is the second-largest museum in New York and something of a buried treasure among the city's cultural institutions. Located far from the boisterous activity of Fifth Avenue's Museum Mile and beside the Brooklyn Botanic Garden at the eastern side of Prospect Park, this grand museum is home to world-renowned permanent collections of Egyptian, Asian, and Islamic art and artifacts, as well as changing exhibits of acclaimed contemporary art, photography, and historic pieces from every culture in the world. Spacious, comfortable, and always quieter than the major museums in Manhattan (except during First Saturdays, the museum's monthly party and program of free events), the Brooklyn Museum makes a noticeable effort to enhance the pleasure of the museum visit—an experience that in other esteemed institutions often suffers from disagreeable atmospheric conditions. In the galleries, there are comfortable, movable chairs for visitors to place in front of pieces they wish to linger over, and the easily negotiable layout encourages visitors to explore without feeling overwhelmed. Don't miss the wonderful fifty-piece collection of Rodin sculptures located on the fifth floor.

200 EASTERN PARKWAY IN BROOKLYN. Open Wednesday through Friday, 10:00 a.m. to 5:00 p.m.; Saturday and Sunday, 11:00 a.m. to 6:00 p.m. Admission (suggested): $10 for adults, $6 for seniors and students; free for children under 12. Subway: 2, 3 to Eastern Parkway-Brooklyn Museum. 718-638-5000. www.brooklynmuseum.org.

293. Spend a day at the **Museum of Modern Art**.

Less classical than the Met, more traditional than the New Museum, and less specialized than the Whitney, the Museum of Modern Art (MoMA) is a wonderful contradiction of a museum. Since its founding in 1929, MoMA has dedicated itself to being the foremost "modern" museum in the world and has done so in both the literal and artistic senses of the term. The museum exhibits and actively pursues contemporary art and pieces by working artists, and an extensive renovation and architectural redesign that took place between 2002 and 2004 has brought MoMA into the twenty-first century; however, the best reason to come here is still to look at the incredible collection of modern masterpieces. This is where you will see Van Gogh's *The Starry Night*, Matisse's *Dance*, and Picasso's *Les Desmoiselles D'Avignon*, which are displayed as part of a wonderful visual survey of artistic movements from the late-nineteenth and twentieth century. Since the renovation, the collection has been reorganized, so now, instead of grouping works by artist, they are presented chronologically by style, unfolding gracefully through two floors of the museum as an exciting tour through Post-Impressionism, Cubism, Surrealism, Dada, Abstract Expressionism, and Pop art. MoMA mounts excellent exhibitions, and in addition to paintings, has galleries for photography and drawings, a film and media department, and a much beloved outdoor sculpture garden. However, unlike many museums, which are either too small or too big to dedicate a day to, MoMA is just the right size and scope to absorb in one marathon visit (which perhaps justifies the steep admission fee).

11 WEST 53RD STREET BETWEEN FIFTH AND SIXTH AVENUES IN MANHATTAN. Open Wednesday through Monday, 10:30 a.m. to 5:30 p.m. (until 8:00 p.m. on Friday). Admission: $20 for adults, $16 for seniors, $12 for students, free for children under 16. Free on Friday from 4:00 p.m. to 8:00 p.m. Subway: E, V to Fifth Avenue/53rd Street. 212-708-9400. www.moma.org.

294. Enjoy the **Cooper-Hewitt**, inside and out.

That a museum known for exhibiting progressive, contemporary design is housed in the stately Carnegie mansion seems a little counterintuitive. But never mind: the collection covers design of all kinds from ancient times through the present day and includes drawings and sketches from examples of decorative art, furniture, jewelry, architectural elements, and industrial and product design, textiles, and wall coverings. The exhibitions focus on modern and contemporary design and development. At the annual Solos exhibition, which showcases contemporary architecture and design, innovative structures—the inaugural edition featured a building made of plastic wrap—are erected in the museum's elegant front garden.

2 EAST 91ST STREET AT FIFTH AVENUE IN MANHATTAN. Open Monday through Friday, 10:00 a.m. to 5:00 p.m; Saturday 10:00 a.m. to 6:00 p.m.; Sunday, noon to 6:00 p.m. Admission: $15 for adults, $10 for students and seniors. Subway: 4, 5, 6 to 86th Street. 212-849-8400. cooper-hewitt.org.

295. Take a kid to the **Forbes Galleries**.

This small, idiosyncratic (and free) museum in a series of rooms on the ground floor of the Forbes Building is filled with the personal possessions of Malcolm Forbes and his family. Many of the exhibits are kid-friendly and are accompanied by written commentary and quotes from Malcolm himself. Although the most famous exhibit, the family's gorgeous collection of Fabergé eggs, is gone, there are still plenty of amusing displays of toys and collectibles, like model ships and toy soldiers, correspondence from famous friends, and the family's extensive trove of Monopoly sets—a fitting collection for the famous capitalist. The best part of the museum, however, is what you see before you go through the front door—an elaborate installation of marbles that is hard to take your eyes off of.

62 FIFTH AVENUE AT 12TH STREET IN MANHATTAN. Open Tuesday through Saturday, 10:00 a.m. to 4:00 p.m. Subway: 4, 5, 6, L, N, Q, R, W to 14th Street-Union Square. Admission is free. For more information, call 212-206-5548 or visit www.forbesgalleries.com.

296. See one of the world's finest personal collections of art at the **Frick Collection**.

By the time of his death in 1919, Henry Clay Frick had accrued a world-renowned collection of fine art that included Oriental rugs, Asian porcelain, furniture, enamels, silver, drawings, prints, and paintings. In his will, he stipulated that these works become part of a museum to be housed in his opulent mansion on the southern end of Museum Mile, which he also bequeathed to the city. Inside are works by some of the world's most famous artists, such as Goya, Rembrandt, Titian, and Holbein, as well as exquisite pieces of Italian Renaissance sculpture and Ming dynasty vases. The Frick Collection has expanded upon Mr. Frick's initial holdings, and there are more works than can be displayed at one time. But walking around these intimate, quiet galleries and charming courtyards is so enjoyable you'll want to visit every time a new exhibit opens.

1 EAST 70TH STREET AT FIFTH AVENUE IN MANHATTAN. Open Tuesday through Saturday,

10:00 a.m. to 6:00 p.m.; Sunday, 11:00 a.m. to 5:00 p.m. Admission: $15 for adults, $10 for seniors, $5 for students; pay what you wish Sundays, 11: a.m. to 1:00 p.m. Subway: 6 to 68th Street-Hunter College. 212-288-0700. www.frick.org.

→ **DID YOU KNOW?** *In the basement of the Frick Museum is the world's most beautiful bowling alley, cast in wood in an oak-paneled hall, which Frick built for himself and which is sadly not open to the public. It's in your interests to befriend someone who works for the museum—they're the only ones who ever get to see it.*

297. Walk around (and around) the **Guggenheim**.

The New York branch of this "chain" museum (the other locations are in Bilbao, Spain; Venice, Berlin, and Las Vegas) is most famous for its exterior. Frank Lloyd Wright's conical design literally put the museum on the map and made it one of the most distinguishable features on the Manhattan architectural landscape. Inside, the curving shape allows for a unique way to view art, as works from temporary shows are displayed along a walkway that spirals up the interior. (Particularly fitting for the *Art of the Motorcycle*, a 1998 exhibition of real motorcycles.) The permanent collection—made up of twentieth- and twenty-first-century art—is displayed in galleries that open along the ramp.

1071 FIFTH AVENUE AT 89TH STREET IN MANHATTAN. Open Friday through Wednesday, 10:00 a.m. to 5:45 p.m., (until 7:45 p.m. on Saturday). Open until midnight on the first Friday of every month. Admission: $18 for adults, $15 for seniors and students, free for children under 12. Subway: 4, 5, 6 to 86th Street. 212-423-3500. www.guggenheim.org.

298. See American art at the **Whitney Museum**.

Though not commonly thought of as a "special interest" museum, the Whitney Museum of American Art contains an extensive collection of modern and contemporary American art and is the best place to see the progression of art in this country over the past century. The permanent collection, displayed on a rotating basis, starts with works by early-twentieth-century masters such as Edward Hopper and Alexander Calder, continues through postwar greats like Jasper Johns and Roy Lichtenstein, and ends with late-twentieth-century and contemporary works by artists who include Kiki Smith and Keith Haring. The Whitney Biennial, held every other spring, showcases new works by contemporary artists.

945 MADISON AVENUE AT 75TH STREET IN MANHATTAN. Open Wednesday, Thursday, Saturday, Sunday 11 a.m. to 6:00 p.m.; Friday 1:00 p.m. to 9.00 p.m. (6:00 p.m. to 9:00 p.m.is pay what you wish). Admission: $15 for adults, $10 for seniors and students, children under 12 free. Subway: 6 to 77th Street. 800-WHITNEY. www.whitney.org.

299. Blow your mind at the **New York Hall of Science**.

Chances are that unless you've got a school-age child, you haven't thought of visiting this Queens museum lately. Too bad. The New York Hall of Science is without a doubt one of the most fun places in the city, provided you're not too cool to get excited about science. It can also, of course, be highly informative—when was the last time you thought about microbes and light particles? The museum boasts more than 400 interactive exhibits, including the world's first hands-on biochemistry lab and a sports center, where you can learn about principles of physics and motion through sports. The museum is definitely geared toward kids, but unlike many children's museums, the exhibits can be just as entertaining (and educational) for adults. So get the kids (or if you don't have any of your own, borrow some) and head out to Queens for a day of mind-bending fun.

7-01 111TH STREET IN QUEENS. For information on visiting hours, visit www.nyscience.org/visitor_info/hours. Admission: $11 for adults, $8 for seniors, students, and children. Subway: 7 to 111th Street. 718-699-0005. www.nyhallsci.org.

300. See what's "new" at the **New Museum of Contemporary Art**.

After exploring the classical masterpieces at the Frick and the Met, the New Museum is the place to check in with today's art scene. From offbeat exhibitions on the photography of John Waters and retrospectives of 1980s East Village art to video and digital displays in the Media Lounge (the only museum space in New York devoted to digital, video, and audio art), the museum definitely has its finger on the pulse. Known for its up-to-date collection and slightly outside-the-mainstream programming—recent shows have included an Elizabeth Peyton retrospective, a collection of Emory Douglas's poster art for the Black Panthers, and Mary Heilman's *To Be Someone*—the New Museum is housed, appropriately enough, in a magnificent new building, which opened in fall 2007. Located on the Lower East Side on the Bowery, the design for the boxy seven-story building looks like the defiant teenage child of the Whitney, another New York museum with a bent toward the contemporary. As well as the exhibitions, the museum has a good café and an excellent (if crowded) gift store—and don't forget to check out the terrace (see page 74).

235 BOWERY AT PRINCE STREET IN MANHATTAN. Subway: 6 to Spring Street; N,R to Prince Street; F,V to Lower East Side/Second Avenue; J,M,Z to Bowery. Open Wednesday, Saturday, and Sunday, noon to 6:00 p.m; Thursday and Friday, noon to 9:00 p.m. Admission: $12 for adults, $10 for seniors, $8 for students, and free for children 18 and under. 212-219-1222. www.newmuseum.org.

301. Visit the other "new museum," the **Neue Galerie**.

Located in an exquisite landmark mansion on Fifth Avenue, the Neue Galerie is a rela-tively recent addition to the New York City museum landscape, but a welcome one. Showing twentieth-century German and Austrian art and design ("neue" is German for new), the museum's small but representative collection is an excellent focused look at the works from this colorful period (including paintings by Klee, Klimt, and Schiele), and the museum is a nice, manageable counterpart to the boundless super-collec-tions at some of the other institutions on Museum Mile. Make sure to save time (and room) for a visit to Café Sabarsky, the museum's excellent Austrian canteen. **Chef Kurt Gutenbrunner** (see pages 196–197) serves excellent renditions of Austrian classics; if liverwurst and goulash are not your thing, then skip right to the *apfelstrudel* and *Linz-ertortes*, or come for the delicious eggs and Viennese pastries served at breakfast. *1048 FIFTH AVENUE AT 86TH STREET IN MANHATTAN. Open Thursday through Monday, 11:00 a.m. to 6:00 p.m. (until 9:00 p.m. on Friday). Admission: $15 for adults, $10 for students and seniors. N.B.: Children under 12 are not admitted and children under 16 must be accompanied by an adult. Subway: 4, 5, 6 to 86th Street. 212-628-6200. www.neuegalerie.org.*

302. See Tibetan art and do tai chi at the **Jacques Marchais Museum** of Tibetan Art.

Staten Island is the unlikely home of the world's largest collection of Tibetan art out-side of Tibet. One of only two Himalaya-style monastery buildings in the Western world, this museum houses permanent and changing exhibits of Tibetan artifacts, from gold-leaf paintings to clothing and earthenware. But the exhibits are only one reason to visit. The museum offers a host of different events all year long, such as classes in Tibetan cuisine, painting and crafts workshops, tai chi classes, and guided meditation. *338 LIGHTHOUSE AVENUE IN STATEN ISLAND. Wednesday to Sunday 1:00 p.m. to 5:00 p.m. Admission: $5 for adults, $3 for seniors and students, children under 6 free. Ferry to St. George; then S74 bus to Lighthouse Avenue. 718-987-3500. www.tibetanmuseum.org.*

303. See the python at the **Brooklyn Children's Museum**.

When it was founded in 1899, the Brooklyn Children's Museum was the first museum of its kind, and it remains one of the most fun and educational places in the city to take a child for a day. Everything in the museum invites active participation, so chil-dren never get bored or feel like they're being dragged around a gallery. In the Music Mix Room, kids can pick up and play all sorts of instruments, from African drums to Fisher-Price xylophones, while the Animal Outpost lets children see, hear, and touch all kinds of animals, with a zoologist on hand to answer questions. The library has books and tapes to keep children thinking, and the museum's educational programming is fun and creative, with regular events like Little Scientist and Artworks, which introduce kids to everything from the joys of drawing with crayons to the physics of wet sand. With ramps and stairs to different exhibits, the museum is fun to walk around, too, and a spectacular water flume runs down the center of the building, teaching children the ways of water and letting them float objects down the stream. The star of the show, though, is Fantasia, the 17-foot Burmese python, who has to be seen to be believed.

145 BROOKLYN AVENUE AT ST. MARK'S AVENUE IN BROOKLYN. Open Wednesday through Friday, noon to 5:00 p.m.; Saturday and Sunday, 10:00 a.m. to 5:00 p.m. Admission: $7.50. Subway: 3 to Kingston Avenue; A, C to Nostrand Avenue. 718-735-4400. www.brooklynkids.org.

304. Play with the exhibits at the **Jewish Children's Museum**.

Where can you bake a challah, participate in a pretend game show, and play miniature golf? At the new Jewish Children's Museum in Brooklyn! Located in Crown Heights, a neighborhood with a history of religious and racial tensions, this one-of-a-kind museum combines the educational and commemorative initiatives of a Jewish museum with the approach and technological influences of secular children's museums. Here, children can touch, taste, make, and climb to learn about Jewish history, culture, and customs. The creative, hands-on exhibits (a walk-through Red Sea, a kosher supermarket kids can "shop" in, and a six-hole mini–golf course that teaches them about the Jewish lifecycle) are fun for all religions, ethnicities, and ages.

792 EASTERN PARKWAY AT KINGSTON AVENUE IN BROOKLYN. Open Sunday through Thursday, 10:00 a.m. to 4:00 p.m. (until 6:00 p.m. on Sunday), and selected Saturday nights. N.B.: The museum is closed on Friday and Saturday in observance of the Sabbath. Admission: $10. Subway: 3 to Kingston Avenue. 718-467-0600. www.jcmonline.org.

305. Visit the **Jewish Museum** on Christmas.

With a location inside an early-twentieth-century Gothic Revival mansion in the heart of Museum Mile, the Jewish Museum would be a pleasure to visit for surroundings alone. The impressive collection straddles the worlds of religious and fine arts, and many exhibitions seek to unite ancient ritual with the present day (such as one recent show on modern synagogue design and another on contemporary ritual objects). While the museum is closed on Jewish holidays, it is open on Christmas, making it one of the few available cultural offerings on that day, should you ever find yourself with some free hours.

1109 FIFTH AVENUE, AT 92ND STREET IN MANHATTAN. Open Thursday through Tuesday, 11 a.m. to 5:45 p.m. (Hours on Fridays are shortened in the winter.) Admission: $12; $10 for seniors; $7.50 for students. (Free all day on Saturdays.) Subway: 4,5,6 to 86th Street. 212-423-3200. www.thejewishmuseum.org.

306. Get a sense of the past and present of Spanish Harlem at the **Museo del Barrio**.

In the nearly forty years since its opening, El Museo del Barrio has evolved into a leading Latino cultural institution. Located in the Spanish-speaking area of East Harlem (also known as *El Barrio*), the museum displays work by young Latin American and Caribbean artists and celebrates the legacies of major influences in Latino art. In celebration of its forty-year anniversary, the museum underwent an extensive renovation in 2009, which added a museum café and updated gallery and shop facilities. Past exhibits have featured a chronicle of Latin American portraiture; a full retrospective of the pioneering Mexican photojournalist Casasola; and the *S-Files* exhibition, a selection of new work by up-and-coming Latin American artists, including an ingenious piece that told the story of a young Puerto Rican's theft of bubble gum from Wal-Mart. (The crime was photographed in stages, the film processed and developed at Wal-Mart's very own photo counter.) There is a beautiful pathos to much of the work exhibited here, touching on themes from the grandeur and romanticism of Latin American colonial life to the strength of the Latino community in struggling Harlem projects, and much of it shares a joyousness that invites visitors to celebrate art and the life that inspires it.

1230 FIFTH AVENUE AT 104ᵀᴴ STREET IN MANHATTAN. Open Wednesday through Sunday, 11:00 a.m. to 5:00 p.m. Admission (suggested): $6. Subway: 6 to 103ʳᵈ Street; 2, 3 to Central Park North (110ᵗʰ Street). 212-831-7272. www.elmuseo.org.

307. Broaden your horizons at the **Museum for African Art**.

Even in a city that prides itself on its multiculturalism, the Museum for African Art is impressive in its expression of a single culture's art and traditions. The largest museum of its kind in America, the museum's collections include examples of sculpture, portraiture, masks, fabrics, and artifacts from across the African continent. Beautiful, accessible, and immediate, much African art has its roots in a spirituality and history that is unfamiliar to Westerners. Past exhibits explored the ways in which ceramics and domestic arts among the Bamana in Mali reflect the conflicting traditions of their colonial heritage, while another featured examples of the vibrant murals, colorful designs, and symbolic carvings of African architecture. At time of press, the museum was in the process of moving from a gallery space in Queens (now closed) to a brand-new home on Museum Mile.

The new location of the museum will be 1280 FIFTH AVENUE, AT 109ᵀᴴ STREET IN MANHATTAN. Subway: 6 to 110ᵗʰ Street.

308. Get a taste of New York history at the **Museum of the City of New York**.

The Museum of the City of New York is an interesting blend of exhibitions and archives, chronicling the history of the city and its culture with a collection of more than 1.5 million objects and images. There are exhibitions in many different mediums (such as wartime photographs by photojournalists, contemporary community art projects, costumes from celebrated Broadway shows, and papers that document political scandals), and every collection and exhibition sheds light on a particular slice of New York, its heritage, and its people.

1220 FIFTH AVENUE AT 103RD STREET IN MANHATTAN. Open Tuesday through Sunday, 10:00 a.m. to 5:00 p.m. Admission (suggested): $10 for adults; $6 for seniors and students. Subway: 6 to 103rd Street. 212-534-1672. www.mcny.org.

309. Brush up your style at the **Museum of the Fashion Institute of Technology**.

The rotating exhibitions at the FIT museum draw on the institute's vast and world-renowned collections of clothing, accessories, and textiles to illuminate every aspect of the fashion world. The exhibits range from whimsical looks at extravagant eighteenth-century haute couture hats to more scholarly examinations of the history of patterned fabrics to sociological evaluations of the miniskirt. The photographic archives contain images of twentieth-century fashion from the obscure to the iconic, and the Fashion and Textile History Gallery chronicles the evolution of fashion and our fascination with it over the last 150 years, and includes fabrics worn as long ago as the sixth century. Go for the glimpse of the priceless Balenciaga but stay for the knowledge of how your wardrobe came to be what it is today.

SEVENTH AVENUE AT 27TH STREET IN MANHATTAN. Open Tuesday through Friday, noon to 8:00 p.m.; Saturday, 10:00 a.m. to 5:00 p.m. Admission is free. Subway: 1 to 28th Street. 212-217-4530. www.fitnyc.edu/museum.

310. Find something you weren't looking for at the **Studio Museum Harlem**.

The newest major arrival to New York's roster of museums is the Studio Museum, housed in an expansive and rambling space on Harlem's main drag, 125th Street. The museum's collections present a focused but open-minded celebration of African-American art in all mediums, from visual arts to music, theater, and installations, and past exhibitions have featured work by such artists as Kalup Linzy, Shinique Smith, and Hurvin Anderson. The museum's brilliant artist-in-residence program turns the relationship between museum and audience into one of mutual support, offering several young emerging artists studio space and exhibition time each year as a part of its larger programs. But the real treats of the Studio Museum are to be found by accident: there is a freedom in the layout of the space that is unlike any other museum in the city, and which can lead you to rooms and hidden works you didn't expect to find.

144 West 125TH STREET IN MANHATTAN. Open Wednesday through Friday, noon to 6:00 p.m.; Saturday 10:00 a.m. to 6:00 p.m.; Sunday noon to 6:00 p.m. Subway: 2,3, 4, 5, 6, A, B, C, D to 125th Street. Admission (suggested): $7 for adults, $3 for seniors and students. 212-864-4500. www.studiomuseum.org.

311. Keep your glass at the **Museum of Art and Design**.

At this forward-looking institution (formerly known as the American Craft Museum) visitors can take in displays of objects created in a wide variety of media, including ceramics, textiles, jewelry, furniture, paper engineering, and porcelain. Regrettably, MAD is now better known amongst some for the controversial redesign of its new home at 2 Columbus Circle (which elicited public protests and formal objections from the likes of Tom Wolfe, Chuck Close, and Frank Stella) than for what it holds inside. This is a shame, for the museum has some interesting offerings. There are open studios on the sixth floor where museum visitors can watch the processes of several artists-in-residence working in a variety of media. And on Thursday evenings, the museum stays open until 9 p.m., and operates a pop-up wine bar in the museum's seventh-floor special-events space (admission is also pay-as-you-wish during this time). Wines from a nearby wine store are served, along with small plates of food, which attendees can nibble while looking through the full-length windows at Columbus Circle below. You can't take your potables down to the gallery with you, but if you buy a drink you do get to keep the glass—a chic plastic tumbler with an ingeniously designed thumbprint. (If you want to complete your set, not surprisingly, the glasses are also sold in the museum's design shop.)

2 COLUMBUS CIRCLE, AT 59TH STREET IN MANHATTAN. Open Tuesday through Sunday, 11 a.m. to 6 p.m. (Thursdays until 9 p.m.) Open studio hours are daily between noon and 2 p.m.; 3 to 5 p.m. and 6:30 to 8:30 on Thursdays. Admission: $15; $12 for seniors and students. (Pay-as-you-wish from 6 p.m. to 9 p.m. on Thursdays.) Subway: A,B,C,D,1 to Columbus Circle. 212-299-7777. www.madmuseum.org.

312. Discover folk art at the **American Folk Art Museum**.

You may think you don't know too much about folk art—a broad categorization of works with traditional, cultural, or regional character, by artists who are usually self-taught and have no formal education—but chances are you know *Girl in Red Dress with Cat and Dog*, Ammi Philips's nineteenth-century portrait of a young round-cheeked girl that appears on posters in many living rooms, doctors' offices, and little girls' rooms. That iconic work is just one of the many pleasing surprises at this unpretentious, extremely rewarding museum. Located a few doors down from **MoMA** (see page 122), the museum sits in a slim slice of real estate, an amazing 85-foot-tall sliver of a structure, clad in stone-like panels that shimmer metallically, which won the prestigious Arup World Architecture Award for "Best New Building in the World" the year it opened. Inside lies a collection of more than 4,500 unusual paintings and crafts.

45 WEST 53RD STREET BETWEEN FIFTH AND SIXTH AVENUES IN MANHATTAN. Open Tuesday through Sunday, 10:30 a.m. to 5:30 p.m. (until 7:30 p.m. on Friday). Admission: adults $9, students and seniors $7, free for children under 12; Friday from 5:30 p.m. to 7:30 p.m. is free. Subway: E, V to Fifth Aveneue/53rd Street. 212-265-1040. www.folkartmuseum.org.

313. Learn about the movies at the Museum of the Moving Image.

New York has lured so many filmmakers to its streets that movie shoots are just part of the neighborhood, and people don't bat an eye when they wake up to a celebrity's trailer parked on their block. The Museum of the Moving Image celebrates the art of film and animation, and is a great place to learn about its technical side and its changing role in our culture. Exhibits at the museum reveal the mechanisms of this glamorous medium, giving visitors a hands-on, behind-the-scenes look at the processes involved in making everything from cartoons and video games to feature films and TV weather bulletins. Besides its engaging exhibitions, the museum also screens movies on a daily basis, with a program that ranges from Hollywood classics to international documentaries and contemporary art-house films.

35TH AVENUE AT 36TH STREET IN QUEENS. Open Tuesday through Friday, 10:00 a.m. to 3:00 p.m. Admission: $7 (children under 8 are free). Subway: R, V, G to Steinway Street. 718-784-0077. www.movingimage.us.

314. Watch old TV shows at the Paley Center for Media.

Watching TV is the thing to do here. The Paley Center—formerly the Museum of Television and Radio—has a collection of more than 120,000 radio and television programs and commercial advertisements, which you can watch at consoles in the museum's library. Keep an eye on their programs for special exhibits, seasonal series, and seminars, where you might get to see your favorite TV stars up close.

25 WEST 52ND STREET BETWEEN FIFTH AND SIXTH AVENUES IN MANHATTAN. Open Wednesday to Friday and Sunday, noon to 6:00 p.m.; Thursday, noon to 8:00 p.m. Admission: $10 for adults, $8 for students and seniors, $5 for children. Subway: E, V to Fifth Avenue/53rd Street. 212-621-6800. www.paleycenter.org.

315. See where George Washington really slept at the
New-York Historical Society.

Calling itself the city's "collective memory," the New-York Historical Society possesses one of the preeminent collections of artifacts, art, and documents of American history, with a focus on New York. The society's library holds more than three million written documents relating to U.S. history, such as newspapers and maps, original Civil War documents, and written correspondence between Alexander Hamilton and Aaron Burr. More than 40,000 items in the society's holdings are on display in the Henry Luce Center, along with furniture, decorative arts, police and military paraphernalia, and other priceless artifacts. Among all of these historic treasures, it's hard to pick out the particularly notable, but favorites include the 132-piece collection of Tiffany lamps (the world's largest) and George Washington's bed from Valley Forge.

170 CENTRAL PARK WEST AT 77ST STREET IN MANHATTAN. Open Tuesday through Thursday and Saturday, 10:00 a.m. to 6:00 p.m; Friday, 10:00 a.m. to 8:00 p.m.; and Sunday, 11:00 a.m. to 5:45 p.m. Admission: $10 for adults, $7 for seniors, teachers, and members of the military; $6 for students; free for children under 12. Subway: B, C to 81st Street-Museum of Natural History. 212-873-3400. www.nyhistory.org.

316. Live a day in the life of a cop and a firefighter at the **New York City Police Museum** and the **New York City Fire Museum**.

For some of us, childhood dreams of heroically fighting fires and valiantly protecting decent citizens from evil villains persist long into adulthood. These museums do a great job of portraying the lives and chronicling the history of New York's emergency forces, and the two can be visited easily in a single day. Exhibits at the New York City Police Museum include a look inside a nineteenth-century police station and a collection of intimidating gear, from uniforms through the ages to the handcuffs and badges used by the earliest New York cops. For further vicarious crime fighting, check out "Suspense in the City," a seasonal series of talks by best-selling mystery writers. The New York City Fire Museum holds a renowned collection of firefighters' equipment and artifacts, which illustrates the history of firefighting in New York from the eighteenth century to the present day, including pre–Civil War hand-pumped fire engines, painted buckets, belts, and the all-important helmets. They also operate an excellent fire safety education program.

NEW YORK CITY POLICE MUSEUM. *100 OLD SLIP BETWEEN WATER AND SOUTH STREETS IN MANHATTAN. Open Monday through Saturday, 10:00 a.m. to 5:00 p.m. Admission: $7 for adults, $5 for seniors and students. Subway: 1 to South Ferry; 2, 3 to Wall Street; 4, 5 to Bowling Green; J, M, Z to Broad Street; N, R, W to Whitehall Street-South Ferry. 212-480-3100. www.nycpolicemuseum.org.*

NEW YORK CITY FIRE MUSEUM. *278 SPRING STREET BETWEEN VARICK AND HUDSON STREETS IN MANHATTAN. Open Tuesday through Saturday, 10:00 a.m. to 5:00 p.m.; Sunday, 10:00 a.m. to 4:00 p.m. Admission (suggested): $5. Subway: C, E to Spring Street. 212-691-1303. www.nycfiremuseum.org.*

317. Have a think in the peaceful gardens at the Noguchi Museum.

Toward the end of his life, the acclaimed (and famously private) sculptor Isamu Noguchi decided in the interests of art and education to convert his working studio in Long Island City into a gallery and learning space. The Noguchi Museum remains a uniquely calm and reflective space, with several rooms and a Japanese garden displaying fine examples of his rock and wood sculpture. It's a meditative place to sit and think in the presence of his soothing art, and on the second Sunday of every month, the museum hosts lectures about Noguchi and his influence on the arts.

9-01 33RD ROAD AT VERNON BOULEVARD IN QUEENS. Open Wednesday through Friday, 10:00 a.m. to 5:00 p.m.; Saturday and Sunday, 11:00 a.m. to 6:00 p.m. Admission: $10, $5 students and seniors. Subway: N, W to Broadway. 718-204-7088. www.noguchi.org.

318. See brand-new modern art at PS1.

PS1, the Queens outpost of the **Museum of Modern Art** (see page 122), is one of the most unusual exhibition spaces in New York. Set in a unique environment in Long Island City that is part converted schoolhouse and part raw installation space, this forward-thinking venue exhibits fresh and creative contemporary art, from light installations that fill entire rooms to pieces of experimental architecture in the museum's outdoor spaces. Galleries of varying shapes and sizes are spread out over the building's five floors, and the eclectic exhibits demand attention in different ways—in one place you're peering down into a dark room full of sculpted figures, and in another you're staring up at a colorful film. Just walking around PS1 can be fun, too: the building is cool and expansive; there are murals in the stairwells; and the views from the windows of the Manhattan skyline and **5Pointz** across the street (see page 139) are surreal and breathtaking.

22–25 JACKSON AVENUE AT 46TH AVENUE IN QUEENS. Open Thursday through Monday, noon to 6:00 p.m. Admission (suggested): $5. Subway: E, V to 23 Street-Ely Avenue; 7 to 45 Road-Court House Square; G to Long Island City-Court Square. 718-784-2084. www.ps1.org.

319. Celebrate New York's vertical landscape at the Skyscraper Museum.

Skyscrapers are New York's signature feature, so it's only fitting that we have a museum dedicated to this particular architectural feat. After operating from several temporary locations, this museum has found a permanent home in the Ritz-Carlton New York,

Battery Park Hotel. Ironically, the museum of tall and majestic structures is in a teeny-tiny space on the ground floor, but you won't feel gypped. The one-room museum showcases the history, engineering, design, and social function of tall buildings through several engaging, kid- and novice-friendly exhibits, like a recent series of shows that juxtaposed twentieth-century American fascination with skyscrapers with images from the new frontier of tall building, China.

39 BATTERY PLACE NEAR LITTLE WEST STREET IN MANHATTAN. Open Wednesday through Sunday, noon to 6:00 p.m. Admission: $5 for adults, $2.50 for students and seniors. Subway: 1 to Rector Street or South Ferry; 4, 5 to Bowling Green; N, R, W to Whitehall Street-South Ferry. 212-968-1961. www.skyscraper.org.

320. Learn about New York nautical history at the **South Street Seaport Museum** and the **Red Hook Waterfront Museum**.

Fourscore years ago and more, when people and goods arrived in New York by boat from overseas, the ports of the East River were hives of business and activity. In the late-eighteenth and early-nineteenth centuries, the port at South Street in downtown Manhattan was the country's leading seaport, and the museum located there preserves the memory of the period, with great exhibits of nautical artifacts like seafarers' maps, ships' bells, and the largest fleet of privately maintained historic vessels in the country. Several of the eight ships are permanently moored to the docks and open to the public, and three others offer sailing tours of the waters around the harbor—imagine the year is 1885 and stand on the deck of the *Wavertree* or sail onboard the *Pioneer*. Afterward, you can cross over to Brooklyn and visit the Waterfront Museum, a small and charming gallery of curiosities and artifacts kept aboard a historic vessel moored at Red Hook's Conover Street harbor.

SOUTH STREET SEAPORT MUSEUM. *207 FRONT STREET AT WATER STREET IN MANHATTAN. Open (summer) Tuesday through Sunday 10:00 a.m. to 6:00 p.m.; (winter) Friday through Monday, 10:00 a.m. to 5:00 p.m. Admission: $10 for adults, $8 for students and seniors, $5 for children ages 5 to 12. Subway: 2, 3, 4, 5, J, M, Z to Fulton Street; A, C to Broadway-Nassau Street. 212-748-8786. www.southstreetseaportmuseum.org.*

RED HOOK WATERFRONT MUSEUM. *290 CONOVER STREET AT PIER 44 IN BROOKLYN. Open Thursday, 4:00 p.m. to 8:00 p.m.; Saturday, 1:00 p.m. to 5:00 p.m. Admission: donations accepted. Subway: F to Smith-9th Streets. Bus: B-77 to Conover Street. 718-624-4719. www.waterfrontmuseum.org.*

321. Take a tour of the **Lower East Side Tenement Museum**.

When the landlord of 97 Orchard Street died in the late 1980s, the five unused stories of the building above the storefronts he controlled were opened for the first time in fifty years. Inside this time capsule were twenty tenement apartments, left exactly as they were when the landlord closed up the residential part of the building. (He was unable to pay for the fireproofing mandated at the time, so he just boarded them up). Using city records, oral histories, and testimonies from descendants of residents, many of the apartments have been restored to look as they did during particular points of the building's seventy-year tenure as a tenement house, from the 1860s through the 1930s. The result is an unusual "museum," where you can tour different apartments and learn about real former tenants, their occupations, and their lifestyles—sort of like Colonial Williamsburg, New York style. And on "Tenement Wednesdays," museum tickets are redeemable at various local bars and restaurants, so you can follow your tour with a taste of old-school Lower-East Side dives. N.B.: The tenement is viewable by guided tour only, and tours do fill up, so it's best to reserve in advance. You can do so online through their Web site or by showing up when the museum opens for same-day tickets.

108 ORCHARD STREET AT DELANCEY STREET (tenement building is 97 Orchard). Tours run daily, from 11:00 a.m. to 6:00 p.m. Admission: $17 for adults, $13 for students and seniors. Subway: F to Delancey; J, M, Z to Essex Street. For more information, call 212-431-0233 or visit www.tenement.org.

322. Ride a trolley car from the past at the **MTA Transit Museum**.

The Metropolitan Transit Authority operates the biggest public transportation system in the world and has been helping people travel all over the city for more than a century. At the Transit Museum, you can learn about the history of the subways, the mechanics of the trains, and the engineering that has helped shape New York as we know it. In addition to amazing photographic exhibitions—such as *On Location*, which used movie stills, photographs, storyboards, film clips, and movie props to explore the pivotal role the MTA has played in New York's cinematic history—there are many engaging interactive permanent exhibits, such as *On the Streets*, a collection of vintage trolley buses that visitors are free to climb aboard.

BOERUM PLACE AT SCHERMERHORN STREET IN BROOKLYN. Open Tuesday through Friday, 10:00 a.m. to 4:00 p.m.; Saturday and Sunday, noon to 5:00 p.m. Admission: $5. Subway: 2, 3, 4, 5 to Borough Hall; A, C, G to Hoyt Street-Schermerhorn Street; F to Jay Street-Borough Hall; M, R to Court Street-Borough Hall. 718-694-1600. www.mta.info/mta/museum/index.html.

Expert Contributor: David Masello

David Masello is the articles editor at *Country Living* magazine and a longtime New York correspondent for *Art & Antiques* magazine. His essays and feature articles about art and architecture have appeared in, among other publications, the *New York Times* and *Boston Globe*, and in several anthologies, including *Best American Essays 2005*. He is the author of two books, *Architecture Without Rules: The Houses of Marcel Breuer* (W.W. Norton) and *Art in Public Places* (City & Company).

MY FIVE FAVORITE WORKS OF ART IN NEW YORK

323. Portrait of Lodovico Capponi *by Bronzino in the Frick Collection* depicts an attractive young man some might consider haughty and imperious. He is dressed in regal, shimmering Florentine garb of the mid-sixteenth century and even sports a conspicuous codpiece (a fashion of the day). The cameo he grasps in his hand includes the word *"sorte"* (fate, in Italian) and refers to the love he felt for an elusive young woman in the Medici court, whom he eventually married. Try to escape the gaze of his wandering eye. *For address and information, see entry on the Frick Collection, pages 123–124.*

324. *Bemelmans Bar,*
located within the Carlyle Hotel, has the feel of an urban version of the Lascaux Caves, the site in France whose rock walls are covered with prehistoric drawings of beasts. Ludwig Bemelmans, the creator and illustrator of the *Madeline* children's books, lived at the hotel in the mid-1940s and his "gift" to the management was to cover the ochre-colored walls with whimsical paintings of humanlike animals in New York City locales. Many of the drawings hearken to famous personalities of the day, including Jackie Gleason and Conrad Hilton. After your third martini, you might consider starting up a conversation with the animals. *35 EAST 76TH STREET AT MADISON AVENUE IN MANHATTAN. Subway: 6 to 77th Street. 212-744-1600. www.thecarlyle.com*

325. It's a remark uttered frequently by both New Yorkers and visitors that the city streets are filled with some of the handsomest people in the world. One of the most dashing permanent citizens is **Nathan Hale, rendered in bronze, in City Hall Park**. The twenty-year-old revolutionary hero is famous for reputedly saying at his hanging by the British on September 22, 1776, "I only regret that I have but one life to lose for my country." The sculpture was fashioned by Frederick MacMonnies (see entry for statue of **Civic Virtue** on page 142) in 1893. The rope-bound Hale maintains a pose of dignity, his beautiful face and coiffed hair set for all to admire.

CITY HALL PARK BETWEEN BROADWAY AND PARK ROW, CHAMBERS AND BARCLAY STREETS IN MANHATTAN. Subway: R, W to City Hall.

326. Depending on your state of mind, **Edvard Munch's The Storm, which is part of the Museum of Modern Art's permanent collection,** is either unnerving or just perplexing. Are those six figures in classic Munch pose (arms raised to the sides of their heads) simply fleeing from the moody storm or are they, well, unbalanced? Perhaps it's those unanswerable, impossible-to-resolve qualities about the painting that make it so intriguing. Whatever the interpretation, though, the colors of the stormy sky juxtaposed with the cozy lighted house make this one of New York City's most alluring public paintings.

For address and information, see entry for MoMA on page 122.

327. It's not uncommon to see people reading the Sunday *New York Times* on one of the benches in the **Astor Court at the Metropolitan Museum of Art.** The tranquil room replicates a Ming Dynasty (1368–1644) residential garden courtyard that is typical of Suzhou, a city in China famous for such spaces. The courtyard is so evocative of the outdoors and of its exotic locale that some New Yorkers use it as an idyllic weekend retreat from the city. And for anyone who doesn't understand the ancient Chinese philosophy of yin and yang, this is the space to learn the lesson: opposites abound, soft and hard surfaces, dark and light areas, natural and man-made details.

For address and more information, see entry for the Met on pages 119–120.

Art

Look for **hidden art.**

In addition to museums, galleries, and open-air public art, New York has some wonderful masterpieces tucked away in less obvious places. Pieces from corporate art collections, commissioned murals in building lobbies, sculptures in plazas, even a decorated piece of the Berlin Wall are all on permanent display in New York—if you know where to look. Accessibility to these semipublic works can be tricky—because many of them belong to corporate collections, they are located in office buildings, banks, and government buildings that do not have specific visiting hours. But rest assured that visiting them—even if you have no other business there—is perfectly legal. That's why they're there. Here are some of our favorites:

328. *Piece of the Berlin Wall, outdoor plaza, 520 Madison.*

Down the block from MoMA is a wonderful piece of contemporary art in an unlikely

place. On 53rd Street, just west of Madison Avenue, there are several rescued sections of the Berlin Wall decorated with two large, angry-looking faces looming over scrawling graffiti. Just don't be tempted to leave your own mark—though the existing graffiti from Germany is considered part of the piece, further additions are not welcome.
PLAZA OF 520 MADISON AVENUE ON 53RD STREET BETWEEN FIFTH AND MADISON AVENUES IN MANHATTAN. Subway: E, V to Fifth Avenue/53rd Street.

329. *Contemporary art, lobby, 520 Madison.*
Just inside the building are several interesting contemporary artworks from the esteemed art collection of the building's owner, Tishman Speyer.
See address above.

330. *Miró paintings and Giacometti sculpture at 9 West 57th Street.*
You may know the bright, red sculpture of the number "9" outside this building, but also on display in the lobby are several large Joan Miró paintings. The security tends to be stiff and snooty, so expect suspicious looks if you try to get a close-up look, but luckily, the lobby has floor-to-ceiling windows and is well lit, so you can get a good view just walking down 57th Street.
9 WEST 57TH STREET BETWEEN FIFTH AND SIXTH AVENUES IN MANHATTAN. Subway: N, Q, R, W to 57th Street; N, R, W to Fifth Avenue/59th Street.

331. *The sculpture garden, 590 Madison Avenue (formerly the IBM Building).*
The atrium at 590 Madison is a true urban oasis, and one of the loveliest, most tranquil spaces in all of Midtown. Located between 56th and 57th Streets, the glass-enclosed public space has both garden and sculptural elements; here, office workers and weary tourists can enjoy a bite to eat amid bamboo trees and a revolving selection of sculpture and large-scale art.
590 MADISON AVENUE BETWEEN 56TH AND 57TH STREETS IN MANHATTAN. Subway: E, V, to Fifth Avenue/53rd Street.

332. Energy, Result, Workmanship and Transportation *in the Chrysler Building.*
Though the Empire State Building may eclipse it in height, the Chrysler Building is the city's architectural darling. Inside the exquisite façade lies another Art Deco masterpiece—Edward Turnbull's elaborate 100-by-72-foot ceiling mural. The work celebrates modernity, depicting the workers during the building's construction. Long obscured by poor lighting, the mural was restored during the building's renovation.
405 LEXINGTON AVENUE AT 42ND STREET IN MANHATTAN. Subway: 4, 5, 6, 7, S to Grand Central-42nd Street.

333. Harbors of the World *in the American Express headquarters.*

Commissioned by American Express in the mid-1980s, this ambitious set of murals depicts the world through its major harbor cities. Artist Craig McPherson traveled around the world for a year and then took another four to complete the artwork. The result is a stunning, intricately detailed, eleven-foot-high panorama of the world's waterways.

3 WORLD FINANCIAL CENTER (BY VESEY STREET) IN MANHATTAN. Subway: E to World Trade Center; A, C to Chambers Street; 2, 3 to Park Place; 1, R, W to Rector Street.

334. *Sculptures at Chase Manhattan Plaza.*

Visitors who make their way through the forest of office buildings that surround this Wall Street complex will be rewarded with several distinguished pieces of public art. The plaza features two large-scale artworks, both referencing the conflict between urban and natural landscapes, and each is stunning in its own way: Jean Dubuffet's forty-two-foot fiberglass sculpture, *Group of Four Trees*, and Isamu Noguchi's *Sunken Plaza*, a circular below-ground water-and-rock garden, visible from the plaza above, and from the surrounding windows on the lower levels. We suggest going on a Sunday, when the financial district is empty and eerily quiet, so you can really see how well these two faux-natural elements enhance the otherwise bleak concrete landscape.

BETWEEN PINE AND LIBERTY STREETS AND BETWEEN NASSAU AND WILLIAM STREETS IN MANHATTAN. Subway: 2, 3, 4, 5 to Wall Street.

→ **DID YOU KNOW?** *Noguchi found the seven heavy basalt rocks (each weighing at least a ton) used in* Sunken Plaza *at the bottom of the Uji River in Japan and had them shipped to the United States.*

335. Paint something for New York to remember you by at 5Pointz, the Institute for Higher Burnin'.

A landmark visible from the windows of the **7 train into Queens** (see page 68), 5Pointz is a unique space dedicated to the appreciation and encouragement of the art of graffiti. Most of the exteriors of this converted warehouse are covered in the colorful murals and tags of talented graffiti artists from all over the world, and director Jan Meres has plans to convert the interiors into galleries and studios for aspiring and seasoned painters alike. While at the time of writing, 5Pointz was closed for renovations, with plans in the offing to convert its interior space into accessible studios, you can still go and walk around the building (including the roof, with spectacular views of Manhattan) to see the work on display.

JACKSON AVENUE AT CRANE STREET AND DAVIS STREET IN QUEENS. Subway: E, V to 23rd Street-Ely Avenue; 7 to 45 Road-Court House Square; G to Long Island City-Court Square. www.5ptz.com.

336. Plunge your hands into fresh soil at the *Earth Room*.

Created by renowned artist Walter De Maria and maintained by the Dia Art Foundation, the *Earth Room* is a quiet space in the heart of SoHo filled with fresh, dark soil that affords New Yorkers a chance to take a break from the busy asphalt streets below. A glass fence separates you from the 250 cubic yards of earth, so you can stand and inhale the clean, moist air, and visitors are free to plunge their hands into the soil. De Maria's installations often play with relationships that exist between the natural and the man-made: he has exhibited earth rooms twice in Germany, and his *Lightning Field* in New Mexico is acclaimed as one of the late-twentieth-century's most significant works of art. Don't be afraid to get your hands dirty—the experience is more refreshing, cathartic, and rewarding than any other hands-on exhibit we can think of.

141 WOOSTER STREET BETWEEN HOUSTON AND PRINCE STREETS IN MANHATTAN. Open Wednesday through Sunday, noon to 6:00 p.m. (Closed in summer.) Admission is free. Subway: N, R, W to Prince Street. www.earthroom.org.

337. Also on permanent exhibit in **SoHo** is another, equally surreal work by Walter De Maria, the ***Broken Kilometer***, a full kilometer's worth of 500 solid brass rods carefully arranged in parallel rows to create a hypnotic illusion of distance and light.

393 WEST BROADWAY BETWEEN SPRING AND BROOME STREETS IN MANHATTAN. Open Wednesday through Sunday, noon to 6:00 p.m. (Closed in summer.) Admission is free. Subway: C, E to Spring Street.www.brokenkilometer.org.

338. See what's new at the **Armory**.

The International Exhibition of Modern Art of 1913—more commonly known as "the Armory Show," for its location in Manhattan's 69th Regiment Armory—was the first of its kind in this country and is credited with introducing America to what we now refer to as modern art, as it was the first time works by Picasso, Kandinsky, and Duchamp were shown in the U.S. Though no longer held in the Armory, the fair's modern incarnation preserves the same spirit, continuing its legacy by presenting new contemporary works from around the world during its annual five-day run. More than 500 galleries from across the globe jockey for fewer than 150 booths, making for a highly selective show of never-before-seen paintings, sculptures, drawings, photography, mixed-media works, installations, and video art.

PIER 94 ON THE HUDSON RIVER (BY 54TH STREET) IN MANHATTAN. Late Winter. Admission: $30 per day or $60 for a 4-day run-of-the-show pass for adults, $10 for students. Subway: C, E to 50th Street. 212-645-6440. www.thearmoryshow.com.

339. Experience creativity at its most free at the **Flux Factory**.

There are no limits to what goes on at the Flux Factory, an ingenious nonprofit artist's workshop in Long Island City, except for the walls of its gallery—and even those don't seem to hold things back. When the gallery moved to a new space in 2008, they celebrated the move with *Everything Must Go*, an exhibition and sale of artworks and props leftover from shows at their old location. The attitude to art at the Flux Factory is that it should always be interactive, engaging, and thought provoking. The *Novel* exhibit saw three writers locked for thirty days and thirty nights in glass isolation booths built by young architects, their only task to have finished a novel when they emerged at the end of the month—an extreme study in the creative potential of solitude. Exhibits and events at the Flux Factory encompass every medium, from sound and film to writing and the visual arts: one recent highlight was *NYNYNY* ("so good they named it thrice"), a multimedia exhibit inspired by the landscape and architecture of the city—and the panorama at the **Queens Museum of Art** (see page 77)—that allowed artists to explore and construct a new cityscape built of both reality and fantasy.

39-31 29TH STREET, LONG ISLAND CITY IN QUEENS. Hours vary according to exhibit. Admission: donations accepted. www.fluxfactory.org.

340. See what's on (any time of day) at **Broadway Windows**.

This 24-hour viewing space bridges the gap between gallery space and public art, showing continuous revolving exhibitions of contemporary artworks in five professionally lighted street-level windows. The site-specific installations stay up for about two months each and have run the gamut from subtle and ambiguous structures of stone or glass, to brightly colored representational paintings and sculptures, and everything in between. Any artist may submit a proposal, and almost all works are for sale. New York University, which operates the space as a nonprofit gallery, sees it as dual-purpose community service: it provides unrepresented artists with an opportunity to have a gallery show of sorts, and it gives the public free exposure to contemporary and unconventional art they may not see otherwise. Note: NYU also operates the Washington Square Windows, a similar street-side gallery of three windows, on the east side of Washington Square Park.

BROADWAY AND 10TH STREET, NORTHWEST CORNER, IN MANHATTAN. Subway: 4, 5, 6, L, N, Q, R, W to 14th Street-Union Square; N, R to 8th Street-New York University. 212-998-5751. www.nyu.edu/pages/galleries.

341. Play among the artwork at **Socrates Sculpture Park**.

This quirky open-air exhibition grounds along the East River holds revolving short-term exhibits of large-scale contemporary sculpture, and also hosts other outdoor events including movies and **tai chi classes** (see pages 229–230), as well as children's programs. *32-01 VERNON BOULEVARD IN QUEENS. Subway: N, W to Broadway. 718-956-1819. www.socratessculpturepark.org.*

342. Get shocked by the statue of *Civic Virtue*.

This 1922 sculpture designed by Frederick MacMonnies was originally erected in Manhattan's City Hall Park. However, its vivid representation of virtue triumphing over temptation (a scantily clad youth with a huge club standing over two trampled sirens languishing at his feet) was deemed by many to be scandalous and insulting to women, which turned the state of *Civic Virtue* into a hotly contested issue around City Hall. "Rough Boy" (or "Tough Boy"), as the sculpture came to be known, was eventually moved to its current location in 1941, when Mayor Fiorello LaGuardia gave it to Queens County on the occasion of the opening of the new Borough Hall, in what can be seen as another example of priceless municipal symbolism.

QUEENS BOROUGH HALL, 120-155 QUEENS BOULEVARD, BY UNION TURNPIKE, IN QUEENS. Subway: E, F to Kew Gardens-Union Turnpike.

→ **DID YOU KNOW?** *Despite the controversy surrounding its allegedly lewd depiction,* Civic Virtue *had quite a prestigious provenance. It was sculpted by the Piccirilli brothers of the Bronx, two of whom also sculpted the lions in front of the* **New York Public Library** *(see page 292) and the Lincoln Memorial in Washington, D.C. The sculpture was, at the time, the largest work designed by an American (MacMonnies) and was said to have come from the largest single block of marble since Michelangelo's* David.

343. Catch a glimpse of the **Keith Haring mural**.

Keith Haring was the artist who made New Yorkers learn to love graffiti. His barking dogs and radiant babies were familiar sights in subway stations in the early '80s and they eventually got him noticed by the art world, but even after he became a star artist, he kept drawing on the streets. By the time of his death in 1990, he had created several outdoor murals around the city, mostly in parks and playgrounds. Some of these were not commissioned and have been erased or destroyed, but his 1986 *Crack is Whack!* mural, which is now maintained by the Parks Department, still exists. A personal riff on "Just Say No," the fluorescent orange mural depicts his typical, faceless characters surrounded by skulls and monsters and was Haring's response to the crack epidemic that plagued the city during those years. Located on a handball court at 128th Street and Second Avenue, it is also visible from the FDR Drive, so keep an eye out if you're stuck in traffic.

128TH STREET BETWEEN SECOND AVENUE AND THE FDR DRIVE IN MANHATTAN. Subway: 4, 5, 6 to 125th Street.

344. Explore the galleries of **West Chelsea**.

In the last decade, the industrial no-man's-land by Chelsea Piers and the West Side Highway has been transformed into a vibrant gallery scene. Today, between two and three hundred galleries lie west of Tenth Avenue, roughly between 20th and 28th Streets, scattered amid taxi depots and warehouses. Attracted initially by lower per-square-foot rents (as compared to SoHo and further uptown) and ample ground-level space (which gallery owners desire), the galleries here also benefit from the large, open spaces that these industrial buildings provide, and visitors benefit from their unbeatable proximity to one another, making it possible to see several shows in a single afternoon—without even having to cross the street.

To plan a walking tour, or to see what's there, visit www.westchelseaarts.com. They have a list of all the galleries in the area, with addresses, hours, and information on artists they represent. For current shows, you can also check the listings in Time Out New York, New York *magazine, or the* New York Times.

345. Peek into **Sotheby's** and **Christie's**.

If you don't have the funds to bid at an **auction** (see page 282), you can still see what's up for sale by visiting the salesrooms of the city's two major auction houses. Both houses display works from major upcoming shows and have pieces from their own holdings on view.

CHRISTIE'S. *20 ROCKEFELLER PLAZA, EAST OF SIXTH AVENUE, IN MANHATTAN. Subway: B, D, F, V to 47th-50th Streets-Rockefeller Center. 212-636-2000. www.christies.com.*

SOTHEBY'S. *1334 YORK AVENUE AT 72ND STREET IN MANHATTAN. Subway: 6 to 68th Street-Hunter College. 541-312-5682. www.sothebys.com.*

346. Go **sculpture spinning**.

Among our many public treasures, New York City is blessed with not one but two outdoor sculptures on rotating axes that turn when pushed. After a mysterious disappearance in 2005, Bernard "Tony" Rosenthal's large black cube titled *Alamo*, which had been on Astor Place since the '60s, was been returned, all tuned up for a lifetime of spinning. The other spinning sculpture is Henry Moore's *Three-Way Piece* on the **Amsterdam overpass** (see page 78) by Columbia University.

ALAMO. *ASTOR PLACE BY FOURTH AVENUE AND LAFAYETTE STREETS IN MANHATTAN. Subway: 6 to Astor Place.*

THREE-WAY PIECE. *AMSTERDAM OVERPASS BETWEEN 116TH AND 118TH STREETS IN MANHATTAN. Subway: 1 to 116th Street-Columbia University.*

347. Dine in the Raleigh Room at **Murals on 54**.

Across the back wall of this small restaurant in the Warwick Hotel, a series of colorful 1937 murals by Dean Cornwall depicts the sixteenth-century British explorer Sir Walter Raleigh and his crew on their way from England to the island of Roanoke. The murals were covered for nearly forty years following a dispute with the hotel's owner, William Randolph Hearst, and an angered Cornwall added some lewd details. In 2004, as part of the restaurant's renovation project, the murals were restored and are once again the focal point of the Warwick's restaurant.

63 WEST 54TH STREET BETWEEN FIFTH AND SIXTH AVENUES IN MANHATTAN. Subway: E, V to Fifth Avenue/53rd Street. 212-314-7700. www.murals54.com.

➜ **DID YOU KNOW?** *William Randolph Hearst built the Warwick as a residential hotel in 1927, designating an entire floor for the apartment of his lover, Marion Davies, the actress and Ziegfeld girl. In a stairwell beyond the front desk, there are photographs of some of the hotel's famous guests, including James Dean, Elvis Presley, Elizabeth Taylor, the Beatles, Audrey Hepburn, and Cary Grant, a twelve-year resident.*

348. **Pick a park** to see some art...

On any given day, there are dozens of outdoor sculptures, installations, and other artworks that you can see for free, thanks to the New York Parks Department, the Public Art Fund, the Mayor's Office, and other organizations. Works by artists, famed and unknown, are displayed in city parks across the five boroughs, many of which you can touch, sit on, or play with. You can find a list of the current works and where they are located on the Parks Department's Web site; then go pick a park (or several!) and admire the work from a sunny spot on the grass.

www.nycgovparks.org/sub_things_to_do/attractions/public_art/public_art.html

349. ...or enjoy Lower Manhattan's "**outdoor museum**" along the Hudson River.

The thirty-plus acres of park area around Battery Park City have one of the city's most interesting public-art programs and several dozen permanent artworks have been incorporated into the layout. Pieces by renowned contemporary artists such as Louise Bourgeois, Jim Dine, Sol LeWitt, Andy Goldsworthy, and Tom Otterness are brilliantly integrated into the park and along the esplanade. Temporary artworks also appear throughout the year. One of the highlights is Brian Tolle's *Irish Hunger Memorial*, an elevated landscape in homage to the Irish potato famine of 1845–54, made of stone and native Irish plants with an authentic nineteenth-century Irish cottage that visitors can climb up and roam around.

Between Battery Park City and the Hudson River, extending from Battery Place to Chambers Street in Manhattan. Subway: 4, 5 to Fulton Street or Bowling Green; N, R to Cortlandt Street; 2, 3 to Park Place; A, C to Chambers Street; E to World Trade Center. www.bpcparks.org. Note: A map with information about the artworks is available at neighborhood museums and businesses.

350. ...And while you are in the neighborhood, **take a tour of downtown art**, at your leisure.

The bottom part of the island is a veritable outdoor museum of public art and sculpture. The Lower Manhattan Cultural Council offers a selection of free downloadable walking tours of public art downtown on their Web site. The audio portion can be downloaded to an iPod or MP3 players, and PDFs maps are available on the site as well. *For listings of current available tours, and to download audio and maps, visit http://www.lmcc.net/art/programs/2006.9.1artwalkingtours/index.html.*

351. See the rock photographs at the **Morrison Hotel**,

the fine-art music photography gallery in SoHo that has bought, exhibited, and sold some of the most famous images in rock music history. Collections of original prints by celebrated music photographers from Henry Diltz to Lynn Goldsmith line the walls, and exhibits change every month or so. The subjects are iconic—recent exhibits have included Elliot Landy's legendary photographs of Bob Dylan and Mick Rock's intimate portrayals of life on the road with David Bowie—and many of the pictures will be familiar to those acquainted with album covers and posters of rock stars. The gallery is popular among musicians, so go on the right day and you might find yourself standing next to some of the famous subjects themselves.

124 PRINCE STREET BETWEEN WOOSTER AND GREENE STREETS IN MANHATTAN. Subway: B, D, F, V to Broadway-Lafayette Street; 6, C to Spring Street. 212-941-8770. www.morrison-hotelgallery.com.

352. Discover a new artist at the **Washington Square Art Show**.

One spring day during the height of the Depression, a young, cash-strapped, aspiring artist named Jackson Pollock and his friend Willem de Kooning set up some paintings to sell on the street, with the hope of raising enough money to pay the rent for the studio (where he lived) just upstairs. The "show" and its artists got the attention of famous modern-art patrons like Whitney and Barr, who worked to turn it into a regular event to showcase the work of living artists. Nearly eighty years later, the Washington Square Outdoor Art Exhibition is a biannual juried event and includes categories for sculpture, photography, and crafts. For two consecutive weekends in May and again in September, the streets around Washington Square Park are lined with booths, where artists display their works, many of which are for sale. Whether or not you're interested in buying, this is a great event, so pick a nice afternoon for a stroll around. Who knows, you might become a collector.

BOOTHS ARE LOCATED ON UNIVERSITY PLACE, FROM 12TH STREET TO WASHINGTON SQUARE PARK, AND THEN ALONG THE EAST SIDE OF THE PARK. Held over two weekends in May and September: Memorial Day and the following weekend; Labor Day and the following weekend. For more information, call 212-982-6255, or visit www.washingtonsquareoutdoorartexhibit.org.

Music & Dance

353. Go to a concert on **the barge**.

Located on a former working barge moored in the East River, this floating concert hall helped put the Brooklyn waterfront on the map. Opened in 1977, Bargemusic has gained a good reputation for its low-cost chamber music concerts. But people aren't going for the novelty—the 125-seat room is one of the best places to hear solos, duets, trios, and quartets in the city, and Bargemusic attracts top musicians who relish the chance to play in this unique and intimate setting.

FULTON FERRY LANDING, BY THE BROOKLYN BRIDGE, IN BROOKLYN. Concerts are held year-round, Thursday through Saturday at 7:30 p.m. and Sunday at 4:00 p.m. Admission: $35 to $40 for adults, $30 for seniors, $20 for full-time students. Reservations required, except for free concerts, which are first-come/first-serve. Subway: 2, 3 to Clark Street; A, C to High Street; F to York Street. For more information and concert schedule, call 718-624-2083 or visit www.bargemusic.org.

354. Take a trip to **Snug Harbor**.

On the north shore of Staten Island, twenty-six historical buildings set within an eighty-three-acre National Historic Landmark district make up one of New York's more unusual cultural centers. Snug Harbor was originally created as a retirement community for sailors, but its impressive array of Greek Revival, Beaux-Arts, Italianate, and Victorian buildings have been turned into exhibition and performance spaces. Stage productions, art exhibitions, classical concerts, and displays of historical artifacts are presented at the many halls, galleries, and theaters across the park, and the Snug Harbor Cultural Center holds educational events, such as lecture series and classes for kids. On top of everything going on inside the buildings, the park that surrounds Snug Harbor's halls is spacious and beautiful and incorporates wonderful sibling institutions including the Noble Maritime Collection, the Staten Island Children's Museum, and the Staten Island Botanical Gardens.

1000 RICHMOND TERRACE IN STATEN ISLAND. Hours and admission vary by attraction; contact the center for details about specific exhibits or performances. Staten Island Ferry to the S40 bus. 718-448-2500. www.snug-harbor.org.

355. Hear a concert at **Carnegie Hall**.

One of the most famous venues in the world, Carnegie Hall has hosted more than 50,000 events in its 115 years of existence. Since it opened in 1891, the most influential musicians, politicians, thinkers, speakers, and singers of the time have ascended to its stages. This is where Antonin Dvorak's *New World Symphony* premiered, Maria Callas sang her last concert in America, Winston Churchill, Woodrow Wilson, Martin Luther King, and Albert Einstein spoke; and every kind of admired musician—from the New York Philharmonic to the Beatles and Ravi Shankar—has played concerts here. The program is as strong and as glamorous as it has ever been, and there is no better place to hear music in the city.

57TH STREET AND SEVENTH AVENUE IN MANHATTAN. Subway: 1, A, C, B, D to 59th Street-Columbus Circle; N, Q, R, W to 57th Street. 212-247-7800. www.carnegiehall.org.

356. Go to the **CMJ Music Marathon**.

The largest event of its kind in the world, the CMJ Music Marathon takes place at various venues across New York at the end of every summer and brings with it many of the world's top music acts. Aiming to bring artists into closer contact with their audiences, CMJ events include live shows, talks by legendary performers, and film screenings, which take place at concert halls, bars, and theaters. Highlights of the 2009 festival included performances by Superdrag, Z-Trip, and Cymbals Eat Guitars, as well as appearances from the ubiquitous Margaret Cho.

Late summer/early fall. For dates, locations, and performance schedules, call 917-606-1908, or visit www.cmj.com/marathon.

357. See opera on a small scale at **Gotham Chamber Opera**.

This nine-year-old company is the **Bargemusic** (see page 146) of opera. Gotham's repertoire concentrates on chamber opera, a term that refers to intimate operas written for small casts, small orchestras, and small theaters, which are seldom performed in the city's larger opera houses. But it's not only the programming that's intimate: most of the performances take place in a 350-seat theater, where the distance from the stage to the last row is roughly the distance between the stage and the third row at Lincoln Center.
466 GRAND STREET AT THE CORNER OF PITT STREET IN MANHATTAN. Subway: F to Delancey Street; J, M, Z to Essex Street. 212-868-4460. www.gothamchamberopera.org.

358. Take your pick of the performing arts at **BAM**.

Originally founded nearly 150 years ago as a hall for the Philharmonic Society of Brooklyn, the Brooklyn Academy of Music has become one of New York's most illustrious and beloved cultural institutions. Enjoying active support from celebrated patrons and bringing some of the world's most renowned artists to its stages, BAM is a center for excellence in all the performing arts—dance, drama, film, and, of course, music. Its programs maintain a careful balance between the modern and the traditional, alternating between provocative new films and nostalgic retrospectives, modern dance premieres and celebrated classical ballets. One of the annual highlights is the Next Wave festival held each November. The ten-week festival is a showcase of the avant-garde, with performances of all shapes, sizes, and kinds.
30 LAFAYETTE AVENUE BETWEEN ASHLAND PLACE AND ST. FELIX STREET IN BROOKLYN. Subway: 2, 3, 4, 5, B, Q to Atlantic Avenue; D, M, R to Atlantic Avenue-Pacific Street; N to Pacific Street; BAMbus to and from various locations in Manhattan (see Web site for more information). 718-636-4100. www.bam.org.

359. Go to the **Time Warner Center for Jazz** at Lincoln Center.

As well as offering the city's most celebrated opera, ballet, and classical music, **Lincoln Center** (see pages 150–153) holds one of New York's best and most diverse jazz programs at **Dizzy's Club** (see page 64), an off-site performance venue in the **Time Warner Center** (see page 64). With renowned house musicians and a roster of incredible performers lighting up its seasons, there is live jazz here every single night of the year. The warm and inviting space has an informal feel that invigorates the performances, from the scheduled weekly acts right through the After Hours Sets, relaxed jams with a wonderful clandestine feel that last well into the night. The Rose Theater and the Allen Room divide between them an eclectic range of visiting acts, from living legends like Yusef Lateef to touring big bands and rising solo stars. An especially fun thing to see is one of the educational shows: as part of the program to teach people to hear, appreciate, and engage in jazz music, artistic director Wynton Marsalis and the Lincoln Center Jazz Orchestra host evenings devoted to legendary artists, genres, or styles of music that let audiences see and hear jazz genius in action. If you arrive early for a show, sit for a moment at the fountains by Columbus Circle and you might catch the house orchestra wheeling their instruments over to the theater.

BROADWAY AT 60TH STREET IN MANHATTAN. Subway: 1, A, C, B, D to 59th Street-Columbus Circle; 1 to 66th Street-Lincoln Center. 212-258-9800. www.jalc.org.

360. See and support dance at the **Joyce Theater**.

The Joyce Theater is one of the nation's premier modern-dance venues, and it holds the rare distinction of being a gentrification venture that New Yorkers actually approve of. As many longtime city residents remember, the beautiful Art Deco building of its Chelsea space used to be the Elgin Theater, a popular revival movie house in the '60s and '70s. The Elgin fell on hard times and was forced to close. In 1982, it reopened as the Joyce, a completely renovated 472-seat theater designed to showcase modern dance. In addition to the theater's technical amenities (it is known for its excellent sightlines), the Joyce is also applauded for its charitable programming schemes, and it subsidizes the in-theater costs of two-thirds of the performing dance companies during their runs. The Joyce operates a second space in SoHo, which offers dance companies rehearsal and performance spaces at discounted rates, and it plans to open the 1,000-seat International Dance Center in the future Freedom Towers.

175 EIGHTH AVENUE AT 19TH STREET IN MANHATTAN. Subway: C, E to 23rd Street. 212-691-9740. JOYCE SOHO: 155 MERCER STREET IN MANHATTAN. Subway: 6 to Spring Street. 212-431-9233. www.joyce.org.

361. See the **American Dance Theater** perform in its new home.

The nation's best-known dance company, the Alvin Ailey American Dance Theater has had an impressive 77,000-square-foot facility to call home since 2006—the largest facility in the country exclusively devoted to dance. The six-story, state-of-the-art Joan Weill Center for Dance is double the size of the company's previous space at City Center, and it includes a 265-seat "black box" theater, as well as studios, classrooms, a library, a costume shop, and physical therapy facilities.

405 WEST 55TH STREET AND NINTH AVENUE IN MANHATTAN. Subway: 1, A, C, B, D to 59th Street-Columbus Circle. 212-405-9000. www.alvinailey.org.

362. Check out the indie rock scene at the **Siren Music Festival**.

This free music festival presented by the *Village Voice* showcases the talents of emerging and alternative bands. The all-day concert features multiple bands on two stages by the water at Coney Island. Many of the indie rock bands go on from there to make it into the mainstream; past concerts have featured Death Cab for Cutie, the Yeah Yeah Yeahs, the Shins, and Peaches.

July. CONEY ISLAND BOARDWALK, MAIN STAGE AND STILLWELL STAGE, IN BROOKLYN. Subway: D, F, N, Q to Coney Island-Stillwell Avenue. For more information, visit www.villagevoice.com/siren.

Theater & Performance

LINCOLN CENTER:

Culture reigns supreme in New York, and Lincoln Center is its kingdom. With a school, a library, several exhibition galleries, shops, restaurants, and nearly two-dozen performance spaces, this expansive complex is a village of the performing arts. An extensive renovation timed with the center's fiftieth anniversary is transforming the grandiose, heavy-seeming plaza and buildings into modern, welcoming spaces full of glass and light, architecturally bringing together Lincoln Center's two raisons d'être: performing the arts and studying them. Lincoln Center is the home of some of the most acclaimed cultural programs in the city (and the world)—including the Metropolitan Opera, the New York Philharmonic, and Juilliard—and hosts annual events, festivals, and, of course, performances of every size, type, and medium under the sun. Its reach, however, extends well beyond the 16.3-acre plaza—there **is Jazz at Lincoln Center** (see pages 148–149) in the Time Warner Center, and the Atrium, a brand-new visitor center located a few blocks southeast of the main campus, which houses a central box office, a café, information desk, and a kiosk offering discounted same-day tickets (similar to **TKTS**, see page 28). Many of the resident organizations also give regular concerts and performances off-site, such as the **Metropolitan Opera's summer concert series in Central Park** (see page 217); and performances can be seen around the country on PBS on *Live from Lincoln Center*, the only televised live performing arts series.

What's best to do at Lincoln Center is subjective and depends on your taste, but the following is a list of our favorite organizations and programs. You can find the full range of offerings (as well as schedules, directions, and additional information) by visiting www.lincolncenter.org. (The following are located on the main campus unless otherwise noted.)

62ND TO 66TH STREETS BETWEEN COLUMBUS AND AMSTERDAM AVENUES IN MANHATTAN.
Subway: 1 to 66th Street-Lincoln Center. Information on all of the following venues and pro-
grams can be found by calling 212-875-5000 or visiting www.lincolncenter.org. For Jazz at
Lincoln Center, located at the Time Warner Center, see page 148.

363. *Metropolitan Opera*

Now almost 125 years old, the Metropolitan Opera is one of the world's preeminent opera companies, drawing some of the best singers, orchestral musicians, and conductors to its stage. Many masterpieces of opera had their American premieres here, from acclaimed new works like John Harbison's *The Great Gatsby* to Puccini's popular *Il Fanciulla del West*, and several of Wagner's classic works. Under the artistic direction of James Levine since 1976, the Metropolitan Opera stages lavish productions of classic works that are always awe-inspiring to watch, from Mozart's *Marriage of Figaro* to Verdi's *Aida* and Gounod's *Romeo and Juliet.* Astonishing sets and enormous casts contribute to consistently powerful and affecting performances—a recent production of Puccini's *La Bohème* featured a set designed by Franco Zeffirelli. A night at the Met feels grand, decadent, and magical: sip champagne during the interval on its stunning balcony overlooking the renovated plaza and fountain.

METROPOLITAN OPERA HOUSE AT LINCOLN CENTER LOCATED BETWEEN 62ND AND 65TH
STREETS AND COLUMBUS AND AMSTERDAM AVENUES IN MANHATTAN. Subway: 1 to 66th
Street-Lincoln Center. For more information, performance schedules, and to purchase tickets,
call 212-362-6000 or visit www.metopera.org.

364. *The New York City Ballet*

The New York City Ballet was founded in 1933 by Leonard Kirstein and George Balanchine, with the mission to create a ballet company on par with those in Europe. Today, NYCB is the largest dance organization in America and one of the leading ballet companies in the world, with ninety dancers and a repertory of over 150 works. They perform at the brand new David H. Koch Theater (formerly the New York State Theater) twenty-three weeks a year, including an annual six-week run of Balanchine's *The Nutcracker.*

For more information, performance schedules, and to purchase tickets, call 212-870-5570 or
visit www.nycballet.com.

365. *New York City Opera*

The New York City Opera is an interesting combination of the contemporary and the traditional, producing unusual pieces of musical theater and inventive interpretations of classic operas on a grand scale. NYCO productions, which take place in the David H. Koch Theater, tend to have smaller casts than those of the Met Opera and an edgier take on costume and set design. (A recent production of *Tosca* was set in fascist Italy, with dramatic blood-red lighting and a terrifying Scarpia dressed in the black of Mussolini's militia.) The theater itself is wonderful, and just like at the Met, intermissions can be spent sipping champagne on the promenade terrace overlooking the fountain and Lincoln Center Plaza.

NEW YORK STATE THEATER AT LINCOLN CENTER LOCATED BETWEEN 62ND AND 65TH STREETS AND AMSTERDAM AND COLUMBUS AVENUES IN MANHATTAN. Subway 1 to 66th Street-Lincoln Center. 212-870-5570. www.nycopera.com.

366. *New York Philharmonic*

Avery Fisher Hall is home to the country's oldest symphony orchestra, the New York Philharmonic, which has been performing classical music domestically and abroad since 1842. The orchestra plays 180 concerts a year; in addition to their official September-through-June season at Avery Fisher Hall, they also put on "**Concerts in the Parks**," an annual series of free outdoor concerts (see page 217). They also hold open rehearsals, which are an interesting and economical way to see a world-class orchestra at work.

For more information, concert schedules, and to purchase tickets, call 212-875-5656 or visit www.nyphil.org.

367. *Film Society of Lincoln Center*

Best known for putting on two of the city's major film festivals—the **New York Film Festival** and **New Directors/New Films** (see pages 156–157)—this eminent cinematic organization holds exciting film-related events all year round and has included nearly every major filmmaker of the past thirty-five years in its programs. They hold regular screenings at the Walter Reade Theater, host conversations, symposia, and discussions, and publish the highly regarded journal, *Film Comment*. Because so many of the events feature advance and exclusive screenings, with high-profile names, many people assume that they're not open to the public. Almost all of them are (with the exception of a handful of annual galas and members-only programs); however, they are extremely popular and often sell out well in advance. The best way to find out what's on is to subscribe to their free e-newsletter, which lets you know about upcoming programs before they are publicized. N.B.: A new home cinema for the Film Society, the Elinor-Bunin-Monroe Center, is part of the last phase of the Lincoln Center renovation, and is planned to open in 2011.

For more information and to sign up for the e-newsletter, call 212-875-5601 or visit www.film-linc.com.

368. *Lincoln Center Presents*

Lincoln Center Presents is the title of the year-round programming that Lincoln Center for the Performing Arts puts on. Featuring more than 400 performances annually in all twenty-two Lincoln Center venues (as well as outdoor events in plazas and Damrosch Park), it includes concerts, theatrical performances, talks, events for kids, and much more: "Great Performers," a classical-music series; "Lincoln Center Festival," their summer performance showcase; "Lincoln Center Out of Doors," a free outdoor summer arts festival; "Live from Lincoln Center"; and "Midsummer Night Swing," a summer-long dance party featuring different performers every night.

For more information on individual programs and schedules, visit www.lincolncenter.org and click on "Lincoln Center Presents."

BROADWAY AND BEYOND

Theaters in New York are classified as "Broadway," "Off-Broadway," and "Off-Off Broadway," but this designation actually has nothing to do with their proximity to the Great White Way. Theaters with more than 500 seats are considered Broadway theaters, 100 to 500 seats are Off-Broadway, and fewer than 100 seats are Off-Off Broadway, regardless of their location. In general, musicals and other popular, large-scale productions appear on Broadway, while serious drama and more off-beat performances start Off-Broadway. (To add to the confusion, successful and critically acclaimed performances will often move to a Broadway theater.) Off-Off Broadway shows tend to be the most experimental and least polished. Many Off-Broadway and Off-Off Broadway theaters are nonprofits, so their productions are usually less commercial than those seen on Broadway. Because going to a show on Broadway is such a classic New York activity in its own right, we've given it its own entry in Chapter 1. But here we give you a short list of other favorite theaters and theater companies.

369. *The Atlantic Theater*

Founded by David Mamet and William H. Macy, the Atlantic Theater Company puts on a broad range of plays, from classic works by Chekhov, Ionesco, and Pinter, to new plays by modern masters like Martin McDonough, in addition to plenty of Mamet plays. They've also put on plays written and directed by Woody Allen, a theatrical adaptation of John Irving's novel *The Cider House Rules*, and originated the Duncan Sheik hit musical *Spring Awakening*, which moved to Broadway. The main theater is located in an old church, which has been converted into a small but well-proportioned theater with good sightlines. (Just make sure to use the bathroom before the play starts—it's located behind the stage.) A new, smaller theater, the Atlantic Stage2, now hosts the edgier performances a few blocks away—a sort of Off-Atlantic Atlantic.

336 WEST 20TH STREET BETWEEN EIGHTH AND NINTH AVENUES IN MANHATTAN. Subway: C, E to 23rd Street. 212-691-5919. ATLANTIC STAGE2: 330 WEST 16TH STREET IN MANHATTAN. www.atlantictheater.org.

370. *Irish Repertory Theater*

For a small country, Ireland has produced a disproportionate number of great play-wrights, and the best place in the city to see their plays performed is the Irish Rep. The theater's mission is to expose American audiences to the wealth of Irish and Irish-American theater, and it puts on an interesting mix of classic and contemporary plays by Samuel Beckett, Brendan Behan, and J. M. Synge, and adaptations of literary works by Yeats and Dylan Thomas. One of its most popular recent productions was *The Irish and How They Got That Way* by the late Pulitzer Prize–winning author Frank McCourt. The theater, located in Chelsea, is typical Off-Broadway, with less-than-spacious seat-ing and a rather awkward layout. But the set designers compensate very well for it, and the acting and direction are typically on par with the impressive plays.

132 WEST 22ND STREET BETWEEN SIXTH AND SEVENTH AVENUES IN MANHATTAN. Subway: 1 to 23rd Street; F, V to 23rd Street. 212-727-2737. www.irishrepertorytheater.com.

371. *New York Theater Workshop*

The New York Theater Workshop is a unique organization that has been developing and producing plays in the East Village for more than twenty-five years. The shows range from innovative interpretations of well-known plays, such as Henrik Ibsen's *Hedda Gabler* and Tennessee Williams's *A Streetcar Named Desire*, to more experimen-tal modern theater, such as Tony Kushner's *Homebody/Kabul*. One of the theater's claims to fame is that it was where *Rent*, Jonathan Larson's hit rock musical based on *La Bohème*, was first staged. The company nurtures new playwrights, actors, and direc-tors, and invites and appreciates the criticism of its patrons in order to further its mis-sion for theatrical growth and improvement. What ties the productions together is the creative influence of artistic director James Nicola (who has presided over the NYTW since 1988) and his dedication to original and intelligent drama.

79 EAST 4TH STREET BETWEEN SECOND AVENUE AND THE BOWERY IN MANHATTAN. Subway: F to Lower East Side-Second Avenue; 6 to Astor Place. 212-780-9037. www.nytw.org.

372. *The Public Theater*

The best known of New York's Off-Broadway venues, the Public Theater is one of the most accomplished theaters in the city, period. Founded in 1954 as the Shakespeare Workshop, the Public is one the premier venues in the city to see Shakespeare, as well as musicals, and contemporary and classical plays. In keeping with its mission as a "public" theater, it offers free performances (such as **Shakespeare in the Park**, see following entry) and makes an effort to appeal beyond the traditional theater-going audience by representing a diverse array of playwrights, actors, and directors in its productions.

425 LAFAYETTE STREET BETWEEN ASTOR PLACE AND EAST 4TH STREET IN MANHATTAN. Sub-way: 6 to Astor Place; N, R to 8th Street-New York University. 212-539-8500. www.publicthe-ater.org.

373. Wait in line to see **Shakespeare in the Park**.

One of New York's most famous theater venues is Central Park's Delacorte Theater, where the **Public Theater** (see previous entry) puts on Shakespeare in the Park. Each summer, hundreds of thousands of people wait in line for countless hours for a chance to see stars like Kevin Kline, Meryl Streep, and Morgan Freeman perform on stage—for free. Tickets for each night's performance become available only on the day of, and the line starts forming around dawn for the box office that opens at 1:00 p.m. For $150, you can be a "summer sponsor," which allows you to reserve a single seat at a performance (proceeds to go toward covering the festival's costs). You can also try your luck on the virtual line, which allows you throw your name into an online pool for tickets to that evening's performance as early as 12 a.m. (There is also a special virtual line for seniors.) Otherwise, take a morning off and get in line; the wait is worth it.

THE DELACORTE THEATER, CENTRAL PARK AT THE SOUTHWEST CORNER OF THE GREAT LAWN (AROUND 81ST STREET) IN MANHATTAN. Tickets available at the Delacorte Theater box office. Subway: B, C to 81st Street-Museum of Natural History; 4, 5, 6 to 86th Street. For more information on becoming a summer sponsor, contact the Public Theater. For virtual line, visit http://vline.publictheater.org.

374. **Volunteer to be an usher** for a night.

Ushering for an Off-Broadway show is not only an economical way to see a play, it can also be a fun experience. Broadway theaters mostly use paid, unionized ushers, but almost all Off-Broadway theaters rely on volunteers. The application process is easy, but the competition can be stiff—there are plenty of veteran volunteers out there, mostly unemployed actors and retirees, who are serious about ushering. The procedure varies from theater to theater, but in general, you show up for the performance you're assigned to about an hour before show time wearing all black (or whatever dress code is specified), help seat people, hand out programs, sell concessions—do whatever needs doing—and then you can watch the show from empty seats or from the back of the theater. The insider feel makes it fun, and it can also be a way to see a sold-out hit. However, one drawback is that if the play isn't great, you don't have the privilege of leaving—ushers are usually required to stay afterward to clean up the theater.

Contact theaters to find out about their specific ushering policies.

Film

Note: Many of the cultural centers listed in Chapter 8 also have film programs. For outdoor movie series, see "Cinema al Fresco" in Chapter 6.

THE SHOCK OF THE NEW (FILM FESTIVALS)

New York probably hosts more film festivals than any other city in the world—pretty much every cultural society, issue group, and cinematic organization puts one on—and they vary enormously in size, structure, content, and purpose. Although retrospectives and film series on one topic can be great if you happen to be interested in the subject matter, the best festivals are generally those that show new and international films, where you can see American and world premieres of movies that may or may not end up getting a wide distribution.

375. *Tribeca Film Festival*

New York's youngest major film festival, the Tribeca was founded in 2002 by neighborhood darling Robert De Niro in an effort to revive optimism following the events of September 11 and to make the New York movie scene more accessible to people in the city. The festival continues to thrive in this spirit, screening an eclectic mix of studio and independent films, foreign and domestic, by first-time filmmakers and well-known directors, from feature films to silent movies to documentaries to freshly restored classics to shorts. For a fortnight each spring, the festival takes over downtown with a series of talks, lectures, and other events accompanying the movies that give new filmmakers a platform to display and discuss their work, and audiences an opportunity to take their favorite directors to task. If you have cinematic ambitions yourself, details of the festival's submission guidelines are listed on its Web site.
Spring. Screenings are held in various locations around Tribeca. For dates, and details of screenings, talks, locations, and show times, visit www.tribecafilmfestival.org.

376. *New York Film Festival*

In the file of "New York's Best Kept Secrets" is the fact that regular people can go to screenings at the New York Film Festival—and that it's not very hard to do. The most prestigious of the city's film festivals, NYFF is the country's preeminent showcase of new and foreign films, and the line-up is always first-rate. Screenings, most of which are held in the newly renovated Alice Tully Hall, often begin with a bonus short film and almost always end with a question-and-answer session with the actors, director, and/or other crew members. The seventeen-day schedule is announced in August and tickets go on sale later that month—first to members of the **Film Society of Lincoln Center** (see page 152). Two weeks later, tickets go on sale to the public, but you have to act fast, since many screenings sell out quickly. If you can't get tickets that way, all is not lost:

show up early at a screening you want to attend and buy a ticket from someone looking to sell. We can say from personal experience that there is never a shortage of people looking to get rid of spare tickets—even to the most coveted screenings—and this is not the kind of crowd who'd try to scalp them for more than they paid.

Late September through early October. Most screenings are held at Alice Tully Hall (at Lincoln Center, see page 150 for more), and tickets are available at the Alice Tully Hall box office, by phone at 212-875-5050, or online at www.lincolncenter.org. For more information and upcoming festival dates and schedules, visit www.filmlinc.com/nyff/nyff.htm.

377. New Directors/New Films

The Film Society of Lincoln Center's other major festival is New Directors/New Films, an annual ten-day festival held in conjunction with the **Film and Media Department of the Museum of Modern Art** (see page 122). As its title suggests, this festival showcases the best films by new directors and filmmakers as chosen by a committee from the two hosting organizations. Filmmakers such as Spike Lee, Richard Linklater, Pedro Almodovar, and Steven Spielberg (yes, you read that right) all made their American debuts at ND/NF, and the festival has also introduced many films that have gone on to attain mainstream success, like *Murderball* and the Academy Award–nominated *My Architect*—an impeccable track record that should allay any fears of going in to see an "unknown."

Spring. Screenings are held in the Walter Reade Theater at Lincoln Center and at the Titus 1 Theater at MoMA. For dates, schedules, and more information, visit www.filmlinc.com/ndnf/ndnf.htm.

378. *Margaret Mead Film and Video Festival.*

Held at the **American Museum of Natural History** (see page 119), this annual festival is the premier venue for new documentary film in the U.S. Named in honor of Margaret Mead, the influential anthropologist who was one of the first in her field to recognize the importance of film, the festival showcases the top nonfiction films from around the world in the past year. Many of the films are American or world premieres, and subjects range from global affairs to small, personal stories.

November. Screenings are $10 each ($9 for members); a twelve-screening "friends of festival" pass is available for $99. Located at the American Museum of Natural History; for dates, schedules, and more information on the museum, visit www.amnh.org.

379. *BAM Cinemafest.*

This brand-new film festival held by Brooklyn's most esteemed performing arts venue is one weekend of movie fun. In addition to showings of new independent films, BAM-Cinemafest also includes outdoor screenings, an all-night movie marathon, and an afternoon dedicated entirely to shorts.

June. BAMcinématek; for schedule, information, and directions, see entry for BAM, page 148.

380. See and learn about independent film at **Anthology Film Archives**.

So what exactly is independent film? At Anthology Film Archives, you can learn about the history and development of this outsider art. This museum-library-screening room is devoted to the showing and the preservation of avant-garde and independent film. Anthology also operates a film preservation center and an exhibition gallery for experimental filmmakers who do other arts. This is an excellent resource for anyone interested in film and an interesting place to visit no matter your taste.

32 SECOND AVENUE AT 2ND STREET IN MANHATTAN. Subway: F, V to Lower East Side-Second Avenue. For more information and screening schedule, call 212-505-5181 or visit www.anthologyfilmarchives.org.

381. Watch movies at **MoMA**.

One of the most impressive holdings of the **Museum of Modern Art** (see page 122) is its film and video collection. Containing more than 22,000 films representing every period and genre, it is considered the strongest international film collection in the U.S. The film-and-media department screens more than 1,000 films annually in the museum's recently renovated, two-screen Roy and Niuta Titus Theater. The programs are much like exhibitions elsewhere in the museum, so films are generally shown in week- or month-long series on particular topics, themes, directors, or eras, and the department often collaborates with institutions in other countries to show their films here. In addition to feature films, animated films, shorts, and even commercials are shown. The theater is well worth a trip, but if you're going to the museum anyway, the deal is terrific: the $20 ticket price includes admission to that day's film.

Located at MoMA; see page 122 for details.

WHEN MAINSTREAM MOVIES GET YOU DOWN, SEE A CLASSIC OR INDEPENDENT FILM.

One thing that New York is blessed with is plenty of places that show movies outside the mainstream, whether it's a good old-fashioned movie (or an obscure art-house film). Here are a few of our favorite venues:

382. *The Angelika:* For years, the Angelika was the city's multiplex alternative: it showed independent, arty, and foreign films and revivals on all four of its screens and served cappuccino and panini in the upstairs café. Now that both Italian-style coffee and indie films have made it into the mainstream, the Angelika doesn't seem quite as avant garde as it once was, but it still shows a good share of foreign films, documentaries, classics, and other movies that a multiplex wouldn't touch with a ten-foot pole. Plus, the Angelika still has one quirk over the newer movie houses: the screens are quite far below street level, so you can feel strong vibrations every time a subway train goes by.

18 WEST HOUSTON STREET AT THE CORNER OF MERCER STREET IN MANHATTAN. Subway: 6 to Bleecker Street; B, D, F, V to Broadway-Lafayette Street. 212-995-2000. www.angelikafilm-center.org.

383. Cinema Village: Cinéastes will feel a warm tingle as soon as they turn the corner from the Union Square multiplex and see the authentic, retro, neon marquee on top, with hand-placed letters spelling out the day's offerings. One of the oldest continually operating movie houses in the city, Cinema Village opened in 1963 as a repertory cinema and made its name as a place to see second-run, cult, and classic movies before the advent of VCRs. Since then, it's changed its format intermittently, and in addition to classic and cult films, it also shows first-run art and indie films, documentaries, shorts, and animated features. In the '90s, before kung fu films went mainstream, Cinema Village was the place to see Hong Kong cinema. Today, it's still a place to see the best of the old, and of the new.

22 EAST 12TH STREET BETWEEN UNIVERSITY PLACE AND FIFTH AVENUE IN MANHATTAN. Subway: 4, 5, 6, L, N, Q, R, W to 14th Street-Union Square. 212-924-3363. www.cinemavillage.com.

384. Loews Village 7: During most of the week, this average-looking multiplex is as mainstream as they go. However, once a week, the Village 7 turns its gaze away from Hollywood's current offerings and looks back at classics like *The Thomas Crowne Affair, Bullitt,* and *The Magnificent Seven.*

66 THIRD AVENUE, CORNER OF ELEVENTH STREET IN MANHATTAN. Subway: 6 to Astor Place. 212-982-2116.

385. Film Forum: This three-screen nonprofit movie theater in the West Village shows contemporary first-run art-house and international films, plus repertories and retrospectives of foreign and American classics. Film Forum also has excellent popcorn.

209 WEST HOUSTON STREET BETWEEN SIXTH AVENUE AND VARICK STREET IN MANHATTAN. Subway: 1 to Houston Street. 212-727-8110. www.filmforum.org.

386. IFC Center: The Waverly Cinema's reincarnation as the Independent Film Channel (IFC) Center was a bittersweet moment for city cinéastes, but most took comfort in the fact that the beloved eyesore didn't change into something entirely different. Now it's a state-of-the art film center, showing independent movies.

323 SIXTH AVENUE AT WEST 3RD STREET IN MANHATTAN. Subway: A, C, E, B, D, F, V to West 4th Street. 212-924-7771. www.ifccenter.com.

387. *The Quad:* This four-screen family-owned cinema shows mainly first-run art-house and foreign films, as well as occasional revivals and retrospectives. A renovation has shined the twenty-five-year-old theater up a bit, but not much has changed. The décor is still retro-'70s *cinematek*, and the movie screens are still the same size—about the width of a large, flat-screen TV.
34 WEST 13TH STREET BETWEEN FIFTH AND SIXTH AVENUES IN MANHATTAN. Subway: F, V to 14th Street; L to Sixth Avenue. 212-255-8800. www.quadcinema.com.

388. *Landmark Sunshine Cinema:* The New York branch of this art-house movie chain mixes classics of all genres into its independent-slanted film program. Located in a restored vaudeville theater, the films here range from the obscure and foreign to almost mainstream and classics of all eras. The Sunshine also does late-night and midnight screenings; for more information, see page 344.
143 EAST HOUSTON STREET BETWEEN FIRST AND SECOND AVENUES IN MANHATTAN. Subway: F, V to Lower East Side-Second Avenue. 212-330-8182. www.landmarktheaters.com.

389. *Leonard Nimoy Thalia:* Remember the scene in *Annie Hall* when Alvy, Woody Allen's character, takes Annie to see *The Sorrow and the Pity*? Well, they see it at the Thalia. (For more **favorite New York movie scenes**, see pages 114–117.) Like **Cinema Village** (see page 159), the Thalia was a revival movie house, beloved by intellectuals and cinephiles, whose role was undermined by the introduction of home video. After years of deterioration, it was reopened as the Leonard Nimoy Thalia, named for the *Star Trek* star, who was a major benefactor. Part of **Symphony Space** (see pages 294–295), the theater is now used for live performances and readings, as well as for showing a mix of classic, revival, art, animated, short, and documentary films.
2537 BROADWAY AT 95TH STREET IN MANHATTAN. Subway: 1, 2, 3 to 96th Street. 212-864-5400. www.symphonyspace.org.

CHAPTER 5:

Eating & Drinking

There's nothing better than a fantastic meal, a great bar, or discovering some delicious new kind of food, and this city has a hearty helping of each of these things. New York has the staple ingredients for a thriving gastronomic culture: sizable populations of pretty much every nationality and ethnicity under the sun; talented chefs, both aspiring and established, with boundless imaginations; and a population that both honors history and embraces the next big thing. This mixture has produced a city filled to the brim with eating and drinking pleasures, from the exotic to the gourmet to the place around the corner that makes a great plate of fries. The variety of food- and drink-related activities here is mind-boggling; you can indulge your passion for street food and have an all-out gourmet splurge in the same afternoon—and then go to a bar to play bocce over drinks.

Like all the great things to do, the best eating and drinking activities in New York are those that give you a delightful experience without much effort or aggravation. Eating well here is a cinch—it can easily take more effort to eat a bad meal than an excellent one. But with the bar set so high, we had to look beyond tasty meals to find the best of the best. Unique offerings, particularly welcoming atmospheres, and gorgeous décor are all things that, along with the food and drink, put the following places and experiences in a separate league. The greatest eating and drinking activities are not necessarily exotic or over the top—spotting a Mister Softee truck while you're walking around on a hot day is a pretty great thing in itself—but they go beyond merely filling you up or quenching your thirst. With such an overwhelming amount of terrific eats and drinks, narrowing them down to a succinct list of "bests" was no easy task, but the ones we've chosen for this chapter are the priceless, wholly satisfying experiences that will make you forget every fast-food outlet and chain restaurant there is.

NOTE: We've selected what we think are the best eating and drinking experiences; however, there are additional food-related listings in other chapters. You can find entries for historic eateries in **The Classics** chapter (page 17), a rundown of 24-hour and late-night restaurants in **24-Hour Fun** (page 315), our favorite street treats in **On the Street & Underground** (page 84), and a few quirky specialty joints in **Only in New York** (page 345). For a full list of restaurants and bars, see the index.

Sample the local cuisine from a **New York chef or restaurateur**.

Several of the city's best (and best-known) chefs and restaurateurs have created mini dining empires, with multiple restaurants to their esteemed names. Some stick to the cuisine that they first made their name with, while others confidently branch out to other styles of food and dining experiences in different places. But what unites them across cuisine, genre, and style is their successful expansion across the city's notoriously fickle dining scene. However, their prevalence doesn't necessarily make it any easier to get a taste—no matter how many restaurants each of the following individuals opens, they all seem to be packed.

390. *Mario Batali.*

"Molto Mario" (as he is affectionately known by millions of Food Network viewers) is the go-to guy for fine Italian food in this city; he's also credited with giving New Yorkers a taste for tripe, offal, pigs' feet, and other exotic meats. But his culinary expertise doesn't stop at the tip of the boot. In addition to his Italian *ristorantes* (Babbo, Lupa, Esca, Otto Enoteca e Pizzeria, and Del Posto), he also runs a pair of excellent adjoining tapas and wine bars, Casa Mono and Bar Jamon. All of his restaurants are wildly popular and perennially cool—and somehow still manage to serve some of the best food in the city.

BABBO: *110 WAVERLY PLACE AT WASHINGTON SQUARE IN MANHATTAN. Subway: B, D, F, V, A, C, E to West 4th Street. 212-777-0303. www.babbonyc.com.*

CASA MONO: *52 IRVING PLACE AT 17TH STREET;* **BAR JAMON,** *125 EAST 17TH STREET, BETWEEN IRVING PLACE AND THIRD AVENUE. Both in Manhattan. Subway: 4, 5, 6, L, N, Q, R, W to 14th Street-Union Square. 212-253-2773. www.casamononyc.com.*

DEL POSTO: *85 TENTH AVENUE AT 16TH STREET IN MANHATTAN. Subway: A, C, E to 14th Street; L to Eighth Avenue. 212-497-8090. www.delposto.com.*

ESCA: *402 WEST 43RD STREET AT NINTH AVENUE IN MANHATTAN. Subway: A, C, E to 42nd Street-Port Authority Bus Terminal. 212-564-7272. www.esca-nyc.com.*

LUPA: *170 THOMPSON STREET BETWEEN HOUSTON AND BLEECKER STREETS IN MANHATTAN. Subwqy: 1 to Houston Street. 212-982-5089. www.luparestaurant.com.*

OTTO ENOTECA E PIZZERIA: *1 FIFTH AVENUE AT 8TH STREET IN MANHATTAN. Subway: N, R, W to 8th Street-New York University. 212-995-9559. www.ottopizzeria.com.*

391. *Daniel Boulud.* Daniel Boulud is the reigning king of French cuisine in New York, ruling over his five restaurants here with deft culinary skills and a captivating personality. Restaurant Daniel, which opened in 1993, revived enthusiasm for *haute cuisine*

with the use of fresh, seasonal ingredients prepared expertly using classic French tech-niques. Five years later, he opened Café Boulud, named for the country café Boulud's family ran in his hometown outside of Lyon. Café Boulud was also a star, charming patrons with its unusual four-category menu of classic country dishes, seasonal spe-cialties, vegetarian dishes, and a rotating celebration of world cuisines called "Le Voy-age." DB Bistro Moderne is a slicked-up bistro whose claim to fame is its **gourmet hamburger** (see page 283). The chef has followed up this trifecta with two compara-tively casual, meat-focused eateries: Bar Boulud and DBGB. Sausages, charcuterie, and pâté abound, as do the crowds.

BAR BOULUD: *1900 BROADWAY BETWEEN 63RD AND 64TH STREETS IN MANHATTAN. 212-595-0303.*

CAFÉ BOULUD: *20 EAST 76TH STREET BETWEEN FIFTH AND MADISON AVENUES IN MAN-HATTAN. Subway: 6 to 77th Street. 212-772-2600.*

DANIEL: *60 EAST 65TH STREET BETWEEN PARK AND MADISON AVENUES IN MANHATTAN. Subway: 6 to 68th Street-Hunter College. 212-288-0033.*

DB BISTRO MODERNE: *55 WEST 44TH STREET BETWEEN FIFTH AND SIXTH AVENUES IN MAN-HATTAN. Subway: B, D, F, V to 42nd Street-Bryant Park; 7 to Fifth Avenue-Bryant Park. 212-391-2400.*

DBGB: *299 Bowery Between Houston and First Streets IN MANHATTAN. Subway: F, V to Sec-ond Avenue. 212-933-5300. www.danielnyc.com*

392. David Bouley. The city's other DB has a lower profile, literally—his longtime com-mitment to lower Manhattan has made him a most beloved neighborhood figure. Bouley opened his eponymous restaurant in 1987, and the eventual four-star rating put Tribeca on the city's foodie map, and paved the way for the chef to expand his offerings in the neighborhood. Several of Bouley's restaurants were forced to close after September 11, but Bouley, unfazed, immediately opened Green Tarp, a tempo-rary canteen that fed workers at Ground Zero around the clock, and later, used the Bouley Bakery for the same purpose. Today, in addition to the upstanding Bouley restaurant, the chef also operates Bouley Bakery & Market, a three-floor multipurpose culinary destination, with a retail store, cooking classes, café, and an informal restaurant on the second floor, appropriately named Upstairs.

BOULEY: *163 DUANE STREET, at HUDSON STREET IN MANHATTAN. Subway: 1, 2, 3, A, C to Chambers Street. 212-964-2525.*

BOULEY BAKERY & MARKET (AND UPSTAIRS): *120 WEST BROADWAY AT DUANE STREET IN MANHATTAN. Subway: 1, 2, 3, A, C to Chambers Street. 212-219-1011. www.davidbouley.com.*

393. Keith McNally: To the bafflement of many restaurateurs, Keith McNally seems to have the golden touch: he is the Rumpelstiltskin of the New York restaurant world, who spins ordinary storefronts into critically acclaimed hits time after time after time. It's as if he were in possession of a magic potion that makes his restaurants and bars irresistible to all, rendering patrons powerless to their charming faux-international style, uniformly chic (but not so elite as to be off-putting) clientele, and simple, tasty food. And the potion doesn't wear off—unlike most hot spots, McNally's restaurants continue to attract crowds even a decade after their opening. McNally, who started his career in the service industry as a bellhop in London and a busboy at **Serendipity** (see page 48), made his name on the New York restaurant scene with **Odeon** (see page 46), the bistro that Jay McInerney, a regular patron, immortalized in *Bright Lights, Big City*. No longer affiliated with Odeon, McNally has since opened a string of stylized restaurants, each one more popular than the last. Lucky Strike is his bistro emeritus, a stylishly comfortable SoHo canteen that continues to pull in a crowd twenty years after its opening—a grand old age that plenty of New York restaurants never reach. McNally opened the fin-de-siècle–style brasserie Balthazar in 1991, and it has been packed every morning, noon, and night since. Russians and Russophiles protest in vain that the polished Soviet-style décor at Pravda is inauthentic while knocking back caviar and shot after shot of house-infused vodka. At Pastis, a lively bistro in the Meatpacking District, the only complaints concern how long the line is to get in, but they barely register over the constant rumbling chatter—all the better for preventing eavesdropping on the conversations of celebrities, who occupy almost every other table (see page 79). Schiller's Liquor Bar is McNally's take on the British gastro-pub; its timeless charm is irresistible to Lower East Side hipsters and serious foodies alike. Morandi reaches over to Italy, where he does Italian trattoria, McNally-style, while Minetta Tavern is a steak-and-red-sauce joint that mines Old New York nostalgia while still managing to be impossibly hip.

BALTHAZAR: *80 SPRING STREET BETWEEN CROSBY STREET AND BROADWAY IN MANHATTAN. Subway: 6 to Spring Street; N, R, W to Prince Street. 212-965-1785. www.balthazarny.com.*

LUCKY STRIKE: *59 GRAND STREET BETWEEN WOOSTER STREET AND WEST BROADWAY IN MANHATTAN. Subway: C, E to Spring Street. 212-941-0772. www.luckystrikeny.com.*

MINETTA TAVERN: *113 MACDOUGAL STREET, AT CARMINE STREET. 212-475-3850. www.minettatavernny.com. Subway: A, B, C, D to West Fourth Street.*

MORANDI: *211 Waverly Place, between Seventh Avenue South and Charles Street. 212-627-7575. www.morandiny.com. Subway: 1 to Christopher Street/Sheridan Square.*

PASTIS: *9 NINTH AVENUE AT LITTLE WEST 12TH STREET IN MANHATTAN. Subway: A, C, E to 14th Street; L to Eighth Avenue. 212-929-4844. www.pastisny.com.*

PRAVDA: *281 LAFAYETTE STREET BETWEEN HOUSTON AND PRINCE STREETS IN MANHATTAN. Subway: 6 to Bleecker Street; B, D, F, V to Broadway-Lafayette Street; N, R, W to Prince Street. 212-226-4944. www.pravdany.com.*

SCHILLER'S LIQUOR BAR: *131 RIVINGTON STREET AT NORFOLK STREET IN MANHATTAN. Subway: F, V to Lower East Side-Second Avenue. 212-260-4555. www.schillersny.com.*

394. _Danny Meyer:_ Though he is not actually a chef (like McNally he's technically a restaurateur), Danny Meyer has contributed more than enough to the city's restaurant landscape to merit him a place at this table. In the mid-'80s, the area around Union Square was not the thriving neighborhood it is today. The only restaurant was McDonald's, and a little operation called the **Greenmarket** (see page 334) had just started putting up stands in a parking lot around the park. Locals brought their kids to Washington Square Park because the overgrown, drug-infested public space by Union Square—pre-playgrounds, pre–dog runs—could hardly qualify as park. Then an affable twenty-seven-year-old guy from St. Louis opened an upscale restaurant serving food prepared from farm-based ingredients, and the rest is history. Union Square Café is the darling of the city's fine-dining scene, a classic that never disappoints, and a place that always makes you feel good about paying it a visit. Meyer used the restaurant's success to bolster the neighborhood by vocally promoting the Greenmarket, using its ingredients at his restaurants, and by slowly peppering the area between Union Square and Madison Square Park with desirable eating establishments: the dark and homey Gramercy Tavern; the grand Eleven Madison Park, with its soaring ceilings, glamorous Art Deco interior, and cosmopolitan atmosphere; Tabla, which serves gourmet Indian food, and its casual, lobby-level Bread Bar, offering Indian street foods; and Blue Smoke, a pitch-perfect pit-barbeque joint, with an adjoining jazz club downstairs called Jazz Standard. In 2005, Meyer ventured out of the neighborhood for the first time to take the helm at the Modern, the fine dining restaurant at the Museum of Modern Art. Four years later, he took to Central Park and launched Public Fare, a casual sandwich and snack concession that now feeds the ravenous masses waiting in line for tickets to **Shakespeare in the Park** (see page 155). N.B. Public Fare is only during the Delacorte Theater's summer season. But Meyer hasn't grown tired of downtown or of revitalizing its amenities: his company, the Union Square Hospitality Group, also operates the Shake Shack, a maddeningly popular, seasonal burger joint that looks like a futuristic roadside dive in Madison Square Park. (There are also outposts on the Upper West Side and at Citi Field, and at time of press, plans are in the works for at least three other Manhattan branches, including one in NoLita on Mulberry and Prince.) The company also sponsors the annual **Big Apple Barbeque** (see page 86), whose proceeds benefit the Madison Square Park Conservancy. Given Meyer's longstanding affiliation with the Union Square and Gramercy areas, it was no surprise when it was announced that he would be taking over the food service and restaurant space in Ian Shrager's posh Gramercy Park Hotel. The Italian restaurant, called Maialino, is named for a nickname Meyer was given when he worked as a tour guide in Rome in his twenties. (It means "little pig.")

BLUE SMOKE/JAZZ STANDARD: _116 EAST 27TH STREET BETWEEN PARK AND LEXINGTON AVENUES IN MANHATTAN. Subway: 6 to 28th Street. 212-447-7733. www.bluesmoke.com._

ELEVEN MADISON PARK: _11 MADISON AVENUE AT 24TH STREET IN MANHATTAN. Subway: 6 to 23rd Street; N, R, W to 23rd Street. 212-889-0905. www.elevenmadisonpark.com._

GRAMERCY TAVERN: *42 EAST 20TH STREET BETWEEN BROADWAY AND PARK AVENUE SOUTH IN MANHATTAN. Subway: 6 to 23rd Street. 212-477-0777. www.gramercytavern.com.*

MAIALINO *is located in the Gramercy Park Hotel. 2 LEXINGTON AVENUE, AT 21ST STREET IN MANHATTAN. Subway: 6 to 23rd Street. 212-920-3300. www.gramercyparkhotel.com.*

THE MODERN: *9 WEST 53RD STREET BETWEEN FIFTH AND SIXTH AVENUES IN MANHATTAN. Subway: E, V to Fifth Avenue/53rd Street. 212-333-1220. www.themodernnyc.com.*

PUBLIC FARE: *81ST STREET AND CENTRAL PARK WEST, BY THE DELACOURT THEATER. Subway: B, C to 81st Street.*

SHAKE SHACK: *SOUTHEAST CORNER OF MADISON SQUARE PARK (MADISON AVENUE AND 23RD STREET) IN MANHATTAN. Subway: 6 to 23rd Street; N, R, W to 23rd Street. 212-889-6600. www.shakeshacknyc.com. 366 Columbus Avenue, at 77th Street. 646-747-8770. Subway: B, C to 81st Street. For information and location of Citi Field, see page 165. www.shakeshacknyc.com.*

TABLA RESTAURANT AND BREAD BAR: *11 MADISON AVENUE AT 25TH STREET IN MANHATTAN. Subway: 6 to 23rd Street; N, R, W to 23rd Street. 212-889-0667. www.tablany.com.*

UNION SQUARE CAFÉ: *21 EAST 16TH STREET BETWEEN FIFTH AVENUE AND UNION SQUARE WEST IN MANHATTAN. Subway: 4, 5, 6, L, N, Q, R, W to 14th Street-Union Square. 212-243-4020. www.unionsquarecafe.com. For more information, visit Union Square Hospitality Group, www.ushgnyc.com.*

395. *Jean-Georges Vongerichten:* He is known simply as Jean-Georges, a chef with whom people all over the world are on a first-name basis. Yet while he has restaurants on three continents, his home is New York, and the city, in turn, has claimed him as its own, as evidenced by the popularity of his restaurants, and the fact that he has earned more *New York Times* stars than any other chef in the city. A bold chef with a shrewd business sensibility, the Alsatian-born Vongerichten has charmed New Yorkers with restaurant after restaurant, and he seems always to have another trick up his sleeve. After introducing himself to the city with a four-star *New York Times* review at Lafayette restaurant, he left the formal, fine-dining milieu to open JoJo, an intimate, paper tablecloth–adorned bistro in an Upper East Side townhouse. After that, he surprised everyone with Vong, where he mixes his ethereal French cooking with spice from the Far East, followed by another four-star venture, Jean-Georges, along with the Lipstick Café (now closed), a casual spot that catered to the business crowd, and Mercer Kitchen for the SoHo set. He then returned to Asian flavors with Spice Market, which serves gourmet renditions of Asian street food in a sexy, dreamlike setting of dark wood and dim lighting, and an upscale Japanese soba house, Matsugen. Just when we thought we had him pegged, he opened a jewel box of a restaurant called Perry Street, a serene, simply designed dining room inside Richard Meier's glass palaces on the Hudson River. According to Vongerichten, Perry Street is his "casual, neighborhood restaurant." Trying telling that to the reservationist.

JEAN-GEORGES AND NOUGATINE: *1 CENTRAL PARK WEST BETWEEN 60TH AND 61ST STREETS IN MANHATTAN. Subway: 1, A, C, B, D to 59th Street-Columbus Circle. 212-229-3900.*

JOJO: *160 EAST 64TH STREET BETWEEN LEXINGTON AND THIRD AVENUES IN MANHATTAN. Subway: 6 to 68th Street-Hunter College. 212-223-5656.*
MATSUGEN: *241 CHURCH STREET BETWEEN WORTH AND LEONARD STREETS IN MANHAT-TAN. Subway: 1 to Franklin Street. 212-925-0202.*
MERCER KITCHEN: *99 PRINCE STREET AT MERCER STREET IN MANHATTAN. Subway: N, R, W to Prince Street. 212-966-5454.*
PERRY STREET: *176 PERRY STREET NEAR THE WEST SIDE HIGHWAY IN MANHATTAN. Subway: 1 to Christopher Street-Sheridan Square. 212-352-1900.*
SPICE MARKET: *403 WEST 13TH STREET AT NINTH AVENUE IN MANHATTAN. Subway: A, C, E to 14th Street; L to Eighth Avenue. 212-675-2322.*
VONG: *200 EAST 54TH STREET AT THIRD AVENUE IN MANHATTAN. Subway: 6 to 51st Street; E, V to Lexington Avenue/53rd Street. 212-486-9592. www.jean-georges.com.*

Splurge on an **incredible meal**.

There are many delightful bargains and delicious cheap eats to be had all over the city, but then there are the indulgences—those famous restaurants whose names are known around the world not for trendiness, longevity, or cool design (though they often have those, too) but for the supreme quality of the food. In addition to many of the restaurants we've already listed, here are some other places that live up to their reputation for delivering incredible dining experiences. Yes, all of the following restaurants fall into the very-expensive-to-small-fortune category, but the meals they serve are worth every penny. If you have the means (and a sweet touch with the reservationists), these are the places to go for out-of-this-world gastronomic splurges. Choose your poison:

396. *Blue Hill:* This petite restaurant has been serving haute fresh-off-the-farm cuisine for ten years, since before "local" was the fashionable way to eat. Proprietors Dan, David, and Laureen Barber ensure utmost quality and freshness of ingredients through their affiliations with the Blue Hill farm in Massachusetts and the Stone Barns Center for Food and Agriculture in Westchester County. The specialties of the house are whatever is freshest and in season, and since that covers nearly every ingredient on the regularly revolving menu, it's hard to go wrong. (Even the butter tastes like it could practically moo.) N.B: While the prices are not as extravagant as some of the other restaurants mentioned in this section, the restaurant is small, and a visit from a certain First Couple catapulted it into the national spotlight. Reserve ahead.
75 WASHINGTON PLACE, BETWEEN MACDOUGAL STREET AND WASHINGTON SQUARE PARK. SUBWAY: A, B, C, D, E, F, V TO WEST FOURTH STREET. 212-539-1776. www.bluehill.com.

397. *Le Bernardin:* If seafood is your weakness, then the four-star fish-focused haute cuisine served here is for you. An offshoot of the equally acclaimed Parisian restaurant of the same name, Le Bernardin holds the distinction of being the only restaurant in New York to have held on to its four-star rating for more than a decade.

155 WEST 51ST STREET BETWEEN FIFTH AND SIXTH AVENUES IN MANHATTAN. Subway: B, D, F, V to 47th-50th Streets-Rockefeller Center. 212-554-1515. www.le-bernardin.com.

398. *Chanterelle:* This Tribeca pioneer does not need to engage in the culinary theatrics of some of the city's other fine restaurants; instead it serves incredible food in a beautiful room with flawless service.

2 HARRISON STREET AT HUDSON STREET IN MANHATTAN. Subway: 1 to Franklin Street. 212-966-6960. www.chanterellenyc.com.

399. *Masa:* Masa is considered the most expensive restaurant in the city at the moment, which is not in itself an illustrious distinction. However, everyone who has eaten here agrees that the money is put to good use (ingredients like truffles and foie gras are thrown around like parsley) and that the experience is never the same twice. (There are no menus; you pay up to $600 for a prix fixe selection of what the kitchen is preparing that day.) That said, getting in is a challenge in itself, in more ways than one—securing one of the twenty-six seats is the holy grail of New York dining as we go to press. But if you are lucky enough to make it onto the reservation list, ask to sit at the bar, where you can watch the master, Masa Takayama, at work. N.B. You can partake of Masa's super-gourmet cuisine without submitting to the main restaurant's $350 base fee at Bar Masa, the comparatively economical offshoot next door, which has menus and does not take reservations.

TIME WARNER CENTER 10 COLUMBUS CIRCLE AT 59TH STREET IN MANHATTAN. Subway: 1, A, C, B, D to 59th Street-Columbus Circle. 212-823-9800. www.masanyc.com.

400. *Nobu:* Nobu can be credited with introducing New York to upscale sushi, and it enjoyed an uncommonly long run as both a hot spot and a foodie mecca. It's been pushed out of the spotlight since Masa and other Japanese mega-restaurants came to town, but even if it's no longer cutting-edge, the sushi is still topnotch. Like Masa, Nobu has a no-reservation offshoot, Nobu Next Door, and it has opened a location in Midtown, Nobu Fifty Seven.

Nobu and Nobu Next Door: 105 HUDSON STREET AT FRANKLIN STREET IN MANHATTAN. Nobu: 212-219-0500; Nobu Next Door: 212-334-4445. Subway: 1 to Franklin Street.
Nobu Fifty Seven: 40 WEST 57TH STREET AT FIFTH AVENUE IN MANHATTAN. Subway: F to 57th Street; N, Q, R, W to 57th Street. 212-757-3000. www.noburestaurants.com.

401. *Per Se:* Eating at Thomas Keller's exclusive nook on the fourth floor of the **Time Warner Center** (see page 64) is like dying and going to epicurean heaven. Considered the country's best chef, Keller's meals are intricately composed and play out like symphonies of hallelujahs. The otherworldly eating experience is heightened by the incredible bird's-eye view of Central Park and the intimacy (the restaurant has only fifteen tables). Even though the lavish multicourse meals can take as long as a transatlantic flight, diners are still reluctant to leave after their meals, unwilling to return to their earthly existence after experiencing such bliss. (Though the signature Per Se experience remains the lavish nine-course prix fixe, the restaurant recently introduced an à la carte menu.) Note: Mortals unable to make it into Per Se can sample some of the heavenly delights one floor below at Keller's more plebian Bouchon Bakery.

10 COLUMBUS CIRCLE AT 59TH STREET, 4TH FLOOR, IN MANHATTAN. Subway: 1, A, C, B, D to 59th Street-Columbus Circle. 212-823-9335. www.perseny.com.

Engage in a legendary New York City food war.
(Choose your camp and defend its honor to the very last bite.)

402. *CHEESECAKE: Junior's vs. Veniero's*

JUNIOR'S *(original location): 386 FLATBUSH AVENUE AT DEKALB AVENUE IN BROOKLYN. Subway: B, M, Q, R to DeKalb Avenue. 718-852-5257. For additional locations, visit www.juniorscheesecake.com.*

VENIERO'S: *342 EAST 11TH STREET BETWEEN FIRST AND SECOND AVENUES IN MANHATTAN. Subway: L to First Avenue. 212-674-7070. www.venierospastry.com.*

403. *BAGELS: Ess-a-Bagel vs. H&H*

ESS-A-BAGEL: *359 FIRST AVENUE AT 20TH STREET IN MANHATTAN. Subway: 6 to 23rd Street. 212-260-2252; 831 THIRD AVENUE AT 50TH STREET IN MANHATTAN. Subway: 6 to 51st Street; E, V to Lexington Avenue/53rd Street. 212-980-1010. www.ess-a-bagel.com.*

H&H: *2239 BROADWAY AT 80TH STREET IN MANHATTAN. Subway: 1 to 79th Street. 212-595-8000; WEST 46TH STREET AT TWELFTH AVENUE IN MANHATTAN. Subway: A, C, E to 42nd Street-Port Authority Bus Terminal. 212-595-8000. www.hhbagels.com.*

404. *STEAK: Smith & Wollensky vs. Peter Luger*

SMITH & WOLLENSKY: *THIRD AVENUE AT 49TH STREET IN MANHATTAN. Subway: 6 to 51st Street; E, V to Lexington Avenue/53rd Street. 212-753-1530. www.smithandwollensky.com.*

PETER LUGER: *178 BROADWAY AT DRIGGS AVENUE IN BROOKLYN. Subway: J, M, Z to Marcy Avenue. 718-387-7400. www.peterluger.com.*

405. *HOT DOGS ON CONEY ISLAND:* Nathan's vs. Ruby's.

NATHAN'S: *CORNER OF SURF AND STILLWELL AVENUES, IN CONEY ISLAND, BROOKLYN.*
RUBY'S: *CONEY ISLAND BOARWALK, BY STILLWELL AVENUE. Subway: D, F, N, Q to Coney Island-Stillwell Avenue.*

406. *CUPCAKES:* Magnolia vs. Billy's

MAGNOLIA BAKERY: *Multiple locations. Visit www.magnoliacupcakes.com.*
BILLY'S BAKERY: *Multiple locations. Visit www.billysbakerynyc.com.*

407. *HOT DOGS:* Gray's Papaya vs. Papaya King

GRAY'S PAPAYA *(all locations in Manhattan): 539 EIGHTH AVENUE AT 37ᵀᴴ STREET. Subway: A, C, E to 34ᵗʰ Street-Penn Station. 212-904-1588; 2090 BROADWAY AT 72ᴺᴰ STREET. Subway: 1, 2, 3 to 72ⁿᵈ Street. 212-799-0243; 402 SIXTH AVENUE AT 8ᵀᴴ STREET. Subway: A, C, E, B, D, F, V to West 4ᵗʰ Street. 212-260-3532.*
PAPAYA KING *(all locations in Manhattan): SEVENTH AVENUE AT 14ᵀᴴ STREET. Subway: 1, 2, 3 to 14ᵗʰ Street. 212-367-8090; 179 EAST 86ᵀᴴ STREET BETWEEN THIRD AND LEXINGTON AVENUES. Subway: 4, 5, 6 to 86ᵗʰ Street. 212-369-0648; 121 WEST 125ᵀᴴ STREET BETWEEN LENOX AVENUE AND ADAM CLAYTON POWELL BOULEVARD. Subway: 2, 3 to 125ᵗʰ Street. 212-678-4268. www.papayaking.com.*

408. *HAMBURGERS:* Corner Bistro vs. Blue 9

CORNER BISTRO: *341 WEST 4ᵀᴴ STREET AT JANE STREET IN MANHATTAN. Subway: 1, 2, 3 to 14ᵗʰ Street; A, C, E to 14ᵗʰ Street; L to Eighth Avenue. 212-242-9502.*
BLUE 9: *92 THIRD AVENUE AT 12ᵀᴴ STREET IN MANHATTAN. Subway: 4, 5, 6, N, Q, R, W to Union Square; L to Third Avenue. 212-979-0053.*

409. *LOBSTER ROLLS:* Pearl Oyster Bar vs. Ed's Lobster Bar

PEARL OYSTER BAR: *18 CORNELIA STREET BETWEEN BLEECKER AND WEST 4ᵀᴴ STREET IN MANHATTAN. Subway: 1 to Christopher Street-Sheridan Square. 212-691-8211.www.pearloysterbar.com.*
ED'S LOBSTER BAR: *222 LAFAYETTE STREET AT SPRING STREET IN MANHATTAN. Subway: 6 to Spring Street. 212-343-3236. www.lobsterbarnyc.com.*

410. *DELIS:* Carnegie vs. Katz's

CARNEGIE: *854 SEVENTH AVENUE AT 55ᵀᴴ STREET IN MANHATTAN. Subway: N, Q, R, W to 57ᵗʰ Street. 212-757-2245.www.carnegiedeli.com.*
KATZ'S: *205 EAST HOUSTON AT LUDLOW STREET IN MANHATTAN. Subway: F, V to Lower East Side-Second Avenue. 212-254-2246.www.katzdeli.com.*

411. Go to a **Greenmarket**.

Fresh, seasonal foods from local farmers, at prices that beat the supermarket—need we say more? Greenmarkets are a bountiful blessing in the concrete jungle. The original Union Square market is the largest and the most popular (it's open four days a week, all year round), but there are more than fifty markets across the five boroughs, many of which operate year-round. Many restaurants buy ingredients there; if you **get to a Greenmarket close to when it opens in the morning** (see page 334), there's a good chance you'll be surrounded by some of the city's best chefs.

UNION SQUARE GREENMARKET: *WEST SIDE OF UNION SQUARE PARK BETWEEN 14TH AND 17TH STREETS IN MANHATTAN. Open Monday, Wednesday, Friday, and Saturday from 8:00 a.m. to 6:00 p.m. Subway: 4, 5, 6, L, N, Q, R, W to 14th Street-Union Square. For a complete list of other Greenmarket locations, schedules, and the farmers that sell there, visit www.cenyc.org.*

Eat on the street at an **outdoor food festival**.

Some of our favorites (for information on other great, non-food-centric street fairs and festivals, please see Chapter 3):

412. *Ninth Avenue International Food Festival.*

As anyone who's ever walked this side of the Port Authority knows, Hell's Kitchen is lined with a more eclectic selection of restaurants than any strip in the city. Get a taste of the melting pot at this massive two-day festival, held each May along Ninth Avenue.

May. NINTH AVENUE BETWEEN 37TH AND 57TH STREETS IN MANHATTAN. Subway: A, C, E to 42nd Street-Port Authority Bus Terminal. www.hellskitchennyc.com.

413. *Taste of Tribeca Street Festival.* This gourmet food festival showcases the gastronomic treasures of lower Manhattan, complete with live music, entertainment, and neighborhood walking tours. The $40 ticket ($45 day of) gets you generously sized tastes of six dishes on offer from more than fifty local restaurants. Sure, it's a bit pricier than a gyro-crêpe combo from a regular street fair, but with participants like Chanterelle, Blaue Gans, and Bouley, it's a relative bargain—and proceeds benefit local public schools.

May. DUANE STREET BETWEEN HUDSON AND GREENWICH STREETS IN MANHATTAN. Subway: 1, 2, 3, A, C to Chambers Street. www.tasteoftribeca.org.

414. *Dine Around Downtown.* If $45 sounds a little steep, Dine Around Downtown offers epicures à la carte tastes of lower Manhattan cuisine at slightly more affordable prices. Admission is free, and you can sample a slew of menu items for $3 to $6 each.

Late Spring. CHASE MANHATTAN PLAZA, BETWEEN LIBERTY AND PINE STREETS AND NAS-SAU AND WILLIAM STREETS IN MANHATTAN. Subway: 2, 3, 4, 5 to Wall Street. 212-835-2789. www.downtownny.com.

415. Another food festival of sorts is the annual **Chocolate Show** at the Metropolitan Pavilion. Probably the most enthusiastically anticipated of all the conventions held in the city, the Chocolate Show is like a Willy Wonka–inspired dream come true: four days of seeing, smelling, and, of course, tasting chocolate from all over the world. Though technically a trade show, the chocolate show has plenty of public offerings, including demonstrations, a chocolate fashion show, and free samples galore.

Early November. THE METROPOLITAN PAVILION, 125 WEST 18TH STREET BETWEEN SIXTH AND SEVENTH AVENUES IN MANHATTAN. Subway: 1 to 18th Street; F, V to 14th Street; L to Sixth Avenue. For more information and ticket prices, visit www.chocolateshow.com.

---

416. Get a taste of the Lower East Side's unique ethnic blend in a single afternoon.

The Lower East Side of New York is a crossroads of three established ethnic enclaves: Chinatown, Little Italy, and the Jewish neighborhoods that surround them. Though these neighborhoods are no longer the homogenous community centers they once were, the cultural influences remain, and in a few blocks, you can sample authentic treats from each. Start with a knish from Yonah Schimmel, followed by Cantonese *congee* (rice porridge) at Congee Village, then walk around the block for dessert at Il Laboratorio del Gelato.

Subway: F to Delancey Street; J, M, Z to Essex Street.

YONAH SCHIMMEL: *137 EAST HOUSTON STREET, BETWEEN FIRST AND SECOND AVENUES IN MANHATTAN. 212-477-2858. www.knishery.com.*

CONGEE VILLAGE: *100 ALLEN STREET BETWEEN DELANCEY AND BROOME STREETS IN MAN-HATTAN. 212-941-1818. www.congeevillagerestaurants.com.*

IL LABORATORIO DEL GELATO: *95 ORCHARD STREET BETWEEN DELANCEY AND BROOME STREETS IN MANHATTAN. 212-343-9922. www.laboratoriodelgelato.com.*

---

417. Staycation to Florida (without leaving the boroughs!) at Steve's Key Lime Pies.

Visit the overgrown, kitschy, waterfront location of this specialty bakery on a summer day and you will swear you are in the Keys. The mouth-watering handmade pies inside are correspondingly authentic, using fresh key lime juice (never bottled) and graham cracker crusts. Pies come in 8-inch and 10-inch sizes and 4-inch single-serving tarts. The house specialty is the Swingle, a dark-chocolate-covered key lime tart on a stick, that some KLP purists (including one of your authors) find is gilding the lily, but others say is a match made in heaven. Park yourself and the treat of your choosing at the wooden picnic benches outside and you have yourself a perfect Florida afternoon in the middle of Red Hook.

204 VAN DYKE STREET, AT THE WATERFRONT, IN BROOKLYN. 718-858-5333. www.stevesauthentic.com. N.B. The closest subway is the Smith-9th Street F/G station, but is a long walk away. The B61 bus has a stop on Van Brunt Street, two blocks away. Another transportation option is the Ikea Water Taxi, which leaves from South Street Seaport's Pier 11 and arrives at the piers by Broad Street and Van Brunt streets, a few blocks from the bakery.

418. Embrace the arepa at Caracas.

More flavorful than a sandwich and easier to carry than a plate of fries, the arepa is a versatile food item that can be snack, lunch, dinner, midnight meal, or even brunch. Caracas's two outposts offers arepas filled with a long list of just-greasy-enough combinations, along with empanadas, salads, side dishes and combination platters for those who want to round out a meal. With generous hours and reasonable prices, you can enjoy their arepas for any meal you like, in whatever fashion strikes you. Just be sure not to leave without applying an extra squirt of the special sauce. You'll thank us.

IN MANHATTAN: 93½ EAST 7TH STREET BETWEEN FIRST AVENUE AND AVENUE A. 212-529-2314. Subway: L to First Avenue in Brooklyn. 291 GRAND STREET BETWEEN HAVEMEYER AND ROEBLING STREETS. 718-218-6050. Subway: L to Bedford Avenue. www.caracasarepabar.com.

 419. Have a midnight kebab at Mamoun's, and eat it in one of their cozy wooden booths. No matter the hour, you will never be alone in Mamoun's.

119 MACDOUGAL STREET BETWEEN BLEECKER AND WEST 3ᴿᴰ STREETS IN MANHATTAN. Subway: A, C, E, B, D, F, V to West 4ᵗʰ Street. 212-674-8685. 22 ST. MARKS PLACE BETWEEN SECOND AND THIRD AVENUES. 212-387-7747. www.mamounsfalafel.com.

420. Devour a cone of Belgian fries from Pommes Frites... smothered in any

one of the many delicious sauces: traditional (ketchup, vinegar, or European mayo) or exotic (Vietnamese pineapple mayo, peanut satay, or parmesan peppercorn, to name a few). They also serve a mean *poutine*, the Canadian specialty of fries, gravy, and cheese curds.

123 SECOND AVENUE BETWEEN 7ᵀᴴ STREET AND ST. MARKS PLACE IN MANHATTAN. Subway: 6 to Astor Place. 212-674-1234. www.pommesfrites.ws.

421. ...then **assuage your grease guilt** at Liquiteria.

Walk by this juice joint (a few blocks up from Pomme Frites) any day of the week and you would be forgiven for thinking that you have passed some exclusive daytime hot spot. Liquiteria is a favorite hangout of some neighborhood celebs (both clean-living and otherwise), and a destination of left-coast movie stars when they're in town, so you never know who you might see there. But beyond the famous faces, and beautiful blessed-out yogis are the most exquisite-tasting fresh juices and smoothies in the city. Offerings range from intensely green to novice-friendly fruit blends. The juices can be pressed-to-order, but the ones in the cooler by the register (made fresh every morning) have a smoother taste, and allegedly have a higher concentration of the good stuff, which hard-core juicers prefer.

170 SECOND AVENUE, CORNER OF 11TH STREET, IN MANHATTAN. Subway: L to First or Third Avenues. 212-358-0300. www.liquiteria.com.

Dinner with **in-house entertainment**.

Now that multiplexes have taken over single-screen movie houses, and tickets cost upward of $12 each, dinner and a movie in New York is no longer as cheap or special as it used to be. Instead, why not try a restaurant that offers a little spectacle along with the meal? The following restaurants cleverly incorporate some signature flourishes into their dinner fare:

422. *Basta Pasta:* Order the pasta with parmesan and prosciutto and wait for the whole restaurant to turn to your table and watch a waiter swirl and toss your pasta inside a giant hollow wheel of cheese and scoop it lavishly onto your plate.
37 WEST 17TH STREET BETWEEN FIFTH AND SIXTH AVENUES IN MANHATTAN. Subway: F, V to 14th Street; L to Sixth Avenue. 212-366-0888. www.bastapastanyc.com.

423. *Churrascaria Plataforma Tribeca:* Order the meat course at this Brazilian restaurant and prepare to eat fifteen different types of meat as they arrive at your table, where steaks, chops, sausages, and ribs are carved and sliced with a flourish before your hungering eyes.
221 WEST BROADWAY BETWEEN FRANKLIN AND WHITE STREETS IN MANHATTAN. Subway: 1 to Franklin Street. 212-925-6969. www.churrascariatribeca.com.

424. *Lucky Cheng's:* We can't remember what the food's like at this drag queen capital of the world; it's the service that's memorable—including comedy, karaoke, and lots and lots of feathers. If you prefer your men *au naturel*, the Savage Men Cover Model Male Revue performs every week on Friday and Saturday nights.

24 FIRST AVENUE BETWEEN 1ST AND 2ND STREETS IN MANHATTAN. Subway: F, V to Lower East Side-Second Avenue. 212-995-5500. www.planetluckychengs.com.

Expert Contributor: Andrea Strong

Andrea Strong is a freelance food writer, reviewer, and self-confessed "eater." She is the author and creator of *The Strong Buzz* (www.thestrongbuzz.com), a twice-weekly newsletter devoted to New York City's food scene. She has a weekly column in the *New York Post*, and her work also appears in other local and national publications. She's the coauthor of *Sparks in the Kitchen* (Knopf) and has been a television guest on *Top Chef* (Bravo) and Gourmet's *Diary of a Foodie* (PBS), among others.

MY FIVE FAVORITE RESTAURANTS IN NEW YORK

425: *Five Points:* This seasonal Greenmarket-driven American restaurant owned by chef Marc Meyer and his wife, Vicki Freeman, is one of those rare gems that will have you planning your next visit shortly after you walk inside. A cozy, bustling bar area opens to a warmly lit dining room with high ceilings, and an open kitchen turns out signatures like wood-oven roasted pizza topped with thinly sliced Yukon potatoes, Sonoma Teleme cheese, and truffle oil; house-cured double pork chops with cauliflower and braised red mustard greens; and chestnut capellacci with preserved cherries and sage butter. Five Points also serves one of the best brunches in the city. I have three words for you: lemon ricotta pancakes.

31 GREAT JONES STREET BETWEEN LAFAYETTE STREET AND BOWERY IN MANHATTAN. Subway: 6 to Astor Place. 212-253-5700. www.fivepointsrestaurant.com.

426: *Tia Pol:* A lively bastion of Madrid awaits you at Tia Pol, a sexy sliver of a tapas bar owned by Mani Dawes and Heather Belz, two friends who lived in Madrid after college and vowed one day to open a place that captured the spirit and cuisine of the city's *taperías*. With Tia Pol, and chef-partner Alexandra Raij, they have succeeded. The place is tiny, so it is often standing room only, but the waiters manage to wind their way through the grinning crowds, serving *terra cotta cazuelas* (Spanish cooking dishes) filled with *patatas bravas, jamon croquetteas, chorizo* finished with sherry, and *tortilla d'españa*. The bar helps keep things buzzing with a great selection of Spanish wines and sherries.

205 TENTH AVENUE BETWEEN 22ND AND 23RD STREETS IN MANHATTAN. Subway: C, E to 23rd Street. 212-675-8805. www.tiapol.com.

427: *Momofuku:* It would be too simple to say that Momofuku serves the best ramen in the city. It would be true, but it would give you only a small picture of what wonders await at this narrow East Village lunch counter washed in blond wood. Chef-owner David Chang learned the art of noodle making in Tokyo, but he is also a classically trained chef who worked under Craft's Tom Collichio. What this means is that you'll find Greenmarket-fresh ingredients in super-fine signature dishes like spicy kimchi stew, addictive little steamed buns filled with pork belly and slicked with sticky-sweet hoisin sauce, and his signature soul-warming Momofuku ramen—braised Berkshire pork swimming in a rich broth filled with silky ramen. Slurping is encouraged.
163 FIRST AVENUE BETWEEN 10TH AND 11TH STREETS IN MANHATTAN. Subway: L to First Avenue. 212-475-7899. www.momofuku.com.

428. *Beppe:* New York is not short on Italian restaurants, but I'll take Beppe over any other. First of all, the place is literally Tuscany in the City, a sun-smudged terra cotta façade that opens to a warm room with a fire-breathing hearth, cathedral wood-beamed ceilings, and sturdy tables set with cheerful gingham napkins. As for the food, it's rustic, simple, and straight from the heart. Don't miss the chef's own *norcino*—a housemade "butcher's spaghetti" tossed with a rich ragú made from crumbled pork, garlic, rosemary, tomatoes, and Chianti; or his fat, spicy grilled sausages made in-house and served in a cast-iron skillet with stewed artisan beans; or the whole roasted *orata* (sea bass) glossed with olive oil and lemon juice and filled to the gills with fresh herbs. And yes, you must have his Tuscan fries, a mile-high pile tossed with freshly fried rosemary.
45 EAST 22ND STREET BETWEEN BROADWAY AND PARK AVENUE SOUTH IN MANHATTAN. Subway: 6 to 23rd Street. 212-982-8422. www.beppenyc.com.

429. *The Spotted Pig:* There is always a wait at the Spotted Pig, but I promise you it is always worth it. This convivial gastropub owned by music industry guru Ken Friedman and his brilliant English chef, April Bloomfield, is jammed with hipsters and hotties who wait (and wait, and wait) for the chef's heartbreakingly good food. Bloomfield is known for her *gnudi*—plump buttons of sheep's milk ricotta sauced in brown butter and sage, but you won't want to miss her roasted beet salad with smoked trout and crème fraîche, or her juicy chargrilled burger, topped with Roquefort and tucked inside a brioche bun the size of a catcher's mitt. The crowds are much tamer at lunch, which is the only time you can get your paws on her killer cubano—a toasted baguette stuffed with slow-roasted pork, prosciutto, cheese, and spicy pickled jalapeños. No reservations.
314 WEST 11TH STREET AT GREENWICH STREET IN MANHATTAN. Subway: A, C, E to 14th Street; L to Eighth Avenue. 212-620-0393. www.thespottedpig.com.

Pick up a tasty snack or get a meal to go at a bakery or gourmet food market.

Ranging from vendors of exotic and high-end gourmet ingredients, to places where you can buy restaurant-quality meals to take home, to specialty stores with in-house cafés, New York has no shortage of epicurean markets—Zagat has even dedicated an entire book to them. The following is a list of some of our favorite places to pick up a gourmet snack or prepared meal.

430. *Agata & Valentina:* This Italian-accented market and café is an established foodie destination, and stands out for exotic seasonal delicacies, such as hybrid fruits like "mandarinquats" and "nectacotums." The fresh meat, fish, and cheese counters are among the finest in the city, and if you want to sit down and enjoy your cubed filet mignon and quail's eggs on the spot, there's a companion restaurant and salad bar across the street from the market.
1505 FIRST AVENUE AT 79TH STREET IN MANHATTAN. Subway: 6 to 77th Street. 212-452-0690. www.agatavalentina.com.

431. *Amy's Bread:* A stop inside one of Amy's outlets inspires nostalgia for a simpler, tastier time, when carbs were healthy and things with words like "artisanal" and "organic" attached to their names were considered good for you. Hearty loaves of white, wheat, semolina, and specialty breads can be bought to take home, while tooth-some sandwiches, quiches, and desserts are best devoured on the spot in the café. Note: The West Village location is right next to the legendary **Murray's Cheese Shop** (see pages 296–297), which makes for an incredible combination.
Multiple locations; visit www.amysbread.com for addresses and information.

432. *Balthazar Bakery:* This tiny storefront next to the imposing Balthazar restaurant is the best-kept (comparatively) secret of the **Keith McNally** empire (see pages 163–164). You can get some of the same menu items served next door (and the famously delicious breads) to take away for less than half the price and unquantifiably less aggravation.
80 SPRING STREET AT THE CORNER OF CROSBY STREET IN MANHATTAN. Subway: 6 to Spring Street; N, R, W to Prince Street. 212-965-1785. www.balthazarbakery.com.

433. *The Chelsea Market:* People started trekking to lower Ninth Avenue to go to the Chelsea Market before the Meatpacking District had anything else to offer besides, well, meat. Inside the indoor market are nearly two dozen restaurants, specialty markets, and stores, including Sarabeth Bakery, Ronnybrook Farm Dairy, and the infamous Fat Witch bakery (which gives small samples, probably because they know that after one taste, you'll buy as much as they ask you to).
75 NINTH AVENUE BETWEEN 15TH AND 16TH STREETS IN MANHATTAN. Subway: A, C, E to 14th

Street; L to Eighth Avenue. Individual retailers are listed on www.chelseamarket.com; visit Web site for hours and information.

434. Eli's & The Vinegar Factory: The son of legendary Upper West Side grocers Louis and Lillian Zabar (see entry on **Zabar's**, page 42), Eli Zabar is well established on the Upper East Side as a purveyor of fine foods and drinks. His multiple-location empire includes restaurants, bakeries, a wine store, and two gourmet supermarkets, inspired by the great food halls of Europe.

Multiple locations on the Upper East Side; for more information on specific outlets, visit www.elizabar.com.

435. Essex Street Market: This former institution of the Lower East Side had fallen into disrepair until the 1990s, when the gentrification of the neighborhood inspired the market's complete rejuvenation. Essex Street ain't much to look at from the outside, but the indoor market is beautiful, and now boasts not only a great mix of fresh meat, fish, cheese, and produce vendors that reflects the area's Italian, Jewish, and Spanish heritage, but also a couple of good sit-down eateries in Essex Restaurant and Shopsins.

120 ESSEX STREET AT DELANCEY STREET IN MANHATTAN. Subway: F,J,M,Z to Essex Street-Delancey Street. 212-388-0449. www.essexstreetmarket.com.

436. Sahadi's: You can't eat in, but you can certainly stock up at this popular (and very reasonably priced) Atlantic Avenue market. Dried fruits, nuts, spices, and Middle Eastern foods, spreads, and ingredients are the specialties here, and the prepared foods are excellent. N.B.: Sahadi's is not open on Sundays.

187 ATLANTIC AVENUE BETWEEN CLINTON AND COURT STREETS IN BROOKLYN. Subway: 2, 3, 4, 5 to Borough Hall; F, G to Bergen Street. 718-624-4550. www.sahadis.com.

437. Sullivan Street Bakery: The breads at this Hell's Kitchen favorite (The original location was on Sullivan Street, in SoHo) combine Italian recipes and organic baking for some mouthwatering results, like the herb-flecked potato pizza.

533 WEST 47TH STREET BETWEEN TENTH AND ELEVENTH AVENUES. Subway: C, E to 50th Street. 212-265-5580. www.sullivanstreetbakery.com.

438. Take a ticket and gorge on samples at DiPalo's.

With more than a century of experience making and selling food in Little Italy, DiPalo's is the true gastronomic gem of the neighborhood. Quite simply the best-stocked Italian deli downtown, DiPalo's is also the unofficial supplier of some of the neighborhood's best restaurants, including Peasant and **L'asso** (see page 207). Shopping here can be exhausting, but only in the same sense that Christmas is: there's simply too much food here to make things easy. Never quiet, the store operates on an old-school ticket system, which means you take a number when you come in and then wait patiently for your turn, all the while watching the cheerful staff slicing cured meats, wrapping up fresh mozzarella, and going into the back room only to emerge with delicious-smelling fresh bread or basil. Fortunately, they're liberal with their samples, so make up for the time in line by getting a taste of whatever looks good at the counter—you'll have worked up quite an appetite by the time you get there.

200 GRAND STREET AT MOTT STREET IN MANHATTAN. Subway: 6 to Spring Street; B to Grand Street. 212-226-1033. www.dipaloselects.com.

439. Play hooky at **Cones** on a sweltering August afternoon.

This Argentinean-owned ice cream shop has developed a cultlike following for its superior scoops—almost chewy, taffylike ice creams and intensely flavored sorbets—which means that the line can get out of control on summer weekends. What better excuse than that to take an afternoon off during the week?

272 BLEECKER STREET BETWEEN MORTON AND JONES STREETS IN MANHATTAN. Subway: 1 to Christopher Street-Sheridan Square; A, C, E, B, D, F, V to West 4th Street. 212-414-1795.

440. Try an ice cream flavor you didn't think existed from the **Chinatown Ice Cream Factory**.

Lychee, red bean, black sesame, and taro are among the exotic offerings at this Chinatown institution, alongside more traditional American staples, such as cookies-and-cream to mint chocolate chip.

65 BAYARD STREET BETWEEN MOTT AND ELIZABETH STREETS IN MANHATTAN. Subway: 6, N, Q, R, W, J, M, Z to Canal Street. 212-608-4170. www.chinatownicecreamfactory.com.

441. Join the **food club**...

Two things that New Yorkers really love are good food and getting to do things before anyone else. Culinary Insiders is a club that combines these two passions by offering rare, one-of-a-kind, private events with New York restaurants, like dinners with chefs, kitchen tours, tastings at not-yet-opened restaurants, and foodie field trips outside of the city. The club works with some of the city's most respected chefs to organize events—including **Daniel Boulud** (see pages 162–163) and **Jean-Georges Vongerichten** (see pages 166–167). Membership gets you early bookings for all events, plus reduced admission fees; events are also open to the public, subject to availability, so you can attend one before you join.

Annual membership: $125 and up. For more information and a schedule of upcoming events, call 212-330-9080 or visit www.culinaryinsiders.com.

442. ...or join the **hamburger club**.

O'Neill's Irish Bar has a burger-of-the-month club, which entitles members to one spe-cial burger at the restaurant each month, served with fries and a matched beer. The burger and beer changes each month, but provided you don't mind toppings like cheese, bacon, or guacamole, you won't be disappointed. You can sign up for a year, a half-year, or a single month—however much your waistline will permit.

729 THIRD AVENUE AT 45TH STREET IN MANHATTAN. Subway: 4, 5, 6, 7, S to Grand Central-42nd Street. 212-661-3530. www.irishpubny.com.

443. Slurp up a **Ralph's Italian ice**.

On a hot, sticky day, enjoying an Italian ice ranks pretty high on the list of all-time best things to do in New York. Though adequately refreshing ices can be procured in sea-son from pushcarts around the city, many locals prefer the ices from Ralph's, which has been selling this delicious treat since 1928. At the original Staten Island location and the other locations in Brooklyn and Queens, you can find dozens of flavors of tradi-tional Italian ice, sherbet, and ice cream. They also have a few low-carb/low-sugar vari-eties, something no self-respecting pushcart would be caught selling.

Multiple locations. For information, visit www.ralphsices.com.

444. Get taken to lunch in the **Condé Nast cafeteria**.

Frank Gehry's sleek, futuristic cafeteria is perennially one of the most exclusive lunch spots in town—no matter who you are, or how much you'll spend, the only way to get in is if someone who works there invites you. But if you can't swing a meeting with Anna Wintour, it's worth trying to bribe one of the numerous editorial assistants for a trip inside. After you've made it past the security desk in the lobby, take the elevators up to the fourth floor and follow the crowd. If you actually want to eat, you'll have to buy a card from one of the machines by the entrance—the only form of payment the cafete-ria accepts—otherwise, you'll have to content yourself with the visual feast. Past the dark servery and cash registers is the glass-and-tan seating area filled with undulating lines of leather booths and blue titanium. The space is small and oddly shaped, but the rise and fall of Gehry's elevated seating areas separated by glass panels make the room look bigger than it is (even when it's packed), and the canteen he created has an eye-catching visual appeal that echoes that of the slick magazine conglomerate. The food offerings are appropriately lavish: an abundant salad bar packed with premium pro-duce and sumptuous prepared dishes; a daily hot meal that reads like the menu of a three-star restaurant; freshly baked breads, bagels, muffins, and pizzas; plus soups, sand-wiches, sushi, fruit, and even a self-serve frozen yogurt machine. Still, that doesn't stop a disproportionate amount of the magazines' staff from congregating around the piles of undressed lettuce and egg whites, so you'll have no problem getting to the more exciting items. Lest you think that you'll blend right in, the aisles up to the bulbous seating areas—compared, inevitably, to catwalks—are sloped and slippery and can send all but the most seasoned fashion editor for a spill in front of the entire staff.

4 TIMES SQUARE AT 42ND STREET, 4TH FLOOR, IN MANHATTAN. Subway: 1, 2, 3, 7, N, Q, R, W, S to Times Square-42nd Street.

445. Escape and rejuvenate at **Hangawi**.

Behind a pair of heavy wooden doors on 32nd Street lies the single most transporting dining experience in the city. Leave your earthly existence along with your shoes at the entrance and let yourself be whisked away by the soothing music, smooth sake and plum wine, and incredible vegetarian Korean cuisine. It is the closest thing to true bliss that is easily accessible by subway.

12 EAST 32ND STREET BETWEEN FIFTH AND MADISON AVENUES IN MANHATTAN. Subway: B, D, F, V, N, Q, R, W to 34th Street/Herald Square. 212-213-0077. www.hangawirestaurant.com.

Have dinner in a restaurant's back garden.

Eating outdoors in the middle of this thriving metropolis always feels like an unusually decadent pleasure. From the first unseasonably warm day in April, any restaurant with decent curb space will throw open the windows, schlep out tables, and string some lights for giddy patrons eager to bask in the long-awaited spring air. However, not all outdoor eateries are created equal. Sidewalk cafés can be good for people-watching, but they've got nothing on the transporting, deliciously smug feeling that comes from eating your meal tucked away in a back garden. Here are a couple of great ones.

446. *Pure Food and Wine:* On a sultry summer day, there's nothing more refreshing than a glass of organic sangria in Pure's backyard, followed by some of the gourmet raw dishes. (Skeptics and carnivores take note—it may not have the heft of a steak, but what these people can do with a tomato will blow your mind.)

57 IRVING PLACE BETWEEN 17TH AND 18TH STREETS IN MANHATTAN. Subway: 4, 5, 6, L, N, Q, R, W to 14th Street-Union Square. 212-477-1010. www.purefoodandwine.com.

447. *Yaffa Café:* One of the few places left in the East Village where you can have a legitimately good meal for under $10. The backyard is loud, lively, and feels kind of like a keg party sometimes—as it should.

97 ST. MARK'S PLACE BETWEEN FIRST AVENUE AND AVENUE A IN MANHATTAN. Subway: L to First Avenue; 6 to Astor Place. 212-677-9001. www.yaffacafe.com.

448. 5 Ninth: This sophisticated restaurant nestled in a townhouse stands out among the many loud, brightly lit attractions of the Meatpacking District. In addition to the far-out meat preparations from acclaimed chef Zak Pelaccio, one of the city's rising-star chefs, the enclosed backyard seating area behind the restaurant is another of its great charms. If you can't get a seat outside, the three-story nineteenth-century brownstone that houses the restaurant is pretty nice, too.
5 NINTH AVENUE BETWEEN GANSEVOORT AND LITTLE WEST 12TH STREETS IN MANHATTAN. Subway: A, C, E to 14th Street; L to Eighth Avenue. 212-929-9460. www.5Ninth.com.

449. DuMont: DuMont's hamburger is considered one of the best in the city, a fact which has obscured not only the rest of the excellent offerings on the menu, but also what we consider to be an even better reason to take a meal there: their cozy, exquisite back garden. This dining space was created with as much care (and with as sharp an eye) as the resto's interior. There's the beautiful contrast between the blonde wood and green plants; the outdoor bar nestled into a nook against the back wall; and a special elevated dining area called the "tree house." A retractable awning and subtle heaters keep the garden available even when the weather isn't totally cooperating.
432 UNION AVENUE, BETWEEN METROPOLITAN AVENUE AND DEVOE STREET. Subway: L, G to Lorimer-Metropolitan. 718-486-7717. www.dumontrestaurant.com.

450. Sherwood Café/Robin des Bois: Hands down, the most romantic garden you can eat in anywhere in the city. Try the Sherwood Special (a combination of the cheese and charcuterie platters), with plenty of wine....
195 SMITH STREET BETWEEN BALTIC AND WARREN STREETS IN BROOKLYN. Subway: F, G to Bergen Street. 718-596-1609.www.sherwoodcafe.com.

451. Home: They have gas lamps on the outdoor deck, so this is a good choice if you just can't wait another night for spring to begin—or if you want to stretch summer out as long as possible. The garden is open year-round, and diners who brave the cold for an al fresco meal in the winter are inducted into the Polar Bear Diner Club, and receive special buttons that congratulate them as "fearless eaters under the heaters."
20 CORNELIA STREET BETWEEN BLEECKER AND WEST 4TH STREETS IN MANHATTAN. Subway: 1 to Christopher Street-Sheridan Square. 212-243-9579. www.homenyc.com.

452. Barolo: Only if the owners opened the gates from the cool Italian-style garden onto Thompson Street would you know you're not in Tuscany.
398 WEST BROADWAY BETWEEN SPRING AND BROOME STREETS IN MANHATTAN. Subway: C, E to Spring Street; N, R, W to Prince Street. 212-226-1102. www.nybarolo.com.

453. Bohemian Hall & Beer Garden: This truly bohemian hangout in Queens (it was started as a community center for Czech and Slovak immigrants in the early twentieth century) is the home of the city's only outdoor beer garden. The décor isn't flashy (picnic tables are pretty much it) and the food's not very fancy (Eastern European staples from the kitchen inside or burgers and dogs from the grill outside), but it's big, lively, and well worth a trip.
29-19 24ᵀᴴ AVENUE IN QUEENS. Subway: N to Astoria Boulevard. 718-274-4925. www.bohemianhall.com.

454. Have a blintz from **Teresa's**.

For some, a blintz has the same power to spark as much passionate competition and unwavering preference as any bagel, steak, pickle, or pizza, and the ones turned out at Teresa's are about as good as they come. Best eaten as soon as they are served, they are warm, crispy, and the soft cheese filling is perfectly balanced between sweet and savory.
80 MONTAGUE STREET AT HICKS STREET IN BROOKLYN. Subway: N, R to Court Street-Borough Hall; 2, 3 to Clark Street. 718-797-3996.

455. Visit the **Brooklyn Brewery**.

Thanks to a large influx of German immigrants, Brooklyn was once one of the nation's beer-producing capitals; one hundred years ago, it was home to nearly fifty breweries. By the second half of the twentieth century, however, all of these family-owned breweries had closed, forced out of business by the bigger breweries in the Midwest. After years of basement brewing, hand labeling, and distributing out of their van, the local brewers who made Brooklyn Lager revived the borough's brewing tradition when the Brooklyn Brewery opened in 1996. You can tour the brewery for free every Saturday (tours run between twenty and thirty minutes and are held hourly from 1:00 p.m. to 6:00 p.m.). The brewery also hosts happy hours (Friday, 6:00 p.m. to 11:00 p.m.; beers are $4 each), concerts, parties, and other events.
1 BREWERS ROW, 79 NORTH 11ᵀᴴ STREET IN BROOKLYN. Subway: L to Bedford Avenue. 718-486-7422. www.brooklynbrewery.com.

456. Try to resist the soft serve at **Milk Bar**.

Part bakery, part lounge area (for the popular Ssam Bar, which Milk Bar is connected to via passageway), part experimental treat lab, Milk Bar resists classification. Though hard to quantify, we can guarantee that you'll find the treats inside unforgettable and one-of-a-kind: offerings revolve according to the chef's imagination, but popular stand-bys include "crack pie" (butter filling in an oat crust), the compost cookie (pretzels, potato chips, ground coffee, oats, and butterscotch and chocolate chips), and the mysterious "cereal milk" (milk infused with toasted cornflakes, sugar, and salt). If you are only going to have one thing, the soft serve is the way to go. The four flavors change monthly, usually inspired by an unexpected theme: one month featured flavors inspired by donuts (jelly, sugar, plain donut, Bavarian cream); lemon verbena, rosemary and other herbal flavors appeared another month. They are as compulsively delicious as they are strange. *MILK BAR SHARES AN ADDRESS WITH SSAM BAR (207 SECOND AVENUE IN MANHATTAN), BUT THE ENTRANCE IS LOCATED AROUND THE CORNER, ON 12TH STREET BETWEEN SECOND AND THIRD AVENUES. Subway: L to First or Third Avenues. 212-254-3500. www.momofuku.com.*

457. Have a champagne date at the **Bubble Lounge**.

Champagne can turn any evening into an occasion. So with the price of a cocktail pushing $20 at hot spots around town, why not let it? This Tribeca lounge offers more than 300 kinds of champagnes and sparkling wines, in a classier, cozier, and more welcoming setting than the trendy bars. Perfect for a romantic rendezvous, a celebration, or a regular after-work drink. *228 WEST BROADWAY BETWEEN FRANKLIN AND WHITE STREETS IN MANHATTAN. Subway: 1 to Franklin Street. 212-431-3433. www.bubblelounge.com.*

458. Swing with your steady on the lovers' seats at **Bowery Bar** and **Down the Hatch**,
probably the only bars left in the city where you can indulge in playground romance. Swing in the breeze in the patio garden at Bowery Bar, or stake out the swing for a whole night at Down the Hatch—it's the only peaceful corner of the bar. *BOWERY BAR, a.k.a. B-BAR & GRILL: 40 EAST 4TH STREET BETWEEN BOWERY AND LAFAYETTE STREET IN MANHATTAN. Subway: 6 to Astor Place; B, D, F, V to Broadway-Lafayette Street. 212-475-2220.*

DOWN THE HATCH: 179 WEST 4TH STREET BETWEEN SIXTH AND SEVENTH AVENUES IN MANHATTAN. Subway: A, C, E, B, D, F, V to West 4th Street. 212-627-9747.

459. Have a rendezvous at the **Cellar Bar** at the Bryant Park Hotel.

Cavernous tiled walls, arched and candlelit hallways, and powerful cocktails mean seduction is inevitable.

40 WEST 40TH STREET BETWEEN FIFTH AND SIXTH AVENUES IN MANHATTAN. Subway: B, D, F, V to 42nd Street-Bryant Park. 212-869-0100. www.bryantparkhotel.com.

460. Have a **pop-up hot dog**.

Only in New York would a hot dog purveyor forgo a bricks-and-mortar operation in favor of a series of regular gigs. The men behind the AsiaDogs fire up the grill at different bars and outdoor spaces on particular nights of the week, offering a menu of seven signature combos to top your choice of dog (beef, chicken, or veggie). The Asia comes from the offerings: there's the Wandang (barbecued pork belly and onions), the Ito (Japanese curry and kimchi apples), and Vietnamese *bánh mi* style, among others. (They also offer a burger Korean BBQ style, topped with kimchi.)

To find out where Asia Dog will be and when, visit their Web site www.asiadog.nyc.com.

Travel the world, table by table.

Many cities boast one or two signature "imported" cuisines, but nowhere else will you have the variety—and for the most part, the authenticity—of so many different types of food, in so many different settings, from so many different places.

With such an abundance of nonindigenous delights, it's hard to contain international food under one heading; we easily could have devoted an entire chapter to the topic. There are excellent restaurants specializing in cuisines both familiar and exotic; there are fancy fine dining establishments, specialty shops, takeout joints, and holes-in-the-wall; there are neighborhoods famous for their authentic foreign food and less-familiar enclaves that boast equally delectable delights. In this section, we've chosen our favorite dining spots for a dozen popular foreign cuisines. However, don't limit your travels to the restaurants whose cuisines you already know—there's so much more out there! **Food-focused walking tours** (see pages 96–97) are a great way to get a taste of the city's hidden gems.

CHINESE

As many food lovers know, "Chinese food" in America is made up of many different regional cuisines and specialties. While there are countless good Chinese restaurants of all kinds all over the city, it can be hard to tell which are authentic (meaning they serve dishes actually eaten in the region). Here are some favorites:

461. Have Hong Kong–style dim sum, a seemingly limitless range of dumplings, spring rolls, and milk teas, with all the flourishes at the **Golden Unicorn**.
18 EAST BROADWAY AT CATHERINE STREET IN MANHATTAN. Subway: 4, 5, 6 to Brooklyn Bridge-City Hall; J, M, Z to Chambers Street. 212-941-0911. www.goldenunicornrestaurant.com.

462. Go celebrity-spotting while you enjoy the best ribs in Chinatown at **Hop Kee**. The famous lemon fried flounder has kept the likes of Bill Cosby, Conan O'Brien, and Bill Clinton coming back time and again.
21 MOTT STREET AT MOSCO STREET IN MANHATTAN. Subway: 1 to Franklin Street; A, C, E to Canal Street. 212-964-8365.

463. Devour a basket of explosive soup dumplings at **Joe's Shanghai**, the restaurant that claims to have invented them. You don't even have to ask for them specifically; they'll know.
9 PELL STREET BETWEEN BOWERY AND MOTT STREET IN MANHATTAN. Subway: B, D to Grand Street; 6, J, M, Z, N, Q, R, W to Canal Street. 212-233-8888. www.joeshanghairestaurants.com. N.B.: There are also locations in Midtown Manhattan and in Queens.

464. Order the duck at the **Peking Duck House**. Even vegetarians have been known to enjoy watching the waiters carve the duck here. (Don't be alarmed by the sleek new look: the décor may say twenty-first-century SoHo, but the food is still Chinatown, all the way.)
28 MOTT STREET AT PELL STREET IN MANHATTAN. Subway: 6, J, M, Z, N, Q, R, W to Canal Street. 212-227-1810. www.pekingduckhousenyc.com. N.B. There is also a location in Midtown Manhattan.

465. Order the Shanghai banquet at **Shanghai Pavilion**. It looks like a regular Chinese restaurant, but critics and aficionados of Chinese cuisine vouch that the dishes at this Upper East Side joint are authentic, and some consider Shanghai Pavilion the best Chinese food outside of Chinatown. You must call a day in advance to request certain specialties, like beggar's chicken, a stuffed chicken baked in clay; but you also won't want to miss the soup dumplings—the restaurant's owner used to work at the venerable dumpling purveyor, **Joe's Shanghai** (see above).
1378 THIRD AVENUE BETWEEN 78TH AND 79TH STREETS IN MANHATTAN. Subway: 6 to 77th Street. 212-585-3388.

ITALIAN

With the extreme variety in look, taste, and price, Italian cuisine in this city defies categorization. Like Chinese cuisine, each region of Italy has its own style and specialties; something that's prepared authentically at a Neapolitan restaurant may not taste the same at a Tuscan trattoria or an enoteca (although they all may be equally good). In addition, the restaurants range broadly in character, from those that specialize in certain foods (pizza, pasta, or panini), to authentic and firmly regional restaurants (like Manducatis or the restaurants on Arthur Avenue in the Bronx), to Italian-inspired fine dining (such as Mario Batali's Babbo, mentioned earlier in this chapter). We've considered each of these under the umbrella of Italian food and selected some of the best. (This being New York, pizza's a whole different story. See also our list of the **best pizza places** on pages 206–208.)

Arthur Avenue.

The neighborhood of Belmont, high in the Bronx between Fordham Road and Crotona Park, has been a dense and popular Italian enclave for close to a century. Running through its center is Arthur Avenue, a street of Italian storefronts and restaurants that has been drawing local residents and traveling epicureans for as long as anyone can remember. Aside from its gastronomic attractions, Belmont is a charming little corner of the Bronx, where church bells ring out every quarter of an hour, Old World traditions meet contemporary American attitudes, and kids play in playgrounds while men and women sit in street cafés talking over cappuccinos. Go by day, and the neighborhood around Arthur Avenue and East 187th Street is a great place to stroll and pick up some of the best quality Italian foods, from fresh pastas to meats, vegetables, breads, cheeses, and herbs. Go by night, and choose from a host of busy restaurants, where you can enjoy these fresh ingredients cooked with genuine Italian-American flair, whether it's a slice to go at **Full Moon** (see page 207) or a sumptuous feast at Pasquale's Rigoletto. Note: All listings below are in the Bronx.

> **466. *Biancardi's:*** An authentic Italian butcher offering everything from rabbit and veal to salami and smoked meats.
> *2350 ARTHUR AVENUE BETWEEN CRESCENT AVENUE AND FRANK SIMEONE SQUARE. 718-733-4058.*

> **467. *Borgatti's:*** A maker of genuine fresh egg pasta and ravioli that has won over locals and food critics alike.
> *632 EAST 187TH STREET BETWEEN HUGHES AVENUE AND BELMONT AVENUE. 718-367-3799.*

468. *Egidio's Patisserie:* A bakery whose windows are so full of extravagant cakes and Italian sweets they're impossible to resist.
622 EAST 187TH STREET AT HUGHES AVENUE. 718-295-6077. www.borgattis.com.

469. *Umberto's Clam House:* One of Arthur Avenue's largest restaurants and the only one devoted entirely to fresh Italian seafood dishes.
2356 ARTHUR AVENUE BETWEEN CRESCENT AVENUE AND FRANK SIMEONE SQUARE. 718-220-2526. www.umbertosclamhousebronx.com.

470. *Pasquale's Rigoletto:* The biggest and liveliest of the restaurants on Arthur Avenue, and the perfect place for a rollicking dinner party.
2311 ARTHUR AVENUE BETWEEN CRESCENT AVENUE AND FRANK SIMEONE SQUARE. 718-365-6644.

The popular part of Arthur Avenue runs from East 184th Street to East 188th Street, and many more great markets and cafés can be found on 187th Street, across Arthur Avenue to Cambrelleng Avenue. Bus: Bx55 from anywhere along Third Avenue to St. Barnabas's Hospital, Third Avenue and East 183rd Street (one block from the base of Arthur Avenue). Subway: 4, D to Fordham Road, then Bx12 bus east; 2, 5 to Pelham Parkway, then Bx12 bus west. N.B.: www.arthuravenuebronx.com has directions, recipes, and facts about Arthur Avenue and Belmont. Information on some of the stores and merchants listed above can also be found there.

471. For true Italian home cooking the way Nonna used to make, head to **Mandu-catis** (rumor has it they close one month each summer to can tomatoes in Italy). Reward yourself for making the trip to Long Island City with exceptional pastas and entrees, rare Italian wines from the owner's collection, and the company of artists from nearby **PS1** (see page 133).
13-27 JACKSON AVENUE AT 47TH AVENUE IN QUEENS. Subway: 7 to Hunters Point Avenue; G to 21st Street. 718-729-4602.

472. For classic Italian cuisine in a more formal setting, head to the darkened dining room of **Il Mulino.** Too far north and west to be part of Little Italy, Il Mulino is located on a busy corner of the Village and is one of the oldest and finest Italian restaurants in the city. While the menu is short and straightforward, the food is carefully and authentically prepared and draws inspiration largely from the recipes and flavors of central Italy's mountainous provinces. Simple pastas with traditional lamb or veal ragús are especially good—differing notably from other restaurants in the quality of the meats used—and the classic, herbed seafood dishes are wonderful.

86 WEST 3RD STREET BETWEEN SULLIVAN AND THOMPSON STREETS IN MANHATTAN. Subway: A, C, E, B, D, F, V to West 4th Street. 212-673-3783. www.ilmulinonewyork.com.

473. For panini and wine, park yourself at the counter at **Bar Veloce**. Offerings at these downtown mainstays are simple, but quality is always excellent. Come for a drink, snack, or meal; with a friend, or on your own—it's also a great place for a solo meal.
Multiple locations in Chelsea, the East Village, and SoHo. www.barveloce.com.

474. For good Italian coffee, go to **Tarallucci e Vino**. Though the name means "biscuits and wines," coffee connoisseurs consider the espresso to be on par with the cafés in Italy.
163 FIRST AVENUE BETWEEN 10TH AND 11TH STREETS IN MANHATTAN. Subway: L to First Avenue. 212-388-1190. 15 EAST 18TH STREET BETWEEN FIFTH AVENUE AND BROADWAY IN MANHATTAN. Subway: 4, 5, 6, L, N, Q, R, W to 14th Street-Union Square. 212-228-5400. N.B. There is also a location in the SoHo Alessi store at 130 Greene Street, between Houston and Prince Streets. www.taralluccievino.net.

FRENCH

Yet again, there's plenty to choose from, along a particularly broad spectrum on the elegance scale. On the high end are those restaurants featuring classic French gourmet cooking mentioned in the "splurges" section (see page 167). But work your way down a bit, and there are bistros, brasseries, patisseries, crêperies, and chocolatiers that excel in particular specialties and regional delights.

475. Get a crêpe from the little window at **Shade To Go** and eat it in **Washington Mews** (see page 301)—Paris without the jet lag.
241 SULLIVAN STREET BETWEEN BLEECKER AND WEST 3RD STREETS IN MANHATTAN. Subway: A, C, E, B, D, F, V to West 4th Street. 212-982-6275.

476. Forget Paris, and have a less traditional but just as scrumptious crêpe at the **Crêperie**. You may not be able to sit, but crêpes like the spinach and feta are worth standing for.
135 LUDLOW STREET BETWEEN RIVINGTON AND STANTON STREETS IN MANHATTAN. Subway: F to Delancey Street; J, M, Z to Essex Street. 212-979-5543. 112 MACDOUGAL STREET BETWEEN BLEECKER AND WEST 3RD STREETS IN MANHATTAN. Subway: A,C,E,B,D,F,V to West 4th Street. 212-253-6705. www.creperienyc.com.

477. Order the *galette des rois* at **Gavroche**. There are many wonderful French bistros in this city, but we wanted to single this one out because it is one of the very few that serve the *galette des rois*, the almond cake with a charm baked inside that the French serve during the Feast of the Epiphany. The person whose slice contains the charm (called "la fève" because they used to use a dry bean; today, charms are usually figurines) is crowned the king or queen of the day, and gets to wear a paper crown. During the first week of January, this bistro serves the cake (which is quite tasty), complete with charms. You can have it by the slice or, to increase your odds, bring a group and buy the entire cake.

212 WEST 14TH STREET BETWEEN SEVENTH AND EIGHTH AVENUES IN MANHATTAN. Subway: 1, 2, 3 to 14th Street; A, C, E to 14th Street; L to Eighth Avenue. 212-646-8553. www.gavroche-ny.com.

478. Get a taste of Provence at **Nice Matin**. Among the many restaurants around this area of the Upper West Side, Nice Matin stands out as a sunny spot of solid regional cooking. Traditional dishes like *soupe au pistou* (a vegetable-and-bean soup) and *pissaladière* (a thin, pizzalike onion tart for which Nice is famous) allow you to experience the Mediterranean flavor that separates the cuisine of southern France from that of the rest of the country.

201 WEST 79TH STREET AT AMSTERDAM AVENUE IN MANHATTAN. Subway: 1 to 79th Street. 212-873-6423. www.nicematinnyc.com.

479. Explore the confections at **Francois Chocolate Bar**. A collective "Mon Dieu" was heard on the Upper East Side when Francois Payard's eponymous and beloved patisserie and bistro shut its doors in 2009. Fortunately for the M. Payard's legions of fans, the swank Mauboussin jewelry store chivalrously provided space for him to resurrect his quintessential patisserie. Here, Payard's signature offerings—pastries, macarons, and *verrines*, exquisite layered parfaits served in glasses—are displayed as elegantly as fine jewels, their decadence concealed by their dainty appearance in that neat trick only the French can pull off.

The Chocolate Bar is located on the fourth floor of Mauboussin. 714 MADISON AVENUE BETWEEN 63rd AND 64th STREETS IN MANHATTAN. Subway: 6 to 63rd Street. 212-759-1600. www.payard.com.

480. Savor a single piece of chocolate from **Maison du Chocolat...** The chocolates made by this Paris-based chocolatier may taste disarmingly bitter to a palette accustomed to Hershey's or Godiva, but anyone who loves the robust flavors of European chocolate will appreciate the satisfying richness of each piece crafted here.

Both locations in Manhattan. 1018 MADISON AVENUE BETWEEN 78TH AND 79TH STREETS. Subway: 6 to 77th Street. 212-744-7117. 30 ROCKEFELLER CENTER AT 49TH STREET. Subway: B, D, F, V to 47th-50th Streets-Rockefeller Center. 212-265-9404. www.lamaisonduchocolat.com.

481. … *Or look past the chocolate at Kee's*. Kee's is a true local gem, and one wh pays an obvious debt to the patisseries of Paris. Kee Ling Tong has been making her unique confections in SoHo since 2002, and while she will ship worldwide (she's developed an international following), the retail store is well worth a trip (all the offerings are made fresh every day). She specializes in chocolate truffles filled with genius, seasonal gourmet combinations (plums and sea salt in dark chocolate; white chocolate filled with fresh lemon and basil), and traditional French *macarons* cookies. While the truffles are fantastic, don't pass up the chance to try one of her *macarons*. They're the best in the city.
80 THOMPSON STREET BETWEEN SPRING AND BROOME STREETS. 212-334-3284. Subway: C, E to Spring Street. 452 FIFTH AVENUE, AT 38TH STREET. (INSIDE HSBC BUILDING) 212-525-6099. Subway: B, D, F, V, 7 to 42nd Street. www.keeschocolates.com.

ENGLISH:

482. Have a proper English tea at ***Tea & Sympathy***, a cozy little tearoom where pots of Yorkshire Gold and tiers of finger sandwiches and scones never look out of place. For heartier appetites, or those craving classic British cooking, they also prepare a nice Yorkshire pudding, bangers and mash, treacle pudding, and, of course, beans on toast.
108 GREENWICH AVENUE BETWEEN SEVENTH AND EIGHTH AVENUES IN MANHATTAN. Subway: A, C, E, to 14th Street; L to Eighth Avenue. 212-989-9735. www.teaandsympathynewyork.com.

483. Get some fish and chips at ***A Salt and Battery***, considered the most authentic taste of home for many wandering Britons (the imported chip-cutter from London helps, as does the Capital Radio and Virgin U.K. soundtrack, broadcast via the Internet).
112 GREENWICH AVENUE BETWEEN SEVENTH AND EIGHTH AVENUES. Subway: A, C, E, to 14th Street; L to Eighth Avenue. 212-691-2713. www.asaltandbattery.com.

484. Step into London at ***Clerkenwell***. Even if the waiters tend to hail from the Antipodes, the recently opened Clerkenwell is an excellent new addition to the British ex-pat palette, with a menu spanning classics like fish and chips, toad in the hole, and an excellent cheese plate, and an atmosphere truly reminiscent of a contemporary yuppie London eatery.
49 CLINTON STREET, NEAR STANTON STREET IN MANHATTAN. Subway: F, J, M, Z to Delancey Street. 212-614-3234. www.clerkenwellny.com.

INDIAN:

The Queens neighborhood of Jackson Heights, which extends beyond Sunnyside up Roosevelt and 37th Avenues between 72nd Street and Junction Boulevard, is known as Little India. While there is a heavy Indian presence in East Midtown and the East Village in Manhattan, Little India is the densest Indian enclave in the five boroughs. Powdered-spice stores, beautiful sari makers, and video shops carrying everything Bollywood line the streets, and the restaurants make this area the place to go for a true and varied taste of Indian food, whether you're looking for a quiet snack in a local curry house, a feast of tandoori meats in one of the larger restaurants, or a sample of authentic Indian desserts to take home.

485. Where else but in Jackson Heights can you find top-notch Indian food in a place that calls itself a diner? Grab a window seat at the enormous **Jackson Diner** and enjoy great South Indian cooking in one of the busiest and most strikingly decorated restaurants in New York.
37-47 74TH STREET BETWEEN 37TH AND ROOSEVELT AVENUES IN QUEENS. Subway: 7 to 74th Street-Broadway; E, F, G, R, V to Jackson Heights-Roosevelt Avenue. 718-672-1232. www.jacksondiner.com.

486. For a quieter experience, visit the **Delhi Palace.** Go hungry—there is such a vast selection of starters and sweets that you'll have no choice but to order a bunch and taste as many as you can.
33-73 74TH STREET IN QUEENS. Subway: 7 to 74th Street-Broadway; E, F, G, R, V to Jackson Heights-Roosevelt Avenue. 718-507-0666.

487. Embrace the madness of Midtown at **Curry in a Hurry**—something of a fast-food place for Indian cuisine, but the food (in particular the chutney) is very good.
119 LEXINGTON AVENUE AT 28TH STREET IN MANHATTAN. Subway: 6 to 28th Street. 212-683-0900.

488. Feast like a king (or a queen) at **Dawat.** Far from the bustling restaurant rows of 6th Street, Murray Hill, and Jackson Heights lies this excellent, upscale Indian fine dining establishment. Dawat means "invitation to a feast," and you should accept. The food is top-notch, the décor refined, and the service on par with the city's most elegant restaurants. Order one of the tasting menus—called "the king" or "the queen"—and then relax as you are served dish after tantalizing dish of the chef's specialties.
210 EAST 58TH STREET BETWEEN SECOND AND THIRD AVENUES IN MANHATTAN. Subway: 4, 5, 6 to 59th Street; N, R, W to Lexington Avenue/59th Street. 212-355-7555. www.dawatrestaurant.com.

489. Let yourself be courted by the "callers" at **Milon** and **Panna II**, two Indian restaurants on First Avenue. Though they allegedly share a common kitchen, the doormen of this neighboring pair of incredibly bright, colorful restaurants do their utmost to make the distinction between dining rooms seem profound. Each has a full and cheap menu of Indian and Bengali dishes, and each is so full of dangling chili lights and tinsel that the world outside seems dull by comparison. Tip: whichever restaurant you choose, make sure you tell the waitstaff that it's someone's birthday—the "surprise" celebrations are elaborate and happen three or four times a night.
Milon (on the left at the top of the stairs) and Panna II (on the right): 93 FIRST AVENUE BETWEEN 6TH AND 7TH STREETS IN MANHATTAN. Subway: L to First Avenue; 6 to Astor Place; F, V to Lower East Side-Second Avenue. Milon: 212-228-4896; Panna II: 212-598-4610. www.panna2.com.

490. Stock up on spices and more at **Kalustyan's**. Though it carries products of all different kinds—snacks, tea, cosmetics, prepared food, chutney, and sweets galore— from all over the world, one sniff inside Kalustyan's will send you straight to the spices. Choose from nearly 900 varieties, from dill, cumin, and nearly a dozen kinds of curry powder to more exotic offerings not found anywhere else.
123 LEXINGTON AVENUE BETWEEN 27TH AND 28TH STREETS IN MANHATTAN. Subway: 6 to 28th Street. 212-685-3451. www.kalustyans.com.

SPANISH:

491. Keep Spanish hours at **Xicala**. Manchego, chorizo, and jamón are all prominently featured on Xicala's menu of tapas, along with authentic but less expected concoctions such as a brilliant stew of chickpeas, spinach, tomato, cheese. The wine list also features a mix of Spanish staples and surprises (as well as a properly lethal sangria). The room is worn in a way that makes it feels like the real thing and also a place where you can stay all night, during the course of which you may be treated to live music or some flamenco dancing. It can be downright peaceful on a lazy late afternoon, but in the great Spanish tradition, it's only after 9 p.m. that Xicala really gets going.
151-B ELIZABETH STREET BETWEEN BROOME AND KENMARE. Subway: 6 to Spring Street; J, M to Bowery; B, D to Grand Street. 212-219-0599. www.xicala.net.

492. Dig into the paella at **El Pote Español**. This excellent Spanish restaurant has been serving an authentic blend of Spanish and South American cuisine for a quarter of a century. The atmosphere is more formal than some of New York's lively sangria-and-tapas bars, and the menu is heavy on rich, savory meat and seafood dishes. The flavorful vegetable dishes (from fresh asparagus to buttery artichokes and stuffed mushrooms)

are outstanding, but it's the colorful and rich paella that keeps people coming back.
718 SECOND AVENUE BETWEEN 38TH AND 39TH STREETS IN MANHATTAN. Subway: 6 to 33rd Street. 212-889-6680. www.elpote.com.

493. Take a date to **El Cid**. Although El Cid is predominantly a tapas bar, it's a great and comfortable place to enjoy an intimate supper. Focus on the chicken or the shellfish dishes, all deliciously garlicky and flavorful, add an order of sweet sangria, and make sure you leave enough room to try the *torrejas*, a traditional Spanish dessert akin to bread pudding in spiced wine and served with ice cream.
322 WEST 15TH STREET BETWEEN EIGHTH AND NINTH AVENUES IN MANHATTAN. Subway: A, C, E to 14th Street; L to Eighth Avenue. 212-929-9332.

RUSSIAN:

Brighton Beach, the stretch of beach and boardwalk that links Coney Island to Sheepshead Bay, is home to one of the largest and most intense ethnic communities in New York. Known locally as "Little Odessa," Brighton is populated almost entirely by Russians and Ukrainians, and it is simply the place to go for borscht, caviar, honey cake, and all things reminiscent of the USSR. (The nightlife's not bad either.) Street signs, papers, and menus are in Russian, delis and street vendors sell fresh sour-cherry and cranberry juices, and everyone brings his or her own bottle of vodka to the table.

494. Eat smoked-fish salad and grilled meat on the boardwalk at **Tatiana**, the grandest and most extravagant of the restaurant-nightclubs in Brighton. They'll bring you blankets if it's windy and umbrellas if it's raining, so you can sit outside and watch the Russians on the beach all year round.
3152 BRIGHTON 6TH STREET AT THE BOARDWALK IN BROOKLYN. Subway: B, Q to Brighton Beach. 718-646-7630.

495. Try a plate of traditional veal dumplings (*pelmeni*) and a bottle of pear soda at **Stolovaya**, the most authentic Russian diner in Brooklyn. Be warned: they do not speak English, but will understand a request for an English menu.
813 AVENUE U BETWEEN 8TH AND 9TH STREETS IN BROOKLYN. Subway: F, Q to Avenue U. 718-787-0120.

496. Indulge in caviar at **Petrossian**. Although it is only twenty-five years old, this sibling of the Paris restaurant founded in the 1920s has already become a Midtown institution. The décor is dark and sophisticated and strongly reminiscent of an indulgent Old Europe, and the service makes you feel positively aristocratic. The menu is

extremely rich and dominated by beluga, osetra, and sevruga caviar, salmon roe, and various smoked fish. The best thing to do is to order the chef's tasting menu and sample a little of everything with a cocktail or glass of cold Champagne.
182 WEST 58TH STREET AT SEVENTH AVENUE IN MANHATTAN. Subway: 1, A, C, B, D to 59th Street-Columbus Circle. 212-245-2214. www.petrossian.com.

497. Have the house-infused vodkas at the **Russian Vodka Room**. This scruffy Theater District haunt doesn't have the look of authenticity one might expect, but rest assured that if vodka's your thing, you've come to the right place. There are many exotic flavors of house-infused vodka—such as apple and pomegranate, and garlic, pepper, and dill—which you can have in a mixed drink or in a generously sized shot.
265 WEST 52ND STREET BETWEEN EIGHTH AVENUE AND BROADWAY IN MANHATTAN. Subway: C, E, to 50th Street; 1 to 50th Street. 212-307-5835. www.russianvodkaroom.com.

POLISH:

The Brooklyn neighborhood of Greenpoint, which bleeds down into Williamsburg and along the East River toward Queens, is the most densely Polish part of New York and the place to go if you've got a hankering for kielbasa and cabbage salad. Walk around the area between Manhattan Avenue, Greenpoint Avenue, and Nassau Avenue, and you'll discover a whole community of Polish butchers, bakeries, cafés, and restaurants serving genuine Polish cuisine with unceremonious authenticity. If you're looking for Polish treats to take home, try Jaslowiczanka Bakery (163 Nassau Avenue, 718-389-0263) for fresh rolls and pancakes, and Poznanski's (668 Manhattan Avenue, 718-383-3908) for delicious smoked and treated meats. If you're looking for a place to sit down and eat Warsaw-style, try one of the following places.
Subway: G to Greenpoint Avenue or Nassau Avenue; L to Bedford Avenue.

498. Raymund's Place. Vegetarians beware: between the goulash, the veal schnitzel, the kielbasa, and the pig's knuckles, the menu at Raymund's revolves around carnivore classics, and only the delicious sides—the pickles, the borscht, and the potato pancakes—might be said to be without animal. Our tip is to come here for an early lunch, when Bedford Avenue is peaceful and the atmosphere of the restaurant transports you to a side street in Warsaw.
124 BEDFORD AVENUE AT NORTH 10TH STREET IN BROOKLYN. Subway: L to Bedford Avenue. 718-383-8993.

499. Antek. Stepping into Antek is like stepping into a Communist cafeteria: the décor is sparse to say the least, and the cheap metal and Formica make you wonder whether the knives, forks, and chairs will be chained to the tables. If that isn't enough to convince you of the authenticity of this Polish treasure, take a tray up to the counter and point out your meat, potato, beet, borscht, and pickle combination of choice. The food is surprisingly good, and with the atmosphere reliant entirely on the conversation of the diners (most of whom will be Polish), you'll find the whole experience thoroughly unique. *105 NORMAN AVENUE AT GREENPOINT AVENUE IN BROOKLYN. Subway: G to Nassau Avenue. 718-383-4382.*

GREEK:

500. If you're looking for fish so fresh it's practically swimming, head to the **Greek Captain Fish Market** in Long Island City.
32-10 36TH AVENUE IN QUEENS. Subway: 7 to 45 Road-Courthouse Square; G to Long Island City-Court Square. 718-786-6015.

501. For an excellent Greek meal that's less fish focused, visit **Periyali**. The atmosphere at this Flatiron restaurant is more subdued than what you might expect of a Greek restaurant, as befitting the excellent, refined renditions of traditional dishes and Greek home cooking.
35 WEST 20TH STREET BETWEEN FIFTH AND SIXTH AVENUES IN MANHATTAN. Subway: N, R, W to 23rd Street; F, V to 23rd Street. 212-463-7890. www.periyali.com.

GERMAN AND AUSTRIAN:

502. Eat upscale Austrian at one of **Kurt Gutenbrunner's restaurants.** A native of Austria, Chef Gutenbrunner has carved a tasty niche in the New York City food scene for this formerly underrepresented cuisine with four high-profile Austrian restaurants. His first, **Wallsé**, named for the small village near the Danube where he grew up, endeared New York foodies to dishes like spätzle, wiener schnitzel, and *kavalierspitz*, a boiled-beef dish. **Blaue Gans** is a casual *würsthaus*, the Austrian equivalent of a brasserie, with lots of sausage, sauerkraut, and schnitzel, along with German and Austrian wines. He also runs **Café Sabarsky,** the elegant Viennese *kaffeehaus* in the **Neue Galerie** (see page 126), one of the loveliest museum eateries in the city, where you can enjoy savory and sweet Viennese treats for breakfast, lunch, or a midday snack. N.B. If you arrive at Wallse and discover there is a wait, head two doors down to the Upholstery Store (713 Washington Avenue), a tiny bar also owned by Gutenbrunner that is not strictly German or Austrian but is mighty charming.
Blaue Gans: 139 DUANE STREET BETWEEN WEST BROADWAY AND CHURCH STREET IN MAN-

HATTAN. *Subway: 1, 2, 3, A, C to Chambers Street. 212-571-8880. Café Sabarsky: 1048 FIFTH AVENUE AT 86*TH *STREET IN MANHATTAN. Subway: 4, 5, 6 to 86*th *Street. 212-288-0665. Wallsé: 344 WEST 11*TH *STREET AT WASHINGTON STREET IN MANHATTAN. Subway: A, C, E to 14*th *Street; L to Eighth Avenue. 212-352-2300. www.wallse.com.*

503. Enjoy the view (and the veal) at **Café Select**. Until Café Select opened in 2008 on the fringes of NoLita, it would have been difficult to say the neighborhood was incomplete without reliable Alpine cuisine. But after only a year or so, the modest-looking middle-European diner has made an indelible stamp on the downtown palette, serving up clean, classic German, Swiss, and Austrian dishes on checkered tablecloths and accompanying them with a suitably Alpine wine list. As tends to be the case with Germanic menus, the simplest dishes are the best: try the veal schnitzel with a glass of white wine recommended by your waiter, or go there for brunch and enjoy perfectly poached eggs with their succulent *rösti* (fried potato patties). In summer, with the front windows wide open onto a pretty and quiet stretch of Lafayette Street—and with its fair share of downtown faces to look out for—Select embodies something of the true spirit of a European café.
212 LAFAYETTE STREET AT KENMARE STREET IN MANHATTAN. Subway: 6 to Spring Street. 212-925-9322. www.cafeselectnyc.com.

SCANDINAVIAN:

504. Enjoy a purist's Scandinavian dining experience at **Aquavit**. To eat at Aquavit is to immerse yourself in Scandinavian culture, from the rich and varied regional menus to the cool, transporting interiors. Aquavit spreads across three separate rooms, each distinguished by the particular type of Scandinavian cuisine it serves. In the bar, small savory snacks like salted herring accompany good European wine and beer, and drinkers lounge on sleek modernist furniture by Arne Jacobsen. The café has an informal, local feel, with a light menu that includes seafood salads and other perfect lunch dishes from cauliflower soup to cold fish sandwiches. The restaurant's main dining room is light and elegant, an austere and refreshing setting for an extravagant menu that mixes Scandinavian tradition with West European flavors, from foie gras with cherry chutney to indulgent seafood samplers, heavily salted ox tongue, and one of the best lobster rolls in the city (served with trout roe, apples, and a bacon and egg dressing). We recommend you try the Sunday smorgasbord buffet, Aquavit's perfect sampler of meats, fish, cheeses, and breads.
*65 EAST 55*TH *STREET BETWEEN PARK AND MADISON AVENUES IN MANHATTAN. Subway: 6 to 51*st *Street; E, V to Lexington Avenue/53*rd *Street. 212-307-7311. www.aquavit.org.*
505. Get out of the weekday lunch rut with an authentic Scandinavian meal at **Smor-**

gas Chef. You can trade in steam tables and salad bars for an authentic smorgasbord, along with other Nordic delicacies like North Sea shrimp, meatballs with jam, and, of course, herring. N.B. Smorgas also operates a beautiful café on the first floor of the ***Scandinavia House*** (see page 302).

All locations in Manhattan. 53 STONE STREET BETWEEN BROAD STREET AND HANOVER SQUARE. 212-422-3500; 283 WEST 12TH STREET AT WEST 4TH STREET. 212-243-7073.

Scandinavia House: 58 PARK AVENUE AT 38TH STREET IN MANHATTAN. 212-847-9745. Subway: 4, 5, 6, 7, S to Grand Central-42nd Street.

For more details on locations and directions visit www.smorgaschef.com.

JAPANESE:

506. Take a trip to ***Village Yokocho.*** This slice of Japan on Stuyvesant Street is like a quiet Tokyo neighborhood that has been transported to the second floor of a building in the East Village, incorporating a restaurant, bar, and grocery store. Yajirobei, the restaurant on the second floor, is lively and comfortable, and the food is authentic and delicious. Though the atmosphere is distinctly Japanese, the menu is pan-Asian and ranges from traditional fish, rice, and noodle dishes to skewered meats and vegetables, which you can eat seated at a wooden bar around the grill. Afterward, walk through the restaurant to the wooden door at the end, which discreetly leads into one of the East Village's best-kept secrets: **Angel's Share**, a dark, sophisticated cocktail bar with a Japanese accent and huge windows overlooking the street (bear in mind that you may have to wait in line: Angel's Share admits on a one-in/one-out basis). Right next door to Yajirobei, above the **St. Mark's Bookshop** (see page 341), is the **Sunrise Mart**, New York's finest Japanese supermarket. Stocking everything from Japanese candy to fresh fish, fruit, vegetables, and prepared foods for lunch, it is the best place for authentic Japanese ingredients—and it's the most colorful grocery store in the city by a mile.

Village Yokocho and Angel Share: 8 STUYVESANT STREET BETWEEN THIRD AVENUE AND EAST 9TH STREET IN MANHATTAN. Village Yokocho: 212-598-3041. Angel Share: 212-777-5415. Sunrise Mart: 4 STUYVESANT STREET BETWEEN THIRD AVENUE AND EAST 9TH STREET IN MANHATTAN. 212-598-3040. Subway: 6 to Astor Place.

507. Have afternoon tea with an Eastern influence at ***Cha An***, a peaceful refuge of restorative tea and freshly prepared food. At Cha An, tea is prepared and served in traditional Japanese style and with meticulous care and precision. Choose a tea from the extensive menu, which explains the background and flavor of each variety. Match it with one of the set teas, which include anything from a Japanese take on scones and clotted cream to fresh salmon, tea-infused rice cakes, vegetable dishes, and culture-clash desserts like a sesame-seed–encrusted crème brulée. The staff is among the most courteous and thoughtful in the city; presentation is beautiful, and there is no calmer atmosphere in town. (Don't miss **Cha An's restrooms**—see page 351.)

230 EAST 9TH STREET BETWEEN SECOND AND THIRD AVENUES IN MANHATTAN. Subway: 6 to Astor Place. 212-228-8030.

508. Quench your craving for ramen at **Rairaiken**. Rairaiken, in the East Village, is one of the few ramen bars in New York to come close to its Japanese counterparts: push through the red curtains at the door and you'll find a short wooden bar, comfy bar stools, excellent music, a warm and informal atmosphere, and a menu that covers everything from tasty *gyoza* (dumplings) to *yaki soba* (fried noodles). But you've come here for the ramen, and one bowl of theirs will cure any wanderer's appetite. The ramen range from the mild and garlicky *miso* to the spicier *curry ramen* and the addictive *shio* (the house special, with roast pork, seaweed, and egg).

214 EAST 10TH STREET AND 1ST AVENUE IN MANHATTAN. Subway: 6 to Astor Place; 4, 5, L, Q, N, R, W to 14th Street. 212-477-7030.

509. Brave the lines at **Tomoe Sushi**. Depression-era lines are usually enough to knock any restaurant out of consideration for this book, but as any local sushi fan will tell you, this reservation-adverse restaurant has the freshest ingredients in the city. If you want the highest quality sushi in the city, well, get in line.

172 THOMPSON STREET BETWEEN BLEECKER AND HOUSTON STREETS. Subway: A, C, E, B, D, F, V to West 4th Street. 212-777-9346.

510. Spend the night eating your fill at **Donguri**. This beautiful and stylish yet traditional Japanese restaurant is small enough to maintain a warm, cozy atmosphere, but offers food that is at once true to Japanese tradition and among the most sophisticated in the city. The décor is coolly soothing, with exposed brick walls and dark wood furniture, and the place feels like an oasis of calm amid the busy blocks of the Upper East Side. Every dish, from finely balanced sashimi to deliciously savory grilled meats and sweet boiled vegetables, is meticulously prepared and beautifully presented. Rather than ordering a full meal at once, the chef's recommendation is that you sit and order one or two dishes at a time. Ask for assorted sashimi, and cross your fingers that the day's special is oysters.

309 EAST 83RD STREET BETWEEN FIRST AND SECOND AVENUES IN MANHATTAN. Subway: 4, 5, 6 to 86th Street. 212-737-5656.

511. Meet a friend for a long, boozy lunch in the middle of the week at **Old Town Bar**.

The "timeless" (read: ungentrified) décor and crew of regulars at the bar are conducive to midweek drinking, and the high-backed wooden booths offer excellent cover in case your boss walks by.

45 EAST 18TH STREET BETWEEN BROADWAY AND PARK AVENUE SOUTH IN MANHATTAN. www.oldtownbar.com. Subway: 4, 5, 6, L, N, Q, R, W to 14th Street-Union Square. 212-529-6732.

512. Pretend you're in the movie business at **Relish**.

A former restaurant that was closed for decades, for a time this diner opened its doors only for directors and cameramen who used its classic interiors as sets for countless New York movies. Now that it's back in business, it's far enough from the Bedford strip to be quieter than most of Williamsburg's hip eateries but still good enough to warrant lines on a weekend, it's as big and spacious as something you'd find on a highway a thousand miles west of the city, and has a menu to fit. Classic diner dishes from eggs and omelets to burgers and tuna melts are infused with spicy Spanish and Cajun flavors, so even the comfort food packs a punch, and the milkshakes are particularly tasty. Come late, approaching the neon lights and the rounded chrome roof in the dark, and hunker down in a cozy booth—you'll feel like you're in a movie yourself. (Note: though Relish is a diner, it's not open round the clock. For our favorite **24-hour diners and eating establishments**, see pages 335–341.)

225 WYTHE STREET AT NORTH 3RD STREET IN BROOKLYN. Subway: L to Bedford Avenue. 718-963-4546. www.relish.com.

513. Have a different hot chocolate shot every day of February at **City Bakery**.

It sounds like a gimmick, but as anyone who's ever tried to take on a full cup can tell you, one shot is really all you need. City Bakery's hot chocolate is sinfully rich and deliriously tasty; a shot topped with one of their homemade marshmallows is pretty much the best thing going in the winter months. During hot chocolate month in February, they offer a different flavor concoction each day, from hot chocolate infused with ginger or vanilla bean to cocao made with malted milk or spiked with bourbon.

3 WEST 18TH STREET BETWEEN FIFTH AND SIXTH AVENUES IN MANHATTAN. Subway: 1 to 18th Street. 212-366-1414. Visit www.hotchocolatefestival.com for a calendar of flavors.

514. Have a cheese plate at Artisanal, New York's favorite fromagerie. This Midtown bistro is dedicated to cheese, from hundreds of varieties available in the cheese cave to the dishes on the menu, which include addictive gougères (French cheese puffs), macaroni and cheese, and excellent fondues. For a real treat, go to the cheese counter, and have them fix you a personalized plate. The menu also includes a section of recommended wine and cheese (and beer and cheese) pairings. But take our advice and plan carefully, or risk waking up the next morning with a fromage hangover.

2 PARK AVENUE AT 32ND STREET IN MANHATTAN. Subway: 6 to 33rd Street. 212-725-8585. www.artisanalbistro.com.

515. Check out a new restaurant during Restaurant Week.

Though we've got four-star restaurants, plenty of celebrity chefs, and some famously inventive cooking, the prices (or the month-long waits for reservations) discourage many of us from trying them out. But twice a year, New Yorkers get a chance to taste what the critics are writing about. During the two Restaurant Weeks, usually held in January and July, restaurants all over the city—from the fanciest and the trendiest to neighborhood joints and old-time classics—offer prix fixe three-course meals at lunch and/or dinner for bargain prices (around $20 for lunch, $35 for dinner). How good a deal it is depends on the restaurant and your taste (the offerings are often from a limited, prix fixe menu, which can make things difficult for vegetarians, those with restricted diets, and picky eaters), and reservations at the more upscale places can be tough to get. (Tip: Be ready to make your reservations as soon as the list is announced.) But a three-course meal for under $40 anywhere in the city is a pretty good deal. N.B. Some restaurants extend the Restaurant Week prix fixe deal past the city's official date and in recent years, the official Restaurant Week has lasted longer than seven days. (In 2009, summer restaurant week was extended through Labor Day.)

For more information, dates, prices, and a list of participating restaurants, visit www.NYCgo.com/restaurantweek.

516. Dinner and a song at Asia Roma...

There are plenty of good karaoke spots around town, but this restaurant and underground karaoke bar on the cusp of Chinatown and Little Italy has a unique bicultural flair. Look out for the resident house singer, a veritable Chinese Sinatra in white gloves, who is only too happy to step up to the mic when the crowd falls quiet.

40 MULBERRY STREET BETWEEN BAYARD AND WORTH STREETS IN MANHATTAN. Subway: 1 to Franklin Street; A, C, E to Canal Street. 212-385-1133. www.asiaroma.com.

517. ...or if you're looking for a seedier sing-song, head to Winnie's, a smaller bar near the courthouse, where Winnie, the glamorous proprietress, presides over a colorful cast of karaoke characters who rock the mic in Mandarin and Michael Jackson.
104 BAYARD STREET BETWEEN MULBERRY AND BAXTER STREETS IN MANHATTAN. Subway: A, C, E to Canal Street. 212-732-2384.

Feast on **bar snacks**...

Bar owners struggle like aspiring Broadway stars to make it on the NYC nightlife scene, so it should come as no surprise that they even get creative about the snacks they serve. Forgo peanuts and potato chips and sample some of following gratis bar-top delights:

518. *Hot dogs at Rudy's Bar & Grill.* Unbelievably, this old-school, red-leather, jukebox-sporting dive bar dispenses free hot dogs—as many as you want, whenever you want them. Order seven, just because you can, then eat them off a paper plate in the pig-themed backyard with a pitcher of Rudy's special red beer. Around $3 a pint, it's a bargain in itself.
627 NINTH AVENUE BETWEEN 44TH AND 45TH STREETS IN MANHATTAN. Subway: 1, 2, 3, 7, N, Q, R, S to Times Square-42nd Street; A, C, E to 42nd Street-Port Authority Bus Terminal. 212-974-9169.

519. *Goldfish crackers and wasabi peas at Tom & Jerry.* If you don't see them on the bar, ask the bartender and you'll get a huge bowl of good old-fashioned Goldfish crackers and wasabi peas to help your beer go down.
288 ELIZABETH STREET BETWEEN HOUSTON AND BLEECKER STREETS IN MANHATTAN. Subway: 6 to Bleecker Street; B, D, F, V to Broadway-Lafayette Street. 212-274-8787.

520. *Pizza at Buttermilk.* On Wednesday nights (and on the occasional quiet Sunday), the staff at this friendly Park Slope bar order pizza from a local take-out place for all to enjoy. To go with your slice, ask for Connect 4, Battleship, or any of the classic board games kept behind the bar, and then grab a booth for a low-key, low-cost evening out.
577 FIFTH AVENUE AT 16TH STREET IN BROOKLYN. Subway: F to 15th Street-Prospect Park. 718-788-6297.

521: *Vegetarian apps at Counter.* Amazingly, this swank East Village veggie restaurant offers all of the appetizers on their regular menu for free at the bar, Sunday through Thursday. The extensive list of small plates includes soups, salads, and gourmet French fries.
105 FIRST AVENUE BETWEEN SIXTH AND SEVENTH STREETS IN MANHATTAN. Subway: L to First Avenue; F, V to Lower East Side-Second Avenue. 212-982-5870. www.counternyc.com.

522. ***The Brazen Head*** on Atlantic Avenue has a weekly roster of free nibbles to go with various activities, so choose your pleasure. Come Mondays for darts and free chicken wings; Wednesday (Ladies' Night) for cheese and discounts on wine; and Sunday mornings for $5 Bloody Marys and a complimentary bagel bar with all the fixings (cream cheese, onions, etc.)

288 ATLANTIC AVENUE, AT COURT STREET IN BROOKLYN. Subway: F, G to Bergen Street. 718-488-0430. www.brazenheadbrooklyn.com.

...or get dinner **delivered to the bar** you're drinking at.

Sometimes you need something more substantial than snacks while you're drinking. Like everywhere else, many New York restaurants have bar menus, and many bars have kitchens. But if you prefer something simple and greasy, you're in luck, too. Plenty of laid-back dives keep a stack of delivery menus behind the bar; all you have to do is ask. They're happy to have you order in from a neighborhood joint if it keeps you drinking there. What you get depends on the area, but when you're two sheets to the wind, it's hard to go wrong with pizza or Chinese. However, there are some bars that benefit from their proximity to some particularly good take-out grub. Two good pairings:

523. Drinking beer in the garden at the ***Gate***, and ordering fish and chips wrapped in newspaper from the ***ChipShop***, Brooklyn's answer to A Salt and Battery and the finest battered sausage and fried Mars bar this side of Blighty.

321 FIFTH AVENUE AT 3RD STREET IN BROOKLYN. Subway: F to 4th Avenue; M, R to 9th Street. Phone: 718-768-4329.

CHIPSHOP: *383 FIFTH AVENUE AT 6TH STREET IN BROOKLYN. Subway as above. 718-832-7701. www.chipshopnyc.com.*

524. Drinking and listening to bands at the legendary ***Arlene's Grocery***, and ordering hot sandwiches from ***Katz's*** (see page 170).

95 STANTON STREET BETWEEN LUDLOW AND ORCHARD STREETS IN MANHATTAN. Subway: F, V to Lower East Side-Second Avenue. 212-995-1652. www.arlenesgrocery.net.

---

525. Find **Freeman's**.

Freeman's is an unusual restaurant in every way, a hidden treasure among the hipster hangouts on the Lower East Side. Finding it is part of the fun: turn off Rivington Street just west of the Bowery onto Freeman Alley. The giant wooden doors at the alley's end open into one of the coolest and most inviting restaurants in the city. The real treat, however, is the spectacular display of taxidermy that decorates the walls. Depending on what you order, you may find a relative of your supper staring down at you while you eat.

END OF FREEMAN ALLEY, OFF RIVINGTON STREET, BETWEEN BOWERY AND CHRYSTIE STREET IN MANHATTAN. Subway: F to Delancey Street; J, M, Z to Essex Street. 212-420-0012. www.free-mansrestaurant.com.

526. Have your sandwich the way they want you to at **The Adore**.

The Union Square area's best-kept secret is this petite sandwich shop, which has a charming upstairs seating area and serves perfect baguette sandwiches. But leave the particular eaters at home: the chef will make only substitutions that he approves of (a request to hold the cheese on a sandwich with grilled squash is OK; the same request on a sandwich with grilled portobello is not), and will not provide condiments other than the ones specified for each sandwich on the menu. Submit to this slight bit of tyranny, and you will be fed well, we promise. All sandwiches are available with a bowl of soup or salad for two dollars extra. If potato leek is on the menu, don't think twice. *17 EAST 13TH STREET IN MANHATTAN. Subway: 4, 5, 6, L, N, R, Q, W. 212-243-8742.*

527. Play bocce while you drink at **Floyd NY**.

In true melting-pot style, this unpretentious Brooklyn bar serves bourbon and beercheese and also sports an indoor bocce court. Try your hand on the forty-foot clay court while you munch on the Kentucky beercheese, a highly addictive blend of cheese, beer, and spices. *131 ATLANTIC AVENUE BETWEEN HENRY AND CLINTON STREETS IN BROOKLYN. Subway: 2, 3, 4, 5 to Borough Hall; N, R to Court Street-Borough Hall. 718-858-5810. www.floydny.com.*

528. Take your time beneath the Williamsburg Bridge at **Marlow & Sons** ...

On a quiet corner of Broadway in South Williamsburg, on the way to the river under the Williamsburg Bridge, Marlow & Sons is one of Brooklyn's gems and one of the best restaurants in the city. With outside seating, a deli full of imported treats in the entrance hall, and a cozy wine bar at the back, the restaurant manages to be everything at once, and is wonderful to eat at whatever the season. When it's warm enough to sit outside, go there for fresh oysters and white wine. In the wintertime, you won't find anywhere more romantic than one of the small wooden tables in the back, where you can order hearty modern American dishes with southern flavors, from corn chowder to the famous brick chicken. And their menu of cold cuts, cheeses, and salads is large and thoughtful enough to make sitting at the bar with a few plates and a bottle of wine as enjoyable as a full meal. Just make sure you leave room for the salted chocolate cake... *81 BROADWAY AT BERRY STREET IN BROOKLYN. Subway: J, M, Z to Marcy Avenue. 718-384-1441. www.marlowandsons.com.*

529. ...or pop in for a cheeseburger at **Diner next door**.

Diner is Marlow & Sons' scruffy elder sibling. Situated right next to Marlow, in a restored old-school diner that has a long wooden bar lined with small and comfy booths along the windows, Diner takes all the love, thought, care, and attention that goes into Marlow's menus and pours it into simple, homely diner fare, from pork and eggs and grits for brunch to their impeccable and juicy burgers for dinner. The burger is the only thing on the dinner menu, but there are different specials every day, from steaks to lamb chops and fish, and the food is always designed to be hearty, filling, and delicious. And best of all, there are crayons and paper place mats.

85 BROADWAY AT BERRY STREET IN BROOKLYN. Subway: J, M, Z to Marcy Avenue. 718-486-3077. www.dinernyc.com.

530. Let sake bring out your literary inclinations, and compose poems **on the wall at Decibel**.

Though this underground sake den has an illicit feel, go ahead and write on the walls. They're cool.

240 EAST 9TH STREET BETWEEN SECOND AND THIRD AVENUES IN MANHATTAN. Subway: 6 to Astor Place; L to Third Avenue; N, R to 8th Street-New York University. 212-979-2733. www.sakebardecibel.com.

531. Have lunch in the **Delegates' Dining Room** at the UN.

Forget Per Se—if you really want to impress someone, take him or her to lunch at the Delegates Dining Room at the **UN** (see page 20). Though it's open to the public (with reservations), this refined commissary feels elite, exclusive, cosmopolitan, and miles away from Midtown midday madness (perhaps that's because the UN is technically an international territory). For $27, you get an abundant lunch buffet, as well as the chance to rub shoulders with some real international superstars—plus a superb view, courtesy of the wall-to-ceiling windows that overlook the East River.

Lunch is served weekdays from 11:30 a.m. to 2:30 p.m. Reservations should be made a day in advance by calling 212-963-7625. No jeans or sneakers allowed; jacket required for men. All diners must bring a photo ID. Use the visitor's entrance on FIRST AVENUE AT 46TH STREET IN MANHATTAN. Subway: 4, 5, 6, 7, S to Grand Central-42nd Street. For more information, visit www.aramark-un.com or www.un.org.

532. Feed nature and yourself at the **New Leaf Café**...

Set in a stone structure between the **Cloisters** (see page 121) and the main entrance of Fort Tryon Park, the New Leaf Café is a uniquely pleasant dining experience that benefits more than just your stomach. Proceeds from the café support the upkeep of the park. *ONE MARGARET CORBIN DRIVE, FORT TRYON PARK IN MANHATTAN. Subway: A to 190th. Street. 212-568-5323. www.nyrp.org/newleaf.*

533. ...or feed your sweet tooth for a good cause at the **Sweet Things Bake Shop**.

This shop is run by the Lower East Side Girls Club, and all the goodies here are made by girls enrolled in an entrepreneurial baking program, Sweet Things. So the cookie you buy supports educational and skill-building programs for local children. And who knows—the girl who baked it might go on to be New York's next master chef. *136 AVENUE C BETWEEN 8TH AND 9TH STREETS IN MANHATTAN. Subway: L to First Avenue. 212-982-1714. www.girlsclub.org/store.*

Slices of New York.

Though we didn't come up with it ourselves, pizza was long ago adopted by New Yorkers and raised as one of our own. The ingenious invention of Italian immigrants more than a century ago, pizza is the perfect meeting of old Italian cuisine and the New York lifestyle. While it can be found all over the world, and different places have different styles, we know that our version is the best. There are pizzerias and take-out pizza parlors all over the five boroughs, and with so many varieties of pie out there, we thought we'd throw in our two cents and give you a shortlist of what we consider the ten best pizzas in town (also see **Lombardi's**, on pages 47–48):

534. *Arturo's:* Almost as old as Lombardi's, and almost as good, eating at Arturo's feels like being in a friend's kitchen. *106 WEST HOUSTON STREET AT THOMPSON STREET IN MANHATTAN. Subway: 6 to Bleecker Street; B, D, F, V to Broadway-Lafayette Street. 212-677-3820.*

535. *Grimaldi's:* You can't get pizza like this in Manhattan—really—the coal ovens they use are illegal in the borough. Go for the meat toppings. *19 OLD FULTON STREET UNDER THE BROOKLYN BRIDGE IN BROOKLYN. Subway: A, C to High Street. 718-858-4300. www.grimaldis.com/Brooklyn.htm.*

536. *John's of Bleecker Street:* Legendarily delicious pies, but remember: they don't sell by the slice.
278 BLEECKER STREET BETWEEN SIXTH AND SEVENTH AVENUES IN MANHATTAN. Subway: 1 to Christopher Street-Sheridan Square; A, C, E, B, D, F, V to West 4th Street. 212-243-1680. www.johnsofbleeckerstreet.com.

537. *Full Moon:* What looks like an unremarkable pie-by-the-slice parlor serves some of the tastiest pizzas in the city.
600 EAST 187TH STREET AT ARTHUR AVENUE IN THE BRONX. See page 188 for full directions. 718-584-3451.

538. *L'asso:* This unassuming pizzeria on the fringes of Little Italy has delicious pies with surprising toppings: try the smoked tartufo.
192 MOTT STREET AT KENMARE STREET IN MANHATTAN. Subway: 6 to Spring Street; F to Delancey Street; J, M, Z to Essex Street. 212-219-2353. www.lassonyc.com.

539. *Franny's:* The garden at this popular spot is as comfortable as your own backyard—if your backyard served some of the best pizza in the city.
FLATBUSH AVENUE BETWEEN ST. MARK'S AVENUE AND PROSPECT PLACE IN BROOKLYN. Subway: 2, 3 to Bergen Street; B, Q to Seventh Avenue. 718-230-0221. www.frannysbrooklyn.com.

540. *Di Fara:* Two-hour lines and $5 slices don't deter local pizza nuts from making pilgrimages to Midwood for a taste of what many claim is the ultimate NYC slice.
1424 AVENUE J BETWEEN 14TH AND 15TH STREETS IN BROOKLYN. Subway: Q to Avenue J. 718-258-1367. www.difara.com.

541. *Artichoke:* The signature spinach-and-artichoke slice weighs a ton and could feed an army, and yet it's still not enough to satisfy this joint's rabid fan base. A brilliant combination of an unexpected flavor with superior pizza-crafting expertise.
328 WEST 14TH STREET BETWEEN FIRST AND SECOND AVENUES IN MANHATTAN. Subway: L to First Avenue. 212-228-2004. www.artichokepizza.com.

542. *Joe's:* Pizza that manages to be both incredibly crispy and amazingly heavy with cheese and toppings.
7 CARMINE STREET AT SIXTH AVENUE IN MANHATTAN. Subway: A, C, E, B, D, F, V to West 4th Street. 212-255-3946.

543. *Viva Herbal Pizzeria:* Pizza purists should not scoff at Viva's unconventional vegetarian pizzas. The monstrous slices are just as messy as those at any of the other joints on our list, and they certainly don't taste virtuous. Try a slice with green tea-infused tofu, mountains of vegetables, and pesto on a spelt crust. (Viva's is kosher, too.)

179 SECOND AVENUE BETWEEN 11TH AND 12TH STREETS IN MANHATTAN. Subway: L to First or Third Avenues. 212-420-8801.

CHAPTER 6:

The Great Outdoors

Despite being the greatest metropolis in the world, New York isn't all sidewalks and skyscrapers. We've got an ocean, rivers, lakes, wildlife refuges, and nearly 30,000 acres of parks and gardens across the five boroughs—not bad for a place known as a concrete jungle. In addition, we've got plenty of people with different athletic pursuits and passions; the same diversity and vivaciousness that's responsible for the city's wide variety of arts and culture also colors the out-of-doors, so along with all of the traditional activities (baseball, basketball, running, cycling, and gardening), we've got cricket leagues, bocce tournaments, and a trapeze school.

In this chapter, we cover the best of outdoor fun, including parks and gardens; nature, wildlife, and zoos; water-related activities; and outdoor sports. One of the interesting things about outdoor activities in New York is how, in different ways, they combine the available natural resources—rivers, beaches, the ocean, and green spaces—with the unique qualities the city has to offer. Outdoor activities in New York are not pathetic, shrunken versions of their natural selves; rather, they are adapted for and enhanced by the particular conditions of city living. We have special Urban Rangers to protect our parks, a state-of-the-art riverfront sports complex on top of a waste treatment plant, and excellent beaches and golf courses only a subway ride away. In fact, one of the most amazing things about the outdoor pursuits around the city is how easily accessible they are. You don't need a car or a long weekend to visit a wildlife center, or go horseback riding, surfing, or canoeing—every activity you can imagine is right here.

Another wonderful part of New York's outdoor culture is how we turn some urban, typically indoor activities outside when the weather gets nice. Outdoor movies, yoga and tai chi classes, concerts, readings, and fairs and festivals abound during the warmer months (for street fairs and festivals, see Chapter 3). Enjoying the arts al fresco can also be a great way to see exciting, world-renowned performances without breaking the bank, since many of these events are free.

There is a wealth of opportunities for enjoying the outdoors across the five boroughs, all year long, from cross-country skiing in the streets after a blizzard to swimming in the ocean or one of the city's public pools during the dog days of summer. The activities we've listed below are the best of hundreds we discovered all over town. So next time you hear someone talking about the lack of open spaces and natural beauty here, just take them outside.

Parks & Gardens

No matter where you are in New York, you're never far from greenery or floral beauty. There are more than 1,700 parks across the city, including playgrounds and ball fields as well as forests and woodlands, and many exquisite gardens, from the botanical gardens found in three of the five boroughs (Brooklyn, the Bronx, and Staten Island) to the lovely community gardens maintained by various volunteer and neighborhood groups.

These bucolic oases are perfect for unstructured retreats, but they also offer organized activities that anyone can take advantage of. The Parks Department, which oversees all of the city parks, runs sports lessons and education programs for kids and adults, gives walks and tours, and puts on hundreds of events, most of which are free. Their Web site (www.nyc.gov/parks) has a list of facilities and programs for all of the parks in the five boroughs, plus maps, opening hours, calendars of events, and much more.

544. Stop and **smell the flowers** all around the city.

If you think that the freshest flowers in New York come from the **Greenmarket** (see page 334), you're in for a shock. Our parks have a surprising amount of floral variety. The Parks Department has created a Citywide Blooming Guide, so you can find out what's in bloom and where to find it. This online guide lists the names of local flora and where they are located (with pictures, for novices), arranged by month. Pick a park, and then see how many you can identify; or, when you come across an unfamiliar blossom in an unlikely place, look it up on the site.

To access the citywide blooming guide, visit www.nycgovparks.org, click on "Things to Do," and visit the "Special Interest" section.

545. Get inside **Gramercy Park**.

This old-fashioned and entirely undemocratic gated park is an exceptional detail on the New York City landscape, and its exclusivity is part of its charm—and history. In 1831, Samuel Ruggles purchased a piece of swampland to develop into real estate. At the time, few New Yorkers wanted to live so far uptown, but Ruggles attracted an elite demographic with the creation of a pristine private park reserved for residents of his development, believing that the well-heeled would be enticed by the promise of a

beautiful, well-manicured outdoor space in Manhattan (this was two decades before Central Park) that was off-limits to the less fortunate. Today it is still New York's only private park, belonging, as per Ruggles's arrangement, to the inhabitants of the homes and apartments surrounding it as a sort of shared front yard. Each building is allotted a certain number of park keys, which residents (renters and owners) are free to use; additional keys for individual residents may be purchased for $350 each. Key holders are understandably protective of their pristine outdoor space, so there are plenty of rules on permissible activities, conduct, and entrants. But though it doesn't welcome the type of freewheeling fun you'll find in most parks, it does offer a rare sense of calm and is a true urban escape—to anyone who can get in. The park is open to the public on Christmas Day, Yom Kippur, and on certain other days of the year for neighborhood events. Otherwise, you'll have to make friends with someone with a home around the park. Just don't try to sneak in behind a key holder—they tend to get litigious.
20ᵀᴴ TO 21ˢᵀ STREETS BETWEEN LEXINGTON AVENUE AND IRVING PLACE IN MANHATTAN. Subway: 6 to 23ʳᵈ Street.

---

546. Walk the length of the **Battery Park City parks**, and explore all the secret coves and hidden harbors along the way.

The parks, pathways, and gardens of Battery Park City cover a long and scenic stretch of the lower West Side, running beside the Hudson River from Wagner Park at the southernmost tip of Manhattan to Rockefeller Park and the piers around Chambers Street. While Battery Park City is a burgeoning neighborhood of new apartments, quiet offices, and cultural offerings, the parks along the Hudson remain relatively peaceful and extremely pleasant to roam around. As well as the popular tree-lined esplanades, there are a number of lesser-known and almost hidden gardens that are great fun to discover along the way. Look out for the old cast-iron benches hidden in the trees above the pathway at South Cove, the chess tables in Rector Park, and the secret "scholar's garden" off the busy harbor at North Cove. There are also some interesting public artworks—for more on those, see page 144.
BATTERY PARK CITY PARKS FROM WAGNER PARK TO ROCKEFELLER PARK IN MANHATTAN. Subway: 1, 2, 3, A, C to Chambers Street (to walk south along the water); 1 to Rector Street (to walk north along the water). www.bpcparks.org.

---

547. Listen to **jazz outdoors** in two of the city's nicest parks.

In honor of Charlie Parker, one of the jazz world's greatest and most lasting influences, a full weekend in late summer each year is devoted to the music he wrote, played, and inspired. Because Parker divided his working life between Harlem and the East Village, the Charlie Parker Jazz Festival begins on Saturday in Marcus Garvey Park and concludes on Sunday in Tompkins Square Park. Although the event draws some of the best and most respected new talent in the world to its stage—recent players have included Vanessa Rubin, Jimmy Heath, and Geri Allen—the weekend is all about being outside in the fresh air, and the musicians seem to enjoy the summer sunshine as much as the audiences. The festival takes place at the same time as the *Howl! Festival* (see pages 87–88), so there are plenty of other things going on in the neighborhood that weekend as well.

The Charlie Parker Jazz Festival is held annually on the last weekend in August. MARCUS GAR-VEY PARK IS JUST SOUTH OF 125TH STREET IN HARLEM. Subway: 2, 3, 4, 5, 6 to 125th Street. TOMPKINS SQUARE PARK IS BETWEEN AVENUES A AND B, RUNNING FROM EAST 7TH TO EAST 10TH STREETS. Subway: F, V to Lower East Side-Second Avenue; L to First or Third Avenues. www.cityparksfoundation.org.

548. Sunbathe on the promenade in **Hudson River Park**.

You can stay on the "shore" (i.e., the promenade and the grassy lawns behind it), or pick a pier and stretch out surrounded by water.

WEST SIDE OF MANHATTAN BETWEEN 59TH STREET AND BATTERY PARK. Subway: A, C, E to 14th Street, 34th Street, 42nd Street-Port Authority Bus Terminal, or 59th Street; 1 to Christopher Street-Sheridan Square, Houston Street, Franklin Street, or Chambers Street. www.hudsonriverpark.org.

549. Skip stones on the water between the Brooklyn and Manhattan Bridges at **Brooklyn Bridge Park**.

This small, little-known public space on the Brooklyn shore was rejuvenated in 2003 and is now one of the most beautiful parks in the city—and one of the only places that brings you within touching distance of the water of the East River. With dramatic views of the bridges, the East River, and the Manhattan skyline in front, and with the striking remains of a nineteenth-century tobacco warehouse and the storehouses of DUMBO behind, the park is a refreshing place to spend an afternoon. Unstructured leisure activities like aimless strolls and skipping stones are great ways to appreciate the gorgeous scenery and secluded feel, but should you desire something more organized, the park hosts a bevy of outdoor events, including **outdoor movies** (see page 215), **yoga classes** (see page 228), performances, and fireworks displays.

EAST RIVER BETWEEN THE BROOKLYN AND MANHATTAN BRIDGES IN BROOKLYN. Subway: 2, 3 to Clark Street; A, C to High Street; F to York Street. For more information on the park and development project, call 718-802-0603 or visit www.bbpc.net.

Borrow a neighborhood park for a **moment of calm**.

They may be big, green, and beautiful, but on a pretty weekend day, the big parks like **Central** and **Prospect** (see pages 219–222 and 222–224) and some of the others listed in this chapter are anything but peaceful. But there are many smaller parks that make excellent escapes from the city hubbub, no matter the day or time. The best are hidden in residential areas, frequented only by locals or those in the know. Here are several particularly beautiful, lesser-known parks and gardens tucked away from busy streets and avenues.

550. *Cobble Hill Park:* Pick up a coffee and a homemade Pop-Tart at Ted & Honey on the corner and then enjoy your breakfast in the park.
VERANDAH PLACE BETWEEN CONGRESS AND CLINTON STREETS IN BROOKLYN. Subway: F, G to Bergen Street.

551. *Tudor City Gardens:* A peaceful retreat from 42nd Street, and the perfect lunch spot for Midtown's desk-bound workers.
SECOND AVENUE AT 42ND STREET IN MANHATTAN. Subway: 4, 5, 6, 7, S to Grand Central-42nd Street.

552. *Gardens of Saint John the Divine:* The grounds are as striking and serene as the Cathedral itself, with herbs, a fountain, a rose garden, and peacocks in the summertime.
1047 AMSTERDAM AVENUE NEAR 110TH STREET IN MANHATTAN. Subway: 1 to 110th Street; B, C to Cathedral Parkway (110th Street). 212-316-7490. www.stjohndivine.org.

553. *Liz Christy Gardens:* The first community garden in New York, named for the local gardener whose efforts brought the park to life more than thirty years ago.
EAST HOUSTON STREET AND BOWERY IN MANHATTAN. Subway: F, V to Lower East Side-Second Avenue. www.lizchristygarden.org.

554. *City Hall Park:* Legend has it that Jack London lived rough for a while in this pretty downtown park, earning his way by telling stories around the fountain at night.
BETWEEN BROADWAY, PARK ROW, AND CHAMBERS STREET IN MANHATTAN. Subway: 4, 5, 6 to Brooklyn Bridge-City Hall; J, M, Z to Chambers Street.

555. Climb the steps in **Morningside Park**.

Carved into the dramatic rock face that defines one side of the park, the steps that lead up to Amsterdam Avenue are a rugged reminder of the city's natural foundations. While you're catching your breath at the top, relax on a bench and gaze out over

Harlem. The view is well worth the trek.

MORNINGSIDE AVENUE AT 110TH STREET IN MANHATTAN. Subway: 1 to Cathedral Parkway (110th Street); B, C to Cathedral Parkway (110th Street).

556. Check out the foliage at **Wave Hill** in Riverdale.

This twenty-eight-acre garden and cultural center includes ten acres of second-growth forest and plenty of native plants and trees. Homesick New Englanders and foliage junkies can celebrate nature's fireworks here each September during the annual Plant Pigment Weekend, with walks, garden demonstrations, and other activities. Afterward, you can check out a nature-focused art exhibit at the Glyndor Gallery, explore the grounds (which include Wave Hill House, a former residence of Mark Twain and the Roosevelts), or enjoy a picnic.

WEST 249TH STREET AND INDEPENDENCE AVENUE IN THE BRONX. Subway: 1 to 231st Street; A to 207th Street, then Bx7 or Bx10 bus. Open year-round, Tuesday through Sunday, though hours vary seasonally. Admission: adults $6, students and seniors $3. Free on Tuesdays and Saturdays from 9:00 a.m. to 12:00 p.m., and throughout December, January, and February. For information on visiting, programs, and hours, call 718-549-3200. www.wavehill.org.

557. Watch a cricket match in **Van Cortlandt Park**.

Believe it or not, cricket's popularity in the U.S. once rivaled that of baseball, and legend has it that Mayor Van Cortlandt designated a portion of his Bronx estate for the purpose of playing cricket. Today, the park that bears his name has thirteen cricket pitches, where you can watch area leagues and teams play this elaborate gentleman's sport. In addition to cricket, the nearly 1,150-acre park has a track stadium, the city's **oldest golf course** (see page 235), a freshwater lake (the Bronx's largest), as well as fields for soccer, football, bocce, and, of course, baseball.

WEST 240TH STREET AND BROADWAY IN THE BRONX. Subway: 1 to Van Cortlandt Park-242nd Street; 4 to Woodlawn.

→ **DID YOU KNOW?** *Stephanus Van Cortlandt was New York's first native-born mayor, who ran the city from 1677 to 1678 and 1686 to 1688.*

558. Take a breather by the **Gandhi statue** in Union Square Park.

The surrounding garden acts as a buffer from the traffic on 14th Street, and the beautiful statue depicting the beloved pacifist will smooth over any rage of the day.

UNION SQUARE PARK WEST BETWEEN 14TH AND 15TH STREETS. Subway: 4, 5, 6, L, N, Q, R, W to 14th Street-Union Square.

559. Soak up the rays beneath the **"Long Island"** and **"Pepsi-Cola"** signs.

You know the ones—you see them all the time across the East River from Manhattan. They're relics from the area's former incarnation as an industrial center, which has been transformed into a waterfront park. If you go early enough on a warm day, you can snag a wooden chaise lounge underneath these beloved New York landmarks. The park is also a great place to **watch the fireworks** on July 4 (see page 26).

GANTRY PLAZA STATE PARK. 474 48TH AVENUE IN QUEENS. Subway: E, V to 23rd Street-Ely Avenue; 7 to 45 Road-Court House Square; G to Long Island City-Court Square.

560. Surf the net at **Bryant Park**...

How appropriate that this Midtown oasis is hooked up for wireless Internet access. On a warm summer day (when the boss is out of the office for the afternoon), take your laptop and work at one of the little tables or sprawl out on the lawn for as long as your battery lasts. (Sorry, no wireless outlets yet.)

40TH TO 42ND STREETS BETWEEN FIFTH AND SIXTH AVENUES IN MANHATTAN. Subway: 7 to Fifth Avenue-Bryant Park; B, D, F, V to 42nd Street-Bryant Park. www.bryantpark.org.

561. ...or downtown.

The Downtown Alliance, a community advocacy group, has rigged nine downtown hot spots for Wi-Fi, including the South Street Seaport and the **Winter Garden** in the World Financial Center (see page 350).

For more information and exact locations, check the map at www.downtownny.com.

Cinema al Fresco

The Big Apple's answer to the classic small-town drive-in is the summer movie series shown in different parks around New York. They are one of the most universally beloved of the city's outdoor activities, and why not? They're fun, free, and an easy, pleasant way to spend a couple of hours in the outdoors, especially after a long day cooped up inside. A few good ones:

562. *Bryant Park:* Probably the best known (and most consistently crowded) of the outdoor movie series. During the ten-week series (late June through August), classic films are screened on the lawn each Monday. The film starts at dusk (usually 8:00 or 9:00 p.m.), but the lawn opens to blanketers at 5:00 p.m., and it's best to get there early and bring a picnic. The park's proximity to Midtown means that it gets pretty packed on not-too-stifling summer nights, but it's a great way to see classics like *The Philadelphia Story, Rear Window,* or *Jaws* on the big screen. (Though screenings tend to be crowded, a perk of this festival is **ample and clean restrooms**—for more information, see pages 351–353.) *For address, see opposite. Subway: 7 to Fifth Avenue-Bryant Park; B, D, F, V to 42nd Street-Bryant Park. For schedules and information, call 212-768-4242 or visit www.bryantpark.org.*

563. *RiverFlicks at Hudson River Park:* RiverFlicks runs two outdoor film series each summer, from the beginning of July through August. On Wednesday nights, they show movies for adults, and on Friday nights there's a special kids' series. The films are shown on Piers 46 (near 10th Street) and 54 (near 14th Street), and there is free popcorn! (Showtime is at dusk. There are public restrooms in the park.)
For address and directions, see page 27. For schedules and information, call 212-627-2020 or visit www.hudsonriverpark.org.

564. *Movies with a View at Brooklyn Bridge Park:* A themed six-week series takes place at this lovely waterfront park. A DJ starts spinning tunes at 6:00 p.m.; movies start at dusk. Plus free bike parking! (Restrooms located near the park's entrance, off Water Street.)
For address and directions, see page 70. For schedules and information, call 718-802-0603 or visit www.bbpc.net.

565. *Rooftop Films:* This nonprofit organization has been showing "underground movies outdoors" for an impressive decade and a half. Every weekend from May through September, films are screened on rooftops around the city. All films are independent, and most are U.S., world, or New York premieres. In addition to the films, evenings usually include live music before the show, and either a Q&A, reception, or after-party following it. The $9 ticket fee goes to support their programs for filmmakers.
For upcoming lineups and more information, visit www.rooftopfilms.com.

Outdoor Music

Like the movies, outdoor concerts are an excellent way to enjoy the out-of-doors in an otherwise urban environment. On evenings and weekends during warmer months, it's hard to find a park that *doesn't* have some music going on, with informal performances by musicians of all kinds playing for your aural enjoyment. Many parks, of course, have extensive, organized concert series, such as:

566. *Summerstage:* A legend, an institution, the festival that started it all. Since 1986, Summerstage has been putting on excellent free events in Central Park all summer long. The schedule also includes dance performances, spoken word events, and a few films, but most of the offerings are musical performances that run the gamut from rock and pop, to classical and instrumental, to experimental, and tributes. Admission is first-come/first-served, so be prepared to line up for more popular acts.

Concerts are held in Central Park on Rumsey Playfield. For more information, visit www.summerstage.org or call 212-360-2756.

567. *Philharmonic in the Park:* Every year, the **New York Philharmonic** (for full entry, see page 152) performs outdoor concerts in parks around the five boroughs. They're both an opportunity to hear the Philharmonic for free and a pleasant way to enjoy a summer evening outside, with soundtrack provided. Tip: the real classical music aficionados tend to sit in the front, and the atmosphere generally gets increasingly more relaxed the farther back you go.

For more information, call 212-875-5656 or visit www.newyorkphilharmonic.org.

568. *Met in the Park:* Like the Philharmonic, the **Met** (see page 151) performs two operas from its current season at a park in each of the boroughs.

For more information, call 212-362-6000 or visit www.metopera.org.

569. During the ***River-to-River*** festival, there are free concerts and musical performances of all kinds almost daily all summer long, at eight lower Manhattan parks.

For more information, call 212-627-2020 or visit www.rivertorivernyc.com.

570. *Bryant Park* hosts several different concert and music series each summer, including "Broadway in Bryant Park," "Piano in the Park," and "Bryant Park after Work."

For more information, call 212-768-4242 or visit www.bryantpark.org.

571. *Midsummer Night Swing and Lincoln Center Out of Doors:* Midsummer Night Swing is a three-week long outdoor dance party that takes place in July. There's a different band every night, Tuesday through Saturday. Following this is Lincoln Center Out of Doors, a series of free concerts and performances, held throughout August. Both are located at Lincoln Center Plaza.

For more information, call 212-875-5000 or visit www.lincolncenter.org.

572. Commune with nature at the **New York Botanical Gardens**.

The largest and best known of the city's three botanical gardens, this 250-acre park has rivers and ponds, hills, rocks, and fifty acres of preserved forest—not to mention forty-eight separate gardens. Take a day and lose yourself in these dramatic and beautiful natural surroundings.

200TH STREET AND KAZIMIROFF BOULEVARD IN THE BRONX. Subway: 4 to Bedford Park Boulevard-Lehman College; B, D to Bedford Park Boulevard, then Bx26 bus east to Garden entrance gate. NYBG is also accessible by Metro-North; take the Harlem line to Botanical Garden station. 718-817-8700. www.nybg.org.

Brooklyn Botanic Gardens.

It's hard to believe that this exquisite, vividly colored piece of land was the site of an ash dump in the nineteenth century. Though not as large as the gardens in the Bronx, there's more than enough floral beauty here to make you forget your urban troubles. Here are our favorite spots.

1000 WASHINGTON AVENUE IN BROOKLYN. Subway: B, Q to Prospect Park; 2, 3 to Eastern Parkway-Brooklyn Museum. 718-623-7200.www.bbg.org.

573. *Follow the Celebrity Path.* Brooklyn's answer to Hollywood's Walk of Fame, featuring plaques for famous Brooklynites. Harvey Keitel is from Brooklyn? Who knew? (New names are added on "Welcome Back to Brooklyn" Day each June.)

574. *Test your sense of smell in the Fragrance Garden.* Originally designed as a place of beauty for the blind, this garden is full of the most wonderfully scented plants around, from chocolate flowers to spearmint leaves and herbs.

575. *Take a walk down the Cherry Esplanade around bloom time.* The site of more than 200 blossoming cherry trees is the perfect way to celebrate spring's arrival. The annual *sakura matsuri* (cherry blossom festival) is one of the garden's most beloved events, a weekend-long Japan-themed celebration that includes samurai sword demonstrations!

576. *Go to Bluebell Wood in May.* A lesser-known rival of to the Cherry Esplanade, Bluebell Wood is a beautiful, secluded spot just south of the cherries that is transformed into the most magical, enchanted glade every spring, when more than 45,000 bluebells cover the forest floor in color. A path wanders between magnificent old oak, birch, and beech trees, and for a stretch of the way, you find yourself surrounded by nothing but bright blues and violets.

577. Lose yourself in thought in the Chinese Scholar's Garden, or just lose yourself in Connie Gretz's Secret Garden at the **Staten Island Botanical Garden**.

Yet another hidden treasure in the low-profile fifth borough is the Staten Island Botanic Garden, which is on the grounds of the **Snug Harbor Cultural Center** (see page 147) and boasts several unique attractions. One is the Chinese Scholar's Garden, which is the only one of its kind in the United States. The garden is a sanctuary of sculptures, waterways, and perennial greens inspired by the traditionally tranquil private gardens of ancient China. Another is Connie Gretz's Secret Garden, which is modeled on the garden in the children's book by Frances Hodgson Burnett. The garden is surrounded by a hedge maze (the only one of its kind in New York), so the "secret" is finding it.

1000 RICHMOND TERRACE IN STATEN ISLAND. Subway: 1 to South Ferry; ferry to Staten Island; then S40 bus to Snug Harbor and the Botanic Gardens. 718-273-8200. www.snug-harbor.org

Central Park.

When people think "outdoors" in New York, chances are the first image that pops into their heads is Central Park. Olmsted and Vaux's 150-year-old park is an urban masterpiece, 843 acres of varied bucolic terrain (including lakes, woodlands, hills, and lawns) that literally runs right through the middle of the city. In addition to the sheer beauty of this verdant oasis, Central Park is also New York City's backyard, and for plenty of Manhattanites, close proximity to "the park" is a nonnegotiable condition of residence. This is where people from all over the city come to play, relax, learn, hang out, work out, and meet up. Here are some of our favorite things about it.

Subway: 1, 4, 5, 6, A, B, C, D, N, R, W to various points; see www.mta.info for subway map. For more information on the park, call 212-310-6600 or visit www.central-parknyc.org.

578. *Watch the giant turtles swim in Turtle Pond.* You can see frogs, fish, and waterbirds there, too.

MIDDLE OF THE PARK, BETWEEN 79TH AND 80TH STREETS (at the base of Belvedere Castle). Subway: B, C to 81st Street-Museum of Natural History.

579. *Go rowboating on the lake.* You'll have to brave the tourists, but it's worth it. It's tons of fun, a great way to cool off, and at $10 an hour, it's a pretty good deal!

EAST SIDE BETWEEN 74TH AND 75TH STREETS. Rowboats can be rented from March through October, weather permitting. Subway: 6 to 77th Street.

580. *Slide your sled down Pilgrim's Hill.* The park is almost at its most beautiful when it's carpeted in snow, and the Upper East Side of the park boasts the best hills for tobogganing. Pilgrim's Hill (above 72nd Street entrance on Fifth Avenue) is steep enough to go fast and level enough to slow down before you hit somebody's mom. All the slopes between here and 79th Street are great to sled on, and luckily for all of us, the park ties bales of hay to the most treacherous tree trunks to cushion any wayward finishes.
ENTER AT FIFTH AVENUE AT 72ND STREET. Subway: 6 to 68th Street-Hunter College. www.centralpark.com/pages/sports/sledding.

581. *Ride the carousel for old times' sake...* The carousel that operates today is actually the fourth to occupy this spot. (The previous ones all burned down.) The first one, built in 1870, was animal powered. The subsequent three, however, have been steam powered.
MIDDLE OF THE PARK, NEAR 64TH STREET. Subway: 6 to 68th Street-Hunter College; B, C to 72nd Street.

582. *...or have a full-fledged amusement park outing at Victorian Gardens.* Think you have to leave the city to ride the teacups? Not anymore. From May through September, Wollman Rink is transformed into a good old-fashioned carnival, with all the cotton candy, face painting, and rides of traditional traveling summer carnivals.
WOLLMAN RINK, EAST SIDE OF THE PARK BETWEEN 62ND AND 63RD STREETS. Subway: N, R, W to Fifth Avenue/59th Street. For more information on hours and admission, visit www.victoriangardensnyc.com.

583. *Watch the "disco skaters" strut their stuff by the Bandshell.* There are no official hours or performance times; just enter the park on the east side, around 64th Street, and follow the music!
Subway: N, R, W to Fifth Avenue/59th Street.

584. *Work on your own skating (and stopping) for free at the Skate Patrol Stopping Clinic.* The Central Park Skate Patrol offers free lessons in inline skate braking on weekends from April through October. They also operate a skate school, offering classes taught by certified Skate Patrol instructors, where you can learn more advanced skills, like turns, crossovers, and skating backward, for a reasonable $25 per class.

Stopping Clinic is open weekends from April through October, 1 p.m. to 5 p.m. WEST 72ND STREET, JUST INSIDE CENTRAL PARK. No reservations. Skate School operates weekends from April through October. Classes are available for beginners through advanced and cost $25 each. Classes meet at BLADES, 120 WEST 72ND STREET, BETWEEN COLUMBUS AVENUE AND BROADWAY. Subway: 1, 2, 3 to 72nd Street. For more information, or to register for Skate School, call 212-439-1234 or visit www.skatepatrol.org.

585. Have drinks at the Boathouse. It's a mob scene at brunch, and dinner is pricey—and the urban lakeside dining idea is pretty gimmicky. But it's a gimmick with a great view, and well worth the price of a cocktail or two. *CENTRAL PARK DRIVE NORTH AT EAST 72ND STREET. Subway: 6 to 68th Street-Hunter College. 212-517-2233. www.thecentralparkboathouse.com.*

586. Watch lawn sports. There are two kept greens in the park reserved for lawn sports like bocce and croquet. If you go on a nice spring or summer day, you can see experienced players, dressed in traditional whites and engaged in intense competition. (If you want to play, however, you need a permit.) *Fields are located near West 69th Street. For more information on permits, call 212-408-0226 or visit www.centralparknyc.org.*

587. Go fishing in the Harlem Meer. Just beyond the Conservatory Gardens at the northeast corner of the park is the Harlem Meer. You can fish there free of charge—poles and corn-kernel bait are available for use at the Dana Center. Fishing is catch-and-release, so everything must be thrown back—not that you'd really be tempted to eat what you catch anyway. *CHARLES A. DANA CENTER, 110TH STREET AND LENOX AVENUE. Subway: 2, 3 to Central Park North (110th Street). Equipment available Tuesday through Sunday from April through October.*

588. Skating at Lasker Rink. Another gem in the lightly traveled northern end of the park. Not surprisingly, it is much less crowded here than at Wollman Rink—and much cheaper. In the summer, the rink converts to a public pool. *MID-PARK BETWEEN 106TH AND 108TH STREETS. Subway: 2, 3 to Central Park North (110th Street). Skating from November through March. For more information, call 917-492-3857 or visit www.wollmanskatingrink.com/main_lasker.htm.*

589. Discover the Conservatory Gardens. Tucked away in the northeast corner of the park, shielded from the commotion of the throngs below, this breathtaking six-acre garden is an oasis of calm in the city's most beloved

open space. The name comes from a huge glass conservatory that stood there from 1898 until 1934, when it was demolished and replaced by the garden. This is the only formal garden in the park, and it is composed of three distinctly landscaped sections: Italian, French, and English. Few park visitors make the trek so far north, so aside from weddings and the occasional painter or two, you'll be able to drink in the exquisite floral beauty in peace. You can enter either by walking up from within the park, or through the gates on Fifth Avenue at 105th Street. The wrought-iron gates once stood at the entrance to the Vanderbilt Mansion on Fifth Avenue and 58th Street (the spot where **Bergdorf Goodman** sits today; see page 243); they were moved to the park in 1927. Just inside lies the Italian garden, with its well-manicured lawns and hedges, crab-apple trees, and a wrought-iron pergola with a fountain in front of it. (Check out the medallions on the walkway under the pergola—they are inscribed with the names of each of the thirteen original colonies.) The French garden to the north has the most stunning floral displays—20,000 tulips bloom each spring, from new bulbs planted the previous fall. There's also the beautiful sculpture of the three dancing maidens that encircles the fountain at the center. The English garden to the south has the best year-round floral display, and a lovely reflecting pool with water lilies and another fountain. This fountain is known as the Burnett Fountain, for the bronze sculpture of two children from Frances Hodgson Burnett's book, *The Secret Garden*—an appropriate touch for the park's own secret garden.
FIFTH AVENUE AND 105TH STREET. Subway: 2, 3 to Central Park North (110th Street).

Prospect Park

Prospect Park is to Brooklyn what Central Park is to Manhattan: a rambling park space overflowing with natural beauty and outdoor amenities. Also designed by Olmsted and Vaux, it shares many similarities with its sister park in Manhattan, but Prospect has its own distinct character and features. Divided by hills, woods, and waterways, the terrain varies from the picturesque lake with its Victorian boathouse to the wilderness of the ravine, the busy field of baseball diamonds, and the small zoo contained in its center. Here we list a few of the very best things to do in Prospect Park.
Subway: 2, 3 to Grand Army Plaza; B, S/Franklin Avenue Shuttle to Prospect Park; F to Seventh Avenue; Q to Parkside Avenue. www.prospectpark.org

590. *Hire a pedal boat on the lake.* Compared to its crowded counterpart in Manhattan, the lake at Prospect Park is like the open sea, a palatial sixty acres of uncharted water for the few happy explorers who make the most of the pedal boats every summer. Follow turtles, watch the herons perched on the islands, and move from open sunlit waters to the shade of bulrushes in a few easy strokes.

Pedal boat rentals at Wollman Rink. Use the Ocean Avenue/Parkside entrance and follow signs to Wollman Rink. Subway: B, S/Franklin Avenue Shuttle to Prospect Park; Q to Parkside Avenue.

591. *Try to catch the prize fish in the annual Macy's fishing contest.*

An annual event since 1947, the Macy's fishing contest sees Brooklyn's youngest fishermen compete to catch a huge, tagged bass named for R. H. Macy. The waters of Prospect Park are full of fish, from bass to porgies, and prizes are awarded for the first and biggest catches of the day, as well as for Macy, the tagged bass (everything caught in Prospect Park must be thrown back). There are exhibits and classes held at the Audubon Center throughout the day to teach kids about the fish they're after.

July. AUDUBON CENTER IS JUST INSIDE THE LINCOLN ROAD/OCEAN AVENUE ENTRANCE TO THE PARK. Subway: B, Q, S/Franklin Avenue Shuttle to Prospect Park.

592. *Ride the carousel.* These painted horses have provided nearly a century of fun for kids, from their original home at Coney Island in 1912 to their beautiful present reincarnation in the "Children's Corner" of Prospect Park.

JUST INSIDE THE WILLINK ENTRANCE AT OCEAN AVENUE, FLATBUSH AVENUE, AND EMPIRE BOULEVARD. Subway: B, Q, S/Franklin Avenue Shuttle to Prospect Park.

593. *Get lost in the wooded ravine.* Brooklyn's only forest runs across the middle of Prospect Park, bringing a glimpse of the rocks, streams, and shady treetops of the Adirondacks to the city.

MIDDLE OF THE PARK BETWEEN LONG MEADOW AND NETHERMEAD; accessible from the Grand Army Plaza entrance or from the Ninth Street entrance on Prospect Park West. Subway: 2, 3 to Grand Army Plaza; F to Seventh Avenue.

594. *Hide undisturbed in the Vale of Cashmere,* a cool, shaded garden and pond sunk down behind the Long Meadow. It is entirely possible to spend a whole day in the Vale of Cashmere without seeing another living soul.

Enter at Grand Army Plaza and head toward the Audubon Center; look for signs to the vale. Subway: 2, 3 to Grand Army Plaza.

595. *See the sun shine through the stained-glass ceiling of the Concert Grove pagoda,* whose Oriental pavilion is one of the prettiest buildings in Brooklyn. The grove is full of whimsical bronze sculptures of famous composers—Beethoven is depicted with a deep frown—which inspires local musicians to play here on warm days.
NEAR THE OCEAN AVENUE/PARKSIDE ENTRANCE. Subway: B, S/Franklin Avenue Shuttle to Prospect Park; Q to Parkside Avenue.

596. *Skate to the best old-school roller-disco music at the "other" Wollman Rink.* Between the Concert Grove and the lake, Prospect Park's popular ice rink has clean ice, floodlights, and the best soundtrack since the Roxy went down.
JUST INSIDE THE OCEAN AVENUE/PARKSIDE ENTRANCE. Follow signs to Wollman Rink. Subway: B, S/Franklin Avenue Shuttle to Prospect Park; Q to Parkside Avenue.

597. *Watch pups splash about on Dog Beach.* No jokes about the doggie paddle—this little pond by the ball fields in the Long Meadow is for canines only. Even if you don't have a dog, it's a quirky urban attraction that's good for at least one "Awwww."
LONG MEADOW, BY 9TH STREET. Off-leash hours and rules apply. Subway: F to Seventh Avenue.

598. Make a rooftop garden (or if your building won't let you, make friends with someone who's got one).

A rooftop garden is a great way to get out of the city without technically leaving your apartment, whether it is full of massive seasonal plantings, or just a few potted plants and a glider chair. Stock up on urban gardening gear at the Chelsea Garden Center.
CHELSEA GARDEN CENTER: *580 ELEVENTH AVENUE AT 13TH STREET IN MANHATTAN. Subway: A, C, E, L, 1, 2, 3 to 14th Street. 212-727-7100.*
CHELSEA GARDEN CENTER (BROOKLYN): *444 VAN BRUNT STREET IN BROOKLYN. Subway: F, G to Smith Street. 718-875-2100. www.chelseagardencenter.com.*

599. Take a canoe ride up the Gowanus Canal.

The Gowanus Dredgers Canoeing Club has canoes, paddles, and life jackets available for public use, and offers tours up and down the canal during the season (May through October). Waterfront tours are by appointment and are 90 minutes long; other tours and special events are 15 to 20 minutes long and are posted on the Web site's calendar. The equipment and tours are free, though contributions are encouraged. (The organization works to maintain the Gowanus Canal and encourages public use and awareness of local waterways). Try to go in the evening—the sunset on the canal is surprisingly romantic.

Most canoeing events depart from 2ND STREET NEAR BOND STREET. Subway: F, G to Carroll Street; R to Union Street. For more information, call 718-243-0849 or visit www.waterfront-museum.org.

600. Go fishing off a real fishing boat in **Sheepshead Bay**.

Catch a boat from one of the piers along Emmons Avenue, and head into the Atlantic for an early-morning or a late-night trip. If you're especially brave, you can try selling your catch to the restaurants along the Bay.

EMMONS AVENUE ALONG SHEEPSHEAD BAY IN BROOKLYN. Prices range from $24 to $40 per trip. Subway: B, Q to Sheepshead Bay.

601. Kayak on the **Hudson or East Rivers** (and don't fall in!).

The Downtown Boathouse offers several public small-crafts programs, the most popular of which is free kayaking on the Hudson. They provide kayaks, paddles, life jackets, and supervision—the only thing you need to know is how to swim. In addition to the public kayak rentals, they also hold three-hour guided trips up the Hudson, and free kayaking lessons on Wednesday evenings. On the other side of the island, the Long Island City Boathouse offers a bunch of free kayaking programs in the East River, including a picturesque Friday evening sunset paddle.

DOWNTOWN BOATHOUSE: *HUDSON RIVER AT PIER 40 IN MANHATTAN (Houston Street: Subway: 1 to Houston Street); PIER 96 (56th Street: Subway: 1, A, C, B, D to 59th Street); 72ND STREET (Subway: 1, 2, 3 to 72nd Street). For more information, call 646-613-0375. www.downtownboathouse.org/links.html.*

Kayaking trips with the Long Island City Boathouse leave at different points in Astoria and Long Island City. For more information, visit www.licboathouse.org.

602. Take the subway to the **beach**.

Take your pick: Brighton Beach, Coney Island, Manhattan Beach, and Rockaway are all accessible by subway, and free, so a day at the beach will cost you only the price of a MetroCard. Each beach has its own character, but they're all fun and well maintained, so choose between the crowded funfair atmosphere of Coney Island, the Russian expanses of Brighton Beach, the quieter Spanish flavor of Manhattan Beach, or the surfer's paradise of Rockaway.

Subways maps at www.mta.info.

603. Take the **Yankee Clipper** to a game.

More peaceful than driving, more comfortable than the train, and much quicker than you would expect.

Departs from various points along the East River in Manhattan. $22 dollars round trip for adults, $18 for children under 12. For more information, call 800-53-FERRY. www.nywaterway.com.

604. Go sailing off **City Island**, the premier resort town of the Bronx.

Many people live in New York for years and never visit City Island, but it's worth the small voyage—especially if you like fish. With all sorts of boats for hire, fishing trips on the nearby waters, and fresh seafood available at cafés along the shore, City Island is a surprisingly lively seaside resort, and a pretty sight from the deck of a sailboat in the sound. Follow up your maritime expedition with fish and chips from **Johnny's Famous Reef** (see page 325).

Subway: 6 to Pelham Bay Park; Bx29 bus to City Island. For information on visiting City Island, sailing, restaurants, and other entertainment, visit www.cityisland.com.

605. See if you can train a telescope on one of the bald-headed eagles that live at the **Inwood Hill Nature Center**.

Inwood Hill Park, the beautiful stretch of land at the northernmost tip of Manhattan, is a great place to visit when you want to get off the beaten path. Walking through its winding forests and along its rocky cliffs, and looking out across the Hudson brings you as close to nature as you can get without leaving the island. The Nature Center within the park is a great place to observe and learn about the few wild animals that make Manhattan their home.

INWOOD HILL PARK, 218TH STREET AND INDIAN ROAD IN MANHATTAN. Open Wednesday through Sunday. Subway: A to Inwood-207th Street. 212-304-2365.

606. Get up close and personal with shorebirds at the **Jamaica Bay Wildlife Refuge**.

More than 300 species of birds spend their summers at this 9,000-acre refuge. From mid- to late-August, the pond is teeming with young birds that aren't yet afraid of people, so you have the rare opportunity to get within petting distance of beautiful wild birds.

GATEWAY NATIONAL RECREATION AREA, FLOYD BENNETT FIELD IN BROOKLYN. Subway: A to Broad Channel. For more information, see entry for Floyd Bennett Field, page 238. 718-318-4340. www.nyharborparks.org/visit/jaba.html

607. Watch an octopus prepare its dinner at the **New York Aquarium**.

To keep the animals as nimble and alert as they would be in the wild, the aquarium staff uses various "enrichment games," like putting food in closed containers or hiding it in a toy. You can watch an octopus use a couple of its arms to open a jar filled with tasty fish at feeding times.

SURF AVENUE AND WEST 8TH STREET IN BROOKLYN. Subway: D to Stillwell Avenue; F, Q to West 8th Street-New York Aquarium. For feeding times, call or check online. 718-265-FISH. www.nyaquarium.com.

608. See lions, tigers, bears, and much more at the **Bronx Zoo**.

The Bronx Zoo is the largest metropolitan zoo in the world, and one of the most important conservation sites. Opened in 1899, the zoo has pioneered many educational and zoological programs, such as taking animals out of cages and putting them into simulations of their natural environments. The zoo's first conservation project was the American bison, whose numbers, by the turn of the century, had dwindled from millions to 1,000. The zoo founded the American Bison Society, which successfully accomplished the breeding and reintroduction of bison into natural habitats all over the country. Now, under the auspices of the Wildlife Conservation Society (WCS), the Bronx Zoo has been integral in preserving species all over the world, and is still on the forefront of zoological technology and design. You can see the fruits of their labor in the highly detailed, replicated natural habitats that fill the 265-acre park, from the Himalayan Highlands, where red pandas, snow leopards, and other rare, endangered animals roam through a forest with authentic natural adornments made by Tibetan monks, to the beautiful Butterfly Garden and greenhouse, where thousands of butterflies roam. The Congo Gorilla Forest is an amazing 6.5-acre replica of an African rain forest that is home to more than 300 native animals (including gorillas, monkeys, and snakes); it is also the first zoo exhibit to involve visitors in the conservation effort by giving them the option to have the zoo donate their admission fee toward rainforest conservation. And that's only the beginning. The number of amazing things to do and see could fill an entire chapter, from daily feedings and enrichment demonstrations where you can watch zookeepers play with the animals, to the Skyfari tram ride that gives an overview of the entire zoo—and of the Bronx river beaver, one of the newest (uninvited!) arrivals to the area.

FORDHAM ROAD AT THE BRONX RIVER PARKWAY IN THE BRONX. Subway: 2 to Pelham Parkway; 2, 5 to West Farms Square-East Tremont Avenue. For hours, admission prices, and other details, call 718-367-1010 or visit www.bronxzoo.com.

609. Go horseback riding **on the beach**.

You can trot up and down a private three-mile stretch of the Brooklyn coast on a horse hired from the Jamaica Bay Riding Academy.

7000 SHORE PARKWAY IN BROOKLYN. Group trail rides and private rides available. Subway: B, Q to Sheepshead Bay; taxi to the academy. For specific directions, call 718-531-8949. www.horsebackride.com/jb/home.html.

Give your yoga a **breath of fresh air**.

In the nicer weather, certain yoga instructors break out of the studio and bring their classes outside to parks around the city. For devoted practitioners, these classes offer a change of pace without changing activity; for newcomers, they are a way to try yoga in a setting that may be less intimidating than a studio. Following is a list of parks that host yoga classes in the warm weather; most are seasonal, but some are offered year-round and shift to indoor spaces elsewhere in the park during the winter months. The days and times of all of these are subject to change, so contact the park or check their Web sites for the most current information.

610. *Brooklyn Bridge Park:* Offers sunset yoga classes on the boardwalk several times during the summer at 7:00 p.m. Classes are free, but you must bring your own mat, and you should arrive half an hour early to sign up.
See full entry on page 70.

611. *Bryant Park:* Hosts a free open class conducted by Lululemon Athletica on Thursday evenings, 6:00 p.m. to 7:00 p.m., May through August. Classes are held on the southwest corner of the lawn. Mats available to borrow.
See full entry on page 215. www.lululemon.com

612. *Central Park:* Central Park Yoga holds public classes on Sunday mornings on the west side of the park, around 81st Street; private or semiprivate lessons can be arranged for other times. Fee is $10 per class; bring your own mat.
For schedule and more information, visit www.centralparkyoga.com.

613. *Greenbelt Nature Center:* Holds an eight-week session July through August, with weekly morning classes. (Cost is per session.)
700 ROCKLAND AVENUE AT BRIELLE AVENUE IN STATEN ISLAND. For information, schedules, and directions, call 718-351-3450 or visit www.sigreenbelt.org, or the Parks Department Web site: www.nyc.gov/parks.

614. *Inwood Hill Park:* Hosts free yoga classes every Thursday evening in the summer. Classes run from 6:15 to 7:30 p.m., and are intended for all skill levels. Bring your own mat.

NEAR 218TH STREET AND INDIAN ROAD IN MANHATTAN. Subway: 1, A to 207th Street. For information and schedules, visit www.nycgovparks.org.

615. *Riverside Park:* Holds a free weekly evening Hatha yoga class for all levels, June through September. (Bring your own mat.)

THE PLAZA, 66TH STREET AND THE HUDSON RIVER IN MANHATTAN. For information on schedule and location, visit www.riversideparkfund.org.

616. *Socrates Sculpture Park:* Holds free Kripalu (a form of Hatha yoga) classes on the park grounds on Saturday mornings from 11:00 a.m. to 12:00 p.m., May through September. (Bring your own mat.)

32-01 VERNON BOULEVARD IN QUEENS. Subway: N, W to Broadway. 718-956-1819. www.socratessculpturepark.org. For more on the park, see page 342.

617. *Union Square Park:* Every year as part of the park's Summer in the Square festival, free weekly yoga classes are held in Union Square Park. The classes are taught by instructors from some of the many studios that surround the park. The time of the classes varies each year, so check the Web site for the most up-to-date listings.

14TH-17TH STREETS BETWEEN PARK AVENUE SOUTH AND BROADWAY IN MANHATTAN. Subway: 4,5,6,L, N, R, Q, W to 14th Street-Union Square. www.unionsquarenyc.org

Outdoor **Tai Chi**.

If you've ever walked through a park in the early morning and noticed a group of people in a trancelike state performing slow, mesmerizing movements in tandem, you've probably witnessed an outdoor tai chi class. Like yoga, there are plenty of studios at which to study tai chi in the city, but going outside can give your practice a pleasant new perspective. Some classes are seasonal, while others are year-round and held outdoors during the warmer months.

618. *Brooklyn Botanic Garden:* Holds weekly classes for different levels on Fridays, in spring, summer, and fall. Beginner classes are held indoors at the Visitor's Center; intermediate and advanced classes are held on the grounds at the Cherry Esplanade, weather permitting. Fees are $62 for 5 classes, or $55 for members.

See full entry on pages 218–219.

619. *Bryant Park:* Holds free open classes on Thursday mornings, 7:30 a.m. to 8:30 a.m., May through October, at the Fountain Terrace.
See full entry on page 215.

620. *Prospect Park:* The Brooklyn Kung Fu and Tai Chi Academy holds classes on Saturday mornings, May through October, on the southwest part of the park, close to the school.
718-768-7762. See full entry for Prospect Park on pages 222–224.

621. *Socrates Sculpture Park:* Holds free weekly classes on Sunday mornings, May through September.
See full entry on page 142.

622. *Wave Hill:* Holds classes on Saturday mornings at 10:00 a.m. (beginners) and 11:00 a.m. (intermediate). Classes are held year-round. The fee is $18 for the public and $10 for members.
See full entry on page 214.

623. Join the New York Road Runners Club.

This nearly fifty-year-old running club is probably most commonly associated with the **New York City Marathon** (see page 29), and membership gives you access to training groups and increases your chances for entry into the marathon. But the club's focus is to facilitate running in the New York area, and it offers plenty for less serious (or complete novice) runners. There are clinics and lectures on running-related topics, and classes in other physical activities like biking, yoga, and strength training to complement your running (open to nonmembers as well). The club can also help you find a running partner or answer your training questions online (members only). The many offerings, flexibility of participation, and supportive community make this a great organization for athletes of any level, with a variety of interests.
Annual membership starts at $40. For information on programs and how to join, call 212-860-4455 or visit www.nyrr.org.

624. Learn to run with Nike.

You may question the company's ethics, but you can't question its commitment to sports. Nike runs free running clinics in **Central Park** (see page 219) all year round, complete with coaches, training plans, and post-run snacks and hydration. In 2009, the clinic met on Tuesdays and Thursdays at 6:30 p.m., and on Saturday mornings at 9:00 a.m. The meeting point is at the Niketown Store (57th and Madison), where everyone starts with a group stretch. Then runners break off into groups, from which you can choose your pace (10-minute mile, 9-minute mile, etc.) and distance (between three and seven miles). The clinics are open to runners of all levels, but this is a particularly good opportunity for novices who want to "learn" how to run. You'll have access to professional trainers, and receive discounts and coupons for things like shoe fittings and free Nike gear. *For more information, call 212-891-6453, or visit www.nikerunning.com.*

625. Run and then refuel with **Team Joe**.

This fun, informal group associated with one of the city's most popular coffee spots welcomes one and all on their weekend runs. Saturday runs leave from the shop on Waverly Place and venture from there down to the tip of Manhattan on the Hudson River path and back up. Sunday runs leave from the Columbus Avenue shop for a runner's choice of distances in Central Park. After the run, coffee is on Joe, and the deal's no joke, as it's some of the best in the city.

Both runs leave at 10 a.m. (9:30 a.m. in summer).

JOE WAVERLY: *141 WAVERLY PLACE WEST OF SIXTH AVENUE. Subway: B, D, F, V to West Fourth Street.*

JOE COLUMBUS: *514 COLUMBUS AVENUE, AT 85TH STREET. For more information, visit www.joetheheartofcoffee.com.*

626. Explore New York **by bike**.

The New York Cycle Club (NYCC) and the Five Borough Bicycle Club (5BBC) offer several rides every weekend day and on certain weekdays to various destinations throughout the five boroughs. Rides range from slow to serious, and some have a strong sightseeing bent. They can be a really great way to see parts of the city that you've never been to (and perhaps never even heard of).

Membership to each of the clubs is about $20 per year. For more information, visit www.nycc.org or www.5bbc.org.

627. The annual **New York Century Ride** is another great way to see New

York by bike, as well as a cycling challenge for riders of all levels. There are five different routes of varying distances—15, 35, 55, 75, and 100 miles—which take you through as many as four of the five boroughs. We prefer the New York Century over the Five Boro Bike Tour, another annual ride popular with cyclists of various levels, because the Century attracts only a fraction of the Five Boro participants (5,000 vs. 30,000), and the starts are staggered by the different distance groups, so there isn't the same backup at the start.

September. Ride start and finish are in Central Park (see page 219–222). For more information and to register, visit www.nyccentury.org.

628. **Ride Manhattan island** from tip to tip.

A continuous bike path running the length of Manhattan was long the Manifest Destiny of city cyclists, but the dream has been realized through a series of interconnecting parks, which allow for an uninterrupted waterfront path. Start at Pier A at Hudson River Park, by Battery Park City, and continue up through Riverside Park, the "Cherry Walk" (a cherry-tree-lined section of the path between 100th and 125th Streets), Fort Washington Park, and arrive at the George Washington Bridge. Stop for a break at the top by the Little Red Lighthouse, the hero of the beloved children's classic, *The Little Red Lighthouse and the Great Gray Bridge*. (You can't miss it—it's directly under the bridge—for more information, see page 74.) Then you can turn around and head back, or, if you're feeling adventurous, you can cross the bridge and continue riding on 9W, a picturesque bike route popular with area cyclists.

629. Walk (run, or ride) in the **middle of the street**.

Each year, for several Saturdays in August, a continuous stretch of streets from the Brooklyn Bridge to Central Park is closed to traffic for several hours, and joggers, walkers, skaters, and cyclists are welcomed into the road. The run or ride along the route (most of which is on Park Avenue) is strangely thrilling—there's a satisfying of feeling of empowerment in conquering a path one has traversed previously only by vehicle. The highlight of the trip is definitely going through the covered passage underneath the Helmsley building and then emerging into the light, and realizing that Park Avenue is there for you to tread.

Saturdays in August. For more information, upcoming dates, and maps, visit www.nyc.gov/summerstreets.

630. Explore the city on a social skate with the **Empire Skate Club**.

Empire Skate is an in-line skating club that holds regular events for skaters of all different levels. It organizes group skates on Tuesday nights around Central Park; day and half-day skates to other boroughs and further afield on weekends; and two- and three-day skating getaways. The events are free, but for $25 you can become a member and receive a free private skating lesson, discounts at local skate shops, and more.

For more information, call 212-774-1774 or visit www.empireskate.org.

631. Put on your blades for **Wednesday Night Skate**.

New York's largest regular group skate is Wednesday Night Skate, a free two-hour evening skate that takes different routes through the city each week. Routes are planned in advance, tested for obstructions and obstacles, and led by volunteers. Each skate covers about ten to twelve miles of city streets, so participants should be comfortable with skating in traffic and with cars, but otherwise, these events are open to anyone—all you have to do is show up.

Skaters meet at 7:45 p.m. (for 8:00 p.m. departure) at UNION SQUARE AND 14TH STREET IN MANHATTAN. Wednesday evenings, from April through October. (Canceled in rain or bad weather.) Subway: 4, 5, 6, L, N, Q, R, W to 14th Street-Union Square. For more information visit www.weskateny.org.

632. Skate with a view at **Riverbank State Park**.

The only state park in Manhattan is a twenty-eight-acre park and recreation area built on top of a wastewater treatment facility. (Yes, you read that right.) But there's nothing second-rate about this park—Riverbank has some of the city's nicest athletic facilities, including a unique elevated ice- and roller-skating rink. The rink boasts panoramic views of the Hudson River for skaters to admire as they whiz around, and it also has a canopy (good for keeping ice skaters safe from sleet in the winter and roller skaters out of the baking sun in the summer). The rink is small, so it does get crowded during prime hours, but even so, it's much calmer than the scene at some of the city's better-known rinks—and is less than half the price.

679 RIVERSIDE DRIVE NEAR 140TH STREET IN MANHATTAN. Subway: 1 to 145th Street. 212-694-3600. http://nysparks.state.ny.us/parks/93/details.aspx

633. Go **cross-country skiing** up and down the empty avenues right after a big snowstorm.

Following a major snowfall, there's a tiny window of opportunity when all regular activity is suspended, and the city is at peace. With cars immobilized, pedestrians scarce, and fresh white powder covering every surface, the best way to enjoy this complete urban calm is to put on some skis and take to the streets. It may not look like Vermont, but this rarity has its own kind of wonderment. If you'd prefer a slightly more bucolic setting, you should go to the Great Lawn or Sheep Meadow in **Central Park** (see pages 219–222).

Anywhere you want!

634. Swim in one of the city's **outdoor pools**.

There are more than fifty pools scattered across the five boroughs, and all of them are free. Many also offer swimming lessons and team training. Try the one in Astoria Park, the nicest and largest in the city system, which hosted the Olympic trials for the U.S. swimming and diving teams in 1936 and 1964. All pools are open from the end of June through Labor Day, usually from 11:00 a.m. to 7:00 p.m.

ASTORIA PARK, BETWEEN DITMARS AVENUE AND HOYT AVENUE SOUTH, AND 19TH STREET AND THE EAST RIVER IN QUEENS. Subway: N, W to Astoria-Ditmars Boulevard. For other pool locations and information, visit: www.nycgovparks.org/sub_things_to_do/facilities/af_pools.html.

635. Surf **Rockaway Beach**.

There's not a palm tree in sight, but this strip between 88th and 90th Streets in Far Rockaway is a bona fide surfing beach. It is New York's only surf-specific spot, the one place where you can take to the waves without having to dodge swimmers. Though the scenery may not be as picturesque as Sunset Beach, surfers say the waves hold their own, and it's an easy subway ride from Manhattan and Brooklyn. Complete the experience by following your surf with some fish tacos from Rockaway Tacos.

SURF BEACH IS BETWEEN THE JETTIES, BETWEEN 88TH AND 90TH STREETS AT ROCKAWAY BEACH IN QUEENS.

ROCKAWAY TACO: 95-19 ROCKAWAY BEACH BOULEVARD, AT 96TH Street. 347-213-7466. www.rockawaybeach.com. Subway: A to Beach 90th Street.

636. Unleash your inner acrobat at **Trapeze School**.

If you want to get "out" of the city but don't have time for a trip upstate, try soaring above it. The Trapeze School of New York offers classes in "aerial arts" on top of Pier 40 on the Hudson River. In the flying trapeze class, students jump from a twenty-three-foot-high platform and fly through the air hanging by their arms or knees, eventually working up to maneuvers like "catches" (the flyer grabs on to a "catcher" and lets go of his trapeze). The benefits (besides fun) include gains in physical fitness, endurance, and self-esteem, as well as stress relief. Can you think of a better way to let loose? You'll feel liberated and invigorated—and far away from the commotion and concrete below.

HUDSON RIVER PARK, WEST STREET AT HOUSTON STREET AND PIER 40. N.B. There is also an indoor location at WEST 30TH STREET AND THE HUDSON RIVER, AT 11TH AVENUE. For information, class schedules, and prices, call 212-242-TSNY or visit www.trapezeschool.com.

637. **Tee off** in the boroughs.

There are a dozen golf courses in four of the five boroughs (all except Manhattan), many of which are accessible by subway or bus. A hop, skip, and a jump from the 86th Street R stop in Brooklyn is the Dyker Beach Golf Course, a favorite destination among area golfers. There are plenty of trees, and even a large lake—you wouldn't know you're in the middle of Brooklyn except for the street noise and exquisite views of the Verrazano-Narrows Bridge. A little further out in Brooklyn is the Marine Park Golf Course. You can still get there by public transportation, but it's a little more complicated—and for that reason, a bit less crowded. The course's proximity to the ocean makes for some gusty breezes from time to time, and on a cool, windy day, you could swear you were at St. Andrew's. In the Bronx, **Van Cortlandt Park** (see page 214) boasts two golf courses: the 110-year-old eighteen-hole Van Cortlandt Golf Course and the smaller nine-hole Mosholu Golf Course. Both of these are also convenient to subway stops. Queens and Staten Island have courses as well.

DYKER BEACH: *86ᵀᴴ STREET AND 7ᵀᴴ AVENUE IN BROOKLYN. Subway: R to 86ᵗʰ Street. 718-836-9722.*

MARINE PARK: *2880 FLATBUSH AVENUE IN BROOKLYN. Subway: 2, 5 to Brooklyn College-Flatbush Avenue, then Q35 Green bus. 718-252-4625.*

Van Cortland & Mosholu Golf Courses are both located in Van Cortlandt Park in the Bronx. Van Cortlandt Golf Course is at VAN CORTLANDT SOUTH AND BAILEY AVENUES. Subway: 1 to Van Cortlandt Park-242nd Street. 718-543-4595. Mosholu is at JEROME AND BAINBRIDGE AVENUES. Subway: 4 to Mosholu Parkway or Woodlawn. 718-655-9164. For a list of all of the city's courses, with information on hours, fees, and directions, visit nycgovparks.org/facilities/golf.

638. **Work yourself out** in the park.

Self magazine's annual health and beauty field day, the Self Workout in the Park, has achieved the highest physical fitness coup there is: it makes working out fun. Really, extremely, surprisingly fun. Now held each spring on Central Park's Rumsey Playfield, the day is packed with activities such as free group exercise classes, massages, personal training sessions, and outdoor rock-climbing simulations, plus a field's worth of sponsors handing out goodies and samples. But what really makes this a great event is that despite the obvious sponsorship, there is a somewhat spontaneous and infectious atmosphere generated by hundreds of people who are clearly having a lot of fun. Well, that and the fact that with all the freebies, you won't have to buy soap or granola bars for at least a year. (Note: While men can attend, it's clearly geared toward women.)

The Self Workout in the Park is held each spring. RUMSEY PLAYING FIELD, CENTRAL PARK, IN MANHATTAN. Tickets are available at the event or online at www.selfworkoutinthepark.com.

639. Swing on the rings at **Riverside Park**.

At this grown-up playground by 105th Street, you can swing on the rings, or do chin-ups or gymnastics on the bars in full view of the patrons of the Hudson Café. Just be warned—it's not as easy as it looks.

TRAVELING RING TOWER, RIVERSIDE PARK AT 105TH STREET IN MANHATTAN. Subway: 1 to 103rd Street. For tips on how to swing for beginners, visit www.swingaring.com.

640. Go to the track for horse races at the **Aqueduct**.

If you prefer watching your horses rather than riding them, spend a day in the sunshine at the thoroughbred races in Queens. Aqueduct is the only racetrack within New York City, and it hosts several great races such as the annual Wood Memorial in April, which is part of the warm-up trail for horses competing for the illustrious Triple Crown. Grandstand admission is only $1—and you could come back a big winner!

110-00 ROCKAWAY BOULEVARD IN QUEENS. Subway: A train to Aqueduct-North Conduit Avenue. 718-641-4700. www.nyra.com/aqueduct.

641. Join a **ZogSports team**.

Combining sports, socializing, and charity, ZogSports organizes activities and sports leagues for regular New Yorkers with a philanthropic bent. You can get a group of friends together to form your own team, or sign up individually and be assigned to one. Each team designates a charity, and the top performing teams in each league receive a donation for their chosen charity. The entry fee, which varies depending on which sport you're interested in, covers equipment, refs, and a contribution. ZogSports runs teams all year long for soccer, softball, kickball, and touch football, among others (they also have indoor leagues), and the divisions vary from very competitive to "extremely casual." Less pressure than a company softball team and more fun than meeting at a bar (though they do that, too), the teams are a great way to have fun, get outside, make friends, and benefit others.

For information and schedules, visit www.zogsports.com.

Take a walk in one of the city's biggest and most beautiful **graveyards**.

If you've never done it, you may find it hard to believe, but taking a walk in a graveyard is a very pleasant thing to do. They're the most reliably peaceful of outdoor spaces—you're pretty much guaranteed that a cell phone won't go off while you're taking your breather. New York cemeteries offer the additional draw of their wide open green spaces—as well as, of course, a roster of impressive inhabitants. Two favorites:

642. *Woodlawn Cemetery:* Woodlawn is well known as one of the most impressive burial grounds in the world, both for the number of notable names it contains and for the grand monuments that adorn the graves. As the first cemetery "local" to the city, Woodlawn was the chosen resting place of many artists, musicians, and other entertainers looking to be among friends. Miles Davis, Lionel Hampton, and Duke Ellington are just three from the long list of jazz legends buried here. Woodlawn was designed on a landscape-lawn plan that encouraged families to create monuments, centerpieces, and sculpture for their loved ones. Take a walk through the winding paths, check out the amazing mausoleums, and explore the memorials (but don't forget to get a photograph permit before you snap).

WEBSTER AVENUE AND EAST 233RD STREET IN THE BRONX. Subway: 4 to Woodlawn; 2 or 5 to 233rd. 718-920-0500. www.thewoodlawncemetery.org.

643. *Green-Wood Cemetery:* This beautiful cemetery sits atop the highest point in Brooklyn; from the top of Battle Hill, you can see downtown Manhattan, the Statue of Liberty, and much of the five boroughs stretching out around you. Late greats who've come to their eternal rest beneath Green-Wood's beautiful lawns include Leonard Bernstein, Jean-Michel Basquiat, Bill "the Butcher" Poole (Daniel Day-Lewis's character in *Gangs of New York*), and one of America's greatest heroes, Charles Feltman (the first guy ever to put a hot dog in a bun).

500 25TH STREET IN BROOKLYN. Subway: R to 25th Street. 718-768-7300. www.greenwood.com.

644. Take a day trip to **Roosevelt Island**.

It is possible (even likely) to have lived in New York for years without ever having considered visiting Roosevelt Island. But this quirky strip of land between Manhattan and Queens has an interesting (and bizarre) history and remnants of some incredible, obscure landmarks, including: Blackwell House, the vacant home of the island's former owners, the Blackwell family; ruins of an infamous lunatic asylum; and a decommissioned lighthouse (whose original purpose was not to direct ships but to light up the aforementioned lunatic asylum and prevent escapes). In the last couple of years, after unrelenting pressure from the Roosevelt Island Conservancy, the legendary neo-Gothic abandoned smallpox hospital at the southern tip of the island has been landmarked, and the nine acres of land around it turned into South Point Park, making the island even more pleasurable (if slightly less mysterious) to explore. You can walk from tip to tip in a couple of hours, and there's a great guide to the island's landmarks online at www.riwalk.com. If you get tired of walking, the bus that runs on the island still operates on a 25-cent fare. To get there, you can take the **tram** (see page 70), drive, or take the F train.

Subway: F to Roosevelt Island.

645. See a sheep-shearing demonstration at the **Queens Farm Museum**.

If days in the city have you longing for some good old-fashioned fun, you can hop on the subway and pay a visit to a farm. The Queens Farm Museum is a real working farm, located on forty-seven acres of undisturbed farmland in eastern Queens. And this is no modern theme-farm for city slickers—it is the longest continually farmed site in the entire state, dating back to 1697. In addition to tours of the historic farmhouse, planting fields, and greenhouse, you can participate in traditional agrarian events and activities: hayrides (April–October), sheep shearing, an Easter Egg hunt, a country fair (September), an Indian powwow (July), a corn maze (late summer–early fall), a haunted house, plus apple and berry festivals, pumpkin picking, and other harvest events.

73-50 LITTLE NECK PARKWAY IN QUEENS. Subway: E, F to Kew Gardens/Union Turnpike. 718-347-3276. www.queensfarm.org.

646. Go on a walk with the **Shorewalkers**.

Think you have to go up (or out of) state for a good hike? Think again. The Shorewalkers is a nonprofit group dedicated to promoting and preserving the city's shore areas—which are much larger than you might think! The group leads walks nearly every weekend to different exotic-sounding destinations, including the Rockaway Peninsula, Inwood Hills, and the **Gowanus Canal** (see pages 224–225). Walks are open to the public with a suggested $3 contribution, or you can join Shorewalkers for around $25 for a year of unlimited walks. The Great Saunter, an annual walk around the perimeter of Manhattan, is the biggest and most popular event. If you still want to get out of the city, no problem: thanks to the Shorewalkers, you can walk from Manhattan to Bear Mountain in the Hudson Valley on the Batt to Bear trail, a fifty-mile scenic hike along the Hudson River.

For information, schedules, and membership policies, visit www.shorewalkers.org.

647. Celebrate New York's contribution to aviation history at **Floyd Bennett Field**.

While it would surprise plenty of New Yorkers to know that there is a 26,000-acre national park within the city limits (also see **Jamaica Bay Wildlife Refuge** on page 226), even lesser known is that within the park, there stands one of the most important landmarks in American aviation history. Named for the man (a New York native) who piloted the first flight over the North Pole, Floyd Bennett Field was the first municipal airport in New York, with runways dating back to the late 1920s. Although it never succeeded as a commercial airport, because of its long runways and isolated location, Floyd Bennett Field was favored by what were then called "experimental pilots" during the golden age of aviation. Many historic and record-breaking flights took off or landed here in the 1930s, such as round-the-world flights by Wiley Post and Howard Hughes, and the "accidental" transatlantic trip that earned "Wrong Way" Corrigan his nickname. In 1941, the airport was turned over to the U.S. Navy, which used it through both World War II and the Cold War, and it was actively used by the Coast Guard until 1998. If you call in advance, you can arrange for a park ranger to give you a tour of the hangar (Tuesday, Thursday, and Saturday), which houses historic aircraft and other aviation memorabilia. Tip: you can drive, but visiting Floyd Bennett Field is a lovely stop on a bike ride around the parkland.

Floyd Bennett Field is located in GATEWAY NATIONAL PARK, JAMAICA BAY UNIT. For directions, maps, and information on visiting, contact the National Park Service at 718-338-3988 or visit www.nps.gov/gate.

→ **DID YOU KNOW?** *Gateway National Recreation Area is also home to a clothing-optional beach that is the only one of its kind in a National Park Service facility. Gunnison Beach is located in the Gateway's Sandy Hook unit, which is actually in northern New Jersey (and therefore can't technically qualify as an entry for our book). However, it is one of the few (if not only) nude beaches in the area, so if you live in New York City and want to sunbathe au naturel, this is your best option. (For more information, visit www.gunnisonbeach.org.)*

Expert Contributor: Francisco Liuzzi

Francisco Liuzzi is a certified personal trainer, cycling coach, and sports nutrition specialist. He is part-owner of Nutri-FitNYC (www.nutri-fitnyc.com), a New York City personal-training company that approaches physical fitness as a combination of proper exercise and proper diet education.

MY FIVE FAVORITE OUTDOOR SPORTS IN NEW YORK:

648. *Pick-up basketball in the park:* The best thing about New York City outdoor basketball is that in almost any park you have the chance to play against someone who can actually do a 360-degree dunk. That and the trash talk. Nothing says New York City ball in the park more than being crossed over and dunked on while being made fun of. It sounds harsh but it's the way they play. To watch a game: the courts at West 4th Street are the best. If you plan to play, bring an A game and a thick skin. One missed lay-up and you inherit a nickname you don't want. Passersby line the fence and they get to hear it all. To play: Tompkins Square Park. The competition can get pretty mean, but more courts mean it's easier to get into a game.

WEST 4TH STREET COURTS: WEST 4TH STREET AND SIXTH AVENUE IN MANHATTAN. Subway: A, C, E, B, D, F, V to West 4th Street. TOMPKINS SQUARE PARK COURTS: BETWEEN 7TH AND 10TH STREETS ON AVENUE A IN MANHATTAN. Subway: L to First Avenue.

649. *Biking through the city:* A view from your bicycle while sliding through pedestrians and traffic will give you an appreciation for the rhythm of the city that you can't really pick up on foot. Though not for everyone, riding uptown in the middle of Sixth Avenue, patting taxis on the side if they get too close and screaming "Heads up!" at pedestrians as they walk across the street staring at cell phones and iPods is strangely relaxing. Less risky is riding "the loop" in Central Park: 6.2 miles of gently rolling hills affords an up-close look at the charms of Central Park, as well as great views of the Midtown skyline. Celebrity sightings are common and even the "regular" people in the park are fun to look at. (For more on **people-watching in the park**, see page 79). *CENTRAL PARK LOOP, BETWEEN 59TH AND 110TH STREETS, FIFTH AVENUE AND CENTRAL PARK WEST IN MANHATTAN. Subway: check map, depending on location.*

650. *Jogging over the Brooklyn Bridge:* Starting at the base of the Manhattan side of the Brooklyn Bridge, run to the Brooklyn side and back. Some of the city's best views come from the middle of the **Brooklyn Bridge** (see page 20): all of Brooklyn, all of the skyscrapers of Midtown and downtown Manhattan, and the South Street Seaport, as well as the Statue of Liberty. The run isn't very long, with slight inclines as you come up both sides. The feeling of crossing the East River while running in the open air of the bridge's top level, as the city unfurls in front of you, is enough to make you forget you're exercising. *Subway: (for Manhattan) 2, 3 to Fulton Street; 4, 5, 6 to Brooklyn Bridge-City Hall; A, C to Broadway-Nassau Street; J, M, Z to Chambers; (for Brooklyn) A, C to High Street.*

651. *Wallball in the city:* "Wallball," or handball as it more commonly known, is one of the more popular activities at nearly all city parks and playgrounds. Few outdoor activities, including basketball, have as competitive a following as handball. Your hand is your racket, so pretty much anyone can play. It's just as fun to watch though, because the small court space gives great advantages to skilled players with a variety of trick serves. Older players frequently compete with younger ones, and trash talk is generational. Wallball is a good way to get a feel for a neighborhood. Any city court or park will have a wall, so there are games all over, but again, the **basketball courts of West 4th Street and Sixth Avenue** (see pages 239–240) are among the most intense. *For a list of parks, visit www.nyc.gov/parks.*

652. *Frisbee on the Great Lawn:* Throwing a Frisbee in the middle of the Great Lawn on a sunny day in the city is hard to beat, regardless of one's athletic ability or taste. The Great Lawn is fun for numerous reasons: endless amounts of grass to run on;

people of all shapes, sizes, and degrees of strangeness to watch; and an ability to make the hectic problems of the city vanish, for a little while. Even when it's crowded, there is plenty of space, and you don't even have to bring your own Frisbee—someone will always let you jump in. Actually, knowing how to throw a Frisbee isn't even required—just watch your head.

CENTRAL PARK BETWEEN 79TH AND 85TH STREETS IN MANHATTAN. Subway: 4, 5, 6 to 86th Street; 6 to 77th Street; B, C to 81st Street-Museum of Natural History or 86th Street.

CHAPTER 7:

Bargains & Splurges

With a countless number of stores in more sizes, shapes, and styles than you can imagine, New York City is truly a shopping mecca, drawing people from around the world eager to escape the monotony of their local malls and familiar chains and partake in the splendid array of exemplary, unique, and thrilling shopping opportunities. But the wonderful thing about shopping in New York is not just the amount and variety of what can be bought; it's also how enchanting the experience can be, whether it is ascending the floors of one of the glamorous department stores, discovering delightful anachronisms like Aphrodisia or The Hat Shop, or scoring a $600 suit for $199 at a sample sale.

In this chapter, we've chosen our favorite New York shopping experiences, from unique treasures that can be found in particular stores, to the best neighborhoods for wandering and window-shopping, to some out-of-the-ordinary retail setups, and the wonderfully eclectic designers' markets. Of course, one of the most distinctive (and intriguing) elements about buying things in New York is the highs and lows. You can buy a beautiful bouquet of flowers for $10 and then spend $100 on a hamburger—and both will exceed your expectations. For this reason, we've also highlighted the city's best bargains and splurges, pitted against each other, to show the manic, crazy, and wonderful niches and extremes that can be found here.

Department Stores

Paris may take credit for inventing the department store, but New York made them her own. Through the twentieth century, New York's department stores touted modernity and luxury, each with its own seductive charm. Although department stores are no longer the epitome of modern shopping, and several of the city's originals (Gimbels, A&S, B. Altman) are now gone, the ones that are left retain a glamorous sheen or have acquired a new patina. Decades after their heyday, they are the grandes dames of New York shopping and occupy a place in city lore, from the specter of the Vanderbilt mansion that haunts the site of today's Bergdorf's to the Macy's of *Miracle on 34th Street*. Unlike the rest of the country, where they are often swallowed up into the bellies of malls, department stores in New York still have a distinct presence and potent allure, different from the other shops and boutiques in the city. Here are our favorite things to do inside them.

653. Use the stairs at **Henri Bendel**.

Though it's named for a man, Bendel is distinctly feminine: petite, ladylike, and perfectly done-up. The ornate architecture, Lalique windows, and diminutive width make it feel more like a private townhouse than a mother ship, making Bendel the most fun of the department stores to explore. There are elevators, but if you ascend via the marble staircases, you're in for a real treat. Each floor unfolds in a series of nooks full of pretty things—fashion, accessories, fragrance, books, exquisite chocolates—and you can easily lose your way wandering from room to dazzling room, which is exactly what we recommend doing. This is not the best place to shop when you need to find something specific quickly, but it is a pleasure to wander around, and the sense of discovery if you do spy something is infinitely more satisfying than if you were to find the same item laid out in plain view at one of the other department stores.

710 FIFTH AVENUE BETWEEN 55TH AND 56TH STREETS IN MANHATTAN. Subway: E, V to Fifth Avenue/53rd Street; N, R, W to Fifth Avenue/59th Street. 212-247-1100. www.henribendel.com.

654. Look but don't touch at **Bergdorf Goodman**.

For pure uptown sophistication, nothing beats a trip to Bergdorf's. The Zola-esque exaltation of luxury retail is apparent from the moment you walk in, when you see the jewelry and fine accessories presented in display cases like works of art. The behind-the-glass atmosphere can take the fun out of shopping (this really doesn't seem like a place where the salespeople like you to try things on), but if you think of it as a museum of luxury rather than a retail outlet, the works on view can be quite thrilling. Our favorite spot is the seventh-floor home department, a mazelike collection of extravagant and stylishly anachronistic décor items, where you can see elaborate taxidermy animals, breathtaking flower arrangements, and sample fancy French chocolates.

754 FIFTH AVENUE BETWEEN 57TH AND 58TH STREETS IN MANHATTAN. Men's store: 745 Fifth Avenue at 58th Street. Subway: E, V to Fifth Avenue/53rd Street; N, R, W to Fifth Avenue/59th Street. 212-753-7300. www.bergdorfgoodman.com.

→ **DID YOU KNOW?** *The Bergdorf building was formerly the site of the mansion of Cornelius Vanderbilt. Before the department store opened in 1928, the mansion's front gates were moved uptown, to Central Park's Conservatory Gardens (see pages 221–222).*

655. Shop and refuel at **Bloomingdale's**.

Though it stands apart from the elite Fifth Avenue retail palaces both in neighborhood and in prestige, Bloomingdale's is well worth a detour. With a large information kiosk situated prominently in the lobby and an entrance to the store located in the subway station, it has a decidedly more plebeian feel than Bendel's or Bergdorf's—although that's not to say that there aren't plenty of items well within splurge territory. Bloomingdale's carries medium- and high-end clothing for men, women, and children, as well as furniture, bedding and housewares, shoes, accessories, and cosmetics, and the atmosphere is welcoming and unpretentious, making it a great place to actually shop. It's also got the best of selection of places to eat. Of the numerous eateries in the store, our favorites are 40 Carrots and David Burke at Bloomingdale's. 40 Carrots is the Bloomie's original, and this health-conscious cafeteria has been serving the same tasty soups, salads with melba toast, and sandwiches served on grainy bread since 1937. 40 Carrots is best known for its frozen yogurt, and it's worth noting New Yorkers have been lining up for cups of coffee and tart plain yogurt since before the word "Pinkberry" was invented. If you're in the mood for something more cutting edge, try Burke in the Box, chef David Burke's prepared-food café on the ground floor, where you can try items like mini-sandwiches served in tennis-ball canisters and cheesecake lollipops.

1000 THIRD AVENUE BETWEEN 59TH AND 60TH STREETS IN MANHATTAN. 212-705-2000. Subway: 4, 5, 6 to 59th Street; N, R, W to Lexington Avenue/59th Street.

Note: Bloomingdale's has a SoHo location, which carries a nice selection of trendy and high-end fashions, but no 40 Carrots or Burke in the Box.

504 BROADWAY BETWEEN SPRING AND BROOME STREETS IN MANHATTAN. Subway: 6 to Spring Street; N, R, W to Prince Street. 212-729-5900. www.bloomingdales.com.

656. Buy something cool at **Barneys**.

Some longtime downtown New Yorkers have never forgiven Barneys for its treasonous act of 1996: forsaking the original 17th Street store to preserve the uptown Madison Avenue location. With its air of exclusivity (some would say snootiness), Barneys fits in quite well among the other upscale Madison Avenue boutiques. Its emphasis on cutting-edge designers gives the feel (or the illusion) that you are getting a glimpse of the latest styles before they go mainstream. And though the vibe is now thoroughly uptown, Barneys has cashed in on its original edgy, downtown image with the edgy, downtown-looking styles of Co-op, the store's "casual" department. Co-op has spawned several freestanding boutiques, including, ironically, a large store within spitting distance of the original Seventh Avenue location.

BARNEYS: *660 MADISON AVENUE AT 61ST STREET IN MANHATTAN. Subway: N, R, W to Fifth Avenue/59th Street. 212-826-8900.*

CO-OP CHELSEA: *236 WEST 18TH STREET BETWEEN SEVENTH AND EIGHTH AVENUE. Subway: 1 to 18th Street. 212-593-7800. For addresses of other Co-op locations, visit www.barneys.com.*

→ **DID YOU KNOW?** *The 17th Street space that used to be the Barneys department store is now a museum of Himalayan art.*

657. Stop and smell the roses **at Takashimaya**.

Takashimaya is an oasis from the madness of Fifth Avenue retail—even Bergdorf's can't compete with the serenity of this exquisite Japanese import. The selection of clothing, accessories, travel items, cosmetics, home items, and gifts is elegantly curated, but the real standout is the store's floral department. If you want to delight someone with a dazzling arrangement, this is the place to come; if you just need a break from the frenzy on the street, it's like a breath of fresh air.

693 FIFTH AVENUE BETWEEN 54TH AND 55TH STREETS IN MANHATTAN. Subway: E, V to Fifth Avenue/53rd Street. 212-350-0100. www.takashimaya-ny.com.

Buy discounted designer clothing at a **sample sale**.

Sample sales are the fashion-conscious New Yorker's best-kept secret. These hidden caches of discounted designer clothing stock plenty of fashionable New York closets, and keep many a young fashion or magazine assistant in office-appropriate apparel. Technically, most of the clothing sold at the sample sales listed here isn't actually designer samples, as they once were when the term "sample sale" was coined. The clothes you find at a sample sale are usually overstock from inventory; after designers ship that season's merchandise to stores, they sell what's left over to what are essentially clearing houses, at a big discount, which offer it to the public through sample sales. This means that, one, the offerings tend to be from the current season; and, two, there's usually a range of sizes.

Sample sales take place all the time. Many are held in the Garment District, at designer showrooms, but others are held in stores or other spaces around the city. *Time Out New York, New York Magazine,* and *DailyCandy* (www.dailycandy.com) often run listings of current sample sales and are good places to check to see who's offering what, where, and when. The following are some favorite places venues and sales:

658. *Clothingline:* This large warehouse in the Garment District gets new merchandise regularly, all year round, from a wide range of well-known labels such as Theory, Tocca, J. Crew, among many, many others. The selection and variety of the sizes are particularly good, and they often have sales featuring children's clothes. You can sign up on their Web site (www.clothingline.com) to receive a weekly e-mail that will notify you about upcoming sales.

*261 WEST 36TH STREET, SECOND FLOOR, BETWEEN SEVENTH AND EIGHTH AVENUES IN MAN-
HATTAN. Opening hours vary; visit www.clothingline.com for upcoming sales and hours. Subway: 1, 2, 3, A, C, E to 34th Street-Penn Station.*

659. *Greenfinds/Ecompassion:* This unusual shopping experience evolved out of
the Find Outlet, a weekend-only boutique that offered a changing selection of deeply
discounted designer clothes at several storefronts across the city. Now located on
Great Jones Street, the clothes are still great, but the operation has changed its name
and shifted its focus—5 percent of all sales is donated to charity, either to an environ-
mental cause, or another cause chosen by the designer whose clothes are being sold.
The list of participating designers changes regularly, so to find out about what's on or
coming, sign up for the weekly e-mail on the Web site.

*2 Great Jones Street between Broadway and Lafayette Streets in Manhattan. Subway: 6 to
Bleecker Street; B, D, F, V to Broadway-Lafayette. www.greenfinds.com.*

660. *Barneys Warehouse Sale:* If you've ever been walking around Chelsea at 7:00
a.m. on a Thursday morning and wondered what throngs of poshly dressed women
could possibly be waiting for at that hour, chances are you've encountered the line for
the opening day of the Barneys Warehouse Sale, the department store's legendary
week-long housecleaning. Twice a year, in February and August, Barneys opens its
warehouse to the public and sells off the remaining stock from that season at incredibly discounted prices to make room for the next season. The difference between this
and a sample sale is that the clothes come from the store rather than the designers, but
in practice there's no difference in merchandise or price, except that the February sale
will feature mostly fall and winter clothes, and the August sale will offer mostly spring
and summer clothes. Basically, you can expect to see all of the designers carried at Barneys and Co-op, and some of the exact clothing that was on the racks just the week
before, for between 50 and 80 percent off, with further markdowns occurring throughout the week. (Shoes and men's clothing available, too.) Caution: this sale is not for the
faint of heart—you need to be a hearty shopper to take it on. You will be pushed and
shoved, you will pick through bins of clothing, you will try on clothes in the aisle, and
you had better keep an eye on whatever treasures you find because everything is fair
game until you hand over your credit card. By the end of the week, they are practically
giving the clothes away, but most of the good stuff is long gone by the second morning. We suggest going on opening day, around 10:00 a.m. or 11:00 a.m.—the initial
opening rush at 8:00 a.m. thins out as people leave for work, so you'll have a good hour
or so before the lunchtime crowd descends.

*August and February. 255 WEST 17TH STREET BETWEEN SEVENTH AND EIGHTH AVENUES IN
MANHATTAN. Subway: 1 to 18th Street. For exact dates and hours, visit www.barneys.com.*

661. Buy designer clothing for a discount at **Century 21**.

Century 21 is a department store—but it's a department store where the merchandise is half the price it would be at other department stores. From Prada and Pucci to Champs and Fruit of the Loom, you can find every type of clothing, shoe, accessory, or houseware, high- and low-end, in a relatively civilized setting. Sure, the racks are crammed with clothes, customer service consists of the promise of a $25 credit if you're not given a receipt, and there is not a dependable selection of size and merchandise, but considering what you're getting (top-quality and high-fashion goods for a fraction of what they're normally sold for), it's amazingly easy to browse the racks. (And browse is what you'll want to do, since inventory varies greatly.) And though it pretty much always feels like the day before Christmas, renovations like an expanded shoe section and women's dressing rooms (well, cubbies) on the third floor have significantly enhanced the shopping experience. It's a particularly good place to stock up on underwear and socks, and for sizable discounts on coats and men's suits. (There's also a location in Bay Ridge, Brooklyn.)

22 CORTLANDT STREET BETWEEN CHURCH STREET AND BROADWAY IN MANHATTAN. Subway: 2, 3, 4, 5, J, M, Z to Fulton Street; A, C to Broadway-Nassau Street; R, W to Cortlandt Street. 212-227-9092. Brooklyn location: 472 EAST 86TH STREET BETWEEN FOURTH AND FIFTH AVENUES. Subway: R to 86th Street. 718-748-3266. www.c21stores.com.

662. Fantasize about your dream house at **ABC Carpet & Home**.

ABC is the king of the city's shelter stores, and a wonderful example of the American dream come true. ABC was born in 1897, out of a pushcart on the Lower East Side, where Max Weinrib, an Austrian immigrant, sold used carpet and odd fabrics. In the generations since, it has grown into the world's biggest rug and carpet store, and today, it is run by Max's grandson and great-granddaughter. Occupying two landmark buildings on opposite sides of lower Broadway, ABC flanks the avenue, as if signaling your arrival downtown, where it rules by taste and confidence (its influence can be seen in the aesthetic and merchandise in many downtown stores and boutiques). On the west side of Broadway, the 881 building houses carpets and rugs, more than 35,000 from around the world, including antiques and Oriental rugs several centuries old, and new, modern rugs from ABC's own collection. At the home store across the street, the riches are laid out over six stories of lavishly designed departments, selling furniture, antiques, vintage and new fabrics, bedding and linens, breathtaking lamps and sconces, toys, books, drapes, scarves, jewelry, spiritual aids...the amount of beautiful merchandise is literally staggering. ABC Home is by far the most opulent store in New York, eschewing minimalist chic in favor of wearing its riches on its sleeves, and while the carpet store may be of interest only to those looking to buy, the home store is actually best visited if you're not looking for anything in particular. Explore, and let yourself be seduced by the treasures that unfold floor after floor. Listen and you may hear a single piece calling your name, beckoning you for a closer look, and—should you have the resources—offering you the privilege of taking it home. (Should you lack the resources, ABC also has an outlet in the Bronx. For more information, visit the Web site below.)

881 AND 888 BROADWAY AT 19TH STREET IN MANHATTAN. Subway: 4, 5, 6, L, N, Q, R, W to 14th Street-Union Square. 212-473-3000. www.abchome.com.

---

663. Take a trip down memory lane (without breaking the bank) at Reminiscence.

Bursting at the seams with kitsch, Reminiscence proves that there is always a steady market for Pez dispensers and Hawaiian shirts. Opened in 1971, it began selling novelty items and vintage camp T-shirts long before other retailers started mass-manufacturing them. Their stuff, however, is authentically tacky. Up front, there is a selection of toys and games right out of *Pee-Wee's Playhouse*, including Tom Tierney paper dolls, plastic Lolita sunglasses, Magic 8-Balls, retro cartoon character lunchboxes, and the largest assortment of car air fresheners we've ever seen. In the back, they sell vintage clothes—and this is a great place to shop for them because, one, unlike most vintage stores, the prices are quite cheap; two, the area with the clothes is roomy and never too crowded; and, three, there isn't an overwhelming amount of stuff, so you can browse through the entire selection easily, without worrying that the Hawaiian shirt you just found will be snatched out from under you.

50 WEST 23RD STREET BETWEEN FIFTH AND SIXTH AVENUES IN MANHATTAN. Subway: F, V to 23rd Street. 212-243-2292. www.reminiscence.com.

---

664. Find the perfect pair of jeans at What Comes Around Goes Around.

Although it's been open only since 1993, WCAGA has revolutionized the way people see and buy vintage clothes in New York. Housing the largest collection of vintage denim in the United States, the SoHo retail location looks more like an uptown boutique than a secondhand store, with shelves upon shelves of pristinely folded jeans, cases of accessories from boots to belt buckles, and racks of well-kept leather and woolen coats and jackets. The store's philosophy is that buying vintage clothes should be more exciting, more reliable, and more selective than picking through the racks at thrift shops, and the success of WCAGA lies in the fact that the selection is so broad and in such good condition that you have the fun of picking out a hard-to-find classic cut without the frustration of sifting through moth-eaten riffraff. Their showroom (open by appointment only) holds one of the most impressive and comprehensive collections of vintage clothing in the world, from western wear to sportswear and military outfits, as well as a library of vintage textiles, periodicals, and historical fashion memorabilia.

The owners have also extended their accessible-vintage philosophy into their own line of casual vintage-inspired clothing for men and women.

WCAGA (RETAIL): *351 WEST BROADWAY BETWEEN BROOME AND GRAND STREETS IN MANHATTAN. Subway: 6 to Spring Street; N, R, W to Prince Street. 212-343-9303.*

WCAGA (SHOWROOM): *13-17 LAIGHT STREET, NO. 28, BETWEEN VARICK AND CANAL STREETS, FIFTH FLOOR, IN MANHATTAN. Subway: 1, 2, 3, A, C, E to Canal Street. 212-274-8340. www.nyvintage.com.*

665. Buy some New York City shoes at **Sacco**.

Why, out of all of the shoe stores in the city, have we chosen this one as the place where you should buy your shoes? Because in New York, you need shoes that look good and you need shoes you can walk in, and Sacco is where you can buy one pair to serve both purposes. Sacco carries beautiful shoes that are designed to be worn (as in walked, run, and subwayed in), but that look like—though not derivative of— shoes from Gucci, Prada, and other high-end designers. Sacco has its own line, designed and manufactured in Italy, and adheres to special design guidelines to make each pump, sandal, and boot comfortable to walk in; the stores also carry styles from a few other brands, specially chosen for their high standards of style and comfort. And it gets better—for the quality, the shoes are shockingly inexpensive, around $100 to $250 for heels and loafers, and $150 to $300 for boots. Sacco adheres to another great European tradition and holds excellent sales in January and July.

Multiple locations throughout Manhattan. Call 212-243-2070 or visit www.saccoshoes.com for store locations.

666. Look like you paid more than you did at **Oak**.

The atmosphere and offerings at this store couple (they're listed as being in an "open relationship" on Facebook) appears at first glance to be in a remote zip code of coolness. But upon inspection of the price tags, you'll find that prices are in the same neighborhood as Banana Republic, making a fashion-mag-inspired look rather easy to experiment with. There's no icy hipster vibe amongst the sales force either, so you can feel free to ask for opinions on a zip-front Lycra minidress, a necklace with a charm in the shape of the Madonna cone bra, or whatever treasure has caught your eye.

OAK WILLIAMSBURG: *208 N. 8TH STREET AT DRIGGS AVENUE IN BROOKLYN. Subway: L to Bedford Street. 718-782-0521.*

OAK BOND: *28 BOND STREET BETWEEN LAFAYETTE AND THE BOWERY IN MANHATTAN. www.oaknyc.com.*

667. Get your dollar back at the **Music Inn**.

The proprietors of this wonderful, museumlike shop have accrued so much musical para-phernalia that to sift through it would take days—and considerable athleticism. All man-ner of musical instruments, from wooden flutes and xylophones to ukuleles and castanets, fill the hallways, clutter the floor, and hang from the ceiling. Shelves of vintage vinyl records line the walls, and sheet music, reeds, metronomes, and other accou-trements take up any leftover space. The owners seem frighteningly knowledgeable on virtually every aspect of music, and will dig around upon request for just about anything you might desire. In order to enter the Music Inn, visitors must pay one dollar, which will be returned if they make a purchase at the store. Our advice is to make the most of this eccentric treasure, make a selection, and get your buck back at the checkout.

169 WEST 4TH STREET BETWEEN SIXTH AND SEVENTH AVENUES. Subway: 1 to Christopher Street-Sheridan Square; A, C, E, B, D, F, V to West 4th Street. 212-243-5715.

668. Seek out the **Manolo Blahnik store**.

The Manolo Blahnik store is hidden in the middle of a quiet block in Midtown, directly behind the **Museum of Modern Art** (see page 122). The store's sign is a tiny plaque, no bigger than those used on street-level doctor's offices, and though shoes are displayed in the window, there is no name-brand fanfare, no autographed pictures from *Sex and the City*, no distinguished marquee, nothing that calls out to shoppers on Fifth Avenue. It's not that they don't want you inside—everyone from the security guard/doorman who lets you in to the well-coiffed salespeople is surprisingly warm and amiable. It's that self-promotion is—apologies to the other stores—clearly beneath them. For this reason, Manolo Blahnik is a truly special store, and one of the few boutiques in the city that radiates luxury without being snooty or offensively exclusive. Even if there's no way in a million years that you'd actually buy a pair of these iconic sartorial treasures, the store is well worth a detour off Fifth Avenue's main drag. Come to experience, admire, and try for yourself, if you dare…

31 WEST 54TH STREET BETWEEN FIFTH AND SIXTH AVENUES IN MANHATTAN. Subway: E, V to Fifth Avenue/53rd Street. 212-582-3007. www.manoloblahnik.com.

669. Check out the competition at **Opening Ceremony**.

This downtown boutique, straddling SoHo and Chinatown, is a store with a mission. Inspired by Pierre de Coubertin, the founder of the modern Olympic Games, OC's own-ers structured their store as something of an international fashion joust, pitting clothes from their favorite American designers against those from designers from a different country each year. The visiting team (past opponents include Hong Kong, Germany,

Japan, and England) is represented by one established brand, several upstarts, and vintage and flea market finds picked up on official scouting trips. Yes, it's high concept, but regular rules of shopping still apply, and the offerings aren't always super highbrow: In 2005, Opening Ceremony became the first U.S. retailer to carry the cultish high-street chain TopShop during their U.K. competition.

35 HOWARD STREET, BETWEEN CROSBY AND BROADWAY IN MANHATTAN. Subway: 6, J, M, Z, N, R, Q, W to Canal Street. 212-226-7930. www.openingceremony.us.com.

---

670. Buy a cool gift from **Auto**.

If you want to impress someone with your good taste, you can't go wrong at Auto. Hanging out on the fringes of the Meatpacking District, Auto is like the cool loner you always wanted to befriend in high school: it's proud to be outside the mainstream, and intriguing and stylish in its own way. Inside the store, you'll find slick, high-design lifestyle accessories like silkscreen cooking aprons, customizable nesting dolls, funky winter caps and mittens, and a well-edited selection of art and design books. The store is definitely geared toward the hip urban family, so you'll see plenty of cool baby gear, like tomato-shaped beanbag chairs, a hyper-stylized bouncy chair, and stuffed animals made of brightly colored cashmere. They also carry jewelry and women's clothing. The prices are about what you'd expect from a place that carries cashmere teddy bears (expensive, though not outrageous), and even if this kind of mod luxury isn't your style, just being in the store will make you feel a little cooler.

805 WASHINGTON STREET BETWEEN GANSEVOORT AND HORATIO STREETS IN MANHATTAN. Subway: A, C, E to 14th Street; L to Eighth Avenue. 212-229-2292. www.thisisauto.com.

---

671. Buy a gift for a kid or something unique for yourself at **Blue Tree**.

When Blue Tree opened up in the space vacated by the beloved toy store Penny Whistle on the Upper East Side, many adults and children who had lamented the loss of the neighborhood's one fun place to shop nearly jumped for joy. Blue Tree isn't exactly a toy store, although it does carry plenty of toys. It's more like a chic curiosity shop, overflowing with unique and exotic treasures scattered about in a delightfully topsy-turvy bi-level space. Children and former children will find something to tickle their fancy, like funky skateboards, a solar-powered rotating globe, ladies' purses made to look like yearbooks and doctor's manuals, and complete sets of Shakespeare's plays in adorable leather-bound mini-books. Store owner Phoebe Cates (a neighborhood mom who is married to the actor Kevin Kline) and her staff dart about the store like little sprites, going up and down the stairs, pulling hidden treasures out of nooks and crannies and chatting with customers. But lest the carefree atmosphere make you forget where you are, one look at the price tags will bring you right back— the cheapest item we found was the $9 pair of cashmere infant socks.

1283 MADISON AVENUE BETWEEN 91ST AND 92ND STREETS IN MANHATTAN. Subway: 4, 5, 6 to 86th Street. 212-369-BLUE. www.bluetreeny.com.

672. Earn a bottle of Cristal at **Sable's**.

The Upper East Side has long been home to many Eastern Europeans, and among the plethora of German and Hungarian delicatessens, Sable's Smoked Fish has for years been the most respected supplier of caviar, salmon, and all manner of Baltic treats. It's best to go on an empty stomach: the exceptionally generous staff will hand you samples of everything from thin slices of smoked mackerel to delicious lashings of lobster salad, served on a crispy square of toast. It's not cheap, but with a vast range of caviar, fish, cheese, bread, and traditional potato pancakes, it's difficult to leave with your wallet intact. That's not to say that there isn't a deal to be had: spend $1,500 in one visit during the holiday season, and you get a bottle of Dom Perignon champagne. Not bad, but we recommend you go the distance—spend $2,000 and earn a gleaming bottle of Cristal as your reward.

1489 SECOND AVENUE BETWEEN 78TH AND 79TH STREETS IN MANHATTAN. Subway: 6 to 77th Street. 212-249-6177. www.sablesnyc.com.

673. Equip yourself like a paparazzo at **B&H Photo**.

A Midtown institution for thirty years, B&H Photo is a photographer's gourmet supermarket, an emporium of camera and film supplies like no other in the world. B&H carries virtually everything a photographer could conceivably need, from a huge range of cameras, flashes, camcorders, and microphones to the broadest selection of film, editing equipment, and Polaroid accessories in the city. The store stocks every new item from every major brand, as well as vintage pieces and secondhand equipment, so there's something to fit every photographer's budget and taste, and amateurs, professionals, and collectors are all catered to. The process of actually purchasing something at B&H is unique as well—orders are placed at different counters and items are then picked up at the checkout, where they arrive by a system of overhead conveyor belts and pulleys.

420 NINTH AVENUE BETWEEN 33RD AND 34TH STREETS IN MANHATTAN. Subway: 1, 2, 3, A, C, E to 34th Street-Penn Station. 212-444-6615. www.bhphotovideo.com.

674. Pluck and strum at **Mandolin Brothers**.

One of Staten Island's lesser-known attractions is Mandolin Brothers, Ltd., one of the greatest guitar stores in the world. With close to a thousand instruments in its vast showroom, Mandolin Brothers really carries every fretted instrument you can imagine, from classic acoustic and electric guitars to banjos, ukuleles, twelve-strings, pedal steels, bass guitars, and, of course, mandolins. There are new and used instruments at reasonable prices and rare collectibles from antique Gibsons to beloved Telecasters and one-of-a-kind Martins, and there is even an entire lefty section devoted to south-paw players. The golden rule of Mandolin Brothers' showroom is that you can pick up and play any instrument you want, without fear of frowns or comments from the staff. *629 FOREST AVENUE BETWEEN PELTON AND OAKLAND AVENUES IN STATEN ISLAND. Staten Island Ferry to Staten Island, then 48 Forest Avenue bus to Pelton Avenue. 718-981-8585. www.mandoweb.com.*

675. Have an intimate encounter with precious jewels at **Harry Winston**.

A block down from **Tiffany** (see page 26) is the flagship store of another legendary jeweler. Harry Winston does not have the same fame or iconic clout as the home of the little blue box, but its jewels are no less impressive. The store is calm and quiet as a boutique, and while that intimacy might make it more intimidating to browse in, it also lends a pleasant, furtive feeling, like being inside a life-size treasure chest right on Fifth Avenue. Winston, who was the last owner of the Hope Diamond (he donated it to the Smithsonian), was known for his intricate, artistic designs, and you can see examples of his masterpieces displayed in the store. (You could also try to strike up a musical number, like **Ed Norton in *Everyone Says I Love You***; for more great movie scenes, see page 114.)
718 FIFTH AVENUE AT 56TH STREET IN MANHATTAN. Subway: E, V to Fifth Avenue/53rd Street; N, R, W to Fifth Avenue/59th Street. 212-245-2006. www.harrywinston.com.

676. See jewels in a less rarefied setting (no pun intended) in the **Diamond District**.

West 47th Street between Fifth and Sixth Avenues is home to more than 2,000 independent jewelers, many of them operating out of "exchanges," which are ground-level halls filled with up to 100 booths where different jewelers operate. The setting isn't luxe, but what it lacks in ambience it makes up for in expertise—since 47th Street is where diamonds come when they arrive in the United States, the jewelers here are some of the most experienced in the world. In addition to diamonds, you can also find wedding bands, watches, and regular gold, silver, and platinum jewelry. (This is also an excellent place for jewelry repairs.) The offerings here are not known for being particularly on the cutting edge (again, pun not intended) of style, but if you want to comparison shop, this is the best way to do it, and even if you're not in the market for a gem, it's fascinating to watch how this enclave of independent merchants does business. To help you navigate, the district operates an excellent Web site (see below) with information about the Diamond District and what is sold there, a directory of jewelers in the area, and buyer's guides for jewelry and diamonds.

WEST 47TH STREET BETWEEN FIFTH AND SIXTH AVENUES IN MANHATTAN. Subway: B, D, F, V to 47th-50th Streets-Rockefeller Center. For more information, visit www.diamonddistrict.org.

677. Get yourself some Rem Koolhaas designs at **United Nude**.

When is a shoe not just a shoe? When it's designed as an interpretation of architecture or an iconic object. To really get the gist, visit United Nude, the New York outpost of this shoe-producing European design company. Co-founded by shoemaker Galahad J.D. Clark and architect Rem D. Koolhaas (nephew of the Pritzker Prize–winning architect of the same name), United Nude produces elegant, architecturally inspired footwear that look as likely to turn up in *Dwell* as in *Vogue*. Their signature "concept" (the United Nude term for style) is the Möbius, a wedge sandal made from a single strip that forms a Möbius band and inspired by Mies van der Rohe's famous Barcelona chair. They also make a high-heeled pump called Naked, which doesn't have any covering over the shoe's construction and reinforcements. Although the design is high-concept, the shoes are surprisingly down-to-earth: all of the styles are comfortable enough to walk around in, and are reasonably priced.

260 ELIZABETH STREET BETWEEN PRINCE AND HOUSTON STREETS IN MANHATTAN. Subway: 6 to Spring Street. 212-274-9010. www.unitednude.com.

678. Spoil your dog at **Trixie and Peanut**.

Trixie and Peanut is the Barneys of the city's pet boutiques, with designer dog clothes, personalized rhinestone collars, "Chewy Vuitton" fuzzy purses, and bottles of "Dog Perignon" (there is also stuff for cats). But what really makes this store stand out is the attention lavished on each and every furry diva. Even if you've got an overweight bulldog with questionable breath, they'll make you feel like he or she is the cutest pet in world.

23 EAST 20TH STREET BETWEEN BROADWAY AND PARK AVENUE SOUTH IN MANHATTAN. Subway: 6 to 23rd Street. 212-358-0881. www.trixieandpeanut.com.

679. Sip and be serenaded while you shop at the **Burgundy Wine Company**...

These twenty-year old Burgundy specialists offer a thorough and well-priced selection of wine from Burgundy, Rhône, and Oregon at their Chelsea store. They hold informal tastings every night of the week from 5 to 7 p.m. (and all day on Saturdays), and on Wednesday nights, there's live jazz as well.

143 WEST 26TH STREET BETWEEN SIXTH AND SEVENTH AVENUES IN MANHATTAN. Subway: 1 to 28th Street. www.burgundywinecompany.com.

680. ...or hang out at the Alphabet City Wine Company.

The gang at this East Village wine shop likes to have fun as much as they like (and know) their vino, and to that end, they usually have a couple of bottles open for customers to try, no matter when you stop by. On Fridays and Saturdays, these informal tastings take on a house party atmosphere, with customers and locals mixing, sipping, browsing, and lounging in the store's comfy chairs. Other in-store happenings have a similar light-hearted spirit (they once held a contest inviting customers to submit crayon drawings on a boxed wine). The owner, Keith Beavers, is also the author of the blog East Village Wine Geek (as well as the owner of the nearby wine bar, In Vino), on which his posts consist of hilarious two-minute videos on wine-related topics. (We're pretty sure he's the only wine-store owner in the city who has done an imitation of Godzilla to make a point about half-bottles of wine.)

100 AVENUE C BETWEEN SIXTH AND SEVENTH STREETS IN MANHATTAN. Subway: L to First Avenue. 212-505-9463. www.abcwineco.com

681. Buy a bottle or two from Acker, Merrall, and Condit.

Many of us would like to know more about wine than we do, and most of us would like to drink more wine than we do. Both goals are possible at Acker, Merrall, and Condit, the oldest wine shop in America and a paradise for anyone with a taste for the grape. Founded in New York in 1820, Acker is still a family-run business and makes its customers' happiness top priority. Shopping for wine at this Upper West Side store is wonderfully unlike looking around a regular liquor store: for one thing, the selection is unrivalled, drawing on wines from most every vintage and continent; and for another, the people who work here are passionate and knowledgeable about wine, and can provide customers with anything from a history of a particular region to good advice on what goes best with butternut squash. AM&C holds a number of live and Internet auctions throughout the year, giving connoisseurs a chance to bolster their collections, and curious newcomers a chance to pick up a good bargain. The company philosophy—that experts and amateurs should enjoy wine together— extends to their Wine Workshop, which holds tastings and other events designed to spread knowledge and enjoyment of wine to as many people as possible.

160 WEST 72ND STREET BETWEEN BROADWAY AND COLUMBUS AVENUE IN MANHATTAN. Subway: 1, 2, 3 to 72nd Street; B, C to 72nd Street. 212-787-1700. www.ackerwines.com.

682. Avoid divulging how much you know about wine (and how much you can spend) at **Discovery Wines**.

It's a gimmick, but it might be the best gimmick in town: this East Village wine store has several computer stations where you can search the inventory by price, type, or region, and avoid the interaction with a store clerk that many people dread. The computers have a food-matching feature, where you enter the type of food and what kind of wine you want to serve (red, white, or sparkling), and it will list all the viable options. Finally, there's a scanner that you use to scan the barcode of a bottle to find out where it's from and what it pairs well with.

10 AVENUE A AT HOUSTON STREET IN MANHATTAN. Subway: F, V to Lower East Side-Second Avenue. 212-674-7833. www.discoverywines.com.

683. If you have to talk to a salesperson at a wine store, the **Chelsea Wine Vault** is the place to do it.

This store is as unpretentious as they come, and with more than 3,000 bottles, there really is something in every price and taste range. The people who work here are unabashedly enthusiastic about wine—a far cry from the aloof oenophiles in many wine stores. Grab a salesperson and describe what you're looking for, and he or she will likely launch into a discussion about a small wine or newly discovered producer. Tastings are similarly lively, with the staff eager to share the featured bottles, and it's hard not be infected by their oeno-exuberance.

75 NINTH AVENUE BETWEEN 14TH AND 15TH STREETS IN MANHATTAN. Subway: A, C, E to 14th Street; L to Eighth Avenue. 212-462-4244. www.chelseawinevault.com.

684. Bring the family to the wine store at **Bottlerocket**.

Believing that "buying wine should be as pleasurable as drinking it," Bottlerocket Wine & Spirits is a user- and family-friendly wine store, with a playspace for kids, treats for dogs and candy for under-agers, a large reading room in back, and some very friendly wine sellers. To keep things easy, the store stocks only 365 bottles at a time, arranging featured wines in several themed kiosks in the middle of the store. Wines for meat, vegetables, chocolate, celebrations, gift-giving, and other occasions are grouped in different stations, with easy-to-read tasting summaries, storage tips (don't keep open bottles of wine on the fridge door!), and edifying facts. There are also sheets of seasonal recipes for customers to take, or if you don't feel like cooking, there's a take-out kiosk, complete with menus from local delivery joints.

5 WEST 19TH STREET BETWEEN FIFTH AND SIXTH AVENUES IN MANHATTAN. Subway: 4, 5, 6, L, N, Q, R, W to 14th Street-Union Square. 212-929-2323. www.bottlerocketwine.com.

685. Add to your wine cellar at **Italian Wine Merchants**.

At the top end of the wine store spectrum is this sophisticated shop, specializing in very fine Italian wines and serving many connoisseurs and collectors. To maintain quality control, only one bottle of each type of wine is on display; the rest is kept in a temperature-controlled cellar. Although the store sells single bottles of "everyday wine," IWM's real strength is in helping people begin or develop their own collections, and as a place to find special gifts (they even have a wine registry for couples). They have an extensive selection of well-chosen gift baskets and wine clubs for the novice through connoisseur. And though IWM is upscale, the attitude is one of appreciation rather than exclusion.

108 EAST 16TH STREET BETWEEN IRVING PLACE AND UNION SQUARE EAST IN MANHATTAN. Subway: 4, 5, 6, L, N, Q, R, W to 14th Street-Union Square. 212-473-2323. www.iwmstore.com.

686. Travel the world without leaving the state at **Idlewild Books**.

Places, travel, and new horizons are the focus of this eclectic specialty bookstore. If you're planning a trip, you can come here to pick up a guidebook, phrase book, or map. If you plan to take your voyage through the mind, there is a selection of interesting and unusual international and foreign-language literature. And because no trip is complete without sampling the local cuisine, they also stock cookbooks from cuisines and cultures around the world. Keep an eye on their Web site for events—the store hosts some of the more interesting book launches downtown, from new travel guides to reissues of foreign-language classics.

12 WEST 19TH STREET, BETWEEN FIFTH AND SIXTH AVENUES IN MANHATTAN. Subway: F, V to 14th or 23rd Streets. www.idlewildbooks.com

→ **DID YOU KNOW?** *Idlewild was the previous name of John F. Kennedy Airport; the airport was renamed in December 1963, after his assassination.*

687. Shop for history at **Argosy**.

For eighty years, Argosy has exhibited and sold valuable autographs, rare books, and antique maps to serious collectors and intrigued passersby in their book-filled storefront. Occupying seven floors of a building near Bloomingdale's, Argosy is a museum, library, gallery, and history lesson rolled into one: you can see centuries-old maps, priceless first editions, rare inscribed copies of works by authors from Hemingway to Boccaccio, and letters from authors, critics, playwrights, composers, and other cultural notables that reveal much more than just a valuable signature. But such illustrious provenances don't come cheap: while some of the more common books and prints are comparatively affordable, you can expect prices for the rarer items to start in the thousands. *116 EAST 59TH STREET BETWEEN PARK AND LEXINGTON AVENUES IN MANHATTAN. Subway: 4, 5, 6 to 59th Street; N, Q, R, W to Lexington Avenue/59th Street. 212-753-4455. www.argosy-books.com.*

688. Fantasize about decorating your apartment with vintage posters from **La Belle Époque**.

Art and advertising have long gone hand in hand, and the classic works on display at this esteemed Upper West Side gallery are testament to the golden age of poster art. La Belle Époque claims to hold the largest collection of rare and vintage advertising posters in the world, with more than three thousand pieces on sale that date from the mid-nineteenth century to the end of the twentieth century. Each poster is an original, and the collection encompasses everything from the earliest English fashion magazine covers to Parisian exhibition posters, Warhol montages, post-Impressionist drawings by Henri de Toulouse-Lautrec, and Art Deco masterpieces by Alphonse Mucha. Prices range from $250 to over $20,000, so shopping at La Belle Époque is serious business—but the colorful gallery is fascinating to visit with or without your checkbook. *280 COLUMBUS AVENUE AT 73RD STREET IN MANHATTAN. Subway: 1, B, C to 72nd Street. 212-362-1770. www.la-belle-epoque.com.*

689. Flip through racks of fine lingerie at **La Petite Coquette**...

Never has buying underwear been more comfortable for girls and easier for their boyfriends than at La Petite Coquette ("the little flirt"), a stylish boutique devoted to fancy lingerie and solid, friendly service. Racks that might otherwise hold paintings, posters, or samples of fabrics display underwear in all shapes, sizes, cuts, and colors, so prospective shoppers can flip through and coordinate exactly which print they want their particular cut of thong to come in. And if G-strings aren't the order of the day, La Petite Coquette carries plenty of other sexy, stylish, and even some comfortable pieces from a wide range of sophisticated brands, from ribbon-decorated creations by Mary Green and slips from La Perla, to comfy pajamas and simple boyshorts from Andre Sarda, and everything in between. *51 UNIVERSITY PLACE BETWEEN 9TH AND 10TH STREETS IN MANHATTAN. Subway: 4, 5, 6, L, N, Q, R, W to 14th Street-Union Square. 212-473-2478. www.thelittleflirt.com.*

690. ...or have some bonbons in **Journelle's dressing rooms**.

This Union Square area lingerie boutique carries only the best and most exquisite lingerie and boudoir items. So it should be no surprise that their dressing rooms are equally as luxurious—and stocked with bottles of Évian and chocolates (French, *bien sûr*). Leaving the questionable wisdom of providing unlimited chocolate in a setting where one will be scrutinizing the body *sans couverture,* this seems a fitting gesture for a store that oozes class and sumptuousness.

3 EAST 17TH STREET, BETWEEN BROADWAY AND FIFTH AVENUE IN MANHATTAN. Subway: 4, 5, 6, L, N, R, Q, W to Union Square. 212-255-7800. www.journelle.com.

691. Stock up on everything Asian at **Pearl River Mart**.

Although **Century 21** (see page 247) coined the motto "New York's Best Kept Secret," Pearl River Mart was for years an underground shopping destination, an emporium of cheap and unusual goods, furniture, and clothes well off the beaten path. For those unacquainted with this strange and wonderful land, Pearl River Mart is a Chinese department store, which started nearly thirty years ago as a small retail outlet for immigrants in Chinatown to get products from home. Pearl's reputation as a place to find exotic and well-priced clothes and gifts eventually traveled uptown, and it became a legendary offbeat shopping stop, until finally, several years ago, it moved from the dingy location on Canal Street to a brand-new, airy, bi-level space complete with a café and **reliably clean public restrooms** (see pages 351–353). For about as much as you would spend at Bed, Bath, and Beyond (or less), you can furnish your home with beautiful porcelain dish sets, colorful lamps, rustic straw hampers, and silk bedding. And speaking of silk, the clothing and apparel section features traditional Chinese jackets, dresses, skirts, pajamas, slippers, and robes. And then there are bags and shoes, food, tea and snacks, toys and dolls, beauty and health products, and, of course, the accessories and gifts. Suffice it to say that pretty much anything you could ever want or need can be found here, including information on feng shui so you can arrange all your new purchases favorably in your home.

477 BROADWAY BETWEEN BROOME STREET AND GRAND STREET IN MANHATTAN. Subway: 6, J, M, Z, N, Q, R, W to Canal Street. 212-431-4770. www.pearlriver.com.

692. Be a mallrat, NYC—style, at the **Williamsburg mini-mall**.

Along the main shopping drag of **Bedford Avenue** (see pages 280–281) is this street-level collection of stores, the Williamsburg version of the suburban strip mall. Just don't expect to find the Gap or Jamba Juice. Located in a converted industrial building (the former Realform Girdle Factory), the utilitarian-looking mini-mall contains a coffee shop (an independent one), a bookstore (also indy, of course), a purveyor of obscure imported and artisan beers and snacks, a store that sells cool electronics accessories like gold-plated flash drives, plus a toy store and a few cute boutiques—but nary a chain in sight. Many of the stores have entrances on the street, but you can also go from one to the other via the enclosed public area, the mall's defining element. Here you'll find a couple of benches, free Wi-Fi, and a Neoprint photo machine, where for $3 you can get a sheet of miniature sticker-photos of you and your friends against animated backgrounds.

BEDFORD AVENUE BETWEEN N. 4TH STREET AND N. 5TH STREET IN BROOKLYN. Subway: L to Bedford Avenue.

---

693. Pretend you're a chef at **Broadway Panhandler**.

Whether your idea of cooking is making a soufflé from scratch or warming up a can of soup, Broadway Panhandler will make you feel like a pro—or that you could be, if you had the right equipment. With top-of-the-line pots and pans, obscure cooking gadgets, sleek kitchen accessories, and the best knife selection in town, this SoHo store will bring out every culinary inclination you have. If that's not enough inspiration, the lively in-store demonstrations by chefs and cookbook authors might convince you to throw away your take-out menus for good.

65 EAST 8TH STREET BETWEEN BROADWAY AND UNIVERSITY PLACE IN MANHATTAN. Subway: N, R, W to 8th Street. 212-966-3434. www.broadwaypanhandler.com.

---

694. Break the mold with something from **Patricia Field**.

Way back in 1966, a young Patricia Field opened an eponymous boutique in Greenwich Village to sell her line of fresh and hip clothes to savvy New Yorkers. Thirty years later, Patricia Field—still younger at heart than most of her fashion contemporaries—moved into a salon in SoHo called Hotel Venus, a haven of sexy, provocative, and chic clothes for the downtown crowd. With a successful history of forays into high fashion, tongue-in-cheek political T-shirts, and an Emmy Award–winning career as a costume designer (she dressed the stars of *Sex and the City* and *The Devil Wears Prada*), Field has achieved legendary status as a true pioneer and visionary of the New York fashion scene. Her designs for women are bright, sassy, and colorful, from tiny miniskirts and iconic T-shirts to tightly cut jeans and striped legwarmers. In addition to a growing range of cool designs for men, her Bowery store stocks a host of accessories ranging from stylish hats, sunglasses, and personalized tote bags to novelty items and other mysterious "white trash treats."

302 BOWERY AT HOUSTON STREET IN MANHATTAN. Subway: 6 to Bleecker Street; B, D, F, V to Broadway-Lafayette Street. 212-925-2741. www.patriciafield.com.

---

695. Bring back a souvenir from **Roberta Freymann**.

If a trip to Kashmir, Marrakech, or Hanoi isn't in your future, a visit to Roberta Freymann can have you looking like you just got back from an exotic holiday. Tucked away on the first and second floors of a townhouse on the Upper East Side, her women's boutique is packed to the brim with colorful clothing and accessories from far-flung reaches of the world. Madison Avenue will feel very far away when you look at the price tags, so you can stock up on gorgeous kimonos and wraps, unusual printed skirts and dresses, jewelry, beach gear and more—without having to worry about how you'll fit everything in your suitcase. A few blocks away is Roberta Roller Rabbit, an even more free-spirited younger sibling that carries casual cotton clothing for men, women, and children, as well as housewares, hand-painted furniture, and gifts. The signature items are block-printed cotton tunics, sheets, and cover-ups, inspired by a fabric Freymann once found in India that illustrated a fable of Roberta Roller Rabbit.

ROBERTA FREYMANN: *153 EAST 70TH STREET BETWEEN LEXINGTON AND THIRD AVENUES IN MANHATTAN. 212-585-3767.*

ROBERTA ROLLER RABBIT: *1019 LEXINGTON AVENUE AT 74TH STREET IN MANHATTAN. 212-772-7200. Subway: 6 to 68th Street or 77th Street. www.robertafreymann.com.*

696. Add some weight to your library at **Bauman Rare Books**.

The Bauman galleries divide their monumental and world-renowned collection of rare and antique books between New York and Philadelphia. Anybody who's serious about getting hold of a particular edition of anything, from Chaucer to Fitzgerald, will be able to find it here—for a hefty price, of course, generally starting in the thousands. Recently seen in the New York gallery: an autographed set of the complete works of James Fenimore Cooper, for $38,000; a first edition of Milton's *Paradise Lost* from 1669, for $35,000; and an inscribed edition of *Walt Disney's Version of Pinocchio*, for $16,800. Besides rare books, the Bauman gallery has original musical scores, handwritten manuscripts from poets, novelists, and playwrights, and autographs.

535 MADISON AVENUE BETWEEN 54TH AND 55TH STREETS IN MANHATTAN. Subway: 6 to 51st Street; E, V to Lexington Avenue/53rd Street. 212-751-0011. www.baumanrarebooks.com.

697. Shop local and sustainable at **Brooklyn Industries**.

This Brooklyn-born clothing store is like the NYC version of American Apparel. Like AA, this local mini-chain offers cool but reasonably priced street wear, outerwear, and bags, and extols the virtue of local production and honest business practices. But our version has more soul, from the graphic tees that exude local pride (such as a Brooklyn version of the iconic I HEART NY shirt with a water tower in place of the heart) to the stores themselves, which are run on wind power.

MULTIPLE LOCATIONS IN MANHATTAN AND BROOKLYN; for information, call 800-318-6061 or visit www.brooklynindustries.com.

698. See stripes at the **Paul Smith boutique**.

One of England's finest fashion exports, Paul Smith has consignments in department stores all over the world, but only a handful of freestanding boutiques. Shopping at Paul Smith can be as fun as the clothes themselves, which stand out as among the most colorful and charismatic in a world of otherwise dark and serious menswear. His store on lower Fifth Avenue—hidden on a quiet corner just south of the big flagship chain stores—is a lively yet comfortable place to browse through wooden shelves of shirts, T-shirts, jeans, suits, and more. The powerful combination of his style and humor shows most in his accessories: everything from hats and ties to wallets and cufflinks is decorated with bright colors, iconic imagery, and the ubiquitous multicolored stripes. The newer and larger store on Greene Street in SoHo also stocks a full range of his women's wear, and both stores have a carefully curated selection of the most interesting art and photography books around—apparently a passion of Sir Paul's.

108 FIFTH AVENUE AT 16TH STREET IN MANHATTAN. Subway: 4, 5, 6, L, N, Q, R, W to 14th Street-Union Square; F, V to 14th Street; L to Sixth Avenue. 212-627-9770.
142 GREENE STREET BETWEEN HOUSTON AND PRINCE STREETS IN MANHATTAN. Subway: N, R, W to Prince Street. 646-613-3060. www.paulsmith.co.uk.

699. Try on shoes at the **Camper store**.

Camper, the stylish Majorcan shoe company, is known for its whimsical sensibility, like its line of "Twins" shoes, where the two shoes in a pair don't quite match. Fittingly, the store in SoHo has a few playful touches as well. The shoes are displayed on a stage against a red painted wall on one side of the store; on the other side is a series of rubbery-looking, slightly inflated disks, which are the seats you can use while trying on shoes. It feels like you're sitting on a whoopee cushion, but don't worry—the air isn't going to come out. It might take a second or two to get your balance, but once you do, you'll be treated to the sweetest seat in the neighborhood.

125 PRINCE STREET AT THE CORNER OF GREENE STREET IN MANHATTAN. Subway: N, R, W to Prince Street. 212-334-0340. N.B. Though it doesn't have inflatable seats, there is an uptown location at 635 MADISON AVENUE, BETWEEN 59TH AND 60TH STREETS. Subway: N, R, W to Fifth Avenue. 212-339-0078. www.camper.com.

700. Sift through forgotten classics at **Left Bank Books**.

Virtually hidden among the winding streets of the far West Village, Left Bank Books is a wonderful old-fashioned bookshop full of first editions, rare old nonfiction books, and tattered copies of classic novels. This shop was known as Bookleaves until 2005, when a former English professor purchased the store from the previous owner. Little besides the store name has changed. It's still cluttered, cozy, and warm, and the selection is so varied that you could leave with a cheap, well-loved paperback thriller or a beautiful vintage hardcover art book. The store has worn leather chairs and a staff with an inexhaustible knowledge of world literature (both previous and current owners can be found in the store). There are few more pleasurable things to do in the colder months than retreat into this little treasure and warm up with a book.

304 WEST 4TH STREET AT BANK STREET IN MANHATTAN. Subway: 1, 2, 3 to 14th Street; A, C, E to 14th Street; L to Eighth Avenue. 212-924-5638. www.leftbankbooksnyc.com.

---

701. Complete your comic book collection (or start one) at **Midtown Comics**.

Among the largest and best-stocked comic book stores in the world, Midtown Comics sells every single trade comic book in print, and a whole lot more besides. Spread out over two huge locations are mainstream brands like Marvel and Dark Horse to manga books, independent publishers, and comic-related trade paperbacks. In addition to their up-to-date selection of new titles, the stores share a collection of more than half a million back issues, as well as toys, statuettes, and figurines of all your favorite characters.

Both locations in Manhattan. **TIMES SQUARE:** *200 WEST 40TH STREET AT SEVENTH AVENUE. Subway: 1, 2, 3, 7, N, Q, R, W, S to 42nd Street-Times Square; A, C, E to 42nd Street-Port Authority Bus Terminal.* **GRAND CENTRAL:** *459 LEXINGTON AVENUE AT 45TH STREET. Subway: 4, 5, 6, 7, S to Grand Central-42nd Street. 800-411-3341. www.midtowncomics.com.*

---

702. Spoil your bicycle at **Conrad's**.

Conrad's is anomalous in several ways: it's a bike store that has thrived in the posh no-man's-land of Tudor City for thirty-five years; it's a mom-and-pop shop, but has a cutting-edge inventory; and despite the notoriously high turnover in retail, it has employed the same mechanics for two and a half decades. But it is exactly these reasons that city cyclists in the know make the trek to Tudor City Place when their precious Treks and Cannondales need some TLC.

25 TUDOR CITY PLACE NEAR 41ST STREET IN MANHATTAN. Subway: 4, 5, 6, 7, S to Grand Central-42nd Street. 212-697-6966. www.conradsbikeshop.com.

---

703. Sip lemonade in the garden at **Darling**.

Darling is without question one of the loveliest boutiques in the city, a special place where you leave yourself in the salesperson's hands, and you'll be cared for like an eagerly anticipated guest. Located in a landmark townhouse at the top of the West Village, the boutique occupies the ground and basement levels, with a beautiful garden out back, where in warmer weather you can drink fresh lemonade (or champagne, which is occasionally available during the evenings) while you chat with the staff. Owner Ann French Emonts, a costume designer and costume teacher whose former students include fashion designer Zac Posen, handpicks every piece in the store, including new, vintage, and her own one-of-a-kind designs. The look is feminine but not cutesy, with an emphasis on pieces with original or hand-sewn details. The women who work here are like no other salespeople in the world—they are enchanting and sweet, like gracious hostesses who make you feel completely at home in their delightful abode.

1 HORATIO STREET AT EIGHTH AVENUE IN MANHATTAN. Subway: A, C, E to 14th Street; L to Eighth Avenue. 646-336-6966. www.darlingny.com.

704. Impress your friends with a bag from **Peter Hermann**.

What's so special about this cramped Thompson Street bag store? Take a closer look at the merchandise inside. Those with a taste for European fashion will surely recognize the names on the labels—and be shocked. This boutique, which carries bags and leather goods from European designers, many of which are hard or impossible to find anywhere else in the U.S., is a well-kept secret among New York Europhiles. Hermann himself is often in the store, but any probing into how he gets the merchandise over here will likely be met with a brush-off or vague explanation, so don't bother. Ten years ago, this was one of the few places where you could find bags from French brands like Longchamp and Hervé Chapellier. Hermann still carries a good selection of both those brands, but today, the hot finds are the bags from Mandarina Duck, an Italian brand whose purses are extremely hard to get in this country.

118 THOMPSON STREET BETWEEN PRINCE AND SPRING STREETS IN MANHATTAN. Subway: C, E to Spring Street. 212-966-9050.

705. Prepare for a trip—pretend or real—at **Flight 001**.

Heading on a trip where laundry facilities may be iffy? Need to arrive in Singapore for a meeting jet-lag free? Make your next stop Flight 001, which specializes in cool travel gear, from sleek luggage and travel accessories to ingenious gadgets that address any traveler's need. Even if you are not going away, you may be tempted by the unusual bags from chic designers like Orla Keily and Un Après-Midi de Chien; leather wallets and accessories from Tusk; and skin care products from Korres and Dr. Hauschka. All told, the selection is a little random, but it's a lot of fun to browse through, and it's a great place to go to feel like part of the jet set.

96 GREENWICH AVENUE AT JANE STREET IN MANHATTAN. Subway: A, C, E to 14th Street; L to Eighth Avenue. 212-989-0001. 132 SMITH STREET AT DEAN STREET IN BROOKLYN. Subway: F, G, to Bergen Street. www.flight001.com.

706. Discover (and rediscover) eyewear at **Silver Lining**.

Before Tom, Ralph, and Donna got into the glasses business, high-fashion eyewear was more notable for craftsmanship than flashy logos. Silver Lining Opticians pays homage to eyewear's more artful history in their chic SoHo boutique, and provides a rare alternative to the identical rows of mass-produced, licensed styles found at Sunglass Huts around the country. The two owners are serious about everything eyewear related: Jordan Silver is a passionate collector of vintage frames, and a connoisseur of eyewear styles and history; Erik Sachler (a licensed optician) fits frames with prescription lenses. The store carries an edited selection of vintage sunglasses from the '60s, '70s, and '80s, as well as eyewear from independent designers, and a few styles from Silver Lining's own line. On the vintage side, you will find familiar fashion names (Ray-Ban, Balenciaga, Dior), but only styles made before these houses farmed out their eyewear lines to licensers. (And if you are not sure what this means, have the owners point out details like python-skin-topped frames from the '80s, or Balenciagas with hand-cut acetate designs.) Not surprisingly, the store caters to a discerning clientele—including some fashion designers who quietly choose their own frames at Silver Lining while overseeing eyewear lines at their own labels.

100 THOMPSON STREET BETWEEN PRINCE AND SPRING STREETS IN MANHATTAN. Subway: C, E to Spring Street. 212-274-9191. www.silverliningsopticians.com.

707. Hook yourself up at **J&R**.

Though much of the technology it started out selling is now obsolete, J&R has remained a fixture of New York retail for thirty-five years. In 1971, J&R opened a store on Park Row selling LPs, eight-tracks, and quadraphonic hi-fi equipment. The J&R stores now occupy an entire block of Park Row, and between them carry absolutely every kind of electronic product imaginable. A rare example of a family-run superstore, J&R is an authorized dealer of virtually everything it carries and yet still maintains the kind of small-business relationships that keep its prices among the lowest in the city. You can get anything from laptops and cameras to iPods, VCRs, stereo equipment, camcorders, DVD players, musical instruments and recording equipment, computer software, CDs, video games…and all those unnamed leads, plugs, and accessories that you need to hook things up. The knowledge of the staff extends beyond the products in the store to great advice on what you have at home and what you might need in the future. On top of all this, J&R holds a special place in the hearts of New Yorkers: it's been a loyal, successful, and dependable retailer integral to the downtown community since it opened, and has been a major player in the support and rejuvenation of lower Manhattan in the wake of 9/11. Keep an eye out for the live music events J&R brings to City Hall Park. N.B. In addition to the main location downtown, J&R also operates an "express" store inside **Macy's** (see page 319 for address and info).

PARK ROW BETWEEN BEEKMAN AND ANN STREETS IN MANHATTAN. Subway: 2, 3 to Park Place or Fulton Street; 4, 5, 6 to Brooklyn Bridge-City Hall; A, C to Broadway-Nassau Street; J, M, Z to Fulton Street; N, R, W to City Hall. 212-238-9000. www.jr.com.

---

708. Sharpen up at **Duncan Quinn**.

After only a couple of years in SoHo, trend-setting menswear designer Duncan Quinn's stylish Spring Street boutique has become one of downtown's hottest shopping destinations. Aptly described by *GQ* magazine as "rock 'n' roll meets Savile Row," Quinn's sense of style is the picture-perfect product of an appreciation for the refinement of traditional English tailoring and a youthful flair for the edgier side of modern fashion. While not straying far from the familiar lines and close-fitting cuts of the classic gentleman's suit, his colorful linings, bold ties, fitted shirts, and lively cufflinks and accessories inject a sharp, modish flavor. Besides suits and formal wear, Duncan Quinn sells a wide range of less serious but equally smart clothing, from brightly colored cashmere sweaters to T-shirts, socks, underwear, and even a small selection of ladies clothes. Best of all, Duncan Quinn offers a bespoke tailoring service, which will fit you with a sharp new look in the hand-cut cloth of your choice.

8 SPRING STREET AT ELIZABETH STREET IN MANHATTAN. Subway: 6 to Spring Street; B, D, F, V to Broadway-Lafayette Street; N, R, W to Prince Street. 212-226-7030. www.duncanquinn.com.

---

709. Have a fragrance made for your sweetheart at **Creed**.

The Creed family has been making beautiful, sophisticated fragrances for its elite clientele in Paris since 1760, counting Oscar Wilde, Audrey Hepburn, and Napoleon Bonaparte as former customers. At their small boutique on Bond Street, and now in a new location on Madison Avenue, New Yorkers can follow in these elegant footsteps and request that the sixth generation of the Creed family—Olivier Creed—make a unique perfume for a lucky someone. The staff will take into account any details of character and taste you wish to share, and will then put centuries of secrets to use in crafting a scent just for the recipient. If the $20,000 price tag seems too high, bottles of Creed's delicious ready-made creations are available for sale at the much friendlier price of $150.

Both locations in Manhattan. 9 BOND STREET AT LAFAYETTE STREET. Subway: 6 to Bleecker Street; B, D, F, V to Broadway-Lafayette Street. 212-228-1940. 897 MADISON AVENUE BETWEEN 71ST AND 72ND STREETS. Subway: 6 to 68th Street-Hunter College. 212-794-4480.

710. Find a replacement for a missing button at **M&J Trimming**.

This Garment District staple has a literally mind-boggling selection of trimming para-phernalia. Ribbons, beading, buttons, buckles, and sequins in every shape, size, color, and material are displayed along ceiling-high racks. For the crafty and DIY set, M&J is the haute couture of trimming, a step above the other trim stores in the area, offering only the best materials (crystal rhinestones, silk jacquard, velvet ribbons) imported from Europe, Asia, and all over the world. For the rest of us, it is a sight to behold, and a store where you are guaranteed to find something you need—or suddenly must have.

1008 SIXTH AVENUE BETWEEN 37TH AND 38TH STREETS IN MANHATTAN. Subway: B, D, F, V, N, Q, R, W to 34th Street-Herald Square. 800-9-MJTRIM. www.mjtrim.com.

711. Treat your dog to happy hour at **Zoomies' biscuit bar**.

You and your pet will feel right at home at Zoomies, thanks to the warm atmosphere and welcome of the owners, Susan and Angelique. Susan, a former executive at Chris-tian Dior, and Angelique, who owned a restaurant in Paris, combined their expertise and love of dogs (they are the proud owners of an adorable pup named Chouchou) to create this charming West Village boutique. Susan designs a line of dog beds and accessories, and Angelique runs the biscuit bar, which is full of homemade dog treats. They will make a fuss over your dog and keep him or her busy as you browse the mer-chandise, displayed on beautiful French antiques (another passion of theirs). After-ward, have a biscuit at the bar (Angelique says they're OK for humans, too), and if the weather's nice, take your pup out to the back garden to run around.

434 HUDSON STREET BETWEEN LEROY AND MORTON STREETS IN MANHATTAN. Subway: 1 to Houston Street. 212-462-4480. www.zoomiesnyc.com.

712. Improve your home with something from the **Vitra Design Store**.

This small showroom offers iconic modern furniture and accessories to design pro-fessionals and discerning Manhattanites. Along one side of the store runs a platform of elegant, utilitarian chairs from designers that include Charles and Ray Eames, Jean Prouvé, Frank Gehry, and George Nelson, and the shop floor is decorated with Karim Rashid tables, Noguchi stools, and Philippe Starck lamps. There is a small selection of highbrow design books, which are housed in a chic shelving system that at first glance looks like an exhibit too carefully arranged to touch, but which can be browsed through in comfortable chairs nearby. Most of the pieces are not only attractive, use-ful pieces of home furniture, but also celebrated artifacts of design history. The prices aren't low, but they aren't extravagant either, so this is a good place to start if you're looking to smarten up your living quarters.

29 NINTH AVENUE BETWEEN 13TH AND 14TH STREETS IN MANHATTAN. Subway: A, C, E to 14th Street; L to Eighth Avenue. 212-463-5750. www.vitra.com.

---

713. Step back in time at the **Lascoff Apothecary**.

Between the Duane Reades on every corner and treasures like **C.O. Bigelow** (see pages 33–34), New York City is a hypochondriac's dream—and Lascoff completes the picture. Housed in a beautiful old room of dark wood shelves and glass casements are Parisian soaps, English bubble baths, Dead Sea salts, Italian flu medicines, and arcane bottles of Swedish mouthwash. Every pharmaceutical taste is catered to, whether you scrub with pumice and oils or shave with a bowl of lather and a badger-hair brush, and the major new brands can be found alongside classic boutique fragrances and little-known international specialties. The Lascoff Apothecary hasn't changed much since moving to its current location in the early 1930s (the store has been in business on Lexington Avenue since 1899, first on 84th Street, and its 82nd Street incarnation is run by the third Lascoff generation), and shopping here is like rummaging through a grandfather's house for treasure. You have to hunt for things by opening the cupboards and drawers around the room (there are even some hidden behind an old leather couch). Be sure to check out the drugstore's history in the beautiful sepia photographs that stand in the windows.

1209 LEXINGTON AVENUE AT 82ND STREET IN MANHATTAN. Subway: 4, 5, 6 to 86th Street. 212-288-9500.

---

714. Get yourself that *schtreimel* you always wanted at **Primo Hats**.

Nowhere else on earth do the forces of style and Orthodox Judaism come together more perfectly than at this Brooklyn men's hat emporium. Primo Hats is a place like no other, an extravaganza of Hasidic headwear that caters to more kinds of religious aesthetics than one would have thought existed. The store, and its charismatic owner, has even been profiled in the *New York Times*. Taking their names from letters of the Hebrew alphabet, Hasidic hats often tend toward the fedora shape and are limited to blacks and browns, but there is a surprising variety of styles, covering everything from wide-brimmed and felt to tall, round, and furry. Whether you're buying your soft velvet *pey*, a trilbyesque rabbit-fur *gimel*, or bowler-style *ayen* out of professional necessity, spiritual enthusiasm, or simple sartorial taste, Primo Hats is a sight to behold, and the only place to go for a sweet *alef beyz*.

366 KINGSTON AVENUE BETWEEN CROWN AND CARROLL STREETS IN BROOKLYN. Subway: 3 to Kingston Avenue; 2, 5 to President Street. 718-804-0770.

Discover a new designer at a **designer market**.

New York has an embarrassment of talented artists and clothing designers whose work has yet to hit the mainstream. You can take advantage of this at two excellent designer markets, regularly occurring flea market–style covered markets brimming with vendors selling clothes, jewelry, handbags, and other pieces of their own design:

715. *TheMarketNYC* is held at two Manhattan locations every weekend. The main market is held at the gym of the Saint Patrick's Youth Center on Mulberry Street every Friday, Saturday, and Sunday, from 11:00 a.m. to 7:00 p.m. A market is also held in the West Village on Saturdays from noon to 7:00 p.m. The vendors are "emerging designers," who sell mostly jewelry and clothes, and the looks do not stray too much from other boutiques in the neighborhood.

Both locations in Manhattan. **NOLITA:** *268 MULBERRY STREET BETWEEN HOUSTON AND PRINCE STREETS. Subway: 6 to Bleecker Street; B, D, F, V to Broadway-Lafayette Street; N, R, W to Prince Street.* **WEST VILLAGE:** *490 HUDSON STREET BETWEEN CHRISTOPHER AND GROVE STREETS. www.themarketnyc.com.*

716. *Artists & Fleas* also holds two markets per weekend, but they are held at adjacent storefronts in Williamsburg. One side is dedicated to art, fashion, jewelry, and accessories created by local artists and designers. The other market is vintage only, and the vendors here are collectors who sell serious vintage and secondhand wares, including clothing, furniture, ceramics and porcelain, accessories, posters, and prints. Both markets are open Saturdays and Sundays from noon until 8 p.m.

125 & 129 N. 6TH STREET BETWEEN BEDFORD AVENUE AND BERRY STREET IN BROOKLYN. Subway: L to Bedford Avenue. 917-541-5760. www.artistsandfleas.com.

717. Go bold or minimalist at the **MoMA Design Store**.

MoMA's museum shop is such a good place to shop that it expanded out of the museum into a freestanding store. In addition to the two locations by the museum (one inside the museum and one across the street), there is one in SoHo, which more than holds it own against the other design heavyweights in the neighborhood, and it is the best of the three to shop in because it's the least crowded. Inside the stores, you'll find traditional gift shop fare (books, calendars, and museum-related tchotchkes) as well as furniture, jewelry, and housewares from cool classic and contemporary designers. There are Eames chairs in bold colors, high-concept kitchen gadgets, contrasting wallets and card cases from the colorful British line Designers Guild, creative games and toys for kids, and products from minimalist cult brand Muji.

Both locations in Manhattan. **MUSEUM LOCATION:** *11 AND 44 WEST 53RD STREET BETWEEN FIFTH AND SIXTH AVENUES. Subway: E, V to Fifth Avenue/53rd Street. 212-767-1050.* **SOHO LOCATION:** *81 SPRING STREET AT THE CORNER OF CROSBY STREET. Subway: 6 to Spring Street; N, R, W to Prince Street. 646-613-1367. www.momastore.org.*

---

718. Try some of Britain's most beloved delicacies at **Myers of Keswick**.

British expats can enjoy a scotch egg and some fresh chipolata sausage, and then stock up on tins of Heinz beans, bottles of H.P. sauce, Walker's crisps, and other treats from home. Those unfamiliar with English gastronomic jewels should start with McVities chocolate digestive biscuits. Myers supplies sausages, meats, and other ingredients to several of the city's **best English restaurants** (see page 191).

634 HUDSON STREET BETWEEN HORATIO AND JANE STREETS IN MANHATTAN. Subway: A, C, E to 14th Street; L to Eighth Avenue. 212-691-4194. www.myersofkeswick.com.

---

719. Set up your own bakery at **New York Cake and Baking Supply**.

This professional-grade supply store has everything you could possibly need to make a dessert. There's no sugarcoating on the store itself, but what it lacks in ambience, it more than makes up for with a selection that will satisfy cooks and pastry chefs, and boggle the minds of everyone else. Even those whose ovens are filled with shoes and wine bottles will want to try their hands at baking when they see things like a cool-but-scary-looking crème brûlée set, complete with mini blowtorch, and the rows of beautiful edible decorations, which can come in handy even if, in the end, you decide to go with store-bought.

56 WEST 22ND STREET BETWEEN FIFTH AND SIXTH AVENUES IN MANHATTAN. Subway: F, V to 23rd Street; N, R, W to 23rd Street. 212-675-2253. www.nycake.com.

---

720. Deck out your studio with art supplies from **New York Central**.

This supplier of the New York art world celebrated its centennial in 2005, and its still the most trusted source of supplies for local artists. New York Central is a wonderful, labyrinthine, old-fashioned art store that has absolutely the best range of art supplies around, from the largest selection of fine arts papers in the country (there are more than 3,000 papers, cards, and vellums) to etching and wood-carving tools, silk-screen supplies, and handmade sketchbooks in every size, shape, and paper weight. They carry more than one hundred canvases and thousands of brushes, many of which are antiques that date back to the 1920s and 1930s. Every member of the staff in the store is an artist, and under the rule of legendary, charming, and outspoken owner Steven Steinberg, the service is second to none, with personal attention and firsthand knowledge doled out in equal measure. Everyone from private enthusiasts to New York nota-bles like Lichtenstein and Warhol has made New York Central their favorite place for art supplies; it would be surprising if it isn't celebrating its bicentennial.

62 THIRD AVENUE AT 11TH STREET IN MANHATTAN. Subway: 4, 5, 6, L, N, Q, R, W to 14th Street-Union Square; L to Third Avenue. 212-473-7705. www.nycentralart.com.

721. Outfit for the outdoors at **Paragon**.

This independent sporting goods store has been around since 1908, so they're experts on New Yorkers' diverse range of athletic needs—from everyday pavement pounding to the most unusual niche sport. The footwear department on the lower level has the best selection of sports shoes in the city, from aqua socks to wrestling shoes. The second floor houses the outdoor department, and there you can pick up some serious camping knives, compare fabric options of different kinds of base layers, or find a winter coat. They've got gear for tennis, baseball, swimming, cycling, soccer and football, too, so whether you're training for the Olympics or just need to keep warm in February (or both), Paragon is the place to go.

867 BROADWAY AT 18TH STREET IN MANHATTAN. Subway: 4, 5, 6, L, N, Q, R, W to 14th Street-Union Square. 212-255-8889. www.paragonsports.com.

→ **DID YOU KNOW?** *Paragon's distinctive black exterior played a supporting role in the sitcom* Mad About You *as Buchman's Sporting Goods, the store owned by Paul's family.*

722. Buy your favorite movie art at **Posteritati**.

With a collection that encompasses many thousands of pieces, Posteritati is a store devoted to the timeless art and iconic imagery of movie posters. The depth of the selection is what sets Posteritati apart—you can find all the quaint and colorful international versions of your favorite movie art here, as well as a rich stock of classic Hollywood and independent movie posters. The gallery hosts changing exhibitions of artwork from different periods and genres of film, from the Eastern European avant-garde to Bollywood, Japanese new wave, and the Hammer horror classics. The store also sells books on film art and other movie memorabilia, which together with the exhibitions, make this a fun place to visit even if you are not in the market to buy.

239 CENTRE STREET BETWEEN BROOME AND GRAND STREETS IN MANHATTAN. Subway: 1, 2, 3, 6, A, C, E, N, Q, R, W to Canal Street. 212-226 2207. www.posteritati.com.

723. Browse artist's books at **Printed Matter**.

Printed Matter is a nonprofit organization whose purpose is to promote and dissemi-
nate works by artists in book format. What that means is that this Chelsea store contains thousands of unusual artworks for you to admire, touch, and explore (and
purchase, too, if you are so inclined). Printed Matter specializes in artists' publications,
what they call "artwork on the page," produced in large, inexpensive editions meant for
dissemination (rather than the more precious "book objects" that artists sometimes
produce). However, "large editions" is a relative term, and you're probably not going to
find too many things that would be in the art section of a regular bookstore. Most
books are priced around $20, though there are many that cost even less.

*195 TENTH AVENUE BETWEEN 21ST AND 22ND STREETS IN MANHATTAN. Subway: C, E to 23rd
Street. 212-925-0325. www.printedmatter.org.*

724. Get a last-minute Halloween costume at **Ricky's**.

The stores we've chosen for this section are almost all New York originals, and for the
most part, we've stayed away from outright, interstate chains, which Ricky's by defini-
tion is. (There are currently twenty-one locations, including two in Miami Beach, which
would not be surprising to anyone who's familiar with Ricky's flamboyant aesthetic.)
However, Ricky's, which recently celebrated its twentieth birthday, is a New York shopping institution and the kind of place that can expand its number of outlets but still
remain one of a kind. Ricky's is a drugstore—you can buy shampoo, toiletries, and cosmetics—but it's a drugstore with a wild streak. When it comes to what they sell, they've
got a very different agenda than CVS: there's a disproportionate amount of hairbrushes
and styling tools, the most extensive hair-dye department we've ever seen (and we're
not talking just Clairol), and a wide selection of wigs and costumes. And while you can't
get a prescription filled, you can get a makeup consultation or a wig fitting from a
transvestite professional behind the counter. In addition to being the best place to
come if, say, you want to cover your gray hair with pink, Ricky's is a great place to shop
for a Halloween costume. Ricky's goes all-out on Halloween, with nearly as good a costume selection as the regular costume stores, and an even better selection of glitter
makeup, hair dye, fake lashes, and risqué hosiery. On the big night, you can still find
ghosts and goblins and French maids at Ricky's putting the finishing touches on their
costumes, long after the other costume shops have closed for the evening.

Various locations in Manhattan. For addresses, visit www.rickys-nyc.com.

725. Pick out a valuable relic at **Skyline Books**.

No matter how many times you've visited, there are always corners of this small and cluttered used bookshop that remain to be discovered. Although there are respectable fiction, poetry, and biography sections, it's the more obscure treasures that stand out: the store has a surprising collection of signed copies and first editions by Beat writers, from Ginsberg to Burroughs, locked in glass cases; and the travel section is a gold mine of charming Victorian travelogues, antiquated guides to New York City, and essays by celebrated traveling raconteurs, from Mark Twain to Bill Bryson. Browse this store and **Books of Wonder** (see page 227), on the same block, for a delightful literary interlude.

13 WEST 18TH STREET BETWEEN FIFTH AND SIXTH AVENUES IN MANHATTAN. Subway: F, V to 14th Street; L to Sixth Avenue. 212-759-5463.

726. Step into the limelight at **Colony Records**.

For nearly sixty years, Colony Records has been supplying Broadway wannabes with all the materials they need to re-create their favorite scenes from smash hit musicals in their own homes. Colony has a vast collection of CDs, sheet music, and special karaoke versions of every Broadway show under the sun—if you've ever seen a show and wanted to take the soundtrack home, this is the place to find it. They even carry the "hardware" for the job, too: microphones and karaoke machines for the living room.

1619 BROADWAY AT 49TH STREET IN MANHATTAN. Subway: 1 to 50th Street; N, R, W to 49th Street. 212-265-2050. www.colonymusic.com.

727. Concoct a witch's brew at **Aphrodisia**.

If it seems improbable that a spice and herb store, of all things, survived the Bleecker Street gentrification, consider that it might have had something to do with the store's merchandise. With jars and vials of alternative remedies lining the wall, each hand-labeled in beautiful, grade-school-teacher–style script, Aphrodisia looks like a musty hippie hangout, and quite frankly, it seems exactly the kind of place that gets taken over by chain stores. Whether it's a coincidence or a great advertisement for whatever concoction they make to ward off evil spirits, we can't say, but it's a priceless relic, and definitely an interesting place to browse whether you're looking for a magic potion or a new tea.

264 BLEECKER STREET BETWEEN CORNELIA AND MORTON STREETS IN MANHATTAN. Subway: 1 to Christopher Street-Sheridan Square; A, C, E, B, D, F, V to West 4th Street. 212-989-6440. www.aphrodisiaherbshoppe.com.

728. Pick a card—any card—at Tannen's Magic Superstore.

Even sorcerers need a place to shop, and for New York's magic circle that place is Tannen's Magic Superstore. Every magic wand, loaded dice, trick sword, multicolored handkerchief, and fifty-one-card deck that an aspiring magician might ever need is here, along with a huge range of bizarre masks and outfits, surprising toys, and any other conjuror's tools you can imagine. The store is unique in the city—and there aren't too many that compare to it anywhere in the world—and it has supplied tricks and treats to everyone from TV show prop departments and professional illusionists to kids looking to master their very first disappearing-coin act. Ask a member of the staff for a demonstration—you'll be blown away.

45 WEST 34TH STREET, SUITE 608, BETWEEN FIFTH AND SIXTH AVENUES IN MANHATTAN. Subway: B, D, F, V, N, Q, R, W to 34th Street-Herald Square. 212-929-4500. www.tannens.com.

→ **DID YOU KNOW?** *Tannen's, which opened in 1929, was featured in Michael Chabon's 2001 novel,* The Amazing Adventures of Kavalier and Clay.

729. Buy organic at Whisker's Holistic Pet Care (and have it delivered).

Whisker's Holistic Pet Care is about as different from the city's pet boutiques as you would expect from a place with the word "holistic" in the name. Instead of designer dog clothes and gourmet treats, this store carries tons of nontoxic and chemical-free food, toys, and supplies for dogs, cats, and birds, all crammed into an East Village storefront. Everything on offer meets high holistic standards, from the organic pet food to the homeopathic remedies, odor neutralizers, and a mysterious potion that even some non-pet owners might be interested in called Mouse-B-Gone. The store has been around since 1988, long before green was cool, and it is definitely the reigning authority on organic pet products. The staff is friendly and knowledgeable, and there is free delivery to anywhere in Manhattan, Brooklyn, Queens, and certain locations in the Bronx.

235 EAST 9TH STREET AT SECOND AVENUE IN MANHATTAN. Subway: 6 to Astor Place. 212-979-1455. www.1800whiskers.com.

730. Curl up with a book at Ursus.

Now that Ursus Rare Books has absorbed its old Chelsea branch into the location upstairs at the Carlyle Hotel, it is indisputably the best place in the city to look for art books of all shapes and sizes. After nearly thirty-five years in the business, the selection is comprehensive, high-end, and up-to-date, with everything from books of critical essays to the latest, glossiest coffee table books and exhibition catalogs from museums around the world. There is a separate room for rare and out-of-print books—one of the most impressive collections of its kind in the city. Inside, it's peaceful and quiet, with soft cushions on the windowsills inviting you to sit back and leaf through the books while gazing out over Madison Avenue. When the shop closes for the night, you can continue the literary theme by heading downstairs to **Bemelmans Bar** to see the Madeline murals (see page 39).

981 MADISON AVENUE BETWEEN 76TH AND 77TH STREETS IN MANHATTAN. Subway: 6 to 77th Street. 212-772-8787. www.ursusbooks.com.

---

731. Buy a hat—and keep the box—at the Hat Shop.

Stocking only hats made by New York milliners—most from the city, some from upstate—the Hat Shop is a bastion of style, taste, and class in the home of the Yankee cap. A Wall Street broker turned millinery maven, owner Linda Pagan believes resolutely in the power of a hat to breathe new life into anybody's look, and the range of styles on display extend from the quiet dignity of a well-made felt fedora to the flamboyant extravagance of a decorated cocktail hat. Although the days are gone when hats were requisites of city society, it is never too late to invigorate your outfits with some snappy headwear, and the Hat Shop is the place to go for anything from a straw summer boater to an elaborate Art Deco–inspired piece. Before you go, brush up on your milliner's lexicon, so instead of fumbling around for an explanation of the feathery thing with ribbons and a hair net at the back, you can ask directly for a *canotier* with *aigrettes*, ruching, and a snood.

120 THOMPSON STREET BETWEEN PRINCE AND SPRING STREETS IN MANHATTAN. Subway: 6 to Spring Street; C, E to Spring Street. 212-219-1445. www.thehatshopnyc.com.

Vinyl Sources

Record collectors and people who amass music as others collect books or antiques will travel all over the world to fill the holes in their libraries, but lucky New Yorkers have no shortage of places carrying classic LPs, EPs, and 45s, if they know where to look. Even as the digital age brings down the giants of CD culture, such as Virgin Megastore, there are still scores of independent, new and used record stores across the city to keep vinyl enthusiasts of all kinds happy—but to find the best ones you'll have to roam the length and breadth of the five boroughs and scour the streets of some unlikely neighborhoods. The five we've chosen to highlight are special not only for keeping astonishing collections of vinyl, from classic oldies to life-changing rarities, but also for being unique places that are worth the journey in itself.

732. Consult the oracles of used CDs and records at **Academy**.

Dividing its vast collections between three locations, Academy Records & CDs is an institution among New York's music and movie hunters. The Chelsea location takes a utilitarian approach, and stocks hundreds of used CDs and DVDs of all genres along-side the traditional collector's choices of classical vinyl LPs; the East Village store is devoted entirely to jazz, pop, rock, soul, and reggae records. The Annex is also record-focused, and even carries new releases from local bands with albums on vinyl. While everything at Academy is likely to be in great working condition, none of the locations stocks too many rarities or mint items, so prices are reasonable, and the selections at both are fluid and comprehensive.

ACADEMY RECORDS & CDS: 12 WEST 18TH STREET BETWEEN FIFTH AND SIXTH AVENUES IN MANHATTAN. Subway: 1 to 18th Street; F, V to 14th Street; L to Sixth Avenue. 212-242-3000. Academy LPs: 414 EAST 12TH STREET BETWEEN FIRST AVENUE AND AVENUE A IN MANHAT-TAN. 212-780-9166. Subway: L to First Avenue.

ANNEX: 96 NORTH SIXTH STREET, BETWEEN BERRY AND WYTHE IN BROOKLYN. Subway: L to Bedford Avenue. 718-218-8200. www.academy-records.com.

733. Stroke chins and spin records at **Big City**.

Big City Records is one of the few DJ-oriented record stores in New York, with a con-cise and carefully chosen selection of albums and singles geared toward the vinyl *cognoscenti*. Going there without an idea of what you might want can be a mistake, therefore—anyone hanging aimlessly around is likely to stand out among a small and elite crowd of knowing musos, whose hungry fingers riffle well-organized racks of obscure funk, disco, soul, hip-hop, and Brazilian gems. But if you know your Daddy O from your O'Jays and you want to find something you might not have heard before, this is the place to come. The store has three turntables available to hear records before you buy them, and while there's a steady turnover of customers, there are seldom more then three people in the shop at once, making it a pleasant place to spend some time and be surprised by what you find.

521 EAST TWELFTH STREET BETWEEN AVENUE A AND AVENUE B IN MANHATTAN. Subway: L to 1st Avenue; 4, 5, 6, N, Q, R, W to 14th Street-Union Square. 212-539-0208.

734. Think of a record, and then find it at **House of Oldies**.

Of the handful of wonderful vinyl record stores that run along Carmine Street, the leg-endary House of Oldies deserves special mention. With a vault of more than a million records in the store itself and in the basement below, you can walk in and request almost any rock, pop, soul, blues, jazz, country, funk, reggae, or dance record from the

1950s through the 1980s and expect to find it. Many of the records are in mint or excellent condition, so prices are suitably high, but the selection is hard to beat, in New York or anywhere.

35 CARMINE STREET BETWEEN BLEECKER AND BEDFORD STREETS IN MANHATTAN. Subway: 1 to Houston Street; A, C, E, B, D, F, V to West 4ᵗʰ Street. 212-243-0500. www.houseofoldies.com.

---

735. Mingle with reggae greats at **Coxsone's Music City**.

In the early 1980s, legendary Studio One reggae producer Coxsone Dodd opened a record store in (appropriately enough) Jamaica, Queens, devoted entirely to reggae, ska, dub, and dancehall records. Although Coxsone is sadly no longer with us, his store remains the best place in New York to look for reggae records, from classic early recordings to brand new Jamaican hits, and albums from big name artists like Bob Marley and Gregory Isaacs to harder-to-find rarities and dub remixes. Many of Coxsone's friends, including reggae icons like Derrick Harriott and the late Alton Ellis, were known to visit the store.

3135 FULTON STREET BETWEEN NORWOOD AND HALE STREETS IN QUEENS. Subway: A, C to Euclid Avenue; J, Z to Norwood Avenue. 718-277-4166.

Expert Contributor: Laura Dave.

Laura is the author of the novels *The Divorce Party* and *London Is the Best City in America*. Her writing has appeared in the *New York Times*, *The Huffington Post*, *ESPN the Magazine*, and the *New York Observer*, as well as on NPR's *All Things Considered*. You can visit her online at www.lauradave.com.

MY FIVE FAVORITE BOOKSTORES IN NEW YORK:

736. *Books of Wonder:* This children's bookstore is just the kind of store that I dreamed of as a little kid. I love perusing the aisles, and will forever hope to bring home one of BOW's hard-to-come-by first editions, like *When We Were Very Young* (for only $4,500!).
18 WEST 18ᵀᴴ STREET BETWEEN FIFTH AND SIXTH AVENUES IN MANHATTAN. Subway: 1 to 18ᵗʰ Street. 212-989-3270. www.booksofwonder.net.

737. *Three Lives and Company:* A West Village touchstone, Three Lives is a favorite stomping ground of mine because the literature-savvy folks behind the counter use words like "chaser" in pairing two books for you. It is a good place for literary stargazing, because many local authors and editors like to frequent the store, and are occasionally invited to do a stint as a guest bookseller. You might see Michael Cunningham checking out the new arrivals, or Jonathan Safran Foer playing salesman for a day. *154 WEST 10TH STREET AT WAVERLY PLACE IN MANHATTAN. Subway: 1 to Christopher Street-Sheridan Square; A, C, E, B, D, F, V to West 4th Street. 212-741-2069. www.threelives.com.*

738. *Housing Works Used Book Café:* You'd be hard-pressed to find a bookstore anywhere doing this much good. One hundred percent of Housing Works' profits go to homeless New Yorkers living with HIV and AIDS. Moreover, the store is spacious and lovely and hosts terrific live events like in-store concerts and performances.
126 CROSBY STREET BETWEEN HOUSTON AND PRINCE STREETS IN MANHATTAN. Subway: 6 to Bleecker Street; B, D, F, V to Broadway-Lafayette Street; N, R, W to Prince Street. 212-334-3324. www.housingworks.org.

739. *McNally Jackson:* Among the many reasons I love this store is that it's a great place to spend an afternoon. You can content yourself for hours browsing books and drinking tea. They also have one of the best "staff recommends" sections in the city!
52 PRINCE STREET, ON THE CORNER OF MULBERRY STREET IN MANHATTAN. Subway: N, R, W to Prince Street; 6 to Spring Street. 212-274-1160. www.mcnallyjackson.com.

740. *The Corner Bookstore:* This intimate Upper East Side establishment is a throw-back to old-school bookshops: full of charm and love, where each book feels hand-picked and gratefully cared for. I have never left here empty-handed. And the in-store readings are among the best and most personal in the city. This may be my favorite bookstore—not just in Manhattan, but anywhere.
1313 MADISON AVENUE AT THE CORNER OF 93RD STREET IN MANHATTAN. Subway: 6 to 96th Street. 212-831-3554. *See page 293 for a list of stores with live reading programs.*

Shopping Excursions

Though all of the stores listed in this chapter offer wonderful individual shopping experiences, perhaps the most special thing about shopping in New York is the pleasant, pedestrian-oriented adventure of strolling the streets, discovering new stores, revisiting favorites, and experiencing the unique atmosphere that each neighborhood has to offer. And despite the ongoing homogenization of retail to the detriment of long-standing independents, and the presence of a few mall-like behemoths, there are still several areas that have retained—and, in some cases, have enhanced—their own special, thoroughly urban shopping character. Here are our five favorites:

741. *Fifth Avenue (part 1):* Though it's become increasingly mallish in recent years, Fifth Avenue has not lost its majesty, and feels anything but run-of-the-mill. From 42nd Street to where the park starts at 59th Street, grand flagship stores grace practically every address. Even stores not known as "luxury brands"(the Gap, H&M, Abercrombie & Fitch) pull out all the stops with their multilevel retail palaces, as if to pay their respects to this legendary shopping strip. Walking up from 42nd Street, you'll hit three legendary department stores (**Saks, Henri Bendel, Bergdorf Goodman**), elegant jewelers (Cartier, H. Stern, **Harry Winston**, and **Tiffany**), famous European designers (Versace, Armani, Louis Vuitton), the exotic and opulent **Takashimaya**, and many more. Should all of this capitalist grandeur inspire a wave of piety (or guilt), you'll also pass the majestic **Saint Patrick's Cathedral** (see page 21).

FIFTH AVENUE BETWEEN 42ND AND 59TH STREETS IN MANHATTAN. Subway: 7 to Fifth Avenue-Bryant Park; B, D, F, V to 42nd Street-Bryant Park; E, V to Fifth Avenue/53rd Street; N, R, W to Fifth Avenue/59th Street.

742. *Madison Avenue:* Barneys (see pages 244–245) marks the passage of Madison Avenue, from its plebeian, middle-of-the road-Midtown strip, to the exclusive-feeling upscale boutiques of the Upper East Side. Between 60th Street and the 80s, Madison has a quiet and stylish grandeur reminiscent of the established shopping districts of Paris or London, with a number of uptown outposts of downtown boutiques, a few major fashion houses, and a handful of single-outpost stores. Along with Armani (760 Madison), Prada (841 Madison), Dolce & Gabbana (825 Madison), Moschino (803 Madison), and Miu Miu (831 Madison) stores, you'll pass the Emanuel Ungaro boutique (792 Madison) and the two huge Ralph Lauren/Polo mansions (867 and 888 Madison), with their luxurious rooms complete with sofas and fireplaces that are like living rooms. There are more specialized boutiques, too, like La Perla (803 Madison) for underwear, Jimmy Choo (716 Madison) for glamorous Upper-East-Side heels, and the wonderful **Maison du Chocolat** (1018 Madison) for hot chocolate and truffles. Other highlights include Sherry-Lehmann (679 Madison), an old-time New York wine store that is a good place to pick up a special bottle; Zitomer (969 Madison), the enormous pharmacy that is like a small department store, with toys, clothes, and all sorts of other baubles; and Ursus Books, inside the **Carlyle Hotel** (at 76th Street; also see page 39). The tranquility breaks briefly at 86th Street, but resumes with a row of small, exquisite shops in Carnegie Hill, including **Blue Tree** (pages 251–252) and the **Corner Bookstore** (opposite). We recommend you start at 60th Street and work your way uptown, so that when you're ready to you're ready to take a break, the frenzy of Midtown is far behind you. You can enjoy tea or a drink at the Mark (just off Madison on 77th) or Carlyle hotels, or find a seat at one of the quiet cafés and restaurants that dot the avenue.

MADISON AVENUE BETWEEN 61ST AND 80TH STREETS IN MANHATTAN. Subway: 4, 5, 6 to 59th Street.

743. *Bleecker Street:* The stretch of Bleecker Street that runs from Hudson Street in the West Village through the eastern edge of SoHo has an eclectic character and a cozy, neighborhood feel that create the perfect setting for shopping or browsing. Start at the corner of Bleecker and Hudson Streets, where a small farmer's market occupies the picturesque intersection on Saturdays, and begin walking east, keeping your eyes open. You'll pass trendy boutiques, cute cafés, gourmet food stores, old music stores, and some great places to find antiques and one-of-a-kind knickknacks all along the way. You can get anything from antique furniture and picture frames to vintage globes and Art Deco lampshades in Les Pierre (369 Bleecker). There are a couple of excellent record stores en route—Rebel Rebel (319 Bleecker), which is better for rock and punk LPs, and Bleecker Street Records (239 Bleecker), which keeps a huge selection of both new and old records—plus one of the city's better guitar shops, Matt Umanov Guitars (273 Bleecker). Take a breather from the serious fashion of Marc Jacobs (Men's and Women's: 403-405; Accessories: 385; Kids: 382), Ralph Lauren (women's store: 380 Bleecker; men's store: 381 Bleecker), and Intermix (365 Bleecker) by stopping in the Lulu Guinness store (394 Bleecker) for a breath of whimsy or Blush (333 Bleecker). Also fun are the offbeat little shops like Verve (353 Bleecker), filled with clothes, accessories, and other odds and ends that are always nice to browse through. If you need snacks along the way, you can brave the lines for the famous cupcakes at **Magnolia** (409 Bleecker), or try the mythic pizzas at **John's** (278 Bleecker, also see page 207), the great Italian meats at **Faicco's** (260 Bleecker; also see pages 42–43), the cheese at **Murray's** (254 Bleecker; also see pages 296–297); or a scoop of gelato at **Cones** (272 Bleecker; see also page 179) or **Grom** (233 Bleecker). Or you can try to revive yourself with some herbs at **Aphrodisia** (264 Bleecker; see page 273). Wherever you go, our advice is to go early on a Saturday or Sunday, when you can see the street and the farmer's market in the prettiest light, and then walk up Bleecker Street before the crowds descend.
BLEECKER STREET BETWEEN HUDSON AND CARMINE STREETS IN MANHATTAN. Subway (to start at Hudson Street): A, C, E to 14th Street or L to Eighth Avenue; (to start at Carmine Street) 1 to Houston Street.

744. *Bedford Avenue:* The vibe on the street of this close-to-Manhattan commercial strip is optimal for browsing and buying: the street is bustling but there's still a sense of being off the beaten path. The Bedford Avenue subway stop lets you out at Bedford Avenue and N. 7th Street. Between there and Metropolitan Avenue (which runs perpendicular to Bedford, right below N. 3rd Street), there are several dozen boutiques, restaurants, and the **mini-mall** (see pages 259–260). The stores cover all the shopping bases, from the delightful and well-equipped kitchenware store Whisk (231 Bedford) to the Bedford Cheese Shop (229 Bedford), known and loved for their interesting selection, knowledgeable staff, and liberal sampling practices; from the bright, flowing Tibetan clothing at Pema (225 Bedford) to the unapologetically girly frills at PinkyOtto (205 Bedford); from independent bookstores (Spoonbill & Sugartown, in the mini-mall) to antique and secondhand furniture at Ugly Luggage (214 Bedford); from hip children's apparel at Sam & Seb (208 Bedford) to grown-up baubles at Catbird (219 Bedford). Take a detour on your way back to the subway and turn east at N. 6th Street, where you'll find another little enclave of shops: The Future Perfect, a cool furniture store that sells a lot of independent designers (115 N. 6th Street); A&G Merch (111 N. 6th Street), Future's equally cool but less pricey spin-off; a secondhand children's shop called Flying Squirrel, where you can get high-fashion kiddie gear at bargain prices (96 N. 6th Street); and **Artists & Fleas** (125 & 129 N. 6th Street; see page 269). Also in the area and worth checking out are Beacon's Closet (88 N. 11th Street, a block east of Bedford), an excellent secondhand store with a wide selection of used, vintage, and contemporary clothing and accessories, and on the other end of the spectrum, a divine boutique called Jumelle (184 Bedford), where the beautiful clothing justifies the highest prices on the avenue. *BEDFORD AVENUE, BETWEEN N. 9TH AND METROPOLITAN AVENUE, AND N. 6TH STREET, BETWEEN BEDFORD AND WYTHE AVENUES, IN BROOKLYN. Subway: L to Bedford Avenue.*

745. *Fifth Avenue (part 2):* Surprise! Manhattan's Fifth Avenue does not have a monopoly on good shopping—Fifth Avenue in Brooklyn also has a great strip. Shopping here is a little like shopping in Williamsburg, with lots of independent boutiques and not a chain store in sight, but whereas Williamsburg has a bit of a gritty feel like North London, Park Slope is more like Notting Hill: well-off, but not ostentatious, with a charming residential feel. Between Flatbush Avenue and Ninth Street (about twenty blocks) lies a quaint, tree-lined stretch of stores. You can easily cover them in one stroll by darting back and forth across the avenue, which is relatively narrow, and has very light traffic. Most of the stores are quite small, even for boutiques, but what they lack in size they more than make up for in charm. Frilly women's clothing shops like Flirt (93 Fifth), Goldy & Mac (219 Fifth), and Eidolon (233 Fifth) are like stepping into a modern boudoir, with friendly feminine chatter that will make girls feel right at home (but might be a little intimidating for a guy). Cog and Pearl (190 Fifth) is a wonderful home store that sells handmade gifts and accessories, while Scaredy Kat (229 Fifth) has great cards—both printed and custom-made—and gifts for children and adults. Speaking of kids, there are also several children's stores, including Romp (145 Fifth), which sells modernist-looking toys, including sleek rocking horses and preservative-free wooden drums, and Lulu's (48 Fifth), a kiddie barber shop that smartly features a big toy selection. 3R Living (276 Fifth) is an interesting home store that carries "future friendly products"—housewares, cookware, toys, pet accessories and cleaning products that are eco-friendly, made with sustainable manufacturing techniques, fairly traded, and packaged in an environmentally conscious way. If you haven't run out of steam, head two blocks east to Seventh Avenue, which also has a lot of stores but is a bit busier and not quite as pleasant to amble around.

FIFTH AVENUE BETWEEN FLATBUSH AVENUE AND 9TH STREET IN BROOKLYN. Subway: 2, 3, 4, 5, B, Q to Atlantic Avenue; D, M, R to Atlantic Avenue-Pacific Street; F to Fourth Avenue; N to Pacific Street.

On the Cheap and All Out

We've got the highest highs, and the lowest lows, and one of the best things to do is to check out what you can get at either end:

746. *One pound of bulk candy of your choice at Economy Candy (around $1.99 to $6.99, depending on selection) vs. a box of Champagne truffles from Jacques Torres ($50 for thirty pieces).* Tip: Economy Candy isn't just for bulk candies. They also have an excellent selection of European chocolate bars and treats available by the bar or piece.

ECONOMY CANDY: *108 RIVINGTON STREET AT ESSEX STREET IN MANHATTAN. Subway: F to Delancey Street; J, M, Z to Essex Street. 800-352-4544. www.economycandy.com.*

JACQUES TORRES: *350 HUDSON STREET AT HOUSTON STREET IN MANHATTAN; Subway: 1 to Houston Street; 212-214-2462; and 66 WATER STREET BETWEEN THE BROOKLYN AND MANHATTAN BRIDGES IN BROOKLYN; Subway: A, C to High Street; F to York Street. 718-875-9772; 285 AMSTERDAM BETWEEN 73RD AND 74TH STREETS IN MANHATTAN; Subway: 1, 2, 3 to 72nd Street. www.mrchocolate.com.*

747. *Bidding on a vintage oak armoire (around $200) or a Gucci jacket (around $60) at the Housing Works auctions vs. bidding on an Impressionist painting at an auction at Christie's or Sotheby's (starting at $20,000 to more than $95,000,000).*

HOUSING WORKS: *Various locations. Check Web site for schedule and locations: www.housingworksauctions.com.*

CHRISTIE'S: *20 ROCKEFELLER PLAZA, 49TH STREET BETWEEN FIFTH AND SIXTH AVENUES, IN MANHATTAN. Subway: B, D, F, V to 47th-50th Streets-Rockefeller Center. 212-636-2000. www.christies.com.*

SOTHEBY'S: *1334 YORK AVENUE AT 72ND STREET IN MANHATTAN. Subway: 6 to 68th Street-Hunter College. 212-606-7000. www.sothebys.com.*

748. *One dozen roses from any corner deli (around $10) vs. an arrangement by Michael George ($100 and up). George's customers include fashion designers, magazine editors, and the doyenne of décor, Martha Stewart.*

MICHAEL GEORGE: *5 TUDOR CITY PLACE, 40TH STREET BETWEEN FIRST AND SECOND AVENUES, IN MANHATTAN. Subway: 4, 5, 6, 7 to Grand Central-42nd Street. 212-883-0304. www.michaelgeorgecustomfloral.com.*

749. *Lunchtime manicure at Bloomie Nails ($12, including a short back rub) vs. Spirit of the Beehive at Jin Soon ($35; includes extra moisturizing treatment and the finest nail painting in the city; see page 312 for full entry).*
BLOOMIE NAILS: *Multiple locations, all over the city. Keep your eyes peeled!*
JIN SOON: *Multiple locations (East Village, West Village, and Upper East Side.) Visit www.jin-soon.com.*

750. *Massage at a street fair ($10 for 10 minutes) vs. Life Dance Journey ($450–$695 for up to three hours of massage, body scrubbing, and stretching) at the Spa at the Mandarin Oriental.*
STREET FAIR MASSAGES: *See page 85.*
THE SPA AT THE MANDARIN ORIENTAL: *80 COLUMBUS CIRCLE AT 60TH STREET IN MANHATTAN. (Also see entry on page 64.) Subway: 1, A, C, B, D to 59th Street-Columbus Circle. 212-805-8880. www.mandarinoriental.com.*

751. *"Recession special" from Gray's Papaya (two franks and a drink for $4.45) vs. the black truffle burger (in season) from DB Bistro Moderne ($75 for a burger with a single portion of truffles; $150 for a double).*
GRAY'S PAPAYA: *Multiple locations. 539 EIGHTH AVENUE AT 37TH STREET: Subway: 1, 2, 3, A, C, E to 34th Street-Penn Station; 212-904-1588. 2090 BROADWAY AT 72ND STREET: Subway: 1, 2, 3 to 72nd Street; 212-799-0243. 402 SIXTH AVENUE AT 8TH STREET: Subway: A, C, E, B, D, F, V to West 4th Street; 212-260-3532.*
DB BISTRO MODERNE: *55 WEST 44TH STREET BETWEEN FIFTH AND SIXTH AVENUES IN MANHATTAN. Subway: B, D, F, V to 42nd Street-Bryant Park. 212-391-2400. www.danielnyc.com. Also see entry on* **Daniel Boulud** *on page 162.*

752. *The AirTrain between Manhattan and JFK ($5 plus subway fare, one way) vs. US Helicopter ($165.10, one way).* AirTrain travel time: about sixty minutes to or from Manhattan via the subway (including the five-minute transfer between subway and AirTrain platforms). Helicopter travel time: less than ten minutes (no transfers).
AirTrain departs regularly from the Howard Beach and Sutphin Boulevard-Archer Avenue stations. Subway: A to Howard Beach or J, Z, E to Sutphin Boulevard-Archer Avenue. For more information on AirTrain, visit www.panynj.gov/airtrain. N.B.: US Helicopter departs every hour on the hour from 7:00 a.m. to 7:00 p.m. from the downtown and Midtown heliports. Reservations are required. For more information and to make reservations, call 877-262-7676 or visit www.flyush.com.

Cheap Thrills: Top five things to do when you are feeling strapped for cash.

753. Go to a museum on a **free** or **pay-what-you-wish day**...

Almost all of the museums in New York designate a couple of hours each week as free or "pay what you wish" time, which is a great way to visit a certain collection or exhibition without feeling like you have to spend the entire day there. Some museums, such as the **Brooklyn Museum** (see pages 121–122) and the **Museum of Arts and Design** (see page 130), offer free programs and performances during these times. Also, the **Met** (see pages 119–120) is always pay-what-you-wish, so if you don't have time to make a marathon visit that would justify the suggested $20 admission fee, you can pop in for an hour and pay what you feel is appropriate.

See Chapter 4 for a list of favorite museums, and contact the museums for information on hours and special programs.

754. ...or pay what you wish anytime, at **Yoga to the People**.

Most yoga studios offer some sort of introductory deal to newcomers, and if you've got the time and energy to studio-hop, there are enough outlets across the five boroughs so that you can keep your per-practice costs pretty low by showing up to a new studio each time. But at YTTP's three Manhattan studios, you can pay whatever you want, every time you show up. Each studio has a particular focus: East Village has Power Vinyasa; 27th Street has traditional hot yoga; 38th Street has heated Power Vinyasa. Suggested donation is between $5 and $10, but anything goes. You'll be treated to the same vigorous practice no matter how many greenbacks you tuck into the basket on your way out of the studio. All locations in Manhattan.

POWER VINYASA: *12 ST. MARKS PLACE, 2ND FLOOR. BETWEEN SECOND AND THIRD AVENUES. Subway: 6 to Astor Place.*
TRADITIONAL HOT: *115 WEST 27TH STREET, 3RD FLOOR. BETWEEN SIXTH AND SEVENTH AVENUES. Subway: 1 to 28th Street; N, R, W to 28th Street.*
HOT POWER VINYASA: *1017 SIXTH AVENUE, 3RD FLOOR. AT 38TH STREET. SUBWAY: N, R, Q, W, B, D, F, V TO 34TH STREET-HERALD SQUARE. 917-573-9642. www.yogatothepeople.com.*

755. Get free haircuts for life at **Bumble & Bumble**.

This one has achieved something of an urban myth status, but we swear it's true— and if you're willing to forsake some control and pampering, it's not that hard to do. Bumble & Bumble, one of the most famous hair companies in the industry, runs an ongoing training school in the Meatpacking District that is constantly in need of models. To become a model, you first have to fill out the online application, which consists mostly of biographical information and a few questions about your hair. Provided you don't have any bizarre hair issues, you should receive an e-mail telling you to attend a model call, where your hair will be assessed for one of about a half-dozen cuts that is being taught at that time. Then you book an appointment for the cut, which occurs in groups of sixteen, with an instructor present. The cuts are free (no tipping either), models get free samples of Bumble & Bumble products, and they will offer you a cut with a pro-fessional if you're unhappy with what you receive. Just don't lose sight of what you're actually doing. The stylists are there for themselves, not for you, so don't expect any pampering, and the appointment is run as a class, so personal attention is at a mini-mum. And most of all, don't be late—they overbook appointments for these classes on purpose, so if you're not among the first sixteen people in the door, you don't get a cut, even though you had an appointment. Once you're in the program, you can call in whenever you want a cut for another of the same style, or come back to the model call to see if you can be assigned a new one.

For more information, call 866-7-BUMBLE or visit www.bbmodelproject.com. The Model Proj-ect is located at 415 WEST 14TH STREET, 6TH FLOOR. BETWEEN NINTH AVENUE AND WASH-INGTON STREETS. Subway: A, C, E, L to 14th Street-Eighth Avenue.

756. Hang out in the "cold room" at **Fairway**.

If it's 100 degrees in the shade, you don't have air-conditioning, and you can practi-cally feel your skin frying, head to Fairway. The 10,000-square-foot "cold room" is a con-tinually refrigerated section, where meat, fish, dairy products, and fresh pasta are kept. It is a sight to behold any time of the year, and a godsend for those without air-condi-tioning in the middle of August. Not only is it free, unlike many other reliable air-con-ditioned venues, but it is really, really cold (around forty degrees) all the time, no matter what's happening outside.

2328 12TH AVENUE BY 129TH STREET IN MANHATTAN. Subway: 1 to 125th Street. 212-234-3883. www.fairwaymarket.com.

757. Gorge on **food freebies**.

Our favorite place for free noshing is **Dean & Deluca** (see pages 41–42), where generous samples of breads, pizzas, prepared food, cakes, and pastries are displayed for the taking, and it's usually too busy for anyone to notice if you're scarfing down a few of each. Both the Gourmet Garage and Garden of Eden also put out trays of free samples sporadically, and both almost always have cheese and bread bits to nibble on. At Williams-Sonoma stores throughout the city, staff members whip up tasty concoctions like chestnut stuffing and chocolate chip blondies throughout the day that you can wash down with a small cup of coffee, mulled cider, hot chocolate, or lemonade. No roundup of city samples would be complete without a mention of Trader Joe's and Whole Foods, both of which reliably provide bite-size teases of their bounty, though the snaking lines and ravenous crowds can leave one with a tint of heartburn. One little-known sample-giving outlet is the Streit Matzo factory on the Lower East Side, which hands out pieces of matzo (fresh from the oven) to bystanders. Finally, to complement your gratis meal, pretty much every wine store has regular tastings, where you pick up some wine freebies and crackers. At Best Cellars on the Upper East Side, there are wine tastings (sometimes with cheese) every night from Monday through Friday, 5:00 p.m. to 8:00 p.m.; and on Saturdays from 2:00 p.m. to 4:00 p.m. They offer free wine and food pairings with dishes made by restaurant chefs from around the city. Speaking of the Upper East Side, some of the best gourmet freebies come from **Sable's** (see page 252), where you will be treated to generous samples of caviar.

DEAN & DELUCA: *See Pages 41–42.*

STREIT MATZO FACTORY: *148-154 RIVINGTON STREET AT SUFFOLK STREET IN MANHATTAN. Subway: F to Delancey Street; J, M, Z to Essex Street. 212-475-7000. www.streitsmatzos.com.*

BEST CELLARS: *1291 LEXINGTON AVENUE BETWEEN 86TH AND 87TH STREETS IN MANHAT-TAN. Subway: 4, 5, 6 to 86th Street. 212-426-4200. www.bestcellars.com.*

GOURMET GARAGE: *Multiple locations. www.gourmetgarage.com.*

WILLIAMS-SONOMA: *Multiple locations. www.williamsonoma.com.*

GARDEN OF EDEN: *Multiple locations. www.edengourmet.com.*

TRADER JOE'S: *In Manhattan: 142 EAST 14TH STREET, BETWEEN THIRD AND FOURTH AVENUES. Subway: 4,5,6, L, N, R, Q, W to 14th Street-Union Square. 212-529-4612. In Brooklyn: 130 COURT STREET, AT ATLANTIC AVENUE. 718-246-8460. Subway: F, G to Bergen Street; 4,5 to Borough Hall. In Queens: 90-30 METROPOLITAN AVENUE, AT WOODHAVEN BLVD. No nearby subway. 718-275-1791. www.traderjoes.com.*

WHOLE FOODS: *Multiple locations in Manhattan. Visit www.wholefoods.com.*

---

758. Wash up at **Kiehl's**.

A not-very-well-kept secret about this 150-year-old apothecary is that they will give you prepackaged samples of anything—and we mean anything—in the store, and as many different products as you want. Cast a look in the skin care direction, and you'll be showered with samples of face wash, moisturizer, and eye cream; step over to the hair care section, and the staff will pick out a shampoo and conditioner for your hair type to try. Fortunately for freeloaders, there is a branch on the Upper West Side now, so you can split your time between there and the Village store to avoid looking too conspicuous. (Kiehl's also has counters in department stores, but those do not offer samples.)

EAST VILLAGE: *109 THIRD AVENUE AT 13TH STREET IN MANHATTAN. Subway: 4, 5, 6, L, N, Q, R, W to 14th Street-Union Square. 212-677-3171.*

Deluxe Treatment: Top five things you can do/buy when money is no object:

759. Order the zillion dollar lobster frittata at **Norma's**.

This gourmet omelet is available for $100 with one ounce of caviar, or with ten ounces for $1,000. The menu dares you to expense it.

LE PARKER MERIDIEN HOTEL, 119 WEST 56TH STREET, BETWEEN SIXTH AND SEVENTH AVENUES IN MANHATTAN. Subway: N, Q, R, W to 57th Street; F to 57th Street. 212-708-7460. www.parkermeridien.com.

760. Have a private dinner at the **Cellar Room at 21**.

Up to twenty-two of your friends and family can have a private meal in the famous Cellar Room at the 21 Club, the famous wine cellar that the Feds never found during Prohibition, with its 2½ -ton door that is unlocked by slipping an eighteen-inch wire through the wall. To have dinner in New York's most famous secret vault costs $485 per person for a seven-course meal. (They also serve lunch in the Cellar Room Monday through Friday at the considerably more reasonable price of $120 per person.)

21 WEST 52ND STREET BETWEEN FIFTH AND SIXTH AVENUES IN MANHATTAN. Subway: E, V to Fifth Avenue/53rd Street. 212-582-7200. www.21club.com.

→ **DID YOU KNOW?** *The Cellar Room at the 21 Club is technically not part of "21" — it's the cellar of the building next door at no. 19. The cellar was "borrowed" from the neighbors during Prohibition to hide their alcohol, so when "21" employees were asked if there was any liquor on the premises, they could truthfully answer no.*

761. Have your jeans custom-made at **Earnest Sewn**.

In a city glutted with high-end denim, the zenith is this Meatpacking District store, where you can have jeans custom-made while you wait. For upward of $300, customers can choose from one of the exclusive denims, and then select pocket designs and buttons, and the jeans are cut and sewn on-site for your personal fit.

Both locations in Manhattan. 821 WASHINGTON STREET AT GANSEVOORT STREET. Subway: A, C, E to 14th Street; L to Eighth Avenue. 212-242-3414. 90 ORCHARD STREET AT BROOME STREET. Subway: F, J, M, Z to Delancey Street. 212-979-5120. www.earnestsewn.com.

762. Have the **World Cocktail** or the **Jewel in the Glass**.

The signature cocktail at the bar in the Trump World Tower is a $50 mix of Veuve Cliquot, Remy XO, and white grape and lemon juices—all topped with a twenty-three-carat garnish.

WORLD BAR: *Trump World Tower, 845 UNITED NATIONS PLAZA, FIRST AVENUE AT 48TH STREET IN MANHATTAN. Subway: 6 to 51st Street; E, V to Lexington Avenue/53rd Street. 212¬935-9361. www.hospitalityholdings.com.*

763. Open a house account with **Posy Floral Design**.

For between $200 and $2,000 per week, this haute Upper East Side floral boutique will deliver fresh flowers to your home and have them arranged by their top-notch floral designers. After an initial personalized consultation with the designers in your home, the designers can also help you choose vessels and vases in which to display the flowers. (They can also do arrangements for hotel rooms.)

145 EAST 72ND STREET NEAR LEXINGTON AVENUE IN MANHATTAN. Subway: 6 to 68th Street-Hunter College. 212-744-7788. www.posyflowers.com.

Five Ways to Live Rich on the Sly.

New Yorkers haven't felt as flush in recent years as they once did, and even in boom times, the opposing pulls of having and have-notting can be wrenchingly palpable. Despite all of the fantastic things to do here, it's not hard to become intermittently fixated with those things that seem monetarily out of reach. Here are five ways to get a taste of the good of life anytime, without breaking the bank:

764. Live by the **Skint**...

A roundup of the best cheap and free happenings around town, covering all areas (food, entertainment, beauty, exercise) and e-mailed daily. Required reading for free-gans and the like.

Visit www.theskint.com to see the day's offerings, or subscribe to the daily newsfeed.

765. ...and eat by the **Dealfeed**.

This excellent Web site specializing in local resto gossip also runs a live feed alerting subscribers to food-related bargains at restaurants all over the city. Listings range from freebie handouts all the way up to complimentary courses and special prix fixe deals at upscale restaurants.

To sign up for the feed or check recent posts, visit eater.com/tags/dealfeed.

766. Figure out how to do pretty much anything cheap (and in style!) by reading Brokelyn.

This local online mag gives new meaning to the phrase sustainable living. Take a flip through their archives to find out the best places to sell clothes for cash, where to go for a cheapo staycation, and how to plan an evening out designed around happy hours and freebies. Much of the content is Brooklyn-focused, though there's plenty on the site that extends beyond the Borough of Kings. The witty articles and regular features will help you find ways to save money you didn't know you had.

www.brokelyn.com.

767. Enter the Met Weekend Ticket Draw.

Perhaps the ultimate lift for cash-strapped culture vultures is the chance to see a performance (in perfectly decent seats) at the Metropolitan Opera for only $25. Drawings for tickets for each weekend's performance are held online every week during the Met's season. To qualify, you must enter the drawing on the Met Web site on Monday. The drawing is held on Tuesday; winners must purchase tickets by 5 p.m. Wednesday; those on the waiting list must purchase tickets by 5 p.m. Thursday. Winners receive up to two tickets per performance, and you may enter as many weeks as like.

For drawing procedures and to enter, visit www.metoperafamily.org/metopera/contests/drawing/index.aspx.

768. Rent for the red carpet at Ilus.

New York City is the world's biggest tease for shoppers on a budget, and for those of us trying to work it on a dime, nothing seems farther from reach than the priceless haute-couture dresses beckoning from boutiques all over town. Ilus is a dream come true for every SATC disciple living on a (Manolo) shoestring: you can rent dresses from top designers for a fraction of their retail price, have them couriered to you anywhere in the city, and wear them for that one big night without a trace of buyer's remorse. Their list of designers includes Abaete, Cynthia Rowley, and Jill Stuart among others, and you can reserve your size in the shop or on their Web site. Rentals last for three days and usually cost between $100 and $150, including a $10 cleaning fee, and you can return the dress in person or by courier. At those prices, you can almost afford to go to brunch the morning after in that little chiffon Carmen Marc Valvo number…

248 ELIZABETH STREET BETWEEN HOUSTON AND PRINCE STREETS IN MANHATTAN. Subway: 6 to Spring Street. 646-454-1678. www.ilus-nyc.com.

CHAPTER 8:

Enrichment & Renewal

Learning, experiencing, and experimenting are an integral part of the culture in New York. This city encourages open minds and active bodies by opening itself to any class, discipline, sport, or pastime that seeks a place, and attracting dynamic, talented people from all over the world to share their creativity and expertise. The experience of trying something new is easy to come by here—so easy, in fact, that you may very well stumble onto something (a bookstore reading, free yoga class, public lecture or performance) without even looking. This in itself is one of the best things about New York.

This chapter is devoted to the best of the city's many wonderful resources for improving one's well-being with education, relaxation, and recreation. From degree programs at prestigious universities to classes in art, dance, language, or martial arts; from lectures, talks, and readings by renowned leaders and scholars to informal discussions and gatherings, the opportunities for learning are limitless and constantly changing. At the same time, there are plenty of ways to refresh, relax, and rejuvenate, whether at spas, meditation sessions, or through exercise. No matter where your interests lie, there's a wealth of resources in this city to help you get what you need to nurture yourself—mind and body.

Note: We've included several forms of exercise and athletics in this chapter, but for more outdoor sports and activities, see Chapter 6, "The Great Outdoors."

Literature & spoken word

769. Listen to stories at **the Moth**.

There are eight million stories in the Naked City, as the saying goes, but only the best ones make it to the Moth. Cooler than a comedy club, more studied than improv, the Moth is an urban storytelling group that showcases this slightly obscure but very particular (and incredibly entertaining) art form. Each season, the organization hosts twelve storytelling events, which feature a different roster of performers, selected by the Moth curator, who deliver unscripted, ten-minute stories on a chosen theme (past themes include "Call of the Wild," "Sex and Money," and "Near-Death Experiences"). Former storytellers have included big-name celebrities, local writers, journalists, and comedians, as well as regular New Yorkers who happen to have a gift for the gab. The Moth also puts on biweekly "Story Slams," in which average Joes compete in an audience-determined storytelling showdown, and runs the brilliant "Story Line" through its Web site, where people are invited to pitch their most memorable (true!) stories by email or by phone. The best might be featured online or chosen to be told in full on the Moth's Radio Hour—or their authors invited to read on stage. All kinds of events are enjoyable and edifying—and their unpredictability makes you realize how thrilling it is to watch a spontaneous, live performance.

Events are held at different venues around the city. For more information and a list of upcoming events, visit www.themoth.org.

---

770. A poetry slam at **the Nuyorican** is another event that explores the possi-

bilities of the spoken word. Even if you haven't read a poem since high-school English, give poetry slams a try—they're anything but dull. The Nuyorican Poets Café started out as a living room poetry salon, and it has evolved into a vibrant, multi-medium art and performance space. And though the poetry slams are still what the venue is best known for, it also holds jazz and hip-hop concerts, theatrical performances, film and video events such as movie screenings, and screenplay readings. With multiple events taking place every night of the week, there's always something on, so either check out the monthly calendar (available online), or just head downtown and see what's happening.

236 EAST 3RD STREET BETWEEN AVENUES B AND C IN MANHATTAN. Poetry slams held Friday night at 10:00 p.m, and on Wednesday nights at 9 p.m. (except for the first Wednesday of every month). Subway: F, V to Lower East Side-Second Avenue. 212-505-8183. www.nuyorican.org.

---

771. Commune with writers at the **Poetry Project at Saint Mark's**.

A longstanding institution of the New York literary scene, the Poetry Project counts Allen Ginsberg, Alice Walker, Patti Smith, and Michael Ondaatje among the many people who have shared their work here. One of the large number of community programs housed in Saint Mark's Church in-the-Bowery, the Poetry Project runs a vibrant roster of literary programs, including three weekly reading and events series; workshops in poetry and writing; and events such as the annual New Year's Day Marathon Reading, which draws in more than a hundred writers and other creative types for a day of performances, discussions, and, of course, readings. There is something for everyone here, no matter how, what, or how often you read.

SAINT MARK'S CHURCH IN-THE-BOWERY: 131 EAST 10TH STREET AT SECOND AVENUE IN MANHATTAN. Subway: 6 to Astor Place. 212-674-0910. www.poetryproject.com.

---

772. Get used to criticism—and fathom the post-Apocalypse—at **Freebird Books**.

This beloved Brooklyn bookstore holds writing workshops with published local authors, inviting aspiring writers, poets, essayists, and dramatists to meet and inspire one another once a week over an eight-week course. At the end of each workshop, participants are guided in the direction of suitable literary journals or publishers for their work at a "publishing party," and the achievements of two months' hard honing of the literary craft are sealed in an envelope and dispatched, possibly to spark a fabulous career. And if you don't want to pop the $230 for the full workshop, you can attend the "Post-Apocalyptic Club," the store's monthly book club whose current theme is the ways in which writers and filmmakers work the post-apocalyptic. Afterward, reward yourself for your intellectual efforts with a selection from the store's large inventory of new and used books, or a treat from the café.

123 COLUMBIA STREET BETWEEN KANE AND DEGRAW STREETS IN BROOKLYN. Subway: F to Bergen Street. 718-643-8484. www.freebirdbooks.com.

---

773. Spend a day in one of the beautiful reading rooms at the **New York Public Library**.

The Humanities and Social Sciences Library, one of four research libraries in the NYPL system, is the one people know best, located in the majestic Beaux-Arts building with the lion sculptures, next to Bryant Park. If you take the small trouble of making an appointment with a legitimate (read "academically sound") motive, you can visit the library's special collections, surround yourself with shelves of wonderful old books, sink into a comfortable chair, and read to your heart's content. Especially recommended is the Pforzheimer Room, an amazing collection of English romanticism in a cozy room with plush, red velvet chairs.

FIFTH AVENUE AND 42ND STREET AT BRYANT PARK IN MANHATTAN. Subway: B, D, F, V to 42nd Street-Bryant Park; 7 to Fifth Avenue-Bryant Park. 212-930-0830. www.nypl.org.

→ ***DID YOU KNOW?*** *The original names of the lions that stand outside the New York Public Library on Fifth Avenue were Leo Astor and Leo Lenox, after the library's founders, John Jacob Astor and James Lenox. During the Great Depression, Mayor Fiorello LaGuardia renamed them Patience and Fortitude.*

Go to a literary reading.

It often seems like everyone in New York has either published a novel, or is working on one. That may be a slight exaggeration, but between the Pulitzer Prize winners and the struggling writers, there are literary readings to attend pretty much any night of the week. The particular setting, caliber of writer, and quality of the audience make some better than others. Our favorite spots:

774. *Housing Works Used Book Café* hosts readings and other literary events year-round. These are interesting because, unlike readings at other bookstores, theirs tend not to be limited to individual authors promoting a new book. Instead, they host discussions between writers, invite several writers to read on a certain theme, or have speakers on topics related to books and literature. (They also have a monthly concert series called "Live From Home.") They attract some fairly big names, but the environment is always cozy and laid-back. Most events are free, but there is a suggested donation to benefit Housing Works, the nonprofit organization that provides services to homeless New Yorkers living with HIV and AIDS. (One hundred percent of the bookstore's profits fund the same cause.)
126 CROSBY STREET BETWEEN HOUSTON AND PRINCE STREETS IN MANHATTAN. Subway: 6 to Spring Street; B, D, F, V to Broadway-Lafayette Street; N, R, W to Prince Street. 212-334-3324. www.housingworks.org/usedbookcafe.

775. *192 Books*, an independent bookstore in Chelsea, hosts readings, signings, and art exhibitions throughout the year. Although the owners call 192 a general-interest bookstore, the store has a distinctly arty vibe (Paula Cooper, one of the store's owners, also operates a nearby gallery) and therefore attracts many artistic types to the readings.
192 TENTH AVENUE AT 21ST STREET IN MANHATTAN. Subway: C, E to 23rd Street. 212-255-4022. www.192books.com.

→ **DID YOU KNOW?** *In 2004, novelist Paul Auster read* Oracle Nights *in its entirety over the course of two four-hour sessions at 192 Books.*

776. *The Corner Bookstore* (see page 278) on the Upper East Side hosts readings and book parties throughout the year, sometimes as many as two or three a week during the fall and spring. The authors that read are often customers, so the events have a cozy, neighborhood feel. Complimentary wine and cheese is another perk. The best way to find out what's scheduled is by picking up a calendar of events at the store.

1313 MADISON AVENUE AT THE CORNER OF 93RD STREET IN MANHATTAN. Subway: 6 to 96th Street. 212-831-3554.

777. At Amanda Stern's **Happy Ending** series, all readers are required to take a "public risk" (in addition to reading from their own work in front of a crowd). Held on the first Wednesday of every month at Joe's Pub, Stern adds a bit of mischief to the typical author reading. Authors at this reading series tend to be on the younger side, many of them first-time novelists, and if they take themselves too seriously, the lively, informal atmosphere, plus the prospect of cracking open a coconut or making sea monkeys perform tricks for the audience, will set them straight.

425 LAFAYETTE STREET AT ASTOR PLACE IN MANHATTAN. Subway: 6 to Astor Place. 212-254-1263. www.amandastern.com/happyending.html.

778. Although **KGB Bar** is only a decade old, it has already joined the ranks of New York's legendary literary haunts. Having grown from modest beginnings in the heart of the Ukrainian East Village, KGB Bar's mildly communist theme recalls its origins with propaganda posters and other memorabilia. It has always relied on the quality of its readings and the prestige of its incumbent authors to sustain its reputation and to justify its cheap and powerful drinks. You can catch readings here almost any night of the week, by authors such as Rick Moody, A. M. Homes, Jonathan Lethem, Joyce Carol Oates, and Luc Sante. KGB also continues to pay homage to its literary roots with readings from well-known Russian-New Yorkers, such as Gary Shteyngart and Michael Idov. Sundays are reserved for poetry, and Mondays for fiction; there are mixed readings and debates most weeknights.

85 EAST 4TH STREET BETWEEN SECOND AND THIRD AVENUES IN MANHATTAN. Subway: F, V to Lower East Side-Second Avenue. 212-505-3360. www.kgbbar.com.

779. If you like your readings big, **Symphony Space** is the place to go. Whereas most venues that host readings (bookstores, bars) tend to be modestly sized, with few professional production amenities, the literary events at Symphony Space are held on the same stages as their concerts, plays, and dance performances, with lighting, a sound system, and ample seating. These events are more "theatrical," so instead of an intimate, informal audience interacting with an author, these feel more like a performance. In addition to "Selected Shorts," the regularly scheduled evening of short stories broadcast on NPR, they also put on readings, discussions, and author Q & A sessions.

The events aren't free (or even that cheap), but they're a fun way to see a favorite author among other fans, kind of like seeing them in concert. *2537 BROADWAY NEAR 95ᵀᴴ STREET IN MANHATTAN. Subway: 1, 2, 3 to 96ᵗʰ Street. 212-864-5400.www.symphonyspace.org.*

780. Can't say much for the setting, but we have to include ***Barnes & Noble*** and Borders on our list. Though they don't feel as special as the independents or as carefree as the bars, these megastores are able to attract the top literary stars—most any author who's anyone reads here. The real big names (Salman Rushdie, David Sedaris) pack the house, which gives you a warm, fuzzy feeling about the future of the written word. And unless they're *really* eccentric, if authors go on a book tour that includes readings, chances are they'll be at an New York location of one of these chains.
For schedules and locations, visit www.barnesandnoble.com or www.borders.com.

Take **a class!**

Opportunities for learning in this city are staggering and seemingly limitless, both for the variety in instruction and the available outlets in which to receive it. At major universities, continuing education programs, and informal classes at community and enrichment centers all over the city, you can learn skills and crafts, earn a certification or degree, or simply indulge in the pleasure of learning.

The following is our selection of places, among the many, that we feel are the best sources of enriching courses and activities, taking into account the quality of instruction, facilities, atmosphere, offerings, and cost. In general, degree and certificate programs tend to be the most serious and most expensive, and involve an admission process. Continuing education classes offer serious learners a less-directed, one-off option for study on a particular topic, field, or skill. There are also plenty of places that offer workshops or single-session classes that are good for an afternoon or evening's entertainment. The classes at the community and enrichment centers tend to be the least formal, and are for the most part recreational in focus. Between them all, the possibilities for personal edification are vast, and it is precisely the boundless array of possibility that makes this a best thing to do.

781. *The 92nd Street Y* enjoys a reputation as one of New York's premier centers for promoting arts, culture, and education. In addition to lectures, it offers instruction in countless subjects, crafts, skills, and pastimes. They have classes for all ages and levels: parenting classes; children's after-school programs; art, fitness, and language classes; personal development classes in home organization or assertiveness training; instruction in playing bridge or mah jong, and even juggling and tarot card reading. Though the 92nd Street Y is affiliated with a Jewish organization and some classes have a Jewish theme or focus, you don't have to be Jewish (or even a member) to take classes there. And despite the name, the Y has a lot going on beyond 92nd Street. 92YTribeca is a 15,000-square-foot community and performance space that offers concerts, film programs, art shows, and more.

MAIN LOCATION: *1395 LEXINGTON AVENUE AT 92ND STREET IN MANHATTAN. Subway: 6 to 96th Street. 212-415-5500.*

92YTRIBECA: *200 HUDSON STREET AT CANAL STREET IN MANHATTAN. Subway: 1, A, C, E to Canal Street. 212-601-1000. www.92Y.org.*

782. The ***Brooklyn Botanic Garden*** (for full entry, see pages 218–219) has a great range of classes in all things horticultural, from serious courses that count toward certificates in floral and landscape design, to one-off classes and short series in seasonal gardening activities. There are also classes in flower arranging, bird-watching, candle making, and even watercolor painting. The conservatories, home to the bonsai and tropical collections, are also a great place to learn about unusual plants and exotic creatures like fruit bats.

1000 WASHINGTON AVENUE IN BROOKLYN. Subway: 2, 3 to Eastern Parkway-Brooklyn Museum; B, Q to Prospect Park. 718-623-7200. www.bbg.org.

783. ***Beads of Paradise***, a jewelry and craft emporium just off Union Square, offers a jewelry-making class on weekends. Participants learn how to use different tools, how to string necklaces and bracelets, and how to make earrings and drop pendants. Also included in the $75 class fee is a set of tools, bead box, and discount card for your next purchase.

16 EAST 17TH STREET BETWEEN UNION SQUARE WEST AND FIFTH AVENUE IN MANHATTAN. Subway: 4, 5, 6, L, N, Q, R, W to 14th Street-Union Square. 212-620-0642. www.beadsofparadisenyc.com.

784. ***The Center for Book Arts*** is a nonprofit arts and education center dedicated to preserving the craft of book making. It holds classes, seminars, and workshops in techniques of traditional and modern bookbinding and printing, including paper marbling, calligraphy, and letterpress. Beginners are welcome. The center also organizes exhibitions and special events.

28 WEST 27TH STREET BETWEEN SIXTH AVENUE AND BROADWAY, THIRD FLOOR, IN MANHATTAN. Subway: 1 to 28th Street; N, R, W to 28th Street. 212-481-0295. www.centerforbookarts.org.

785. You can eat your way through ***a cheese class at Murray's, the Artisanal Premium Cheese Center, or the Institute of Culinary Education***. You can take classes on regional cheeses or cheese and wine pairing, or learn to make your own in a cheese-making class.

MURRAY'S: *254 BLEECKER STREET BETWEEN SIXTH AND SEVENTH AVENUES IN MANHATTAN. Subway: 1 to Christopher Street-Sheridan Square. 212-243-3289. www.murrayscheese.com.*

ARTISANAL PREMIUM CHEESE CENTER: *500 WEST 37ᵀᴴ STREET AT TENTH AVENUE, SECOND FLOOR, IN MANHATTAN. Subway: 1, 2, 3, A, C, E to 34ᵗʰ Street-Penn Station. 877-797-1200. www.artisanalcheese.com.*

ICE: *50 WEST 23ᴿᴰ STREET BETWEEN FIFTH AND SIXTH AVENUES IN MANHATTAN. Subway: F, V to 23ʳᵈ Street; N, R, W to 23ʳᵈ Street/Broadway. 212-847-0700. www.iceculinary.com. For more information, see following page.*

786. Cooper Union is one of the pioneers of continuing education in this country, having offered courses to New York residents since 1898. Today, you can study fine arts, languages, writing, history, and art history through their continuing education program, as well as try a class in more unusual disciplines, such bookbinding, calligraphy, and green building design.

COOPER SQUARE BY ASTOR PLACE AND LAFAYETTE STREET IN MANHATTAN. Subway: 6 to Astor Place. 212-353-4195. www.cooper.edu.

787. The French Culinary Institute offers a small menu of amateur cooking classes focused on technique. It also offers courses in restaurant management, food writing, and wine.

462 BROADWAY AT GRAND STREET IN MANHATTAN. Subway: 6 to Spring Street; 6, N, Q, R, W, J, M, Z to Canal Street. 212-219-8890. www.frenchculinary.com.

788. Gotham Writers' Workshop runs classes and one-session workshops in many genres: fiction and nonfiction, screenplay, memoir, writing for television, travel writing, humor, and more. The instructors are professional writers and teachers. It isn't glamorous, but the egalitarian feel makes it a comfortable environment in which to work on and share your writing.

Classes held at various locations around the city. For more information, class schedules, and locations, call 212-WRI-TERS or visit www.writingclasses.com.

789. The recreation division at the Institute of Culinary Education gives a full range of cooking classes covering everything from basic technique to specific topics, skills, and cuisines, many in one- or two-evening sessions. It also offers diploma programs in culinary arts, pastry and baking arts, and culinary management, and classes for professional development in restaurant and catering, food media, and more.

50 WEST 23ᴿᴰ STREET BETWEEN FIFTH AND SIXTH AVENUES IN MANHATTAN. Subway: F, V to 23ʳᵈ Street; N, R, W to 23ʳᵈ Street. 212-847-0700. www.iceculinary.com.

790. *The Jewish Community Center* on the Upper West Side offers classes for all ages in the visual arts, photography, media, sports and exercise, cooking, and subjects of Jewish interest. The facilities are immaculate and state-of-the-art, and include a gymnasium and fitness center, swimming pool, an entire floor of arts and media studios, along with classrooms and auditoriums. Classes are open to members and non-members of any religion, race, or ethnicity.

334 AMSTERDAM AVENUE AT 76ᵀᴴ STREET IN MANHATTAN. Subway: 1, 2, 3 to 72ⁿᵈ Street; B, C to 72ⁿᵈ Street. 646-505-4444. www.jccmanhattan.org.

791. *Joe* is considered by many to serve the best coffee in the city. Every year, their perfectly brewed coffee and espresso beverages top local "best of" lists. You can learn how they do it at their coffee classes, which are held throughout the year at their various locations in the West Village, Union Square area, and Chelsea. They offer classes on the basics of coffee and espresso preparation and presentation, milk steaming, and home-brewing techniques. To find out more, call, check the Web site, or just pop in—theirs is the friendliest, most mellow staff we've ever encountered in a coffee shop, and it's a good excuse to get a cup of coffee.

Classes are held on weeknights and cost between $20 and $25 each. Reservations required. For more information, current class schedule, and class locations, visit www.joetheartofcoffee.com.

792. The cooking classes at *Miette Culinary Studio* in the West Village feel like a potluck dinner at a good friend's house, except that your host is a chef, and everyone is cooking the same thing at the same time. Housed in a nineteenth-century townhouse, the airy studio is more like someone's dream apartment than a cooking school. Paul Vandewoude formerly owned Tartine, the charming BYOB restaurant in the West Village (Tartine still exists, but Paul, who has a young son, moved on to start a more family-friendly venture). The classes are limited to twelve students, are held on weekday evenings, and last between two and three hours. Each class teaches the preparation of classic but manageable meals, like marinated salmon in ginger with green beans and roasted potatoes, or a roasted root vegetable salad with pumpkin risotto. The focus is on classic French cooking, but there are also special classes on specific techniques, other cuisines, and special themes. Afterward, the class sits down together to enjoy the food, and, adding to the homey, convivial atmosphere, participants are encouraged to bring bottles of wine to contribute to the meal.

109 MACDOUGAL STREET BETWEEN BLEECKER AND WEST 3ᴿᴰ STREETS IN MANHATTAN. Subway: A, C, E, B, D, F, V to West 4ᵗʰ Street. 212-460-9322. www.mietteculinarystudio.com.

793. The *Manhattan Neighborhood Network*, a local community access channel, offers one of the best deals in the city. In keeping with its mission of promoting free speech through the medium of television, it gives free classes in its studios. Classes include studio production, control-room basics, camera technique and more; students are also allowed to use their equipment during the term of the class. Classes are first-come/first-served, and you must show proof of residency.

537 WEST 59TH STREET BETWEEN TENTH AND ELEVENTH AVENUES IN MANHATTAN. Subway: 1, A, C, B, D to 59th Street-Columbus Circle. 212-757-2670. www.mnn.org.

794. Proudly proclaiming itself "the leader in adult education," the **New School** is considered the premier institution of continuing education in the country. Most classes at the New School of General Studies, Parsons School of Design, and Mannes College for Music are open to both credit and noncredit students. This means that you can take a regular university class with matriculating students, but because of the university's dedication to continuing education, you won't be made to feel like an anomaly. They also offer certificate programs in several disciplines.

66 WEST 12TH STREET BETWEEN SIXTH AND SEVENTH AVENUES IN MANHATTAN. Subway: F, V to 14th Street; L to Sixth Avenue. For phone numbers of specific schools and departments, visit www.newschool.edu.

795. The New York Film Academy has classes and workshops that range in length and intensity from a few weeks to one year. In addition to traditional filmmaking, it offers classes in digital film, screenwriting, editing, producing, animation, and screen acting.

100 EAST 17TH STREET AT UNION SQUARE IN MANHATTAN. Subway: 4, 5, 6, L, N, Q, R, W to 14th Street-Union Square. 212-674-4300. www.nyfa.com.

796. The New York Open Center is a holistic learning center that offers courses in just about any creative, physical, emotional, psychological, sociological, and spiritual topic you can imagine. From aromatherapy to Ayurveda, photography to psychology—you name it, they teach it. (We even found a listing for a class on canine acupressure.) A look through the online course catalog is quite an enriching experience in itself.

22 EAST 30TH STREET BETWEEN FIFTH AND MADISON AVENUES. Subway: 6 to 28th Street or N, R, W to 28th Street. 212-219-2527. www.opencenter.org.

797. New York University's School of Continuing and Professional Studies gives adults of any educational background a chance to study pretty much any topic, field, or discipline imaginable. Among the more than 2,500 courses are classes in all the traditional liberal arts (history, literature, social sciences); skills (arts, editing, accounting, languages); professional interests; plus classes in leadership skills, emergency management, and other highly targeted areas of study. There are enough different certificate and degree programs for graduates and professionals to accommodate any educational goal. Whether you are looking to take a college-level literature class for fun, pick up a new skill, or get a license to boost your career, or you are considering a graduate degree but not quite ready to invest in a master's program, NYU has a class to meet your needs. *145 FOURTH AVENUE, ROOM 201, IN MANHATTAN. Subway: 4, 5, 6, L, N, Q, R, W to 14th Street-Union Square. 212-998-7200. www.scps.nyu.edu.*

798. *PhotoManhattan* offers photography classes at a fraction of the cost of the ones at other schools and institutes around the city. They have classes in introductory-level photography, darkroom technique, lighting, street photography and more that offer the same level of instruction as the others at half the price. Equipment rentals are similarly affordable.
51 WEST 14TH STREET BETWEEN FIFTH AND SIXTH AVENUES IN MANHATTAN. Subway: F, V to 14th Street; L to Sixth Avenue. 212-929-3302. www.photomanhattan.com.

799. *The Pratt Institute*, one of New York's most celebrated art and architecture schools, offers continuing education and certificate programs in the arts in addition to its undergraduate and graduate degree programs. The Center for Continuing and Professional Studies provides a wide range of classes in fields such as computer skills, technical art skills, fashion design, and feng shui. Classes are held on the main Brooklyn campus, or on the satellite campus in Manhattan.
BROOKLYN: *200 WILLOUGHBY AVENUE NEAR HALL STREET. Subway: G to Clinton-Washington Avenue. 718-636-3600.* **MANHATTAN:** *144 WEST 14TH STREET BETWEEN SIXTH AND SEVENTH AVENUES. Subway: F, V to 14th Street; L to Sixth Avenue. 212-647-7775. www.pratt.edu.*

800. *The School of Visual Arts* runs terrific continuing education programs in advertising, animation, computer arts, film and video, fine arts, graphic design, illustration and cartooning, interior design, and photography, as well as graduate and undergraduate degree courses.
209 EAST 23RD STREET BETWEEN SECOND AND THIRD AVENUES IN MANHATTAN. Subway: 6 to 23rd Street. 212-592-2000. www.schoolofvisualarts.edu.

801. *Craigslist*. It's true that Craigslist exists in many cities here and abroad, but like food, arts, and pretty much everything else in New York, the diversity and ingenuity of our locals really work in your favor. The combination of constant Internet access and the large number of highly skilled but underemployed (or underpaid) New Yorkers makes this city a buyer's market for instruction and tutelage (the excellent public transportation system helps, too—services can often be delivered in under an hour). A quick look at the postings under "classes" reveals offers for lessons in art, dance, languages, music, yoga, computer skills—and that's just one day's listings. The quality of the lessons, of course, is not guaranteed, but if you want to try something out for the hell of it (or you really need to learn HTML right now), this is the place to go.
http://newyork.craigslist.org.

Another valuable resource for education and enrichment opportunities in New York is *international institutes.* Most have language classes, with some of the major cultural centers offering more comprehensive curriculums in literature, business, and cultural studies, and the classes tend to be less strictly utilitarian than at regular language schools. These institutes also tend to have many other cultural resources, such as film and lecture programs, art exhibits, and libraries. Some of these include:

802. *The French Institute/Alliance Française* offers classes in French language for all levels, as well as more advanced classes in writing, literature, film, history, politics, and business.
22 EAST 60TH STREET AT FIFTH AVENUE IN MANHATTAN. Subway: N, R, W to Fifth Avenue/59th Street. 212-355-6100. www.fiaf.org.

803. *The China Institute* runs fun and informative courses in a range of Chinese cultural pursuits, from calligraphy and languages to painting and *taijiquan* (tai chi). Most classes are taught in the evening and can be taken on a night-by-night basis or as a full program.
125 EAST 65TH STREET IN MANHATTAN. Subway: 4, 5, 6 to 59th Street; F to Lexington Avenue/63rd Street; N, R, W to Lexington Avenue/59th Street. 212-744-8181. www.chinainstitute.org.

804. *The Deutsches Haus* holds classes on a quarterly basis in German language, with special courses on reading, business German, and other topics. There is also a language-focused book club for contemporary German literature to help students practice their German in a more relaxed setting. (For an additional fee, the book club is open to nonstudents who speak German or are in the process of learning.) Another plus is the center's lovely setting by the Washington Mews.
42 WASHINGTON MEWS BETWEEN UNIVERSITY PLACE AND FIFTH AVENUE IN MANHATTAN. Subway: N, R, W to 8th Street-New York University. 212-998-8660. www.deutcheshaus.as.nyu.edu.

805. *The Japan Society* maintains a comprehensive program of Japanese language classes for children and adults, from beginner on up. It also offers classes in ESL, business Japanese, and *shodo*, an art form using Japanese calligraphy.
333 EAST 47TH STREET BETWEEN FIRST AND SECOND AVENUES IN MANHATTAN. Subway: 4, 5, 6, 7, S to Grand Central-42nd Street. 212-832-1155. www.japansociety.org.

806. *The Instituto Cervantes* offers Spanish language classes for adults, from beginner on up. It also runs special classes for children, as well as classes on Spanish culture and history, business Spanish, and classes with a reading or writing focus. Students receive a free six-month membership to the institute's library, and are given access to other educational support.

211-215 EAST 49TH STREET AT AMSTER YARD IN MANHATTAN. Subway: 6 to 51st Street; E, V to Lexington Avenue/53rd Street. 212-308-7720. www.nuevayork.cervantes.es.

807. Scandinavia House offers a wide range of language classes, including a super program for kids. There is also an exhibition space for works by Scandinavian artists, sculptors, and photographers, where lecture and film series are held throughout the year. Get the events calendar and try to make it to one of the parties—Scandinavians know how to have fun.
58 PARK AVENUE BETWEEN 37TH AND 38TH STREETS IN MANHATTAN. Subway: 4, 5, 6, 7, S to Grand Central-42nd Street. 212-879-9779. www.scandinaviahouse.org.

Lectures

As a center for arts, politics, international relations, history, and culture, New York attracts authorities on every field imaginable, a great number of whom will be speaking about something, somewhere, on any given night. If the word lecture is off-putting to you, take note: most bear no resemblance to the stuffy, sleep-inducing assemblies of your school days (some even serve food and drink). Most of the schools and community and cultural centers listed earlier in this chapter also have lecture series, symposia, panel discussions, and other speaking programs that are open to the public. The following are other places around the city that compile interesting programs:

808. Museum at the Fashion Institute of Technology. Most of the lectures and debates that take place in New York's top school of fashion and textile design are free and open to the public. Topics vary from the history of textiles around the world to more specific elements of contemporary fashion, and they often relate to the current exhibitions at the museum. A little time here can provide an interesting perspective on the hours spent schlepping around boutiques uptown and in SoHo. (See page 129 for more information on visiting the museum.)
SEVENTH AVENUE AT 27TH STREET IN MANHATTAN. Subway: 1 to 28th Street. 212-217-5800. www.fitnyc.edu.

809. The Interfaith Center is a secular organization whose goal is to celebrate New York's religious and cultural diversity through education, entertainment, and enrichment. It hosts a broad range of lectures, seminars, and workshops on topics of local and cultural interest. It also holds exhibitions and performances at various locations around the city.
475 RIVERSIDE DRIVE BETWEEN 119TH AND 120TH STREETS IN MANHATTAN. Subway: 1, A, B, C, D to 125th Street. 212-870-3510. www.interfaithcenter.org.

810. ***The Tibet House*** holds speaking events related to Tibet and Buddhism and has an on-site gallery for exhibitions of visual art. Classes are offered as part of the Tibetan studies program at the New York Open Center (see page 299), and there are weekly meditation sessions.

22 WEST 15TH STREET BETWEEN FIFTH AND SIXTH AVENUES IN MANHATTAN. Subway: F, V to 14th Street; L to Sixth Avenue. 212-807-0563. www.tibethouse.org.

811. ***AIA Center for Architecture.*** The New York headquarters of the American Institute for Architects is a wonderful and underused resource. The building itself is unique in the city because, by virtue of a deep well that was dug out beneath, it is the only structure in New York with an ecofriendly geothermal heating and cooling system. The library is a nice, quiet place to work; it is well stocked with glossy volumes of contemporary and historic architecture, and allows for eavesdropping on university classes that take place here. Almost all lectures are free, and range from debates on important issues of contemporary urban planning to retrospective talks from renowned architects. The guests are often world famous, the after-parties are great, and there are always interesting faces in the crowd.

536 LAGUARDIA PLACE BETWEEN BLEECKER AND WEST 3RD STREETS IN MANHATTAN. Subway: 6 to Bleecker Street; A, C, E, B, D, F, V to West 4th Street. 212-683-0023. www.aiany.org. See AIA President Ric Bell's favorite classic New York buildings on page 54.

812. Attend an organized **meditation session**.

The focus, relaxation, and calm achieved through meditation are just what every New Yorker needs, right? Meditation sessions are a sure way to nourish a weary psyche, and they are as prevalent as hot dog vendors, if you know where to look. In addition to Tibet House (see above for more information), which offers weekly meditation on Tuesday nights, sessions can be found at yoga studios, wellness centers, and at some of the community centers listed earlier in this chapter. The **Museum of Tibetan Art** (see page 126) also offers free meditation sessions each Saturday, led by monks from the Staten Island Vihara. You may think you don't have time, or that you're too "type A" to go in for this kind of stuff, but isn't the chance of improving your mental well-being worth a try?

Sessions take place all over the city; check local listings for specific times and venues

813. Tell a story to **StoryCorps**, and be a part of American History! StoryCorps is a program that aims to record a people's history of the United States, voice by voice, from city to city. For $10, anyone can sit in front of a microphone in a booth with a sound engineer and just talk—the tapes will be saved in the Library of Congress, you get to keep a recording of your story on CD, and the most intriguing tales will be

played on NPR. Since the first booth was opened in Grand Central in 2003, more than 50,000 New Yorkers have told their tales into the StoryCorps microphone. Now the booth resides downtown close to City Hall, and the waiting list is as long as ever—so make a reservation as soon as you can and use the time you have to prepare for your contribution to history!

STORYCORPS BOOTH, FOLEY SQUARE, CENTRE STREET BETWEEN DUANE STREET AND WORTH STREET IN MANHATTAN. Subway: 4, 5, 6 to Brooklyn Bridge-City Hall; 1, 2, 3, J, M, Z to Chambers Street; R, W to City Hall. Reservations can be made by phone on 1-800-850-4406 or online at www.storycorps.org.

814. Learn to focus on the task at hand at a **Japanese tea ceremony**.

Urasenke Chanoyu is one of the most prestigious tea schools in the world. Based in Japan, the school teaches the art of Japanese tea ceremonies at various outposts around world. The New York branch is an uncommonly tranquil spot in the city, hidden on a quiet block on the Upper East Side. A small door in the middle of the block opens onto a peaceful Japanese rock garden courtyard, which is surrounded by kitchens, classrooms, libraries, and storerooms. To be a full-time student here is serious business (training to be a tea master can take years), and there is a long waiting list to be approved for entry. But the center holds monthly tea ceremony demonstrations for the public, which include an introductory lecture on the practice and etiquette of the Japanese tea ceremony, the tea ceremony itself, and a question-and-answer session. Focusing on the task at hand is an integral part of a tea ceremony, and you are supposed to perform the movements of pouring and serving tea by treating these tasks as the most important in the world. The experience shows how concentration can elevate ordinary-seeming actions into meaningful parts of life—a lesson from which most of us could surely benefit.

153 EAST 69TH STREET BETWEEN THIRD AND LEXINGTON AVENUES IN MANHATTAN. Subway: 6 to 68th Street-Hunter College. 212-988-6161. www.urasenkeny.org.

→ **DID YOU KNOW?** *The 130-year-old building the center is located in was formerly the studio of the artist Mark Rothko.*

815. For about two months in the fall, beginner lessons in quilting are taught at the Queens Botanical Garden. Classes take place in various locations

indoors and out around the gardens, are taught by an experienced quilter, and can be an inspiring alternative to knitting on the subway.

43-50 MAIN STREET IN QUEENS. Subway: 7 to Flushing-Main Street. For details and specific dates, call 718-886-3800 or visit www.queensbotanical.org.

816. Hone your mind against the smartest hustlers in the world at the chess tables in **Washington Square Park**.

It's a different kind of focus, but one that will sharpen your mind (and your reflexes) like none other. Washington Square Park's tables (also known as the "snake pit") are legendary, but remarkably, even after a scare in 2009 when the park was renovated and a renewed spirit of conservatism threatened, this technically illegal chess racket hasn't been shut down. A mixture of serious amateurs, college chess club dropouts, and the occasional unwitting novices play against seasoned regulars for three dollars and up per game. Look out for "the Lithuanian," an anonymous master in a trench coat— he never loses. N.B. Formidable opponents can also be found at the tables in the East Village in Tompkins Square Park, where the chess is not as flashy but equally as serious. *WASHINGTON SQUARE PARK AT THOMPSON STREET IN MANHATTAN. Subway: A, C, E, B, D, F, V to West 4th Street.*

Also: **Chess Forum** (219 Thompson Street) and the **Village Chess Shop** (230 Thompson Street) are great places to engage in anything from idle games to competitive championships with other would-be grand masters. See page 330 for details.

817. Recharge with a **midday nap**.

Going somewhere to conk out in the middle of the day may sound illicit, but if you find yourself feeling a little groggy in the West 50s, take a peek inside Yelo. This unique business venture offers short-term rentals of private sleep cabins called "Yelo Cabs," in which a client can briefly nod off and enjoy the many proven restorative benefits of a nap. (Nap sessions can be topped off by short reflexology sessions or massage.) The entire experience is choreographed to maximize the positive physical effects of a nap—legs are elevated to help slow down the heart rate; naps are capped at forty minutes to avoid grogginess on waking—so while the hushed voices and low lights give off a bit of a speakeasy feel, there's nothing shady about the increase in energy and productivity you'll feel afterward. *315 WEST 57TH STREET BETWEEN EIGHTH AND NINTH AVENUES IN MANHATTAN. Subway: 1, A, B, C, D to Columbus Circle. Drop-ins welcome, and reservations are taken online and by phone. 212-245-8235. www.yelonyc.com.*

818. **Use a Pass** to take a Class.

The American Health Fitness Alliance has a brilliant solution for NYC locals with crippling fitness indecision. They have put together three types of PassBooks that contain vouchers for free classes or admission at hundreds of studios and gyms across the five boroughs. For $75 (less than the price of an initiation fee at many local gyms), you can try every form of exercise this city offers, without making a long-term commitment. The FitnessPass contains 600 passes for everything from regular gyms to martial arts studios, pools, and even bowling. The YogaPass and PilatesPass both contain vouchers for classes at studios all across the city. Each pass is good for a minimum of two classes at the venue, with some offering unlimited access for a week or even a month.

For more information and to order online, visit www.health-fitness.org.

Learn to **dance**.

Taking a dance class is a refreshing (and socially empowering) way to get some exercise, and, not surprisingly, there is no shortage of classes offered around the city. Here are some favorites:

819. Started in 1979 by ballroom dance champion Sandra Cameron, the **Sandra Cameron Dance School** offers classes in all types of Latin, swing, hip-hop, and, of course, ballroom dancing. For beginners, the Basic Six course is a great introduction to ballroom dancing, where you learn the steps of six popular dances (foxtrot, swing, waltz, tango, rhumba, and salsa), as well as basic dance principles. The month-long course, which is given all year round, meets once a week for an hour, and also includes a free review class near the end of the term. After Basic Six, you can go on to more advanced classes in these or other dances, such as salsa or merengue. The center also holds open practice sessions every night of the week, which are free for enrolled students. (The Friday evening sessions feature complimentary wine and cheese.) During these sessions, students can work on your steps with an instructor present.
199 LAFAYETTE STREET BETWEEN BROOME AND KENMARE STREETS IN MANHATTAN. Subway: 6 to Spring Street. 212-431-1825. www.sandracameron.com.

820. Founded in 1992 as a nonprofit cultural organization, the **Djoniba Dancing & Drum Centre**'s mission is to provide a home for the teaching and performance of multiethnic dance and drumming, and to that end, they offer classes in over thirty styles of dance from around the world, including African dance, reggae, belly dance, and capoeira. After losing the lease on its space, the Djoniba formed a partnership with another downtown dance school, **Peridance**, which itself was about to expand into a new space in the East Village. Today, curious movers and shakers can find Djoniba's eclectic offerings in the same building as Peridance's more mainstream curriculum of ballet, tap, and modern.
126 EAST 13TH STREET, BETWEEN THIRD AND FOURTH AVENUES. Subway: 4, 5, 6, L, N, Q, R, W to 14th Street-Union Square. 212-505-0886 (Peridance phone) www.djoniba.com or www.peridance.com.

821. There are many studios that teach **partner dancing** around the city, and most have comparable offerings like packages for beginners, free introductory classes, wedding packages, and complimentary practice sessions and parties. The biggest dance center in New York is **DanceSport**, located near the Empire State Building, famous for the celebrities and Broadway stars they've worked with. (The center's claim to fame is that its founders choreographed the tango scene in *Scent of a Woman*.) DanceSport offers classes in dozens of types of partner dances at all levels. The Chelsea studios **Dance Manhattan** and **Stepping Out** are also good places for lessons, as is **Sandra Cameron** (see entry above).

All studios located in Manhattan. **DANCESPORT:** *22 WEST 34TH STREET BETWEEN FIFTH AND SIXTH AVENUES IN MANHATTAN. Subway: B, D, F, N, Q, R, V, W to 34th Street-Herald Square. 212-307-1111. www.dancesport.com.* **DANCE MANHATTAN:** *39 WEST 19TH STREET BETWEEN FIFTH AND SIXTH AVENUES. Subway: 4, 5, 6, L, N, Q, R, W to 14th Street-Union Square.212-807-0802.www.dancemanhattan.com.* **STEPPING OUT:** *37 WEST 26TH STREET BETWEEN BROADWAY AND SIXTH AVENUE. Subway: N, R, W to 28th Street. 646-742-9400. www.steppingoutstudios.com.*

Study a **martial art**.

The organized systems of movement and postures that characterize martial arts were developed originally as means of self-defense, but their individual principles, philosophies, and focus techniques provide benefits beyond fighting skills. Like yoga, martial arts can enhance both physical and mental fitness, and though the styles vary in approach and specifics, they are all quite beautiful to watch and perform. Karate, tai chi, and tae kwon do are only some of the many kinds of martial arts practiced in New York, and each of these can found at gyms and studios all around the city. Following are several places that offer less well-known varieties. We've also included listings for outdoor tai chi classes on pages 229–230 in Chapter 6, "The Great Outdoors."

822. *The Japanese Swordsmanship Society* is an organization dedicated to preserving ancient Japanese martial arts. They offer classes in several types of swordsmanship: *iado, naginata*, and *jodo*. They welcome beginners and are eager to introduce anyone to the art of the sword.

Classes, times, and locations vary; see Web site for details. www.ny-jss.org.

823. Grappling, or Brazilian jujitsu, is a cross-cultural martial art that resembles wrestling. It was developed in Brazil in the early twentieth century by a family that received instruction in traditional Japanese jujitsu from a visiting master. In Manhattan, you can study it at the **_Renzo Gracie Academy_** with a member of the original Brazilian family and an international martial arts champion.

224 WEST 30TH STREET, SUITE 100, IN MANHATTAN. Subway: 1 to 28th Street. 212-279-6724. www.renzogracie.com.

824. At the **USA Shaolin Temple**, you can visit the origins of all martial arts and be instructed in various disciplines of ancient Chinese practices. There are classes in various styles of kung fu, tai chi, chi kung, plus teachings in Chan Buddhism and the rich history of the Shaolin Temple.
446 BROADWAY, SECOND FLOOR, BETWEEN GRAND AND HOWARD STREETS IN MANHATTAN. Subway: N, Q, R, W, 6 to Canal Street. 212-358-7876. www.usashaolintemple.com.

825. Pick a sport at **Chelsea Piers**.

This thirty-acre waterfront sports complex has literally transformed physical activity in New York since it opened ten years ago, and it remains one of the best places in the city for unbridled recreation. Nowhere else in the city can you find this much space for so many different kinds of activities, and some of the facilities are the only ones of their kind. There's a forty-lane bowling alley; a **golf club** (see page 347); an ice-skating rink; a roller rink and skate park; the Field House, with an indoor rock-climbing wall, batting cages, soccer and basketball courts, and gymnastics; a fitness center with a pool; a spa; plus restaurants, shops, studios, and more. (To some New Yorkers, the most exotic amenity, however, might be the on-site parking.) Finally, there are also camps, after-school activities, training programs, and extensive adult sports programs—including the world's largest adult gymnastics program.
23RD STREET AND THE HUDSON RIVER IN MANHATTAN. Subway: C, E to 23rd Street. For information, hours, prices, and phone numbers of specific facilities, call 212-336-6666 or visit www.chelseapiers.com.

Expert contributor: Pavia Rosati

Pavia Rosati is a journalist who has been living in New York for fifteen years. She is the executive editor of DailyCandy.com, and she writes about food and travel. She travels extensively for work, but finds special pleasure in her favorite New York escapes.

MY FAVORITE RETREATS IN NEW YORK:

826. *Balthazar:* Everyone is beautiful at Balthazar. The restaurant is New York at its best: buzzy, sceney, cool, and usually insanely (and annoyingly) packed, which is why I only go for breakfast or a late midweek supper. The tables in the back left corner are perfect for hiding out in plain sight.

80 SPRING STREET BETWEEN BROADWAY AND CROSBY STREET IN MANHATTAN. Subway: 6 to Spring Street. 212-965-1785. www.balthazarny.com. For more information on Balthazar, see page 164.

827. *Rose Reading Room at the New York Public Library:* I love to play hooky from the office and spend the day working here. Soaring ceilings, pink cloud murals, long tables, plus a mishmash of students, tourists, and researchers—easily the most inspiring yet quiet place in town. Plus there's free Internet access, and Wi-Fi right outside in Bryant Park.
FIFTH AVENUE AND 42ND STREET AT BRYANT PARK IN MANHATTAN. Subway: B, D, F, V to 42nd Street-Bryant Park; 7 to Fifth Avenue-Bryant Park. www.nypl.org. For more information on the New York Public Library, see page 292.

828. *Housing Works Used Book Café:* I work in a creative, noisy office in SoHo. When I can't hear myself think, I head to Housing Works Café, an oasis in an otherwise zoo-like neighborhood. That Crosby is the sexiest, gritty street in the city only adds to the charm.
126 CROSBY STREET BETWEEN HOUSTON AND PRINCE STREETS IN MANHATTAN. Subway: 6 to Spring Street; B, D, F, V to Broadway-Lafayette; Street N, R, W to Prince Street. 212-334-3324. www.housingworks.org. For full entry, see page 293.

829. *Juvenex Spa:* Now this is a miracle: a 24-hour spa in the middle of the city. It's for women only from 7:00 a.m. until 5:00 p.m.; co-ed thereafter. There's no better chaser to an overly rich dinner than the jade igloo sauna.
25 WEST 32ND STREET BETWEEN FIFTH AND SIXTH AVENUES IN MANHATTAN. Subway: B, D, F, V, N, Q, R, W to 34th Street-Herald Square. For full entry, see page 326. www.juvenexspa.com.

830. *Williamsburg Bridge:* As much as I love to travel, I love coming home more. I always tell the driver to take the BQE (Brooklyn-Queens Expressway) from the airport so I can stare at the skyline and cross the Williamsburg Bridge on my way home to the East Village.

Massages, baths, acupuncture, spas, herbal remedies and other ways to relax

Along with exercising your mind and body with classes, sports, and entertainment, part of improving yourself and your well-being involves taking time to relax and recharge. In New York, there are innumerable ways to do just that, such as spa visits, massages and body treatments, and alternative medicine, to name a few. Here we've listed the particularly notable options for bolstering your inner health.

831. Float for an hour in the tanks at **La Casa Day Spa**.

The mission of this Flatiron spa is to draw on the healing powers of the five earthly elements (earth, water, fire, air, and sky) to draw pesky toxins out of the body, and to restore balance and well-being. So it follows that one of the signature treatments is flotation. Inside a private tank, you rest peacefully in water saturated with 800 pounds of Epsom salts. The salts draw toxins from the body, so they can be washed away. The water is heated to the precise temperature of your skin, which prevents nerve transmissions from skin to brain. What results is a relaxing and purifying experience more profound than a regular massage.

41 EAST 20TH STREET BETWEEN PARK AVENUE SOUTH AND BROADWAY IN MANHATTAN. One-hour float is $80, or $50 when combined with another treatment. Subway: 6 to 23rd Street; N, R, W to 23rd Street. 212-673-CASA. www.lacasaspa.com.

832. Have someone walk on your back at **Osaka**.

During the famous sixty-minute shiatsu acupressure massage, which has been enjoyed by movie stars, politicians, and plenty of other celebrities not usually found in west Midtown, the therapist walks on your back (while holding on to ropes hanging from the ceiling), expertly releasing hidden tension with her toes. It sounds strange, but it does the trick, and is the perfect way to end a long day, no matter when your days ends (the 46th Street location is open until midnight; 56th Street location is open until 2:00 a.m.).

Both locations in Manhattan. OSAKA 46: 37 WEST 46TH STREET BETWEEN FIFTH AND SIXTH AVENUES. Subway: B, D, F, V to 47th-50th Streets-Rockefeller Center. 212-575-1303. OSAKA 56: 50 WEST 56TH STREET BETWEEN FIFTH AND SIXTH AVENUES. Subway: F to 57th Street; N, R, W to Fifth Avenue/59th Street. 212-956-3422. www.osakahealthspa.com.

833. Meet a friend and sweat out the toxins after a hard day's work in the "igloo" at **Athena Spa**.

This tri-level Midtown sanctuary combines the services of a spa with the luxuriating amenities of a bathhouse, with one additional special feature: an igloo-shape sauna made with *hwangto*. Hwangto is a special yellow soil from Korea used in purifying and cleansing treatments; it has special properties that filter out toxins and boost circulation and metabolism. The igloo at Athena also has amethysts and jades embedded in the wall, which, in addition to looking pretty, have restorative properties. The air has a cleaner, lighter feel than most saunas, so despite the heat, you can lie there for quite a while without feeling stifled, as the impurities seep out of your body (really, you can feel them!). Use of both the igloo and the wet spa is included when you opt for a massage ($80), as well as the use of the steam room, showers, soaking tub, and lounge area for an unlimited time. Make an appointment, grab a friend, and spend a couple of hours at Athena letting yourselves really relax. (N.B.: **Juvenex Spa**, listed on pages 309 and 326, also has an igloo.)

32 EAST 31ST STREET BETWEEN PARK AND MADISON AVENUES IN MANHATTAN. Subway: 6 to 33rd Street. 212-683-4484. www.athenaspany31.com.

834. Have a facial at **Sava Spa**.

Why is having a facial at this tiny Washington Heights spa such a treat? Because when owner Joanna Czech works on your face, she's not merely giving a treatment; she's practicing a craft. Her warm demeanor and artistlike dedication to her clients' faces make this often uncomfortable beauty ritual a personal and pleasant experience. If the Washington Heights location makes you balk, consider how rare it is that a famed and highly sought-after craftsperson in New York eschews the limelight in favor of opening her own place, in her neighborhood, where she can work on customers herself, as well as hand-pick and personally train everyone she hires. You'd be hard-pressed to find either the homey, relaxed manner of Joanna and her staff, or the quality of their work, at any other spa closer to home.

211 PINEHURST AVENUE BETWEEN 186TH AND 187TH STREETS IN MANHATTAN. Subway: A to 181st Street. 212-543-0008. www.savaspa.com.

835. Experience reflexology at **Angel Feet**...

Nestled between the brownstones on Perry Street, this tiny West Village reflexology parlor is about as far from a spa as you can get. The sterile, businesslike feel that more chic operations can't quite escape is entirely absent here. In lieu of a high-tech check-in desk and lots of tools and machines, there is a table up front where someone takes appointments by hand, plus overstuffed armchairs, and a staff that *really* knows reflexology. The cozy, off-the-beaten-path setting and the single-minded focus on the treatments offered make a trip to Angel Feet one of the most genuinely therapeutic treatments around—not to mention an unusually pleasurable experience.

77 PERRY STREET BETWEEN BLEECKER AND WEST 4TH STREETS IN MANHATTAN. Subway: 1 to Christopher Street-Sheridan Square; A, C, E, B, D, F, V to West 4th Street. 212-924-3576. www.angelfeet.com.

836. ...and then pamper your nails at Jin Soon.

It is almost absurdly easy to get one's nails done in this city, where salons of all sizes and price ranges seem to occupy as many storefronts as delis and Starbucks combined. But rare is the venue where one can receive superior care, at a reasonable price, in a tranquil environment. In fact, we can think of only three. At Jin Soon's trio of tiny, delicate salons, everything from the creams, salves, and essential oils used during treatments to the choice of light bulbs (no harsh fluorescent lighting here!) appears to have been selected with great sensitivity. Rather than having your treatment in the middle of a busy room with the bustling street in full view, at Jin Soon, you get to relax on silk pillows, sipping the signature citrus tea, with the rest of the city invisible behind a half wall. Staff members are all trained by Soon herself, who is renowned in beauty circles for her exquisite shaping, buffing, and painting techniques. This experience of quality and comfort is even more remarkable when you consider that the price of a regular pedicure at Jin Soon ($32) is on par with the rest of the city. (Manicures start at $18.) If you feel like you need some additional pampering, there are more luxurious offerings as well—see page 283.

Multiple locations in the East Village, West Village, and Upper East Side. Visit www.jinsoon.com for locations and hours, or call 212-249-9144.

837. Open your mind to a *platza* and salt scrub at the Russian and Turkish baths in the East Village...

The first is an oddly relaxing thrashing with oak twigs soaked in olive oil, and the second is a natural exfoliation to rid you of excess body weight. For the courageous, there are single-sex days when everyone in the baths can go naked.

268 EAST 10TH STREET BETWEEN FIRST AVENUE AND AVENUE A IN MANHATTAN. Subway: 6 to Astor Place; L to First Avenue. 212-505-0665.

838. ...or relax like a Russian at Royal Palace Baths.

If the East Village baths aren't serious enough for you, then go to Royal Palace, the largest of Russian Brooklyn's many *banya*. Baths here serve the same purpose they do in Russia—as places to clean up, shave, relax, eat, and be social—so the atmosphere is busier and more family oriented than at other baths in the city. Renovated and reopened in 2008—with a spectacular giant shark sculpture hanging ominously over the pool—the Royal Palace is allegedly the biggest Russian bathhouse in the country. For the complete experience: order a drink and a plate of fresh Mediterranean fruit, try each of the steam rooms (which are styled after Russian, Finnish, Roman, and Turkish baths), take a dip in the ice water, swim in the pool, ask to be smacked with a soapy *besom* (a bundle of leaves and branches), and finally get doused with cold water in the hottest sauna.

614 SHEEPSHEAD BAY ROAD AT WEST 8TH STREET IN BROOKLYN. Subway: F to Neptune Avenue. 718-373-3002.

839. Storm the Spa Castle in the depths of Queens.

If you really need to escape the stress and grime of the city, and the steam and *platza* of the Russian and Turkish baths aren't quite your cup of tea, make the trek out to the New York Spa Castle, located in the heart of Queens. The Castle—whose vast and palatial site entirely merits the name—is simply the largest and best-equipped spa the city has to offer, with five floors and a hundred thousand square feet full of saunas, hot tubs, plunge pools, swimming pools, flotation tanks, massage centers, and any and every relaxing treatment you care to think of. It's a little farther out than most city-dwellers are prepared to go—the journey involves going beyond the scope of the subway, and taking a special bus provided by the spa—but the journey is worth it for the glorious outdoor pools alone, which are heaven in summer. Indoors, you can move from body scrubs and lavender body massages to the crowded food court, which has everything from fresh juice and a Starbucks to sushi and an Italian restaurant, before you wander off through the Castle's hallways to sweat it out in one of the many steam rooms. Be prepared, though, to share your hot tub with the odd rowdy child: the Castle is one of Flushing's biggest family destinations.

131-10 11 AVENUE IN COLLEGE POINT, QUEENS. Subway: 7 to Flushing, then connect with the Spa Castle shuttle bus. 718-939-6300. For driving directions, shuttle bus times, and more information, visit www.nyspacastle.com.

840. Make like a mafioso at **Spa 88**.

With an interior decked out like a shabby Miami beach club, this is probably the most garish of all the spas in Manhattan—there's even a kitschy smoking room upstairs. But where else can you lounge by a pool surrounded by fake palm trees with a large cocktail in your hand after your choice of saunas, mud treatments, massages, or ear candling?

88 FULTON STREET BETWEEN WILLIAM AND GOLD STREETS IN MANHATTAN. Subway: 4, 5, J, M, Z to Fulton Street. 212-766-8600. www.spa88.com.

841. Have your ailment diagnosed and healed with natural remedies at Kamwo Herb and Tea Shop, the largest authentic Chinese herbal medicinal store on the East Coast. No medical knowledge is required on your part—just name your ailment, and the professionals will pull leaves, roots, and powders from the rows of drawers that line the walls, and chop and grind them together into a neat little paper packet for you to take home. There are more than 1,000 items to choose from, from magnolia and ginseng to peppermint leaves and dried seahorses. The traditional remedies purport to cure everything from headaches to stiff joints, from a blocked nose to insomnia, and there are mixtures designed for general relief from stress, fatigue, or other symptoms of urban malaise.

211 GRAND STREET BETWEEN MOTT AND ELIZABETH STREETS IN MANHATTAN. Subway: B, D to Grand Street. 212-966-6370. www.kamwo.com.

842. Try an acupuncture session at Lin Sisters in Chinatown.

Acupuncture is the other specialty of Chinese natural medical practitioners, and it is believed by many to be the ultimate way to relax and, literally, let the pressure out. Of course you know it's not supposed to hurt, but for those with needle fears, Lin Sisters is among the quainter, more genuine and reassuring places to be pricked. Adjoining a respected herb and tea store, Lin Sisters charges $55 per session and treats each customer with great care and respect; you can sip a bowl of tea until you're relaxed and ready to begin. N.B.: Chinatown is home to the most authentic and least expensive practitioners of acupuncture in the city, but be careful—check for certification either by New York State or by the National Certification Commission for Acupuncture and Oriental Medicine. You can find a list of all certified acupuncture practitioners in New York City at www.nccaom.org.

LIN SISTERS: 4 BOWERY AT PELL STREET IN MANHATTAN. Subway: N, R, Q, W, J, M, Z, 6 to Canal Street. 212-962-5417.

CHAPTER 9:

24-Hour Fun

New York is wide awake at all hours of the day, and even if it's 11:00 p.m. on a Sunday or eight o'clock in the morning on Thanksgiving Day, there are more things to do, see, and take advantage of here than in most places on a typical weekday afternoon. In this city of schemers, dreamers, high rollers, and people struggling to get by, one person's bedtime is another's graveyard shift, and the start of someone else's night on the town. Subways, taxis, and even the Staten Island ferry Ferry run around the clock, coursing up, down, and around the city, bringing life and activity wherever they go. Traffic lights tick away all through the night, ushering vehicles and pedestrians from rush hour to the break of dawn without missing a beat, while all-night diners, coffee shops, and delis beckon to wanderers with fluorescent lights, coffee, and ATMs.

This chapter celebrates New York's unique, unceasing vibrancy, its inexhaustible spirit that does not discriminate between early birds and night owls; the lunch crowd and the after-hours bunch; morning people and insomniacs. We've found the best of the always-open and odd-hour amenities, as well as plenty of places and activities that offer something special at a time when most people are asleep—not just the kinds of things you want only if you're in a fix. Sure, New York has resources for emergencies of all kinds just like everywhere else, but in our opinion, just because you can get something at a certain hour doesn't necessarily mean that it is a great thing to do. Here you'll find 24-hour diners and restaurants; late-night movies, dance parties, and yoga; early-morning bird-watching and late-night stargazing, and many other wonderful things to do and see that are worth staying up—or rising early—for.

N.B.: Although everything we list here is ostensibly safe, and we don't hesitate to make these recommendations, it should go without saying that if you are out late at night or in the early morning, you should be alert and be extra careful, especially if you are alone.

843. Take the **subway anytime** you want...

Even if you wouldn't get on the train at 5:00 a.m. in a million years, consider how great it is that you can, and appreciate what it means for a transit system to provide that level of service, when so many others do not.

For schedules and routes, visit www.mta.info.

844. ...or hail **a cab**...

Cabs also run 24/7, which is helpful if you find yourself out late at night in an unfamiliar place, if you need to make an early-morning plane, train, or bus, or if you just want someone to talk to at a rate of $2.50 plus $.40 for every 1/5 mile.

Anywhere you can find them!

845. ...or take **the ferry**.

In addition to being one of the best deals in New York, the ***Staten Island Ferry*** (see page 69) is also the most reliable form of mass transit. Running every hour or half-hour 24 hours a day, 7 days a week, 365 days a year, the ferry offers free transportation and sightseeing with the highest on-time performance of any form of mass transit in the city—over 96 percent.

Manhattan: WHITEHALL TERMINAL AT 1 WHITEHALL STREET AND SOUTH STREET. Staten Island: 1 BAY STREET AT RICHMOND TERRACE. For more information on the ferry and ferry service, visit www.nyc.gov/html/dot/html/ferrybus/statfery.shtml.

846. Look at the night sky from inside **Grand Central**.

Late at night is the best time to view the incredible painted ceiling in the main hall, a glittering astrological motif by French artist Peter César Helleu. Obscured by dirt and disrepair, Helleu's 1912 masterpiece was revealed after a 1990s renovation. During the day, the constant commotion of the terminal distracts from the ceiling's subtle beauty, but at night, after the shops and restaurants close and the last commuter goes home, the main hall becomes still and eerily quiet, and you can drink in the gold-painted constellations and the ornate decorated windows as peacefully as if you were stargazing in the country—except that the sky is painted backward, because that's how it looked in the medieval manuscript that the artist relied on (the manuscript presented the sky from the perspective of someone looking down at it instead of gazing upward). You can visit until 1:30 a.m., when the terminal closes, or show up when it reopens at 5:30 a.m., when the commuters begin charging in again. See if you can find the dark patch left over from before the renovation (see page 113).

42ND STREET BETWEEN LEXINGTON AVENUE AND PARK AVENUE IN MANHATTAN. Subway: 4, 5, 6, 7, S to Grand Central-42nd Street. For full entry on Grand Central Terminal, see page 23.

847. Walk the **Great White Way** after dark.

Times Square, and the neighboring stretch of Broadway between 40th and 47th Streets, is one of the signature images of New York, almost as widely recognized as the skyline and its skyscrapers. Named for the city's most famous newspaper—it opened its offices here a little over a century ago—Times Square remains the heart of New York, pumping life into the city with lights, sounds, and crowds twenty-four hours a day, every day of the year. Although its most famous attractions are the tourist stalls, the **Broadway shows** (see pages 153–154) that entertain daytime and evening crowds, and the New Year's Eve festivities, the place is bright and busy all about, all the time. In addition to late-night haunts like the View Lounge in the Marriot Marquis and **Sephora** (see page 319), and the nightlong pull of the **Broadway City Video Arcade** (see page 343), there are enough dazzling lights, blazing billboards, and unexpected street entertainment to make a nighttime stroll around the Square exhilarating. The light from storefronts and advertisements is so bright that Times Square never approaches darkness, making it a surreal place to get a cup of coffee and snack in the middle of the night. Amuse yourself with diversions like the Cup of Noodles billboard, whose steam wafts out above the street; the Reuters news ticker that keeps the streets abreast of breaking news; the NYPD station that's lit up like a diner; and the McDonald's on 42nd Street that projects cartoons on the walls of the restaurant all day and all night.

TIMES SQUARE IN MANHATTAN. Subway: 1, 2, 3, 7, N, Q, R, W to Times Square-42nd Street; A, C, E to 42nd Street-Port Authority Bus Terminal.

848. Watch the lights go out on the **Empire State Building**.

An eerie urban sight if ever there was one, and a good piece of trivia. The lights on the **Empire State Building** (see page 19), often colored to commemorate certain holidays or occasions, go off at 2:00 a.m. You can check the lighting schedule on the Web site, which tells what color the building will be and what occasion the lights are honoring, or check the current issue of *Time Out*, which lists the coming week's lighting schedule in their "Around Town" section.

FIFTH AVENUE AT 34TH STREET IN MANHATTAN. Subway: B, D, F, V, N, Q, R, W to 34th Street-Herald Square. 212-736-3100. www.esbnyc.com.

849. See what happens at **night court in Chinatown**.

The Criminal Courts Building is where New Yorkers under arrest are formally charged with a crime—and since arraignments are required by law to be open to the public, anyone can drop in and watch the proceedings. Show up for the night session, which runs from 5:30 p.m. to past 1:00 a.m., and you'll take in one of the city's most under-appreciated and unlikely forms of entertainment. To watch the cases come and go is to see real-life dramas play out before your eyes. The judges hear the stories of the cases, the attorneys arrive to argue with one another, and a succession of characters step up to the bench—and eventually are released on bail or led away into the sinister hallways behind the courtroom. If you can feel comfortable sitting next to the family of the accused, you can join the few law students, insomniacs, and other curious New Yorkers on the benches in the back. The court officers are aware of their audience, and will even (on occasion) recommend one court over another depending on the drama of the cases that night. (On a recent visit, one officer advised, "You ought to check out AR2. There's a cocaine bust going on in there.") Just around the corner from some of the best restaurants in Chinatown, night court is the perfect (free) after-dinner show.

100 CENTRE STREET BETWEEN LEONARD AND FRANKLIN STREETS IN MANHATTAN. Subway: 1, 6, A, C, E to Canal Street; 4, 5, 6 to Brooklyn Bridge-City Hall; B to Grand Street. 646-386-4511. www.courts.state.ny.us/courts/nyc/criminal.

Go early-bird or night-owl shopping.

Most retail stores and boutiques in the city have generous hours, and are open seven days a week from around ten or eleven in the morning until seven or eight at night, with slightly shorter hours on Sunday, and sometimes slightly longer hours in the evening one or two days a week. However, a few stores have carved out off-hours niches for themselves by deviating from these unofficial rules. For shoppers, this means less time constraints on an otherwise busy day; for others, it means more places to visit, hang out in, and explore if you happen to be in the neighborhood when everything else is closed up.

850. *American Apparel:* The Lower East Side branch is open until midnight Thursday through Saturday, and a still-respectable 11:00 p.m. from Monday through Wednesday (it closes at a cowardly 10:00 p.m. on Sunday). It's a great place to pick up trendy, affordable leisurewear, and browsing the store is a good way to pass the time before a midnight movie at the **Sunshine** (see page 344).

183 EAST HOUSTON STREET AT ORCHARD STREET IN MANHATTAN. Subway: F, V to Lower East Side-Second Avenue. 212-598-4600. www.americanapparel.net.

851. *Lowe's and Home Depot:* You can pick up lumber on your way to work at the local branches of these national chains, which all open at the extremely go-getter time of 6:00 a.m. every day except Sunday. If you find yourself needing a late-night home improvement fix, two of the Brooklyn locations (the HD on Hamilton Avenue and the Lowe's nearby on Second Avenue) stay open until midnight (except on Sundays).

Multiple locations in the five boroughs. Visit www.lowes.com or www.homedepot.com for all addresses.

852. *Sephora:* Need to primp before heading out to a club? The Times Square store is open until midnight, with plenty of makeup stations, where you can touch up, try out, get a free consultation, and, of course, buy products.
1500 BROADWAY BETWEEN 42ND AND 43RD STREETS IN MANHATTAN. Subway: 1, 2, 3, 7, N, Q, R, W, S to Times Square-42nd Street; A, C, E to 42nd Street-Port Authority Bus Terminal. 212-944-6789. www.sephora.com.

853. *The Flower District:* Manhattan's Flower District, which has been located in the West 20s for over one hundred years, has been threatening extinction for a while now, to the extent that many New Yorkers aren't even sure it's still there. Yet while the number of shops has diminished over the past few years, the remaining cluster on 28th Street is still bustling enough to constitute a district. (In fact, the shop owners' peril is a boon for walk-ins, as many wholesalers will now sell to the public as well as the trade.) It's an early-bird paradise, with shops throwing open their doors before 6:00 a.m. to showcase new arrivals from Europe, South America, and Asia, and the best blooms long gone by 9:00 a.m. Even if you're not in the market for orchids and cherry blossoms, the market is still a sight to behold: —a microcosm of the city, hustling and bustling according to its own schedule, and one of the few industries left that must cater to the demands of its goods, rather than the preferences of its clients.
28TH STREET BETWEEN SIXTH AND SEVENTH AVENUES IN MANHATTAN. Subway: 1 to 28th Street or N/R/WN, R, W to 28th Street.

---

854. Shopping in New York around the holidays is, generally speaking, not such a great thing to do, but many stores offer extended holiday hours in the weeks before Christmas, which, when taken advantage of at the extremes, can actually make last-minute shopping kind of fun. These extra hours vary by store, and change from year to year (and day to day): Macy's in Herald Square, for instance, opens at 7:00 a.m. on selected days between Thanksgiving and Christmas, and stays open some nights until midnight. If you get there when the store opens, you'll feel like you have it pretty much to yourself for a good two hours before the craziness begins, at which point you'll be ready to head home for a nap. (This is also a good time to see **Santa**—see page 346).
151 WEST 34TH STREET BETWEEN BROADWAY AND SEVENTH AVENUE IN MANHATTAN. Subway: 1, 2, 3, A, C, E to 34th Street-Penn Station; B, D, F, V, N, Q, R, W to 34th Street-Herald Square. For information and specific hours, call 212-695-4400 or visit www.macys.com. For other stores with extended holiday hours, check listings during the season.

855. Get your laptop looked at in the wee hours at the **Apple Store**.

The mighty gleaming cube of glass and light at the corner of 59th Street and Fifth Avenue is a beacon that draws every digitally dependent New Yorker to its door—and that's a lot of people, because New York is one of the most laptop-happy and iPod-heavy cities in the world. The biggest of the three Apple stores in the city, the flagship is also the only one to stay open 24 hours a day. Aside from the irresistible appeal of checking your e-mail on a pristine new computer, there are more serious draws that keep bring the late crowds in. The Genius Bar operates 24/7, so you can expect to see desperate students and panicking businessmen lining up at all hours of the night to get those files retrieved by any of the store's roster of smart-alec salesclerks. And on summer nights the Midnight Mix brings top-flight DJs in to keep everyone moving from 12:00 midnight to 2:00 a.m.—mixing on Macs and iPods only, of course…

767 FIFTH AVENUE AT 59TH STREET IN MANHATTAN. Subway: N, R, W, 4, 5, 6 to 59th Street. 212-336-1440. www.apple.com/retail/fifthavenue.

856. Get that **prescription filled** at 4:30 a.m. in Manhattan…

Thanks to the many **Duane Reade** drugstores that keep their doors open round the clock, New Yorkers can get all the pharmaceuticals they need at any time of night. Aside from the obvious practical advantages of 24-hour drugstores—besides medicine, they carry snacks, condoms, cigarettes, and many other lifestyle essentials— browsing around the empty, sterile, white stores after dark is oddly compelling. Check online for your nearest all-night savior.

N.B. While many Duane Reade stores are open around the clock, not all of their pharmacies are 24-hour. To check locations and hours, visit www.duanereade.com.

857. …or in Brooklyn.

Brooklyn residents can be smug about the fact that when they get their late-night pre-scriptions filled, they do so without resorting to a chain. The family-owned **Neergaard** pharmacies have been serving Brooklynites since 1888. There are two branches, but only the Fifth Avenue location is open 24 hours; they also deliver until 9:00 p.m.

454 FIFTH AVENUE BETWEEN 9TH AND 10TH STREETS IN BROOKLYN. Subway: F to Fourth Avenue; M, R to 9th Street. 718-768-0600. (The other branch is at 120 SEVENTH AVENUE BETWEEN CARROLL AND PRESIDENT STREETS IN BROOKLYN. Subway: F to Seventh Avenue. 718-857-1600.) www.neergaardpharmacies.com.

858. Launder anytime you like at **Baby Girl's Bubbles & Cleaners**.

A washer and dryer are standard equipment in residences in almost every other area of the country except New York City, and many apartment dwellers have a hard time getting used to the fact that they can't throw in a load any time they splatter some red sauce. While admittedly not as convenient as having a machine in the next room (or even in the basement), this 24-hour Laundromat does provide round-the-clock access to washers and dryers, a comparative luxury in a city where the clothing of so many residents is subject to the restrictions of someone else's idea of business hours.
2212-14 EIGHTH AVENUE BETWEEN 119TH AND 120TH STREETS IN MANHATTAN. Subway: B, C to 116th Street. 212-662-1080.

859. Find out how to get anything you want at any hour with **Quintessentially**.

An anonymous warehouse building in the Meatpacking District is the suitably clandestine home of Quintessentially, a concierge company so secretive and so effective that it deserves to be referred to in the same hushed breath as James Bond or the CIA. For a hefty annual fee, members can call on Quintessentially any time of the day or night to advise on any problem they might have, wherever they might be in the city. The staff—skilled researchers and publicists with myriad guides, references, and public and private directories at their fingertips—can address clients' needs, and can tell them where to go, whom to see, and what to do. Whether directing you to round-the-clock pet food suppliers in Harlem, locating emergency tailors in the Financial District, booking same-day front-row tickets to a hit Broadway show, or getting your name on the guest list at the hottest club of the moment, the people at Quintessentially have the answers. If the fee doesn't put you off (depending on your level of membership, it's around $2,000), this is a truly great resource for the 24-hour New Yorker.
25 NINTH AVENUE AT 14TH STREET, SUITE 201, IN MANHATTAN. Subway: A, C, E to 14th Street; L to Eighth Avenue. 212-206-6633. www.quintessentially.com.

860. Find out if the early birds **really do** get the worm.

Birds are busiest in the morning, so instead of sleeping in one Sunday, make your way to Prospect Park for an Early Bird Walk, a monthly guided tour of the park's feathered friends given for free by the Audubon Center. Trekking around the park's nature trails, you'll see some of the 200 species of birds that reside in the park at different points during the year, and learn about different species and migration patterns.
The Audubon Center is located in Prospect Park;. ENTER AT LINCOLN ROAD AND OCEAN AVENUE IN BROOKLYN. First Sunday of every month, from 8:00 a.m. to 10:00 a.m. Meet at the Boathouse. Subway: B, Q, S/Franklin Avenue Shuttle to Prospect Park. 718-287-3400. www.prospectpark.org.

→ **DID YOU KNOW?** *Prospect Park's Audubon Center is the first urban Audubon Center in the nation. One of the reasons that Prospect Park was chosen as the site was its position along the Atlantic Flyway, a major route for bird migration.*

New Year's Fun

Every year, three-quarters of a million people migrate to Times Square to watch the ball drop at midnight. To each their own, but standing in a pen in the freezing cold, corralled with hundreds of thousands of people, with no access to food, drink, or restrooms (alcohol, backpacks, and large bags are not permitted; there are no public toilets or food vendors on New Year's; and if you leave, you lose your space) for up to ten hours (space is first-come/first-served, and people usually begin arriving in the early afternoon) doesn't sound like a best thing to do, in our opinion. Instead, here are our favorite New Year's activities:

861. Do the midnight run in **Central Park**...

Start the New Year off on the right foot, literally and figuratively, with this annual four-mile run through Central Park, sponsored by the New York Road Runners Club. If you don't expect to be in top shape come midnight, there's also a dance party, a costume show for the runners, and a fireworks display at midnight.

MEET AT THE BANDSHELL, LOCATED ON THE CENTRAL PARK TRANSVERSE NEAR 72ND STREET IN MANHATTAN. To participate in the race costs $30 to $40 in advance or $45 to $50 on the day of, depending on availability. Dance party begins at 10:00 p.m.; costume parade and contest begins at 11:00 p.m.; race starts at midnight. Subway: 1, 2, 3 to 72nd Street. 212-860-4455. www.nyrr.org.

862. ...or in **Prospect Park**.

The Brooklyn Road Runners Club also puts on a midnight run in Prospect Park that is slightly shorter than the Manhattan counterpart (3.3 miles, which is one loop around the park). But the Brooklyn version has everything else—free food and drink, and fireworks at the finish line.

MEET AT GRAND ARMY PLAZA ENTRANCE TO PROSPECT PARK AT FLATBUSH AVENUE IN BROOKLYN. $15 in advance or $20 on the day of. Race starts at 11:15 p.m. Subway: 2, 3 to Grand Army Plaza. 917-238-9447. www.brooklynroadrunners.org.

863. Ring in the New Year in silence at **Jivamukti**...

This popular downtown yoga center holds a free annual New Year's Eve "celebration," where they observe *mauna*, the yogic practice of silence. From 9:00 p.m. until midnight, they open the studio to silent individual practice and meditation. At midnight, the silence is broken with chanting led by the center's directors, followed by vegan snacks.

841 BROADWAY AT 13ᵀᴴ STREET IN MANHATTAN. Subway: 4, 5, 6, L, N, Q, R, W to 14th Street-Union Square. 212-353-0214. www.jivamuktiyoga.com.

864. ...or hear the steam whistles at Pratt on New Year's Eve.

Brooklyn's **Pratt Institute** (see page 300) maintains one of the world's largest collections of steam whistles—and a power plant and steam engine to blow them. On New Year's Eve, nearly 2,000 whistles of all shapes and sizes—some tiny, some over eight feet tall with flanges more than three inches wide—are brought into the quadrangle, and at midnight, they start the new year with a blast! Arrive early and spend the evening eating and drinking while you check out the whistles (and their unlikely enthusiasts), listen to the legendary steam calliope's jolly piping music, and try in vain to prepare your ears for the cacophony that strikes at midnight—it's one of the strangest, loudest noises you'll ever hear. Pratt also supplies steam and compressed air for energetic spectators who bring their own horns to participate.

200 WILLOUGHBY AVENUE IN BROOKLYN. Subway: G to Clinton-Washington Avenues. 718-636-3600. www.pratt.edu.

865. Party on the Brooklyn Bridge.

Celebrate the crossing of one year into the next by crossing from one borough to another on the annual "Walk into the New Year." This guided walk starts with a history talk about the bridge, and then leads you across, when, if the timing is right (and you can bear the cold), you will see fireworks displays from Central Park, Grand Army Plaza, Staten Island, New Jersey, and the Empire State Building light show.

MEET AT POPEYE'S: *143 FULTON STREET BETWEEN NASSAU STREET AND BROADWAY IN MANHATTAN. $30 per person in advance or $60 day of. Walks start between 10:30 p.m. and 11:15 p.m. Subway: 4, 5, 6 to Brooklyn Bridge-City Hall. 718-591-4741. www.newyorktalksandwalks.com.*

866. Milonga!

Milongas, or tango socials, are parties where dancers come to hang out and practice their moves. In New York, there are milongas almost every night of the week, held at different places around the city. Each milonga does its own thing, but most start around 9:00 p.m. or 10:00 p.m. and can go until any time between 1:00 a.m. and 5:00 a.m. Some of the more novice-friendly gatherings start with a free lesson. New York milongas are held at dance studios, restaurants, and clubs, and most occur regularly, on the same night each week, and many have live music or DJs. A good source for learning more is www.dancetango.com, which has an up-to-date calendar with milonga listings, addresses, and details.

Various locations; visit www.dancetango.com for current locations and times.

867. Go **clubbing.**

Nightclubs, bars, and lounges are what most people think of when they say "the city that never sleeps," and no chapter on 24-hour New York would be complete without a mention of nightlife. From the glitzy, star-studded Cotton Club and famous Prohibition-era joints like the **21 Club** (see page 287), to the notoriously wild times at Studio 54 in the '80s and the scandalous happenings at Limelight, the Tunnel, and Twilo in the '90s, New York nightlife has long been a potent mix of glamour, scandal, and late-night decadence, and every night promises the potential for excitement. Movies, books, celebrity magazines, and TV shows like *Sex and the City* have mythologized the experience of going out in New York, making names like Lotus, Tao, and Bungalow 8 familiar to people well outside taxi range.

Bars, clubs, and lounges are generally open until 4:00 a.m.; clubs usually don't open until 10:00 p.m. or even 11:00 p.m., but many bars are open all day, and lounges fall somewhere in between. The difference between the three types of venue is a little vague, but as a rule, clubs have a cover (anywhere from $10 to $30) and usually a bouncer; bars for the most part do not have either; and lounges, again, fall some-where in between. There are also after-hours venues that stay open until 5:00 a.m. and later (or earlier, depending on how you think of it). What constitutes a great club is subjective, and depends on your taste in music, preference for environment, crowd, and décor—and, of course, what's hot at the moment (which, lately, is anything in the Meat-packing District or west Chelsea). There are many, many Web sites devoted to New York bars and clubs, and an equally inexhaustible number of nightlife guides with listings and addresses. *Time Out New York* (www.timeoutny.com), *Citysearch* (http://newyork.citysearch.com), and *Shecky's* (www.sheckys.com) are all thorough sources for finding information on different places, but our recommendation for figuring out where to go is word of mouth, and trial and error. The adventure of winding up somewhere new is part of the fun.

Every night of the week, all over town.

Expert contributor: Wendy Mitchell

Wendy Mitchell is an entertainment journalist, and the author of *New York City's Best Dive Bars*.

MY FIVE FAVORITE DIVES:

868. *Nancy Whiskey Pub:* Avoid the chic Tribeca crowd at this neighborhood pub (established in 1967), a favorite of cops and postal workers. Make sure you try your hand at Manhattan's only bank shuffleboard table. If you don't know the rules, an affable regular or bartender will be glad to show you the ropes.
1 LISPENARD STREET AT WEST BROADWAY IN MANHATTAN. Open 9:00 a.m. to 4:00 a.m., Monday through Saturday; noon to 4:00 a.m. on Sunday. Subway: A, C, E to Canal Street. 212-226-9943. www.nancywhiskeypub.com.

869. *Mars Bar:* Even if you are a very tough guy (or gal), you might still be scared to walk into this bar, which is probably the creepiest hole in New York. It long had a reputation as a heroin addict hangout, and even if that's no longer true, there will definitely be some unsavory characters at the bar, some ear-splitting punk blaring from the jukebox, and a cockroach or two crawling around. Explore at your own risk!
25 EAST 1ST STREET AT SECOND AVENUE IN MANHATTAN. Open noon to 4:00 a.m. daily. Subway: F, V, to Lower East Side-Second Avenue. 212-473-9842.

870. *Hogs & Heifers:* Shed your bra, your necktie, or just your inhibitions at this classic biker bar. Julia Roberts famously took her bra off and danced on the bar here; you may very well be inspired to do the same.
859 WASHINGTON STREET BETWEEN 13TH AND WASHINGTON STREETS IN MANHATTAN. Open 11:00 a.m. to 4:00 a.m. Monday through Friday; 1:00 p.m. to 4:00 a.m. Saturday; 2:00 p.m. to 4:00 a.m. Sunday. Subway: A, C, E to 14th Street; L to Eighth Avenue. 212-929-0655. www.hogsandheifers.com.

871. *Johnny's Famous Reef:* A daytrip to City Island wouldn't be complete without dining and drinking at this fish shack at the tip of the island. Grab some no-frills fried seafood, a cheap can of beer, and try to avoid the predatory seagulls.
2 CITY ISLAND AVENUE NEAR BELDON AVENUE IN THE BRONX. Open 11:00 a.m. to 1:00 a.m. (Closed December through February). Subway: 6 to Pelham Bay Park; Bx29 bus to City Island. 718-885-2086.

Sadly, one of Wendy's original picks, the legendarily grungy Siberia—a dive so stalwart that it survived a change of venue without losing an inch of grime — finally boarded its own train to nowhere in 2007. The original location lurked in the shadows of a subway stop on 50th Street; in its place, we humbly offer one of Midtown's last lingering ungentrified gems, which fittingly is also associated with subterranean mass transit.

872. *The Subway Inn.* While a bar doesn't have to be old to qualify as a dive, it helps. The Subway Inn opened in 1937, and it appears that nothing's been changed, repaired, or wiped down since then (including the bathrooms). But no matter. One comes to Subway because of and not despite the dinginess. Requests for lychee martinis will fall on deaf ears, but if it's beer, booze, and darkness you crave, you'll be well served. Subway stays open until 4:00 a.m. on weekends (2:00 a.m. on weeknights), but like any decent dive, they start serving early in the morning, too—an aging hair-of-the-dog crew can be found there from from around 10:00 or 11:00 most mornings.

143 EAST 60TH STREET, BETWEEN THIRD AND LEXINGTON AVENUES. Subway: 4,5,6,N, R, W to 59th Street-Lexington Avenue.

873. Enjoy live music until the **wee hours** of the morning.

Every big city has its share of bars and clubs with crowded floors and hallowed stages, but New York is a place apart, where names are made and legends are forged, and where one night in a bar can range from a great little party to a date memorialized for a lifetime. As longtime haunts like the Bowery Ballroom, Mercury Lounge, and the Bitter End are continually surrounded by new venues, and as the music halls of Williamsburg and Greenpoint have grown to outshine their Manhattan counterpoints, the best thing to do is to keep an eye on the listings in magazines like *Time Out New York* and *New York* magazine, then pick the ones you like the sound of, and try them out.
All over town.

874. Forgo sleep in favor of a different kind of nocturnal revitalization at **Juvenex**.

At this midtown oasis, you can enjoy massages, facials, manicures, pedicures, and body treatments any time of day or night. You can also visit the steam room, saunas, showers, and special soaking tubs, which are infused with purifying elements that include seaweed, ginseng, and tea tree oil. During the day (7:00 a.m. to 5:00 p.m.), the spa is women only; but in the evenings, the doors open to couples as well. Who goes to a day spa after midnight, you may ask? Juvenex says that its late-night clientele consists of Broadway stars who come to unwind after a show, people who drop by after a night of clubbing, and couples enjoying an extended romantic evening.

25 WEST 32ND STREET, FIFTH FLOOR, BETWEEN FIFTH AND SIXTH AVENUES IN MANHATTAN. Subway: B, D, F, V, N, Q, R, W to 34th Street-Herald Square. 646-733-1330. www.juvenexspa.com.

875. Get a manicure during cocktail hour at **Beauty Bar**.

The original Beauty Bar on 14th Street was so named because of its location in an old-fashioned beauty salon; when the new owners converted the salon into a bar, they kept the salon's retro front signage, the egg-shaped hair drying stations, and one of the formers tenants' services. Today, you can still get your nails done long after most salons have shuttered (until 11:00 p.m. every night of the week at the Manhattan location; the new Brooklyn location extends the service until midnight on Saturdays). The $10 price also includes one cocktail, which can be an apéritif or nightcap depending on when you time it.

IN MANHATTAN: 231 EAST 14TH STREET BETWEEN FIRST AND SECOND AVENUES IN MANHATTAN. Subway: L to First Avenue. 212-539-1389. IN BROOKLYN: 921 BROADWAY, AT MELROSE STREET IN BROOKLYN. Subway: J/M/ZJ, M, Z to Myrtle Avenue. 347-529-0370. www.beautybar.com.

Take advantage of your insomnia and hit the gym.

What would the city that never sleeps be without 24-hour gyms? There are a handful of gyms around the city that are open continuously throughout the week (though most close for a few hours on Friday, Saturday, and/or Sunday nights).

876. *24/7 Fitness Club:* This utilitarian gym lacks many of the amenities of other gyms in the city (including, most prominently, multiple locations), but it is the only gym in the city that is open 24/7, as its name suggests.

47 WEST 14TH STREET BETWEEN FIFTH AND SIXTH AVENUES IN MANHATTAN. Subway: F, V, to 14th Street; L to Sixth Avenue. 212-206-1504.

877. *New York Sports Clubs:* Several NYSC clubs are open twenty-four hours through the week (meaning that they're open continuously from 5:00 a.m. on Monday through 10:00 p.m. on Saturday), and close only from 10:00 p.m. on Saturday through 8:00 a.m. on Sunday and again from 10:00 p.m. Sunday through 5:00 a.m. on Monday.

For 24-hour locations and membership information, visit www.mysportsclubs.com.

878. *Crunch:* The Lafayette Street location is open continuously between 5:00 a.m. on Monday and 9:00 p.m. on Saturday, for members only (no guests are permitted late at night for security reasons).

404 LAFAYETTE STREET AT EAST 4TH STREET IN MANHATTAN. Subway: 6 to Astor Place. 212-614-0120. www.crunch.com.

879. *24-Hour Fitness.* New Yorkers can thank Derek Jeter for more than just his work on the Yankees. Jeter partnered with 24-Hour Fitness to bring this round-the-clock chain gym to the city that never sleeps. At time of press, three locations in Manhattan are poised to open (in SoHo, Midtown East, and by Madison Square Park), and more in the works.

For addresses and additional locations, visit www.24hourfitness.com.

880. Squeeze in the some midnight sets at the courts in Hudson River Park.

Playing tennis in the city is a tricky venture to be sure, and the public courts in Hudson River Park, just below Canal Street, are no exception. The wait for an hour on the two doubles courts and one singles court, which operate on a first-come/first-serve basis and do not require a permit, is daunting during prime times. But come nightfall, the crowds thin, the lights come on, and the courts offer the closest thing the city has to private tennis, with matches going on until 12:30 a.m.

HUDSON RIVER, NEAR CANAL STREET IN MANHATTAN. Subway: A, C, E to Canal Street; 1 to Houston Street.

881. Go on a moonlight bike ride...

If you're curious about what goes on in the park after dark, or you want to ride without those pesky joggers getting in your way, here's your opportunity. Time's Up! has free late-night group rides in Central and Prospect Parks. (Rollerbladers are welcome, too, but should be very competent to keep up with the bikes.) Cyclists of all levels can join, and the pace is leisurely, with plenty of ride leaders lighting the way.

FOR CENTRAL PARK RIDE, MEET AT COLUMBUS CIRCLE IN MANHATTAN; FOR PROSPECT PARK RIDE, MEET AT GRAND ARMY PLAZA IN BROOKLYN. Rides are held at 10:00 p.m. on the first Friday of every month and at 9:00 p.m. on the second Saturday of every month. For more information, call 212-802-8222 or visit www.times-up.org.

882. ...or take an early-morning ride, jog, or roll in the park before it opens up to cars.

In both Central and Prospect Parksparks, the drives are closed to cars from 7:00 p.m. to 7:00 a.m. on weekdays, and from 7:00 p.m. on Friday to 7:00 a.m. on Monday. (Note: the parks are officially closed between 1:00 a.m. and 5:00 a.m.)

For address information and directions, see entries for Central and Prospect parks in Chapter 6.

883. Pick up some midnight reading at the **Lafayette Smoke Shop**.

In order to remain as fashion-conscious, politically aware, and culturally literate as they are, New Yorkers are insatiable consumers of papers, journals, quarterlies, reviews, and periodicals. How do they fit it all in? While bookstore chains like Barnes & Noble and Borders help out during daylight hours, this small, unassuming store in SoHo has pretty much every magazine from all corners of the world available from 7:00 a.m. to 12:30 a.m. With a surprisingly diverse selection of publications, from European fashion magazines to local papers and political and literary journals, Lafayette Smoke Shop has something for every nighttime reader.

63 SPRING STREET AT LAFAYETTE STREET IN MANHATTAN. Subway: 6 to Spring Street; B, D, F, V to Broadway-Lafayette Street; N, R, W to Prince Street. 212-226-3475.

Also worth a mention is **Universal News**, an independent chain of news stores with ten locations south of Central Park that are stuffed full of publications in every genre and in every language. All stores are open from 5:00 a.m. to midnight daily.

Multiple locations. For more information, visit www.universalnewsusa.com.

884. Play pool at **Amsterdam Billiards**...

Amsterdam Billiards, an Upper West Side institution since 1989 of the Upper West Side, (from where it took its name), relocated in 2007 to the space in the East Village formerly occupied by its celebrated but shabbier predecessor, Corner Billiards. Where once sneakered feet shambled about on musty carpet and skinny jeans perched on high stools, now an eclectic mix of spendthrift students and slumming Midtown suits bump elbows at a brushed steel bar and compete for plush velvet armchairs in between games. Amsterdam is about as classy as pool halls get, with immaculate tables (including a VIP section roped off in the middle of the room), an upscale atmosphere, and a fancier bar than any other gaming establishment in town. The hall stays open until 3:00 a.m. on weeknights and until 4:00 a.m. on weekends, so you can settle in for the night and take your time with the hustle.

110 EAST 11TH STREET BETWEEN THIRD AND FOURTH AVENUES IN MANHATTAN. Subway: 4, 5, 6, L, N, Q, R, W to 14th Street-Union Square. 212-995-0333. www.amsterdambilliardclub.com.

885. ...or play Ping-Pong at **Spin**.

The most glamorous manifestation to date of the renaissance of table tennis, Spin is the first Ping-Pong club in New York to lend the game the style and the status of pool. Playing here is expensive—prices start at $15 per half-hour for nonmembers, and go up to $50 per half-hour on the "stadium court," should you wish to play for an audience—but you're paying for something seldom associated with the game: class. The tables and equipment are Olympic-standard, the rooms are lit beautifully, and there's a bar and café for post-game meals and drinks that make Spin as much a social club as a sports club. Private or group lessons with top-class coaches are available during the daylight hours;, and until midnight through the week and until 4:00 a.m. on weekends you can indulge your urge to Ping-Pong whenever it strikes you.

10 EAST 21ST STREET BETWEEN BROADWAY AND FIFTH AVENUE IN MANHATTAN. Subway: N, R, W to 23rd Street. 212-388-1582.

886. Play chess **at midnight**.

The two long-standing rivals of New York's chess capital on Thompson Street—**Chess Forum** and the **Chess Shop**—both stay open until around midnight, hosting games between keen amateurs and sleepless masters alike. On busy nights, each place can fill up, and small crowds have been known to gather to watch the more interesting games. If there's a slow game going on and it's time to close, you'll see players sketching the board so that the following night, they can resume where they left off. Each place supplies all the essentials—boards, pieces, clocks, and cheap coffee—all you have to bring is an impregnable defense.

CHESS FORUM: *219 THOMPSON STREET BETWEEN WASHINGTON SQUARE AND WEST 3RD STREET IN MANHATTAN. 212-475-2369.*

CHESS SHOP: *230 THOMPSON STREET BETWEEN WASHINGTON SQUARE AND WEST 3RD STREET IN MANHATTAN. 212-475-9580. www.chess-shop.com.*

Subway (for both): A, C, E, B, D, F, V to West 4th Street.

887. Get a late-night 'do at **Hair24**.

This salon is exactly what it sounds like: the only place in the city where you can get your hair done any way you want, any time of day or night. Founded on the worthy principle that New Yorkers work hard and play hard, the salon caters to those of us who need to look one way during the day and another way at night, and offers a full range of hair and beauty services geared toward transforming a working Midtowner into a partying Downtowner and back again—and all without having to skip out of the office early with the spurious excuse of a doctor's appointment. The range of services is amazingly comprehensive and includes everything from hair coloring and extensions to waxing, makeup treatments, manicures and pedicures, and a variety of massages. Whether you need to get out of your work look and into something fancier for an impromptu night out, or you've been burning the midnight oil and you just need a massage before you head home, Hair24 is the place to go.

76 MADISON AVENUE AT 28TH STREET IN MANHATTAN. Subway: 6 to 28th Street; R, W to 28th Street. 212-213-0056. www.hair24hours.com.

888. Ride the night loop and see the city **after dark**.

While there aren't too many city bus tours that we'd recommend, the Nightline (operated by Grayline Tours) deserves a mention. Following the traditional route of the Manhattan tour, the double-decker Nightline buses whisk passengers around the city, from Midtown on the West Side up around the top of Central Park, then down past the UN building to the East Village, SoHo, and Chinatown, and up through Greenwich Village and Chelsea, then back to Rockefeller Center, the Empire State Building, and Times Square. They offer the same tours during the day, but the difference, of course, is that by night everything is much more exciting! (And you'll move a lot faster.) From the roof of the Nightline bus, you'll see how great the city looks after dark: the luminescent tips of the skyscrapers in Midtown, paths carved through the park with lanterns, skies glowing orange above Harlem and Downtown, searchlights illuminating the city's most beautiful buildings, and an endless parade of bright storefronts, and drinkers and diners posing in neon-lit windows. On its route downtown, the bus goes over the Manhattan Bridge for a stop in Brooklyn and a look back across the East River at the Manhattan skyline in full effect. Tours run every half hour from 6:00 p.m. to 9:00 p.m., and last around two and a half hours. Try to sit on the top deck, even (or especially) during the winter; the snow, Christmas trees, and seasonal street decorations only make the ride brighter. *GRAYLINE VISITORS CENTER: 777 EIGHTH AVENUE BETWEEN 47TH AND 48TH STREETS IN MANHATTAN. Subway: C, E to 50th Street. 888-609-5665. www.grayline.com.*

889. See where the **Meatpacking District** gets its name.

Although its heyday as one of the most thriving markets on the East Coast has passed, there are still enough wholesalers, butchers, and warehouses operating in the Meatpacking District—otherwise known as the Gansevoort Market—to make a nighttime stroll worthwhile. Around four or five in morning—when most bars and clubs in the area are emptying out—the market stirs into action, and the austere warehouses and building fronts that provide the silent backdrop to the trendy neighborhood at night spring into life. Then, if you can stay awake, go to one of the nearby diners for a really fresh bacon breakfast. *MEATPACKING DISTRICT (BORDERED BY WEST 14TH STREET, HUDSON STREET, GANSEVOORT STREET, AND ELEVENTH AVENUE) IN MANHATTAN. Subway: A, C, E to 14th Street; L to Eighth Avenue.*

890. Party at the **Guggenheim**.

On the first Friday of most months, the **Guggenheim** (see page 124) throws a dance party from 9:00 p.m. to 1:00 a.m., with DJs, drinks, and, of course, art to view. All galleries are kept open for the evening, although drinks are off-limits outside of the lobby. *$25 dollars entry; cash bar. 1071 FIFTH AVENUE AT 89TH STREET IN MANHATTAN. Subway: 4, 5, 6 to 86th Street. 212-423-3500. www.guggenheim.org.*

891. Get food **delivered to you**...

When we polled New Yorkers about their absolute favorite things about the city for this book, food delivery was the single most popular answer. At any hour of the day, you can dial up a meal of any shape, size, or cuisine, from basic pizza or Chinese, to exotic ethnic food, to meals from trendy places like **Pastis** (see page 79). Although all restaurants don't deliver 24/7, most neighborhoods have plenty of places that deliver on both the early and late sides, and at least one or two that deliver around the clock, so there's never an hour when you can't get a hot meal brought to your door. If you don't already have a couple of staples, visit the Web site **www.menupages.com** to investigate the selection in your area. Once you've selected an area, click on "Delivery" in the features tab on the bottom left. That will bring up the names and menus of all of the listings in the area that offer delivery, along with user reviews, hours, and delivery minimum if there is one.

892. ...or **go out** to grab a bite.

Hankering for a midnight snack but not sure where to go? **Menupages.com** also has a list of 24-hour restaurants (with menus), including delis, cafés, ethnic restaurants, and diners (for our **favorite late-night spots**, see pages 335–341). With listings for more than 8,000 restaurants (and counting) in Manhattan and Brooklyn, you're bound to find something that hits the spot.

Anywhere you are!

893. Do your **grocery shopping** in the middle of the night.

Not the most glamorous of the city's nocturnal activities, to be sure, but when you stop and think about it, there's something extremely intriguing (and romantic) about being able to buy a ripe cantaloupe in the middle of the night. There are many delis and grocery stores in the city that stay open all night—too many to list here, or to single out, although there are more downtown than uptown—that make it possible to live as nourishing a life by night as by day. If you're up late working, if you've just come back from a long night on the town, or if you're simply sleepless and hungry, try stepping out for a snack, and you'll probably feel much better.

All over the city.

894. Get a hot dog (or two) from **Gray's Papaya**.

For some people, there's never a bad time for a hot dog. For them, there's Gray's Papaya. With locations scattered all over the city and open round the clock, with delicious, crispy dogs for sale, and prices friendly enough for any budget, Gray's Papaya has it sewn up and is king of the Papaya family (although fans of Papaya King would dis-agree—for more on **classic New York food wars**, see pages 169–170). You can get one hot dog for under a dollar, or try the "**recession special**" (see page 283): two dogs and a cup of ice-cold juice for $4.75—the perfect midnight snack.

All locations in Manhattan. 539 EIGHTH AVENUE AT 37TH STREET. Subway: A, C, E to 34th Street–Penn Station. 212-904-1588. 2090 BROADWAY AT 72ND STREET. Subway: 1, 2, 3 to 72nd Street. 212-799-0243. 402 SIXTH AVENUE AT 8TH STREET. Subway: A, C, E, B, D, F, V to West 4th Street. 212-260-3532.

895. Get a late-night cupcake from **Magnolia**.

The absurd lines and constant crowds keep this mini-chain of bakeries out of the running for a best thing to do during most hours of the day, but its late-night hours—unusual for a bakery—make it impossible for us to resist. At midnight, when most bakeries are tak-ing a rest before an early morning of baking, Magnolia is still open for business. In the realm of after-hours street treats, the fresh, hand-frosted cupcakes are a big step up from day-old pizza or a bag of chips from a deli. But don't think that you'll beat the lines by coming at night—the dessert crowds are in full force right up until closing.

Open until 12:30 a.m., Friday and Saturday; open until 11:30 p.m., Sunday through Thursday. 401 BLEECKER STREET AT 11TH STREET IN MANHATTAN. Subway: A, C, E to 14th Street; L to Eighth Avenue. 212-462-2572. Rockefeller Center location: 1240 AVENUE OF THE AMERICAS AT 49TH STREET. Subway: B, D, F, V to 47-50th Streets – Rockefeller Center. 212-767-1123. Uptown location: 200 COLUMBUS AVENUE AT 69th STREET. Subway: 1 to Lincoln Center; B, C to 72nd Street. 212-724-8101. www.magnoliabakery.com.

896. Go ice skating **off-hours**.

A seasonal treat, ice skating at any of the city's rinks is often frustratingly crowded, especially around Christmas. However, the most famous of them all, the **rink in Rock-efeller Center** (see page 33) helps thin the crowds by offering generous hours. The rink is open until midnight every night of the week during the holiday season (from November through New Year's), and on Friday and Saturday nights during the rest of the season (mid-October through April). On the other end, the rink opens by 9:00 a.m. all season long (by 8:30 during the holiday season), so you can squeeze a little bit of ice time before heading to work.

Both locations in Manhattan. THE ICE RINK IS LOCATED IN THE MIDDLE OF ROCKEFELLER CENTER IN MANHATTAN. Subway: B, D, F, V to 47th-50th Streets-Rockefeller Center. Call 212-332-7654 for information and current schedules. www.therinkatrockcenter.com.

897. Shop with the chefs at the **Union Square Greenmarket**.

The **Greenmarket** (see page 165) isn't just a grocery store alternative for New York residents; it's also the source of many of the ingredients that wind up in dishes at the city's finest restaurants. Any chef worth his or her salt comes to the main Greenmarket in Union Square to pick up specific items from favorite vendors, chat with farmers, and be inspired by seasonal offerings. Wednesday and Friday are the big days for chefs, who usually arrive right when the market opens to beat the crowds and get first pick of the day's bounty. So come early and keep your ears open: you can pick up some tips about what's fresh and the best way to prepare it.

Opens at 8:00 a.m., Monday, Wednesday, Friday, and Saturday. NORTH AND WEST SIDES OF UNION SQUARE PARK BETWEEN 14TH AND 17TH STREETS IN MANHATTAN. Subway: 4, 5, 6, L, N, Q, R, W to 14th Street-Union Square.

898. Regress on a Sunday night at **Southpaw**.

Since opening in 2002, Southpaw has become one of Brooklyn's best-known music venues, attracting big names and fun crowds. On some Sunday nights, from about six or seven in the evening until well after midnight, the space turns into an after-hours playground for kids of legal drinking age, with games, toys, and a killer juke-box. There's a Ping-Pong table, some classic pinball machines, a basketball hoop affixed to the wall, and usually a skateboard or two rolling around. It's always a terrific place to see a band, but on Sundays, it's a great place to let your inner kid enjoy some low-key fun.

Contact bar for upcoming dates. 125 FIFTH AVENUE BETWEEN BUTLER STREET AND SAINT JOHN'S PLACE IN BROOKLYN. Subway: 2, 3 to Bergen Street; 4, 5, Q to Atlantic Avenue; F to Fourth Avenue; M, N, R to Union Street. 718-230-0236. www.spsounds.com.

899. Borrow a telescope in **Central Park**.

On clear, mild nights, scores of amateur lunar enthusiasts and more serious astronomers emerge from their homes and labs to set up telescopes of all shapes and sizes in clearings around Central Park. Even in the depths of night, the city is so bright that visible stars are few and far between; but knowledgeable astronomers can train their glass on anything from constellations to shooting stars. Most of the park's nocturnal viewers are amenable to the curious, and will happily trade telescope time for an audience eager to share in the delights of the sky at night. Here's a hint: to guarantee a good turnout of telescopes, look for tips in the newspaper's weather section for good nights for stargazing before you head out.

For the best chances of finding a glass, scout Central Park's Great Lawn (enter through the entrances at 72nd Street). Subway: B, C to 72nd Street; 6 to 68th Street-Hunter College. See note on page 328 regarding closing hours of the park. See page 219 for more on Central Park.

900. Get something printed at the **24-hour Village Copier**.

With top-quality equipment and an intelligent and helpful staff, the Village Copier has acquired a legendary status among students, writers, designers, and others frequently in need of late-night printing facilities. The branch by Columbia University stays open until 11:00 p.m. on weeknights through Thursday, while the original downtown location keeps the printers on until midnight Monday through Friday. (Both locations open at 8:00 in the morning.) Both have a student clientele, so they're experts at taking care of stubborn dissertations that won't print out at home, or whipping up a thousand color flyers for a birthday party. (They will also loan out computers to anyone whose laptop has folded under pressure.) On top of the practical advantages, these copy shops also feature an amazing cast of nocturnal New Yorkers: a few hours here and you'll understand where all the posters tacked to streetlamps come from, and why all of those bootleg DVD covers sold on Canal Street look so good.

COLUMBIA UNIVERSITY: *2872 BROADWAY BETWEEN 111TH AND 112TH STREETS IN MANHATTAN. Subway: 1, B, C to Cathedral Parkway (110th Street). 212-666-0600.* **DOWNTOWN:** *20 EAST 13TH STREET BETWEEN UNIVERSITY PLACE AND FIFTH AVENUE. Subway: 4, 5, 6, L, N, Q, W to 14th Street-Union Square. 212-924-3456. For information and addresses of other locations with more limited hours, visit www.villagecopier.com.*

Get a meal anytime you want.

Round-the-clock diners and coffee shops are a great odd-hours thing to do anywhere, and have long been supplying food and coffee to truck drivers, cab drivers, and other night crawlers at hours when no one else will take them in. In New York, we've got plenty, and when you're starving at 4:00 a.m., the best one in the city is whichever is closest. However, not all are created equal, and there's quite a range in type of place and quality of experience. If you can make the trip, here are the places you should seek out for off-hours eating. From authentic Greek coffee shops to French bistros, we've managed to narrow it down to a dozen places, with a greasy spoon or two thrown in for good measure.

901. Mourn the passing of Florent over a late-night feast at **Gansevoort 69**.

When Florent closed in 2008, the Meatpacking District lost one of its most beloved and colorful staples—and a beacon of 24-hour downtown nightlife downtown. In the fall of 2009, however, after a long hiatus, its shoes have finally been filled by something worth talking about. Gansevoort 69 has retained much of the aesthetic that made Florent so attractive in the early hours of the morning: the long, cool metal bar, and the spacious and well-lit restaurant floor filled with tables that are pleasingly close together and invite conversation to run over from party to party. The menu is half good ol'e American comfort food and half light French cuisine—not far from its predecessor in tone and flavor, with fanciful touches applied to traditional diner favorites such as the incredibly savory truffled grilled cheese. And while it turns off the stove at midnight Mondays through Wednesdays, it's open all night from Thursday through Sunday, making it the perfect place to stop for supper (or breakfast) and a drink after a night of dancing at the clubs in the **Meatpacking District** (see page 324).

69 GANSEVOORT STREET BETWEEN WASHINGTON AND GREENWICH STREETS IN MANHATTAN. Subway: A, C, E to 14th Street; L to Eighth Avenue. 212-989-5779. www.gansevoortcafe.com.

902. Eat a hearty midnight snack at **Big Nick's**.

One of the best places on the Upper West Side to satisfy nighttime appetites, Big Nick's is a small diner with a huge menu and one of the biggest burgers in New York City. Decorated in classic diner style, with small tables covered by red-and-white checked tablecloths and faded photographs adorning the walls, the space is cozy in a nostalgic sort of way, and the staff does its best to keep patrons amused. If you think you're up to the challenge, discard the weighty menu and order the sumo burger— it's one of the largest, best-cooked, and tastiest sandwiches in the city.

2175 BROADWAY BETWEEN 75TH AND 76TH STREETS IN MANHATTAN. Subway: 1, 2, 3 to 72nd Street. 212-362-9238. www.bignicksnyc.com.

903. People-watch at **Cafeteria**.

Some 24-hour joints are great for winding down after a long night; this is where to come when you want to keep the action going. No matter the hour, this upscale Chelsea eatery is a place to see and be seen, and, as evidenced by the large plaque on the corner warning patrons to keep the noise down and the street clear, it's always a party. And though the cravings satisfied here tend to be more visual and audible than edible, the macaroni and cheese tempts even the most ascetic of New York waifs.

119 SEVENTH AVENUE AT 17TH STREET IN MANHATTAN. Subway: 1 to 18th Street. 212-414-1717. www.cafeteriagroup.com.

904. Try to get in to **Chelsea Square**.

Of all the late-night eateries in Chelsea, this one offers the most deliciously incongru-ous, only-in-New-York type of experience—if you can get in. For years, this classic (in the least polished sense of the word) diner has been located on the corner of 23rd Street and Ninth Avenue, an unremarkable structure with unmemorable food. But when nightclubs started popping up around the neighborhood in the '90s, Chelsea Square acquired a new image: a bustling after-hours spot. By day and into the evening, it still serves a neighborhood crowd, but on weekend nights, it performs a Superman-style quick change, and by the time the kids start leaving the clubs, it's sporting bouncers and a makeshift velvet rope. Waiting in line to get into a Greek coffee shop at 4:00 a.m. may not be everyone's cup of tea, but if you persevere, you will be treated to the unusual sight of made-up and decked-out club kids fighting over well-worn booths, and feast-ing on plates of shrimp cocktail, Jell-O and cottage cheese salads, and London broil. *368 WEST 23RD STREET AT NINTH AVENUE IN MANHATTAN. Subway: C, E to 23rd Street. 212-691-5400.*

905. Have a snack at the other Empire State Building at the **Empire Diner**.

The West Side of Manhattan is something of a haven for America's favorite kind of eatery, and this sparkling 1950s-style diner in Chelsea is the best of the bunch. With comfy booths, a long row of high stools at the bar, and a proud replica of the city's most celebrated skyscraper sitting on top of its chrome roof, the Empire Diner is the perfect blend of classic and kitsch. As its popularity has grown among the young, hip, late-night Chelsea crowd, so its prices have risen and its traditional diner dishes have taken on trendy new twists—you now have to specify if you want American cheese on your tuna melt—but the food is still great, and it's the liveliest and most welcoming place to find breakfast after a night on the tiles. *210 TENTH AVENUE AT 22ND STREET IN MANHATTAN. Subway: C, E to 23rd Street. 212-924-0011.*

906. See the inside of **Tom's Restaurant**.

Anyone who's ever watched an episode of *Seinfeld* will recognize the famous exterior of Tom's. In reality, Tom's looks different on the inside from the restaurant you see on the TV show, but it's a great place to eat, and an institution of the Columbia University area. As a rule, comfort food gets better the farther uptown you go, and the melts, shakes, and fried chicken at Tom's are close to perfect. Always busy and always friendly, a late-night snack or an early breakfast here is worth a trip from just about anywhere in the city. Go at dawn on a summer weekend, and you can watch the market setting up on the street outside the diner.

2880 BROADWAY AT 112ᵀᴴ STREET IN MANHATTAN. Subway: 1, B, C to Cathedral Parkway (110th Street). 212-864-6137.

→ **DID YOU KNOW?** *The "other" diner frequented by the characters in Seinfeld was actually the Munson Diner. The Munson stood on the corner of Eleventh Avenue and 49th Street for more than half a century, until 2005, when its stainless-steel façade was packed up and transferred upstate. A group of investors bought the sixty-year-old diner, and then loaded it—deep fryers, industrial-size refrigerators, and all—on a flatbed truck, and moved it up to the Catskills, where it began its new life as, well, a 1950s diner-themed restaurant. For information on visiting the "new" Munson Diner, visit www.munsondiner.com.*

907. Get a good deal, anytime you like, at **Waverly Restaurant**.

The old neon sign waving at the corner of Waverly and Sixth begs the question: is the Waverly Restaurant as old fashioned as it looks? The answer is a resounding yes. This is a coffee shop in the most old-fashioned sense of the word, from the epic, plastic-laminated menus to the prices. You can feast like a king on $3 egg sandwiches and $7 burgers, which for a mere 50 cents more can become deluxe platters, with fries and garnishes. But equally as enticing are its never-ending hours, which can bring together boisterous NYU students and a posher, West Village nightlife elite in the common joy of a proper late-night meal, white paper place mat and all.

385 SIXTH AVENUE, CORNER OF WAVERLY PLACE IN MANHATTAN. Subway: A, B, C, D, E, F, V to West Fourth 4th Street. 212-675-3181.

908. Find your savior at **Remedy**.

Remedy is strategicically placed on East Houston Street, at the crossroads between the Lower East Side and the East Village, two neighborhoods with plenty of nighttime action and tons of restaurants, but a surprising lack of refueling resources after a certain hour. Remedy is the beacon of all-night offerings for many blocks, its neon sign calling out to depleted revelers above and below it. After a night of belligerent bouncers and exorbitant cover charges, the cozy vinyl booths will feel as luxurious as velvet, and the simple plates of eggs, burgers, salads, and sandwiches will taste like manna from heaven.

245 EAST HOUSTON STREET AT NORFOLK. Subway: F, V to Lower East Side-Second Avenue. 212-677-5110.

909. Have late-night lyonnais at **L'Express**...

If you happen to be hungry at 3:00 a.m. in the Union Square area, you are in luck. Just a few blocks north is a restaurant that far and away exceeds the usual expectations of a 24-hour joint. No matter what hour you arrive at L'Express, you'll never feel like you've arrived at an off time: the food is always good, and the atmosphere is never dead. Other pluses include the lighting (or lack thereof), which is just right for hunkering down after a big night on your feet, and the speedy service, which at night is fast even by diner standards (Sunday brunch is a different story). Burgers, salads, croque monsieur, and an excellent French onion soup are all good choices day or night, but if you're in the mood for something more unusual at an odd hour, try one of the *spécialités lyonnaises*, such as the charcuterie plate or *tripe à l'ancienne* (tripe in tomato sauce).

249 PARK AVENUE SOUTH AT 20ᵀᴴ STREET IN MANHATTAN. Subway: 4, 5, 6, L, N, R, Q, W to 14ᵗʰ Street-Union Square; 6 to 23ʳᵈ Street. 212-254-5858. www.lexpressnyc.com.

910. ...or borscht for breakfast at **Veselka**.

If hearty Eastern European fare is what you crave come midnight, check out this East Village greasy spoon, where you can feast on pierogis, borscht, and blintzes at any hour of the day or night. The diner-size menu has something for everyone, including soups, salads, and sandwiches, and plenty of hearty vegetarian options, from the meatless stuffed cabbage to veggie burgers. A sentimental favorite that has been on the same well-traveled corner for fifty years, Veselka may not stand out on today's Second Avenue restaurant row in the light of day. But late at night and in the early morning, the unpretentious food and old-time atmosphere seem mighty appealing, and if you come in the wee hours of the morning, you'll appreciate how the harsh, garish lighting knocks the sleep right out of your eyes.

144 SECOND AVENUE AT 9ᵀᴴ STREET IN MANHATTAN. Subway: 6 to Astor Place. 212-228-9682. www.veselka.com.

⟶ **DID YOU KNOW?** *Veselka means "rainbow" in Ukrainian.*

911. Go to a **Greek diner** in Astoria.

If you want an old-fashioned 24-hour Greek diner, plastic-covered booths and all, Astoria is the place to go. The **Neptune** is a local favorite, beloved for its homey atmosphere, retro tableside jukeboxes, and faithful renditions of Greek diner classics, from tuna melts to spinach pie.

3105 ASTORIA BOULEVARD AT 31ˢᵀ STREET IN QUEENS. Subway: N to Astoria Boulevard. 718-278-4853.

912. Beat the crowds at the **Carnegie Deli**.

Technically, the **Carnegie Deli** (see page 170) doesn't belong with the eateries above, since it's open only twenty-two hours a day. But discounting the hours between 4:30 a.m. and 6:30 a.m., this historic restaurant is a great place to have a decadent late-night or early-morning meal. Polish off a mountainous Reuben sandwich or triple-decker deli meat combo that you might not be caught dead eating during the day at this tourist trap. Under cover of night, luxuriate in the elbow room, and worry about your arteries in the morning.

854 SEVENTH AVENUE AT 55ᵀᴴ STREET IN MANHATTAN. Subway: N, Q, R, W to 57ᵗʰ Street. 212-757-2245. www.carnegiedeli.com.

913. Buy a bagel at **H&H**...

You can top off a midnight stroll or get a head start on the day with breakfast from one of New York's **most beloved bagel purveyors** (see page 169) because, as the nice man who answered the phone when we called said in a weary voice, "We never close."

Both locations in Manhattan:. 2239 BROADWAY AT 80ᵀᴴ STREET., Subway: 1 to 79ᵗʰ Street, 212-595-8000. 639 WEST 46ᵀᴴ STREET AT TWELFTH AVENUE., Subway: A, C, E to 42ⁿᵈ Street-Port Authority Bus Terminal, 212-595-8000. www.hhbagels.net.

914. ...or at **Fifth Avenue Bageltique Café**,

Brooklyn's best 24-hour bagelry, and a favorite late-night eatery of both cops and night crawlers. It looks like a deli, but the large selection of cream cheeses shows its true *raison d'être*; or you can have the best of both worlds by ordering a sandwich or burger served on a bagel.

242 FIFTH AVENUE BETWEEN CARROLL AND PRESIDENT STREETS IN BROOKLYN. Subway: 2, 3, 4, 5, B, Q to Atlantic Avenue; D, M, R to Atlantic Avenue-Pacific Street; N to Pacific Street. 718-638-1866.

915. Eat Chinese at **Wo Hop**...

Many Chinatown restaurants have surprisingly generous hours, often staying open until four or five in the morning, but Wo Hop marries two New York passions—Chinese food and 24-hour service—in what is one of the neighborhood's only round-the-clock restaurants.

15 MOTT STREET AT MOSCO STREET IN MANHATTAN. Subway: 6 to Canal Street. 212-962-8617.

916. ...or an early-morning burger at **Pop Burger**.

It's not open a full twenty-four hours (it closes at 4:00 a.m.), but Pop Burger still merits a mention among the all-hours eateries because one, in any other city but New York, being open as late as it is would qualify as "after-hours"; two, the burgers and shakes are great, morning, noon, and night; and three, with the number of clubs, bars, and other late-night entertainment in the Meatpacking District and west Chelsea, hungry nightcrawlers need all the options they can get. Although the place looks more posh than the average fast-food joint (there's a lounge in back), the menu is simple and crowd pleasing: burgers, fries, milkshakes, and onion rings.

58-60 NINTH AVENUE AT 15TH STREET IN MANHATTAN. Subway: A, C, E to 14th Street; L to Eighth Avenue. 212-414-8686. 14 EAST 58TH STREET BETWEEN MADISON AND FIFTH AVENUES. Subway: 4, 5, 6 to 59th Street. 212-991-6644. www.popburger.com.

917. Read after dark at **St. Mark's Bookshop**.

This brilliant bookshop in the East Village comes as close as you can get to a late-night bookstore, closing around midnight seven days a week. With so many restaurants, clubs, and watering holes around NoHo and the East Village, there are always plenty of tired revelers wandering the store looking for something good to read on the train home or simply passing time before their night-on-the-town begins. Even if you're not searching for something in particular, the store has an excellent selection, including a lot of new fiction, wonderful art books, an impressive collection of nonfiction titles, and a full stock of American and international magazines, so it's a great place to browse for something to take home and curl up in bed with.

31 THIRD AVENUE AT EAST 9TH STREET IN MANHATTAN. Subway: 6 to Astor Place; L to Third Avenue. 212-260-7853. www.stmarksbookshop.com.

918. Camp out at the **NYHoS**...

Ever take kids to a museum and have to pull them out kicking and screaming at closing time? OK, maybe not every museum captures children's attention quite like that, but the **New York Hall of Science** (see page 125) is one they'll definitely be reluctant to leave. Luckily, the museum has come up with the perfect solution: a sleepover! Starting at 6:00 p.m. and finishing at 9:00 a.m. the next day, the Science Sleepover is an adventure that kids will never forget. For three or four hours, the museum belongs to the sleepover kids, who can explore the entire hall at their own pace and with staff at their disposal. When they're through making giant bubbles, playing games with light, and learning how sound travels through space, they can have a snack, roll out their sleeping bags, and camp out among the exhibits. On summer evenings, kids can play in the outdoor science playground, where swings, slides, and monkey bars all serve to demonstrate different scientific concepts. And maybe, after having breakfast and sewing a NYHoS patch onto their shirt in the morning, the kids will be ready to go home.

47-01 111TH STREET IN QUEENS. Subway: 7 to 111th Street. 718-699-0005. www.nyhallsci.org. Note: There is usually a minimum of 200 guests required for a sleepover, with a charge of $40 per person, so check online for available open dates, or organize the trip with your kids' school or with other parents in the community.

919. ...or have a late-night party at **FAO Schwarz**.

This sounds like something from the mind of Roald Dahl—a child's fantasy come to life in a way that's almost too stupendous to believe. For $25,000, you and up to nine other of your children and friends can have a private party at this iconic toy store. The party starts at 9:00 p.m. and ends at 3:00 in the morning. Between those hours, you and your guests will have the store to yourselves. The package includes food, a toy-soldier host, a scavenger hunt, a show on the famous piano from *Big*, plus a choice of numerous other activities using the store's mind- boggling resources of toys.

767 FIFTH AVENUE AT 58TH STREET IN MANHATTAN. Subway: F to 57th Street; N, R, W to Fifth Avenue/59th Street. 212-644-9400. www.fao.com.

920. Midnight yoga at **Laughing Lotus**.

As the name suggests, Laughing Lotus takes a playful approach to practicing yoga. It teaches serious yoga, but with a welcoming and enthusiastic attitude, which makes the classes as fun as they are enriching, perfect for beginners and dabblers, as well as experienced yogis. The popular midnight yoga session on Friday nights is a lively prac-tice that runs from 10:00 p.m. to midnight with live music. The late-night class is both relaxing and invigorating, and unlike other, more indulgent Friday nights out, you won't regret it in the morning.

59 WEST 19TH STREET, THIRD FLOOR, IN MANHATTAN. 212-414-2903. www.laughinglotus.com.

921. Bowl until you fall asleep at **Night Strike** at Bowlmor Lanes . . .

On Monday nights, this popular and historic bowling alley (it's been open in the same location since 1938, making it one of the oldest bowling alleys in the country) offers a $24 all-you-can-bowl deal (including shoe rental) between 9:00 p.m. and 1:00 a.m. Other perks include glow-in-the-dark bowling balls and a live DJ.

110 UNIVERSITY PLACE BETWEEN 12TH AND 13TH STREETS IN MANHATTAN. Subway: 4, 5, 6, L, N, Q, R, W to 14th Street-Union Square. 212-255-8188. www.bowlmor.com. N.B.: Night Strike is open to those twenty-one and older; ID required.

922. ...or at Extreme Bowling at **Harlem Lanes**.

On Friday and Saturday nights, Harlem's premier bowling alley stays open until three in the morning as well, and in addition to glow-in-the-dark balls and DJs, they've got a lounge full of comfy couches in case you need to take a snooze mid-game.

2110-2118 ADAM CLAYTON POWELL BOULEVARD AT 126TH STREET IN MANHATTAN. Subway: 2, 3, A, C, B, D to 125th Street. 212-678-BOWL. www.harlemlanes.com.

923. ...or among the hipsters at **Brooklyn Bowl**.

The newest addition to New York's late-nite night bowling scene is Brooklyn Bowl. This expensive hipster venue brings together four of every New Yorker's favorite pursuits under one beautifully designed roof: eating, drinking, music, and bowling. With sixteen stunning lanes backed by banks of shabby-chic Chesterfield sofas, it's hard to imagine a more enjoyable place to play Lebowski's game. And with food by Blue Ribbon and one of Williamsburg's best-stocked bars, there's plenty to do in between strikes—or if you just feel like being a spectator. And to top it off, Brooklyn Bowl functions as one of the neighborhood's liveliest music venues, hosting live music two or three nights every week. The lanes are open until 2:00 a.m. during the week and until 4:00 a.m. on weekends,

61 WYTHE AVENUE BETWEEN NORTH 11TH STREET AND NORTH 12TH STREET IN BROOKLYN. Subway: L to Bedford Avenue. 718-963-3369. www.brooklynbowl.com.

924. Hammer joysticks until your fingers bleed at **Broadway City Video Arcade**.

Nothing says midnight like the blinking neon of a video game arcade. Broadway City, an enormous arcade in the heart of the city's own neon wonderland, is far and away the best place to satisfy the late-night yearning for bright lights and constant motion. Every classic arcade attraction is here, from fairground hoops and basketball nets to old-school fighting games and shoot-'em-ups, as well as newer editions, with cutting-edge video-game technology. There are Japanese dancing games with dance steps mapped out on flashing disco floors, fake one-armed bandits, and banks of multi-player racing games, so entire teams of friends and strangers can yell at one another in competitive fury. There's a whole level devoted to sports games housed in a mock Yankee Stadium, a fleet of pristine air hockey tables, brand-new pinball machines, and something for pretty much anyone with a taste for gaming. It's so bright in here that you can easily lose track of time—you may be amazed to see dark skies outside when you eventually leave.

241 WEST 42ND STREET AT TIMES SQUARE IN MANHATTAN. Subway: 1, 2, 3, 7, N, Q, R, W, S to Times Square-42nd Street; A, C, E to 42nd Street-Port Authority Bus Terminal. 212-997-9797. www.broadwaycity.net.

Attend a midnight movie.

For some years the province solely of *Rocky Horror* fans, the midnight movie has again become, if not mainstream, at least a bit more common, and the offerings more diverse. You can catch midnight shows of everything from classics and cult films to special one-night-only engagements to showings of first-run films on occasion. The following theaters have regular midnight shows; other NYC movie theaters also run them from time to time, so check current listings.

925. *The Village East:* This fascinating movie house housed in a grand, former Yiddish-language theater has midnight shows every weekend that range from current releases to cult classics and occasionally the obligatory *Rocky Horror*.
181-181 SECOND AVENUE, CORNER OF 12ᵀᴴ STREET IN MANHATTAN. Subway: L to First or Third Avenues. 212-529-6799.

926. *The Sunshine:* The glorious **Landmark Sunshine Cinema** (see page 160) runs a series of midnight movies for the hip, indie Lower East Side crowd that congregates around Houston Street. On Friday and Saturday nights, the "Sunshine at Midnight" shows always pull the biggest audiences, and the choices are real crowd pleasers, from cult classics like *Dog Day Afternoon* to nostalgic favorites like *Heathers* and *Clue*. Selections change every week, but if you become a regular, you'll start to see many familiar faces in the crowd.
143 EAST HOUSTON STREET BETWEEN FIRST AND SECOND AVENUES IN MANHATTAN. Subway: F, V to Lower East Side-Second Avenue. 212-330-8182. www.landmarktheatres.com.

927. *Loews Village 7:* This generic-looking multiplex quietly shows revivals of horror and suspense flicks most weekends.
66 THIRD AVENUE, CORNER OF 11ᵀᴴ STREET, IN MANHATTAN. Subway: 6 to Astor Place, L to Third Avenue. 212-982-2116.

928. *IFC Center:* In tribute to its former incarnation as the beloved Waverly, the splendid new **IFC Center's** (see page 159) series of late-night movies, "Waverly Mid-nights," runs themed programs of independent-flavored modern classics. The theme varies by season—the recent "Midnight Rocks" series revived rockumentaries and pop-influenced films like *A Hard Day's Night, Purple Rain, Sid and Nancy,* and the New York disco epic *The Apple*—but every show is edgy, nostalgic, and ideal for late-night viewing.
323 SIXTH AVENUE AT WEST 3ᴿᴰ STREET IN MANHATTAN. Subway: A, C, E, B, D, F, V to West 4ᵗʰ Street. 212-924-7771. www.ifccenter.com.

CHAPTER 10:

Only in New York

"**O**nly in New York, kids, only in New York," is the signature sign-off of the *Post*'s famous gossip columnist, Cindy Adams, and a phrase that—whether they read her or not—echoes in New Yorkers' ears each time they see an oven filled with wine bottles; refer without irony to a 650-square-foot apartment as "palatial"; hear about a members-only luxury social club for babies, a yoga class for dogs, and a recreational juggling team, all in the same neighborhood; or catch themselves nearly getting into fisticuffs over who makes the best bagels or pizza. In this, our final chapter, we celebrate New York's great idiosyncrasies. Here you'll find offbeat activities (learning the secret manufacturing techniques on a tour of the world's finest piano factory; a finishing school for drag queens; and the last great things to do at the city's diminishing hub of eccentricity, Coney Island), unique or signature NYC services, and a handful of oddities that defy categorization (elephants marching through the Midtown Tunnel).

Throughout the book, we've tried to pick out the city's best features—the sites, entertainment, and activities that stand out from the multitude of simply wonderful things here as experiences worth taking a detour for. In this chapter, we hope to convey what makes just being in New York one of the best things to do in and of itself.

---

929. Get a little extra protection from erratic cab drivers at the Blessing of the Bikes at the Cathedral of Saint John the Divine.

In April, right around the time when many of them take to the streets for the season, cyclists and their bikes are invited to **Saint John** (see page 21) to receive a blessing for good health and no accidents during the coming year. Cyclists of all religions (and levels) are welcome. If you aren't a hardcore biker, it is still worth the trip to witness this hearty group of weekend warriors in skin suits ringing their bike bells inside the majestic cathedral.

Another blessing event worth checking out is the annual **Blessing of the Animals**, held on the Feast of Saint Francis of Assisi in October. During this spectacular occasion, Saint John turns into an unlimited-capacity Noah's Ark, opening its doors to thousands of pets of all shapes and sizes, whose owners bring them to receive a protective blessing and a sprinkling of holy water. After the service, the animals—which include both common house pets as well as snakes, farm animals, and, one year, a camel—proceed down the aisle and out to the cathedral grounds for an animal fair.

1047 AMSTERDAM AVENUE NEAR 110TH STREET IN MANHATTAN. Subway: 1 to 110th Street; B, C to Cathedral Parkway (110th Street). 212-316-7490. www.stjohndivine.org.

930. Visit Santa at Macy's.

This is the only place in the world where you can see the real one—don't you remember *Miracle on 34th Street*? After making the trip down from the North Pole for the **Thanksgiving Day Parade** (see page 90), Santa takes up residence at Santa's Village on the eighth floor of Macy's from the Friday after Thanksgiving through Christmas Eve. There is also a puppet show there, which is fun for kids (as opposed to visiting Santa, which is an imperative activity for all ages). Tip: Depending on when you go, the line of impatient visitors who are corralled around the store and through Santaland can threaten Santa's status as a best thing to do. Macy's has **extended hours** (see page 319) during the holidays, so if you can, try to get there right when the store opens at 7:00 a.m., and you and your little one can move through Santaland at your own pace, and have an audience with Santa while he's fresh.

Santaland is located on the eighth floor. 151 WEST 34TH STREET BETWEEN BROADWAY AND SEVENTH AVENUE IN MANHATTAN. Subway: 1, 2, 3, A, C, E to 34th Street-Penn Station; B, D, F, V, N, Q, R, W to 34th Street-Herald Square. 212-494-4495. www.macys.com.

931. Excuse me, Mr. Science Man—what's this?

Excuse me, Mr. Science Man—what's this? Ever come across a creature in the park and wonder what it is? Ever wonder what the real story is behind some of the treasures in your grandparents' cupboard? For all those with a hunger for knowledge, there's the **American Museum of Natural History's Identification Day**, an annual event during which an expert panel drawn from the museum's staff—including biologists, archaeologists, historians, and paleontologists—is available to the public to examine and explain any natural object or man-made curiosity you care to bring in. Each of the museum's representatives is a specialist in some field or other, so a kid who unearths an antique board game might be referred to one person for an authoritative answer, and a sunbather who stumbles on an unusual rock at the beach might be sent to another. As well as the identifications—which are as fascinating to observe for passersby as it is for the discoverers—there are special lectures, films, and events, and the museum staff is around to answer questions about pretty much anything that's in the museum as well.

Contact the museum for dates and more information. 79ᵀᴴ STREET AND CENTRAL PARK WEST IN MANHATTAN. Subway: 1 to 79ᵗʰ Street; B, C to 81st Street-Museum of Natural History. 212-769-5100. www.amnh.org. For more information on the museum, see page 119.

932. **Watch the elephants** come out of the tunnel on the way to the circus.

Why did the elephants cross the road? For the punch line, join the spectators (and ASPCA protestors) on the night when the circus comes to town. Each year, a night or two before the circus opens, the Queens-Midtown Tunnel closes to traffic to allow the Ringling Brothers' largest performers to march through on their way to Madison Square Garden. This is no publicity gimmick—there's really no other way to get the elephants into the city. The procession usually occurs between 11:00 p.m. and 1:00 a.m., although the start and end time are subject to change due to the unpredictability of the performers. If you're in the area around that time, it's hard to miss them, but the best place to watch is right by the tunnel entrance on First Avenue. You can also try to follow the pachyderms along their journey to MSG—but good luck. They may look like they're moving slowly, but with legs that long, they're not so easy to keep up with.

March. For exact date of the procession, contact the circus. 34ᵀᴴ STREET AND FIRST AVENUE IN MANHATTAN. Subway: 6 to 33ʳᵈ Street. www.ringling.com.

933. Smack golf balls at **New Jersey**.

With space at a premium in New York City, a golfer can get pretty frustrated. You can release your aggression (without hitting anybody) at the **Chelsea Piers Golf Club**, the only place to putt in Manhattan. The ingenious conversion of disused piers at the Chelsea harbor into an outdoor driving range allows space-deprived city dwellers to practice their swings without fear of breaking windows or injuring passersby. With 200-yard Astroturf fairways, state-of-the-art automated tees that disappear after each drive and then rise again with each new ball, and unobstructed views of glorious sunsets over the neighboring state, the driving range is a fun and surprisingly scenic alternative to a trek out to a course in the country. As well as the outdoor range, the center offers group and individual instruction and other amenities to improve your game, including electronic swing simulators, small picket-fenced greens for putting practice, and indoor sandpits to perfect those vital bunker escapes. And although resolute netting keeps the balls from doing any damage, for city sophisticates, there may be something cathartic about aiming a strong drive at their neighbors across the Hudson.

PIER 59 AT 23ᴿᴰ STREET AND THE HUDSON RIVER IN MANHATTAN. Subway: C, E to 23ʳᵈ Street. 212-336-6400. www.chelseapiers.com/gc. For more information on Chelsea Piers, see page 308.

934. Try to catch a glimpse of **Pale Male and Lola**, and their luxury nest.

Of all the beloved **New York characters** (see pages 361–363), one of Gotham's most unique longtime residents is Pale Male, a red-tailed hawk. Since he was first spotted in the mid-'90s, Pale Male has become a familiar sight to bird-watchers and pedestrians, who used to congregate in Central Park and around his posh digs on upper Fifth Avenue hoping for a glimpse. But like so many high-profile New Yorkers, he has also been the subject of controversy—and a victim of the city's strict co-op boards. In 2004, the board of 927 Fifth Avenue voted to dismantle Pale Male's nest, a 200-pound structure anchored by pigeon wire where he had lived for years, and where he and his mate, Lola, had produced several offspring, on the grounds that it was unsafe. Immediately, there was a virulent public outcry protesting the eviction, and a few weeks later, the board acquiesced, and reinstalled the nest, along with a safety rail. Unflappable as ever, Pale Male and Lola moved back in time for the 2005 nesting season. Today, the lovebirds freely roam the neighborhood, and can be seen flying around the park and perched on buildings on the Upper East Side, or at their newly renovated nest on the twelfth-floor ledge of 927 Fifth.

The nest is located on FIFTH AVENUE BETWEEN 73RD AND 74TH STREETS IN MANHATTAN. Subway: 6 to 77th Street. Best viewing locations are in Central Park, or along Fifth Avenue in the neighborhood. Check on their progress at www.palemale.com.

Putting the Fun in Funeral

Several years ago, when we wrote the first edition of this book, we introduced Coney Island as "the best one-of-a-kind attraction in the city, hands down," and we declared it a gem of Brooklyn history that could never be rendered obsolete. "Long live Coney!" we cried. Now, barely five years on, it is our sad duty to record that a surge of redevelopment along the Brooklyn coast has brought an end to much that made Coney Island what it used to be—and what it *should* be. Not all is lost just yet, though. The shabby games and old-school fairground rides of Astroland are gone, and new tents and markets are going up and coming down all over the site. But make your way down to the boardwalk and you'll see that Coney is still home to **one of the world's oldest and most famous roller coasters**, a **world-famous hot-dog–eating competition**, and a genuine **old-school sideshow**.

SURF AVENUE AND WEST 12TH STREET IN BROOKLYN. Subway: D, F, N, Q to Coney Island-Stillwell Avenue.

935. See the last of the **great sideshows**—and learn the tricks of the trade.

The Amusement Park at Coney Island is home to one of America's last great circus sideshows, a strange theater of outrageous acts, revolting tricks, and feats of unimaginable oddity. With a cast of characters that includes Donny Vomit (the human pin-cushion), Heather Holliday (the youngest female sword swallower in the world), and Serpentina (a contortionist and snake charmer), the sideshow's acts range from freak-show staples, such as fire-breathing and hammering a nail into someone's face, to more postmodern variations and innovative tricks, such as the "bed of nails sandwich" or the "neon sword swallowing." Founded by Yale Drama MFA graduate Dick D. Zigun, the sideshow is one of Coney Island's priceless contributions to New York City culture, and judging from the packed houses it draws every summer weekend, it's not going any-where anytime soon. If you think you've got what it takes, sign up for a semester at the sideshow school, an acclaimed instructional program where you will learn to walk on glass, lie on nails, and swallow fire with the best of them.

1208 SURF AVENUE IN BROOKLYN. 718-372-5159. www.coneyisland.com/sideshow.shtml.

936. Watch the Nathan's Famous July Fourth **hot-dog–eating contest**.

Watch the world's top hot-dog "gurgitators" (as they are known within the competi-tive eating circuit) vie for the sport's highest honor, the Mustard Yellow International Belt, at this annual event, which has been held at Nathan's since 1916. Twenty top eaters from around the world go head-to-head on the beach to see how many hot dogs (and buns) each one can down in twenty minutes (current record: 68).

Contest is held every year on July 4, at noon, at NATHAN'S FAMOUS, CORNER OF SURF AND STILLWELL AVENUES IN BROOKLYN. For more information, visit www.nathansfamous.com.

937. Ride the **Cyclone**.

The crown jewel of the sadly departed Astroland, the Cyclone is probably the only National Historical Landmark it's okay to throw up on. Though it was built in 1927, the Cyclone is still beloved by New Yorkers and roller-coaster aficionados alike, and for more than just nos-talgic reasons. Admittedly, the changes to the Coney Island landscape have taken some of the fun out of the view from the top. But with twelve drops, six 108-degree turns, and sixteen changes of directions at 60 miles per hour during the course of the two-minute ride, the Cyclone holds its own against the newer, sleeker models at more modern amuse-ment parks. (Don't worry—despite the rickety-looking wooden structure, the owners of the park work very hard to maintain it.) Afterward, if you're not feeling too queasy, you can follow the ride with a hot dog and curly fries from the original **Nathan's** (see above) on Surf Avenue, which has been serving them since before the Cyclone was built.

→ *DID YOU KNOW? Though the Cyclone has many distinctions, it is not the first roller coaster. It was, however, built on the site of what is considered to have been the first roller coaster in the world: LaMarcus A. Thompson's Switchback Railway.*

938. See a puppet show at the **Swedish Cottage Marionette Theater**.

For thirty years, the hands behind the stage at the Swedish Cottage have been making puppets dance around to the delight of children and parents from all over the city. Imported from Sweden in the late nineteenth century and moved to Central Park by Frederick Law Olmsted, the cottage houses what is now the only performing public marionette theater in the country. With charming performances of classic children's stories from *Cinderella* to *Jack and the Beanstalk*, a trip to the cottage is a fairy tale for kids from their very first sight of the charming log cabin to the puppets' last bow.

CENTRAL PARK NEAR THE 79TH STREET ENTRANCE ON THE WEST SIDE IN MANHATTAN. Subway: 1 to 79th Street; B, C to 81st Street-Museum of Natural History. 212-988-9093. www.centralparknyc.org/virtualpark/thegreatlawn/swedishcottage.

939. See the palm trees at the **Winter Garden**...

If you're sick of snow, and February seems like it's never going to end, one of the best cures for the winter blues is a visit to the sixteen *Washingtonia robusta* palm trees in the World Financial Center's Winter Garden. The trees, which come from the Mojave Desert, stretch an impressive forty feet high. They are a lovely backdrop for the performances and events that regularly take place in the Winter Garden (this is where the final competition took place in the film *Mad Hot Ballroom*), but they're worth a visit on their own. If you look at the trees from the steps on the north side of the atrium, the Hudson River is visible through the glass wall behind them, and if you squint a little, it almost looks like a Caribbean beach scene. (Note: the Winter Garden is one of the **Wi-Fi hotspots** sponsored by the Downtown Alliance. For more information, see page 215.)

THE WORLD FINANCIAL CENTER IS BORDERED BY WEST STREET, VESEY STREET, LIBERTY STREET, AND THE HUDSON RIVER IN MANHATTAN. Subway: 1 to Rector Street; 2, 3, 4, 5, J, M, Z to Fulton Street; A, C to Broadway-Nassau Street; E to World Trade Center. www.worldfinancial-center.com.

940. ...or step into the jungle at the **Ford Foundation Building**.

A well-kept secret in the heart of Midtown, the stunning lobby of the Ford Foundation is one of the city's most pleasant surprises. A three-tier landscaped garden occupies the building's 160-foot atrium, with thousands of colorful exotic plants covering the terraces, vines climbing all over the interiors, and seventeen fully grown trees looming above. Vast glass walls let in an amazing amount of sunlight, and the atmosphere is a warm, moist, and refreshing antidote to the oppressive asphalt world outside. The gardeners in charge of this horticultural microcosm vary the vegetation by season, ensuring vibrant springs of tulips and daffodils and restful autumns of dahlias and chrysanthemums. For those who know it's there, the Ford Foundation is one of the city's most cherished eccentricities.

320 EAST 43RD STREET BETWEEN LEXINGTON AND THIRD AVENUES IN MANHATTAN. Subway: 4, 5, 6, 7, S to Grand Central-42nd Street. 212-573-5000.

The best places to go

When we first started to work on this book, one suggestion that came up repeatedly was that we include a list of the city's nicest restrooms. And why not? This is a city of pedestrians and amblers of all kinds, who need amenities while en route or aimlessly exploring on foot, and although it's never difficult to find a public restroom wherever you happen to be in the city (department stores, hotel lobbies, and Starbucks are reliable sources in a pinch), it's true that some are (much) better than others. Whether boasting design elements that make them worth a detour or simply offering clean, convenient facilities that are easy to pop in and use on your way, the following is a list of our favorite restrooms in the city. Note: All of these are technically open to the public, except for the three in restaurants—Cha An, Peep, and Pukk—which can be used only if you are a patron.

941. *Cha An:* This quiet, traditional teahouse in Manhattan's **Japanese Village** (see pages 198–199) happens to have some of the most high-tech bathrooms in the city. Built seamlessly into the subtle, dark décor of the ladies' room is an elegant, electronically operated toilet-cum-bidet imported from Japan, which will leave you feeling cleaner and more refreshed than in your own bathroom at home.
230 EAST 9TH STREET BETWEEN SECOND AND THIRD AVENUES IN MANHATTAN. Subway: 6 to Astor Place. 212-228-8030.

942. *Pearl River Mart:* This recently renovated Asian emporium gives shoppers more than an amazing array of unusual, well-priced clothing, goods, furniture, and miscellany. **Pearl River Mart** (see page 259) has, somewhat surprisingly, the best public bathrooms in SoHo. Painted a cheery yellow, they literally sparkle, and located on the lower level just to the side of the stairs, they are perfectly placed—easy to find on your own, but not so prominent that you won't be able to slip in from the street unnoticed.
477 BROADWAY BETWEEN BROOME STREET AND GRAND STREET IN MANHATTAN. Subway: 6, J, M, Z, N, Q, R, W to Canal Street. 212-431-4770. www.pearlriver.com.

943. *Crate and Barrel:* The bathrooms at this megalith of home furnishings remain a remarkably little-known haven of downtown relief. Standing at one of the busiest intersections in Manhattan, at the crossroads of Broadway and Houston Street, the Crate and Barrel store is within dashing distance of anywhere in SoHo and NoHo, which means it's accessible from some of the most overcrowded and frantic shopping areas in the city. The bathrooms are hidden upstairs and are spacious, clean, and quiet, and you'll get no dirty looks from staff or security for rushing straight in there from the street. What makes it a perfect place to go is that before you walk back out into the maelstrom, you can pause for a few moments' peace "trying out" one of their many inviting couches…

611 BROADWAY AT HOUSTON STREET IN MANHATTAN. Subway: 6, F, V to Broadway-Lafayette Street. 212-780-0004. www.crateandbarrel.com.

944. *Peep:* This SoHo Thai restaurant's R-rated bathrooms aren't for the shy, but if you're up for a cheap thrill, give them a try. The walls are done in one-way glass, so the occupant (it's a single-occupant bathroom) can see out into the restaurant, but the people in the restaurant only see mirrored glass. If that weren't risqué enough, there is a video screen above the sink in the bathroom that plays steamy films like *sex, lies, and videotape* on an ongoing loop. (There are also one-way-glass bathrooms at **Pukk**, an excellent vegetarian Thai restaurant in the East Village.)

PEEP: *177 PRINCE STREET BETWEEN SULLIVAN AND PRINCE STREETS IN MANHATTAN. Subway: C, E, to Spring Street. 212-254-7337. www.peepsoho.net.*
PUKK: *71 FIRST AVENUE BETWEEN 4TH AND 5TH STREETS IN MANHATTAN. Subway: F, V to Lower East Side-Second Avenue. 212-253-2741. www.pukknyc.com.*

945. *Bar 89:* These days, there are enough shaky videos from mischievous customers on YouTube to spoil the surprise, but for a long time the misty bathroom doors at Bar 89 in SoHo were a secret that had to be experienced firsthand to be believed. The bathrooms at this emblem of 1990s New York are unisex, which adds a mild frisson to the leap of faith required to trust that the fog in the glass will cloud you from view in time. And you don't need to go there just for the bathrooms: the cocktails are trustworthy, too.

89 MERCER STREET BETWEEN SPRING STREET AND BROOME STREET IN MANHATTAN. Subway: 6 to Spring Street; N, R to Prince Street. 212-274-0989. www.bar89.com.

946. *The Waldorf-Astoria:* The public restrooms at the **Waldorf** (see pages 37–38) deserve a mention because one, compared to efficient, no-frills, or high-concept modern bathrooms, they are pretty special, in an anachronistic sort of way; and two, there is so much going on in the hotel's lobby, these are really easy to slip in and use (they are across the hall from Sir Harry's Bar, near to the Park Avenue side). The décor is not stylish (some might even call it garish), but neither is it shabby nor worn-looking, and there's a cozy lounge area with couches where you can hang out and rest your feet. One anachronism that may not charm everyone: the stalls are considerably narrower than most modern ones, so they can seem slightly cramped.

301 PARK AVENUE BETWEEN 49TH AND 50TH STREETS IN MANHATTAN. Subway: 6 to 51st Street; E, V to Lexington Avenue/53rd Street. 212-255-3000. www.waldorfastoria.com.

947. *Bryant Park:* Nicely kept bathrooms in city facilities are few and far between, but the public toilets in Bryant Park are among the greatest marvels of Midtown. Housed in a small but majestic stone building behind the New York Public Library, the bathrooms are under constant supervision and are kept wonderfully clean, fresh smelling, and adorned with pretty bouquets. There are simply no better public restrooms in the city.

42ND STREET AT FIFTH AVENUE IN MANHATTAN. Subway: B, D, F, V to 42nd Street-Bryant Park; 7 to Fifth Avenue-Bryant Park.

948. Find your way to Sakagura.

New Yorkers grumble all the time about the spatial constraints of living in such a packed city, which makes the few establishments that manage to draw inspiration from these limitations all the more exciting. One of the best examples is this Midtown sake den, which is tucked away in the basement of an office building. You'd never know it from the outside, but if you make your way past the elevators and down a set of fire stairs, you will uncover a subterranean jewel, and one of the best sake lists in the city. The food and drink are terrific regardless, but what really makes Sakagura special is the glorious audacity of the entire venture—one has the sense that the restaurant demanded its privacy, trusting that it would be sought out even in this city of myriad choice.

211 EAST 43RD STREET BETWEEN SECOND AND THIRD AVENUES. Subway: 4, 5, 6, 7 to Grand Central. 212-953-7253. www.sakagura.com.

Famous faces in the bar

Celebrity-owned bars aren't unique to New York—there was the infamous Viper Room in Los Angeles owned by Johnny Depp, the pharmacy-themed Damien Hirst bar in London, and U2 owns a hotel in Dublin. But in New York, where movie shoots are practically as common as street vendors, celeb-cred alone does not a destination make. There have been ventures nominally affiliated with a high-profile name or two, many of which closed once the initial buzz died down (the Fashion Café and the Britney Spears restaurant come to mind); then there are some really great places that just happen to be run or owned by someone of note. Here are the best of the latter, the ones that would be worth going to, no matter whose name was on the door, but whose backstory edges them up a notch or two.

949. Risk playing the jukebox at Jimmy's Corner, a dive bar run by an ex-boxing manager of some repute. The walls are covered with photos of Jimmy with Ali, Tyson, and other legends of the ring, past and present, and Jimmy hovers around looking formidable and telling stories to regulars and (pretty) newcomers at the bar. The jukebox is one of the best in the city—but if you put something on that Jimmy doesn't like, he'll let you know. *140 WEST 44TH STREET BETWEEN SIXTH AVENUE AND BROADWAY IN MANHATTAN. Subway: B, D, F, V to 42nd Street-Bryant Park. 212-221-9510.*

950. Commune with writers at the Half King.

This casual pub is owned by the writers Sebastian Junger (author of *A Perfect Storm*) and Scott Anderson. The two friends wanted to open a bar that resembled in atmosphere the journalist hangouts the two frequented while covering wars in Chechnya, Bosnia, and Sierra Leone. In 2000, they opened a modest bar in what was then a barren no-man's-land in west Chelsea, attracting both writers and journalists from around the city, as well as people from the galleries that were beginning to crop up in the neighborhood. Today, although the area is no longer considered on the fringe, the Half King remains deliberately unpretentious right down to its understated oak structure (made from a collapsed Mennonite barn in Pennsylvania) and excellent pub grub (try the fish and chips). Exhibits by photojournalists line the walls, and at the Monday night readings, expect to hear excerpts from books about child soldiers in Asia, or an exposé about the self-help industry in America. Other nights, the conversation may not be quite as heavy, but anytime you go, you'll be surrounded by a thinking crowd taking refuge from the chaos on the frontlines and the headlines. *505 WEST 23RD STREET AT TENTH AVENUE IN MANHATTAN. Subway: C, E to 23rd Street. 212-462-4300. www.thehalfking.com.*

951. Dance with hip-hop stars at the **40/40 Club**.

Jay-Z is one of the biggest things to have come out of New York hip-hop, and 40/40, the dance club he co-owns in the Flatiron District, is becoming quite a big thing itself. If Mr. Z isn't there in person, you're sure to hear his tunes on every floor, and you won't be starved of other hip-hop celebrities either. The seats are leather, the bar is slate, the plasma screens are enormous, and the block is a landing strip for limos. Look your best.

6 WEST 25TH STREET BETWEEN BROADWAY AND SIXTH AVENUES IN MANHATTAN. Subway: 1 to 23rd Street; F, V to 23rd Street; N, R, W to 23rd Street. 212-832-4040. www.the4040club.com.

952. Go dancing with the celebs at **Santos Party House**.

The best thing about Santos—one of the coolest and most enjoyable clubs down-town, and the brainchild of rocker Andrew WK—is that even with all the celebrity DJs and paparazzi-trailed clientele competing for your attention, it's impossible not to lose yourself dancing to some of the best hip-hop, R&B, and dance music you'll hear in the city. With surprise guests and regular DJ spots from the likes of Lady Gaga and Q-Tip, the club has earned a devoted following of discerning clubbers that manages to incor-porate everyone from hardcore hip-hop heads to bridge-'n'-tunnel glitterati. And when a club's Web site makes a point of detailing its audio equipment, you know they take their sound seriously.

96 LAFAYETTE STREET AT WALKER STREET IN MANHATTAN. Subway: 6, J, M, Z, N, Q, R, W to Canal Street. 212-584-5492. www.santospartyhouse.com.

953. Karaoke with one of the great Jews in sports at **Tracey J's**.

Emblazoned across this popular karaoke spot and watering hole is a banner touting the owner, Art Heyman. Duke basketball fans will know him as the player who led the Blue Devils to their first-ever Final Four appearance in 1963; native New Yorkers may know him as a local kid from Long Island who went on to play for the Knicks. Heyman is also the only Jew ever chosen as the NBA's overall number-one draft pick. His bar is a dive of the best kind: dark, with no obvious gesture toward style, and authentically rowdy, especially on Fridays, when happy hour starts at noon. The after-work crowd gives way to the karaoke scene on Thursday, Friday, and Saturday nights, and then it kicks up again in the morning, with sports fans gathering to watch the day's games. During the day, Art often sits on a stool outside the bar reading the papers, so if you're in the neighborhood, wave as you go by.

106 EAST 19TH STREET BETWEEN IRVING PLACE AND PARK AVENUE SOUTH IN MANHATTAN. Subway: 4, 5, 6, L, N, Q, R, W to 14th Street-Union Square. 212-674-5783. www.tracyjs.com.

Have a meal at a **grilled cheese restaurant**, followed by dessert from a **rice pudding restaurant**...

New York is probably the only place on the planet where a restaurant that serves only rice pudding has a better shot at making it than a Wendy's. The city has a bunch of restaurants that focus on one item—and we're not talking about donuts or ice cream. Inspired by tastes, practical concerns, or who knows what, the owners of the following restaurants decided that these particular foodstuffs were exactly what the city needed.

954. *Say Cheese:* Say Cheese is a favorite Hell's Kitchen lunch spot, offering a long menu of variations on the American classic, the grilled cheese sandwich. Say Cheese departs from the traditional preparation by offering a variety of imported cheeses such as Gouda and Gruyère, and fancy flavored breads from **Amy's** (see page 177). But you can also get a plain old American cheese and tomato, grilled in butter, just the way Mom used to make.

649 NINTH AVENUE BETWEEN 44TH AND 45TH STREETS IN MANHATTAN. Subway: A, C, E to 42nd Street-Port Authority Bus Terminal. 212-265-8840. www.saycheese.cc.

955. *Rice to Riches:* Who would have thought that a restaurant that serves only—and we mean only—rice pudding would be a hit? But Rice to Riches is a New York darling and the unofficial queen of the city's eccentric specialty restaurants. Just looking at the restaurant will make you smile—with its sleek, pod-shape exterior, it looks like something out of *The Jetsons*. And apparently in the future, at least according to R-to-R, people have forsaken South Beach and gone back to ingesting all-American staples like cream, white sugar, and carbs. Twenty different flavors are whipped up daily, from basic vanilla and cinnamon to wild concoctions like chocolate hazelnut, maple and blueberry, French toast, and Rocky Road. The puddings can be topped with cocoa, espresso, pound cake, graham crackers, and more, and are served in colorful plastic tubs that look like futuristic Tupperware. Sizes come in solo (one person), sumo (five people), and the Moby, a ten-person pudding vat.

37 SPRING STREET BETWEEN MOTT AND MULBERRY STREETS IN MANHATTAN. Subway: 6 to Spring Street. 212-274-0008. www.ricetoriches.com.

956. *Peanut Butter & Co.:* Forget mashed potatoes and macaroni-and-cheese— PB&J is the real American comfort food, at least according to the folks here. Peanut Butter & Co. serves a dozen versions of the lunch-box staple made with freshly ground peanut butter. Classic sandwiches include the Lunchbox Special, with your choice of strawberry or grape jelly, and the Elvis, a grilled sandwich with bananas, honey, and bacon (optional), both served with your choice of chunky or smooth peanut butter.

There are also sandwiches made with special flavored peanut butters (spicy, cinnamon raisin, white chocolate, and dark chocolate), plus peanut butter milk shakes (with jelly or without), a host of peanut butter desserts, and the preschool snack-time favorite, Ants on a Log. Oh, and they'll cut the crusts off for no extra charge.

240 SULLIVAN STREET BETWEEN BLEECKER AND WEST 3RD STREETS IN MANHATTAN. Subway: A, C, E, B, D, F, V to West 4th Street. 212-677-3995. www.IlovePeanutButter.com.

957. Stuffed Artisan Cannolis: Grammarians may quibble with the redundancy in the name, but we dare even the purest dessert lover to try to resist the crazily vast selection of cannolis at this Lower East Side shop. The modus operandi behind the concoctions (thirty varieties in all) is to interpret traditional American treats as Italian cannoli. Thus flavor offerings include red licorice, root beer float, apple pie, and the rainbow-sprinkle-topped birthday cake. For the aforementioned purists, there is the traditional, plain ricotta, a kind of "control" sweet against which numerous, more exotic samples can be compared.

176 STANTON STREET, BETWEEN CLINTON AND ATTORNEY STREETS IN MANHATTAN. Subway: F, J, M, Z to Essex Street-Delancey. 212-995-2266. www.stuffedcannoli.com.

958. The Hummus Place: The name says it all. At these holes-in-the-wall, the only things you can get are heaping plates of hummus, and pita to sop it up with. But don't let the narrowness of the menu dissuade you: the hummus is so tasty that serious foodies (it was a chef who tipped us off) come from around the city to feast on one of the three preparations: plain with tahini, or topped with whole chickpeas or *foul* (cooked fava beans and soft-boiled egg). You can get it to go, and they do deliver, but we highly recommend that you eat in—the taste of warm hummus with a sprinkle of fresh paprika on a warm pita is heavenly.

All locations in Manhattan. 99 MACDOUGAL STREET AT BLEECKER STREET. Subway: A, C, E, B, D, F, V to West 4th Street. 212-924-2022; 109 SAINT MARK'S PLACE NEAR FIRST AVENUE. Subway: 6 to Astor Place; L to First Avenue. 212-529-9198; 71 SEVENTH AVENUE SOUTH AT BLEECKER STREET. Subway: 1 to Christopher Street, A, B, C, D, E, F, V to West 4th Street. 212-924-2022; 305 AMSTERDAM AVENUE BETWEEN 74TH AND 75TH STREETS. Subway: 1, 2, 3 to 72nd Street. 212-799-3335.

959. Fresh yogurt from the Yoghurt Place II: Gorge on rich, sinful-tasting Mediterranean yogurt covered in fresh strawberries, nuts, or honey, or get a giant tub to take home. But take our advice and stock up—after this, you'll never again be satisfied by the offerings at the supermarket.

71 SULLIVAN STREET BETWEEN SPRING AND BROOME STREETS IN MANHATTAN. Subway: C, E to Spring Street. 212-219-3500. www.yoghurtplacenyc.com.

960. *Risotteria:* A true New York original if ever there was one—a place where food-ies, vegetarians, and celiacs can eat together! The Risotteria serves more than fifty kinds of risotto, made with three different kinds of rice. But if that weren't enough to merit an entry in this category, there's more: almost all the dishes are strictly gluten-free, so people with celiac disease (a severe intolerance to gluten that prevents sufferers from eating wheat, rye, barley, and most grains) can order most anything off the menu with-out thinking twice. There are also many vegetarian dishes. (Menu items are clearly marked as gluten-free, vegetarian, or prepared with chicken stock.) In addition to risotto, they also serve lots of gluten-free goodies, such as pizza, panini, breadsticks, and desserts, all made with rice-flour dough.

270 BLEECKER STREET AT MORTON STREET IN MANHATTAN. Subway: 1 to Christopher Street-Sheridan Square; A, C, E, B, D, F, V to West 4th Street. 212-924-6664. wwwrisotteria.com.

961. *Chikalicious:* Perhaps best not to tell the kids about this one. This East Village restaurant serves dessert, and only dessert, in three-course prix fixe meals, starting with an *amuse-bouche*, and finishing with petit fours. For the main course, you choose among the menu's half-dozen gourmet dessert plates (complete with side dishes of ice cream and garnishes like toasted pecans), which change regularly. The meals cost $12 per person; you can also add wine or coffee/tea pairings ($7 and $3.50, respectively). But if you want a breadbasket, you'll have to go elsewhere.

203 EAST 10TH STREET BETWEEN FIRST AND SECOND AVENUES IN MANHATTAN. Subway: L to First Avenue. 212-475-0929. www.chikalicious.com.

...or try some **one-of-a-kind fusion.**

New York is a melting pot—no surprise there. Yet only a few intrepid operations have taken that fact to its literal, delectable conclusion. Mix diversity and creativity and add cheese is the recipe for the two offbeat culinary mash-ups below.

962. *Pizza and macaroni-and-cheese at Pinch & S'MAC:* Stroke of genius or lethal combination? Leaving aside the guilt-inducing potential of copious carbs and cheese, this joint venture between pizza innovators Pinch and macaroni-and-cheese special-ists S'MAC is an only-in-New-York brilliant merge of business identity. Pinch made its name by selling its pizza by the inch, rather than the slice; S'MAC presaged the local comfort food revival when it launched a mac-and-cheese-only menu at its original (and still perpetually mobbed) East Village restaurant. But at Pinch & S'MAC (appro-priately located in the kid-friendly Upper West Side), you don't have to choose between a pepperoni pie and a bowl of mac and cheese with buffalo chicken (or masala spices, or brie and figs)—even though your doctor might wish you would.

474 COLUMBUS AVENUE BETWEEN 82ND AND 83RD STREETS IN MANHATTAN. Subway: B, C to 81st Street. 646-438-9494. www.pinchandsmac.com.

963. *Cream puffs and cheese bread at Puff & Pao:* This West Village snack shop serves bite-size morsels of two foreign specialties: Brazilian *pão de queijo* (cheese bread) and French *choux* buns, more commonly known as cream puffs. The cream puffs are piped to order with your choice of cream fillings, while the *pãolitos*, as they are called, come in a variety of savory flavors. To add to the multicultural mix, the shop has put a modern, American finish on these two traditional snacks: they offer sugar- and gluten-free options, and you can get an egg-and-pãolito breakfast sandwich that's like a spiffed-up Egg McMuffin.

105 CHRISTOPHER STREET BETWEEN BLEECKER AND HUDSON STREETS IN MANHATTAN. Subway: 1 to Christopher Street-Sheridan Square. 212-633-PUFF (7833). www.puffandpao.com.

964. Pickle yourself at the **Pickle Day Festival**.

Every year at the beginning of fall, a sunny corner of the Lower East Side is invaded by delicatessens and foodies from around the country, whose specialty lies in pickling cucumbers and other treats. As well as local stalwarts such as the Pickle Guys on Essex Street, Russ & Daughters on Houston, and the brilliant Brooklyn Brine, there are also suppliers from farther afield such as McClure's from Detroit, and the Grey Mouse Farm upstate. Wander around the block-wide lot and sample to your heart's vinegary (dis)content: there is something for even a fickle pickle palette here, from the exotic (jalapeño-pickled white beans) to the downright shocking (mustard- and cider-infused pickled turnips). Just make sure you save room for a cool, classic pickle on a stick—the ice-cream cone of the true New Yorker.

For more information and event date, contact the New York Food Museum at the Web site below. Event takes place in the PARKING LOT BETWEEN BROOME, LUDLOW, AND ESSEX STREETS IN MANHATTAN. Subway: F, J, M, Z to Delancey Street / Bowery. www.nyfoodmuseum.org.

965. Root for your favorite tug in the **Annual Tugboat Race**.

Each September, the top tugboats in the area go nose-to-nose (that's tugboat speak) for a day of nautical-themed competition on the Hudson. The main event is a one-nautical-mile race, which starts at the 79th Street Boat Basin and ends at Pier 84 (by 42nd Street). There are also competitions for best-looking tugboat, a line-throwing contest, and a Popeye-inspired spinach-eating contest.

For more information and event date, contact the Working Harbor Committee at 212-757-1600 or www.workingharbor.org.

966. See a professional magic show at **Monday Night Magic**.

Many people think that New York is a magical city, but until fairly recently, there was-n't any place where you could actually see magic performed. Every Monday night, Monday Night Magic puts on a live show at a theater off Lafayette Street—the only regular magic show in town. Each show features a different group of live performers, who pull off mystifying feats of escape, strength, and illusion, as well as card tricks, jug-gling, and comedy.

Monday at 8:00 p.m. THE BLEECKER STREET THEATRE, 45 BLEECKER STREET AT LAFAYETTE STREET IN MANHATTAN. Subway: 6 to Broadway-Lafayette Street. 212-615-6432. www.mon-daynightmagic.com.

967. **Race to the top** of the Empire State Building.

High-speed elevators will whisk you up in seconds; but if you feel like you need to climb your monuments to really appreciate them, there's an annual run up the 1,576 steps to the observatory of the **Empire State Building** (see page 19). Current record: 9 minutes and 33 seconds.

FIFTH AVENUE AT 34TH STREET IN MANHATTAN. Subway: B, D, F, V, N, Q, R, W to 34th Street-Her-ald Square. Observatory open daily. For more information on hours, ticket prices, and the run, visit www.esbnyc.com.

968. Nominate your favorite street vendor for a **Vendy**.

If you asked us to name New York's single signature cuisine, we would have to say **street food** (see pages 111–112 for some of our favorite offerings from carts and trucks). The proliferation of food trucks in recent years is evidence of a thriving scene. Yet, as many loyal cart-followers would agree, until recently, the vendors were the unsung heroes of the city's culinary scene. To remedy this, the Street Vendor Project put on the first annual Vendy Awards in 2005, and this event has been unanimously embraced the city, judg-ing from its coverage by local food pubs and blogs and its popularity with the cart-lov-ing public. (The 2009 event sold out well in advance, no small feat when you consider that tickets rivaled the cost of a restaurant dinner with wine). Finalists in several differ-ent categories are selected via public voting from hundreds of nominees, and then compete in a live cook-off and taste-test at the event. The Vendy Cup is decided by a ros-ter of judges with ties to the local food and restaurant scene. Awards in the other cate-gories—best dessert truck and "rookie of the year"—are decided by attendee voting. If $60 or $100 seems a lot to pay for street nibbles and voting, know that the event is a fundraiser for the Street Vendor Project, a nonprofit social justice organization that helps provides vendors with legal resources and representation.

September. Tickets: Prices vary according to time of purchase, $60–$100. For more informa-tion on the Vendys, upcoming dates, and location, visit streetvendor.org.

969. Take a **hybrid**.

Town Car, meet your match. Those familiar black sedans that have long ferried high-pow-ered execs around the city now have a formidable opponent: OZOcar, New York's eco-friendly luxury-car service. The fleet is composed of hybrid vehicles, which produce up to 89 percent less emissions than other cars. But that's not the only way they differ from the lumbering black dinosaurs: each car has satellite radio, and a wireless Internet con-nection. If you're not in a position to ride in them to work each day, you can still enjoy them on your next trip to the airport, or to Westchester, Long Island, or Connecticut. *For reservations, call 866-OZO-5966 or visit www.ozocar.com.*

970. Go **bike jousting** in Brooklyn.

The Black Label Bicycle Club is a citywide society devoted to manic, violent fun on bicycles. Held in suitably sparse industrial parts of Brooklyn and Queens, the Black Label club draws masochistic cyclists from all around the country to events that resem-ble medieval fairs, where anyone can take part in crazy contests from bicycle polo and bike-hurling to the Whiplash, in which two bikers joined at the hip by a long rope pedal in opposite directions until the weaker is thrown from his seat. The king of these games is the joust, which involves two cyclists, armed with giant rubber lances, racing at each other to an obvious and spectacular end. The club, whose members are largely Brook-lynites and who vary from city-loving cycling fanatics to *Jackass* fans, also organizes all manner of races, scavenger hunts, and rollicking dance parties. Even if you don't fancy being a competitor, it's worth turning up to an event just to see the amazing fleet of customized, vandalized, and bastardized two-wheelers that roll in. *For details of upcoming parties, events, and locations, visit www.blacklabelnewyork.com.*

Try to catch a glimpse of an all-time favorite **New York character**.

New York is full of interesting (and interesting-looking) people, but there are a few who stand out from the rest as local celebrities. These are people whose faces or names are not necessarily recognizable outside—or, in some cases, even inside—the city but who, for whatever reason, are well known here, by profession or reputation or distinctive look. We've chosen our five favorites: a mysterious chauffeur, a drag queen extraordi-naire, an heir to an old-school salesman, a photogenic weatherman, and a very strik-ing man with avian delusions. Unlike regular celebrities, these people can regularly be seen walking the streets, so keep your eyes open!

971. *The tambourine-playing limo driver:* Delighted passengers of one particular downtown limo service can find themselves being driven around town by a chauffeur celebrated for beating a tambourine against the steering wheel and blowing a whistle in time to the classic '80s pop tunes that bang from his speakers. Many who claim to have seen him have really only *heard* him; but for the lucky few who've sneaked a peek through his window, or glanced down from a balcony through his open sunroof, the image of his tambourine glittering around the dashboard as he steers the limo one-handed is a hard one to forget.
Anywhere, late at night.

972. *Amanda Lepore:* Explaining it-girl transvestite, party-hopper, and fashion muse Amanda Lepore is kind of like Justice Potter's famous description of pornography: hard to describe, but you'll know her when you see her. With her signature white-face makeup, bulbous breasts, and enormous red lips, she looks like a comic-book villainess come to life. She dabbles in many creative and business pursuits—singing, modeling, merchandising—and is a regular on the New York club scene, but she's probably best known for the photographs of her taken by David LaChappelle. When she's not on photo or movie shoots, attending parties, or otherwise indisposed, she resides at the Hotel 17, from which she roams the otherwise sleepy strips of Second and Third Avenues in the teens by day (we once spotted her coming out of a dry cleaner's), and by night, she drops in on one lavish party after another.
For more on Amanda, visit www.hotel17ny.com.

973. *The Vegetable-Peeling Ades in Union Square:* Joe Ades—better known to many as the peeler guy in Union Square—was perhaps the most enigmatic character that the city has ever called her own. Mr. Ades sold vegetable peelers—or to be precise, a specific kind of vegetable peeler—from a three-legged stool in the Union Square Park. Though sitting close to the ground and without a proper booth or even a table to attract customers to his wares, he was impossible to miss for his dress (he was always impeccably turned out in suit and tie) and booming, circus-barker-pitch–style. His accent suggested British upper crust; his dress would not look out of place in Carnegie Hill. Yet his day-in-and-day-out persistence in boasting the particular effectiveness of his peeler by slicing perfect mounds of carrots and potatoes counteracted his appearance, and fueled the mystery. Had he made his fortune from peelers? Was it true that he lived on Park Avenue? (A 2006 *Vanity Fair* profile revealed that Ades was a self-made man who developed his performance style on the streets of Manchester as a teenager and later sold goods out of a truck in Australia before moving to the United States.) Ades passed away in February 2009, but his daughter has taken up the family trade, so you can still procure one of Ades's magic peelers and watch the demonstration-entertainment he developed.
UNION SQUARE PARK IN MANHATTAN. Subway: 4, 5, 6, L, N, R, Q, W to 14th Street-Union Square.

974. Sam Champion: The golden weather boy of WABC shines like a star among the drab mortals of downtown Manhattan. Living proof that television weathermen can be celebrities, too, Champion can all too often be seen (or his unmistakable broadcaster's voice overheard) in the trendiest bars and restaurants of Chelsea and the Meatpacking District. Unlikely as it is, Sam is a true local icon, a Big Apple Adonis who divines the fates of our days by proclaiming sun or rain. We dare you to ask him for a forecast. *For more on Sam, visit www.7online.com.*

975. The Birdman: If you find yourself in Times Square on a busy afternoon and you hear—over the traffic and the crowds—a squawking, twittering, or whistling from an eccentric-looking man with wings tattooed across his chest and feathers in his fedora, don't be alarmed: he is the Birdman of Times Square. This ornithological stranger is a familiar face around the area, and like all rare birds, should be photographed quickly upon sighting.
TIMES SQUARE, BROADWAY AND 42ND STREET. Subway: 1, 2, 3, 7, N, Q, R, W, S to Times Square-42nd Street.

976. Watch the masters at the International **Yo-Yo Open**.

Cosmopolitan center that it is, New York's got a slew of glamorous awards ceremonies and championships, so many that some of the more offbeat ones can slide under the radar of the average city resident. This, at least, is how we explain why the Yo-Yo Open, an international competition and championship, has taken place in the city for the past several years with little publicity. This is not to say that the event is a sedate affair. Over the two days of competition, the world's top yo-yo talents compete and perform the most complicated sequences in yo-yoing, interspersed with exhibition performances and live music. At the highest rankings, the competition works like Olympics ice-skating, as there's a technical program (contestants must perform a list of specific tricks, which is called the Sport Ladder) and then a freestyle one (contestants improvise a routine to several minutes of music). Watching the event is free and open to the public, and unlike many sporting events, you don't need to know the rules well to have a good time watching.
August. Event takes place at PIER 17 AT SOUTH STREET SEAPORT IN MANHATTAN. Subway: 2, 3, 4, 5, J, M to Fulton Street or A, C to Broadway-Nassau Street. For upcoming dates and schedule, visit www.yoyoopen.com.

977. See the famous fan mail at **Steinway Hall**.

In addition to three floors displaying some of the finest musical instruments in the world, there is the Rotunda, a dome-topped room filled with art, paintings, and memorabilia from Steinway's illustrious 150-year history, including displays of fan mail from everyone from Rachmaninoff to Thomas Edison. Below ground, there is the famous piano bank, where loaner pianos for traveling concert musicians are kept. N.B. Also of interest to piano lovers is the **Steinway Piano factory** in Queens. A factory tour is offered intermittently, but if you like pianos, it's worth contacting the factory see when the next one is. (One of the tour highlights is a visit to the "pounder room," where a machine bangs on all of the keys of each piano 10,000 times to make sure the sound is correct.)

109 WEST 57TH STREET AT SIXTH AVENUE IN MANHATTAN. Subway: N, Q, R, W to 57th Street. 212-246-1100. www.steinwayhall.com. The piano factory is located at 1 STEINWAY PLACE (NINETEENTH AVENUE AND 38TH STREET) IN QUEENS. To inquire about factory tours, call 718-721-2600, ext. 3164. Subway: N, W to Astoria-Ditmars Boulevard. www.steinway.com.

→ **DID YOU KNOW?** *Ninety-eight percent of concert pianists play on Steinway pianos.*

978. See the gold at the **Federal Reserve Bank of New York**.

Eighty feet below Liberty Street in the heart of downtown Manhattan, locked in a maximum security vault to which no one individual holds all the keys and codes, sits nearly a third of the world's monetary gold reserves. The Federal Reserve Bank has held the U.S. reserves on these premises for nearly a century, since it was decided in 1924 that the very bedrock of Manhattan, fifty feet below sea level, was the safest place to hide all that bullion (and the strongest, because a vault like this needs a sturdy floor). Call in advance and reserve a place on a tour of the Gold Vault, and you'll come as close as you will ever get to ten billion dollars' worth of solid gold bars—and you'll learn something of the history of the city while you're at it.

33 LIBERTY STREET BETWEEN BROAD AND WILLIAM STREETS IN MANHATTAN. Subway: J, M, Z to Broad Street. 212-720-6130. www.ny.frb.org.

979. Hang out in the limo at **David Burke & Donatella**...

This is a best thing to do only if you're a smoker, although it's quite a sight and a clever gimmick. To attract patrons in the wake of the city's smoking ban in restaurants, this upscale Midtown restaurant has a stretch limo parked outside the restaurant every night during the winter months (except Sundays), so smokers can puff away out of the cold. With seating for eight to ten people, the limo often evolves into its own social scene, as people climb in with their drinks and sit shoulder-to-shoulder with their fellow smokers. Note: The chef David Burke also has a restaurant across the street, on the ground floor of **Bloomingdale's** (see page 244).

133 EAST 61ST STREET BETWEEN LEXINGTON AND THIRD AVENUES IN MANHATTAN. Subway: 4, 5, 6 to 59th Street; F to Lexington Avenue/63rd Street; N, R, W to Lexington Avenue/59th Street. 212-813-2121. www.dbdrestaurant.com.

980. See a movie on the big screen at **Village East Cinema**.

Now a six-screen first-run cineplex, this East Village theater was built in 1926 and hosted performances of Yiddish-language plays. In addition to lovely architectural details and some Yiddish inscriptions in the lobby, the theater has held on to its grand, full-size auditorium, complete with boxes, orchestra, and mezzanine seating. Five other small screens have been added in the basement, and it's not always easy to guess which one you'll end up in, so if your movie isn't in the big theater, at least make sure to pop your head in. It's a beautiful space in which to watch a movie, with comfortable and roomy seats, and if the movie's dull, you can always look up at the intricately decorated dome ceiling.

181-189 SECOND AVENUE, CORNER OF 12TH STREET IN MANHATTAN. Subway: L to First or Third Avenues. 212-529-6799. www.villageeastcinema.com.

981. Learn everything you want to know about living in New York (and then some) through **Manhattan User's Guide**.

Quick, what's the city's largest park? Where were the original Oreos made? And who is Donna Faske? The answers to these questions and countless others can be found on Manhattan User's Guide, or MUG, an unrivaled source of information on everything and anything New York. Every weekday, it publishes an informative e-newsletter on a subject of particular local interest, from entertainment and goings on (i.e., upcoming sample sales and restaurant reviews) to practical information (instructions on how to register a complaint with the city, for instance), to things you never would have thought to ask (like the number of unsolved murders). The articles are then archived on the site, where you can look them up any time you feel the urge. There is also a monthly quiz of New York trivia (with some questions that stumped even your authors), and photos by **Joseph O. Holmes** (see page 80) of a different New York scene each day. MUG covers everything—arts, dining, sports, shopping—but the most interesting articles are in the "Services" and "Info" categories, where you'll find information on topics like organ donation, how to take your landlord to court, or where to find someone to clean a hat, fix a typewriter, disassemble a sofa, or sharpen knives. P.S.: The answers to the questions above are Pelham Bay Park, the old Nabisco factory (now the Chelsea Market), and Donna Karan.

Subscription is free. Visit www.manhattanusersguide.com for more information or to subscribe.

At our service.

New York is a mecca for those with an entrepreneurial spirit, and thanks to the surplus of creative people looking for a niche, the city supports a bunch of eccentric-sounding services that are geared toward the idiosyncrasies of a Big Apple lifestyle. We've also included one popular service that New Yorkers can use to provide something for others.

982. *Give your clothes all the comforts of home by sending them to the Ladies Who Launder.* "Even better than your mom" proclaims this lovely laundry service. When we asked New Yorkers to name their favorite thing about the city, a disproportionate number replied, "Having your laundry done and delivered." (Almost as many as those who chose **food delivery**—see page 332.) The combination of childhood nostalgia and the paucity of on-site laundry facilities in apartment buildings makes this posh-sounding service a nonnegotiable luxury to many New Yorkers. But not all wash-and-deliver services are of the same caliber, and few do the job with the TLC you remember from your youth. The Ladies Who Launder are like moms with a delivery van: women who wash your clothes with care, and bring them to your doorstep. They do far more than separate the lights from the darks: they are experts at stain removal, know what delicates are and how to treat them, and will follow any special instructions you provide. The basic service is competitive with most other laundries; for an additional fee, they will also hand-wash or iron. They pick up anywhere in Manhattan, whether or not you have a doorman, and bring back items within 48 hours. They also do dry cleaning, something even mom couldn't pull off.

For more information, schedules, and rates, call 347-820-6627 or visit www.ladywholaunder.com.

983. *Order reflexology from Cloud Nine.* Masseuses who make house calls? Old news. Cloud Nine can bring reflexology—a healing and relaxation treatment that stimulates organs through pressure points in the hands and feet—directly to you. These practitioners will travel to your home or office, anywhere in Manhattan, and to certain locations in Brooklyn and Queens.

$100 for sixty minutes. For information and to make an appointment, call 212-714-3921.

984. *Ask and receive with MaxDelivery.* The ideal service for the downtown idler, MaxDelivery.com is a deli, drugstore, video store, and novelty shop. Customers below 34th Street on the West Side and 26th Street on the East

Side can call MaxDelivery and arrange for an immediate delivery of anything from shampoo and soda to fresh food, cigarettes, razor blades, and DVD rentals. Orders are guaranteed to arrive within the hour, and they even carry cards, gifts, and wrapping paper for urgent, last-minute forgotten birthday, holiday, or anniversary presents. They have also put together special packages for different occasions, such as "Sick in Bed," "Exam Cram," and "Date Night." Outside of Max's range? Zip codes are added regularly, so check www.maxdelivery.com.

Check online for details of stock, delivery rates, and delivery locations.

985. *Get your sweaters rewoven at French-American.* Reweaving—the meticulous process of mending other woven garments by hand—is a dying art. French-American Reweaving is one of the few places in the country where you can get sweaters, jackets, and other clothing items repaired by professional reweavers. French-American has been around since 1930, and has fixed the torn and moth-eaten garments of Leonard Bernstein, Gloria Swanson, and Mrs. Lionel Hampton. Each tear is evaluated and then repaired using one or more of a variety of methods. Because of the labor involved, jobs take much longer than alterations at a local tailor, and can cost anywhere from $50 to $500 (depending on the work needed), but if you're attached to the article, a few days and few extra bucks is a small price to pay for a service that produces such results—and is nearly impossible to find anywhere else.

119 WEST 57TH STREET, ROOM 1406, BETWEEN SIXTH AND SEVENTH AVENUES IN MANHATTAN. Subway: N, Q, R, W to 57th Street. 212-765-4670.

986. *Start your own business at Your Neighborhood Office.* New York is full of entrepreneurs who spend their lives in line at the post office, freelancers who don't leave their apartments for fear of missing a package, and a whole lot of other people who can't afford the cost of office space. Your Neighborhood Office is a genius niche service that caters to these atypical professionals by making available to them the office services that a business needs to survive in this town. It messengers packages, receives mail, writes and prints brochures, sorts, labels and sends out mailings, sends and receives faxes, provides supplies and legal forms, and performs virtually any other office service you could ever need—so you can toil away on your screenplay/business plan/first novel without a care.

332 BLEECKER STREET BETWEEN WEST 10TH AND CHRISTOPHER STREETS IN MANHATTAN. Subway: 1 to Christopher Street-Sheridan Square. 212-989-8303. www.neighborhoodoffice.com.

987. *Get the closet of your dreams from GardeRobe.* GardeRobe is a luxury clothing storage company that fulfills the number-one wish of New Yorkers: more closet space. Clients can store "racks" of clothing (up to fifty items per rack, which also includes a special storage box for accessories and ten shoe boxes) in the temperature-controlled, air-purified, video-monitored GardeRobe loft. The items are photographed, cataloged, and then posted online in the Cyber Closet, where you can search, review, and request items. Items can be requested anytime, as often as you want; they are delivered at no extra charge, within hours, at your convenience, and then get picked up, professionally cleaned with any repairs or alterations needed, and returned to your rack. At $350 per rack, per month, it may sound extravagant to people with a basement or a garage, but consider that it costs over $300 per month for a medium-size storage cube here, and that doesn't come with delivery! GardeRobe's services aren't just for New Yorkers—frequent travelers can use them as a way of keeping the fashion equivalent of a pied-à-terre. *For more information, and to sign up, call 212-255-3047. www.garderobeonline.com.*

988. *Help out Santa and the post office on Christmas.* In the 1920s, inspired by the number of letters they received for Santa, postal workers in New York asked the public to assist them with Operation Santa, inviting them to come to the General Post Office to pick out letters and answer the children's wishes. Today, the post office receives more than 150,000 letters each year, from all over the world, mostly from poor, inner-city kids. All you have to do is go to the post office sometime in December, select as many letters as you want, and fill the children's requests by Christmas Day. (If you don't live in New York, you can still participate by requesting letters from the post office here, or by contacting your local post office to see if it runs a similar charity.) *421 EIGHTH AVENUE AT 33RD STREET IN MANHATTAN. Subway: 1, 2, 3, A, C, E to 34th Street-Penn Station. 212-330-3084. www.operationlettertosanta.com.*

989. Decorate like a TV star at **Props for Today**.

Every hit television show filmed on location in New York City needs props, and no one wants the same props twice. Props for Today takes care of the problem. When Carrie Bradshaw is through with her pillows and David Letterman is done with his couches, Props for Today moves in for the kill, picks up the debris, and sells it to their adoring public. Thanks to moderate prices and helpful tags that detail the merchandise's televised life—which episode of *CSI* or *Saturday Night Live* a piece was used on, say, or which celebrity's behind warmed it up for you—you, too, can decorate your home to resemble the set of your favorite TV show.

330 WEST 34TH STREET BETWEEN EIGHTH AND NINTH AVENUES IN MANHATTAN. Subway: 1, 2, 3, A, C, E to 34th Street-Penn Station. 212-244-9600. www.propsfortoday.com.

990. Enroll in Miss Vera's Finishing School for **Boys Who Want to be Girls**.

The name of this prestigious Manhattan academy says it all. A veteran of the adult entertainment industry and a tireless researcher into the preferences and practices of modern Americans, Miss Vera opened her transvestite's finishing school to boost the confidence of those who feel held back and to polish up the acts of those already living the life. With a faculty of experts to offer individual or group instruction, and with classes that cover everything from walking in heels and applying makeup to focusing a more feminine sexual energy and refining a suitable voice, Miss Vera's school aims to improve every aspect of the "Cinderfella experience." Classes cost between $500 and $4,000 and take place on campus, with occasional field trips around the city.

For more information, class descriptions, and locations, call 212-242-6449 or visit www.missvera.com.

991. Take the **Great Saunter**.

Once a year in early summer, a group of seasoned amblers meets at the South Street Seaport to begin a daylong walk along the entire perimeter of Manhattan. The **Shorewalkers** (see page 238), a nonprofit organization dedicated to the preservation, improvement, and above all, the appreciation of the city's coastal walkways and vistas, have been holding walks, tours, and other events for likeminded city enthusiasts for twenty-five years, and the annual Great Saunter is their greatest adventure. A thirty-two-mile hike taken at a strolling pace, the walk begins at 7:30 a.m. and usually lasts a full twelve hours, moving from the island's southernmost tip up the West Side, around Inwood Hill Park at the northernmost end, along the Harlem River, down the East Side and back to the Seaport by suppertime. Hardened amblers can make the full tour, while part-timers are welcome to join the walk at any point for any length to enjoy the route's beautiful vistas.

For more information and updates on events like the Great Saunter, visit www.shorewalkers.org.

Citizens: Know your subway entertainers!

New York's rambling and irrepressible subway system is a perpetual stage for the most eclectic and prolific cast of buskers and street entertainers in the world. With each train characterized by the neighborhoods and ethnic enclaves along its route (as well as the amount of tourist spots it runs through), each line has its own brand of entertainment, its own set of characters, and its own trademark sights and sounds. The world of busking is a fickle one: while some performers forge careers that span decades, new acts arrive on the scene almost daily; and though there are some amazingly talented types working the MTA circuit, not everybody would agree that a mariachi band clamoring inside a packed commuter train is a good idea. Look out for these stalwarts of the underground scene and judge for yourself:

992. *The Brighton Trumpeter:* An inexhaustible old man with a poor grasp of English, this experienced trumpet player blows traditional, rousing Russian melodies over backing tracks that blare from a CD player strapped to his chest. *Q train.*

993. *Hip-Hop Acrobats:* An impressive duo of athletic kids who get in a subway car, set down a stereo, and perform amazing turns and break dancing moves in the impossibly narrow walkways between seats—all while the train is moving. Their signature move is a linked somersault, during which they grab each other's ankles to form a ball and roll from one end of the car to the other, swerving unerringly past poles and passengers to the sound of "Thriller." *A train.*

994. *Museum Mile Mariachi:* Targeting tourists as their primary audience, this Mexican three-piece has perfected the art of the two-minute fiesta, striking up as the doors close in one station and reaching a passionate climax as the train draws to a halt at the next. They are a tight outfit, from well rehearsed performances to the ornately sequined authentic mariachi jumpsuits. *4, 5, 6 trains.*

995. *Midtown Break-dancers:* If you come upon a circle of people congregated in the concourses of Midtown's bigger terminals, it's probably the crowd surrounding one of the city's teams of break-dancers who commandeer corners of the station to perform elaborate choreographed routines, dressed in matching Adidas jackets, accompanied by loud, old-school hip-hop. *Times Square and Grand Central stations.*

996. *Gospel Barbershop Quartet:* A relic, perhaps, of the soulful subways of the '60s and '70s, this group of beautiful and varied voices reworks classic Motown hits in the barbershop quartet style. When they're performing formally (standing together by a doorway), the spectacle is enthralling; but catching them rehearsing on quiet rides, when they sit apart, move around, and don't even look at each other while they sing and work out new harmonies, is a genuine thrill. *A train.*

Expert contributor: A. J. Jacobs

A. J. Jacobs is a writer and New York native. He is the editor-at-large of *Esquire* and the author of several books, including *The Know-It-All: One Man's Humble Quest to be the Smartest Person in the World*, *The Year of Living Biblically*, and *The Guinea Pig Diaries*. (You can read more about him at www.ajjacobs.com.)

MY FIVE FAVORITE THINGS I LEARNED ABOUT NEW YORK FROM THE ENCYCLOPEDIA:

997. Short story writer **O. Henry** came up with one of the all-time greatest nicknames for New York: ***"Baghdad on the Subway"*** (sometimes misquoted as "Baghdad on the Hudson," after another one of his NYC pet names, "Yaptown on the Hudson"). He meant it as a compliment, referring to the magical, cosmopolitan, and culturally rich city of Scheherazade's *1001 Arabian Nights*. Still, we doubt that the Chamber of Commerce will be adopting it anytime soon.
For more on O. Henry, see entry on Pete's Tavern, page 43.

998. In New York, everyone's got a real-estate horror story. But in 1667, the Dutch engaged in the ***single worst real-estate deal in history***. They traded Manhattan to Britain, in exchange for the South American country of Suriname. However, a bit of the Dutch legacy can still be seen at the **Collegiate School**, an elite secondary school for boys, which is the oldest educational institution in the country (it was founded in 1628). The school mascot is "the Dutchman."
Collegiate is located at the **WEST SIDE COLLEGIATE CHURCH:** *260 WEST 78TH STREET AT WEST END AVENUE IN MANHATTAN. Subway: 1 to 79th Street. www.collegiateschool.org.*

999. With a street, hotel, parkway, bridge, and 300-mile river named after him, **Henry Hudson** is ***one of the city's most popular pre-Revolutionary celebrities***. Unfortunately, he wasn't so beloved by his crewmembers. In 1611, during a voyage up the waters in Canada, his crew mutinied and sent him off to die in a rowboat.
For more activities on the Hudson River, see Chapter 6, "The Great Outdoors."

1000. We all know *The New York Times'* famous motto: "All the News That's Fit to Print." But I actually prefer the paper's slogan from the early twentieth century: "***It will not soil the breakfast cloth.***"
THE NEW YORK TIMES BUILDING *is located at 229 WEST 43RD STREET BETWEEN SEVENTH AND EIGHTH AVENUES IN MANHATTAN. Subway: 1, 2, 3, 7, N, Q, R, W, S to Times Square-42nd Street. 212-556-1234. www.nytimes.com.*

1001. The **Empire State Building** *shrank eighteen feet in 1985*—from 1,472 feet to 1,454—because the old antenna was replaced. That doesn't make the ride—or run—to the top any shorter.

FIFTH AVENUE AT 34TH STREET IN MANHATTAN. Subway: B, D, F, V, N, R, Q, W to 34th Street-Herald Square. 212-736-3100. www.esbnyc.com. For more information, see full entry on page 19. For Empire State Building lights, see page 317. For Empire State Building Run, see page 360.

THE BEST NEW YORK WEBSITES

General Information:

www.hopstop.com
See page 13.

www.lowermanhattan.info
An invaluable Web site devoted to the communities and development of downtown Manhattan, and a great place to find out about new places to go and things to do south of Canal Street.

www.manhattanusersguide.com
See page 365.

www.mta.info
The Web site for the Metropolitan Transit Authority, with maps, schedules, and information about subways, buses, Metro-North, and the Long Island Railroad. You can also check for night and weekend services advisories.

www.nycgovparks.org
The Department of Parks and Recreation Web site, with information on events, facilities and programs in parks in all five boroughs.

www.newyork.timeout.com
The NY annex of the world's most popular what's-on guide. A good place to find out about events around town for the coming week.

www.nymag.com
NYMetro.com, the online version of New York magazine, is hands-down the best source on the web for listings (stores, restaurants, services, museums, parks, etc), information, and addresses. It beats comparable sites for its thoroughness, up-to-date and informative content, and straightforward and user-friendly layout.

www.smalltownbrooklyn.com
This Web site has up-to-date street-by-street listings of Brooklyn storefronts. It also marks where the subways are.

Dining:

www.menupages.com
See page 332.

www.ny.eater.com
Everything you want to know and more on dining out in NYC.

www.opentable.com
Free online reservation service with more than 600 area restaurants.

www.thestrongbuzz.com
News, reviews, and articles and restaurants and food-related events around the city by Andrea Strong (see pages 175–176).

Entertainment:

www.brooklynpaper.com
An excellent resource for finding out about events in Brooklyn, organized by day. Also has a Brooklyn dining guide.

www.cityparksfoundation.org
The Web site for the foundation that organizes programming in city parks. The Web site includes information and events on their programs, including concerts and events, sports, and education. Lots of stuff for kids.

www.freenyc.net
Everything free in New York: Concerts, parties, museums, film screenings, and other events. Updated daily.

www.jimsdeli.com
Information and listings for hotels, Broadways shows, museums, music and dance, nightlife, sports, and other events.

www.nycstreetfairs.com
This is the Web site for Mardi Gras Productions, the company that puts on most of the street fairs around the city. The Web site has a calendar of all their fairs for the current or upcoming season.

www.playbill.com

The best source for information on theater in New York, and online ticketseller. Discounts on tickets, restaurants and hotels are available to members (membership is free).

Miscellaneous & Fun

www.barrypopik.com

Contains information, history, commentary, about New York, edited by Barry Popik, an administrative judge and etymologist credited with discovering the origin of the nickname "the Big Apple."

www.Brokelyn.com

While officially covering thrifty living in the borough of Kings, this extensive site has information on shopping, eating, entertainment, and outings that can be of interest no matter what budget or borough you're in.

www.craigslist.com

See page 300.

www.forgotten-ny.com

See pages 98–99.

www.movie-locations.com

This Web site has a list of movies shot in New York, with places and addresses from them.

www.songlines.com

See page 98.

www.streeteasy.net

Thorough source for all things related to the city's favorite sport, real estate.

www.thebathroomdiaries.com

This site has listings of public restrooms around the world, rated by users. You can search for ones in different neighborhoods in all of the five boroughs.

www.theskint.com

A daily roundup of free and cheap things to do around the city.

www.watsonadventures.com/culture.html

The Web site for this walking tour company (see pages 112–113) issues a monthly online newsletter with lots of New York trivia.

INDEX

A

A60 at 60 Thompson Hotel, 60
ABC Carpet & Home, 247–248
Academy Records & CDs, 276
Accomplice, 104–105
Acker, Merrill, and Condit, 255
acupuncture, 314
Ades, Joe, 362
African Burial Grounds, 107
African Dancing, 306
Aga Kahn, 38
Agata & Valentina, 177
AIA Center for Architecture, 303
AirTrain, 283
Alamo sculpture, 143
Algonquin Hotel, 47
Alice Austen House, 70
Alliance Française, 88, 300
Allen, Mel, 30
Allen, Steve, 31
Allen, Woody, 34, 39, 102, 115, 153
Alma, 61
Alvin Ailey American Dance
   Theater, 148
American Apparel, 318
American Express hq, 139
American Family Immigration
   history center, 19
American Folk Art Museum,
   130–131
American Museum of Natural
   History, 119
   Identification Day, 346
Amsterdam Avenue, overpass, 78,
   144
Amsterdam Billiards, 329
Amy's Bread, 177, 356
Anderson, Scott, 354
Angel Feet, 311–312
Angelika, 40, 158–159
Angel's Share, 198
Annie Hall, 115
Antek, 195–196
Anthology Film Archives, 158
Aphrodisia, 273
Apollo Theater, Amateur Night at,
   45
Apple Store, 320
Aquavit, 197
Aqueduct, 236
arepa, 173
Argosy, 257–258
Arlene's Grocery, 203
The Armory Show, 140
Arms & Armor exhibit, at the Met,
   120

Armstrong, Louis, 112
art, 137–139. *See also specific*
   museums
   graffiti, 139
Arthur Avenue, 187–188
Artichoke, 207
Artisanal, 201
The Artisanal Premium Cheese
   Center, 296
Artists and Fleas, 269
Arturo's, 206
Asia Roma, 201
Asiate, 64
Astor Court at the Metropolitan
   Museum of Art, 137
Astor Court, St. Regis Hotel, 37
Astor, John Jacob, 22, 292
Astroland, 349
Athena Spa, 311
Atlantic Antic, 86
Atlantic Theater, 153
auctions, 143, 282
Audubon Center, 223
Audubon, John James, 22
Austrian cuisine, 196–197
Auto, 251
Ava Lounge, 60
aviation history, 238–239

B

B train over the Manhattan
   Bridge, 69
B-52's, 52
B61, 61
Babbo, 162
Baby Girl's Bubbles & Cleaners,
   321
bagels, 169
bakeries, 114, 163, 170, 172,
   177–178, 188, 195, 200, 333
Baldwin, James, 46
balloons, inflating of Thanksgiv-
   ing Day floats, 91
Balthazar, 164, 308
Balthazar Bakery, 177
BAM, 148
BAMcinématek, 157
Bar 89, 352
Bar Boulud, 163
Bar Jamon, 162
Bar Veloce, 189
Baratz, Richard, 35
barge concerts, 146
Bargemusic, 146
Barnes & Noble, 295
Barneys, 244–245
   Christmas windows, 32
   Warehouse Sale, 246
Barolo, 183

Barrymore, Ethel, 99
Bartók, Bela, 101
basketball, 239
Basta Pasta, 174
Bastille Day Festivals, 88
Batali, Mario, 162
Battery Park City Parks, 211
Battery Park Promenade, 66
Bauman Rare Books, 261
beaches, 225, 234
Beads of Paradise, 296
the Beatles, 144, 147
Beauty Bar, 327
Beaux, Cecilia, 99
Bedford Avenue, 280–281
Beekman Hotel, 58
Behan, Brendan, 154
Bell, Ric, 54–56
Bellows, George, 99
Belly dancing, 306
Belvedere Castle, 73
Belz, Heather, 175
Bemelman, Ludwig, 39, 43, 136
Bemelmans Bar, 136
Beppe, 176, 359
Bergdorf Goodman, 69, 243
   Christmas windows, 32
Berlin Wall, pieces of, 137–138
Berra, Yogi, 30
Berry Park, 63
Best Cellars, wine tastings, 286
B&H Photo, 252
Biancardi's, 187
bicycling activities, 12, 20, 66, 71,
   231–232, 238, 240, 328, 345, 361
   jousting, 361
   through Manhattan, 240
   moonlight, 328
Big, 25
Big Apple Barbeque Block Party,
   86, 165
Big City, 276
Big Nick's, 336
Big Onion Walking Tours, 96
Billy's Antiques & Props, 110
Billy's Bakery, 170
Birdland, 44–45
Birdman of Times Square, 363
Black Label Bicycle Club, 361
Blaue Gans, 196
Bleecker Street, 280
Blessing of the Animals, 345–346
Blessing of the Bikes, 345
Block Beautiful, 99
Bloomfield, April, 176
Bloomie Nails, 283
Bloomingdale's, 244
Blue Hill, 167

Blue 9, 170
Blue Smoke/Jazz Standard, 165
Blue Tree, 251–252
Bluebell Wood, Brooklyn Botanical Gardens, 218
Boat Basin Café, 62
Boathouse, Central Park, 221
Bob Marley and the Wailers, 52, 277
Bobby Wagner Walkway at Carl Schurz Park, 67
Bohemian Hall & Beer Garden, 183
Bonaparte, Napoleon, 266
Books of Wonder, 277
books, used, 273, 278, 292, 309
bookstores, 100, 247, 251, 257, 261, 262, 263, 269, 272, 273, 274–275, 277–278, 293, 295, 341
Borders, 295
Borgatti's, 187
Bottlerocket, 256
Bouley, 163
Bouley Bakery & Market, 163
Bouley, David, 163
Boulud, Daniel, 162-163, 179
Bourne, Jason, 115
Bow Bridge, 75
Bowery Bar, 184
Bowie, David, 145
bowling, 342–343
Branagh, Kenneth, 40
Brazen Head, The, 203
Brazil Day Festival, 89
Bridge Café, 50–51
bridges, 20, 23, 62–63, 67–68, 69, 70–71, 74, 75, 82, 212, 240, 309, 323
Brighton Beach Boardwalk, 79
Broadway City Video Arcade, 343
Broadway Panhandler, 260
Broadway shows, 153–154
    day-of tickets, 28
Broadway Windows, 141
Broken Kilometer, 140
Bronx Zoo, 113, 227
Brooklyn Academy of Music, 148
Brooklyn Botanic Garden, 82, 218–219, 229, 296
Brooklyn Book Festival, 87
Brooklyn Bowl, 343
Brooklyn Brewery, 183
Brooklyn Bridge, 20, 67, 228, 323
Brooklyn Bridge Park, 70, 212, 228
    movies at, 216
Brooklyn Children's Museum, 126–127
Brooklyn Dodgers, 52

Brooklyn Heights Promenade, 66
    watching fireworks from, 27
Brooklyn House Tours, 97–98
Brooklyn Industries, 261
Brooklyn Museum, 121–122
Brown, James, 45
Bryant Park, 81, 215, 217, 228, 230
    bathrooms, 353
    concerts, 217
    movie series, 215–216
Bryant Park Hotel, 185
Bubble Lounge, 184
Bumble & Bumble, 284–285
Bunshaft, Gordon, 55
Burgee, John, 55
burger-of-the-month club, 180
Burgundy Wine Company, 254
Burke, David, 244, 364
Burke in the Box, 244
Burr, Aaron, 50, 132
Burroughs, William, 40
Bush, George H. W., 49
Butterfly Garden, 227
Buttermilk bar, 202

C
C. O. Bigelow, 33–34
cabs, 316
Café Boulud, 163
Café des Artistes, 53–54
Café Doma, 80
Café Lalo, 116
Café Sabarsky, 125, 196
Café Select, 197
Cafeteria, 336
Caine, Michael, 34
Callas, Maria, 147
Campbell Apartment, 24
Campbell, John W., 24
Camper store, 262
cannoli, 48, 85, 357
canoe rides, 224
capture the flag, 105
Caracas, 173
car service, eco-friendly luxury, 361
Carl Schurz Park, 67
Carlyle Hotel, 279
    Woody Allen at, 39
Carnegie Deli, 170, 340
Carnegie Hall, 147
Caroline's, 43–44
carousels, 89, 220, 223
carriage rides, in Central Park, 27–28
the Cars, 52
Carson, Johnny, 31
carved mango flowers, 112
Casa Mono, 162

Casasola, 128
Cassavetes, John, 116
Cates, Phoebe, 251
Cathedral of Saint John the Divine, 21, 213, 345
CBGB, 52
Celebrity path, 218
celebrity sightings, 79
Cellar Bar, Bryant Park Hotel, 185
Cellar Room, The, at 21, 287
cemeteries, 107, 236–237
The Center for Book Arts, 296
Central Park, 27, 217, 228, 230–231, 322
    carriage rides, 27–28
    telescopes in, 334–335
Central Park Drive, 79
Century 21, 244–247
Cha An, 198–199
Champion, Sam, 363
Chang, David, 176
Chanterelle, 168
Chapel of the Seven Tongues, 21
Chappelle, Dave, 44
Charlie Parker Jazz Festival, 211–212
Chase Manhattan Plaza, 139
cheesecake, 169
chefs of New York, 162–167
Chelsea Garden Center, 224
Chelsea Highline, 77
Chelsea Hotel, 39–40
The Chelsea Market, 177–178
Chelsea Piers, 308
Chelsea Piers Golf Club, 347
Chelsea Square, 337
Chelsea Wine Vault, 256
Cher, 114
Cherry Esplanade, 218
chess, 305
    at midnight, 330
Chess Forum, 330
Chess Shop, 330
Chikalicious, 358
Childs, David, 55
The China Institute, 301
Chinatown Ice Cream Factory, 179
Chinatown, night court, 317–318
Chinese food, 186
Chinese New Year, 93
Chinese Scholar's Garden, 219
ChipShop, 203
chocolate, 48, 97, 111, 113, 172, 184, 190, 191, 200, 204, 218, 243, 258–259, 270, 282, 285–286, 356–357
    European, 282
Chocolate Show, 172

Christie's, 143, 282
Christmas tree
    lighting ceremony, Park
    Avenue, 110
    at Rockefeller Center, 32
Christmas windows, 31–32
Christy, Howard Chandler, 54
Chrysler Building, 138
Chumley's, 53
Churchill, Winston, 20, 147
Churrascaria Plataforma Tribeca,
    174
cinema al fresco, 215–216
Cinema Village, 159
cinemas, *see movies*
Cipriani Dolce, 63
Cipriani Downtown, 38
Cipriani, Giuseppe, 38
Cipriani, Harry, 38
Circle Line tour, 23, 73
Citi Field, 30
City Bakery, 200
City Hall Park, 136, 213
City Hall Station, 104
Citywide Blooming Guide, 210
Civic Virtue, 142
Clark, Galahad J. D., 254
classic buildings, 54–56
Clerkenwell, 191
Clinton, Bill, 186
Clinton Diner, 116
clocks, of NYC, 74, 108–109
Cloisters, 71, 121
Cloisters' Medieval Festival, 88
Clothingline, 244
Cloud Nine, 366
clubbing, 324
CMJ Music Marathon, 147–148
Cobble Hill Park, 213
Cocktail Terrace, Waldorf-Astoria, 37
coffee, 111, 116, 158, 189, 213, 231,
    244, 258, 298, 337, 358
Colgate clock, 74
Collegiate School, 370
Collichio, Tom, 176
Colony Records, 273
Coltrane, John, 44, 45
Columbus Circle, 80
comic-book store, 263
Coming to America, 114
Concert Grove Pagoda, 224
Condé Nast Cafeteria, 180–181
Cones, 179
Coney Island, 65, 348–349
Coney Island/Brighton Beach
    Boardwalks, 66
Coney Island–Stillwell Avenue Ter-
    minal, 104

Congee Village, 172
Congo Gorilla Forest, 113, 227
Connie Gretz's Secret Garden, 219
Conrad's bike store, 263
Conservatory Gardens, 221–222
cooking classes, 296–297
Cooper, Paula, 293
Cooper Union, 297
Cooper-Hewitt museum, 86, 122–
    123
Van Corlaer, Anthony, 75
corn maze, Queens Farm
    Museum, 238
Corner Billiards, 329
Corner Bistro, 170
The Corner Bookstore, 278, 293
Cornwall, Dean, 144
corporate art collections, 137–139
costume parade, 80, 91
Count Basie, 44
Counter Bar, 202
country fair, Queens Farm
    Museum, 238
courses, enrichment, 295–303
Coxsone's Music City, 277
Craigslist, 300
Crate and Barrel, 352
Creed, 266
Creed, Olivier, 266
Creperie, 189
crepes, 85, 86, 189
cricket matches, 69
Criminal Courts Building, 317–318
cross-country skiing, 233
Crunch, 327
Culinary Insiders, 179–180
Culkin, Macauley, 25
Cunningham, Michael, 277
cupcakes, 170, 332
Curry in a Hurry, 192
cyclists, 79
Cyclone, Coney Island, 349
D
D train over the Manhattan
    Bridge, 69
Dachshund Festival, 89–90
Dachshund Spring Fiesta, 89–90
Dachtober Fest, 89–90
The Daily Show with Jon Stewart, 31
Dakota, 100, 116
Damon, Matt, 115
Dance Manhattan, 307
DanceSport, 307
dancing, 149, 193, 306–307, 335
Daniel, 163
Danube, 196
Darling, 263–264
Dave, Laura, 277–278

David Burke & Donatella, 364
Davies, Marion, 144
Davis, Miles, 45
Dawat, 192
Dawes, Mani, 175
DB Bistro Moderne, 163, 283
DBGB, 163
De Maria, Walter, 140
De Niro, Robert, 116, 156
Dean & Deluca, 41–42
    noshing at, 285–286
Dean, James, 144
Death Cab for Cutie, 150
Decibel, 205
Del Posto, 162
Delegates Dining Room, 20, 205
Delhi Palace, 192
delicatessens, 170
department stores, 242–245
Depp, Johnny, 354
designer markets, 269
The Deutsches Haus, 301
DeVito, Danny, 55–56
Di Fara, 207
Diamond District, 253–254
Diltz, Henry, 145
DiMaggio, Joe, 30
Dine Around Downtown, 171–172
Dine, Jim, 145
Diner, 205
Di Palo's, 178
disco skaters, 220
Discovery Wines, 256
Dizzy's Jazz Club Coca-Cola, 64
The Djoniba Dancing & Drum
    Centre, 306
Dodd, Coxsone, 277
Dog Beach, 224
Donguri, 199
Doonan, Simon, 32
dosas, 112
Down the Hatch, 184
drawings collection, at the Met, 120
Dream Hotel, 60
drugstores, 33–34, 268, 272, 320,
    366–367
Duane Reade, 320
DuBuffet, Jean, 139
Duchamp, Marcel, 53
DUMBO, Brooklyn, 82–83
DuMont, 182
Duncan, Isadora, 53
Duncan Quinn, 266
Dylan, Bob, 39, 52, 102, 145
E
eagles, bald-headed, 226
Eames, Charles and Ray, 267
Early Bird Walk, Prospect Park, 321

early-bird shopping, 318–319
Earnest Sewn, 287
Earth Room, 140
Ebbets Field, 51–52
Economy Candy, 282
Eddie Davis New Orleans Jazz
    Band, 39
Ed's Lobster Bar, 170
Egidio's Patisserie, 188
Egyptian galleries, at the Met, 120
85 Broad Street, 106
"86 it," origination of phrase, 53
Eighth Avenue "catwalk," 80
Einstein, Albert, 147
El Cid, 194
El Museo del Barrio, 86
El Pote Espanol, 193–194
Elaine's, 34
elephant procession, Queens-
    Midtown Tunnel, 347
Eleven Madison Park, 165
Eli's & The Vinegar Factory, 178
Ellington, Duke, 44, 45
Ellis, Alton, 277
Ellis Island, 19, 66
Ellis Island Museum, 19
Eloise, 25
Emonts, Ann French, 264
Empire Diner, 337
Empire Skate Club, 232
Empire State Building, 19, 76, 81,
    317, 360, 371
Empire-Fulton Ferry State Park, 70
Energy, Result, Workmanship and
    Transportation, 138
English cuisine, 191
Esca, 162
Ess-a-Bagel, 169
Essex Street Market, 178
ethnic eating, 185–199
European & American paintings,
    at the Met, 120
Everyone Says I Love You, 115, 253

F
F Train to Brooklyn, 69
facials, 310–311, 326–327
Faicco's Pork Butcher, 42–43
fairs and festivals, 84–90
Fairway, "cold room," 285
FAO Schwarz, 25, 342
Far Rockaway, 65
Farrow, Mia, 116
fashion, 81
Fashion Institute of Technology,
    129, 302
Fashion Week, 81
FDR Boardwalk, 66
FDR Drive, watching fireworks

from, 26–27
Feast at San Gennaro, 85
Federal Reserve Bank of New York,
    364
ferry, Staten Island, 69, 315
festivals, 84–90
    Brazil Day, 89
    Brooklyn Book, 87
    film, 156–157
    food, 171–172
    Margaret Mead Film and
        Video, 157
    New Directors/New Films, 157
    New York is Book Country, 87
    Ninth Avenue International
        Food, 171
    Pickle Day, 359
    San Gennaro, 85
    Taste of Tribeca Street, 171
    Tribeca Film, 156
Fifth Avenue, Brooklyn, 281
Fifth Avenue, Manhattan, 279
Fifth Avenue Bageltique Café, 340
Fifty-Five (55), 45
film festivals, 156–160
Film Forum, 40, 159
Film Society of Lincoln Center,
    newsletter, 152
Find Outlet, 246
fireworks, Macy's, 26–27
Fisher, Carrie, 116
fishing, 223, 225
    in Harlem Meer, 224
Fitzgerald, Ella, 45
Five Borough Bicycle Club, 231
Five Points, 175
5 Ninth, 182
5Pointz, 139
flea markets, 93–95
Flight 001, 264
Florent, 336
Flower District, 319
Floyd Bennett Field, 238–239
Floyd NY, 204
Flux Factory, 141
Foer, Jonathan Safran, 278
food clubs, 179–180
food delivery, 332, 366
food festivals, 171–172
food focused walking tours,
    96–97
food freebies, 285–286
Forbes Galleries, 123
Forbes, Malcolm, 123
Ford Foundation building, gar-
    dens at, 350
forests, 226
Forgotten NY, 98, 105–106

40 Carrots, 244
40-40 Club, 355
Four Seasons, 47
4 Train into Bronx, 69
Fragrance Garden, 218
Franny's, 207
Fraunces, Samuel, 33
Fraunces Tavern, 33
free concerts, Lincoln Center, 217
Freebird Books, 292
Freeman, Vicki, 175
Freeman's, 203
French cuisine, 189-191
The French Culinary Institute, 297
The French Institute/Alliance
    Française, 88, 301
French-American Reweaving, 367
Frick Collection, 123–124, 136
Frick, Henry Clay, 123–124
Friedman, Ken, 176
frisbee, 240-241
Full Moon, 185, 207
Fulton, Robert, 22

G
galette des rois at Gavroche, 189
galleries
    subterranean art, 103
    West Chelsea, 143
    whispering, 24
Gandhi statue, 214
Gansevoort 69, 336
Gansevoort Market, 331
Gantry Plaza State Park, watching
    fireworks from, 27
Garage, 94
Gard, Alex, 35
Garden of Eden, samples, 285
gardens, 78, 121, 133, 147, 211,
    213, 218, 221, 304
Gardens of Saint John the Divine,
    213
GardeRobe, 368
Gate, 203
Gateway National Park, 238–239
Gavroche, 187–188
Gay Pride Parade, 80, 92
Gehrig, Lou, 30
Gehry, Frank, 180, 267
George Washington Bridge, 68, 74
German cuisine, 196–197
Ghostbusters, 115
Giacometti, 138
Giando on the Water, 62–63
Ginsberg, Allen, 46, 87, 102, 291
Giuliani, Rudolph, 110
Gleason, Jackie, 136
Golden Unicorn, 186
Goldsmith, Lynn, 145

Goldsworthy, Andy, 145
golf courses, 235
Goodfellas, 116
Gotham Chamber Opera, 148
Gotham Writer's Workshop, 297
gourmet food markets, 41–43, 177–178
Gourmet Garage, samples, 285
Governors Island, 71–72
Gowanus Canal, 224–225, 238
graffiti art, 139
Gramercy Park, 210–211
Gramercy Tavern, 166
Grand Central, 23–25, 316
    dark patch on the ceiling, 113
Grant, Cary, 25, 51, 142
Grant's Tomb, 76
graveyards, 236–237
Gray's Papaya, 170, 283, 333
The Great Lawn, 240
The Great Saunter, 238, 369
Great White Way, 317
Greek Captain Fish Market, 196
Greek cuisine, 196
Green-Wood Cemetery, 237
Greenbelt, 228
Greenbelt Nature Center, 228
Greenfinds Ecompassion, 246
Greenflea Market, 94–95
Greenmarket, 95, 165, 334
greenmarkets, 171
Grimaldi's, 20, 206
grocery shopping 24/7, 332
Group of Four Trees, 139
Growler Submarine, 20
Guggenheim Museum, 124, 331
Guggenheim, Peggy, 38
Gutenbrunner, Kurt, 126, 196–197
gyms, 24-hour, 327–328

H
hair, 330
haircuts, free, 284–285
Half King, 354
Half Moon Overlook, 75–76
Halloween Carnival, 89
hamburgers, 170
Hamilton, Alexander, 22, 132
handball, 240
Hangawi, 181
Hanks, Tom, 25
Hannah and Her Sisters, 102, 116
Happy Ending, 294
Harbors of the World, 139
Haring, Keith, 21, 142–143
Harlem Lanes, 343
Harlem Meer, 221
Harriott, Derrick, 277
Harry Cipriani, 38–39

Harry, Deborah, 52
Harry Winston, 115, 253
Hat Shop, 275
hayrides, Queens Farm Museum, 238
Hayworth, Rita, 100
Hearst, William Randolph, 144
helicopter tours, 73
Hemingway, Ernest, 38, 257
Henri Bendel, 243
Hepburn, Audrey, 144, 266
Hermann, Peter, 264
Hess estate plaque, 105–106
Heyman, Art, 355
H&H bagels, 169, 340
High Bridge Water Tower, 70–71
Highline, 72, 77
Hill, Lauryn, 45
Hilton, Conrad, 136
Hoffman, Abbie, 52
Hoffman, Dustin, 100, 115
Hogs & Heifers, 325
Holiday, Billie, 44, 96
Holiday Market, Union Square, 95
holiday shopping, 24-hour, 319
Holmes, Joseph O., 80, 365
Holzer, Jenny, 56
Home, 182
Home Depot, 318
Hood, Raymond, 54
Hop Kee, 186
horse races, 236
horseback riding, 228
hot chocolate month at City Bakery, 200
hot dog eating contest, Coney Island, 94
hot dogs, 66, 111, 170, 185, 202, 237, 333, 349
Hotel Chelsea, 39–40
Hotel Gansevoort, 59
Hotel Metro Rooftop Bar, 59
House Beautiful, 99
House of Oldies, 276–277
houses, of distinction, 101–102
Housing Works, 282
Housing Works Used Book Café, 278, 293, 309
Howl! Festival, 87–88
Hudson, Henry, 370
Hudson Hotel Sky Terrace, 60
Hudson River Park, 212–216
    tennis courts, 328
    watching fireworks from, 27
The Hummus Place, 357
Hungarian Pastry Shop, 80
hybrid, 361

I

IBM Building, 138
Ibsen, Henrik, 154
ice cream, 48, 111, 112, 179–180, 194
ice-skating
    Lasker Rink, 221
    Rockefeller Center, 333
Idlewild Books, 257
IFC Center, 159, 344
igloo, 311
Il Laboratorio Del Gelato, 172
Il Mulino, 188
Independent Film Channel (IFC) Center, 159, 344
Indian food, 192–193
Indian powwow, Queens Farm Museum, 238
Indochine, 47
inline skate braking lessons, 220
inner health, spas, 310–314
Institute of Culinary Education, 96–97
    recreation division of, 297
The Instituto Cervantes, 301
The Interfaith Center, 302
International Cannoli Eating Championship, 85
International Exhibition of Modern Art of 1913, 140
internet access, 215, 309
Intrepid, 20
Inwood Hill Nature Center, 226
Inwood Hill Park, 229
Irish Hunger Memorial, 145
Irish Repertory Theater, 154
Irving, John, 153
Isaacs, Gregory, 277
Italian cuisine, 187–189
Italian Wine Merchants, 257
Ivory, Merchant, 40

J
Jackie Robinson Apartments, 52
Jackson Diner, 192
Jacobs, A. J., 370–371
Jacques Marchais Museum of Tibetan Art, 126, 303
Jacques Torres, 282
Jagger, Mick, 104
Jamaica Bay Riding Academy, 228
Jamaica Bay Wildlife Refuge, 226
The Japan Society, 301
Japanese food, 198–199
The Japanese Swordsmanship Society, 307
Japanese Tea Ceremony, 304
Japanese Village, 351
Jaslowiczanka Bakery, 195
Jay-Z, 355

jazz
  clubs, 44–46
  at Lincoln Center, 150
Jean-Georges and Nougatine, 166
Jewish Children's Museum, 127
The Jewish Community Center, 298
Jimmy's Corner, 354
Jin Soon Salon, 283, 312
Jivamukti, 322
Joan Weill Center for Dance, 149
Joe Allen, 28
Joe, 298
Joe's, 207
Joe's Shanghai, 186
jogging
  over Brooklyn Bridge, 240
John Paul, II (Pope), 106
Johnny's Famous Reef, 226, 325
John's of Bleecker Street, 207
John's of 12th Street, 43
Johnson, Philip, 47, 55
JoJo, 167
Journelle, 258–259
Joyce Theater, 149
Junger, Sebastian, 354
Junior's cheesecake, 169
Juvenex Spa, 309, 326

K
Kalustyan's, 193
Kamwo Herb and Tea Shop, 314
karaoke, 174, 201, 202, 272, 355
Katz's, 1114, 170, 203
Kaufman, Elaine, 34
Kaufman, George, 47
kayaking, 225
kayaking/kayaking lessons, 225
Keaton, Diane, 100, 115
Kennedy, John F., 106
Kee's, 191
Kerouac, Jack, 46, 74, 102
kettle corn, 85
KGB Bar, 294
Kiehl's, samples, 286–287
Kim's Video, 52–53
King Cole Bar, St. Regis Hotel, 36
King, Martin Luther, 147
Kline, Kevin, 251
Knickerbocker, 36
Koolhas, Rem D., 254
de Kooning, Willem, 146
Kripalu, Socrates Sculpture Park, 229
Kristal, Hilly, 52

L
La Belle Epoque, 258
La Casa Day Spa, 310

La Petite Coquette, 258
Ladies Who Launder, 366
Lady Mendl's Tea Salon, 38
Lafayette Smoke Shop, 329
Lafayette's feet, 75
LaGuardia, Fiorello, 142, 292
Landmark Sunshine Cinema, 160, 344
landmarks, no longer with us, 51–54
Landy, Elliot, 145
language classes, 301–302
Larson, Jonathan, 154
Lascoff Apothecary, 268
L'asso, 206
Late Show with David Letterman, 31
Laughing Lotus, 342
laundry facilities, 24/7, 321
lawn sports, 221
L'Express, 339
Le Bernardin, 167–168
lectures, 302–303
Left Bank Books, 262–263
Lenin statue, Red Square building, 106
Lennox Lounge, 44
Lenox, James, 292
Leonard Nimoy Thalia, 160
Lepore, Amanda, 362
Lethem, Jonathan, 294
Letterman, David, 31
Lever House, 55
Lever House Restaurant, 46, 55
LeWitt, Sol, 145
Liberty Helicopter tours, 73
Liberty State Park, 18
Library Walk, 107
Lichtenstein, Roy, 52, 103, 124
Lin Sisters in Chinatown, 314
Lincoln Center, 148, 150–153
Lincoln Center Out of Doors, 217
Lindbergh, Charles, 107
lingerie, fine, 258
Lipstick Building, 55
Liquiteria, 174
literary readings, 290–295
Little Italy, 85
Little Red Lighthouse, 74, 232
The Little Restaurant, 34
Liuzzi, Francisco, 239–240
Live From Lincoln Center, 150
Liz Christy Gardens, 213
Lobby Lounge, 64
lobster rolls, 170
Loews Village 7, 159, 344
Lombardi, Gennaro, 47
Lombardi's, 47–48, 203

"Long Island" sign, 58, 215
Lord & Taylor, Christmas windows, 32
Louis Armstrong House, 112
Lounge at the Pierre Hotel, 37
Lower East Side Girls Club, 206
Lower East Side Tenement Museum, 135
Lowe's, 318
Lucky Cheng's, 174–175
Lucky Strike, 164
Lupa, 162

M
MacMonnies, Frederick, 142
Macy, William H., 153
Macy's
  Christmas windows, 31
  fishing contest, 223
  July 4 fireworks, 26
  Santa at, 346
  Thanksgiving Day Parade, 90
Madeline murals, 39
Madison Avenue, 279
Madison Square Garden, 31
magic shows, 360
Magnolia Bakery, 170, 333
Mailer, Norman, 46
Maison du Chocolat, 190
Mamet, David, 153
Mamoun's, 173
Mandolin Brothers, 252–253
Manducatis, 188
mango flowers, carved, 112
Manhattan Bridge, 68
  walkway of, 82
Manhattan Neighborhood Network, 298–299
Manhattan User's Guide, 365
Manolo Blahnik Store, 250
Mantle, Mickey, 30
Marathon Man, 115
Marcus Garvey Park, 211
Margaret Corbin Drive, 71
Margaret Mead Film and Video Festival, 157
marionette theatre, 350
markets
  designer, 269
  flea, 93–95
  Gansevoort, 331
  gourmet food, 41–43, 177–178
  green, 164, 171, 334
Marley, Bob, 52, 277
Marlow & Sons, 204
Marriott Marquis, 60
Mars Bar, 325
Marsalis, Wynston, 149
martial arts, 307

Masa, 64, 168
Masello, David, 136–137
massage, 285, 305, 310–313, 330
MaxDelivery, 366
Max's Kansas City, 52
McCourt, Frank, 154
McDonough, Martin, 153
McGraw-Hill Building, 54
McGriff, Jimmy, 44
McKim Mead & White, 55
McNally, Keith, 46, 79, 163–164, 177
McNally Jackson, 278
McSorley's Old Ale House, 50
Meatpacking District, 331
meditation sessions, 322–323
menupages.com, 332
Mercer Kitchen, 167
Meriwether, Roy, 44
Mermaid Parade, 91
Met in the Park, 217
Met Weekend Ticket Draw, 289
Metrazur, 63, 78
Metropolitan Museum of Art, 59, 78–79, 114, 119–120, 137
Metropolitan Opera, 151
Meyer, Danny, 165–166
Meyer, Marc, 175
Michael George, 282
Michael's, 49
midday naps, 305
midnight movies, 344
midnight runs, 322
midnight yoga, 342
Midsummer Night Swing, 153, 217
Midtown Comics, 263
Miette Culinary Studio, 298
Mighty Mutts, 110
Milk Bar, 184
Milon, 193
Milonga, South Street Seaport, 323–324
Minetta Tavern, 164
Ming Dynasty, 123, 137
Miracle on 34th Street, 346
Miró, 138
Miss Vera's Finishing School, 369
Mister Softee ice cream, 112
Mitchell, Wendy, 325–326
M&J Trimming, 267
The Modern, 165
Modern Lovers, 52
Molto Mario. See Batali, Mario
MoMA Design Store, 269–270
MoMA (Roy and Niuta Titus Theater), 158
Momofuku, 176
Monday Night Magic, 360

Monk, Thelonius, 45
Monroe, Marilyn, 114
Monument Park, 30
Moody, Rick, 294
moonlight bike ride, 328
Moonstruck, 114
Moore, Clement Clark, 22
Moore, Henry, 78, 144
Morandi, 164
Morningside Park, 215
Morrison Hotel, 145
Moscow on the Hudson, 115
Moses, Robert, 36
the Moth, 290–291
Mount Vernon Hotel and Garden, 102
movies, see also festivals
    Angelika, 158–159
    Anthology Film Archives, 150
    BAMcinematek, 157
    cinema al fresco, 215–216
    Cinema Village, 159
    famous sites, 114–117
    Film Festivals, 156–160
    Film Forum, 159
    Film Society of Lincoln Center, 156
    IFC Center, 159, 344
    independent theaters, 159-160
    Kim's, 52–53
    Leonard Nimoy Thalia, 160
    Loews Village, 344
    midnight, 344
    MoMA (Roy and Niuta Titus Theater), 158
    outdoor, 215–216
    Paris Theater, 40, 344
    The Quad, 160
    Sunshine Landmark Cinema, 40, 160, 344
    Village East, 344
    Walter Reade Theater, 152
    Ziegfeld, 17, 40–41
movie sites, famous, 114–117
MTA Transit Museum, 104, 135
Mud Trucks, 111
Munch, Edvard, 137
Municipal Art Society Walking Tours, 97
Municipal Building, 54–55
Munson Diner, 338
Murals on 54, 144
Murphy, Eddie, 114
Murray's Cheese Shop, 177, 296–297
Museo del Barrio, 128
museum(s), 118–135, 284. See also galleries;

specific museums
    for African Art, 128
    American Folk Art, 130–131
    American Museum of Natural History, 119
        Identification Day, 346
    of Art and Design, 130
    Astor Court at the Metropolitan Museum of Art, 137
    Brooklyn, 121–122
    Brooklyn Children's, 126–127
    of the City of New York, 86, 129
    Cooper-Hewitt, 84, 121–122
    Ellis Island, 19, 70, 71
    Fashion Institute of Technology, 129, 302
    free or pay-what-you-wish day, 284
    free programs, 118–135
    Guggenheim, 84, 124, 331
    highlights tour, at the Met, 119–120
    Jacques Marchais, of Tibetan Art, 126, 303
    Jewish Children's, 127
    Lower East Side Tenement, 135
    Metropolitan, of Art, 59, 78–79, 114, 137
    Mile Festival, 86–87
    of Modern Art, 122, 133, 137, 158
    Mount Vernon Hotel and, 102, 116
    of the Moving Image, 131
    MTA Transit Museum, 103, 135
    New Museum of Contemporary Art, 125
    New York City Fire, 132
    New York City Police, 132
    Noguchi, 133
    Paley Center for Media, 131
    Queens Farm, 238
    Red Hook Waterfront, 134
    Skyscraper, 133–134
    South Street Seaport, 134
    of Tibetan Art, 303
    Whitney, 124
Music Inn, 250
music, outdoor, 216–217
Myers of Keswick, 270
N
N Train over the Manhattan Bridge, 69
Nancy Whiskey Pub, 325
Nathan Hale, rendered in bronze, 136

Nathan's, 66, 170
National Historic Landmarks
   Grand Central Terminal, 23–24
   Little Red Lighthouse, 74
   The Plaza, 25
   Snug Harbor, 147
NBC's *Today Show*, 31
Neergaard, 323
Nelson, George, 267
Neptune, 339
Neue Galerie, 86, 126, 196
New Directors/New Films
   (festival), 152
New Leaf Café, 206
New Museum of Contemporary
   Art, 74, 125
New School, 299
New Year's fun, 323
New York Aquarium, 227
New York Botanical Gardens, 218
New York Cake and Baking Sup-
   ply, 270
New York Central, 270–271
New York Century Ride, 231–232
New York character, 361–362
New York City Ballet, 151
New York City Fire Museum, 132
New York City Marathon, 29, 230
New York City Opera, 151–152
New York City Police Museum, 132
New York City Public Library, 107,
   292
New York Cycle Club, 231
New York Dosa, 112
New York Film Academy, 299
New York Film Festival, 152, 156–
   157
New York Hall of Science, 125, 341
New York Historical Society, 132
New York Knicks, at Madison
   Square Garden, 31
New York Liberty, 31
New York Marathon, 29
New York Open Center, 299, 303
New York Panorama, 77–78
New York Philharmonic, 145, 152
New York Public Library, 292
New York Road Runners Club, 230
New York Sports Club, 327
New York Theater Workshop, 154
New York Transit Museum, 183
New York Times slogan, 370
New York University's School of
   Continuing and Professional
   Studies, 299
Newson, Mark, 46
Next Wave Festival, Brooklyn
   Academy of Music, 148

Nice Matin, 190
nicknames, for NY, 370
night court, in Chinatown,
   317–318
Night Strike, 342
Nightline, 331
night-owl shopping, 318–319
Nike running clinics, 230–231
The 92nd Street Y, 295
Ninth Avenue International Food
   Festival, 171
Nobu, 168
Noguchi, Isamu, 133, 267
Noguchi Museum, 133
Norma's, 287
Norton, Ed, 115, 253
Nutri-FitNYC, 239
the Nuyorican, 291
NYC, after dark, 317, 328, 331
NYC parks, for art, 144

O
O. Henry, 43, 370
O' Keefe, Michael "Buzzy," 61
Oak, 249
Oates, Joyce Carol, 294
O'Brien, Conan, 30, 186
Odeon, 46, 164
O'Donnell, Rosie, 44
Off-Broadway/Off-Off Broadway.
   See Broadway shows
Old Town Bar, 200
Once Upon a Time in America, 117
Ondaatje, Michael, 291
One if by Land, Two if by Sea, 50
192 Books, 293
O'Neill's Irish Bar, 180
OpenHouseNewYork, 71, 72
Opening Ceremony, 250–251
opera, 151
Operation Santa, 368
organic options, 178, 180, 274
Osaka, 310
Otterness, Tom, 145
Otto Enoteca E Pizzeria, 162
Otto gelato cart, 112
outdoor eating, 171–173
outdoor museum, 144–145
outdoor music, 216–217
outdoor pools, 234
Oyster Bar, 25
OZOcar, 361

P
Pale Male and Lola (red-tailed
   Hawks), 348
Paley Center for Media, 131
The Palm, 49–50
palm trees, at Winter Garden, 350
Panna II, 193

Papaya King, 170
parades, 90–93
Paragon, 271
Paris Theater, 40
Park Avenue view, 78
Parker, Charlie, 45, 211–212
Parker, Dorothy, 47
parks and gardens, 210–215
partner dancing, 306
Pasquale's Rigoletto, 188
Pastis, 46, 79, 164, 332
Patricia Field, 260
Paul Molé Barber Shop, 34
Paul Smith Boutique, 262
Payard Patisserie & Bistro, 190
Peaches, 150
Peanut Butter & Co., 357
Pearl River Mart, 259, 351
Pearl Oyster Bar, 170
Peasant, 178
pedal boating, 222–223
Peep, 352
Peking Duck House, 186
Pelaccio, Zak, 182
people watching, 78–81
"Pepsi-Cola" sign, 58, 215
Per Se, 64, 168–169
A Perfect Storm, 354
perfume, 266
Peridance, 306
Periyali, 196
Perry Street, 167
Pétanque, 88
Peter Hermann bag store, 264
Peter Luger steak, 169
Pete's Tavern, 43
Petrossian, 194–195
Philharmonic in the Park, 217
Philips, Ammi, 130
Photography spots, 82–83
PhotoManattan, 300
The Pickle Guys, 359
Pilgrim's Hill, 220
pizza, 20, 47–48, 175, 178, 180, 190,
   202, 206–208, 280, 285, 358
Plant Pigment Weekend, Wave
   Hill, 214
platza, 313
Playbill's official website, 28
playgrounds, 81, 236
The Plaza, 25
poetry, 291
Poetry Project at Saint Mark's,
   291–292
Polar Bear Diner Club, 182
Polish food, 195
Pollack, Jackson, 146
The Polo Grounds, 30, 57

Polshek Partnership, 55
Pommes Frites, 173
pools, 234
Pop Burger, 341
Pop-up hot dog, 185
Porter, Cole, 37
Portrait of Lodovico Capponi, 136
post office, 24/7, 319
Posteritati, 271
posters, vintage, 258
Posy Floral Design, 288
Poznanski's, 195
The Pratt Institute, 300
Pravda, 164
Presley, Elvis, 144
Primo Hats, 260
Printed Matter, 272
Props for Today, 368
Prospect Park, 36, 89, 213, 222–224, 230, 322
Prouve, Jean, 267
PS1 (outpost of Museum of Modern Art), 133
public restrooms, 351–353
The Public Theater, 154
Puff & Pao, 359
Pukk, 352
Pure Food and Wine, 181
Pushcarts, 111

Q
Q Train in Brooklyn, 69
Q Train over the Manhattan Bridge, 69
The Quad, 160
Queens Botanical Gardens, 304
Queens Farm Museum, 238
Quintessentially, 321

R
Radio City Music Hall, 23
Raij, Alexandra, 175
Rairaiken, 199
Raleigh, Sir Walter, 144
Ralph's Italian Ice, 180
Ramones, 52
Rao's, 49
Rare View, 58–59
Rashid, Karim, 267
Raymund's Place, 195
real-estate horror story, 371
record stores, 273, 275–277
Red Hook waterfront, 76
Red Hook Waterfront Museum, 134
reflexology, 305, 311–312, 366
Relish, 200
Remedy, 338
Reminiscence, 248
Renzo Gracie Academy, 307

Restaurant Week, 201
restrooms, 199, 257, 351–353
Rice to Riches, 356
Ricky's, 272
Riley, Ronnette, 55
Risotteria, 358
River Café, 61–62
River to River, 217
Riverbank State Park, 233
RiverFlicks, Hudson River Park, 216
Riverside Church, 73
Riverside Park, 229, 236
Rizzuto, Phil, 30
Roberta Freymann, 260–261
Rock, Mick, 145
rock star photographs, 145
Rockaway Beach, 234
Rockefeller Center (the Rock), 76–77
Rockettes, 23
van der Rohe, Mies, 254
roller-coaster. See Cyclone, Coney Island
roller-disco skating, 220, 224
romance, 27, 66–67, 99–101, 114–115, 182, 184, 185, 326
rooftop bars, 58–60
Rooftop Films, 216
Rooftop sculpture garden, at the Met, 121
Roosevelt, Franklin Delano, 24
Roosevelt Island, 67, 74, 237
tram ride, 70
Rosati, Pavia, 308
Rose Center for Earth and Space, 119
Rose Reading Room at the New York Public Library, 309
Rosemary's Baby, 116
Rosenthal, Bernard "Tony," 143
Rotunda, Pierre Hotel, 37
rowboating, in Central Park, 219
Royal Palace Baths, 312
Ruby's, 66, 170
Rudy's Bar & Grill, 202
Ruiz, Rosie, 29
Rumsey Playing Field, Self Workout in the Park, 235
running
midnight, 322
Nike, clinics, 230–231
Rushdie, Salman, 295
Ruskin, Mickey, 52
Russ & Daughters, 42
Russian and Turkish Baths, 312
Russian food, 194–195
Russian Vodka Room, 195
Ruth, Babe, 30

Rutherford Observatory, 65
Ryan, Meg, 116

S
Sable's, 252
Sacco, 249
Sahadi's, 86, 178
sailing, 134, 226
Saint John the Divine (cathedral), 21
Saint Patrick's Old Cathedral, 21
Outdoor Market, 95
Sakagura, 353
Saks Fifth Avenue, Christmas windows, 32
A Salt and Battery, 191
salt scrubs, 312
Salon de Ning, 58
sample sales, 245–246
Sandra Cameron, 306
The Sandra Cameron Dance School, 306
Santa, at Macy's, 346
SantaLand, 31
Sante, Luc, 294
Santos Party House, 355
Sardi, Vincent, 34
Sardi, Vincent Jr., 35
Sardi's, 34–35
Saturday Night Fever, 114
Sava Spa, 311
Say Cheese, 356
Scandinavia House, 198, 302
Scandinavian cuisine, 197–198
scavenger hunts, 104–105
Schein, Françoise, 108
Schiller's Liquor Bar, 164
The School of Visual Arts, 300
sculptures, spinning, 143–144
Sedaris, David, 295
Seinfeld, Jerry, 44, 337–338
Self Workout in the Park, 235
Sephora, 317, 319
Serendipity, 48, 164
The Seven Year Itch, 114
7 Train to Queens, 68
7WTC, 55–56
Sex Pistols, 52
Shade To Go, 189
Shake Shack, 30, 166
Shakespeare in the Park, 73, 155
Shanghai Pavilion, 186
Shankar, Ravi, 147
Shearwater, 73
sheep-shearing demo, 238
Sheik, Duncan, 153
Sherry-Netherland, 38–39
Sherwood Café/Robin des Bois, 182
shiatsu, 310

the Shins, 150
shopping, 242–289, see also
    specific stores
    early bird, 318–319
    excursions, 278–282
    night-owl, 318–319
Shorewalkers, 238, 369
Siberia, 326
Silver Lining, 265
Sinatra, Frank, 20
Siren Music Festival, 150
60 Thompson Hotel, 60
Skate Patrol Stopping Clinic, 220
skating, 220
    off hours, 333
    at Rockefeller Center, 33
Skidmore Owings & Merrill, 55
Skyline Books, 273
Skyscraper Museum, 133
sleepover parties, 341–342
S'MAC, 358
Smith & Wollensky steak, 169
Smith, Hildegarde H., 74
Smith, Patti, 52, 290
Smith, Paul, 262
Smorgas Chef, 198
Snug Harbor, 147
Snug Harbor Cultural Center, 147
Socrates Sculpture Park, 142, 229
Songlines, 98
The Sorrow and the Pity, 160
Sotheby's, 143, 282
South Street Seaport, 73
    Museum, 134
Southpaw, 334
Spa Castle, 313
Spa 88, 313
The Spa at the Mandarin Oriental,
    283
Spanish cuisine, 193–194
spas, 282, 283, 310–314
Spears, Britney, 354
Spice Market, 167
Spin, 329–330
The Spotted Pig, 176
Springsteen, Bruce, 52
Spuyten Duyvil Shorefront Park,
    75
St. Mark's Bookshop, 198, 341
St. Nick's Pub, 45
St. Patrick's Cathedral, 21
St. Vincent Millay, Edna, 102
Stapleton, Maureen, 35
Starck, Phillippe, 267
Staten Island Botanical Garden,
    219
Staten Island Ferry, 69, 316
Staten Island Yankees game, 113

Statue of Liberty, 18, 66
steaks, 169
Steinway Factory Tour, 364
Steinway Hall, fan mail at, 363
Stepping Out, 307
Stern, Amanda, 294
Sterner, Frederick J., 99
Steve's Key Lime Pie's, 172–173
Stewart, Jon, 31
Stilettos (band), 52
Stolovaya, 194
stoop sales, 96
Storm, The, 137
StoryCorps, 303–304
storytelling, 290–291
Strawberry Fields, 107–108
Street Fair Massages, 85
street fairs and festivals, 85–90
street food, 111–112
Street Vendor Project, 361
StreetWars, 105
Streit Matzo Factory, tastings, 286
Strong, Andrea, 175–176
Studio Museum of Harlem,
    129–130
Stuffed Artisan Cannolis, 357
Stylowa, 194
subterranean art gallery, 104
The subway, 68–69, 83, 103–105
    biggest map of, 108
    and subway stations, 103–104
    system of, 84
Subway Inn, 326
Sullivan, Ed, 31
Sullivan Street Bakery, 178
summer movie series, 215–216
Summerstage, 217
Sunken Plaza, 139
Sunrise Mart, 198
The Sunshine Landmark Cinema,
    40, 160, 344
surfing, 234
Swedish Cottage Marionette The-
    ater, 350
Sweet Things Bake Shop, 206
swimming, 234, 298, 313
Symphony Space, 160, 294–295
Synge, J. M., 154

T
Tabla Restaurant and Bread Bar,
    166
Tai Chi, 142, 229–230
Takashimaya, 245
The Taking of Pelham One Two
    Three, 116
talk shows, late night, 31
tango socials, 324
Tannen Magic Superstore, 274

Tarallucci e Vino, 189
Taste of Tribeca Street Festival, 171
Tatiana, 194
Tavern on the Green, 35–36
Taylor, Elizabeth, 144
Tea and Sympathy, 191
tea ceremonies, 304
Tea time, 36–38
Team Joe, 231
Television (band), 52
Temple of Dendur, 120
10 Downing Street, 102
Teresa's, 183
Terrace, 61
Terrace in the Sky, 61
Thalia theatre, 115
The Adore, 204
theaters, 40–41, 45, 115, 147,
    148–149, 150–160, 348, 350,
    365. See also cinemas
TheMarketNYC, 269
Thomas, Dylan, 40, 46, 154
Thompson, LaMarcus A., 349
Thompson Street playground, 81
Three Lives and Company,
    277–278
Three Way Piece sculpture, 78, 144
Tia Pol, 175
The Tibet House, 302–303
Tierney, Tom, 248
Tiffany, 26
Time Warner Center, 64, 168
Times Square, 83
    Birdman of, 363
TKTS booths, 28
Tolle, Brian, 145
Tom & Jerry, 202
Tomoe Sushi, 199
Tompkins Square Park Courts,
    239–240
Tom's Restaurant, 338–339
Tonight Show, 31
Tracey J's, 355
trains, 68–69
Transit Museum, 104
transvestite finishing school, 369
Trapeze School, 234
Travolta, John, 114
Tribeca Film Festival, 156
Trinity Cemetery, 22
Trinity Church, 22, 107
Trixie and Peanut, 254
Trump World Tower, 288
Tudor City Gardens, 213
tugboat race, 359
Turnbull, Edward, 138
Turtle Pond, 219
Twain, Mark, 33, 40, 214

21 Club, 287, 324
24/7 Fitness Club, 327
24-hour drugstores, 320
24-hour eating, 335–341
24-hour fun, 316–344
24-hour Village Copier, 335
25th Street Market/Garage, 94

U
Umberto's, 188
unicorn tapestries, Cloisters, 121
Union Square Café, 166
Union Square Greenmarket, 171, 334
Union Square Park, 229
United Nations, 20
    tour, 20
United Nude, 254
Urasenke Chanoyu, 304
Ursus, 274
US Helicopter, 283
U.S. Open, 29–30
USA Shaolin Temple, 308
ushering, for performances, 155

V
Vale of Cashmere, 223
Van Cortlandt Park, 214, 235
Vanderbilt, Cornelius, 243
Vandewoude, Paul, 298
vegetarian options, 111, 162, 180, 202, 208, 339, 352, 358
Velvet Underground, 52
vendors, at Union Square, 110
Vendy Awards, 360–361
Veniero's, 48
    cheesecake, 169
Verrazano-Narrows Bridge, 29, 68
Veselka, 339
View Lounge, 60
Village Cigar Shop, 105
Village Copier, 335
Village East Cinema, 344
Village Halloween Parade, 92–93
Village Halloween Party, 92
Village Vanguard, 45
Village Yokocho, 198
vintage, 93, 248-249, 250, 251, 280–282
Virgin Megastore, 275
Vitra Design Store, 267
Viva Herbal Pizzeria, 208
Vong, 167
Vongerichten, Jean-Georges, 166–167, 179

W
Wagner Park, 65
Waldorf-Astoria, 353
Walter Reade Theater, 156, 157
Walk into the New Year, 323

Walker, Alice, 291
walking tours, 96–99, 145, 321
Walkway of Manhattan Bridge, 82
Wall of Honor, 19
wallball, 240
Wallsé, 196
Warhol, Andy, 40, 48, 52
Warwick Hotel, 144
Washington, George, 22, 33, 50, 132
Washington Mews, 189
Washington Square Art Show, 146
Washington Square Hotel, 39
Washington Square Park, 305
Water Club, 62
Water Taxi Beach, 72
Water's Edge, 62
Waters, John, 88
Waterston, Sam, 102, 116
Watson Adventures, 112–113
    scavenger hunt, 104
Watson, Bret, 112–113
Wave Hill, 214, 230
Waverly Restaurant, 338
Weaver, Sigourney, 99
weddings
    Empire-Fulton State Park, 70
    on board the *Intrepid*, 21
    Tavern on the Green, 35
Wednesday Night Skate, 233
Welles, Orson, 38
West 4th Street Courts, 239–240
West Indian-American Day Parade & Carnival, 91
What Comes Around Goes Around, 248–249
When Harry Met Sally, 114
Whisker's Holistic Pet Care, 274
whispering gallery, 24
White Horse Tavern, 46
Whitney Museum, 124
Whole Foods, 71
Wiest, Dianne, 116
Wilde, Oscar, 266
Williams, Robin, 115
Williams, Tennessee, 154
Williamsburg Bridge, 309
Williams-Sonoma, samples, 285
Williamsburg mini-mall, 259–260
Wilson, Woodrow, 147
wine, 161, 254–255
Winnie's, 202
Winter Garden, 215, 350
wireless internet access, 215, 309, 350
Wo Hop, 340
de Wolfe, Elsie, 38
Wollman Rink, 224

carnival, 220
Wonder, Stevie, 45
Wonder Wheel, at Coney Island, 65
Woodlawn Cemetery, 237
Working Girl, 99
World Bar, 288

X
Xicala, 193

Y
Yaffa Café, 181–182
Yajirobei, 198
Yankee Clipper, 226
Yankee Stadium, 30, 113
Yeah Yeah Yeahs, 150
yoga, 228, 230, 284, 300, 322–323, 342
    at Bryant Park, 228
    at Greenbelt Nature Center, 228
    midnight, 342
Yoghurt Place II, 357
Yonah Schimmel, 172
Your Neighborhood Office, 367
You've Got Mail, 116
Yo-Yo Open, 363

Z
Zabar, Eli, 178
Zabar, Lillian, 42
Zabar, Louis, 42
Zabar's, 42, 178
Zeffirelli, Franco, 40, 151
Ziegfeld, Florenz, 41
Ziegfeld Theater, 17, 40–41
Zigun, Dick D., 349
ZogSports team, 236
Zoomie's biscuit bar, 267

BY NEIGHBORHOOD

BRONX

CITY ISLAND
The Great Outdoors
sailing, 226
24-Hour Fun
Johnny's Famous Reef, 325

FORDHAM/BELMONT/
BEDFORD PARK
Eating & Drinking
Arthur Avenue, Italian cuisine on, 187–188
Biancardi's, 187
Borgatti's, 187
Egidio's Patisserie, 188
Full Moon, 207
Pasquale's Rigoletto, 188
Umberto's, 188
The Great Outdoors
Bronx Zoo, 227
New York Botanical Gardens, 218
On the Street & Underground
Bronx Zoo, 113
HIGHBRIDGE
Views & Sights
4 Train (view of Yankee Stadium), 69

RIVERDALE
The Great Outdoors
Wave Hill, 214
Wave Hill, Tai Chi, 230

VAN CORTLANDT PARK
The Great Outdoors
cricket matches, 214
Mosholu Golf Course, 235
Van Cortlandt Golf Course, 235

WOODLAWN
The Great Outdoors
Woodlawn Cemetery, 237

BROOKLYN

BAY RIDGE
Bargains & Splurges
Century 21, 247
On the Street & Underground
86th Street strut (Travolta in SNF), 114
Views & Sights
Verrazano Bridge, 29, 68
BOERUM HILL

On the Street & Underground
Atlantic Antic, 86
Williamsburg Bank Building's clock, 109

BRIGHTON BEACH
Eating & Drinking
Stolovaya, 194
Tatiana, 194
Views & Sights
Brighton Beach boardwalk, 66

BROOKLYN HEIGHTS
Arts & Culture
MTA Transit Museum, 135
The Classics
Brooklyn Bridge, 20
Brooklyn Heights Promenade, 66
Eating & Drinking
Bridge Cafe, 50–51
Chip Shop, 203
Floyd NY, 204
Grimaldi's, 206
Sahadi's, 178
Teresa's, 183
The Great Outdoors
Brooklyn Bridge, 228
Brooklyn Bridge Park, 212
Brooklyn Bridge Park, movies, 216
Brooklyn Bridge Park, yoga classes, 228
Beautiful Blocks, 99
On the Street & Underground
Brooklyn Heights Promenade, 66
house tours, 66
Views & Sights
Brooklyn Bridge, 67
Brooklyn Bridge Park, 70
Brooklyn Heights Promenade, 66
promenade, 66

CARROLL GARDENS/
COBBLE HILL
Eating & Drinking
Brazen Head, The, 203
Sherwood/Robin des Bois, 182
Enrichment & Renewal
Freebird Books, 292
The Great Outdoors
Cobble Hill Park, 213
Gowanus Canal, 224–225
Gowanus Dredgers Canoeing Club, 224–225
On the Street & Underground
Bastille Day, 88
Café Naidre's, 114
Moonstruck Cafe, 114
24-Hour Fun

Neergaard Pharmacy, 323

CLINTON HILL/FORT GREENE
Enrichment & Renewal
Pratt Institute, 300
24-Hour Fun
Pratt Institute, 323

CONEY ISLAND
Arts & Culture
Siren Music Festival, 150
The Great Outdoors
New York Aquarium, 227
Only in New York
Astroland, 349
Coney Island, 348–349
Nathan's Hot Dog Eating Contest, 349
On the Street & Underground
Mermaid Parade, 91
Stillwell Avenue station, 104
Views & Sights
Coney Island boardwalk, 66
Wonder Wheel, 65

CROWN HEIGHTS
Arts & Culture
Brooklyn Children's Museum, 126–127
Jewish Children's Museum, 127
Enrichment & Renewal
Brooklyn Botanic Garden, 296
The Great Outdoors
Brooklyn Botanic Garden, 218–219
Views & Sights
Brooklyn Botanic Garden, 82

DOWNTOWN BROOKLYN
Arts & Culture
Brooklyn Academy of Music, 148
Bargains & Splurges
Brooklyn Museum, 121–122
Eating & Drinking
Franny's, 207
Junior's Cheesecake, 169
On the Street & Underground
West Indian-American Day Parade & Carnival, 91

DUMBO
Arts & Culture
concert on the barge, 146
On the Streets & Underground
Once Upon a Time in America, 117
Views & Sights
Empire State - Fulton Ferry Park (Brooklyn Bridge Park), 70

Manhattan Bridge, 68
River Café, 61–62

DYKER HEIGHTS
The Great Outdoors
Dyker Beach Golf Course, 235

GREENPOINT
Eating & Drinking
Antek, 195–196
Brooklyn Brewery, 183
Poznanski's, 195
Raymund's Place, 195
Stylowa, 194

MARINE PARK
The Great Outdoors
golf, 232

MIDWOOD
Eating & Drinking
Di Fara, 207

PARK SLOPE
Bargains & Splurges
Fifth Avenue (shopping excursion), 279–281
Eating & Drinking
Buttermilk bar, 202
Chip Shop, 203
Gate, 203
On the Street & Underground
beautiful blocks, 99
24-Hour Fun
Fifth Avenue Bageltique Cafe, 340
Neergaard Pharmacy, 323
Southpaw, 334
Views & Sights
Lafayette statue at Prospect Park West, 75

PROSPECT PARK
The Great Outdoors
carousel, 223
Concert Grove pagoda, 224
Dog Beach, 224
forest/hiking, 226
Macy's fishing contest, 223
pedal boating, 222–223
Vale of Cashmere, 223
Wollman Rink, 224
On the Street & Underground
Halloween Carnival, 89
24-Hour Fun
Audubon Center, 321
Prospect Park, 321

RED HOOK
Arts & Culture
Red Hook Waterfront Museum, 134
Eating & Drinking
Steve's Key Lime Pies, 172–173
The Great Outdoors
Red Hook waterfront, 76

SHEEPSHEAD BAY/MILL BASIN
The Classics
Jamaica Bay Riding Academy, 228
Enrichment & Renewal
Royal Palace Baths, 312
The Great Outdoors
fishing, 222

SUNSET PARK
The Great Outdoors
Green-Wood cemetery, 237
24-Hour Fun
Lowe's, 318

WILLIAMSBURG
Bargains & Splurges
Artists and Fleas, 269
Bedford Avenue (shopping excursion), 280–281
Oak, 249
Williamsburg mini-mall, 259–260
Eating & Drinking
Caracas, 173
Diner, 205
DuMont, 182
Peter Luger, 169
Relish, 200
Enrichment & Renewal
Williamsburg Bridge, 309
Only in New York
Black Label Bicycle Club, 361
24-Hour Fun
Brooklyn Bowl, 343
Views & Sights
Giando on the Water, 63

MANHATTAN

CENTRAL PARK
Arts & Culture
Delacorte Theater, 155
The Classics
horse drawn carriage rides, 27–28
Tavern on the Green, 35–36
The Great Outdoors
amusement park at Victorian Gardens, 220
Boathouse, 221

carousel, 220
Central Park Loop, biking, 240
Conservatory Gardens, 221–222
cross-country skiing, 233
disco skaters, Bandshell, 220
Fishing, Harlem Meer, 222
The Great Lawn, 240
The Great Lawn, frisbee, 240
Lasker Rink, 221
lawn sports, 221
Nike free running clinics, 230–231
rowboating, 219
Rumsey Playing Field, 235
Sheep Meadow, 233
Skate Patrol Stopping Clinic, 220
skating, Lasker Rink, 221
Summerstage, 217
Tai Chi, 229–230
Turtle Pond, 219
yoga classes, 228–229
Only in New York
Swedish Cottage Marionette Theater, 350
On the Street & Underground
reservoir, 115
Strawberry Fields, 107–108
24-Hour Fun
telescope viewing, 334–335
Views & Sights
Belvedere Castle, 73
Bow Bridge, 75
Central Park Drive, 79

CHELSEA
Arts & Culture
Atlantic Theater, 153
galleries, 143
Irish Repertory Theater, 154
Joyce Theater, 149
Museum of the Fashion Institute of Technology, 129
Bargains & Splurges
Academy Records & CDs, 276
Barnes & Noble, 295
Barneys Co-op, 244–245
Barneys Warehouse Sale, 246
Burgundy Wine Company, 254
Chelsea Wine Vault, 256
Find Outlet, 246
Flower District, 319
Printed Matter, 272
25th Street Market/Garage, 94
The Classics
Chelsea Hotel, 39–40
Eating & Drinking
Basta Pasta, 174
Billy's Bakery, 170
The Chelsea Market, 177–178

Chocolate Show, 172
Del Posto, 162
El Cid, 194
Gavroche, 189–190
Tia Pol, 175
Enrichment & Renewal
192 Books, 293
The Center for Book Arts, 295
Chelsea Piers, 308
Museum at the Fashion Institute
   of Technology, 302
Stepping Out, 307
The Great Outdoors
Chelsea Garden Center, 224
Hudson River Park, 212
RiverFlicks at Hudson River Park,
   216
Only in New York
Chelsea Piers Golf Club, 347
The Half King, 354
24-Hour Fun
Cafeteria, 336
Chelsea Square, 337
Empire Diner, 337
Views & Sights
Chelsea Highline, 77

CHINATOWN
Bargains & Splurges
Greenfinds/Ecompassion, 246
Oak, 249
Posteritati, 271
Eating & Drinking
Asia Roma, 201
Chinatown Ice Cream Factory, 179
Golden Unicorn, 186
Hop Kee, 186
Joe's Shanghai, 186
Peking Duck House, 186
Santos Party House, 355
Winnie's, 202
Enrichment & Renewal
Kamwo Herb and Tea Shop, 314
Lin Sisters, 314
On the Street & Underground
Chinese New Year Celebration, 93
24-Hour Fun
night court, 317–318
Wo Hop, 340

EAST VILLAGE
Arts & Culture
Alamo, 143
Anthology Film Archives, 158
New York Theater Workshop, 154
The Public Theater, 154
Kim's Video, 52–53
Village East Cinema, 344

Bargains & Splurges
Academy Records & CDs, 276
Alphabet City Wine Company, 255
Discovery Wines, 256
Kiehl's, 286–287
New York Central, 270–271
Whisker's Holistic Pet Care, 274
The Classics
McSorley's Old Ale House, 50
Veniero's, 48
Eating & Drinking
Angel's Share, 198
Bowery Bar, 184
Caracas, 173
Cha An, 198–199
Counter, 202
DBGB, 163
Decibel, 205
Five Points, 175
Indochine, 47
John's of 12th Street, 43
Liquiteria, 174
Lucky Cheng's, 174–175
Milk Bar, 184
Milon, 193
Momofuku, 176
Panna II, 193
Pommes Frites, 173
Rairaiken, 199
A Salt and Battery, 191
Sunrise Mart, 198
Sweet Things Bake Shop, 206
Tarallucci e Vino, 189
Teresa's, 183
Tom & Jerry, 202
Veniero's cheesecake, 169
Village Yokocho, 198
Viva Herbal Pizzeria, 208
Yaffa Café, 181–182
Enrichment & Renewal
KGB Bar, 294
Nuyorican, 291
Peridance, 306
Russian and Turkish baths, 312
Saint Mark's Church in the Bow-
   ery, 291
The Great Outdoors
Tomkins Square Park Courts,
   239–240
Only in New York
Cha An, 351
Chikalicious, 358
Hummus Place, 357
Pukk, 352
S'MAC, 358
On the Street & Underground
Allen Ginsberg's stoop, 102
Howl! Festival, 87–88

24-Hour Fun
Corner Billiards, 329
Crunch (Lafayette Street location),
   327
St. Mark's Bookshop, 341

ELLIS ISLAND
Ellis Island, 19

FINANCIAL DISTRICT
Arts & Culture
Battery Park City, outdoor
   museum, 144–145
Chase Manhattan Plaza, 139
85 Broad Street, 106
Harbors of the World, 139
Nathan Hale statue, City Hall Park,
   136
New York City Police Museum,
   132
sculpture, Chase Manhattan Plaza,
   139
Skyscraper Museum, 133
South Street Seaport Museum,
   134
Bargains & Splurges
Century 21, 247
J&R, 265–266
The Classics
Bridge Café, 50–51
Fraunces Tavern, 33
Municipal Building, 54–55
7WTC, 56
Trinity Church, 22
Eating & Drinking
Dine Around Downtown, 171–172
Smorgas Chef, 198
Enrichment & Renewal
Spa 88, 313
The Great Outdoors
Battery Park City Parks, 211
City Hall Park, 213
Downtown Alliance, 215
Hudson River Park, 212, 216, 378
Only in New York
Federal Reserve Bank of New York,
   364
Winter Garden, 350
On the Street & Underground
African Burial Grounds, 107
Canyon of Heroes, 106
City Hall Station, 104
New York Sun Clock, 109
River to River festival, 217
sidewalk clock, 109
24-Hour Fun
Milonga, South Street Seaport,
   323–324

Views & Sights
Battery Park Promenade, 66
Liberty Helicopter Tours, 73
Shearwater, 73
South Street Seaport, 73
Wagner Park, 65

GREENWICH VILLAGE & WEST VILLAGE
Arts & Culture
Broadway Windows, 141
Cinema Village, 159
Film Forum, 159
Forbes Galleries, 123
IFC Center, 159
Kim's, 52–53
New York City Fire Museum, 132
The Quad, 160
Washington Square Art Show, 146
Bargains & Splurges
Aphrodisia, 273
Bleecker Street (shopping excursion), 280
Darling, 263–264
Flight 001, 264
Gray's Papaya, 2
House of Oldies, 276–277
Jacques Torres, 282
Left Bank Books, 262–263
Music Inn, 250
Myers of Keswick, 270
Three Lives and Company, 277–278
Zoomie's biscuit bar, 267
The Classics
Chumley's, 53
C.O. Bigelow, 33–34
Faicco's Pork Butcher, 42–43
One if by Land, Two if by Sea, 50
Village Vanguard, 45
Washington Square Hotel, 39
White Horse Tavern, 46
Eating & Drinking
Babbo, 162
Blue Hill, 167
Café Select, 197
Cones, 179
Corner Bistro, 170
Down the Hatch, 184
Gray's Papaya, for hotdogs, 170
Home, 182
Il Mulino, 188
Joe's pizza, 207
John's of Bleecker Street, 204
Lupa, 162
Magnolia Bakery, 170
Mamoun's, 173
Minetta Tavern, 164

Otto Enoteca E Pizzeria, 162
Pearl's Oyster Bar, 170
Perry Street, 167
A Salt and Battery, 191
Shade To Go, 187
The Spotted Pig, 176
Tea and Sympathy, 191
Tomoe Sushi, 199
Wallse, 196
Enrichment & Renewal
AIA Center for Architecture, 303
Angel Feet, 312
The Deutsches Haus, 301
Miette Culinary Studio, 298
Murray's, 296–297
USA Shaolin Temple, 308
Washington Square Park, 305
The Great Outdoors
kayaking on the Hudson, 225
Laughing Lotus, rooftop yoga classes, 342
West 4th Street and Sixth Avenue, wallball, 246
West 4th Street Courts, 239–240
Only in New York
Hummus Place, 357
Peanut Butter & Co., 356–357
Puff & Pao, 359
Risotteria, 358
Union Jack at 10 Downing Street, 102
Your Neighborhood Office, 367
On the Street & Underground
Dachsund Festival, 89–90
Greenflea Market, 94–95
Isaacs-Hendricks House, 102
New York Dosa cart, 112
Otto Gelato Cart, 112
PrideFest, 92
75½ Bedford Street, 102
Village Halloween Parade, 92–93
Washington Square North, 100–101
24-Hour Fun
Chess Forum, 330
Chumley's, 53
The IFC Center, 344
Magnolia, 176, 333
Village Chess Shop, 305
Waverly Restaurant, 338
Views & Sights
Café Doma, 80

HARLEM, EAST HARLEM & MORNINGSIDE HEIGHTS
Arts & Culture
Crack is Whack!, 142
Museo del Barrio, 128

Museum of the City of New York, 86, 129
Bargains & Splurges
Fairway cold room, 285
The Classics
Apollo Theater, 45
Cathedral of Saint John the Divine, 21, 213
Lenox Lounge, 44
Rao's, 49
St. Nick's Pub, 45
The Great Outdoors
Gardens of Saint John the Divine, 213
Marcus Garvy Park, 212
Morningside Park, 213
Only in New York
Cathedral of Saint John the Divine, 345
24-Hour Fun
Baby Girl's Bubbles & Cleaners, 321
Harlem Lanes, 343
Tom's Restaurant, 338–339
24-hour Village Copier, 335
Views & Sights
Amsterdam Avenue Overpass, 78
Grant's Tomb, 76
Hungarian Pastry Shop, 80
Riverside Church, 73
Rutherford Observatory, 65
Terrace in the Sky, 61
Three Way Piece, 78

INWOOD
Arts & Culture
Cloisters, 21, 121
Eating & Drinking
New Leaf Café, 206
The Great Outdoors
Inwood Hill Nature Center, 226
Inwood Hill Park, yoga classes, 229
Views & Sights
Cloisters, 71, 121
Margaret Corbin Drive, 71

LIBERTY ISLAND
Statue of Liberty, 18

LITTLE ITALY/NOLITA
Arts & Culture
New Museum of Contemporary Art, 125
Bargains & Splurges
Creed, 266
Find Outlet, 246
TheMarketNYC, 269
United Nude, 254

The Classics
Lombardi's, 46–47
Eating & Drinking
L'asso, 206
DiPalo's, 178
On the Street & Underground
San Gennaro, 85
Saint Patrick's Old Cathedral
    Outdoor Market, 95
Only in New York
Rice to Riches, 356

LOWER EAST SIDE
Arts & Culture
Gotham Chamber Opera, 148
Lower East Side Tenement
    Museum, 135
Landmark Sunshine Cinema, 160,
    344
Bargains & Splurges
Economy Candy, 282
Essex Street Market, 178
Patricia Field, 260
Streit Matzo Factory, 286
The Classics
Russ & Daughters, 42
Eating & Drinking
Arlene's Grocery, 203
Congee Village, 172
Creperie, 189
Freeman's, 203
Il Laboratorio Del Gelato, 172
Katz's, 114, 170, 203
The Pickle Guys, 359
Remedy, 338
Schiller's Liquor Bar, 164
Stuffed Artisan Cannolis, 357
Yonah Schimmel, 172
Enrichment & Renewal
Happy Ending, 294
The Great Outdoors
Liz Christy Gardens, 213
On the Street & Underground
Billy's Antiques & Props, 110
Lenin statue, Red Square Building,
    106
24-Hour Fun
American Apparel, 318
CBGB, 52
Landmark Sunshine Cinema, 344
Mars Bar, 325
Veselka, 339

MARBLE HILL
Views & Sights
Half Moon Overlook, 75–76
Spuyten Duyvil, 75

MEATPACKING DISTRICT
Bargains & Splurges
Auto, 251
Earnest Sewn, 287
Vitra Design Store, 267
Eating & Drinking
5 Ninth, 182
Gansevoort 69, 336
Pastis, 163
Spice Market, 167
24-Hour Fun
Hogs & Heifers, 325
Pop Burger, 341
Quintessentially, 322
Views & Sights
Hotel Gansevoort, 59

MIDTOWN
Arts & Culture
9 West 57th Street, art at, 138
520 Madison Ave, 137–138
American Dance Theater, 148
American Folk Art Museum,
    130–131
Armory Show, 140
Carnegie Hall, 147
Christie's, 143, 282
*Energy, Result, Workmanship, and
    Transportation*, 138
Museum of Modern Art, 122, 133,
    137, 158
New Directors/New Films, 152
Paley Center for Media, 131
sculpture garden, 590 Madison
    Ave., 138
Bargains & Splurges
Apple Store, 320
Bauman Rare Books, 261
Bergdorf Goodman, 243
B&H Photo, 252
Bloomingdales, 244
Cellar Room at 21, 287
Christie's, 143, 282
Clothingline, 244
Colony Records, 273
Conrad's, 263
DB Bistro Moderne, 163, 283
Diamond District, 253–254
Fifth Avenue (shopping excur-
    sion), 279, 281
Gray's Papaya, 283
Harry Winston, 115, 253
Henri Bendel, 243
Manolo Blahnik store, 250
Michael George, 282
Midtown Comics, 263
M&J Trimming, 267
MoMA Design Store (museum),

269–270
Norma's, 287
Takashimaya, 245
Tannen's Magic Superstore, 274
World Bar, 288
The Classics
Algonquin Hotel, 47
Astor Court, 37
Barneys Christmas Windows, 32
Bergdorf Goodman Christmas
    Windows, 32
Birdland, 45
Broadway Shows, 28, 153-154
Caroline's, 44
The Circle Line, 43–44
Empire State Building, 19
FAO Schwarz, 25
Four Seasons, 47
Grand Central Terminal, 23–25
Harry Cipriani, 38–39
Intrepid, 20
King Cole Bar, 36
late night talk shows, 31
Lever House, 46, 55
Lipstick Building, 55
Lord & Taylor Christmas Windows,
    32
Macy's Christmas Windows, 31
Macy's July 4 Fireworks, 26
Madison Square Garden, 31
McGraw-Hill Bu ilding, 54
Michael's, 49
The Palm, 49–50
Paris Theater, 40
Radio City Music hall, 23
Rockefeller Center, 76–77
Saks Fifth Avenue Christmas Win-
    dows, 32
Sardi's, 34–35
St. Patrick's Cathedral, 21
St. Regis Hotel, 36, 37
Subway Inn, 326
Tiffany, 26
United Nations, 20
Waldorf-Astoria, 353
The Ziegfeld, 40–41
Eating & Drinking
Aquavit, 197
Artisanal, 201
Carnegie Deli, 170
Cellar Bar, Bryant Park Hotel, 185
Condé Nast Cafeteria, 180–181
Dawat, 192
DB Bistro Moderne, 163, 283
Delegates Dining Room, 205
Esca, 162
Hangawi, 181
H&H bagels, 169

Le Bernardin, 167–168
Maison du Chocolat, 190
Masa, 168
The Modern, 165
Ninth Avenue International Food
    Festival, 171
Nobu Fifty Seven, 168
O'Neill's Irish Bar, 180
Per Se, 168–169
Petrossian, 194–195
Rudy's Bar & Grill, 202
Russian Vodka Room, 195
Sakagura, 353
Salon de Ning, 58
Scandinavia House, 198
Smith & Wollensky, 169
Smorgas Chef, 198
Sullivan Street Bakery, 178
Vong, 167
Enrichment & Renewal
Alliance Française, 88, 301
Athena, 311
The Instituto Cervantes, 301
The Japan Society, 301
Juvenex Spa, 309
Manhattan Neighborhood Net-
    work, 298–299
New York Public Library, 292
Osaka, 310
Renzo Gracie Academy, 307
Scandinavia House, 302
The Great Outdoors
Bryant Park, 215, 217
Bryant Park outdoor movie series,
    215–216
Bryant Park, Tai Chi, 230
Bryant Park, yoga classes, 228
Tudor City Gardens, 213
Only in New York
Bryant Park, 353
elephants, walking to Madison
    Square Garden, 347
Empire State Building, 360, 371
Ford Foundation Building, 350
French-American, 367
Jimmy's Corner, 354
Macy's, Santa, 346
Monday Night Magic, 360
New York Times Building, 370
Props for Today, 368
Say Cheese, 356
Steinway Hall, 363
Waldorf-Astoria, 353
On the Street & Underground
Annex/Hell's Kitchen flea market,
    94
Bela Bartók plaque, 101
Harry Winston, 115, 253

Library Walk, 107
Seth Thomas clock, 109
The Seven Year Itch grate, 114
Sherry-Netherland, 38–39
24-Hour Fun
Broadway City Video Arcade, 343
Carnegie Deli, 340
Duane Reade, 320
Empire State Building, 317
FAO Schwarz, 342
Grand Central, 316
Great White Way, 317
H&H, 340
Juvenex Spa, 326
The Paris Theater, 40
Rockefeller Center, 76–77
Sephora, 317, 319
Siberia, 326
Times Square, 317
Views & Sights
Asiate, 64
Ava Lounge, 60
Bergdorf Goodman, 69
Cipriani Dolce, 63
Columbus Circle, 80
Dream Hotel, 60
Empire State Building, 81
Hotel Metro Rooftop Bar, 59
Hudson Hotel Sky Terrace, 60
Masa, 64
Metrazur, 63, 78
Per Se, 64, 168–169
Terrace 5, 61
Time Warner Center, 64
Times Square, 83
Top of the Rock, 76
View Lounge, 60

MURRAY HILL
The Classics
Fireworks from FDR Drive, 26–27
Eating & Drinking
Curry in a Hurry, 192
El Pote Espanol, 193
Ess-a-Bagel, 169
Kalustyan's, 193
On the Street & Underground
28th Street subway station, 116
Schwarzenbach Building, 109
Views & Sights
Rare View, 58–59
The Water Club, 62

ROOSEVELT ISLAND
The Great Outdoors
Roosevelt Island, 237
Views & Sights
lighthouse, 74

SOHO
Arts & Culture
Angelika, 158–159
Broken Kilometer, 140
Earth Room, 140
Morrison Hotel, 145
Bargains & Splurges
Broadway Panhandler, 260
Camper, 262
Dean & Deluca, 285–286
Duncan Quinn, 266
Hat Shop, 275
Housing Works Used Book Café,
    278
MoMA Design Store (museum),
    269–270
Opening Ceremony, 250-251
Peter Hermann, 264
What Comes Around Goes
    Around, 248–249
The Classics
Dean & Deluca, 41–42
Eating & Drinking
Arturo's, 206
Balthazar, 164
Balthazar Bakery, 177
Barolo, 183
Ed's Lobster Bar, 170
Kee's, 191
Lucky Strike, 164
Mercer Kitchen, 167
Papaya King, for hotdogs, 170
Pravda, 164
Sullivan Street Bakery, 178
Wallsé, 196
Xicala, 193
Enrichment & Renewal
Balthazar, 308
French Culinary Institute, 88, 297
Housing Works Used Book Café,
    293, 309
New York Open Center, 299
Sandra Cameron Dance School, 306
Only in New York
Bar 89, 352
Pearl River Mart, 351
Peep, 352
Yoghurt Place II, 357
On the Street & Underground
*Subway Map Floating on a New
    York Sidewalk*, 108
24-Hour Fun
Lafayette Smoke Shop, 329
Views & Sights
A60 at 60 Thompson Hotel, 60
Thompson Street playground, 81

TRIBECA
Arts & Culture
Tribeca Film Festival, 156
Bargains & Splurges
What Comes Around Goes
  Around showroom, 248–249
The Classics
Odeon, 46
Eating & Drinking
Blaue Gans, 196
Bouley, 163
Bouley Bakery & Market, 163
Bubble Lounge, 184
Chanterelle, 168
Churrascaria Plataforma Tribeca,
  174
Danube, 196
Nobu, 168
Nobu Next Door, 168
Odeon, 46
Taste of Tribeca Street Festival, 171
The Great Outdoors
Hudson River Park, 212–216
Trapeze school, 234
On the Street & Underground
Ghostbusters fire station, 45
Tribeca Grand Clock, 109
24-Hour Fun
Nancy Whiskey Pub, 325

UNION SQUARE AREA &
FLATIRON & GRAMERCY
Bargains & Splurges
ABC Carpet & Home, 247–248
Academy Records & CDs, 276
Books of Wonder, 277
Bottlerocket, 256
Idlewild Books, 257
Italian Wine Merchants, 257
Jivamukti, 322-323
Journelle, 258–259
La Petite Coquette, 258
New York Cake and Baking Sup-
  ply, 270
Paragon, 271
Paul Smith Boutique, 262
Reminiscence, 248
Skyline Books, 273
Trixie and Peanut, 254
The Classics
Lady Mendl's Tea Salon, 38
Pete's Tavern, 43
Eating & Drinking
Artichoke, 207
Bar Jamon, 162
Beppe, 176
Blue 9, 170
Blue Smoke/Jazz Standard, 165

Casa Mono, 162
City Bakery, 200
Eleven Madison Park, 165
Gramercy Tavern, 165
Old Town Bar, 200
Periyali, 196
Pure Food and Wine, 181
Shake Shack, 166
Tabla Restaurant and Bread Bar, 166
Tarallucci e Vino, 189
The Adore, 204
Union Square Café, 166
Union Square Greenmarket, 171
Enrichment & Renewal
Beads of Paradise, 296
Cooper Union, 297
Dance Manhattan, 307
Djoniba Dancing & Drum Centre,
  306
Joe, 298
La Casa Day Spa, 310
New School, 299
New York Film Academy, 299
New York University's School of
  Continuing and Professional
  Studies, 299
PhotoManhattan, 300
Pratt Institute, 300
School of Visual Arts, 300
The Tibet House, 303
The Great Outdoors
Gandhi statue, 214
Gramercy Park, 210–211
Union Square Park, 229
Only in New York
40-40 Club, 355
Tracey J's, 355
On the Street & Underground
Big Apple Barbeque Block Party,
  86
"The Block Beautiful," 99
The Golden Clock, 109
Holiday Market, 95
Metronome, 108
street vendors, 111–112
24-Hour Fun
Bowlmor Lanes, 342
Greenmarket, 334
Hair, 24, 330
Jivamukti, 322–323
Laughing Lotus, 342
L'Express, 339
Spin, 329–330
24/7 Fitness Club, 327
Village Copier, 335
Views & Sights
Whole Foods, 71

UPPER EAST SIDE
Arts & Culture
Bemelman's Bar, 136
The Cooper Hewitt, 122–123
The Frick Collection, 122 124
The Guggenheim, 124
Metropolitan Museum of Art,
  119–120
The Neue Galerie, 126
Sotheby's, 143
The Whitney Museum of Ameri-
  can Art, 124
Bargains & Splurges
Argosy, 252–253
Barneys, 244–245
Best Cellars, 286
Blue Tree, 251–252
The Corner Bookstore, 278, 293
Creed, 266
Lascoff Apothecary, 268
Madison Avenue (shopping
  excursion), 279
Posy Floral Design, 288
Roberta Freymann, 260–261
Sable's, 252
Sotheby's, 282
Ursus, 274
The Classics
Barneys Christmas Windows, 32
Carlyle Hotel, 279
Elaine's, 34
Paul Molé Barber Shop, 34
Pierre Hotel, 37
Serendipity, 48
Eating & Drinking
Agata & Valentina, 177
Café Boulud, 163
Café Sabarsky, 196
Daniel, 163
Donguri, 199
Eli's & the Vinegar Factory, 178
JoJo, 167
Maison du Chocolat, 190
Payard Patisserie & Bistro, 190
Shanghai Pavilion, 186
Enrichment & Renewal
The China Institute, 301
The Corner Bookstore, 293
French Institute/Alliance Fran-
  caise, 301
The Interfaith Center, 302
The 92nd Street Y, 295
Urasenke Chanoyu, 304
The Great Outdoors
Gardens of Saint John the Divine,
  213
Only in New York
David Burke & Donatella, 364

Pale Male and Lola, 348
On the Street & Underground
Bastille Day Festival, 88
Mount Vernon Hotel Museum
and Garden, 102
Museum Mile Festival, 86–87
Park Avenue Christmas Tree Light-
ing Ceremony, 110
The Temple of Dendur, 114
Yorkville Clock, 109
24-Hour Fun
Duane Reade, 320
Guggenheim, 331
Views & Sights
Bobby Wagner Walkway, 67
Carl Schurz Park, 67
Metropolitan Museum, 59

UPPER WEST SIDE
Arts & Culture
American Museum of Natural His-
tory, 119
Film Society of Lincoln Center, 152
Jazz at Lincoln Center (Frederick P.
Rose Hall), 150
Kim's, 52–53
Leonard Nimoy Thalia, 160
Lincoln Center, 150–153
Lincoln Center Presents, 152–153
Margaret Mead Film and Video
Festival, 157
Metropolitan Opera, 151
New Directors/New Films, 152
New York City Ballet, 151
New York City Opera, 151–152
New York Film Festival, 156–157
New York-Historical Society, 132
New York Philharmonic, 152
Rose Center for Earth and Space,
119
Bargains & Splurges
Acker, Merrill, and Condit, 255
Gray's Papaya, 283
Greenflea market, 94–95
Kiehl's, 286–287
La Belle Epoque, 258
Mandarin Oriental, 64, 283
The Classics
Café des Artistes, 53–54
Zabar's, 42, 178
Eating & Drinking
Bar Boulud, 163
H&H Bagels, 169
Jean-Georges and Nougatine, 166
Nice Matin, 196
Enrichment & Renewal
DanceSport, 307
Jewish Community Center, 298

The 92nd Street Y, Makor/Stein-
hardt Center, 295
Symphony Space, 294–295
The Great Outdoors
Lincoln Center Out of Doors, 217
Met in the Park, 217
Philharmonic in the Park, 217
Riverside Park, 229,236
Riverside Park, yoga classes, 229
Only in New York
American Museum of Natural
History, 346
West Side Collegiate Church, 370
On the Street & Underground
Café Lalo, 116
Central Park West, 100
Greenflea Market, 94–95
Leonard Nimoy Thalia, 160
Views & Sights
Boat Basin Café, 62
Dizzy's Jazz Club Coca-Cola, 64
24-Hour Fun
Amsterdam Billiards, 329
Big Nick's, 336
Duane Reade, 320
H&H Bagels, 340

WASHINGTON HEIGHTS
The Classics
Trinity Cemetery, 22
Enrichment & Renewal
Sava Spa, 311
The Great Outdoors
Riverbank State Park, 233
Views & Sights
High Bridge Water Tower, 70–71

QUEENS

ASTORIA
Eating & Drinking
Bohemian Hall & Beer Garden, 183
The Great Outdoors
Astoria Pool, 234
24-Hour Fun
Neptune, 339

BROAD CHANNEL
The Great Outdoors
Floyd Bennett Field, Gateway
National Park, 238–239
Jamaica Bay Riding Academy, 228
Jamaica Bay Wildlife Refuge (in
Gateway National Recreation
Area), 226

COLLEGE POINT
Enrichment & Renewal
Spa Castle, 313

ELMHURST
On the Street & Underground
Wendy's ("MacDowell's"), 114
Enrichment & Renewal
Queens Botanical Gardens, 304

FAR ROCKAWAY
The Great Outdoors
Rockaway Beach, 234
Views & Sights
beach at nightfall, 65
Rockaway Beach, 65

FLUSHING MEADOWS/CORONA
Arts & Culture
Louis Armstrong House, 112
New York Hall of Science, 341
The Classics
US Open, 29–30
Enrichment and Renewal
Queens Botanical Gardens, 304
On the Street & Underground
Louis Armstrong House, 112
24-Hour Fun
New York Hall of Science, 341
Views and Sights
New York Panorama, 77–78

JACKSON HEIGHTS
Eating & Drinking
Delhi Palace, 192
Jackson Diner, 192

JAMAICA
Bargains & Splurges
Coxsone's Music City, 277
The Great Outdoors
Aqueduct, 236

KEW GARDENS
Arts & Culture
Civic Virtue statue, 142
The Great Outdoors
Queens Farm Museum, 238

LONG ISLAND CITY/HUNTER'S
POINT
Arts & Culture
5 Pointz, 139
Flux Factory, 141
Museum of the Moving Image,
131
Museum for African Art, 128
Noguchi Museum, 133

PS1, 133
Socrates Sculpture Park, 142
The Classics
Gantry Plaza State Park, 27
Eating & Drinking
Greek Captain Fish Market, 196
Manducatis, 188
The Great Outdoors
"LONG ISLAND" and "PEPSI-COLA"
  signs, 215
Socrates Sculpture Park, Tai Chi,
  230
Socrates Sculpture Park, yoga
  classes, 229
Only in New York
Steinway Factory, 364
Views & Sights
7 train into Queens, 68
Water Taxi Beach, 72
Water's Edge, 62

MASBETH
On the Street & Underground
The Clinton Diner, 116

STATEN ISLAND
Arts & Culture
Snug Harbor, 147
Bargains & Splurges
Mandolin Brothers, 252–253
Eating & Drinking
Ralph's Italian Ices, 180
Enrichment & Renewal
Jacques Marchais Museum of
  Tibetan Art, 303
The Great Outdoors
Greenbelt Nature Center, yoga
  classes, 228
Staten Island Botanical Garden, 219
On the Street & Underground
Staten Island Yankees, 113
24-Hour Fun
Lowe's, 318
Views & Sights
Alice Austen House, 70
FDR Boardwalk, 66

CALENDAR OF EVENTS

JANUARY
Chinese New Year, celebration
  (date varies), 93
galette des rois at Gavroche, 189
New Year's Day Marathon Reading, 291
Restaurant Week, 201

Sacco shoe sale, 249
Wave Hill, free admission, 211

FEBRUARY
The Armory Show, 140
Barneys Warehouse Sale, 246
Chinese New Year, celebration
  (date varies), 93
Fashion Week, 81
hot chocolate month at City Bak-
  ery, 200
Wave Hill, free admission, 214

MARCH
Astroland, Coney Island
  (opens Palm Sunday through
  early fall):
  The Cyclone, 348–349
  Wonder Wheel, 65
elephant procession, Queens-
  Midtown Tunnel, 347
rowboating, in Central Park
  (through October), 219

APRIL
Boat Basin Café, 62
Dachshund Spring Fiesta, 89–90
fishing for free, Harlem Meer, 224
hayrides, Queens Farm Museum
  (through October), 238
inline skating lessons, Central Park
  (through October), 220
Shearwater, sail around Manhattan
  (through October), 73
Tribeca Film Festival, 156
Wednesday Night Skate, 233

MAY
Blessing of the Bikes, 345
Dine Around Downtown, 171–172
Gowanus Canal tours (through
  October), 224–225
Kripalu (through August),
  Socrates Sculpture Park, 229
Milonga (through October), South
  Street Seaport, 323–324
Ninth Avenue International Food
  Festival, 171
Tai Chi (through August), Bryant
  Park, 230
Taste of Tribeca Street Festival,
  171
Tribeca Film Festival, 156
Washington Square Art Show, 146
Water Taxi Beach (through
  October), 72
Victorian Gardens (through
  September), 220

yoga classes (through August),
  Bryant Park, 228

JUNE
concerts, Bryant Park (through
  August), 217
Gay Pride Parade, 80, 92
movie series (through August),
  Bryant Park, 215
Museum Mile Festival, 86–87
outdoor pool (through Labor
  Day), Astoria Park, 234
Summerstage (through August),
  217

JULY
Bastille Day celebrations, 88
fireworks, Macy's, 26–27
hot dog-eating contest, Nathan's
  Famous, 349
Indian powwow, Queens Farm
  Museum, 238
Philharmonic in the Park, 217
Restaurant Week, 201
RiverFlicks (through August), Hud-
  son River Park, 216
Sacco shoe sale, 249
Siren Music Festival, Coney Island,
  150
yoga (through August), Greenbelt
  Nature Center, 228

AUGUST
Barneys Warehouse Sale, 246
Charlie Parker Jazz Festival,
  211–212
Lincoln Center Out of Doors
  (through September), 217
Metropolitan Opera in the Park,
  217
Yo-Yo Open, 363

SEPTEMBER
Atlantic Antic, 86
Brazil Day Festival, 89
Brooklyn Book Festival, 87
corn maze, Queens Farm Museum
  (through October), 238
country fair, Queens Farm
  Museum, 238
Fashion Week, 81
Feast at San Gennaro, 85
New York Century Ride, 231–232
New York Film Festival (through
  October), 152, 156–157
Plant Pigment Weekend, Wave
  Hill, 214
Tai Chi (through November),

Brooklyn Botanic Garden,
229–230
Washington Square Art Show, 146
West Indian-American Day Parade
& Carnival, 91

OCTOBER
Blessing of the Animals, 345–346
Dachtober Fest, 89–90
ice-skating
Rockefeller Center (through
April), 333
Milonga, South Street
Seaport, 323–324
OpenHouseNewYork, 71, 72
Village Halloween Parade, 92–93

NOVEMBER
Chocolate Show, 172
Christmas tree, at Rockefeller Cen-
ter (through January), 32
Christmas windows (through
January), 31–32
Holiday Market, Union Square
(through December), 95
ice-skating
Lasker Rink (through March),
221
Margaret Mead Film and Video
Festival, 157
New York City Marathon, 29, 132
Next Wave Festival, Brooklyn
Academy of Music, 148
Vendy Awards, 360–361

DECEMBER
Christmas tree lighting ceremony,
Park Avenue, 110
Jivamukti New Year's Celebration,
322
Midnight Run, Central Park, 322
Midnight Run, Prospect Park, 322
New Year's Eve Steam Whistle
Blow at Pratt, 323
Operation Santa, 368
Walk into the New Year, 323
Wave Hill, free admission (through
February), 214

FREE ACTIVITIES

A
African Burial Grounds, 107
AIA Center for Architecture,
lectures, 303
Amsterdam Avenue, overpass, 78

B
balloons, inflating of Thanksgiving
Day floats, 91
barge concerts, 146
Bastille Day Festival, 88
Battery Park City Parks, 211
Battery Park Promenade, 66
Best Cellars, wine tastings, 286
bike ride, moonlight, 328
Billy's Antiques & Props, 110
Blessing of the Bikes, 345
Block Beautiful, 99
Bobby Wagner Walkway at Carl
Schurz Park, 67
Bow Bridge, 75
Brazil Day Festival, 89
Brighton Beach Boardwalk, 79
Broken Kilometer, 140
Brooklyn Brewery, tours of, 183
Brooklyn Bridge, 20, 67
Brooklyn Bridge Park, 70, 212
Brooklyn Heights Promenade, 66
Brooklyn Museum, free events,
121–122
Bryant Park, 81
Bumble & Bumble, 284–285

C
Carl Schurz Park, 67
Cathedral of Saint John the
Divine, 21
cemeteries, walking through,
236–237
Central Park, 217
Central Park Drive, 79
Chelsea Hotel, 39–40
Chelsea Market, samples, 177–178
Chinatown, night court, 317–318
Christmas tree lighting ceremony,
110
Christmas windows, 31–32
City Hall Park, 213
clocks, of NYC, 74, 108–109
Cloisters' Medieval Festival, 88
Cobble Hill Park, 213
Colgate clock, 74
Columbus Circle, 80
Coney Island/Brighton Beach
Boardwalks, 66

D
Dachsund Festival, 88–90
Dean & Deluca, noshing at, 285–
286
DUMBO, Brooklyn, 82–83

E
Early Bird Walk, guided tour, 321
Earth Room, 140
Eighth Avenue "catwalk," 80
elephants, on way to circus, 347

Ellis Island, 19
Empire Skate Club, 232
Empire-Fulton Ferry State Park, 70
F
Fairway, "cold room," 285
Far Rockaway, 65
FDR Boardwalk, 66
Feast at San Gennaro, 85
Film Society of Lincoln Center,
newsletter, 152
fishing, in Harlem Meer, 224
Flux Factory, 141
food freebies, 285–286
Forgotten NY, 98
G
Garden of Eden, samples, 285
Gardens of Saint John the Divine,
213
Gay Pride Parade, 92
George Washington Bridge, 68, 74
Gourmet Garage, samples, 285
Gowanus Canal tours, 224–225
graffiti art, 139
Gramercy Park, 210–211
Grand Central Terminal, 23–25
Grant's Tomb, 76
H
haircuts, 284–285
Half Moon Overlook, 75–76
Halloween Carnival, 89
High Bridge Water Tower, 70–71
houses, of distinction, 101–102
Howl! Festival, 87–88
Hudson River Park, 212, 216
I
The Instituto Cervantes, member-
ship for students, 301
internet access, 215, 309
J
Jivamukti, New Year's Eve, 322
K
kayaking/kayaking lessons, 225
kettle corn, 85
Kiehl's, samples, 286–287
L
Lafayette's feet, 75
Lenin statue, Red Square building,
106
Library Walk, 107
Lincoln Center Out of Doors, 217
literary readings, 290–295
Liz Christy Gardens, 213
M
Macy's
Santa, 346
Thanksgiving Day Parade, 90
Manhattan Bridge, 68
walkway of, 82

Manhattan Neighborhood Network classes, 298–299
Manhattan's User Guide subscription, 365
Margaret Corbin Drive, 71
Mermaid Parade, 91
Metropolitan Museum of Art stairs, 78–79
Morningside Park, 213
movie sites, famous, 114–117
Museum Mile Festival, 86–87
museums, 284
  free or pay-what-you-wish day, 284
  free programs, 118–135
  highlights tour at the Met, 119–120
music, outdoor, 216–217

N
New York City Marathon, as spectator, 29
New York Panorama tours, 77–78
Nike running clinic, 230–231
Ninth Avenue International Food Festival, 171
NYC parks, for art, 144

P
Pale Male and Lola (red-tailed Hawks), 348
Park Avenue view, 78
parks and gardens, 210–215
partner dancing, introductory classes, 306
people watching, 78–81
Petanque, 88
Philharmonic in the Park, 217
PhotoManattan, Artist's Exchange Program, 300
pools, outdoor, 234
Prospect Park, 222–224

R
Red Hook waterfront, 76
River to River, 217
Riverside Church, 73
Rudy's Bar & Grill, hot dogs, 202

S
Santa, at Macy's, 346
sculptures, spinning, 143–144
Sephora, consultation, 317, 319
Shakespeare in the Park, 155
Siren Music Festival, 150
Skate Patrol Stopping Clinic, 220
Songlines, 98
Spuyten Duyvil Shorefront Park, 75
St. Patrick's Cathedral, 21
Staten Island Ferry, 69, 316
Statue of Liberty, 18
stoop sales, 96

Strawberry Fields, 107–108
Streit Matzo Factory, samples, 286
subway map, biggest, 108
Summerstage, 217

T
Tai Chi classes, 229–230
tango socials, lessons, 323–324
Thompson Street playground, 81
Times Square, 83
Trinity Cemetery, 22
Trinity Church, 22
Tudor City Gardens, 213

U
ushering, for performances, 155

V
vendors, at Union Square, 110
Verrazano-Narrows Bridge, 68
Village Halloween Parade, 92–93

W
Wagner Park, 65
Walkway of Manhattan Bridge, 82
Water's Edge, free ferry service, 62
Wednesday Night Skate, 233
West Indian-American Day Parade & Carnival, 91
Williams-Sonoma, samples, 285

Y
yoga classes, 228, 230, 284, 300, 322–323, 342

KID-FRIENDLY ACTIVITIES

A
Alvin Ailey American Dance Theater, 148
American Folk Art Museum, 130–131
American Museum of Natural History, 119
American Museum of Natural History Identification Day, 346
Arms & Armor exhibit, at the Met, 120
Arthur Avenue, 187–188
Astroland, 349
Atlantic Antic, 86

B
balloons, inflating of Thanksgiving Day floats, 91
Barge music, 146
Barney's, Christmas windows, 32
basketball, 239
Bastille Day Festival, 88
Battery Park City Parks, 211
beaches, 225, 234
Bergdorf Goodman, Christmas windows, 32

Berlin Wall, pieces of, 137–138
Big Apple Barbeque Block Party, 86, 165
biking, through Manhattan, 240
Blessing of the Bikes, 345
Blue Tree, 251–252
Bluebell Wood, 218
Books of Wonder, 277
Bottlerocket, 256
Brazil Day Festival, 89
Broadway shows, 28, 153–154
Broadway Windows, 141
Bronx Zoo, 113, 227
Brooklyn Academy of Music, 148
Brooklyn Botanic Garden, 82, 218–219, 229, 296
Brooklyn Bowl, 343
Brooklyn Bridge, 228
Brooklyn Bridge Park, 70, 212, 228
  movies at, 216
Brooklyn Children's Museum, 126–127
Brooklyn Heights Promenade, 66
  watching fireworks from, 27
Brooklyn Museum, 121–122
Bryant Park, 228, 230
  movie series, 215, 216
Butterfly Garden, 227

C
canoe rides, 224
Carnegie Hall, 147
carousels, 89, 220, 223
Cathedral of Saint John the Divine, 21, 345
Celebrity path, 213
Central Park, 217, 228, 230–231
  carriage rides, 27–28
Charlie Parker Jazz Festival, 211–212
Chelsea Piers, 308
Chelsea Piers Golf Club, 347
Cherry Esplanade, 218
chess, 305
Chinese Scholar's Garden, 219
Chocolate Show, 172
Christmas tree lighting ceremony, 110
Christmas windows, 31–32
Circle Line tour, 23, 73
City Hall Park, 213
clocks, of NYC, 108–109
Cloisters, 121
Cloisters' Medieval Festival, 88
Cobble Hill Park, 213
Concert Grove Pagoda, 224
Coney Island, 65, 348–349
Congo Gorilla Forest, 113, 227
Connie Gretz's Secret Garden, 219

Conservatory Gardens, 221–222
Cooper-Hewitt museum, 122–123
cricket matches, 69
cross-country skiing, 233
Cyclone, Coney Island, 349

D
Dachshund Festival, 89–90
dance, 149, 306–307
disco skaters, 220
The Djoniba Dancing & Drum
   Centre, 306
Dog Beach, 224

E
Egyptian galleries, at the Met, 120
elephants, on way to circus, 347
Ellis Island, 19, 66
Empire Skate Club, 232
Empire State Building, 76, 371
Empire-Fulton Ferry State Park, 70
European & American paintings,
   at the Met, 120

F
fairs and festivals, 89–90
FAO Schwarz, 25, 342
FDR Drive, watching fireworks
   from, 26–27
Federal Reserve Bank of New York,
   364
Fifth Avenue, 279, 281
fishing, 223, 225
flea markets, 93–95
Floyd Bennett Field, 238–239
Flux Factory, 141
Forbes Galleries, 123
Ford Foundation building, gar-
   dens at, 350
forests, 226
Fragrance Garden, 218
Frick Collection, 123–124, 136
frisbee, 240–241

G
Gandhi statue, 214
Gantry Plaza State Park, watching
   fireworks from, 27
Gardens of Saint John the Divine,
   213
Gateway National Park, 238–239
Gay Pride Parade, 80, 92
Gowanus Canal, 224–225, 238
graffiti art, 139
Gramercy Park, 210–211
Grand Central, dark patch on the
   ceiling, 113
The Great Lawn, 240
Greenbelt Nature Center, 228
Guggenheim, 124

H
Halloween Carnival, Prospect Park, 89

handball, 240
High Bridge Water Tower, 70–71
horse races, 236
horseback riding, 228
hot dog eating contest, Coney
   Island, 349
Howl! Festival, 87–88
Hudson River Park, 212, 216
   watching fireworks from, 27

I
inline skate braking lessons, 220
The Instituto Cervantes, 301
Intrepid, 20
Inwood Hill Nature Center, 226
Inwood Hill Park, 229
Irish Hunger Memorial, 145

J
Jacques Marchais Museum, 303
Jamaica Bay Wildlife Refuge, 226
The Japan Society, 301
Jewish Children's Museum, 127
Joan Weill Center for Dance, 149

K
kayaking, 225

L
lawn sports, 221
Lincoln Center, 148, 150–153
Liz Christy Gardens, 213
"Long Island" sign, 58, 215
Lord & Taylor, Christmas windows,
   32
Lower East Side Tenement
   Museum, 135

M
Macy's
   Christmas windows, 31
   fishing contest, 223
   July 4 fireworks, 26
   Santa at, 346
   Thanksgiving Day Parade, 90
Marcus Garvey Park, 211
marionette theater, 350
Mermaid Parade, 91
Metropolitan Museum of Art,
   119–120
Midtown Comics, 263
Monday Night Magic, 360
Monument Park, 30
Morningside Park, 213
movie sites, famous, 114–117
MTA Transit Museum, 103–104,
   135
Museo del Barrio, 128
Museum for African Art, 128
museum highlights tour, at the
   Met, 119–120
Museum of Modern Art, 122, 133,
   137, 158

Museum of the City of New York,
   86, 129
Museum of the Fashion Institute
   of Technology, 129, 302
Museum of the Moving Image, 131
museums. *See specific museums*

N
Neue Galerie, 126
New Museum of Contemporary
   Art, 125
New York Aquarium, 227
New York Botanical Gardens, 218
New York City Fire Museum, 132
New York City Police Museum,
   132
New York Hall of Science, 123, 341
New York Historical Society, 132
New York Knicks, at Madison
   Square Garden, 31
New York Marathon, 29
New York Panorama, 77–78
New York Public Library, 292
New York Road Runners Club, 230
New York Transit Museum, 183
The 92nd Street Y, 230
Ninth Avenue International Food
   Festival, 171
Noguchi Museum, 133
NYC parks, for art, 144

O
Off-Broadway/Off-Off Broadway.
   See Broadway shows
OpenHouseNewYork, 71, 72
Operation Santa, 368

Pale Male and Lola (red-tailed
   Hawks), 348
Paley Center for Media, 131
palm trees, at Winter Garden, 350
pedal boating, 222–223
"Pepsi-Cola" sign, 58, 215
Petanque, 88
Pilgrim's Hill, 220
playgrounds, 81, 236
Prospect Park, 222–224
PS1 (outpost of Museum of Mod-
   ern Art), 133
The Public Theater, 154

Q
Queens Farm Museum, 238

R
Radio City Music Hall, 23
Red Hook Waterfront Museum,
   134
Riverbank State Park, 233
RiverFlicks, Hudson River Park, 216
Riverside Park, 229, 230
rock star photographs, 145

roller-coaster. *See Cyclone, Coney Island*
roller-disco skating, 220, 224
Rooftop sculpture garden, at the Met, 121
Roosevelt Island, 237
Rose Center for Earth and Space, 119
rowboating, 219
Rutherford Observatory, 65

S
sailing, 226
Sak's Fifth Avenue, Christmas windows, 32
Santa, at Macy's, 346
Scandinavia House, 302
Shakespeare in the Park, 73, 155
sheep-shearing demo, 238
skating, 220
     off hours, 333
     at Rockefeller Center, 33
Skyscraper Museum, 133
sleepover parties, 341–342
Snug Harbor, 147
Socrates Sculpture Park, 142, 229
South Street Seaport, 73
     Museum, 134
Spuyten Duyvil, 75
St. Patrick's Cathedral, 21
Staten Island Botanical Garden, 219
Staten Island Yankees game, 113
Statue of Liberty, 66
Steinway Factory Tour, 364
Steinway Hall, fan mail at, 363
stoop sales, 96
Strawberry Fields, 107–108
Studio Museum of Harlem, 129–130
subway map, biggest, 108
Swedish Cottage Marionette Theater, 350
Sweet Things Bake Shop, 206
swimming, 234, 298, 313

T
Tannen Magic Superstore, 274
Taste of Tribeca Street Festival, 171
Tompkins Square Park Courts, 239–240
Trapeze School, 234
Trinity Church, 22, 107
Tudor City Gardens, 213
Turtle Pond, 219

U
unicorn tapestries, Cloisters, 121

V
Vale of Cashmere, 223
Van Cortlandt Park, 214, 235
vendors, at Union Square, 110

Victorian Gardens, 220
Village Halloween Parade, 92–93

W
wallball, 246
Washington Square Art Show, 146
Washington Square Park, 305
Wave Hill, 214, 230
West 4th Street Courts, 239–240
West Indian-American Day Parade & Carnival, 91
whispering gallery, 24
Whitney Museum, 124
Winter Garden, 350
Wollman Rink, 224

Y
Yankee Clipper, 226
Yankee Stadium, 30, 113

RESTAURANTS, FOOD MAR-
KETS, AND BARS
═══════════════════════

A
A60 at 60 Thompson Hotel, 60
Agata & Valentina, 177
Algonquin Hotel, 47
Alma, 61
Amy's Bread, 177, 356
Angel's Share, 198
Antek, 195–196
Aquavit, 197
Arlene's Grocery, 203
Arthur Avenue, Italian cuisine on, 187–188
Artichoke, 207
Artisanal, 201
Arturo's, 206
Asia Roma, 201
Asiate, 64
Astor Court, St. Regis Hotel, 37

B
B61, 61
Babbo, 162
Balthazar, 164, 308
Balthazar Bakery, 177
Bar 89, 352
Bar Boulud, 163
Bar Jamon, 162
Bar Veloce, 189
Barolo, 183
Basta Pasta, 174
Beauty Bar, 327
Bemelmans Bar, 136
Beppe, 176, 359
Berry Park, 63
Biancardi's, 187
Big Nick's, 336
Billy's Bakery, 170

Birdland, 44
Blaue Gans, 196
Blue 9, 170
Blue Hill, 167
Blue Smoke/Jazz Standard, 165
Boat Basin Café, 62
Boathouse, Central Park, 221
Bohemian Hall & Beer Garden, 183
Borgatti's, 187
Bouley, 163
Bouley Bakery & Market, 163
Bowery Bar, 184
Brazen Head, The, 203
Bridge Café, 50–51
Bubble Lounge, 184
Burke in the Box, 244
Buttermilk, 202

C
Café Boulud, 163
Café des Artistes, 53–54
Café Doma, 80
Café Sabarsky, 196
Cafeteria, 336
Campbell Apartment, 24
Carnegie Deli, 170, 340
Caroline's, 43–44
Casa Mono, 162
Cellar Bar, Bryant Park Hotel, 185
Cellar Room at 21, 287
Cha An, 198–199, 351
Chanterelle, 168
The Chelsea Market, 177–178
Chelsea Square, 337
Chikalicious, 358
Chinatown Ice Cream Factory, 179
ChipShop, 203
Chumley's, 53
Churrascaria Plataforma Tribeca, 174
Cipriani Dolce, 63
Cipriani Downtown, 9
City Bakery, 200
Cocktail Terrace, Waldorf-Astoria, 37
Cones, 179
Congee Village, 172
Corner Bistro, 170
Creperie, 189
Curry in a Hurry, 192

D
Daniel, 163
Danube, 196
David Burke & Donatella, 364
Dawat, 192
DB Bistro Moderne, 163, 283
DBGB, 163
Dean & Deluca, 41–42, 285–286
Decibel, 265

Del Posto, 162
Delegates Dining Room, 20, 205
Delhi Palace, 192
Diner, 205
DiPalo's, 178
Donguri, 199
Down the Hatch, 184
Dream Hotel, 60
DuMont, 182
E
Ed's Lobster Bar, 170
Egidio's Patisserie, 188
El Cid, 194
El Pote Espanol, 193–194
Elaine's, 34
Eleven Madison Park, 165
Eli's & The Vinegar Factory, 178
Empire Diner, 337
Esca, 162
Ess-a-Bagel, 169
Essex Street Market, 178
F
Fifth Avenue Bageltique Café, 340
Five Points, 139, 175
5 Ninth, 182
Florent, 336
Floyd NY, 204
food trucks, 111
40 Carrots, 244
40-40 Club, 355
Four Seasons, 47
Franny's, 207
Fraunces Tavern, 33
Freeman's, 203
Full Moon, 185, 207
G
Gansevoort 69, 336
Gate, 203
Gavroche, 189–190
Giando on the Water, 62–63
Golden Unicorn, 186
Gramercy Tavern, 165
Gray's Papaya, 170, 283, 333
Greek Captain Fish Market, 196
Greenmarket, 334
Grimaldi's, 20, 206
H
Half King, 354
Hangawi, 181
Harry Cipriani, 38–39
H&H bagels, 169, 340
Hogs & Heifers, 325
Home, 182
Hop Kee, 186
Hotel Gansevoort, rooftop, 59
Hotel Metro Rooftop Bar, 59
Hudson Hotel Sky Terrace, 60
The Hummus Place, 357

Hungarian Pastry Shop, 80
I
Il Laboratorio Del Gelato, 172
Il Mulino, 188
Indochine, 47
J
Jackson Diner, 192
Jean-Georges and Nougatine, 166
Jimmy's Corner, 354
Joe Allen, 28
Joe's, 207
Joe's Shanghai, 186
Johnny's Famous Reef, 226, 325
John's of Bleecker Street, 207
John's of 12th Street, 43
JoJo, 167
Junior's cheesecake, 169
K
Kalustyan's, 193
Katz's, 114, 170, 203
Kee's, 191
King Cole Bar, St. Regis Hotel, 36
L
Lady Mendl's Tea Salon, 38
L'Express, 339
L'asso, 206
Le Bernardin, 167–168
Lennox Lounge, 44
Lever House Restaurant, 46, 55
Liquiteria, 174
Lobby Lounge, 64
Lombardi's, 47–48, 203
Lounge at the Pierre Hotel, 37
Lucky Cheng's, 174–175
Lucky Strike, 164
Lupa, 162
M
Magnolia Bakery, 176, 333
Maison du Chocolat, 190
Mamoun's, 173
Manducatis, 188
Mars Bar, 325
Masa, 64, 168
McSorley's Old Ale House, 50
Mercer Kitchen, 167
Metrazur, 63, 78
Metropolitan Museum Rooftop
    Terrace, 59
Michael's, 49
Milk Bar, 184
Milon, 193
Minetta Tavern, 164
The Modern, 165
Momofuku, 176
Murray's, 177, 286–287
N
Nancy Whiskey Pub, 325
Nathan's, 66, 170

Neptune, 339
New Leaf Café, 206
Nice Matin, 196
Nobu, 168
Norma's, 287
O
Odeon, 164
Old Town Bar, 200
One if by Land, Two if by Sea, 50
O'Neill's Irish Bar, 180
Otto Enoteca E Pizzeria, 162
Oyster Bar, 25
P
The Palm, 49–50
Panna II, 193
Papaya King, 170
Pasquale's Rigoletto, 188
Pastis, 46, 79, 164, 332
Payard Patisserie & Bistro, 190
Peanut Butter & Co., 356–357
Pearl Oyster Bar, 170
Peasant, 178
Peep, 352
Peking Duck House, 186
Per Se, 64, 168–169
Periyali, 196
Perry Street, 167
Peter Luger, 169
Pete's Tavern, 43
Petrossian, 194–195
The Pickle Guys, 359
Pommes Frites, 173
Pop Burger, 341
Poznanski's, 195
Pravda, 164
Puff & Pao, 359
Pukk, 352
Pure Food and Wine, 181
R
Rairaiken, 199
Rao's, 49
Rare View, 58–59
Raymund's Place, 195
Relish, 200
Remedy, 338
Rice to Riches, 356
Risotteria, 358
River Café, 61–62
Rotunda, Pierre Hotel, 37
Rudy's Bar & Grill, 202
Russian Vodka Room, 195
S
Sable's, 252
Sahadi's, 86, 178
Salon de Ning, 58
A Salt and Battery, 191
Santos Party House, 355
Sardi's, 34–35

Say Cheese, 356
Scandinavia House, 198, 302
Schiller's Liquor Bar, 164
Serendipity, 48, 164
Shade To Go, 189
Shake Shack, 30, 166
Shanghai Pavilion, 186
Sherwood Café/Robin des Bois, 182
Siberia, 326
S'MAC, 358
Smith & Wollensky steak, 169
Smorgas Chef, 198
Spice Market, 167
The Spotted Pig, 176
St. Nick's Pub, 45
Stolovaya, 194
Stylowa, 194
Sullivan Street Bakery, 178
T
Tabla Restaurant and Bread Bar, 166
Tarallucci e Vino, 189
Tatiana, 194
Tavern on the Green, 35–36
Tea and Sympathy, 191
10 Downing Street, 102
Teresa's, 183
Terrace 5, 61
Terrace in the Sky, 61
The Adore, 204
Tia Pol, 175
Tom & Jerry, 202
Tomoe Sushi, 199
Tom's Restaurant, 338–339
Tracey J's, 355
Trump World Tower, 288
25th Street Market/Garage, 94
21 Club, 324
U
Umberto's, 188
Union Square Café, 166
V
Veniero's, 48, 169
Veselka, 339
View Lounge, 60
Village Vanguard, 45
Village Yokocho, 198
Viva Herbal Pizzeria, 208
Vong, 167
W
Wallsé, 196
Water Club, 62
Water's Edge, 62
Waverly Restaurant, 338
White Horse Tavern, 46
Whole Foods, 71
Winnie's, 202
Wo Hop, 340

World Bar, 288
X
Xicala, 193
Y
Yaffa Café, 181–182
Yajirobei, 198
Yoghurt Place II, 357
Yonah Schimmel, 172
Z
Zabar's, 42

CAITLIN LEFFEL, a native New Yorker, is a writer and editor who has contributed to *Daily Candy*, *Metro*, and *Publishers Weekly*.

JACOB LEHMAN, a more recent arrival to the Big Apple, works in the editorial division of a major New York publisher.

They are also the authors of *NYC: An Owner's Manual*.